The Li Ki

Translated by James Legge

The Li Ki

Table of Contents

The Li Ki

Table of Contents

Table of Contents

Table of Contents

The Li Ki

Table of Contents

Table of Contents

The Li Ki

Translated by James Legge

- BOOK XLVI. SANG FÛ SZE KIH, OR THE FOUR PRINCIPLES UNDERLYING THE DRESS OF MOURNING[1].

PREFACE.

I MAY be permitted to express my satisfaction that, with the two volumes of the Lî Kî now published, I have done, so far as translation is concerned, all and more than all which I undertook to do on the Chinese Classics more than twenty–five years ago. When the first volume was published in 1891, my friend, the late Stanislas Julien, wrote to me, asking if I had duly considered the voluminousness of the Lî Kî, and expressing his doubts whether I should be able to complete my undertaking. Having begun the task, however, I have pursued it to the end, working on with some unavoidable interruptions, and amidst not a few other engagements.

The present is the first translation that has been published in any European language of the whole of the Lî Kî. In 1853 the late J. M. Callery published at the Imprimerie Royale, Turin, what he called 'Lî Kî, ou Mémorial des Rites, traduit pour la première fois du Chinois, et accompagné de Notes, de Commentaires, et du Texte Original.' But in fact the text which P. Callery adopted was only an expurgated edition, published by Fan Sze–tang, a scholar of the Yüan dynasty, as commented on and annotated by Kâu Kih, whose well–known work appeared in 1711, the 50th year of the Khang–hsî reign or period[1]. Callery has himself called attention to this in his introduction, and it is to be regretted that he did not indicate it in the title–page of his book. Fan's text omits entirely the 5th, 12th, 13th, 19th, 28th, 31st, 32nd, 33rd, 34th, 35th, 37th, and 39th Books in my translation, while of most of the others,

[1. The for which Callery gives—Combinaison des Commentaires Ta Tsüen (le Grand Complet) et Chu (I'explication), d'apris le sens original du Mémorial des rites.' Kâu Kih *has the alias of Kâu Tan–lin.]

'a good third' has been expurgated. I do not think that Callery's version contains above one half of the Lî Kî, as it is found in the great editions of the Thang and present dynasties. The latter of these was commanded in an imperial rescript in 1748, the 13th year of the Khien–lung period. The committee charged with its execution consisted of 85 dignitaries and scholars, who used the previous labours of 244 authors, besides adding, on many of the most difficult passages, their own remarks and decisions, which are generally very valuable.

My own version is based on a study of these two imperial collections, and on an extensive compilation, made specially for my use by my Chinese friend and former helper, the graduate Wang Thâo, gathered mostly from more recent writers of the last 250 years. The Khien–lung editors make frequent reference to the work of Khan Hâo, which appeared in 1322 under the modest title of, 'A Collection of Remarks on the Lî Kî[1].' This acquired so great a celebrity under the Ming dynasty, that, as Callery tells us, an edict was issued in 1403 appointing it the standard for the interpretation of the Classic at the public examinations; and this pre–eminence was accorded to it on to the Khien–lung period. The whole of the Lî Kî is given and expounded by Khan, excepting the 28th and 39th Books, which had long been current as portions of 'The Four Books.' I may say that I have read over and over, and with much benefit, every sentence in his comments. Forming my own judgment on every passage, now agreeing with him and now differing, and frequently finding reason to attach a higher value to the views of the Khien–lung editors, I must say that 'he deserves well' of the Lî Kî. His volumes are characterised by a painstaking study of the original text, and an honest attempt to exhibit the logical connexion of thought in its several parts.

[1. The author has the aliases for Hâo of Kho Tâ Yün–wang and Tung Hui; the last, I suppose, from his having lived near the lake so called.]

P. Callery's translation of his expurgated text is for the most part well executed, and his notes, of which I have often made use, are admirable. I have also enjoyed the benefit of the more recent work, 'Cursus Litteratura o Sinicae,' by P. Angelo Zottoli, in whom the scholarship of earlier Jesuit missionaries has revived. In his third the earlier volume, published at Shang–hâi in 1880, there are good translations of the 1st, 5th, 10th, 20th, 21st, and 22nd Books; while the 28th and 39th are in his second volume. In the Latin which he employs, according to the traditions of his church and what is still a practice of some scholars, he is able to be more brief in his renderings than Callery and myself, but perhaps not so satisfactory to readers generally. I also referred occasionally to Signor Carlo Puini's 'Lî–Kî: Instituzioni, Usi e Costumanze della Cina antica; Traduzione. Commento e Note (Fascicolo Primo; Firenze, i883Y

The present translation is, as I said above, the first published in any European language of the whole of the Lî Kî; but another had existed in manuscript for several years, the work of Mr. Alexander Wylie, now unhappily, by loss of eye–sight and otherwise failing health, laid aside from his important Chinese labours. I was fortunate enough to obtain possession of this when I had got to the 35th Book in my own version, and, in carrying the sheets through the press, I have constantly made reference to it. It was written at an early period of Mr. Wylie's Chinese studies, and is not such as a Sinologist of his attainments and research would have produced later on. Still I have been glad to have it by me, though I may venture to say that, in construing the paragraphs and translating the characters, I have not been indebted in a single instance to him or P. Callery. The first six Books, and portions of several others, had been written out, more than once, before I finally left China in 1873; but I began again at the beginning, early in 1883, in preparing the present version. I can hardly hope that, in translating so extensive and peculiar a work. descriptive of customs and things at so remote a period of time, and without the assistance of any Chinese graduate with whom I could have talked over complicated and perplexing paragraphs, I may not have fallen into some mistakes; but I trust they will be found to be very few. My simple and only aim has been, first, to understand the text for myself and then to render it in English, fairly and as well a I could in the time attain to, for my readers.

J. L.

OXFORD,

July 10, 1885.

INTRODUCTION.

CHAPTER I.

THREE DIFFERENT LÎ KING, OR RITUAL BOOKS, ACKNOWLEDGED IN CHINA. THE RECOVERY OF THE FIRST TWO, AND FORMATION OF THE THIRD, UNDER THE HAN DYNASTY.

How Confucius spoke of the Lî.

1. Confucius said, 'It is by the Odes that the mind is aroused; by the Rules of Propriety that the character is established; from Music that the finish is received[1].' On another occasion he said, 'Without the Rules of Propriety, respectfulness becomes laborious bustle; carefulness, timidity; boldness, insubordination; and straightforwardness, rudeness[1].'

These are two specimens of the manner in which Confucius expressed himself about the Lî, the Rules of Propriety or Ceremonial Usages, recognised in his time. It is a natural inference from his language that there were Collections of such Rules which could be read and studied; but he does not expressly say so.

How Mencius spoke of them.

The language of Mencius was more definite. In at least two passages of his works we find the usual form of quotation Lî Yüeh, 'The Lî says[2],' which, according to the analogy of Shih Yüeh, 'The Shih King, or Book of Poetry, says,' might be rendered,

[1. Confucian Analects, Book VIII, 8 and 2.

2. Works of Mencius, II, Part ii, 2. 5; III, Part ii, 3. 3.]

'The Lî. King says.' In another passage, he says to a Mr. King Khun, 'Have you not read the Lî?' It does not appear that Mencius was always referring to one and the same collection of Lî; but it is clear that in his time there were one or more such collections current and well known among his countrymen.

Now there are three Lî King, or three Rituals.

There are now three Chinese classics into which the name Lî enters:—the Î Lî, the Kâu Lî, and the Lî Kî, frequently styled, both by the Chinese themselves and by sinologists, 'The Three Rituals[2] ' The first two are books of the Kâu dynasty (B.C. 1122–225). The third, of which a complete translation is given in the present work, may contain passages of an earlier date than either of the others; but as a collection in its present form, it does not go higher than the Han dynasty, and was not completed till our second century. It has, however, taken a higher position than those others, and is ranked with the Shû, the Shih, the Yî, and the Khun Khiû, forming one of 'The Five King,' which are acknowledged as the books of greatest authority in China. Other considerations besides antiquity have given, we shall see, its eminence to the Lî Kî.

State of the Lî books at the rise of the Han an dynasty.

2. The monuments of the ancient literature, with the exception, perhaps, of the Yi King, were in a condition of disorder and incompleteness at the rise of the Han dynasty. (B.C. 206). This was the case especially with the Î Lî and Kâu Lî. They had suffered, with the other books, from the fires and proscription of the short–lived dynasty of Khin, the founder of which was bent especially on their destruction[3]; and during the closing centuries of Kâu, in all the period of 'The Warring Kingdoms,' they had been variously mutilated by the contending princess[4].

[1. Works of Mencius, III, ii, 2. 2.

2. See Wylie's Notes on Chinese Literature, p.4, and Mayers' Chinese Reader's Manual, p. 300.

3. Sze–mâ Khien's Biographies, Book 61, p. 5b. Other testimonies to the fact could be adduced.

4. Mencius V, ii, 2. 2. See also the note of Liû Hsin, appended to his catalogue of Lî works, in the Imperial library of Han.]

Work of the ancient emperors of Han in recovering the books.

The sovereigns of Han undertook the task of gathering up and arranging the fragments of the ancient books, and executed it well.. In B.C. 213 Shih Hwang Tî of Khin had promulgated his edict forbidding any one to hide and keep in his possession the old writings. This was repealed in B.C. 191 by the emperor Hui, so that it had been in existence only twenty–two years, during most of which, we may presume, it had been inoperative. Arrangements were also made to receive and preserve old tablets which might be presented[1], and to take down in writing what scholars might be able to repeat. In B.C. 164, the emperor Wan ordered 'the Great Scholars' of his court to compile 'the Royal Ordinances,' the fifth of the Books in our Lî Kî[2].

Recovery of the Î Lî.

i. Internal evidence shows that when this treatise was made, the Î Lî, or portions of it at least, had been recovered; and with this agrees the testimony of Sze–mâ Khien, who was born perhaps in that very year[3], and lived to between B.C. 90 and 80. In the 61st Book of his Biographies, referred to in a note above, Khien says, 'Many of the scholars repeated (parts of) the Lî; but no other of them so much as Kâo Thang of Lû; and now we have only the Shih Lî, which he was able to recite.' In harmony with this statement of the great historian, is the first entry in Liû Hsin's Catalogue of Lî books in the Imperial library of Han:—'56 küan or sections of Lî in the old text, and 17 phien in the (current) text (of the time);' forming, as is universally believed, the present Î Lî, for which the Shih Lî of Khien is merely another name.

That Kâo Thang should have been able to dictate so much of the work will not be thought wonderful by those who

[1. Such was the 'Stone–Conduit Gallery,' which Mayers (Manual, p. 18,5) describes as a building erected by Hsiâo Ho at Khang–an for the reception of the records of the extinct Khin dynasty, about B.C. 200, adding that 'in B.C. 51, the emperor Hsüan appointed a commission of scholars to assemble in this building, and complete the revision of the classical writings.' But it had also been' intended from the first as a repository for those writings as they were recovered.

2. See the General Mirror of History under that year.

3. Mayers puts his birth 'about B.C. 163,' and his death 'about 86.']

are familiar with the power of memory displayed by many Chinese scholars even at the present day. The sections in the old text were found in the reign of the emperor Wû (B.C. 140–87), and came into the possession of his brother, known as king Hsien of Ho–kien. We do not know how much this mass of tablets added to the Î Lî, as we now have it, but they confirmed the genuineness of the portion obtained from Kâo.

King Hsien of Ho–kien, and his recovery of the Kâu Lî.

ii. The recovery of the Kâu Lî came not long after, and through the agency of the same king Hsien. No one did so much as he in the restoration of the ancient of literature. By name Teh, and one of the fourteen sons of the emperor King (B.C. 156–141), he was appointed by his father, in B.C. 155, king of Ho–kien, which is still the name of one of the departments of Kih–lî, and there he continued till his death, in 129, the patron of all literary men, and unceasingly pursuing his quest for old books dating from before the Khin dynasty. Multitudes came to him from all quarters, bringing to him the precious tablets which had been preserved in their families or found by them elsewhere. The originals he kept in his own library, and had a copy taken, which he gave to the donor with a valuable gift. We are indebted to him in this way for the preservation of the Tâo Teh King, the works of Mencius, and other precious treasures; but I have only to notice here his services in connexion with the Lî books[1].

Some one [2] brought to him the tablets of the Kâu Lî, then called Kâu Kwan, 'The Official Book of Kâu,' and purporting to contain a complete account of the organised government of the dynasty of Kâu in six sections. The sixth section, however, which should have supplied a list of the officers in the department of the minister of Works,

[1. See the account of king Hsien in the twenty–third chapter of the Biographies in the History of the first Han dynasty. Hsien was the king's posthumous title, denoting 'The Profound and Intelligent.'

2 The Catalogue of the Sui Dynasty's (A. D. 589–618) Imperial library says this was a scholar of the surname Lî. I have been unable to trace the authority for the statement farther back.]

with their functions, was wanting, and the king offered to pay 1000 pieces of gold to any one who should supply the missing tablets, but in vain[1]. He presented the tablets which he had obtained at the court of his half–brother, the emperor Wû; but the treasure remained uncared for in one of the imperial repositories till the next century; when it came into the charge of Liû Hsin. Hsin replaced the missing portion from another old work, called Khâo Kun Kî, which Wylie renders by 'The Artificers' Record.' This has ever since continued to appear as the sixth section of the whole work, for the charge of which Hsin obtained the appointment of a special board of scholars, such as had from the first been entrusted with the care of the Î Lî. The Kâu Lî is a constitutional and not a ritual work. The last entry in Hsin's Catalogue of Lî Books is:—'The Kâu Kwan in six sections; and a treatise on the Kâu Kwan in four sections.' That is the proper name for it. It was not called the Kâu Lî till the Thang dynasty[2].

Formation of the Lî Kî.

iii. We come to the formation of the text of the Lî Kî, in which we are more particularly interested. We cannot speak of its recovery, for though parts of it had been in existence during the Kâu dynasty, many of its Books cannot claim a higher antiquity than the period of the Han. All that is known about the authorship of them all will be found in the notices which form the last chapter of this Introduction;

After the entry in Lia Hsin's Catalogue about the recovered

[1. This is related in the Catalogue of the Sui dynasty, It could not be in Khien's sixty–first chapter of Biographies, because the Kâu Kwan was not known, or, at least, not made public, in Khien's time. The Sui writers, no doubt, took it from some biography of the Han, which has escaped me.

2. A complete translation of the Kâu Lî appeared at Paris in 1851, the work of Edward Biot, who had died himself before its publication, before his fiftieth year. According to a note in Callery's 'Memorial des Rites' (p. 191), the labour of its preparation hastened Biot's death. There are some errors in the version, but they are few. I have had occasion to refer to hundreds of passages in it, and always with an increasing admiration of the author's general resources and knowledge of Chinese. His early death was the greatest loss which the cause of sinology has sustained. His labours, chiefly on Chinese subjects, had been incessant from 1835. The perusal of them has often brought to my memory the

words of Newton, 'If Mr. Cotes had lived, we should have known something.' Is there no sinologist who will now undertake a complete translation of the Î Lî?]

text of the Î Lî, 'there follows—'131 phien of Kî,' that is, so many different records or treatises on the subject of Lî. These had also been collected by king Hsien, and Kû Hsî's note about them is that they were 'Treatises composed by the disciples of the seventy disciples,' meaning by 'the seventy disciples' those of Confucius' followers who had been most in his society and, profited most from his instructions. These 131 phien contained, no doubt, the germ of our Lî Kî; but there they remained for about a century in the imperial repositories, undigested and uncared for, and constantly having other treatises of a similar nature added to them.

Council of B.C. 511.

At last, in B.C. 51, the emperor Hsüan (B.C. 71–47) convoked a large assembly of Great Scholars to meet in the Stone–Conduit Gallery, and discuss the text of the recovered classics[1]. A prominent member of this assembly, the president of it I suppose, was Liû Hsiang, himself a celebrated writer and a scion of the imperial house, who appears to have had the principal charge of all the repositories. Among the other members, and in special connexion with the Lî works, we find the name of Tâi Shang, who will again come before us[2].

B.C. 26.

We do not know what the deliberations of the Great Scholars resulted in, but twenty–five years later the emperor Khang caused another search to be made throughout the empire for books that might hitherto have escaped notice; and, when it was completed, he ordered Hsiang to examine all the contents of the repositories, and collate the various copies of the classics. From this came the preparation of a catalogue; and Hsiang dying at the age of seventy–two, in B.C. 9, before it was completed, the work was delegated to his third and youngest son Hsin. His catalogue we happily possess. It mentions, in addition to the Î Lî and

[1. See the Details in the General Mirror of History, under B.C. 51.

2. See the 58th Book of Biographies in the History of the first Han, and the Catalogue of the Sui Library.]

Kâu Lî, 199 phien of Lî treatises. The résumé appended to the Lî books in the Catalogue of the Su i Dynasty, omitting works mentioned by Hsin, and inserting two others, says that Hsiang had in his hands altogether 214 phien. What was to be done with this mass of tablets, or the written copies made from them?

Hâu Zhang and the two Tâis

The most distinguished of the Lî scholars in the time of the emperors Hsüan and Khang was a Hâu Zhang, the author of the compilation called in Hsin's Catalogue Khü Tâi Kî; and two of his disciples, Tâi Teh and Tâi Shang, cousins[1], the name of the latter of whom has already been mentioned as a member of the council of B.C. 51, were also celebrated for their ability. Teh, the older of the two, and commonly called Tâ Tâi, or 'the Greater Tâi,' while Hsiang was yet alive, digested the mass of phien, and in doing so reduced their number to 85. The younger, called Hsiâo Tâi, or 'the Lesser Tâi,' doing the same for his cousin's work, reduced it to 46 treatises. This second condensation of the Lî documents met with general acceptance, and was styled the Lî Kî. Shang himself wrote a work in twelve chapters, called 'A Discussion of the Doubts of Scholars about the Lî Kî,' which, though now lost, was existing in the time of Sui.

Mâ Yung and Kang Hsüan.

Through Khiâo Zan and others, scholars of renown in their day, the redaction passed on to the well-known Mâ Yung (A.D. 79–166), who added to Shang's books the Yüeh Ling, the Ming

[1. Sinologists, without exception I believe, have called Shang a 'nephew' of Teh, overlooking the way in which the relationship between them is expressed in Chinese. Shang is always Teh's, and not simply. Foreign students have overlooked the force of the phrase and, more fully, . Teh and Shang's father had the same grand-father, and were themselves the sons of brothers. They were therefore what we call first cousins, and Teh and Shang were second cousins. The point is unimportant, but it is well to be correct even in small matters. Not unimportant, however, is the error of Callery (Introduction, p. 6), who says, 'Le neveu, homme dépravé, beaucoup plus adonné aux plaigirs, qu'à l'étude, retrancha encore davantage et fixa le nombre des chapitres à 46.' No such stigma rests on the character of Taî Shang, and I am sure translators have reason to be grateful to him for condensing, as he did, the result of his cousin's labours.]

Thang Wei, and the Yo Kî making their number in all forty–nine, though, according to the arrangement adopted in the present translation, they still amount only to forty–six. From Mâ, again, it passed to his pupil Kang Hsüan (A.D. 127–200), in whom be was obliged to acknowledge a greater scholar than himself.

Thus the Lî Kî was formed. It is not necessary to pursue its history farther. Kang was the scholar of his age, and may be compared, in scholarship, with the later Kû Hsî. And he has been fortunate in the preservation of his works. He applied himself to all the three Rituals, and his labours on them all, the Kâu Lî, the Î Lî, and the Lî Kî, remain. His commentaries on them are to be found in the great work of 'The Thirteen King' of the Thang dynasty. There they appear, followed by the glosses, illustrations, and paraphrases of Khung Ying–tâ.

Zhâi Yung and his manusculpt.

In A.D. 175, while Kang was yet alive, Zhâi Yung, a scholar and officer of many gifts, superintended the work of engraving on stone the text of all the Confucian classics. Only fragments of that great manusculpt {*sic*} remain to the present day, but others of the same nature were subsequently made. We may feel assured that we have the text of the Lî Kî and other old Chinese books, as it was 1800 years ago, more correctly than any existing Manuscripts give us that of any works of the West, Semitic, or Greek, or Latin, of anything like equal antiquity.

Lî of the Greater Tâi.

3. A few sentences on the Lî of the Greater Tâi will fitly close this chapter. He handed down his voluminous compilation to a Hsü Liang of Lang Yeh in the present Shan–tung[1], and in his family it was transmitted; but if any commentaries on it were published, there is no trace of them in history. As the shorter work of his cousin obtained a wide circulation, his fell into neglect, and, as Kû Î–zun says, was simply put upon the shelf. Still there appears in the Sui Catalogue these two entries:—'The Lî Kî of Tâ Tâi, in 13 Sections,' and 'The Hsiâ

[1. .]

Hsiâo Kang, in 1 Section,' with a note by the editor that it was compiled by Tâ Tâi. This little tractate may, or may not, have been also included in one of the 13 Sections. There are entries also about Tâ Tâi's work in the catalogues of the Thang and Sung dynasties, which have given rise to many discussions. Some of the Sung scholars even regarded it as a 14th King. In the large collection of 'Books of Han and Wei,' a portion of the Lî of Tâ Tâi is still current, 39 Book in 10 Sections, including thc fragment of the Hsiâ dynasty, of which a version, along with the text, was published in 1882 by Professor Douglas of King's College, under the title of 'The Calendar of the Hsiâ Dynasty.' I have gone over all the portion in the Han and Wei Collection, and must pronounce it very inferior to the compilation of the Hsiâo or Lesser Tâi. This inferiority, and not the bulk, merely, was the reason why from the first it has been comparatively little attended to.

CHAPTER II.

SIGNIFICANCE OF THE CHINESE CHARACTER CALLED LÎ. MEANING OF THE TITLE LÎ KÎ. VALUE OF THE WORK.

Lî is a symbol of religious import.

1. The Chinese character Lî admits of a great variety of terms in translating a work where it abounds into any of our western languages. In order fully to apprehend its significance, we must try to get bold of the fundamental ideas which it was intended to convey. And these are two. First, when we consult the Shwo Wan, the oldest Chinese dictionary, we find Lî defined as 'a step or act; that whereby we serve spiritual beings and obtain happiness.' The character was to the author, Hsü Shan, an ideagram of religious import; and we can see that he rightly interpreted the intention of its maker or makers. It consists of two elements, separately called khih and lî[1]. That on the left is the symbol,

[1. .]

determining the category of meaning to which the compound belongs. It was the earliest figure employed to indicate spiritual beings, and enters into characters denoting spirits, sacrifices, and prayer[1]. That on the right, called lî, is phonetic, but even it is the symbol for (a vessel used in performing rites;' and if, as the Khang–hsî dictionary seems to say, it was anciently used alone for the present compound, still the spiritual significance would attach to it, and the addition of the khih to complete the character, whensoever it was made, shows that the makers considered the rites in which the vessel was used to possess in the first place a religious import.

Lî is a symbol for the feeling of propriety.

Next, the character is used, in moral and philosophical disquisitions, to designate one of the primary constituents of human nature. Those, as set forth by Mencius, are four; 'not fused into us from without,' not produced, that is, by any force of circumstances, but 'belonging naturally to us, as our four limbs do.' They are benevolence (zan), righteousness (î), propriety (lî), and understanding (kîh). Our possession of the first is proved by the feeling of distress at the sight of suffering; of the second, by our feelings of shame and dislike; of the third, by our feelings of modesty and courtesy; of the fourth, by our consciousness of approving and disapproving[2].

Thus the character lî, in the concrete application of it, denotes the manifestations, and in its imperative use, the rules, of propriety. This twofold symbolism of it—the religious and the moral—must be kept in mind in the study of our classic. A life ordered in harmony with it would realise the highest Chinese ideal, and surely a very high ideal, of human character.

But never and, nowhere has it been possible for men to maintain this high standard of living. In China and elsewhere the lî have become, in the usages of society in. its various relationships, matters of course, forms without the

[1. E.g. (shan),, (kî), (khi).

2. Mencius, II, i, 6; VI, i, 6. 7.]

spirit, and hence we cannot always translate the character by the same term. It would be easy to add to the number of words, more or less synonymous, in French or English or any other Aryan language, which Callery has heaped together in the following passage:—'Autant que possible, j'ai traduit Lî par le mot Rite, dont le sens est susceptible à une grande étendue; mais il faut convenir que, suivant les circonstances où il est employé, il peut signifier—Cérémonial, Cérémonies, Pratiques cérémoniales, L'étiquette, Politesse, Urbanité, Courtoisie, Honnêteté, Bonnes manières, Égards, Bonne éducation, Bienséance, Les formes, Les convenances, Savoir–vivre, Décorum, Décence, Dignité personnelle, Moralité de conduite, Ordre Social, Devoirs de Société, Lois Sociales, Devoirs, Droit, Morale, Lois hiérarchiques, Offrande, Usages, Coutumes[1].' I have made little use in my translation of the word Rite or Rites, which Callery says he had endeavoured to adhere to as much as possible, but I do not think I have allowed myself so much liberty in other terms in my English as he has done in his French. For the symbol in the title I have said 'Rules of Propriety or Ceremonial Usages.'

Translation of the title.

2. The meaning of the title—Lî Kî–need not take us so long. There is no occasion to say more on the significance of Lî; the other character, Kî, should have a plural force given to it. What unity belongs to the Books composing it arises from their being all, more or less, occupied with the subject of Lî. Each one, or at least each group, is complete in itself. Each is a Ki; taken together, they are so many Kîs. Only into the separate titles of seven of them, the 13th, 16th, 17th, 18th, 19th, 27th, and 29th, does the name of Kî enter. That character is the symbol for 'the recording of things one by one,' and is often exchanged for another Kî[2], in which the classifying element is sze, the symbol for 'a packet of cocoons,' the compound denoting the unwinding

[1. Introduction, p. 16.

2. The classifier of Kî in the title is (yen), the symbol of words; that of this this Kî is (sze).]

and arrangement of the threads'. Wylie's 'Book of Rites' and Callery's 'Mémorial des Rites' always failed to give me a definite idea of the nature of our classic. Sze–mâ Khien's work is called Sze Kî [2], or 'Historical Records,' and Lî Kî might in the same way be rendered 'Ceremonial Records,' but I have preferred to give for the title, 'A Collection of Treatises on the Rules of Propriety or Ceremonial Usages.'

The value of the Lî Kî.

3. The value of the work has been discussed fully by P. Callery in the sixth paragraph of the Introduction to his translation of an abbreviated edition of it, and with much of what he has said I am happy to feel myself in accord. I agree with him, for instance, that the book is 'the most exact and complete monography which the Chinese nation has been able to give of itself to the rest of the human race.' But this sentence occurs in a description of the Chinese spirit, which is little better than a caricature. 'Le cérémonial,' he says, 'résume l'esprit Chinois. . . . Ses affections, si elle en a, sont satisfaites par le cérémonial; ses devoirs, elle les remplit au moyen du cérémonial; la vertu et le vice, elle les reconnait au cérémonial; en un mot, pour elle le cérémonial c'est l'homme, l'homme moral, l'homme politique, l'homme religieux, Dans ses multiples rapports avec la famille, la société, l'état, la morale et la religion.'

To all this representation the first sentence of our classic is a sufficient reply:—'Always and in everything let there be reverence.' In hundreds of other passages the same thing is insisted on,—that ceremony without an inspiring reverence is nothing. I do not deny that there is much attention to forms in China with a forgetfulness of the spirit that should animate them. But where is the nation against whose people the same thing may not be charged? The treaties of western nations with China contain an article stipulating for the toleration of Chinese Christians on the ground that, 'The Christian religion, as professed by

[1. Structure of Chinese Characters, p. 132.

2. .]

Protestants or Roman Catholics, inculcates the practice of virtue, and teaches man to do as he would be done by[1].' Scores of Chinese, officers, scholars, and others, have, in conversations with myself, asked if such were indeed the nature of Christianity, appealing at the same time to certain things which they alleged that made them doubt it. All that can be said in the matter is this, that as the creeds Of men elsewhere are often better than their practice, so it is in China. Whether it be more so there or here is a point on which different conclusions will be come to, according to the knowledge and prejudices of the speculators.

More may be learned about the religion of the ancient Chinese from this classic than from all the others together. Where the writers got their information about the highest worship and sacrifices of the most ancient times, and about the schools of Shun, we do not know. They expressed the views, doubtless, that were current during the Han dynasty, derived partly from tradition, and partly from old books which were not gathered up, or, possibly, from both those sources. But let not readers expect to find in the Lî Kî anything like a theology. The want of dogmatic teaching of religion in the Confucian system may not be all a disadvantage and defect; but there is a certain amount of melancholy truth in the following observations of Callery:—'Le Lî Kî, celui de tous les King où les questions religieuses auraient dû être traitécs tout naturellement, à propos des sacrifices au Ciel, aux Dieux tutélaires, et aux ancêtres, glisse légèment sur tout ce qui est de pure spéculation, et ne mentionne ces graves matières qu'avec une extrême indifférence. Selon moi ceci prouve deux choses: la première, que dans les temps anciens les plus grand génies de la Chine n'ont possédé sur le créateur, sur la nature et les destinées de l'âme, que des notions obscures, incertaines et souvent contradictoires; la seconde, que les Chinois possèdent à un trés faible degré le sentiment religieux, et qu'ils n'éprouvent pas, comme les races de

[1. From the eighth article in the Treaty with Great Britan, 1858.]

l'occident, le besoin impérieux de sonder les mystères du monde invisible.'

The number of the Kî that are devoted to the subject of the mourning rites shows how great was the regard of the people for the departed members of their families. The solidarity of the family, and even the solidarity of the race, is a sentiment which has always been very strong among them. The doctrine of filial piety has also the prominence in several Books which we might expect.

As to the philosophical and moral ideas which abound in the work, they are, as Callery says, 'in general, sound and profound.' The way in which they are presented is not unfrequently eccentric, and hedged about with absurd speculations on the course of material nature, but a prolonged study of the most difficult passages will generally bring to light what Chinese scholars call a tâo–li, a ground of reason or analogy, which interests and satisfies the mind.

The Lî Kî as one of the Five King.

4. The position that came gradually to be accorded to the Lî Kî as one of 'The Five King,' par excellence, was a tribute to its intrinsic merit. It did not, like the Kâu Lî, treat of matters peculiar to one dynasty, but of matters important in all time; nor like the Î Lî, of usages belonging to one or more of the official classes, but of those that concerned all men. The category of 'Five King' was formed early, but the 'Three Rituals' were comprehended in it as of equal value, and formed one subdivision of it. So it was early in the Thang dynasty when the collection of 'The Thirteen King' was issued; but ere the close of that dynasty our classic had made good its eminence over the other two Rituals. In the 29th chapter of the Monographs of Thang, page 17, it is said, 'To the charge of each of the Five King two Great Scholars were appointed. The Yî of Kâu, the Shang Shû, the Shih of Mâo, the Khun Khiû, and the Lî Kî are the Five King.'

CHAPTER III.

BRIEF NOTICES OF THE DIFFERENT BOOKS WHICH MAKE UP THE COLLECTION.

BOOK I. KHÜ LÎ.

This first Book in the collection is also the longest, and has been divided because of its length into two Books. In this translation, however, it appears only as one Book in two Sections, which again are subdivided, after the Khien–lung editors, into five Parts and three Parts respectively.

The name Khü Lî is taken from the first two characters in the first paragraph, and the first sentence, 'The Khü Lî says, 'extends over all that follows to the end of the Book. P. Callery, indeed, puts only the first paragraph within inverted commas, as if it alone were from the Khü Lî, and the rest of the Book were by a different hand. He translates the title by 'Rites Divers,' and to his first sentence, 'Le Recueil des rites divers dit,' appends the following note :—'This work, that for a very long time has been lost, was, so far as appears, one of those collections of proverbs and maxims with which philosophy has commenced among nearly all peoples. Although the author does not say so, it is probable that this chapter and the next contain an analysis of that ancient collection, for the great unconnectedness which we find in it agrees well with the variety indicated by the title Khü Lî.' My own inference from the text, however, is what I have stated above, that the

Book is a transcript of the Khü Lî, and not merely a condensation of its contents, or a redaction of them by a different author.

It is not easy to translate the title satisfactorily. According to Kang Hsüan (or Kang Khang-khang), the earliest of all the great commentators on the Lî Kî, 'The Book is named Khü Lî, because it contains matters relating to all the five ceremonial categories. What is said in it about sacrifices belongs to the "auspicious ceremonies;" about the rites of mourning, and the loss or abandonment of one's state, to the "inauspicious;" about the payment of tributory dues and appearances at the royal court, to "the rites of hospitality;" about weapons, chariots, and banners, "to those of war;" and about serving elders, reverencing the aged, giving offerings or presents, and the marriage of daughters, to the "festive ceremonies."' On this view the title would mean 'Rules belonging to the different classes of ceremonies,' or, more concisely, the 'Rites Divers' of Callery; and Mr. Wylie has called the Book 'The Universal Ritual.'

But this rendering of the title does not suit the proper force of the character Khü, which is the symbol of 'being bent or crooked,' and is used, with substantival meaning, for what is small and appears irregularly. Mention is made in Book XXVIII, ii, 23, Of 'him who cultivates the shoots of goodness in his nature,' those 'shoots' being expressed by this character Khü; and in a note on the passage there I have quoted the words of the commentator Pâi Lü:—'Put a stone on a bamboo shoot, or where the shoot would show itself, and it will travel round the stone, and come out crookedly at its side.' Thus Khü is employed for what is exhibited partially or in a small degree. Even Kang Hsüan on that passage explains it by 'very small matters;' and the two ablest in my opinion of all the Chinese critics and commentators., Kû Hsî and Wû Khang (of the Yüan dynasty, A.D. 1249–1333), take our title to mean 'The minuter forms and smaller points of ceremony.' P. Zottoli is not to be blamed for following them, and styling the Book—'Minutiores Ritus.' Still even this does not satisfy my own mind. Great rites are mentioned in the treatise as well as small ones. Principles of ceremony are enunciated as well as details. The contents are marked indeed by the 'unconnectedness' which Callery mentions; but a translator cannot help that. The Book may not be as to method all that we could wish, but we must make the best we can of it as it stands; and I have ventured to call it 'A Summary of the Rules of Ceremony.' It occupies very properly the place at the beginning of the collection, and is a good introduction to the treatises that follow.

Among the Lî books in Lâo Hsin's Catalogue of the Imperial Library of Han, is a Treatise in nine chapters (phien), compiled by Hâu Zhang, and called Khü Thâi Ki, or 'Record made in the Khü Tower.' The Khü Tower was the name of an educational building, where scholars met in the time of the emperor Hsüan to discuss, questions about ceremonies and other matters connected with the ancient literature, and Hâu Zhang (mentioned in the preceding chapter) kept a record of their proceedings. I should like to think that our Khü Lî is a portion of that Khü Thâi Kî, and am sorry not to be able to adduce Chinese authorities who take the same view. It would relieve us of the –difficulty of accounting for the use of Khü in the title.

BOOK II. THAN KUNG

The name Than Kung given to this Book is taken from the first paragraph in it, where the gentleman so denominated appears attending the mourning rites for an officer of the state of Lû. Nowhere else in the Treatise, however, is there any mention of him, or reference to him. There can be no reason but this, for calling it after him, that his surname and name occur at the commencement of it. He was a native, it is understood, of Lû; but nothing more is known of him.

The Than Kung, like the Khü Lî, is divided into two Books, which appear in this translation as two Sections of one Book. Each Section is subdivided into three Parts.

The whole is chiefly occupied with the observances of the mourning rites. It is valuable because of the information which it. gives about them, and the views prevailing at the time on the subject of death. It contains also many historical incidents about Confucius and others, which we are glad to possess. Some of the commentators, and especially the Khien–lung editors, reject many of them as legendary and fabulous. The whole Book is reduced to very small compass in the expurgated editions of the Lî Kî. We are glad, however, to have the incidents such as they are. Who would not be sorry to want the account of Confucius' death, which is given in I, ii, 20? We seem, moreover, to understand him better from accounts which the Book contains of his intercourse with his disciples, and of their mourning for him.

Dze–yû[1], an eminent member of his school, appears in the first paragraph much to his credit, and similarly afterwards on several occasions; and this has made the Khien–lung editors throw out the suggestion that the Book was compiled by his disciples. It may have been so.

BOOK III. WANG KIH.

According to Lû Kih (died A.D. 192)[2], the Wang Kih, or 'Royal Regulations,' was made by the Great Scholars of the time of the emperor Wan (B.C. 179–157), on the requisition of that sovereign[3]. It professes to give the regulations of the early kings on the classes of the feudal nobles and officers and their emoluments, on their sacrifices, and their care for the aged. The emperor ordered it to be compiled after the death of Kiâ Î, a Great scholar and highly esteemed by the sovereign, which event must have taken place about B.C. 170, when Kih was only thirty–three. The Book is said to have contained, when it first appeared, an account of the royal progresses and of the altars and ceremonies of investiture, of which we do not now find any trace. Parts of it are taken from Mencius, from the Shû, and from the Commentaries of Kung–yang and Zo on the Khun Khiû; other parts again are not easily reconciled with those authorities.

[1. .

2. See the 54th Book of the Biographies in the History of the Second Han Dynasty.

3. In B.C. 164. See the Mirror of History on that year.]

The Khien–lung editors deliver their judgment on it to the following effect: When it was made, the Î Lî must have appeared, but not the Kâu Lî. Hence the Banquet and Missions appear among the 'Six Subjects of Teaching,' and no mention is made of the minister of Religion, as one of the six great ministers, nor is anything said of the minister of War's management of the army. On a general view of it, many subjects are evidently based on Mencius, and whole paragraphs are borrowed from him. Nothing is said of the peculiar position of the son of Heaven, because in the Han dynasty, succeeding immediately to that of Khin, the emperor was to be distinguished from, and not named along with, the feudal princes. In what is said about the reports of the Income and fixing the Expenditure, only the Grand ministers of Instruction, War, and Works are mentioned, because these were the three ducal ministers of the Han dynasty, and the ancient arrangements were represented so as to suit what had come into existence. That nothing is said about altars and investitures arose from Wan's having disregarded in that matter the advice of Hsin–yüan Phing[1]. It only shows how much the information of the compilers exceeded that of Shû–sun Thung[2] and Sze–mâ Hsiang–zû[3]. The Book was received into the collection of the Lî Kî, because it was made at no great distance from antiquity. It is foolish in later scholars to weigh and measure every paragraph of it by its agreement or disagreement with Mencius and the Kâu Lî.

This account of the Wang Kih must commend itself to unprejudiced readers. To myself, the most interesting thing in the Book is the information to be gathered from it about the existence of schools in the earliest times. We see at the very commencement of history in China a

[1. A Tâoistic charlatan, honoured and followed for a few years by the emperor Wan; put to death in B.C. 163.

2. A scholar of Khin; was a counsellor afterwards of the first and second emperors of Han.

3 An officer and author. Died B.C. 126.]

rudimentary education, out of which has come by gradual development the system of examinations of the present day.

BOOK IV. YÜEH LING.

The Yüeh Ling, or 'Proceedings of Government in the different Months,' appears in the Khien–lung edition of the Lî Kî in six Sections; but it has seemed to me more in, harmony with the nature of the Book and more useful for the student to arrange it in four Sections, and each Section in three Parts, a Section thus comprehending a season of the year, and every month having a part to itself. There is also a short supplementary Section in the middle of the year, at the end of the sixth month, rendered necessary by the Tâoist lines on which the different portions are put together.

Zhâi Yung (A. D. 133–192)[1] and Wang Sû[2], somewhat later (in our third century), held that the Book was the work of the duke of Kâu, and must be assigned to the eleventh or twelfth century B.C. But this view of its antiquity may be said to be universally given up. Even King Hsüan saw in the second century that it was a compilation from the Khun Khiû of Lü Pû–Wei[3], still foolishly said by many Chinese writers to have been the real father of the founder of the Khin dynasty, and who died in B.C. 237. Lû Teh–ming[4], writing in our seventh century, said, 'The Yüeh Ling was originally part of Lü's Khun Khiû, from which some one subsequently compiled this Memoir. The Khien–lung editors unhesitatingly affirm this origin of the Yüeh Ling; as indeed no one, who has compared it with–thc work ascribed to Lü, can have any doubts on the matter. Of that work, Mayers says that 'it is a collection of quasi–historical notices, and, although nominally Lü's production, really compiled under his direction by an assemblage of scholars.' Mayers adds, that on the completion of the work, Lü Pû–wei suspended 1000 pieces of gold at the gate of his palace, which he offered as a reward to any one who could suggest an improvement of it by adding or expunging a single character[1].

Such was the origin of the Yüeh Ling. We do not know who compiled it from the Khun Khiu of Lü, but it was first received into the Lî Kî by Mâ Yung. It can be explained only by noting the Khin peculiarities in the names of titles and other things. It is in itself full of interest, throwing light on the ancient ways and religious views, and showing how the latter more especially came to be corrupted by the intrusion among them of Tâoistic elements.

The Book has sometimes been called 'A Calendar of the Months of Kâu.' Callery translates the name Yüeh Ling by 'Attributs des Mois.' My own translation of it is after King Hsüan, who says, 'The Book is called, Yüeh Ling, because it records the proceedings of Government in the twelve months of the year.'

BOOK V. ZANG–DZE WAN.

This Book is named from the first three characters in it, meaning 'The Questions of Zang–dze.' Most of the different paragraphs or chapters in the two Sections of it commence in the same way. It is not found at all in the expurgated editions of the classic.

Zang–dze, or Mr. Zang[2], about fifty years younger than Confucius, was one of the chief disciples of his school, perhaps the ablest among them. He was distinguished for his filial piety, and straightforward, honest simplicity.

[1. Mayers 'Chinese Reader's Manual, p. 145. The 1000 pieces of gold suspended at Lü's gate are probably only a variation of what has been related in the preceding chapter of what was done by king Hsien of Ho–kien towards the recovery of the missing Book of the Kâu Kwan.

2. ; his name was (Shan,), and that which he received in his maturity, Dze–yü.]

There is an interesting account of his death in Book II, i, Part i, 18. In the department of Liû Hsin's Catalogue, which contains 'Works of the Literati' there are entered '18 Treatises (phien) of Zang–dze,' but without any further specification of them. Ten of those treatises, or fragments of them, are found in the Lî of the Greater Tâi, but this Book is not among them, nor have I seen it anywhere ascribed to him as the writer of it. It must have been compiled, however, from memoranda left by him or some of his intimate disciples. The names of only two other disciples of the Master occur in it–those of Dze–yû and Dze–hsiâ[1]. The reference to the disciples of the former in Section ii, 19, must be a note by the final compiler. The mention of Lâo–dze or Lâo Tan, and his views also, in Section ii, 22, 24, 28, strikes us as remarkable.

If it were necessary to devise a name for the Book, I should propose—'Questions of Casuistry on the subject of Ceremonial Rites.' Zang–dze propounds difficulties that have struck him on various points of ceremony, especially in connexion with the rites of mourning; and Confucius replies to them ingeniously and with much fertility. Some of the questions and answers, however, are but so much trifling. Khung Ying–tâ says that only Zang–dze could have proposed the questions, and only Confucius have furnished the answers. He applies to the Book the description of the Yî in the third of the Appendixes to that classic, i, 40, as 'Speaking of the most complex phenomena under the sky, and having nothing in it to awaken dislike, and of the subtlest movements under the sky, and having nothing in it to produce confusion.'

BOOK VI. WAN WANG SHIH–DZE.

No hint is given, nothing has been suggested, as to who was the compiler of this Book, which the Khien–lung editors publish in two Sections. Its name is taken from the first

[1. and .]

clause of the first paragraph, which treats of king Win, the founder of the Kâu dynasty, as he demeaned himself in his youth, when he was Shih–dze, or son and heir of his father. This is followed by a similar account of his son, who became king Wû; and in paragraph 3 the writer goes on to the duke of Kâu's training of king Khing, the young son of Wû. In the last paragraph of the second Section, the subject of king Wan as prince is resumed.

But the real subject–matter of the Book lies between those portions, and treats of three things.

First; Section i, paragraph 5 to the end, treats of the education and training of the eldest sons of the king and feudal princes, and of the young men of brightest promise throughout the kingdom, chosen to study with these. We learn much from it as to the educational institutions and methods of ancient times.

Second; in Section ii, paragraphs 1 to 15, we have the duties of the Shû–dze, the head of an official Section, belonging to the department of the premier, whose special business was with the direction of the young noblemen of the royal and feudal courts in all matters belonging to their instruction.

Third; from paragraph 17 to 23 of Section ii, we have an account of the various ceremonies or observances in the king's feasting and cherishing of the aged, and of his care that a similar course should be pursued by all the princes in their states.

BOOK VII. LÎ YUN.

Lî Yun means, literally, 'The Conveyance of Rites.' P. Callery translates the name, not unsuccessfully, by 'Phases du Cerémonial;' but I prefer my own longer rendering of it, because it gives the reader a better idea of the contents of the Book. Kang Hsüan said it was called the Conveyance of Rites, because it records how the five Tîs and three Kings made their several changes in them, and how the Yin and the Yang, or the twofold movement and operation of nature, produced them by their revolutions. The whole is difficult and deep; and no other portion of the collection has tasked the ablest commentators more. The Khien–lung editors say that we have in the Book a grand expression of the importance of ceremonial usages, and that, if we are on our guard against a small Tâoistic element in it, it is pure and without a flaw. That depraving element, they think, was introduced by the smaller Tâi, who ignorantly thought he could make the Treatise appear to have a higher character by surreptitiously mixing it up with the fancies of Lâo, and Kwang. But the Tâoistic admixture is larger than they are willing to allow.

Some have attributed the Book to Dze–yû, who appears, in the first of its Sections, three times by his surname and name of Yen Yen, as the questioner of Confucius, and thereby giving occasion to the exposition of the sage's views; others attribute it to his disciples. The second Section commences with an utterance of Confucius without the prompting of any interlocutor; and perhaps the compiler meant that all the rest of the Treatise should be received as giving not only the Master's ideas, but also his words. Whoever made the Book as we now have it, it is one of the most valuable in the whole work. Hwang Kan (in the end of the Sung dynasty) says of it, that notwithstanding the appearance, here and there, of Tâoistic elements, it contains many admirable passages, and he instances what is said about creation or the processes of nature, in iii, 2; about government, in ii, 18; about man, in iii, 1, 7; and about ceremonial usages, in iv, 6.

But the Tâoistic element runs through the whole Book, as it does through Book IV. There is an attempt to sew the fancies about numbers, colours, elements, and other things on to the common–sense and morality of Confucianism. But nevertheless, the Treatise bears important testimony to the sense of religion as the first and chief element of ceremonies, and to its existence in the very earliest times.

BOOK VIII. LÎ KHÎ

Book VII, it was said, has been attributed to Dze–yû. I have not seen this ascribed to any one; but it is certainly a sequel to the other, and may be considered as having proceeded from the same author. The more the two are studied together, the more likely will this appear.

Callery has not attempted to translate the title, and says that the two characters composing it give the sense of 'Utensils of Rites,' and have no plausible relation with the scope of the Book in which there is no question in any way of the material employed either in sacrifices or in other ceremonies; and he contends, therefore, that they should not be translated, but simply be considered as sounds[1].

But the rendering which I have given is in accordance with an acknowledged usage of the second character, Khî. We read in the Confucian Analects, V, 3:—'Dze–kung asked, "What do you say of me?" The Master answered, "You are a vessel." "What vessel?" "A sacrificial vessel of jade."' The object of the Book is to show how ceremonial usages or rites go to form 'the vessel of honour,' 'the superior man,' who is equal to the most difficult and important services. Kang Hsüan saw this clearly, and said, 'The Book was named Lî Khi, because it records how ceremonies cause men to become perfect vessels.' 'The former Book shows the evolution of Rites; this shows the use of them:'—such was the dictum in A.D. 1113 of Fang Küeh, a commentator often quoted by Khan Hâo and by the Khien–lung editors.

Throughout the Book it is mostly religious rites that are spoken of; especially as culminating in the worship of God. And nothing is more fully brought out than that all rites are valueless without truth and reverence.

[1. .]

BOOK IX. KIÂO THEH SANG.

The name of the Book is made up of the three characters with which it commences, just as the Hebrew name for the Book of Genesis in our Sacred Scriptures is Beraishith ({*BeRAShiTh*}). From the meaning, however, of Kiâo Theh Sang the reader is led to suppose that he will find the Treatise occupied principally with an account of the great Border Sacrifice. But it is not so.

The main subject of the Book is sacrifice generally; and how that which is most valuable in it is the reverence and sincerity of the worshipper, finding its exhibition in the simplicity of his observances. In the preceding Book different conditions have been mentioned which are of special value in sacrifice and other ceremonies. Among them is the paucity of things (Section i, paragraph 8); and this consideration is most forcibly illustrated by 'the Single Victim' employed in the Border Sacrifice, the greatest of all ceremonies. At the same time various abuses of the ancient sincerity and simplicity are exposed and deplored.

The ceremonies of capping and marriage are dealt with in the third Section; and we are thankful for the information about them which it supplies. In the end the writer returns to the subject of sacrifices; and differences in the different dynasties, from the time of Shun downwards, in the celebration of them are pointed out.

The Khien-lung editors say that this Book was originally one with the last, and 'was separated from it by some later hand.' I had come to the same conclusion before I noticed their judgment. Books VII, VIII, and IX must have formed, I think, at first one Treatise.

BOOK X. NÊI ZEH.

The title of this book, meaning 'The Pattern of the Family,' rendered by Callery, 'Réglements Intérieurs,' approximates to a description of its contents more than most of the titles in the Lî Kî. It is not taken, moreover, from any part of the text near the commencement or elsewhere. It is difficult to understand why so little of it is retained in the expurgated editions, hardly more than a page of P. Callery's work being sufficient for it.

Kang Hsüan says:—'The Book takes its name of Nêi Zeh, because it records the rules for sons and daughters in serving their parents, and for sons and their wives in serving her parents-in-law in the family-home. Among the other Treatises of the Lî Kî, it may be considered as giving the Rules for Children. And because the observances of the harem are worthy of imitation, it is called Nêi Zeh, "the Pattern of the Interior."' Kû Hsî says, that 'it is a Book which was taught to the people in the ancient schools, an ancient Classic or Sacred Text.'

Because the name of Zang-dze and a sentence from him occur, the Khien-lung editors are inclined to ascribe the authorship to his disciples; but the premiss is too narrow to support such a conclusion.

The position of the wife, as described in Section i, will appear to western readers very deplorable. Much in this part of the Treatise partakes of the exaggeration that is characteristic of Chinese views of the virtue of filial piety.

The account in Section ii of the attention paid to the aged, and the nourishing of them, is interesting, but goes, as the thing itself did, too much into details. What is it to us at the present time how they made the fry, the bake, the delicacy, and the other dishes to tempt the palate and maintain the strength? The observances in the relation of husband and wife, on the birth of a child, and the education and duties of the young of both sexes, which the Section goes on to detail, however, are not wanting in attraction.

BOOK XI. YÜ ZÂO.

The name of the Book, Yü Zâo, is taken from the first clause of the first paragraph. The two characters denote the pendants of the royal cap worn on great occasions, and on which beads of jade were strung. There were twelve of those pendants hanging down, before and behind, from the ends of the square or rectangular top of the cap, as in the cardinal cap which is the crest of Christ Church, Oxford. But we read nothing more of this cap or its pendants after the first paragraph; and the contents of all the three Sections of the Book are so various, that it is impossible to give an account of them in small compass.

King Hsüan said that the Book was named Yü Zâo, because it recorded the dresses and caps warn by the son of Heaven; but it is not confined to the king, but introduces rulers also and officers generally. It treats also of other matters besides dress, which it would be difficult to speak of in so many categories. Much, moreover, of the second Section seems to consist of disjecta membra, and the paragraphs are differently arranged by different editors. Here and there the careful reader will meet with sentiments and sentences that will remain in his memory, as in reading Book I; but he will only carry away a vague impression of the Book as a whole.

BOOK XII. MING THANG WEI.

Readers will turn to this Book, as I did many years ago, expecting to find in it a full description of the Ming Thang, generally called by sinologists, 'The Brilliant Hall,' and 'The Hall of Light;' but they will find that the subject–matter is very different. I have here translated the name by 'the Hall of Distinction,' according to the meaning of it given in paragraph 5, taking 'distinction' in the sense of separation or discrimination.

The Treatise commences with, but does not fairly describe, the great scene in the life of the duke of Kâu, when a regent of the kingdom, he received all the feudal lords and the chiefs of the barbarous tribes at the capital, on occasion of a grand audience or durbar. The duke was the ancestor of the lords or marquises of the state of Lû,—part of the present province of Shan–tung. He was himself, indeed, invested with that fief by his nephew, king Khang, though, remaining for reasons of state at the royal court, he never took possession of it in person, but sent his son Po–khin to do so in his room. Because of his great services in the establishment and consolidation of the new dynasty, however, various privileges were conferred on the rulers of Lû above the lords of other states. These are much exaggerated in the Book; and after the sixth paragraph, we hear no more of the Hall of Distinction. All that follows is occupied with the peculiar privileges said to have been claimed, and antiques reported to have been possessed, by the marquises of Lû. What is said has no historical value, and the whole Book is excluded from the expurgated editions.

The Khien–lung editors say that its author must have been an ignorant and vainglorious scholar of Lû in the end of the Kâu dynasty. Some have imagined that it was handed on, with additions of his own, by Mâ Yung to Kang Hsüan; but the latter says nothing about the other in his brief prefatory note.

The Hall of Distinction was a royal structure. Part of it was used as a temple, at the sacrifices in which peculiar honour was done to king Wan (The Shih, IV, i, 7). It was also used for purposes of audience, as on the occasion referred to in this Book; and governmental regulations were promulgated from it (Mencius, I, ii, 5). To this third use of it would belong the various references to it in Book IV of this collection.

The principal Hall was in the capital; but there were smaller ones with the same name at the four points where the kings halted in their tours of inspection to receive the feudal lords of the different quarters of the kingdom. It was one of these which Mencius had in his mind in the passage referred to above.

In the 67th Book of the Lî of the Greater Tâi there, is a description of the building and its various parts; and among the 'Books of Kâu' said to have been found in A.D. 279 in the grave of king Hsiang of Wei, the 55th chapter has the title of Ming Thang, but it is little more than a rifacimento of the first four paragraphs of this Book of the Lî Kî.

In Morrison's Chinese Dictionary, vol. i, p. 512, there is a ground–plan of the Hall according to a common representation of it by Chinese authorities.

BOOK XIII. SANG FÛ HSIÂO KÎ.

This 'Record of Smaller Points in connexion with the Dress of Mourning,' is the first of the many treatises in our collection, devoted expressly to the subject of the mourning rites, and especially of the dress worn by the mourners, according to the degree of their relationship. The expurgated editions do not give any part of it; and it is difficult—I may say impossible—to trace any general plan on which the compiler, who is unknown, put the different portions of it together. Occasionally two or three paragraphs follow one another on the same subject) and I have kept them together after the example of Khung Ying–tâ; but the different notices are put down as if at random, just as they occurred to the writer.

Kû Hsî says that Dze–hsiâ made a supplementary treatise to the 11th Book of the Î Lî, and that we have here an explanation of many points in that Book. It is so; and yet we may not be justified in concluding that this is a remnant of the production of Dze–hsiâ.

BOOK XIV. TÂ KWAN.

This Book, 'the Great Treatise,' has been compared to the Hsî Zhze, the longest and most important of the Appendixes to the Yî King, which is also styled Tâ Kwan.

It is short, however, as compared with that other; nor is it easy to understand, the subjects with which it deals being so different in the conceptions of Chinese and western minds. 'It treats,' said Khan Hsiang–tâo (early in the Sung dynasty), 'of the greatest sacrifice,—that offered by the sovereign to all his ancestors; of the greatest instance of filial piety,—that of carrying back to his forefathers the title gained by the sacrificer; of the greatest principle in the regulation of the family,—that expressed by the arrangement of the names of its members according to their relations to one another; and of the course of humanity as the greatest illustration of propriety and righteousness. On account of this it is called The Great Treatise.'

From this summary of its contents the importance of the Book will be seen. We know nothing either of its author or of the date of its compilation.

BOOK XV. SHÂO Î.

The Shâo Î, or 'Smaller Rules of Conduct,' is akin to much of the first Book in our collection, 'the Summary of the Rules of Ceremony.' Shâo means 'few,' and often 'few in years,' or 'young;' and hence some have thought that the subject of the Book is 'Rules for the Young.' So Callery, who gives for the title, 'Règles de Conduite des Jeunes Gens.'

But the contents cannot be so restricted; and since the time of King Hsüan, shâo has been taken by most Chinese commentators as equivalent to hsiâo[1], which occurs in the title of Book XIII. The difference between the two Chinese characters is not so great as that between these alphabetic exhibitions of their names. Lû Teh–ming says, 'Shâo is here equivalent to hsiâo;' and Kang says, that the Book is named Shâo Î 'because it records the small rules of demeanour at interviews and in bringing in the provisions for a feast.' But the observances described are very various, and enable us to form a life–like picture of manners in those early days.

According to Kû Hsi, the Book was intended to be a branch of the smaller learning, or lessons for youth; but

[1. and .]

was extended to a variety of subjects in daily life and the intercourses of society. When and by whom it was compiled is not known.

BOOK XVI. HSIO KÎ

The Hsio Kî, or 'Record of Studies,' is a treatise of very considerable interest and importance. Khang–dze, whom Kû Hsî was accustomed to call his 'Master,' considered it to be, after Books XXVIII and XXXIX, the Kung Yung and Tâ Hsio, the most correct and orthodox Book in the Lî Kî.

The Khien–lung editors say that in paragraphs 4 and 5 we have the institutions of the ancient kings for purposes of education; in 6 to 19, the laws for teachers; and in what follows, those for learners. The summary is on the whole correct, but the compiler (who is unknown) did not always keep his subjects distinct. In the three commencing paragraphs the importance of education to the moral well–being of the people is strikingly exhibited. The whole displays an amount of observation and a maturity of reflection on the subject, which cannot but be deemed remarkable. The information about ancient schools and higher institutions may be found in the earlier Books, but we are glad to have this repetition of it.

BOOK XVII. YO KÎ

The Yo Kî, or 'Record of Music,' will be found to have more interest for general readers than most of the other Books of the Lî. Khang–dze speaks of it in terms similar to those quoted from him in the preceding notice about the Hsio Kî. That, so far as correctness and orthodoxy are concerned, is next to the Kung Yung and Tâ Hsio; this is near to them. Its introduction into our collection is ascribed to Mâ Yung.

The old documents on music that, had been recovered during the earlier Han dynasty, appear in Liû Hsin's Catalogue after those of the Lî, amounting in all to 165 phien, distributed in, six collections. The first of these was the Yo Kî, in 23 phien; the second, the Kî of Wang Yü[1], in 24 phien. Khung Ying–tâ, deriving his information from a note in Hsin's Catalogue and other sources, sums up what he has to say about this Book in the following way:—On the rise of the Han dynasty, the treatises of former times on music, as well as the practice of the art, were in a state of special dilapidation. In the time of the emperor Wû, his brother Teh, with the help of many scholars, copied out all that remained on the subject of music, and made a Yo Kî, or 'Record of Music,' in 24 phien or books, which Wang Yü presented to the court in the time of the emperor Khang (B.C. 32–7);—but it was afterwards hardly heard of. When Liû Hsiang (died B.C. 9) examined the books in the Imperial library, he found a 'Record of Music' in 23 phien, different from that which Wang Yü had presented. Our present Yo Kî contains eleven of those phien, arranged with the names of their subjects. The other twelve are lost, though their names remain.

Most of the present text is found in Sze–mâ Khien's Monograph on Music; and as he was so long before Liû Hsiang (Khien died between B.C. 90 and 80), the Khien–lung editors suppose that it is one of the portions of Khien's work, supplied by Khû Shâo–sun[2], who was a contemporary of Hsiang.

Kû Hsî had a great admiration of many passages in the Yo Kî, and finds in them the germs of the views on the constitution of humanity, and on the action and interaction of principle and passion, reason and force, in the economy of what we call Providence, on which he delighted to dwell in his philosophical speculations. We expect from the title, as Hwang Kan-hsing (Ming dynasty) says, that music will be the chief subject of the Treatise, but everywhere we find ceremonial usages spoken of equally and in their relation to it; for, according to the view of the author, the framework of society is built on the truth

[1. .

2. ; see Wylie's Notes, p. 14.]

underlying ceremonies, and music is the necessary expression of satisfaction in the resulting beauty and harmony.

BOOK XVIII. ZÂ KÎ.

Book XVII is given nearly complete in the expurgated edition translated by Callery, while the 18th or 'Miscellaneous Records,' happily rendered by him by the one French word 'Mélanges,' is reduced to about a third of its length in the Chinese text. Notwithstanding its name of 'Miscellanies,' the greater part is occupied with the observances of the Mourning Rites. Interesting questions concerning them are discussed, and information is given on customs which we do not find in such detail elsewhere,—such, for instance, as those relating to the gifts of grave-clothes and other things for the burial of the dead. Towards the end other customs, besides those of the mourning rites, are introduced. It would be a mistake, however, to suppose that this is done to justify the name of Miscellaneous Records given to the whole. It is a peculiarity of many of the other Books that the writer, or writers, seem to get weary of confining themselves to one subject or even to a few subjects, and introduce entries of quite a different nature for no reason that we can discover but their arbitrary pleasure.

The correctness and integrity of many paragraphs have been justly called in question. The authority of the Book does not rank high. It must be classed in this respect with the Than Kung.

BOOK XIX. SANG TÂ KÎ.

Book XIII deals with smaller points in connexion with the dress of mourning; Book XVIII, with miscellaneous points in mourning; and this Book with the greater points, especially with the two dressings of the dead, the coffining, and the burial. Beginning with the preparations for death in the case of a ruler, a Great officer, or an ordinary officer, it goes methodically over all the observances at and after death, until the burial has taken place. It takes us into the palace, the mansion, and the smaller official residence, and shows us what was done at the different steps that intervened between death and the committing of the coffin to the grave. Some of the observances differ in minor points from details in those other Books, and in the Than Kung or Book II; but taking them all together, we get from them a wonderfully minute account of all the rites of mourning in ancient China. Wû Khang says, 'This Book relates the greater rules observed in each event which it mentions.' It was not, intended to supplement the information elsewhere given about smaller details; and hence it is named 'The Greater Record of Mourning Rites.'

BOOK XX. KÎ FÂ.

Ki Fâ, so named from the first two characters in the Book, and meaning 'Laws or Rules of Sacrifices,' is the first of three treatises, all on the subject of sacrifices, that come together at this part of the collection of the Lî. They were not, perhaps, the production of the same hand; but the writer of this one evidently had before him the 17th article in the first Part of the Narratives connected with the state of Lû, which form the second Section of 'the Narratives of the States[1].' That article contains an exposition of the subject of sacrifices by a Ken Khin, in deprecation of a sacrifice ordered by Zang Wan-kang, who had been for about fifty years one of the ministers of Lû. Zang died in B.C. 617.

Difficulties attach to some of the historical statements in the Book, which cannot be cleared up from our want of sufficient documents. The whole consists of two Parts,—paragraphs 1–8, and paragraph 9. All the former is excluded from the expurgated editions; but in it, as well as in the other, the sacrifices are mainly those to departed worthies. There is no idea of deprecation in them; much less of atonement. They are expressions of gratitude, and commemorative of men whose laws and achievements were

[1. .]

beneficial to their own times, and helped on the progress of civilisation, so that they would be beneficial also to all ages.

In the conclusion, the sacrifices to the sun, moon, and other parts of nature appear; and it is said that they were instituted because the action of those bodies contributed to promote the comfort and agency of men. So far those sacrifices were a species of nature–worship; but the question arises whether they were not really offered to the spirits under whose guardianship those objects operated.

BOOK XXI. KÎ Î.

The Kî Î, or 'The Meaning of Sacrifices,' 'Sens des Sacrifices' in Callery, embraces a wider extent of subjects than the last Book. It treats first of the sacrifices to Heaven, and to the sun and moon in connexion with it, as well as of those in the ancestral temple, though the latter are the principal subject. The writer, whoever he was, goes fully into the preparations of the sacrificer, and the spirit of reverence in which the services should be conducted.

No idea of deprecation or expiation is expressed as belonging to the sacrifices. It is said, indeed, in Section i, A, that the sacrifice in the suburb of the capital was the great expression of gratitude to Heaven.

In Section ii other subjects besides sacrifice are treated of. It commences with a remarkable conversation between Confucius and his disciple Zâi Wo, on the constitution of man, as comprehending both the Kwei and Shin, the former name denoting the animal soul, which, with the bones and flesh, 'moulders below and becomes the dust of the fields;' while the latter denotes the intelligent soul or spirit, which issues forth at death, and is displayed on high in a condition of glorious brightness.

The ploughing of the special fields by the king and rulers of states, and the regulations for the nourishment of silkworms and the preparation of silk by their wives, are set forth, both operations being to provide the sacrificial grain and robes.

After this we have the views of Zang–dze and one of his disciples on filial piety, which subject again passes into the submission of the younger brother to the elder, and the respect to be paid generally by juniors to their elders.

BOOK XXII. KÎ THUNG.

The 'Summary Account of Sacrifices' is the last and longest, and, it may be added, the most interesting, of the treatises, specially on that subject. We find nothing in it, any –more than in the others, of the idea of propitiation; but it gives many details of the purposes which the institution of sacrifices served in the Chinese state. The old commentators took the character Thung[1] in the sense of 'Root' or 'Origin[2],' and hence some English sinologists have named the book 'The Origin of Sacrifices,' and P. Zottoli gives for the title 'Sacrificii Principium.' Callery calls it, better, 'Généralités sur les Sacrifices.' The very able commentator Khan Hsiang tâo compares the Treatise to 'the large rope which controls the meshes of a net,' saying, that it commences with sacrifice as coming from the feeling of the heart, and ends with the display of its influence in the conduct of government.

The concluding. paragraph shows that it was written while the state of Lû still had an existence; and if the whole Book proceeded from the same hand, it must have been composed some time after the death of Confucius and before the extinction of Lû, which was consummated by Khû in B.C. 248. I think we may refer it to the fourth century B.C.

The doctrine of Filial Piety occupies a prominent place in it. Paragraph 13 and the ten that follow, on the connexion between sacrifice and the ten relationships of men, are specially instructive. The author writes forcibly and often subtilely; and can hardly do himself justice in the

[1. .

2. .]

expression of his ideas. What he says on the subject of Inscriptions towards the conclusion is interesting. He was a true Lû man, and his views on the sacrifices of his state are contrary to the standard of Chinese orthodoxy about them.

BOOK XXIII. KING KIEH.

King Kieh has been translated 'Explanations of the Classics,' and Callery gives for the title 'Sens Général des Livres Canoniques.' A slight attention to the few paragraphs which compose the Book, however, will satisfy the reader that these translations of the name are incorrect. No explanation is attempted of passages in the different King. The true meaning of King Kieh was given by Hwang Khan in A.D. 538. 'Kieh,' he says, 'is to be taken in the sense of "separation" or "division;" and the Treatise describes the difference between the subjects dealt with in the different King.'

The Book, though ingenious, is not entitled to much attention. The first two paragraphs, assigned to Confucius, could not have come from him. They assume that there were six King; but that enumeration of the ancient writings originated with the scholars of the Han dynasty. And among the six is the Khun Khiû "the work of Confucius himself, which he compiled only a year or two before his death. It was for posterity, and not for him, to raise it to the rank of a King, and place it on the same level with the Shû, the Shih, and the Yî. It may be doubted, moreover, if there were ever a Yo King, or 'Classic of Music.' Treatises on music, no doubt, existed under the Kâu dynasty, but it does not appear that there was any collection of them made till the attempts that have been referred to in the introductory notice to Book XVII.

Who the ingenious, but uncritical, compiler of the King Kieh was is unknown.

BOOK XXIV. ÂI KUNG WAN.

'Questions of Duke Âi' is a translation of the three characters with which the Book commences, and which mean there 'Duke Âi asked;' and the title is so far descriptive of the contents of the Book,—two conversations on ceremonies and the practice of government between the marquis Ziang of Lû, posthumously called duke Âi, and Confucius. The sage died in the sixteenth year of Ziang's marquisate. As an old minister of the state, after he had retired from public. life, he had a right of entrance to the court, which, we know, he sometimes exercised. He may have conversed with the marquis on the subjects discussed in this Treatise; but whether he held the particular conversations here related can only be determined by the consideration of their style and matter. I am myself disposed to question their genuineness.

There are other recensions of the Treatise. It forms the third of the Books in the current editions of 'the Lî of the Greater Tâi,' purporting to be the forty–first of those which were in his larger collection; and is the same as in our Lî Kî, with hardly a variation. The second conversation, again, appears . as the fourth article in the collection called the 'Narratives of the School[1],' but with considerable and important variations, under the title of Tâ Hwan, 'The Grand Marriage.' The first conversation is found also in the same collection, as part of the sixth article, called Wan Lî, or 'Questions about Ceremonies.' There are also variations in, it; but the questioner in both articles is duke Âi.

The most remarkable passages of the Book are some paragraphs of the second conversation towards its conclusion. P. Callery translates Thien Tâo, 'the Way of Heaven,' in paragraph 16, by 'La Vérité Céleste,' and

says in a note that Confucius speaks of this Tâo in a way not unlike Lâo–dze in the Tâo Teh King, adding that 'these two fathers of Chinese philosophy had on this mysterious Being ideas nearly similar.' But a close examination of the passage, which is itself remarkable, shows that this resemblance between it and passages of the Tâoist classic does not exist. See my concluding note on the Book. If there were a Tâoist semblance in the phraseology, it would make us refer the composition of the Treatise to the time of Khin or the early days of Han, when Tâoism had taken a place in the national literature which it had not had under the dynasty of Kâu.

BOOK XXV. KUNG–NÎ YEN KÜ.

The title of this Book is taken from the four characters with which it commences. Confucius has returned from his attendance at the court of Lû, and is at home in his own house. Three of his disciples are sitting by him, and his conversation with them flows on till it has reached the subject of ceremonial usages. In reply to their questions, he discourses on it at length, diverging also to the subjects of music and the practice of government in connexion with ceremonies, in a familiar and practical manner.

He appears in the title by his designation, or name as married, Kung–nî, which we find also two or three times in Book XXVIII, which is received as the composition of his grandson Khung Kî, or Dze–sze. This Treatise, however, is much shorter than that, and inferior to it. The commentator Wang of Shih–liang[1], often quoted by Khan Hâo, says, that though this Treatise has a beginning and end, the style and ideas are so disjected and loose, that many of the utterances attributed to Confucius cannot be accepted as really his.

[1. .]

BOOK XXVI. KHUNG-DZE HSIEN KÜ.

The title of this Book is akin to that of the last, the characters of that leading us to think of Confucius as having returned from court to 'his case,' and those of this suggesting nothing of his immediate antecedents, but simply saying that he was 'at home and at leisure.' Instead of being called, as there, by his designation, he appears here as Khung-dze, 'the philosopher Khung,' or' Mr. Khung.'

The Book also relates a conversation, but only one disciple is present, and to him the Master discourses on the description of a sovereign as 'the parent of the people,' and on the virtue of the founders of the three dynasties of Hsiâ, Shang, and Kâu, illustrating his views by quotations from the Book of Poetry. His language is sometimes strange and startling, while the ideas underlying it are subtle and ingenious. And the poetical quotations are inapplicable to the subjects in connexion with which they are introduced. If the commentator Wang could not adopt the speeches attributed to Confucius in the last Book as really his, much less can we receive those in this as such.

From their internal analogies in form and sentiment, I suppose that the two Books were made by the same writer; but I have met with no guess even as to who he was.

BOOK XXVII. FANG KÎ.

'The Dykes,' which is the meaning of the title of this Book, is suggestive of its subject-matter. We have in it the rules or usages of ceremony presented to us under the figure of dykes, dams, or barriers; defensive structures made to secure what is inside them from escaping or dispersion, and to defend it against inundation or other injurious assault and invasion from without. The character, called fang, is used for the most part with verbal force, 'acting as a dyke or barrier;' and it would often be difficult to say whether the writer was thinking of the particular institution or usage spoken of as fulfilling the purpose of defence against peril from within, or violence from without.

The illustrations are numerous, and they are all given as if they came from the lips of Confucius himself; but we cannot suppose that they were really from him. They are not in his style, and the reasonings are occasionally unworthy of him. Many paragraphs carry on their front a protest against our receiving them as really his. Nevertheless, the Book, though sometimes tedious, is on the whole interesting, and we like the idea of looking on the usages as 'dykes.' We do not know to whom wc arc indebted for it. One of the famous brothers Khang of the Sung dynasty has said:–We do not know who wrote the Treatise. Since we find such expressions in it As "The Lun Yü says," it is plainly not to be ascribed to Confucius. Passages in the Han scholars, Kiâ Î and Tung Kung–shû, are to the same effect as what we find here; and perhaps this memoir was their production.'

BOOK XXVIII. KUNG YUNG.

The Kung Yung would be pronounced, I think, by Chinese scholars to be the most valuable of all the Treatises in the Lî Kî; and from an early time it asserted a position peculiar to itself. Its place in the general collection of Ritual Treatises was acknowledged by Mâ Yung and his disciple Kang Hsüan; but in Liû Hsin's Catalogue of the Lî Books, we find an entry of 'Observations on the Kung Yung, in two phien;' so early was the work thought to be deserving of special treatment by itself. In the records of the Sui dynasty (A.D. 589–617), in the Catalogue of its Imperial library, there are the names of three other special works upon it, one of them by the emperor Wû (A. D. 502–549) of the Liang dynasty.

Later on, under the Sung dynasty, the Kung Yung, the Tâ Hsio, or 'Great Learning,' which is also a portion of the Lî Kî, the Confucian Analects, or the Lun Yü, and the works of Mencius, were classed together as 'The Four Books,' which have since that time formed so important a division of Chinese literature; and ' the Kung Yung, in chapters and sentences, with a digest of commentaries on it,' was published by Kû Hsî early in A.D. 1189. About 125 years afterwards, the fourth emperor of the Yüan dynasty enacted that Kû's edition and views should be the text–book of the classic at the literary examinations. From that time merely the name of the Kung Yung was retained in editions of the Lî Kî, until the appearance of the Imperial edition of the whole collection in the Khien–lung period of the present dynasty. There the text is given in two Sections according to the old division of it, with the ancient commentaries from the edition of 'The

Thirteen King' of the Thang dynasty, followed at the end of each paragraph by the Commentary of Kû.

The authorship of the Kung Yung is ascribed to Khung Kî, better known as Dze–sze, the grandson of Confucius. There is no statement to this effect, indeed, in the work itself; but the tradition need not be called in question. It certainly existed in the Khung family. The Book must have been written in the fifth century B.C., some time, I suppose, between 450 and 400. Since A.D. 1267, the author has had a place in the temples of Confucius as one of 'The Four Assessors,' with the title of 'The Philosopher Dze–sze, transmitter of the Sage.' I have seen his tomb–mound in the Confucian cemetery, outside the city of Khü–fû in Shantung, in front of those of his father and grandfather. There is a statue of him on it, bearing the inscription, 'Duke (or Prince) of the State of Î.'

It is not easy to translate the name of the Treatise, Kung Yung. It has been represented by 'Juste Milieu;' 'Medium Constans vel Sempiternurn;' 'L'Invariable Milieu;' 'The Constant Medium.' 'The Golden Medium;' 'The True Medium,' and otherwise. I called it, in 1861, 'The Doctrine of the Mean,' which I have now changed for 'The State of Equilibrium and Harmony,' the reasons for which will be found in the notes on the first chapter of the present version.

I do not here enter on an exhibition of the scope and value of the Book. It gives the best account that we have of the Confucian philosophy and morals, and will amply repay careful study, and hold its place not only in China, but in the wider sphere beyond it. The writer had an exaggerated conception of the sage; but he deserves well of his own country and of the world.

BOOK XXIX. PIÂO KÎ.

The character called Piâo is the symbol for the outer garments, and is used to indicate whatever is external in opposition to what is internal; the outside of things, what serves to mark them out and call attention to them. Hence comes its use in the sense which it bears in the title of this Book, for what serves as an exàmple or model. Callery renders that title by 'Mémoire sur l'Exemple;' Wylie, by 'The Exemplar Record.'

Piâo is also used for the gnomon of a dial; and the Khien–lung editors fix on this application of the character in explaining the name of the Book. 'Piâo,' they say, 'is the gnomon of a dial, by which the movement of the sun is measured; it rises up in the Centre, and all round is regulated by it. The Fang Kî shows men what they ought to be on their guard against; the Piâo Kî, what they should take as their pattern.' Then they add—'Of patterns there is none so honourable as benevolence (or humanity proper), and to aid that there is righteousness, while, to complete it, there is sincerity or good faith, and reverence is that by which the quest for humanity is pursued.' This second sentence may be considered a summary of the contents of the Book, which they conclude by saying, they have divided into eight chapters after the example of the scholar Hwang; meaning, I suppose, Hwang Khan, who has been already mentioned as having published his work on our classic in A. D. 538.

That division into eight chapters lies on the face of the Treatise. We have eight paragraphs commencing with the characters which I have rendered by 'These were the words of the Master;' and these are followed by a number of others, more or fewer as the case may be, in which the words of the Master ('The Master said') are adduced to substantiate what has been stated in that introductory passage. The arrangement is uniform, excepting in one instance to which I have called attention in a note, and suitably divides the whole into eight chapters.

But no one supposes that 'the words of the Master' are really those of Confucius, or were used by him in the connexion which is here given to them. They were invented by the author of the Treatise, or applied by him, to suit his own purpose; and scholars object to many of them as contrary to the sentiments of the sage, and betraying a tendency to the views of Tâoism. This appears, most strikingly perhaps, in the fifth chapter. On the statement, for instance', in paragraph 32, that the methods of Yin and Kâu were not equal to the correction of the errors produced by those of Shun and Hsîa, the Khien–lung editors say:—'How could these words have come from the mouth of the Master? The disciples of Lâo–dze despised forms and prized the unadorned simplicity, commended what was ancient, and condemned all that was of their own time. In the beginning of the Han dynasty, the principles of Hwang and Lâo were widely circulated; students lost themselves in the stream of what they heard, could not decide upon its erroneousness, and ascribed it to the Master. Such cases were numerous, and even in several paragraphs of the Lî Yun (Book VII) we seem to have some of them. What we find there was the utterance, probably, of some disciple of Lâo–dze.'

No one, so far as I have noticed, has ventured to assign the authorship of this Book on example. I would identify him, myself, with the Kung–sun Nî–dze, to whom the next is ascribed.

BOOK XXX. DZE Î

It is a disappointment to the reader, when he finds after reading the title of this Book, that it has nothing to do with the Black Robes of which he expects it to be an account. That phrase occurs in the second paragraph, in a note to which its origin is explained; but the other name Hsiang Po, which is found in the same paragraph, might with equal appropriateness, or rather inappropriateness, have been adopted for the Treatise.

It is really of the same nature as the preceding, and contains twenty–four paragraphs, all attributed to 'the Master,' and each of which may be considered to afford a pattern for rulers and their people. It ought to form one Book with XXIX under the title of 'Pattern Lessons.' I have pointed out in the notes some instances of the agreement in their style and phraseology, and the intelligent reader who consults the translation with reference to the Chinese text will discover more. Lû Teh–ming (early in the Thang dynasty) tells us, on the authority of Liû Hsien, that the Dze Î was made by a Kung–sun Ni–dze. Liû Hsien was a distinguished scholar of the early Sung dynasty, and died about A. D. 500; but on what evidence he assigned the authorship of the Book to Kung–sun Ni–dze does not, in the present state of our knowledge, appear. The name of that individual is found twice in Liû Hsin's Catalogue, as belonging to the learned school, and among 'the Miscellaneous writers,' with a note that he was 'a disciple of the seventy disciples of the Master.' The first entry about him precedes that about Mencius, so that he must be referred to the closing period of the Kâu dynasty, the third century B.C. He may, therefore, have been the author of 'The Black Robes,' and of the preceding Book as well, giving his own views, but attributing them, after the fashion of the time, to Confucius; but, as the commentator Fang Î (? Ming dynasty) observes:—'Many passages in the Book are made to resemble the sayings of a sage; but the style is not good and the meaning is inferior.'

BOOK XXXI. PAN SANG.

This Book refers to a special case in connexion with the mourning rites, that of an individual who has been prevented, from taking part with the other relatives in the usual observances at the proper time. It might be that he was absent from the state, charged by his ruler with public business, or he might be in the same state but at a distance, and so occupied that he had been unable to take part in the mourning services.

But they were too sacred to be entirely neglected, and we have here the rules applicable to such a case, in a variety of circumstances and different degrees of consanguinity. Some other matter, more or less analogous, is introduced towards the end.

We have seen how the first of the 'Three Rituals' recovered in the Han dynasty was seventeen Books that now form the Î Lî. Kang Hsüan supposed that the Pan Sang had been another Book of that collection, and was afterwards obtained from the tablets found in the village of Yen–kung in Lû. It has been decided, however, that the style determines it to be from another hand than the Î Lî.

Here it is, and we have only to make the best of it that we can, without knowing who wrote it or when it came to light. The Khien–lung editors say :—'Anciently, in cases of mourning for a year or shorter period even, officers left their charges and hurried to the rites. In consequence of the inconvenience arising. from this, it was enacted that officers should leave their charge only on the death of a parent. It was found difficult, however, to enforce this. The rule is that a charge cannot be left, without leave asked and obtained.'

BOOK XXXII. WAN SANG.

The Wan Sang, or 'Questions about Mourning Rites,' is a short Treatise, which derives its name from inquiries about the dressing of the corpse, the putting off the cap and replacing it by the cincture, and the use of the staff in mourning. Along with those inquiries there are accounts of some of the rites, condensed and imperfect. The Book should be read in connexion with the other Books of a similar character, especially XIII.

Much cannot be said in favour of the style, or of the satisfactoriness of the replies to the questions that arc propounded. The principal idea indeed in the mind of the author, whoever he was, was that the rites were the outcome of the natural feelings of men, and that mourning was a manifestation of filial piety. The most remarkable passage is that with which the Treatise concludes, that the use of the staff was not to be sought in any revelation from heaven or earth, but was simply from the good son's filial affection. The way in which the sentiment is expressed has often brought to my mind the question of the Apostle Paul about faith, in Romans x. 6–8.

BOOK XXXIII. FÛ WAN.

Like the last two Books and the two that follow, the Fû Wan is omitted in the expurgated editions. It is still shorter than the Wan Sang, and treats also of the mourning rites, and specially of the dress in it, and changes in it, which naturally gave rise to questioning.

The writer, or compiler, often quotes from what he calls the Kwan, a name which has sometimes been translated by 'Tradition.' But the Chinese term, standing alone, may mean what is transmitted by writings, as well as what is handed down by oral communication. It is used several times in Mencius in the sense of 'Record' and 'Records.' I have called it here 'The Directory of Mourning.' Wû Khang says rightly that the Book is of the same character as XIII; that the mourning rites were so many, and some of them so peculiar, that collisions between different rites must have been of frequent occurrence. The Fû Wan takes up several such cases and tells us how they were met satisfactorily, or, as we may think, unsatisfactorily.

BOOK XXXIV. KIEN KWAN.

The Kien Kwan is a Treatise on subsidiary points in the mourning rites, It is not easy to render the name happily in English. I have met with it as 'The Intermediate Record.' Kwan is the character spoken of in the preceding notice; Kien is the symbol for the space between two things, suggesting the idea of distinction or difference. Kang Hsüan says that 'the name has reference to the distinctions suitably made in mourning, according as it was lighter or more important.'

However we translate or explain the name, we find the Book occupied with the manifestations of grief in the bearing of the mourners; in the modulation of their voices; in their eating and drinking; in their places; in the texture of their dress; and in the various changes which were made in it till it was finally put off. Some points in it are difficult to understand at this distance of time, and while we are still imperfectly acquainted with the mourning usages of the people at the present day.

BOOK XXXV. SAN NIEN WAN.

The 'Questions about the Mourning for three years' is occupied principally with the mourning for parents for that period, but it touches on all the other periods of mourning as well, explaining why one period differs in its duration from the others.

Mourning, it is said, is the outcome of the relative feeling proper to man; the materials of the dress, the duration of the rites, and other forms are from the ancient sages and legislators, to regulate and direct the expression of the feeling.

What is said in paragraph 4 about the mourning of birds and beasts is interesting, but fantastical. Though the mourning for a parent is said to last for three years, the western reader is not to suppose that it continues to the end of that time, but simply that it extends into the third year. Virtually it terminates with the twenty–fifth month, and positively with the twenty–seventh. It is the eastern mode in speaking of time to say that it lasts for three years. Similarly, I have often been told that a child, evidently not more than six months, was two years old, when a little cross–questioning has brought out the fact that it had been born towards the end of the previous year, that it had. lived in two years, and was, therefore, spoken of as two years old.

BOOK XXXVI. SHAN Î.

The Shan Î is what we should expect from the name, a description of the dress so–called. It was the garment of undress, worn by all classes of the people, from the highest to the lowest, when they were at home and at ease. What distinguished it from other dresses was that in those the jacket or upper garment was in one piece, and the skirt or lower garment in another, whereas in this they were joined together, so that it could be put on and off with ease.

In the Khien–lung edition of the Lî Kî, chapter 29, second collection of Plates, there are pictures of the Shan Î, taken from Kû Hsî's 'Rules for the Family,' but they do not correspond with the description here. More accurate plates are to be found in a monograph on the subject by Yung Kiang, a senior licentiate of the present dynasty, which forms the 251st chapter in the 'Explanations of the Classics under the Imperial dynasty of Khing.' The proper meaning of Shan Î is 'The Deep Dress;' but the garment was also called 'The Long Dress,' which suits our nomenclature better; and 'The Inner Dress,' when it was worn under another.

The reasons assigned for fashioning it after the description in paragraphs 3 and 4 are of course fanciful; but M. Callery is too severe on the unknown author, when he says:–'On est tenté de rire en voyant les rapprochements que Pauteur cherche à établir entre la forme de cet habit et les principes les plus abstraits de la morale. Je suis porté à croire que toutes ces allegories ont été imaginées après coup; car si elles avaient dirigé la coupe primitive du Shan Î, il faudrait dire que les ateliers des anciens tailleurs de la Chine étaient des écoles de mysticisme.'

BOOK XXXVII. THÂU HO.

The Thâu Hû, or 'Pitching into a jar,' gives the description of a game, played anciently, and probably at the present day also, at festal entertainments. It was a kind of archery, with darts instead of arrows, and the hand instead of a bow; 'the smallest,' as Kang says, 'of all the games of archery,' and yet lessons for the practice of virtue and for judging of character might be learned from it. It is interesting to us, however, simply as a game for amusement, and a sufficient idea of it may be gained from this Book.

Two might play at it, or any number. The host and guest in the text are the representatives of two sides or parties. It was a contest at pitching darts into the mouth of a pot or vase, placed at a short distance from the players,—too short a distance, it appears to us. There was nothing peculiar in the form of the vase of which we have an account in paragraph 10. We are surprised to read the description of it in the late Dr. Williams' Syllabic Dictionary, under the character for Hû:—'One ancient kind (of vase) was made with tubes on each side of the mouth, and a common game, called Thâu Hû, was to pitch reeds into the three orifices.' This would have been a different jar, and the game would have been different from that here described, and more difficult.

The style of the Treatise is like that of the Î Lî, in the account of the contests of archery in Books VIII–XI, to which we have to refer to make out the meaning of several of the phrases.

The Book should end with paragraph 10. The three paragraphs that follow seem to have been jotted down by the compiler from some memoranda that he found, that nothing might be lost which would throw light on the game.

Then follows a paragraph, which may be pronounced unintelligible. The whole Book is excluded from the expurgated editions.

BOOK XXXVIII. ZÛ HSING.

The Zû Hsing, or 'Conduct of the Scholar,' professes to be a discourse delivered to duke Âi of Lû on the character and style of life by which scholars, or men claiming to possess literary acquirements, ought to be, and were in a measure, distinguished. Even so far back, such a class of men there was in China. They had certain peculiarities of dress, some of which are alluded to in Odes of the Shih. The duke, however, had not been accustomed to think highly of them; and struck by something in the dress of Confucius, he asks him if he wore the garb of a scholar. The sage disclaims this; and being questioned further as to the conduct of the scholar, he proceeds to dilate on that at great length, and with a remarkable magnificence of thought and diction. He pourtrayed to his ruler a man sans peur et sans reproche, strong in principle, of cultivated intelligence, and animated by the most generous, patriotic, and benevolent spirit. We are told in the conclusion that the effect on duke Âi was good and great. It made him a better man, and also made him think more highly of the class of scholars than he had done. The effect of the Book on many of the literati must have been great in the ages that have intervened, and must still be so.

But did such a conversation really take place between the marquis of Lû and the sage? The general opinion of' Chinese scholars is that it did not do so. Lü Tâ–lin (of the eleventh century, and a contemporary of the brothers Khang), as quoted by the Khien–lung editors, while cordially approving the sentiments, thinks the style too grandiloquent to allow of our ascribing it to Confucius. Another commentator of the Sung period, one of the Lîs[1], holds that the language is that of some ambitious scholar of the period of the Warring States, who wished. to stir up the members of his order to a style of action worthy of it. P. Callery appends to his translation the following note:—'In general, the maxims of this chapter are sufficiently profound to justify us in ascribing them to Confucius, in preference to so many other passages which the author of this work places to the credit of the great philosopher. We find nevertheless in it some ideas of which the really authentic works of Confucius do not offer any trace.'

BOOK XXXIX. TÂ HSIO.

Like the Kung Yung (XXVIII), the Tâ Hsio has long been published separately from the other Books of the Lî Kî, and is now. the first of the well–known 'Four Books.' As it appears in this translation, we follow the arrangement of the text given by the Khien–lung editors from that in the Thirteen King published by Khung Ying–tâ, who himself simply followed King Hsüan. Early in the Sung dynasty the brothers Khang occupied themselves with the Treatise; and thinking that errors had crept into the order of the paragraphs, and that portions were missing, made various alterations and additions. Kû Hsî entered into their labours, and, as he thought, improved on them. It is now current in the Four Books, as he published it in 1189, and the difference between his arrangement and the oldest one may be seen by comparing the translation in the first volume of my Chinese Classics and that in the present publication.

Despite the difference of arrangement, the substance of the work is the same.

There can be no doubt that the Tâ Hsio is a genuine monument of the Confucian teaching, and gives us a sufficient idea of the methods and subjects in the great or higher schools of antiquity. The enthusiasm of M. Pauthier is not to be blamed when he says:—'It is evident that the aim of the Chinese philosopher is to exhibit the duties of political government as the perfecting of self and the practice of virtue by all men.'

Pauthier adopts fully the view of Kû, that the first chapter is a genuine relic of Confucius himself, for which view there really is no evidence. And he thinks also that all that follows should be attributed to the disciple, Zang–dze, which is contrary to the evidence which the Treatise itself supplies.

If it were necessary to assign an author for the work, I should adopt the opinion of Kiâ Kwei (A.D. 30–101), and assign it to Khung Kî, the grandson of Confucius, and author of the Kung Yung. 'When Khung Kî,' said Kiâ, 'was still alive, and in straits, in Sung, being afraid that the lessons of the former sage (or sages) would become obscure, and the principles of the ancient Tîs and Kings fall to the ground, he made the Tâ Hsio, as the warp of them, and the Kung Yung as the woof.' This would seem to have been the opinion of scholars in that early time, and the only difficulty in admitting it is that Kang Hsüan does not mention it. Notwithstanding his silence, the conviction that Khung Ki wrote both treatises has become very strong in my mind. There is that agreement in the matter, method, and style of the two, which almost demands for them a common authorship.

BOOK XL. KWAN Î

A fuller account of the ceremony of capping is obtained from portions of the ninth and other Books, where it comes in only incidentally, than from this Book in which we might expect from the title to find all the details of it brought together. But the object of the unknown writer was to glorify the rite as the great occasion when a youth stepped from his immaturity into all the privileges and responsibilities of a man, and to explain some of the usages by which it had been sought from the earliest times to mark its importance. This intention is indicated by the second character in the title called Î, which we have met with only once before in the name of a Book,–in Kî Î, 'the Meaning of Sacrifices,' the title of XXI. It is employed in the titles of this and the five Books that follow, and always with the same force of 'meaning,' 'signification,' 'ideas underlying the ceremony.' Callery renders correctly Kwan Î by 'Signification de la Prise du Chapeau Viril.'

The Chinese cap of manhood always suggests the toga virilis of the Romans; but there was a difference between the institutions of the two peoples. The age for assuming the toga was fourteen; that for receiving the cap was twenty. The capped Chinese was still young, but he had grown to man's estate; the gowned Roman might have reached puberty, but he was little more than a boy.

Until the student fully understands the object of the Treatise, the paragraphs seem intricate and heavy, and the work of translation is difficult.

BOOK XLI. HWAN Î.

After capping comes in natural order the ceremony of marriage; and we are glad to have, in the first portion of this Book, so full an account of the objects contemplated in marriage, the way in which the ceremony was gone about, and the subsequent proceedings by which the union was declared to be established.

The writer made much use of the chapters on marriage in the Î Lî. Nothing is said of the age at which it was the rule for a young man to marry; and this, we have seen, is put down, in other parts of this collection, as thirty. The same age is mentioned in the Kâu Lî, XIII, 55, on the duties of the marriage–contractor. But marriage, we may assume from the case of Confucius himself, actually took place earlier in ancient times, as it does now. The Dze[1], or name of maturity, which was given at the capping, is commonly said to be the name taken at marriage, as in Morrison's Dictionary, I, i, page 627.

The duties set forth in the Book, however, are not those of the young husband, but those of the wife, all comprised in the general virtue of 'obedience.' After the tenth paragraph, the author leaves the subject of marriage, and speaks of the different establishments of the king and queen and of their functions. So far what is said on these topics bears on marriage as it sets forth, mystically, that union as analogous to the relations of heaven and earth, the sun and moon, and the masculine and feminine energies of nature; and the response made by these to the conduct of the human parties in their wedded union.

BOOK XLII. HSIANG YIN KIÛ Î

Hsiang was anciently the name for the largest territorial division of the state. Under the dominion of Kâu, from the hamlet of five families, through the lü, the zû, the tang, and the kâu, we rise to the hsiang, nominally containing 12,000 families, and presided over by a 'Great officer.' The royal domain contained six hsiang, and a feudal state three.

In more than one of these territorial divisions, there were festive meetings at regular intervals, all said to be for the purpose of 'drinking.' There was feasting at them too, but the viands bore a small proportion to the liquor, called by the name of Kiû, which has generally been translated wine, though the grape had nothing to do with it, and whether it was distilled or merely fermented is a disputed point.

The festivity described in this Book was at the true Hsiang meeting, celebrated once in three years, under the superintendence of 'the Great officer' himself, when, in the, principal school or college of the district, he assembled the gentlemen of accomplishments and virtue, and feasted them. His object was to select, especially from among the young men, those who were most likely to prove useful to the government in various departments of service. There was in the celebration the germ of the competitive examinations which have been for so long a characteristic feature of the Chinese nation.

The writer had before him the sixth and seventh Books of the Î Lî on the same subject, or their equivalents. He brings out five things accomplished by the ceremony, all of a moral and social nature; but in trying to explain the arrangements, he becomes allegorical or mystical, and sometimes absurd.

BOOK XLIII. SHÊ Î

There were various games or competitions of archery; at the royal court, at the feudal courts, at the meetings in the country districts which form the subject of the last Book, and probably others of a less public and distinguished character. We have references in this Book to at least one of the archery trials at the royal court; to that at the feudal courts; and to one presided over by Confucius himself, of which it is difficult to assign the occasion. The object of the author is to show the attention paid to archery in ancient times, and how it was endeavoured to make it subservient to moral and educational purposes.

He had before him the accounts of the archery for officers in Books VIII, IX, and X of the Î Lî; but he allows himself more scope, in his observations on them, than the authors of the two preceding Books, and explains several practices in his own way,—unsatisfactorily, as I have pointed out in my notes.

BOOK XLIV. YEN Î

The Yen Î, or 'Meaning of the Banquet,' is a fragment of only five paragraphs, which, moreover, are inartistically put together, the first having no connexion with the others. The Book should begin with paragraph 2, commencing: 'The meaning of the Banquet at the feudal courts was this.' It was of this banquet that the compiler intended to give his readers an idea.

The greatest of all the ancient banquets was that which immediately followed the sacrifices in the ancestral temple, given to all the kindred of the same surname as the ruler, and to which there are several references in the Shih King. Thang San-zhâi (Ming dynasty) specifies four other occasions for the banquet besides this:—It, might be given by a feudal prince, without any special occasion,—like that described in the second of the Praise Songs of Lû; or to a high dignitary or Great officer, who had been engaged in the royal service,—like that in the Minor Odes of the Kingdom, iii, 3; or when a high dignitary returned from a friendly mission,—like that also in the Minor Odes, i, 2; or when an officer came from one state to another on a friendly mission. Many other occasions, however, can be imagined on which public banquets were appropriate and might be given. The usages at them would, for the most part, be of the same nature.

The eleventh and twelfth chapters of the Î Lî are occupied with the ceremony of the banquet. The author of this Treatise quotes passages here and there from them, and appends his own explanation of their educational significance. Two lessons, be says, were especially illustrated in them:—the right relations to be maintained between superiors and inferiors, and the distinction between the noble and the mean.

BOOK XLV. PHING Î

The subject of the Phing Î is the interchange of missions between the ancient feudal states. It was a rule of the kingdom that those states should by such interchange maintain a good understanding with one another, as a means of preventing both internal disturbances and aggression from without. P. Callery gives for the title:—'Signification (du Rite) des Visites.' I have met with it rendered in English by 'The Theory of Embassies;' but the Phing was not an embassy on any great state occasion, nor was it requisite that it should be sent at stated intervals. It could not be long neglected between two states without risk to the good fellowship between them, but events might at any time occur in any one state which would call forth such an expression of friendly sympathy from others.

A mission occasioned a very considerable expenditure to the receiving state, and the author, with amusing ingenuity, explains this as a device to teach the princes and their peoples 'to care little for such outlay in comparison with the maintenance of the custom and its ceremonies.

Those visits are treated with all the necessary details in the Î Lî, Books XV–XVIII; and though the extracts from them are not many, we get from the author a sufficiently intelligible account of the nature of the missions and the way in which they were carried through.

In paragraph 11, however, be turns to another subject, and writes at some length about archery, while the concluding paragraphs (12 and 13) give a conversation between Confucius and his disciple Dze–kung on the reasons why jade is thought so much of. The three paragraphs have no connexion with those that precede on the subject of the missions; and the question arises–Whence were they derived? The previous paragraphs, taken from or based on the Î Lî, are found in one of the surviving Treatises of the larger collection of the Greater Tâi, the thirty–sixth Book, called Khâo–sze, in consequence of which the Khien–lung editors suggest that these concluding paragraphs were an addition made by his relative, Tâi Shang. It may have been so, but we should not thereby be impressed with a high idea of the skill or judgment with which Shang executed his work.

BOOK XLVI. SANG FÛ SZE KIH.

This Book, with which the collection of the Lî Kî concludes, is an attempt to explain the usages of the mourning rites, and especially of the dress, wherein they agree, and wherein they differ, by referring them to the four constituents of man's nature,—love, righteousness, the sentiment of propriety, and knowledge, in harmony with the operations of heaven and earth in the course of nature. We do not know who was the author of it, but the Khien–lung editors contend that it could not have been in the original compilation of the Smaller Tâi, and owes its place in the collection to Kang Hsüan.

The greater part of it is found in the thirty–ninth, or last but one[1], of the Books still current as the Lî of the Greater Tâi; and another part in the 'Narratives of the School,' the third article in the sixth chapter of that Collection[2], the compilation of which in its present form is attributed to Wang Sû in the first half of our third century. But this second fragment must have existed previously, else Kang

himself could not have seen it. The argument of those editors, therefore, that some scholar, later than the Smaller Tâi, must have incorporated it with what we find in the Greater Tâi, adding a beginning and ending of his own, so as to form a Book like one of those of Tâi Shang, and that Kang thought it worth his while to preserve it as the last portion of Shang's collection,—this argument is inconclusive. The fragment may originally have formed part of Tâi Teh's thirty–ninth Book or of some other, and the whole of this Book have been arranged, as we now have it by Shang himself, working, as he is reported to have done, on the compilation or digest of his cousin. However this be, the views in the Book are certainly ingenious and deserve to be read with care.

A few lines in Callery's work are sufficient to translate all of the Book which is admitted into the expurgated editions.

BOOK 1. KHÜ LÎ. SUMMARY OF THE RULES OF PROPRIETY.

SECTION I. PART I.

Ch. 1. 1. The Summary of the Rules of Propriety says:–Always and in everything let there be reverence; with the deportment grave as when

[On the names of the whole work and of this book, see the Introduction, pp. 9–12 and 15–17.

Part I is occupied with general principles and statements about Propriety rather than with the detail of particular rules. It may be divided into seven chapters, containing in all thirty–one paragraphs,

Ch. 1. 1, tells how reverence and gravity, with careful speech, are essential in Propriety; and shows its importance to a community or nation. 2. 2, specifies habits or tendencies incompatible with Propriety. 3. 3–5, gives instances of Propriety in superior men, and directions for certain cases. 4. 6, 7, states the rules for sitting, standing, and a mission to another state. 5. 8–22, sets forth how indispensable Propriety is for the regulation of the individual and society, and that it marks in fact the distinction between men and brutes. 6. 23–26, indicates how the rules, unnecessary in the most ancient times, grew with the progress of society, and were its ornament and security. 7. 27–31, speaks of the different stages of life, as divided into decades from ten years to a hundred; and certain characteristics belonging to them.]

one is thinking (deeply), and with speech composed and definite. This will make the people tranquil.

2. 2. Pride should not be allowed to grow; the desires should not be indulged; the will should not be gratified to the full; pleasure should not be carried to excess.

3. 3. Men of talents and virtue can be familiar with others and yet respect them; can stand in awe of others and yet love them. They love others and yet acknowledge the evil that is in them. They accumulate (wealth) and yet are able to part with it (to help the needy); they rest in what gives them satisfaction and yet can seek satisfaction elsewhere (when it is desirable to do so). 4. When you find wealth within your reach, do not (try to) get it by improper means; when you meet with calamity, do not (try to) escape from it by improper means. Do not seek for victory in small contentions; do not seek for more than your proper share. 5. Do not positively affirm what you have doubts about; and (when you have no doubts), do not let what you say appear (simply) as your own view[1].

4. 6. If a man be sitting, let him do so as a personator of the deceased[2]; if he be standing, let him do so (reverently), as in sacrificing. 7. In

[1. The text in the second part of this sentence is not easily translated and interpreted. I have followed in my version the view of Kang, Kû Hsi,.and the Khien–lung editors. Callery gives for'the whole sentence, ' Ne donnez pas comme certain ce qui est douteux, mais exposez–le clairement sans arrière–pensée.' Zottoli's view of the meaning is probably the same as mine: 'Dubiu's rerurn noli praesumere, sed sincerus ne tibi arroges.'

2 On the personator of the deceased, see vol. iii, pp. 300, 301, According to the ritual of Kau, the representatives of the dead always sat, and bore themselves with the utmost gravity.]

(observing) the rules of propriety, what is right (for the time and in the circumstances) should be followed. In discharging a mission (to another state), its customs are to be observed.

5. 8. They are the rules of propriety, that furnish the means of determining (the observances towards) relatives, as near and remote; of settling points which may cause suspicion or doubt; of distinguishing where there should be agreement, and where difference; and of making clear what is right and what is wrong. 9. According to those

rules, one should not (seek to) please others in an improper way, nor be lavish of his words, 10. According to them, one does not go beyond the definite measure, nor encroach on or despise others, nor is fond of (presuming) familiarities. 11. To cultivate one's person and fulfil one's words is called good conduct. When the conduct is (thus) ordered, and the words are accordant with the (right) course, we have the substance of the rules of propriety. 12. I have heard that it is in accordance with those rules that one should be chosen by others (as their model); I have not heard of his choosing them (to take him as such). I have heard in the same way of (scholars) coming to learn; I have not heard of (the master) going to teach. 13. The course (of duty), virtue, benevolence, and righteousness cannot be fully carried out without the rules of propriety; 14. nor are training and oral lessons for the rectification of manners complete; 15. nor can the clearing up of quarrels and discriminating in disputes be accomplished; 16. nor can (the duties between) ruler and minister, high and low, father and son, elder brother and younger, be determined; 17. nor can students for office and (other) learners, in serving their masters, have an attachment for them; 18. nor can majesty and dignity be shown in assigning the different places at court, in the government of the armies, and in discharging the duties of office so as to secure the operation of the laws; 19. nor can there be the (proper) sincerity and gravity in presenting the offerings to spiritual Beings on occasions of supplication, thanksgiving, and the various sacrifices[1]. 20. Therefore the superior man is respectful and reverent, assiduous in his duties and not going beyond them, retiring and yielding;–thus illustrating (the principle of) propriety. 21. The parrot can speak, and yet is nothing more than a bird; the ape can speak, and yet is nothing more than a beast 22. Here now is a man who observes no rules of propriety; is not his heart that of a beast? But if (men were as) beasts, and without (the principle of) propriety, father and son might have the same mate. 22. Therefore, when the sages arose, they framed the rules of propriety in order to teach men, and cause them, by

[1. Four religious acts are here mentioned, in connexion with which the offerings to spiritual Beings were presented. What I have called 'various sacrifices' is in Chinese Kî sze. Wû Khang says: 'Kî means sacrificial offerings to the spirit (or spirits) of Earth, and sze those to the spirits of Heaven. Offerings to the manes of men are also covered by them when they are used together.'

2 We know that the parrot and some other birds can be taught to speak; but I do not know that any animal has been taught to enunciate words even as these birds do. Williams (Dict. p. 8og) thinks that the shang shang mentioned here may be the rhinopithecus

Roxellana of P. David, found in Sze-khüan; but we have no account of it in Chinese works, so far as I know, that is not evidently fabulous.]

their possession of them, to make a distinction between themselves and brutes.

6. 23. In the highest antiquity they prized (simply conferring) good; in the time next to this, giving and repaying was the thing attended to[1]. And what the rules of propriety value is that reciprocity. If I give a gift and nothing comes in return, that is contrary to propriety; if the thing comes to me, and I give nothing in return, that also is contrary to propriety. 24. If a man observe the rules of propriety, he is in a condition of security; if he do not, he is in one of danger. Hence there is the saying, 'The rules of propriety should by no means be left unlearned.' 25. Propriety is seen in humbling one's self and giving honour to others. Even porters and pedlers are sure to display this giving honour (in some cases); how much more should the rich and noble do so (in all)! 26. When the rich and noble know to love propriety, they do not become proud nor dissolute. When the poor and mean know to love propriety, their minds do not become cowardly.

7. 27. When one is ten years old, we call him a boy; he goes (out) to school. When he is twenty, we call him a youth; he is capped. When he is thirty, we say, 'He is at his maturity;' he has a wife[2]. When

[1. Compare with this paragraph the state of 'the highest antiquity' described in the Tâo Teh King, chapters 18, 19, et al.

2 When it is said that at thirty a man has a wife, the meaning must be that he ought not to reach that age without being married. Early marriages were the rule in ancient China, as they are now. Confucius was married when barely twenty. In the same way we are to understand the being in office at forty. A man might take office at thirty; if he reached forty before he did so, there was something wrong in himself or others.]

he is forty, we say, 'He is in his vigour;' he is employed in office. When he is fifty, we say, 'He is getting grey;' he can discharge all the duties of an officer. When he is sixty, we say, 'He is getting old;' he gives directions and instructions. When he is seventy, we say, 'He is old;' he delegates his duties to others. At eighty or ninety, we say of him, 'He is very old.' When he is seven, we say that he is an object of pitying love. Such a child and one who is very old, though they may be chargeable with crime, are not subjected to punishment. At a hundred, he is called a centenarian, and has to be fed. 28. A great officer, when he is seventy, should resign (his charge of) affairs. 29. If he be not allowed to resign, there must be given him a stool and staff. When travelling on service, he must have the attendance of his wife[1]; and when going to any other state, he will ride in an easy carriage[2]. 30. (In another state) he will, style himself 'the old man;' in his own state, he will call himself by his name. 31. When from another they ask (about his state), he must tell them of its (old) institutions[3].

[1. Perhaps we should translate here in the plural—'his women,' which would include his wife.

2. An 'easy carriage' was small. Its occupant sat in it, and did not stand.

3. It is supposed here that the foreign envoys first question the ruler, who then calls in the help of the aged minister.]

PART II

1. 1. In going to take counsel with an elder, one must carry a stool and a staff with him (for the elder's use). When the elder asks a question, to reply without acknowledging one's incompetency and (trying to) decline answering, is contrary to propriety[1].

2. 2. For all sons it is the rule :—In winter, to warm (the bed for their parents), and to cool it in summer; in the evening, to adjust everything (for their repose), and to inquire (about their health) in the morning; and, when with their companions, not to quarrel.

3. 3. Whenever a son, having received the three (first) gifts (of the ruler), declines (to use) the carriage and horses, the people of the hamlets and smaller districts, and of the larger districts and neighbourhoods, will proclaim him filial; his brothers and relatives, both by consanguinity and affinity, will proclaim him

[Part II enters more into detail about the rules of Propriety. It has been divided into seven chapters, containing in all thirty–two paragraphs.

Ch. 1. 1, speaks of a junior consulting an elder. 2. 2, describes services due from all sons to their parents. 3. 3, shows a filial son when raised to higher rank than his father. 4. 4–16, contains rules for a son in various circumstances, especially with reference to his father. 5. 17–26, gives the rules for younger men in their intercourse with their teachers and elders generally, and in various cases. 6. 27, is the rule for an officer in entering the gate of his ruler or coming out by it. 7. 28–32, deals with a host and visitor, and ceremonious visiting and intercourse generally.

3. The reply of Tsang Shan to Confucius, as related in vol. iii, pp. 465, 466, is commonly introduced in illustration of this second sentence.]

loving; his friends who are fellow–officers will proclaim him virtuous; and his friends who are his associates will proclaim him true[1].

4. 4. When he sees an intimate friend of his father, not to presume to go forward to him without being told to do so; nor to retire without being told; nor to address him without being questioned:—this is the conduct of a filial son, 5. A son, when he is going abroad, must inform (his parents where he is going); when he returns, he must present himself before them. Where he travels must be in some fixed (region); what he engages in must be some (reputable) occupation. 6. In ordinary conversation (with his parents), he does not use the term 'old' (with reference to them)[2]. 7. He should serve one twice as old as himself as he serves his father, one ten years older than himself as an elder brother; with one five years older he should walk shoulder to shoulder, but (a little) behind him. 8. When five are sitting together, the eldest must have a different mat (by himself)[3]. 9. A son should not occupy the south–west corner of the apartment, nor sit in the

[1. The gifts of distinction, conferred by the sovereign on officers, ministers, and feudal princes, were nine in all; and the enumerations of them are not always the same. The three intended here are the appointment to office, or rank; the robes belonging to it; and the chariot and horses. We must suppose that the rank placed the son higher than the father in social position, and that he declines the third gift from humility,—not to parade himself as superior to his father and others in his circle.

2. Some understand the rule to be that the son is not to speak of himself as old; but the meaning in the translation is the more approved.

3. Four men were the proper complement for a mat; the eldest of the five therefore was honoured with another mat for himself.]

middle of the mat (which he occupies alone), nor walk in the middle of the road, nor stand in the middle of the doorway[1]. 10. He should not take the part of regulating the (quantity of) rice and other viands at an entertainment. 11. He should not act as personator of the dead at sacrifice[2]. 12. He should be (as if he were) hearing (his parents) when there is no voice from them, and as seeing them when they are not actually there. 13. He should not ascend a height, nor approach the verge of a depth; he should not indulge in reckless reviling or derisive laughing. A filial son will not do things in the dark, nor attempt hazardous undertakings, fearing lest he disgrace his parents. 14. While his parents are alive, he will not promise a friend to die (with or for him)[3], nor will he have wealth that he calls his own. 15. A son, while his parents are alive, will not wear a cap or (other) article of dress, with a white border[4]. 16. An orphan son, taking his father's place, will not wear a cap or (other article of) dress with a variegated border[5].

5. 17. A boy should never he allowed to see an

[1. The father is supposed to be alive; the south–west part of an apartment was held to be the most honourable, and must be reserved for him. So of the other things.

2. This was in the ancestral worship. A son, acting such a part, would have to receive the homage of his father.

3. I have known instances of Chinese agreeing to die with or for a friend, who wished to avenge a great wrong. See the covenant of the three heroes of the 'romance of the Three Kingdoms,' near the beginning.

4. White was and is the colour worn in mourning.

5. The son here is the eldest son and heir; even after the regular period of mourning is over, he continues to wear it in so far. The other sons were not required to do so.]

instance of deceit[1]. 18. A lad should not wear a jacket of fur nor the skirt[2] . He must stand straight and square, and not incline his head in hearing. 19. When an elder is holding him with the hand, he should hold the elder's hand with both his hands. When the elder has shifted his sword to his back and is speaking to him with the side of his face bent, down, he should cover his mouth with his hand in answering[3]. 20. When he is following his teacher 4, he should not quit the road to speak with another person. When he meets his teacher on the road, he should hasten forward to him, and stand with his hands joined across his breast. If the teacher speak to him, he will answer; if he do not, he will retire with hasty steps. 21. When, following an elder, they ascend a level height, he must keep his face towards the quarter to which the elder is looking. 22. When one has ascended the wall of a city, he should not point, nor callout[5]. 23. When he intends to go to a lodging–house, let it not be with the feeling that he must get whatever he asks for. 24. When about to go up to the hall (of a house), he must raise his voice. When outside the door there are two (pairs

[1. This maxim deserves to be specially noted. It will remind the reader of Juvenal's lines:—

'Maxima debetur puero, reverentia. Si quid
Turpe paras, nec tu pueri contempseris annos.'

To make him handy, and leave him free to execute any service required of him.

2. The second sentence here is difficult to construe, and the critics differ much in dealing with it. Zottoli's version is—'Si e dorso vel latere transverso ore (superior) eloquatur ei, tunc obducto ore respondebit.'

3. 'Teacher' is here I the one born before him,' denoting I an old man who teaches youth.'

4. And thus make himself an object of general observation.]

of) shoes[1], if voices be heard, he. enters; if voices be not heard, he will not enter. 25. When about to enter the door, he must keep his eyes cast down. As he enters, he should (keep his hands raised as high as if he were) bearing the bar of the door. In looking down or up, he should not turn (his head). If the door were open, he should leave it open; if it were shut, he should shut it again. If there be others (about) to enter after him, while he (turns to) shut the door, let him not do so hastily. 26. Let him not tread on the shoes (left outside the door), nor stride across the mat (in going to take his seat); but let him hold up his dress, and move hastily to his corner (of the mat). (When seated), he must be careful in answering or assenting.

6. 27. A great officer or (other) officer should go out or in at the ruler's doors[2], on the right of the middle post, without treading on the threshold.

7. 28. Whenever (a host has received and) is entering with a guest, at every door he should give place to him. When the guest arrives at the innermost door (or that leading to the feast–room),

[1. It was the custom in China, as it still is in Japan, to take off the shoes, and leave them outside the door on entering an apartment. This paragraph and the next tell us how a new–comer should not enter an apartment hastily, so as to take those already there by surprise.

2. It is necessary to translate here in the plural. Anciently, as now, the palace, mansion, or public office was an aggregate of courts, with buildings in them, so that the visitor passed from one to another through a gateway, till he reached the inner court which conducted to the hall, behind which again were the family apartments. The royal palace had five courts and gates; that of a feudal lord had three. Each gate had its proper name. The whole assemblage of buildings was much deeper than it was wide.]

the host will ask to be allowed to enter first and arrange the mats. Having done this, he will come out to receive the guest, who will refuse firmly (to enter first). The host having made a low bow to him, they will enter (together). 29. When they have entered the door, the host moves to the right, and the guest to the left, the former going to the steps on the cast, and the latter to those on the west. If the guest be of the lower rank, he goes to the steps of the host (as if to follow him up them). The host firmly declines this, and he returns to the other steps on the west[1]. 30. They then offer to each other the precedence in going up, but the host commences first, followed (immediately) by the other. They bring their feet together on every step, thus ascending by successive paces. He who ascends by the steps on the cast should move his right foot first, and the other at the western steps his left foot. 31. Outside the curtain or screen[2] (a visitor) should not walk with the formal hasty steps, nor above in the hall, nor when carrying the symbol of jade. Above, in the raised hall, the foot–prints should be alongside each other, but below it free and separate. In the apartment the elbows should not be held out like wings in bowing. 32. When two (equals) are sitting side by side, they do not have their elbows extended crosswise. One should not kneel in handing anything to a (superior) standing, nor stand in handing it to him sitting.

[1. The host here is evidently of high dignity, living in a mansion.

2 The screen was in front of the raised hall, in the courtyard; until they passed it visitors might not be in view of their host, and could feel at ease in their carriage and movements.]

PART III.

1. In all cases of (a lad's) carrying away the dirt that has been swept up from the presence of an elder, it is the rule that he (place) the brush on the basket, keeping his sleeve before it as he retires. The dust is not allowed to reach the elder, because he carries the basket with its mouth turned towards himself. 2. He carries the (elder's) mat in his arms like the cross–beam of a shadoof 3. If it be a mat

[Part III continues to lay down the rules for various duties and classes of duties. It extends to sixty–seven paragraphs, which may be comprised in twenty–one chapters.

Ch. 1. 1–4, describes a youth's ways in sweeping for an elder and in carrying and placing his mats. 2. 5–7, relates to host and guest. 3. 8–19, is about a youth, especially a pupil, in attendance on his elders. 4. 20–26, is about his ways in serving a superior. 5. 27–29, is about the shoes in visiting. 6. 30–39, gives rules about not interfering with people's private affairs, and avoiding, between male and female, what would cause suspicion. 7. 40, is a message of congratulation to a friend on his marriage. 8: 41, is about consideration for the poor and the old. 9. 42–46, gives rules for the naming of sons and daughters. 10. 47–51, describes the arrangement of the dishes, and the behaviour of the host and guests, at an entertainment. 11. 52, we have a youth and his host eating together. 12. 53, shows how people, eating together, ought to behave. 13. 54–58, is about things to be avoided in eating. 14. 59, shows us host and guest at the close of the entertainment. In 15. 6o, we have a youth and elder drinking together. 16. 6 1, is about a gift from an elder. 17. 62, shows how the kernel of a fruit given by an elder is to be dealt with in his presence. 18. 63, 64, relates to gifts at a feast from the ruler, and how they are to be used. 19. 65, is about a ruler asking an attendant to share in a feast. 20. 66, is about the use of chopsticks with soup. 21. 67, gives the rules for paring a melon for the ruler and others.]

to sit on, he will ask in what direction (the elder) is going to turn his face; if it be to sleep on, in what direction he is going to turn his feet. 4. If a mat face the south or the north, the seat on the west is accounted that of honour; if it face the east or the west, the seat on the south.

2. 5. Except in the case of guests who are there (simply) to eat and drink, in spreading the mats a space of ten cubits should be left between them[1]. 6. When the host kneels to adjust the mats (of a visitor), the other should kneel and keep hold of them, declining (the honour)[2]. When the visitor (wishes to) remove one or more, the host should firmly decline to permit him to do so. When the visitor steps on his mats, (the host) takes his seat. 7. If the host have not put some question, the visitor should not begin the conversation.

3. 8. When (a pupil) is about to go to his mat, he should not look discomposed. With his two hands he should hold up his lower garment, so that the bottom of it may be a cubit from the ground. His clothes should not hang loosely about him, nor should there be any hurried movements of his feet. 9. If any writing or tablets of his master, or his lute or cithern be in the way, he should kneel down and remove them, taking care not to disarrange them. 10. When sitting and doing nothing, he should keep quite at the back (of his mat); when eating, quite at the front of it[3] . He should sit quietly and keep

[1. To allow space and freedom for gesticulation.

2. Two or more mats might be placed over each other in honour of the visitor.

3. The dishes were placed before the mats.]

a watch on his countenance. If there be any subject on which the elder has not touched, let him not introduce it irregularly. 11. Let him keep his deportment correct[1], and listen respectfully. Let him not appropriate (to himself) the words (of others), nor (repeat them) as (the echo does the) thunder. If he must (adduce proofs), let them be from antiquity, with an appeal to the ancient kings. 12. When sitting by his side, and the teacher puts a question, (the learner) should not reply till (the other) has finished. 13. When requesting (instruction) on the subject of his studies, (the learner) should rise; when requesting further information, he should rise. 14. When his father calls, (a youth) should not (merely) answer 'yes,' nor when his teacher calls. He should, with (a respectful) 'yes,' immediately rise (and go to them). 15. When one is sitting in attendance on another whom he honours and reveres, he should not allow any part of his mat to keep them apart[2], nor will he rise when he sees others (come in) of the same rank as himself. 16. When the torches come, he should rise; and also when the viands come in, or a visitor of superior rank[3]. 17. The torches should not (be allowed to burn) till their ends can be seen. 18. Before an honoured visitor we should not shout (even) at

[1. Here, and in some other places, we find the second personal pronoun; as if the text were made up from different sources. I have translated, however, as if we had only the third person.

2. He should sit on the front of his mat, to be as near the other as possible.

3. The torches were borne by boys. They were often changed, that the visitors might not be aware how the time was passing.]

a dog. 19. When declining any food, one should not spit.

4. 20. When one is sitting in attendance on another of superior character or rank, and that other yawns or stretches himself, or lays hold of his staff or shoes, or looks towards the sun to see if it be early or late, he should ask to be allowed to leave. 21. In the same position, if the superior man put a question on a new subject, he should rise up in giving his reply. 22. Similarly, if there come some one saying (to the superior man), 'I wish, when you have a little leisure, to report to you,' he should withdraw to the left or right and wait. 23. Do not listen with the head inclined on one side, nor answer with a loud sharp voice, nor look with a dissolute leer, nor keep the body in a slouching position[1]. 24. Do not saunter about with a haughty gait, nor stand with one foot raised. Do not sit with your knees wide apart, nor sleep on your face. 25. Have your hair gathered up, and do not use any false hair[2]. 26. Let not the cap be laid aside; nor the chest be bared, (even) when one is toiling hard; nor let the lower garment be held up (even) in hot weather.

5. 2 7. When (going to) sit in attendance on an elder, (a visitor) should not go up to the hall with his shoes on, nor should he presume to take them off in front of the Steps. 28.

(When any single visitor is leaving), he will go to his shoes, kneel down and take them up, and then move to one side. 29. (When the visitors retire in a body) with their

[1. The style and form of 23–26 differ from the preceding. Perhaps they should form a paragraph by themselves.

2. Which women were accustomed to do.]

faces towards the elder, (they stand) by the shoes, which they then, kneeling, remove (some distance), and, stooping down, put on[1].

6 . 30. When two men are sitting or standing together, do not join them as a third. When two are standing together, another should not pass between them. 31. Male and female should not sit together (in the same apartment), nor have the same stand or rack for their clothes, nor use the same towel or comb, nor let their hands touch in giving and receiving. 32. A sister–in–law and brother–in–law do not interchange inquiries (about each other). None of the concubines in a house should be employed to wash the lower garment (of a son)[2]. 33. Outside affairs should not be talked of inside the threshold (of the women's apartments), nor inside (or women's) affairs outside it. 34. When a young lady is; promised in marriage, she wears the strings (hanging down to her neck)[3]; and unless there be some :great occasion, no (male) enters the door of her apartment[4]. 35. When a married aunt, or sister, or daughter returns home (on a visit), no brother (of the family) should sit with her on the same mat or eat with her from the same dish. (Even) the father and daughter should not occupy the same mat[5]. 36.

[1. The host would be seeing the visitors off, and therefore they would keep their faces towards him.

2. Concubines might be employed to wash clothes; delicacy forbade their washing the lower garments of the sons.

3. Those strings were symbolic of the union with and subjection to her husband to which she was now pledged.

4. Great sickness or death, or other great calamity, would be such ant occasion.

5. This is pushing the rule to an extreme. The sentence is also (but wrongly) understood of father and son.]

Male and female, without the intervention of the matchmaker, do not know each other's name. Unless the marriage presents have been received, there should be no communication nor affection between them. 37. Hence the day and month (of the marriage) should be announced to the ruler, and to the spirits (of ancestors) with purification and fasting; and (the bridegroom) should make a feast, and invite (his friends) in the district and neighbourhood, and his fellow–officers :—thus giving its due importance to the separate position (of male and female). 38. One must not marry a wife of the same surname with himself. Hence, in buying a concubine, if he do not know her surname, he must consult the tortoise–shell about it[1]. 39. With the son of a widow, unless he be of acknowledged distinction, one should not associate himself as a friend.

7. 40. When one congratulates (a friend) on his marrying, his messenger says, 'So and So has sent me. Having heard that you are having guests, he has sent me with this present.'

8. 41. Goods and wealth are not to be expected from the poor in their discharge of the rules of propriety; nor the display of sinews and strength from the old.

9. 42. In giving a name to a son, it should not be that of a state, nor of a day or a month, nor of any hidden ailment, nor of a hill or river[2]. 43.

[1. Not to find out what her surname is, but to determine whether it be the same as that of the gentleman or not.

2. Such names were so common, that if it became necessary to avoid them, as it might be, through the death of the party or on other grounds, it would be difficult and inconvenient to do so.]

Sons and daughters should have their (relative) ages distinguished[1]. 44. A son at twenty is capped, and receives his appellation[2]. 45. Before his father a son should be called by his name, and before his ruler a minister[3]. 46. When a daughter is promised in marriage, she assumes the hair–pin, and receives her appellation.

10. 47. The rules for bringing in the dishes for an entertainment are the following:—The meat cooked on the bones is set on the left, and the sliced meat on the right; the rice is placed on the left of the parties on the mat, and the soup on their right; the minced and roasted meat are put outside (the chops and sliced meat), and the pickles and sauces inside; the onions and steamed onions succeed to these, and the drink and syrups are on the right. When slices of dried and spiced meat are put down, where they are folded is turned to the left, and the ends of them to the right. 48. If a guest be of lower rank (than his entertainer), he should take up the rice[4], rise and decline (the honour he is receiving). The host then rises and refuses to allow the guest (to retire). After this the guest will resume his seat. 49. When the host leads on the guests to present an offering (to the father of cookery), they will begin

[1. As primus, prima; secundus, secunda, &c.

2 The appellation was thus the name given (at a family meeting) to a youth who had reached man's estate. Morrison (Dict. i. 627) calls it the name taken by men when they marry. Such a usage testifies to the early marriages in ancient China, as referred to in note 2, p. 65.

3. There might be some meaning in the appellation which would seem to place its bearer on the level of his father or his ruler.

4. The rice is called 'the principal article in a feast.' Hence the humbler guest takes it up, as symbolical of all the others.]

with the dishes which were first brought in. Going on from the meat cooked on the bones they will offer of all (the other dishes)[1]. 50. After they have eaten three times, the host will lead on the guests to take of the sliced meat, from which they will go on to all the other dishes. 51. A guest should not rinse his mouth with spirits till the host has gone over all the dishes.

11. 52. When (a youth) is in attendance on an elder at a meal, if the host give anything to him with his own hand, he should bow to him and eat it. If he do not so give him anything, he should eat without bowing.

12. 53. When eating with others from the same dishes, one should not try to eat (hastily) to satiety. When eating with them from the same dish of rice, one should not have to wash his hands[2].

13. 54. Do not roll the rice into a ball; do not bolt down the various dishes; do not swill down (the soup). 55. Do not make a noise in eating; do not crunch the bones with the teeth; do not put back fish you have been eating; do not throw the bones to the dogs; do not snatch (at what you want). 56. Do not spread out the rice (to cool); do not use chopsticks in eating millet[3].

[1. This paragraph refers to a practice something like our 'saying grace.' According to Khung Ying–tâ, a little was taken from all the dishes, and placed on the ground about them as an offering to 'the father of cookery.'

2 As all ate from the same dish of rice without chopsticks or spoons, it was necessary they should try to keep their hands clean. Some say the 'washing' was only a rubbing of the hands with sand.

3 A spoon was the proper implement in eating millet.]

57. Do not (try to) gulp down soup with vegetables in it, nor add condiments to it; do not keep picking the–teeth, nor swill down the sauces. If a guest add condiments, the host will apologise for not having had the soup prepared better. If he swill down the sauces, the host will apologise for his poverty[1]. 58. Meat that is wet (and soft) may be divided with the teeth, but dried flesh cannot be so dealt with. Do not bolt roast meat in large pieces.

14. 59. When they have done eating, the guests will kneel in front (of the mat), and (begin to) remove the (dishes) of rice and sauces to give them to the attendants. The host will then rise and decline this service from the guests, who will resume their seats.

15. 60. If a youth is in attendance on, and drinking with, an elder, when the (cup of) spirits is brought to him, he rises, bows, and (goes to) receive it at the place where the spirit–vase is kept. The elder refuses (to allow him to do so), when he returns to the mat, and (is prepared) to drink. The elder (meantime) lifts (his cup); but until he has emptied it, the other does not presume to drink his.

16. 61. When an elder offers a gift, neither a youth, nor one of mean, condition, presumes to decline it.

17. 62. When a fruit is given by the ruler and in his presence, if there be a kernel in it, (the receiver) should place it in his bosom[2].

[1. The sauce should be too strong to be swallowed largely and hurriedly.

2. Lest he should seem to throw away anything given by the ruler.]

18. 63. When one is attending the ruler at a meal, and the ruler gives him anything that is left, if it be in a vessel that can be easily scoured, he does not transfer it (to another of his own); but from any other vessel he should so transfer it[1].

19. 64. Portions of (such) food should not be used as offerings (to the departed). A father should not use them in offering even to a (deceased) son, nor a husband in offering to a (deceased) wife[2].

20. 65. When one is attending an elder and (called to) share with him (at a feast), though the viands may be double (what is necessary), he should not (seek) to decline them. If he take his seat (only) as the companion of another (for whom it has been prepared), he should not decline them.

21. 66. If the soup be made with vegetables, chopsticks should be used; but not if there be no vegetables.

22. 67. He who pares a melon for the son of Heaven should divide it into four parts and then into cight, and cover them with a napkin of fine linen. For the ruler of a state, he should divide it into four parts, and cover them with a coarse napkin. To a great officer he should (present the four parts) uncovered. An inferior officer should receive it (simply) with the stalk cut away. A common man will deal with it with his teeth.

[1. A vessel of potter's ware or metal can be scoured, and the part which his mouth has touched be cleansed before the ruler uses it again.

2. The meaning of this paragraph is not clear.]

PART IV.

1. When his father or mother is ill, (a young man) who has been capped should not use his comb, nor walk with his elbows stuck out, nor speak on idle topics, nor take his lute or cithern in hand. He should not eat of (different) meats till his taste is changed, nor drink till his looks are changed'. He should not laugh so as to show his teeth, nor be angry till he breaks forth in reviling. When the illness is gone, he may resume his former habits. 2. He who is sad and anxious should sit with his mat

[Part IV contains fifty–two paragraphs, which have been arranged in ten chapters, stating the rules to be observed in a variety of cases.

Ch. 1. 1, 2, treats of the ways of a young man who is sorrowful in consequence of the illness or death of a parent. 2. 3–26, treats of the rules in giving and receiving, and of messages connected therewith. The presentations mentioned are all from inferiors to superiors. 3. 27, 28, does not lay down rules, but gives characteristics of the superior man, and the methods by which he preserves his friendships unbroken. 4. 29, 30, refers to the arrangement of the tablets in the ancestral temple, and to the personators of the dead. 5. 31, tells how one fasting should keep himself from being excited. 6. 32–34, sets forth cautions against excess in the demonstrations of mourning. 7. 35, 36, speaks of sorrowing for the dead and condoling with the living. 8. 37, 38, gives counsels of prudence for one under the influence of sympathy and benevolent feeling. 9. 39–48, describes rules in connexion with mourning, burials, and some other occasions. 10. 49–52, describes gradations in ceremonies and in the penal statutes; and how a criminal who has been punished should never be permitted to be near the ruler.

1. Does the rule about eating mean that the anxious son should restrict himself to a single dish of meat?]

spread apart from others; he who is mourning (for a death) should sit on a single mat[1].

2. 3. When heavy rains have fallen, one should not present fish or tortoises (to a superior)[2]. 4. He who is presenting a bird should turn its head on one side; if it be a tame bird, this need not be done. 5. He who is presenting a carriage and horses should carry in his hand (to the hall) the whip, and strap for mounting by[3]. 6. He who is

presenting a suit of mail should carry the helmet (to the hall). He who is presenting a staff should hold it by its end[4]. 7. He who is presenting a captive should hold him by the right sleeve[5]. 8. He who is presenting grain unhulled should carry with him the left side of the account (of the quantity); if the hull be off, he should carry with him a measure–drum[6]. 9. He who is presenting cooked food, should carry with him the sauce and pickles for it. 10. He who is presenting fields and tenements should carry with him the writings about them, and give them up (to the superior). 11. In every case of giving a bow to another, if it be bent, the (string of) sinew should be kept upwards; but if unbent, the horn.

[1. Grief is solitary. A mourner afflicts himself.

2 Because the fish in such a case are so numerous as not to be valuable, or because the fish at the time of the rains are not clean. Other reasons for the rule have been assigned.

3. The whip and strap, carried up to the hall, represented the carriage and horses, left in the courtyard.

4. For convenience; and because the end, going into the mud, was not so honourable.

5. So that he could not attempt any violence.

6. The account was in duplicate, on the same tablet. The right was held to be the more honourable part. 'Drum' was the name of the measure.]

(The giver) should with his right hand grasp the end of the bow, and keep his left under the middle of the back. The (parties, without regard to their rank as) high and low, (bow to each other) till the napkins (at their girdles) hang down (to the ground). If the host (wish to) bow (still lower), the other moves on one side to avoid the salutation. The host then takes the bow, standing on the left of the other. Putting his hand under that of the visitor, he lays hold of the middle of the back, having his face in the same direction as the other; and thus he receives (the bow). 12. He who is giving a sword should do so with the hilt on his left side[1]. 13. He who is giving a spear with one hook should do so with the metal end of the shaft in front, and the sharp edge behind. 14. He who is presenting one with two hooks, or one with a single hook and two sharp points, should do so with the blunt shaft in front. 15. He who is giving a stool or a staff should (first) wipe it. 16. He who is presenting a horse or a sheep should lead it with his right hand. 17. He who is presenting a dog should lead it with his left hand. 18. He who is carrying a bird (as his present of introduction) should do so with the head to the left[2]. 19. For the ornamental covering of a lamb or a goose, an embroidered cloth should be used. 20. He who receives a pearl or a piece of jade should do so with both his hands. 21. He who receives a bow or a sword should do so (having his hands covered) with his sleeves[3]. 22. He who has

[1. That the receiver may take it with his right hand.

2. Compare paragraph 4. In this case the bird was carried across the body of the donor with its head on his left.

3. A different case from that in paragraph 11. It is supposed that here the two things were presented together, and received as on a cushion.]

drunk from a cup of jade should not (go on to) shake it out[1]. 23. Whenever friendly messages are about to be sent, with the present of a sword or bow, or of (fruit, flesh, and other things, wrapped in) matting of rushes, with grass mats, and in baskets, round and square, (the messenger) has these things (carried with him, when he goes) to receive his commission, and deports himself as when he will be discharging it[2]. 24. Whenever one is charged with a mission by his ruler, after he has received from him his orders, and (heard all) he has to say, he should not remain over the night in his house. 25. When a message from the ruler comes (to a minister), the latter should go out and bow (to the bearer), in acknowledgment of the honour of it. When the messenger is about to return, (the other) must bow to him (again), and escort him outside the gate. 26. If (a minister) send a message to his ruler, he must wear his court–robes when he communicates it to the bearer; and on his return, he must descend from the hall, to receive (the ruler's) commands.

3. 27. To acquire extensive information and remember retentively, while (at the same time) he is modest; to do earnestly what is good, and not become weary in so doing:—these are the characteristics of him whom we call the superior man. 28. A superior man does not accept everything by which another would express his joy in him, or his devotion to him[3]; and thus he preserves their friendly intercourse unbroken.

[1. Because of the risk to a thing so valuable.

2. A rehearsal of what he would have to do.

3. E. g., it is said, festive entertainments and gi fits.]

4. 29. A rule of propriety says, 'A superior man may carry his grandson in his arms, but not his son.' This tells us that a grandson may be the personator of his deceased grandfather (at sacrifices), but a son cannot be so of his father[1]. 30. When a great officer or (other) officer sees one who is to personate the dead (on his way to the ancestral temple), he should dismount from his carriage to him. The ruler himself, when he recognises him, should do the same[2]. The personator (at the same time) must bow forward to the cross–bar. In mounting the carriage, he must use a stool.

5. 31. One who is fasting (in preparation for a sacrifice) should neither listen to music nor condole with mourners[3].

6. 32. According to the rules for the period of mourning (for a father), (a son) should not emaciate himself till the bones appear, nor let his seeing and hearing be affected (by his privations). He should not go up to, nor descend from, the hail by the steps on the east (which his father used), nor go in or out by the path right opposite to the (centre of the) gate. 33. According to the same rules, if he have a scab on his head, he should wash it; if he have a sore on his body, he should bathe it. If he be ill, he should drink spirits, and eat flesh, returning to his former

[1. The tablets of a father and son should not be in the same line of shrines in the ancestral temple; and the fact in the paragraph—hardly credible—seems to be mentioned as giving a reason for this.

2. The personator had for the time the dignity of the deceased whom he represented.

3. The fasting and vigil extended to seven days, and were intended to prepare for the personating duty. What would distract the mind from this must be eschewed.]

(abstinence) when he is better. If he make himself unable to perform his mourning duties, that is like being unkind and unfilial. 34. If he be fifty, he should not allow himself to be reduced (by his abstinence) very much; and, if he be sixty, not at all. At seventy, he will only wear the unhemmed dress of sackcloth, and will drink and eat flesh, and occupy (the usual apartment) inside (his house).

7. 35. Intercourse with the living (will be continued) in the future; intercourse with the dead (friend) was a thing of the past[1]. 36. He who knows the living should send (a message of) condolence; and he who knew the dead (a message also of his) grief. He who knows the living, and did not know the dead, will send his condolence without (that expression of) his grief; he who knew the dead, and does not know the living, will send the (expression of) grief, but not go on to condole.

8. 37. He who is condoling with one who has mourning rites in band, and is not able to assist him with a gift, should put no question about his expenditure. He who is enquiring after another that is ill, and is not able to send (anything to him), should

[1. This gives the reasons for the directions in the next paragraph.. We condole with the living—to console them; for the dead, we have only to express our grief for our own loss. P. Zottoli's translation is:—'Vivis computatur subsequens dies; mortuo computatur praecedens dies;' and he says in a note :—'Vivorum luctus incipit quarta a morte die, et praecedente die seu tertia fit mortui in feretrum depositio; luctus igitur et depositio, die intercipiuntur; haec precedit ille subsequetur.' This is after many, critics, from Kang Khang-khang downwards; but it does great violence to the text. I have followed the view of the Khien-lung editors.]

not ask what he would like. He who sees (a traveller), and is not able to lodge him, should not ask where he is stopping. 38. He who would confer something on another should not say, 'Come and take it;' he who would give something (to a smaller man), should not ask him what he would like.

9. 39. When one goes to a burying-ground, he should not get up on any of the graves. When assisting at an interment, one should (join in) holding the rope attached to the coffin[1]. 40. In a house of mourning, one should not laugh. 41. In order to bow to another, one should leave his own place. 42. When one sees at a distance a coffin with the corpse in it, he should not sing. When he enters among the mourners, he should not keep his arms stuck out. When eating (with others), he should not sigh. 43. When there are mourning rites in his neighbourhood, one should not accompany his pestle with his voice. When there is a body shrouded and coffined in his village, one should not sing in the lanes. 44. When going to a burying-ground, one should not sing, nor on the same day

when he has wailed (with mourners). 45. When accompanying a funeral, one should not take a by–path. When taking part in the act of interment, one should not (try to) avoid mud or pools. When presenting himself at any mourning rite, one should have a sad countenance. When holding), the rope, one should not laugh, 46. When present on an occasion of joy, one should not sigh. 47. When wearing his coat of

[1. The rope here may also be that, or one of those, attached to the low car on which the coffin was drawn to the grave. Compare paragraph 45.]

mail and helmet, one's countenance should say, 'Who dares meddle with me?' 48. Hence the superior man is careful to maintain the proper expression of his countenance before others.

10. 49. Where the ruler of a state lays hold of the cross–bar, and bends forward to it, a great officer will descend from his carriage. Where a great officer lays bold of the bar and bends forward, another officer will descend. 50. The rules of ceremony do not go down to the common people[1]. 51. The penal statutes do not go up to great officers[2]. 52. Men who have suffered punishment should not (be allowed to) be by the side of the ruler[3].

[1. Not that the common people are altogether freed from the rules. But their occupations are engrossing, and their means small. Much cannot be expected from them.

2. It may be necessary to punish them, but they should be beyond requiring punishment. The application of it, moreover, will be modified by various considerations. But the regulation is not good.

3. To preserve the ruler from the contamination of their example, and the risk of their revenge.]

PART V.

1. 1. A fighting chariot has no cross–board to assist its occupants in bowing; in a war chariot the

[Part V contains forty–eight paragraphs, which may be arranged in ten chapters.

Ch. 1. 1–10, relates to carriages, especially to war chariots, and the use of them with their banners and other things in an expedition. 2. 10, gives the rules in avenging the deaths of a father, brother, and friend. 3. 11, shows the responsibility of ministers and officers generally in maintaining the defence and the cultivation of their country. 4. 12–14, relates to sacrifices,—the sacrificers, their robes, the victims, &c. 5. 15–21, gives rules about avoiding the mention of certain names. 6. 22–27, is on the subject of divination,—of divining, especially, about the days for contemplated undertakings. 7. 28–33, describes thc yoking the horses to a ruler's chariot, his taking his seat, and other points. 8. 34–35, is about the strap which the driver banded to parties who wished to mount the carriage. 9. 36, gives three prohibitive rules:—about a visitor's carriage; a woman riding in a carriage; and dogs and horses. 10. 37–48, relates various rules about driving out, for the ruler and people generally.]

banner is fully displayed; in a chariot of peace it is kept folded round the pole. 2. A recorder should carry with him in his carriage his implements for writing[1]; his, subordinates the (recorded) words (of former covenants and other documents). 3. When there is water in front, the flag with the green bird[2] on it should be displayed. 4. When there is (a cloud of) dust in front, that with the screaming kites. 5. For chariots and horsemen, that with wild geese in flight[3]. 6. For a body of troops, that with a tiger's (skin). 7. For a beast of prey, that with a leopard's (skin). 8. On the march the (banner with the) Red Bird should be in front; that with the Dark Warrior behind; that with the Azure Dragon on the left; and that with the White Tiger on the right; that

[1. The original character denotes what is now used for 'pencils;' but the ordinary pencil had not yet been invented.

2. Some kind of water–bird.

3. A flock of geese maintains a regular order in flying, and was used to symbolise lines of chariots and horsemen. Khung Ying–tâ observes that chariots were used in the field before cavalry, and that the mention of horsemen here looks like the close of the Kin dynasty. One of the earliest instances of riding on horseback is in the Zo Kwan under the year B.C. 517.]

with the Pointer of the Northern Bushel should be reared aloft (in the centre of the host):—all to excite and direct the fury (of the troops)[1]. 9. There are rules for advancing and retreating; there are the various arrangements on the left and the right, each with its (proper) officer to look after it.

2. 10. With the enemy who has slain his father, one should not live under the same heaven. With the enemy who has slain his brother, one should never have his sword to seek (to deal vengeance). With the enemy who has slain his intimate friend, one should not live in the same state (without seeking to slay him).

3. 11. Many ramparts in the country round and near (a capital) are a disgrace to its high ministers and great officers[2]. Where the wide and open country is greatly neglected and uncultivated, it is a disgrace to the officers (in charge of it).

4. 12. When taking part in a sacrifice, one should not show indifference. 13. When sacrificial robes are worn out, they should be burnt: sacrificial vessels in the same condition should be buried, as should the tortoise-shell and divining stalks, and a victim that has died. 14. All who take part with the ruler in a sacrifice must themselves remove the stands (of their offerings).

[1. 'The Red Bird' was the name of the seven constellations of the southern quarter of the Zodiac; 'the Dark Warrior' embraced those of the northern; 'the Azure Dragon,' those of the eastern; and 'the Tiger,' those of the western. These flags would show the direction of the march, and seem to suggest that all heaven was watching the progress of the expedition.

2. As showing that they had not been able to keep invaders at a distance.]

5. 15. When the ceremony of wailing is over[1], a son should no longer speak of his deceased father by his name. The rules do not require the avoiding of names merely similar in sound to those not to be spoken. When (a parent had) a double name, the avoiding of either term (used singly) is not required. 16. While his parents (are alive), and a son is able to serve them, he should not utter the names of his grandparents; when he can no longer serve his parents (through their death), he need not avoid the names of his grandparents. 17. Names that would not be spoken (in his own family) need not be avoided (by a great officer) before his ruler; in the great officer's, however, the names proper to be sup pressed by the ruler should not be spoken. 18. In (reading) the books of poetry and history, there need be no avoiding of names, nor in writing compositions. 19.

In the ancestral temple there is no such avoiding. 20. Even in his presence, a minister need not avoid the names improper to be spoken by the ruler's wife. The names to be avoided by a wife need not be unspoken outside the door of the harem. The names of parties for whom mourning is worn (only) nine months or five months are not avoided[2]. 21. When one is crossing the boundaries (of a state), he should ask what are its prohibitory laws; when he has fairly entered it, he should ask about its customs; before entering the door (of a house), he should ask about the names to be avoided in it.

[1. After the burial. Till then they would not allow themselves to think of the departed as dead.

2. As, in the first place, for uncles; and in the second, for cousins and grand-uncles.]

6. 22. External undertakings should be commenced on the odd days, and internal on the even[1]. 23. In all cases of divining about a day, whether by the tortoise-shell or the stalks, if it be beyond the decade, it is said, 'on such and such a distant day,' and if within the decade, 'on such and such a near day.' For matters of mourning a distant day is preferred; for festive matters a near day[2]. 24. It is said, 'For the day we depend on thee, O great Tortoise-shell, which dost give the regular indications; we depend on you, O great Divining Stalks, which give the regular indications.' 25. Divination by the shell or the stalks should not go beyond three times. 26. The shell and the stalks should not be both used on the same subject[3]. 27. Divination by the shell is called pû; by the stalks, shih. The two were the methods by which the ancient sage kings made the people believe in seasons and days, revere spiritual beings, stand in awe of their laws and orders; the methods (also) by which they made them determine their perplexities and settle their misgivings. Hence it is said, 'If you doubted, and have consulted the stalks, you need not (any longer) think that you will do wrong. If the day (be clearly indicated), boldly do on it (what you desire to do).'

7. 28. When the ruler's carriage is about to have the horses put to it, the driver should stand before

[1. The odd days are called 'strong,' as belonging to the category of yang; the even days 'weak,' as of the category of yin.

2. 'A distant day' gave a longer period for cherishing the memory of the departed; 'a near day' was desired for festive celebrations, because at them the feeling of I respect' was supposed to predominate.

3. To reverse by the one the indication of the other.]

them, whip in hand. 29. When they are yoked, he will inspect the linch pin, and report that the carriage is ready. 30. (Coming out again), he should shake the dust from his clothes, and mount on the right side, taking hold of the second strap[1]. he should (then) kneel in the carriage[2]. 31. Holding his whip, and taking the reins separately, he will drive the horses on five paces, and then stop. 32. When the ruler comes out and approaches the carriage, the driver should take all the reins in one hand, and (with the other) hand the strap to him. The attendants should then retire out of the way. 33. They should follow quickly as the carriage drives on. When it reaches the great gate, the ruler will lay his hand on that of the driver (that he may drive gently), and, looking round, will order the warrior for the seat on the right to come into the carriage[3]. In passing through the gates (of a city) or village, and crossing the water–channels, the pace must be reduced to a walk.

8. 34. In all cases it is the rule for the driver to hand the strap (to the person about to mount the carriage). If the driver be of lower rank (than himself) that other receives it. If this be not the case, he should not do so[4]. 35. If the driver be of the lower rank, the other should (still) lay his own

[1. In a carriage the ruler occupied the seat on the left side; the driver avoided this by mounting on the right side. Each carriage was furnished with two straps to assist in mounting; but the use of one was confined to the chief occupant.

2. But only till the ruler had taken his seat.

3. This spearman occupied the seat on the right; and took his place as they were about to pass out of the palace precincts.

4. That is, I suppose, he wishes the driver to let go the strap that he may take hold of it himself.]

hand on his (as if to stop him). If this be not the case (and the driver will insist on handing it), the other should take hold of the strap below (the driver's hand).

9. 36. A guest's carriage does not enter the great gate; a woman does not stand up in her carriage dogs and horses are not taken up to the hall[1].

10. 37. Hence[2], the ruler bows forward to his cross–board to (an old man of) yellow hair; he dismounts (and walks on foot) past the places of his high nobles (in the audience court)[3] . He does not gallop the horses of his carriage in the capital; and should bow forward on entering a village. 38. When called by the ruler's order, though through a man of low rank, a great officer, or (other) officer, must meet him in person, 39. A man in armour does not bow, he makes an obeisance indeed, but it is a restrained obeisance. 40, When the carriage of a deceased ruler is following at his interment, the place on the left should be vacant. When (any of his ministers on other occasions) are riding in (any of) the ruler's carriages, they do not presume to leave the seat on the left vacant, but he who occupies it should bend forward to the cross–board[4]. 41. A charioteer

[1. The carriage halted outside in testimony of the guest's respect. A man stood up in the carriage; a woman, as weaker, did not do so. For horses, see the rules in Part IV, 5. Dogs were too insignificant to be taken up.

2. We do not see the connexion indicated by the 'hence.'

3. Leaving the palace, he walks past those places to his carriage. Returning, he dismounts before he comes to them.

4. The first sentence of this paragraph has in the original only four characters; as P. Zottoli happily renders them in Latin, 'Fausti currus vacante sinistra;' but they form a complete sentence. The left seat was that of the ruler in life, and was now left vacant for his spirit. Khung Ying–tâ calls the carriage in question, 'the Soul Carriage' (hwan kü). A ruler had five different styles of carriage, all of which might be used on occasions of state; as in the second sentence.]

driving a woman should keep his left hand advanced (with the reins in it), and his right hand behind him[1]. 42. When driving the ruler of a state, (the charioteer) should have his right hand advanced, with the left kept behind and the head bent down. 43. The ruler of a state should not ride in a one–wheeled carriage[2]. In his carriage one should not cough loudly, nor point with his hand in an irregular way. 44. Standing (in his carriage) one should look (forward only) to the distance of five revolutions of the wheels. Bending forward, he should (do so only till he) sees the tails of the horses. He should not turn his head round beyond the (line of the) naves. 45. In the (streets of the) capital one should touch the horses gently with the brush–end of the switch. He should not urge them to their speed. The dust should not fly beyond the ruts. 46. The ruler of a state should bend towards the cross–board when he meets a sacrificial victim, and dismount (in passing) the ancestral temple. A great officer or (other) officer should descend (when he comes to) the ruler's gate, and bend forward to the ruler's horses[3]. 47.

[1. The woman was on the driver's left, and they were thus turned from each other as much as possible.

2. Common so long ago as now, but considered as beneath a ruler's dignity. So, Wang Tâo. See also the Khang–hsî dictionary under (kî).

3. The text says that the ruler should dismount before a victim, and bow before the temple. The verbal characters have been misplaced, as is proved by a passage of the commentary on the Official Book of Kâu, where one part is quoted. The Khien–lung editors approve of the alteration made in the version above.]

(A minister) riding in one of the ruler's carriages must wear his court robes. He should have the whip in the carriage with him, (but not use it). He should not presume to have the strap handed to him. In his place on the left, he should bow forward to the cross–board. 48. (An officer) walking the ruler's horses should do so in the middle of the road. It he trample on their forage, he should be punished, and also if he look at their teeth, (and go on to calculate their age).

SECTION II. PART I.

1. When a thing is carried with both hands, it should be held on a level with the heart; when with one hand, on a level with the girdle. 2. An article belonging to the son of Heaven should be held higher than the heart; one belonging to a ruler of a state, on a level with it; one belonging to a Great officer, lower than it; and one belonging to an (inferior)

[This Part I contains thirty-three paragraphs, which have been arranged in sixteen chapters.

Ch. 1. 1–5, describes the manner of carrying things belonging to superiors, and standing before them. 2. 6, relates to the not calling certain parties by their names. 3. 7, 8, to designations of themselves to be avoided or used by certain other parties. 4. 9, prescribes modesty in answering questions. 5. 10, 11, gives rules about the practice of ceremonies in another state. 6. 12, is a rule for an orphan son. 7. 13, 14, is for a son in mourning for his father, and other points. 8. 15–17, describes certain offences to be punished, and things to be avoided in the palace; and in private. 9. 18, shows us a superior man in building, preparing for sacrifice and cognate matters; 10. 19–21, a great or other officer, leaving his own state to go to another, and in that other 22, 23, officers in interviews with one another and with rulers. 12. 24–26, gives the rules for the spring hunting; for bad years; and for the personal ornaments of a ruler, and the music of officers. 13. 27, is about the reply of an officer to a question of his ruler; 14. 28, about a great officer leaving his state on his own business. 15. 29, tells how parties entreat a ruler, and others, not to abandon the state. 16. 30–33, gives rules relating to the king: his appellations, designations of himself, &c.]

officer should be carried lower still. 3. When one is holding an article belonging to his lord, though it may be light, he should seem unable to sustain it. In the case of a piece of silk, or a rank-symbol of jade, square or round, he should keep his left hand over it. He should not lift his feet in walking, but trail his heels like the wheels of a carnage. 4. (A minister) should stand (with his back) curved in the manner of a sounding-stone[1], and his girdle-pendants hanging down. Where his lord has his pendants hanging at his side, his should be hanging down in front; where his lord has them hanging in front, his should descend to the ground. 5. When one is holding any symbol of jade (to present it), if it be on a mat, he leaves it so exposed; if there be no mat, he covers it with (the sleeve of) his outer robe[2].

2. 6. The ruler of a state should not call by their names his highest ministers, nor the two noble ladies of her surname, who accompanied his wife to the harem[3]. A Great officer should not call in that way an officer who had been employed by his father, nor

[1. The sounding-stone which the writer had in mind could not have been so curved as it is ordinarily represented to be in pictures, or the minister must have carried himself as

Scott in his 'Fortunes of Nigel,' ch. 10, describes Andrew the Scrivener.

2 p. Zottoli translates this paragraph by.—'Deferens gemmas, si eae habent sustentaculum, tunc apertam indues diploidem; si non habent sustentaculum, tunc clausam.' The text is not easily construed; and the commentaries, very diffuse,.are yet not clear.

3. When a feudal prince married, two other states, of the same surname as the bride, sent each a daughter or their ruling house to accompany her to the new harem. These are 'the noble ladies' intended here.]

the niece and younger sister of his wife (members of his harem)[1]. (Another) officer should not call by name the steward of his family, nor his principal concubine[2].

3. 7. The son of a Great officer (of the king, him self equal to) a ruler, should not presume to speak of himself as 'I, the little son[3]. The son of a Great officer or (other) officer (of a state) should not presume to speak of himself as 'I, the inheriting son, so–and–so[4].' They should not so presume to speak of themselves as their heir–sons do. 8. When his ruler wishes an officer to take a place at an archery (meeting), and he is unable to do so, he should decline on the round of being, ill, and say, 'I, so–and–so, am suffering from carrying firewood[5].'

4. 9. When one, in attendance on a superior man, replies to a question without looking round to see (if any other be going to answer), this is contrary to rule[6].

5. 10. A superior man[7], in his practice of ceremonies

[1. The bride (what we may call the three brides in the preceding note) was accompanied by a niece and a younger sister to the harem.

2. This would be the younger sister of the wife, called in the text the oldest concubine.'

3. So the young king styled himself during mourning.

4. The proper style for the orphan son of such officer was, 'I, the sorrowing son.'

5. Mencius on one occasion (I. ii. 2. 1) thus excused himself for not going to court. The son of a peasant or poor person might speak so; others, of higher position, adopted the style in mock humility.

6. The action of Dze–lû in Analects 9, 5. 4, is referred to as an instance in point of this violation of rule.

7. The 'superior man' here must be an officer, probably the head of a clan or family. Does not the spirit of this chapter still appear in the unwillingness of emigrants from China to forget their country's ways, and learn those of other countries?]

(in another state), should not seek to change his (old) customs. His ceremonies in sacrifice, his dress during the period of mourning, and his positions in the wailing and weeping, will all be according to the fashions of–his former (state). He will carefully study its rules, and carry them exactly into practice. 11. (But) if he (or his descendants) have been away from the state for three generations, and if his dignity and emoluments be (still) reckoned to him (or his representative) at the court, and his outgoings and incomings are announced to the state, and if his brothers or cousins and other members of his house be still there, he should (continue to) send back word about himself to the representative of his ancestor. (Even) after the three generations, if his dignity and emoluments be not reckoned to him in the court, and his outgoings and incomings are (no longer) announced in the state, it is only on the day of his elevation (to official rank) that he should follow the ways of his new state.

6. 12. A superior man, when left an orphan, will not change his name. Nor will he in such a case, if he suddenly become noble, frame an honorary title for his father[1].

7. 13. When occupied with the duties of mourning and before the interment of (a parent), (a son) should study the ceremonies of mourning, and after

[1. The honorary title properly belonged to men of position, and was intended as a condensed expression of their character and deeds. A son in the position described would be in danger of styling his father from his own new standpoint.]

the interment, those of sacrifice. When the mourning is over, let him resume his usual ways, and study the pieces of music. 14. When occupied with the duties of mourning, one should not speak of music. When sacrificing, one should not speak of what is inauspicious. In the ruler's court, parties should not speak of wives and daughters.

8. 15. For one to have to dust his (collection of). written tablets, or adjust them before the ruler, is a punishable offence; and so also is it to have the divining stalks turned upside down or the tortoiseshell turned on one side, before him[1]. 16. One should not enter the ruler's gate, (carrying with him) a tortoise–shell or divining stalks, a stool or a staff, mats or (sun–)shades, or having his upper and lower garments both of white or in a single robe of fine or coarse hempen cloth[2]. Nor should he do so in rush sandals, or with the skirts of his lower garment tucked in at his waist, or in the cap worn in the shorter periods of mourning. Nor, unless announcement of it has been made (and permission given), can one take in the square tablets with the written (lists of articles for a funeral), or the frayed sackcloth, or the coffin and its furniture[3]. 17. Public affairs should not be privately discussed.

9. 18. When a superior man, (high in rank), is about to engage in building, the ancestral temple should

[1. These things indicated a want of due preparation and care.

2 All these things were, for various reasons, considered inauspicious.

3. A death had in this case occurred in the palace, and the things mentioned were. all necessary to prepare for the interment; but still they could not be taken in without permission asked and granted.]

have his first attention, the stables and arsenal the next, and the residences the last. In all preparations of things by (the head of) a clan, the vessels of sacrifice should have the first place; the victims supplied from his revenue, the next; and the vessels for use at meals, the last. Those who have no revenue from lands do not provide vessels for sacrifice. Those who have such revenue first prepare their sacrificial dresses. A superior man,. though poor, will not sell his vessels of sacrifice; though suffering from cold, he will not wear his sacrificial robes; in building a house, he will not cut down the trees on his grave–mounds.

10. 19. A Great or other officer, leaving his state[1], should not take his vessels of sacrifice with him across the boundary. The former will leave his vessels for the time with another Great officer, and the latter his with another officer. 20. A Great or other officer, leaving his state[2], on crossing the boundary, should prepare a place for an altar, and wail there, looking in the direction of the state. He should wear his upper garment and lower, and his cap, all of white; remove his (ornamental) collar, wear shoes of untanned leather, have a covering of white (dog's–fur) for his cross–board, and leave his horses manes undressed. He should not trim his nails or beard, nor make an offering at his (spare) meals. He should not say to any one that he is not chargeable with guilt, nor have any of his women approach him. After three months he will return to his usual dress. 21. When a Great or other officer has an interview with the ruler of the state (to whom he has been sent),

[1. And expecting to return.

2. This is in case of exile.]

if the ruler be condoling with him on the toils of his journey, he should withdraw on one side to avoid (the honour), and then bow twice with his head to the ground. If the ruler meet him (outside the gate) and bow to him, he should withdraw on one side to avoid (the honour), and not presume to return the bow.

11. 22. When Great or other officers are having interviews with one another, though they may not be equal; in rank, if the host reverence (the greater worth of) the guest, he should first bow to him; and if the guest reverence the (greater worth of the) host, he should first bow. 23. In all cases but visits of condolence on occasion of a death, and seeing the ruler of one's state, the parties should be sure to return the bow, each of the other. When a Great officer has an interview with the ruler of (another) state, the ruler should bow in acknowledgment of the honour (of the message he brings); when an officer has an interview with a Great officer (of that state), the latter should bow to him in the same way. When two meet for the first time in their own state, (on the return of one from some mission), the other, as host, should bow in acknowledgment (of the service). A ruler does not bow to a (simple) officer; but if it be one of a different state, he should bow to his bow. A Great officer should return the bow of any one of his officers, however mean may be his rank. Males and females do (? not) bow to one another[1].

[1. The text says that they do bow to one another; but it is evident that Kang Khang-Khang understood it as saying the very opposite. Lû Teh-ming had seen a copy which had the character for 'not.']

12. 24. The ruler of a state, in the spring hunting, will not surround a marshy thicket, nor will Great officers try to surprise a whole herd, nor will (other) officers take young animals or eggs. 25. In bad years, when the grain of the season is not coming to maturity, the ruler at his meals will not make the (usual) offering of the lungs[1], nor will his horses be fed on grain. His special road will not be kept clean and swept[2], nor when at sacrifices will his musical instruments be suspended on their stands. Great officers will not eat thc large grained millet; and (other) officers will not have music (even) at their drinking. 26. Without some (sad) cause, a ruler will not let the gems (pendent from his girdle) leave his person, nor a Great officer remove his music-stand, nor an (inferior) officer his lutes.

13. 27. When an officer presents anything to the ruler of his state, and another day the ruler asks him, 'Where did you get that?' he will bow twice with his head to the ground, and afterwards reply[3].

14. 28. When a Great officer wishes to go beyond the boundaries (of the state) on private business, he must ask leave, and on his return must present some offering. An (inferior) officer in similar circumstances,

[1. The offering here intended was to 'the father of cookery;' see the first note on p. 80. Such offering, under the Kâu dynasty, was of the lungs of the animal which formed the principal dish. It was not now offered, because it was not now on the ground, even the ruler not indulging himself in such a time of scarcity.

2. The road was left uncared for that vegetables might be grown on it, available to the poor at such a time.

3. The offering must have been rare and valuable. The officer had turned aside at the time of presenting it to avoid an), compliment from his ruler.]

must (also) ask leave, and when he comes back, must announce his return. If the ruler condole with them on their toils, they should bow. if he ask about their journey, they should bow, and afterwards reply.

15. 29. When the ruler of a state (is proposing to) leave it, they should (try to) stop him, saying, 'Why are you leaving the altars of the spirits of the land and grain?' (In the similar case of) a Great officer they should say, 'Why are you leaving your ancestral temple?' In that of an (inferior) officer, they should say, 'Why are you leaving the graves (of your ancestors)?' A ruler should die for his altars; a Great officer, with the host (he commands); an inferior officer, for his charge.

16. 30. As ruling over all, under the sky, (the king) is called 'The son of Heaven[1].' As receiving at court the feudal princes, assigning (to all) their different offices, giving out (the laws and ordinances of) the government, and employing the services of the able, he styles himself, 'I, the one man[2].' 31. When he ascends by the eastern steps, and presides at a sacrifice, if it be personal to himself and his family[3], his style is, 'I, so–and–so, the filial king;' if it be external to himself[4], 'I, so–and–so, the inheriting king.' When he visits the feudal princes[5], and sends to make announcement (of his

[1. Meaning, 'Heaven–sonned; constituted by Heaven its son, its firstborn.'

2. An expression of humility as used by himself, 'I, who am but a man;' as used of him, 'He who is the one man.'

3. In the ancestral temple.

4 At the great sacrifices to Heaven and Earth.

5 On his tours of inspection.]

presence) to the spirits (of their hills and streams), it is said, 'Here is he, so–and–so, who is king by (the grace of) Heaven.' 32. His death is announced in the words, 'The king by (the grace of) Heaven has fallen[1].' In calling back (his spirit), they say, 'Return, O son of Heaven[2].' When announcement is made (to all the states) of the mourning for him, it is said, 'The king by (the grace of) Heaven has gone far on high[3].' When his place is given to him in the ancestral temple, and his spirit–tablet is set up, he is styled on it, 'the god[4].' 33. The son of Heaven, while he has not left off his mourning, calls himself, 'I, the little child.' While alive, he, is so styled; and if he die (during that time), he continues to be so designated.

[1. A great landslip from a mountain is called pang, which I have rendered 'has fallen.' Like such a disaster was the death of the king.

2. This ancient practice of calling the dead back is still preserved in China; and by the people generally. There are many references to it in subsequent Books.

3. The body and animal soul went downward, and were in the grave; the intelligent soul (called 'the soul and spirit,' 'the essential breath') went far on high. Such is the philosophical account of death; more natural is the simple style of the text.

4 The spirit–tablet was a rectangular piece of wood, in the case of a king, a cubit and two inches long, supposed to be a resting–place for the spirit at the religious services in the temple. Mang says that the deceased king was now treated as 'a heavenly spirit,'—he was now deified. p. Zottoli translates the character here—Tî—by imperator; but there was in those times no 'emperor' in China.]

PART II.

1. The son of Heaven has his queen, his helpmates, his women of family, and his ladies of honour. (These) constituted his wife and concubines[1].

2. 2. The son of Heaven appoints the officers of Heaven's institution[2], the precedence among them belonging to the six grandees:—the Grand–governor; the Grand–minister of the ancestral temple; the Grand–historiographer; the Grand–minister of prayers; the Grand–minister of justice; and the Grand–divine These are the guardians and superintendents of the six departments of the statutes. 3. The five (administrative) officers of the son of Heaven are:—the minister of instruction; the minister of war; the

[Part Il consists of twenty–one paragraphs, which are distributed in eight chapters.

Ch 1, describes the members of the royal harem. 2. 2–6, relates to the various ministers and officers appointed by the king with their departments and duties. 3. 7–10, gives the names and titles, applied to, and used by, the chiefs of regions, provinces, and of the barbarous tribes. 4. 11–16, is about audiences, meetings, and covenants, and the designations of the princes and others in various circumstances. 5. 17, is about the demeanour of the king and others. 6. 18, 19, is about the inmates of the harems, and how they designated themselves. 7. 20, is about the practice of sons or daughters, and various officers, in designating themselves. 8. 21, is about certain things that should not be said of the king, of princes, and of superior men.

1. See the very different translation of this paragraph by p. Zottoli in his Cursus, iii. p. 653. It is confessed out of place here, should belong to paragraph 18, and is otherwise incomplete.

2. So described, as 'Powers that be ordained' by the will of Heaven, equally with the king, though under him these grandees are not all in the Kâu Kwan.]

minister of works; the minister of offices; and the minister of crime. These preside over the multitude in (each of) their five charges. 4. The six treasuries of the son of Heaven are under the charge of the superintendent of the land; the superintendent of the woods; the superintendent of the waters; the superintendent of the grass; the superintendent of articles of employment; and the superintendent of wares. These preside over the six departments of their charges. 5. The six manufactures of the son of Heaven are under the care of (the superintendents of) the workers in earth; the workers in metal; the workers in stone; the workers in wood; the workers in (the skins of) animals; and the workers in twigs. These preside over the six departments of stores. 6. When the five officers give in their contributions, they are said to 'present their offerings[1].'

3. 7. Chief among the five officers are the presidents[2], to whom belong the oversight of quarters (of the kingdom). In any message from them transmitted to the son of Heaven, they are styled 'ministers of the son of Heaven.' If they are of the same surname as he, he styles them 'paternal uncles;' if of a different surname, 'maternal uncles.' To the feudal princes, they designate themselves, 'the ancients of the son of Heaven.' Outside (their own states), they are styled 'duke;' in their states, 'ruler.' 8. The head prince in each

[1. Who are the five officers here? Those of paragraph 3? Or the feudal dukes, marquises, earls, counts, and barons? Both views have their advocates. The next paragraph favours the second view.

2. Such presidents were the dukes of Kâu and Shâo, at the commencement of the Kâu dynasty.]

of the nine provinces, on entering the state of the son of Heaven, is styled 'pastor.' If he be of the same surname as himself, the son of Heaven calls him 'my paternal uncle;' if he be of a different surname, 'my maternal uncle.' Outside(his own state) he is called 'marquis;' in it, 'ruler,' 9. The (chiefs) among (the wild tribes of) the Î on the east, the Tî on the north, the Zung on the west, and the Man on the south, however great (their territories), are called 'counts.' In his own territories each one calls himself. 'the unworthy one;' outside them, 'the king's ancient.' 10. Any of the princelets of their various tracts[1], on entering the state of the son of Heaven, is styled, 'Such and such a person.' Outside it he is called 'count,' and calls himself 'the solitary.'

4. 11. When the son of Heaven stands with his back to the screen with axe-head figures on it, and the princes present themselves before him with their faces to the north, this is called kin (the autumnal audience). When he stands at the (usual) point (of reception) between the door and the screen, and the dukes have their faces towards the east, and the, feudal princes theirs towards the west, this is called Khâo (the spring audience)[2]. 12. When feudal, princes see one another at a place and time not agreed on beforehand, the interview is called 'a meeting.' When they do so in some open place agreed on beforehand, it is called 'an assembly.'

[1. It is held, and I think correctly, that these princelets were the chiefs of the wild tribes.

2. There were other audiences called by different names at the other two seasons.]

When one prince sends a great officer to ask about another, it is called 'a message of friendly inquiry.' When there is a binding to mutual faith, it is called 'a solemn declaration.' When they use a victim, it is called 'a covenant.' 13. When a feudal prince is about to be introduced to the son of Heaven, he is announced as 'your subject so-and-so, prince of such-and-such a state.' He speaks of himself to the people as 'the man of little virtue.' 14. If he be in mourning (for his father), he is styled 'the rightful eldest son, an orphan;' if he be taking part at a sacrifice in his ancestral temple, 'the filial son, the prince of such-and-such a state, the prince so-and-so.' If it be another sacrifice elsewhere, the style is, 'so-and-so, prince of such-and-such a state, the distant descendant.' 15. His death is described by the character hung (disappeared). In calling back (his spirit), they say, 'Return, sir so–and–so.' When he has been interred and (his son) is presented to the son of Heaven, the interview, (though special), is said to be 'of the same kind as the usual interviews.' The honorary title given to him is (also) said to be 'after the usual fashion.' 16. When one prince sends a message to another, the messenger speaks of himself as 'the ancient of my poor ruler.'

5. 17. The demeanour of the son of Heaven should be characterised by majesty; of the princes, by gravity; of the Great officers, by a regulated composure; of (inferior) officers, by an easy alertness; and of the common people, by simplicity and humility.

6. 18. The partner of the son of Heaven is called 'the queen;' of a feudal prince, 'the helpmate;' of a Great officer, 'the attendant;' of an (inferior) officer, 'the serving woman;' and of a common man ' 'the mate[1].' 19. A duke and (one of) the feudal princes had their helpmate, and their honourable women, (which) were their mates and concubines. The helpmate called herself, before the son of Heaven, 'the aged servant;' and before the prince (of another state), 'the small and unworthy ruler.' To her own ruler she called herself 'the small maid.' From the honourable women downwards (each member of the harem) called herself 'your handmaid.'

7. 20. To their parents, sons and daughters called themselves by their names. A Great officer any of the states, entering the state of the son Heaven, was called 'the officer of such–and–such state)' and styled himself 'your subsidiary minister.' Outside (his own state), he was called 'sir;' and in that state, 'the ancient of our poor ruler.' A messenger (to any state) called himself 'so–and–so.'

8. 21. The son of Heaven should not be spoken of as 'going out (of his state)[2].' A feudal prince should not be called by his name, while alive. (When either of these things is done), it is because the superior man[3] will not show regard for wickedness. A prince who loses his territory is named, and also one who extinguishes (another state ruled by) lords of the same surname as himself.

[1. Here should come in paragraph 1.

2. All the states are his. Wherever he may flee, he is still in what is his own land.

3. This 'superior man' would be an upright and impartial historiographer, superior to the conventions of his order.]

PART III.

1. 1. According to the rules of propriety for a minister, he should not remonstrate with his ruler openly. If he have thrice remonstrated and is still not listened to, he should leave (his service). In the service of his parents by a son, if he have thrice remonstrated and is still not listened to, he should follow (his remonstrance) with loud crying and tears. 2. When a ruler is ill, and has to drink medicine, the minister first tastes it. The same is the rule for a son and an ailing parent. The physic of a doctor in whose family medicine has not been practised for three generations at least, should not be taken.

2. 3. In comparing (different) men, we can only do so when their (circumstances and conditions) are of the same class.

[Part Ill contains twenty paragraphs, which may be comprised in eleven chapters.

Ch. 1. 1, 2, contains the rules for a minister and a son in remonstrating with a ruler or parent; and also in seeing about their medicine when ill. 2. 3, gives the rule in making comparisons. 3. 4, 5, gives the rules to be observed in asking about the age and wealth of different parties from the king downwards. 4. 6–10, is about sacrifices: those of different parties, the sacrificial names of different victims, &c. 5. 11, 12, gives the terms in which the deaths of different men, and of animals, are described. 6. 13, 14, gives the names of near relatives, when they are sacrificed to, and when they are alive. 7. 15, tells how different parties should look at others. 8. 16, 17, is about executing a ruler's orders, and things to be avoided in the conduct of business. 9. 18, is about great entertainments. 10. 19, is about presents of introduction. 11. 20, contains the language used in sending daughters to different harems.]

3. 4. When one asks about the years of the son of Heaven, the reply should be—'I have heard that he has begun to wear a robe so many feet long[1].' To a similar question about the ruler of a state, the reply should be—'He is able to attend to the services in the ancestral temple, and. at the altars of the spirits of the land and grain,' if he be grown up; and, if he be still young, 'He is not yet able to attend to the services in the ancestral

temple, and at the altars of the spirits of the land and grain.' To a question about the son of a Great officer,—the reply, if he be grown up, should be—'He is able to drive;' and, if he be still young, 'He is not yet able to drive.' To a question about the son of an (ordinary) officer, the reply, if he be grown up, should be—'He can manage the conveying of a salutation or a message;' and, if he be still young, 'He cannot yet manage such a thing.' To a question about the son of a common man, the reply, if he be grown up, should be—'He is able to carry (a bundle of) firewood;' and, if he be still young, 'He is not yet able to carry (such a bundle).' 5. When one asks about the wealth of the ruler of a state, the reply should be given by telling the extent of his territory, and the productions of its hills and lakes. To a similar question about a Great officer, it should be said, 'He has the lands allotted to him, and is supported by the labour (of his people). He needs not to borrow the vessels or dresses for his sacrificial occasions.' To the

[1. This would seem to imply that the king was still young.]

same question about an (ordinary) officer, the reply should be by giving the number of his carriages; and to one about a common man, by telling the number of the animals that he keeps.

4. 6. The son of Heaven sacrifices (or presents oblations) to Heaven and Earth[1]; to the (spirits presiding over the) four quarters; to (the spirits of) the hills and rivers; and offers the five sacrifices of the house,—all in the course of the year. The feudal princes present oblations, each to (the spirit pre-siding over) his own quarter; to (the spirits of) its hills and rivers; and offer the five sacrifices of the house,–all in the course of the year. Great officers present the oblations of the five sacrifices of the house,—all in the course of the year. (Other) officers present oblations to their ancestors[2]. 7. There should be no presuming to resume any sacrifice which has been abolished (by proper authority)[3], nor to abolish any which has been so established. A sacrifice which it is not proper to offer, and which yet is offered, is called a licentious sacrifice. A licentious sacrifice brings no blessing. 8. The son of Heaven uses an ox of one colour, pure and unmixed; a feudal prince, a fatted ox; a Great officer, an ox selected for the occasion; an (ordinary) officer, a sheep or a pig. 9. The son of an inferior

[1. There were various sacrifices to Heaven and also to Earth. The great ones were—that to Heaven at the winter solstice, and that to Earth at the summer solstice. But all the sacrifices to Heaven and Earth were confined to the king.

2. The king offered all the sacrifices in this paragraph. The other parties only those here assigned to them, and the sacrifices allowed to others of inferior rank. The five sacrifices of the house will come before the reader in Book IV and elsewhere.

3. The 'proper authority' would be the statutes of each dynasty.]

member of the harem cannot offer the sacrifice (to his grandfather or father); if (for some reason) he have to do so, he must report it to the honoured son, (the head of the family). 10. According to the 'rules for all sacrifices in the ancestral temple, the ox is called 'the creature with the large foot;' the pig, 'the hard bristles;' a sucking–pig, 'the fatling;' a sheep, 'the soft hair;' a cock, 'the loud voice;' a dog, 'the soup offering;' a pheasant, 'the wide toes;' a hare, 'the clear seer;' the stalks of dried flesh, 'the exactly cut oblations;' dried fish, 'the well–considered oblation;' fresh fish, 'the straight oblation.' Water is called 'the pure cleanser;' spirits, 'the clear cup;' millet, 'the fragrant mass;' the large–grained millet, 'the fragrant (grain);' the sacrificial millet, 'the bright grain;' paddy, 'the admirable vegetable;' scallions, 'the rich roots;' salt, 'the saline, briny substance;' jade, 'the admirable jade;' and silks, 'the exact silks.'

5. 11. The death of the son of Heaven is expressed by pang (has fallen); of a feudal prince, by hung (has crashed); of a Great officer, by zû (has ended); of an (ordinary) officer, by pû lû (is now unsalaried); and of a common man, by sze (has deceased). (The corpse) on the couch is called shih (the laid–out), when it is put into the coffin, that is called kiû (being in the long home). 12. (The death of) a winged fowl is expressed by hsiang (has fallen down); that of a quadruped, by zhze (is disorganised). Death from an enemy in fight is called ping (is slain by the sword).

6. 13. In sacrificing to them, a grandfather is called 'the sovereign grandfather;' a grandmother,' the sovereign grandmother;' a father, 'the sovereign father;' a mother, 'the sovereign mother; a husband, 'the sovereign pattern.' 14. While (they are) alive, the names of father (fû), mother (mû), and wife (khî) are used; when they are dead, those of 'the completed one (khâo),' 'the corresponding one (pî),' and 'the honoured one (pin).' Death in old age is called 'a finished course (zû);' an early death, 'being unsalaried (pû lû).'

7. 15. The son of Heaven does not look at a person above his collar or below his girdle; the ruler of a state looks at him a little lower (than the collar); a Great officer, on a line

with his heart; and an ordinary officer, not from beyond a distance of five paces. In all cases looks directed above to the face denote pride, and below the girdle grief; directed askance, they denote villainy.

8. 16. When the ruler orders (any special business) from a Great officer or (other) officer, he should assiduously discharge it; in their offices speaking (only) of the official business; in the treasury, of treasury business; in the arsenals, of arsenal business; and in the court, of court business. 17. At court there should be no speaking about dogs and horses. When the audience is over, and one looks about him, if he be not attracted by some strange thing, he must have strange thoughts in his mind. When one keeps looking about him after the business of the court is over, a superior man will pronounce him uncultivated. At court the conversation should be according to the rules of propriety; every question should be so proposed, and every answer so returned.

9. 18. For great entertainments[1] there should be no consulting the tortoise–shell, and no great display of wealth.

10. 19. By way of presents of introduction, the son of Heaven uses spirits of black millet; feudal princes, their symbols of jade; a high minister, a lamb; a Great officer, a goose; an (ordinary) officer, a pheasant; a common man, a duck. Lads should bring their article, and withdraw. In the open country, in the army, they do not use such presents;—a tassel from a horse's breast, an archer's armlet, or an arrow may serve the purpose. For such presents women use the fruits of the hovenia dulcis, or of the hazel tree, strings of dried meat, jujube dates, and chestnuts.

11. 20. In presenting a daughter for (the harem of) the son of Heaven it is said, 'This is to complete the providers of sons for you;' for that of the ruler of a state, 'This is to complete the providers of your spirits and sauces;' for that of a Great officer, 'This is to complete the number of those who sprinkle and sweep for you.'

[1. Instead of 'for great entertainments,' p. Zottoli has 'summo sacrificio;' but the Khien–lung editors decide in favour of the meaning which I have followed.]

BOOK II. THE THAN KUNG.

SECTION I. PART I.

I. At the mourning rites for Kung–î Kung–dze, Than Kung (was there), wearing the mourning cincture for the head, Kung–dze had passed over his grandson, and appointed one of his (younger) sons as his successor (and head of the family). Than Kung said (to himself), 'How is this? I never heard of such a thing;' and he hurried to Dze–fû Po–dze at the right of the door, and said, ' How is it that Kung–dze passed over his grandson, and made a (younger) son his successor?' Po–dze replied, 'Kung–dze perhaps has done in this, like others, according to the way of antiquity. Anciently, king Wan passed over his eldest son Yî–khâo, and appointed king Wû; and the count of Wei passed over his grandson Tun, and made Yen, his (own) younger brother, his successor. Kung–dze perhaps did also in this according to the way of antiquity.' Dze–yû asked Confucius (about the matter), and he said, 'Nay, (the rule is to) appoint the grandson[1].'

[On the name and divisions of this Book, see the Introduction, pp., 17, 18.

1. Important as showing the rule of succession to position and property. We must suppose that the younger son, who had been made the head of the family, was by a different mother, and one whose position was inferior to that of the son, the proper heir who was dead. Of course the succession should have descended in the line of the rightful heir. Po–dze evaded the point of Than Kung's question; but Confucius did not hesitate to speak out the truth. On other matters which the paragraph might suggest we need not enter.]

2. In serving his father, (a son) should conceal (his faults), and not openly or strongly remonstrate with him about them; should in every possible way wait on and nourish him, without being tied to definite rules; should serve him laboriously till his death, and then complete the mourning for him for three' years. In serving his ruler, (a minister), should remonstrate with him openly and strongly (about his faults), and make no concealment (of them); should in every possible way wait on and nourish him, but according to definite rules; should serve him laboriously till his death, and should then wear mourning for him according to rule for three years. In serving his master, (a learner) should have nothing to do with openly reproving him or with concealing (his faults); should in every

possible way wait upon and serve him, without being tied to definite rules; should serve him laboriously till his death, and mourn for him in heart for three years[1].

3. Kî Wû-dze had built a house, at the bottom of the western steps of which was the grave of the Tû family. (The head of that) asked leave to bury (some member of his house) in it, and leave was granted to him to do so. (Accordingly) he entered the house (with the coffin), but did not dare to wail (in the usual fashion). Wû-dze said to him, 'To bury in the same grave was not the way of antiquity. It was begun by the duke of Kâu, and has not been

[1. On differences in the services rendered to a parent, a ruler, and a master or instructor.]

changed since. I have granted you the great thing, and why should I no tgrant the less?' (With this) he ordered him to wail[1].

4. When Dze-shang's mother died, and he did not perform any mourning rites for her, the disciples of (his father) Dze-sze asked him, saying, 'Did your predecessor, the superior man, observe mourning for his divorced mother?' 'Yes,' was the reply. (And the disciples went on), 'Why do you not make Pâi also observe the mourning rites (for his mother)?' Dze-sze said, 'My progenitor, a superior man, never failed in pursuing the right path. When a generous course was possible, he took it and behaved generously; and when it was proper to restrain his generosity, he restrained it. But how can I attain to that? While she was my wife, she was Pâi's mother; but when she ceased to be my wife, she was no longer his mother.' It was in this way that the Khung family came not to observe mourning for a divorced mother; the practice began from Dze-Sze[2].

5. Confucius said, 'When (the mourner) bows to (the visitor), and then lays his forehead to the ground,

[1. This Wû-dze was a great-grandson of Kî Yû, the third son (by an inferior wife) of duke Kwang of Lû (B.C. 693-662), and the ancestor of the. Ki-sun, one of the three famous families of U. It would appear that he had appropriated to himself the burying ground of the Tû family.

2. Dze-shang, by name, Pâi, was the son of Dze-sze, and great-grandson of Confucius. What is related here is important as bearing on the question whether Confucius divorced

his wife or not. If I am correct in translating the original text by 'your predecessor, the superior man,' in the singular and not in the plural, and supposing that it refers to Confucius, the paragraph has been erroneously supposed to favour the view that he did divorce his wife.]

this shows the predominance of courtesy. When he lays his forehead to the ground, and then bows (to his visitor), this shows the extreme degree of his sorrow. In the three years' mourning, I follow the extreme (demonstration)[1].'

6. When Confucius had succeeded in burying (his mother) in the same grave (with his father) at Fang, he said, 'I have heard that the ancients made graves (only), and raised no mound over them. But I am a man, who will be (travelling) east, west, south, and north. I cannot do without something by which I can remember (the place).' On this, he (resolved to) raise a mound (over the grave) four feet high. He then first returned, leaving the disciples behind. A great rain came on; and when they rejoined him, he asked them what had made them so late. 'The earth slipped,' they said, 'from the grave at Fang.' They told him this thrice without his giving them any answer. He then wept freely, and said, 'I have heard that the ancients did not need to repair their graves.'

7. Confucius was wailing for Dze–lû in his courtyard. When any came to condole with him, he bowed to them. When the wailing was over, he made the messenger come in, and asked him all about (Dze–lû's death). 'They have made him into pickle,' said the

[1. In the former case the mourner first thought of his visitor; in the latter, of his dead and his own loss. The bow was made with the hands clasped, and held very low, the head being bowed down to them. They were then opened, and placed forward on the ground, on each side of the body, while the head was stretched forward between them, and the forehead made to touch the ground. In the second case the process was reversed.]

messenger; and forthwith Confucius ordered the pickle (in the house) to be thrown away[1].

8. Zang–dze said, 'When the grass is old[2] on the grave of a friend, we no (longer) wall for him.'

9. Dze–sze said, 'On the third day of mourning, when the body is put into the coffin, (a son) should exercise sincerity and good faith in regard to everything that is placed with it, so that there shall be no occasion for repentance[3]. In the third month when the body is interred, he should do the same in regard to everything that is placed with the coffin in the grave, and for the same reason. Three years are considered as the extreme limit of mourning; but though (his parents) are out of sight, a son does not forget them. Hence a superior man will have a lifelong grief, but not one morning's trouble (from without); and thus on the anniversary of a parent's death, he does not listen to music.'

10. Confucius, being quite young when he was left fatherless, did not know (his father's) grave. (Afterwards) he had (his mother's) body coffined in the street of Wû–fû. Those who saw it all thought that it was to be interred there, so carefully was (everything done), but it was (only) the coffining. By inquiring of the mother of Man–fû of Zâu, he succeeded

[1. Dze–lû had died in peculiar circumstances in the state of Wei, through his hasty boldness, in B.C. 480. It was according to rule that the Master should wail for him. The order about the pickled meat was natural in the circumstances.

2. The characters in the text imply that a year had passed since the friend's death.

3. The graveclothes and coverlet. The things placed in the grave with the coffin were many, and will by–and–by come before the reader at length.]

in burying it in the same grave (with his father) at Fang[1].

11. When there are mourning rites in the neighbourhood, one should not accompany his pestle with his voice[2]. When there is a body shrouded and coffined in his village, one should not sing in the lanes[2]. For a mourning cap the ends of the ties should not hang down.

12. (In the time of Shun) of Yü they used earthenware coffins[3]; under the sovereigns of Hsiâ, they surrounded these with an enclosure of bricks. The people of Yin used wooden coffins, the outer and inner. They of Kâu added the surrounding curtains and the feathery ornaments. The people of Kâu buried those who died between 16 and 19 in the coffins of Yin; those who died between 12 and 15 or between 8 and 11 in the brick enclosures of

Hsiâ; and those who died (still younger), for whom no mourning is worn, in the earthenware enclosures of the time of the lord of Yü.

13. Under the sovereigns of Hsiâ they preferred what was black. On great occasions (of mourning), for preparing the body and putting it into the coffin, they used the dusk; for the business of war, they used black horses in their chariots; and the victims which they used were black. Under the Yin dynasty they preferred what was white. On occasions

[1. This paragraph is generally discredited. The Khien–lung editors say it is not to be relied on.

2. These two rules are in Book I, i. Pt. iv, 43, page 89.

3. In a still earlier time, according to the third Appendix of the Yî (vol. xvi, p. 385), they merely covered the body on the ground with faggots.]

of mourning, for coffining the body, they used the midday; for the business of war they used white horses; and their victims were white. Under the Kâu dynasty they preferred what was –red. On occasions of mourning, they coffined the body at sunrise; for the business of war they used red horses, with black manes and tails; and their victims were red.

14. When the mother of duke Mû of Lû[1] died, he sent to ask Zang–dze[2] what (ceremonies) he should observe. Zang–dze said, 'I have heard from my father that the sorrow declared in the weeping and wailing, the feelings expressed in the robe of sackcloth with even or with frayed edges, and the food of rice made thick or in congee, extend from the son of Heaven to all. But the tent–like covering (for the coffin) is of (linen) cloth in Wei, and of silk in Lû.'

15. Duke Hsien of Sin, intending to put to death his heir–son Shan–shang, another son, Khung–r, said to the latter, 'Why should you not tell what is in your mind to the duke?' The heir–son said, 'I cannot do so. The ruler is happy with the lady Kî of Lî. I should (only) wound his heart.' 'Then,' continued the other, 'Why not go away?' The heir son replied, 'I cannot do so. The ruler says that I wish to murder him. Is there any state where the (sacredness) of a father is not recognised? Where should I go to obviate this charge?' (At the same time) he sent a man to take leave (for him) of Hû

[1. Duke Mû was marquis of Lû from B.C. 409 to 376.

2. This was not the disciple of Confucius, but his son, also named Shin like him; but the characters for the names are different.]

Tû, with the message, 'I was wrong in not thinking (more) of your words, my old friend, and that neglect is occasioning my death. Though I do not presume to grudge dying, yet our ruler is old, and his (favourite) son is (quite) young. Many difficulties are threatening the state, and you, old Sir, do not come forth (from your retirement), and consult for (the good of) our ruler. If you will come forth and do this, I will die (with the feeling that I) have received a (great) favour from you.' He (then) bowed twice, laying his head to the ground, after which he died (by his own hand). On this account he became (known in history as)'the Reverential Heir–son'.'

16. There was a man of La, who, after performing in the morning the ceremony which introduced the 25th month of his mourning, began to sing in the evening. Dze–lû laughed at him, (but) the Master said, 'Yû, will you never have done with your finding fault with people? The mourning for three years is indeed long.' When Dze–lû went out, the Master said, 'Would he still have had to wait long? In another month (he might have sung, and) it would have been well.'

17. Duke Kwang of Lû fought a battle with the men of Sung at Shang–khiû. Hsien Pan–fû was driving, and Pû Kwo was spearman on the right. The horses got frightened, and the carriage was broken, so that the duke fell down[2]. They handed the strap

[1. The marquis of Zin, who is known to us as duke Hsien, ruled from B.C. 676 to 651. Infatuated by his love for a barbarian captive from among the Lî, he behaved recklessly and unnaturally to his children already grown up. One very tragical event is the subject of this paragraph.

2. The text would seem to say here that the army of the duke was defeated; but the victory was with the duke. See the Zo Kwan, under B.C. 684, and there was a different reading, to which Lû Teh–ming refers on the passage, that leaves us free to translate as I have done.]

of a relief chariot (that drove up) to him, when he said, 'I did not consult the tortoise–shell (about the movement).' Hsien Pân–fû said, 'On no other occasion did such a disaster occur; that it has occurred to–day is owing to my want of courage. Forthwith he died (in the fight). When the groom was bathing the horses, a random arrow was found (in one of them), sticking in the flesh under the flank; and (on learning this), the duke said, 'It was not his fault; and he conferred on him an honorary name. The practice of giving such names to (ordinary) officers began from this.

18. Zang–dze was lying in his chamber very ill. Yo–kang Dze–khun was sitting by the side of the couch; Zang Yüan and Zang Shan were sitting at (their father's) feet; and there was a lad sitting in a corner holding a torch, who said, 'How beautifully coloured and bright! Is it not the mat of a Great officer?' Dze–khun (tried to) stop him, but Zang–dze had heard him, and in a tone of alarm called him, when he repeated what he had said. 'Yes,' said Zang–dze, 'it was the gift of Kî–sun, and I have not been able to change it. Get up, Yüan, and change the mat.' Zang Yüan said, 'Your illness is extreme. It cannot now be changed. If you happily survive till the morning, I will ask your leave and reverently change it! Zang–dze said, 'Your love of me is not equal to his. A superior man loves another on grounds of virtue; a little man's love of another is seen in his indulgence of him. What do I seek for? I want for nothing but to die in the correct way.' They then raised him up, and changed the mat. When he was replaced on the new one, before he could compose himself, he expired.

19. When (a father) has just died, (the son) should appear quite overcome, and as if he were at his wits' end; when the corpse has been put into the coffin, he should cast quick and sorrowful glances around, as if he were seeking for something and could not find it; when the interment has taken place, he should look alarmed and. restless, as if he were looking for some one who does not arrive; at the end of the first year's mourning, he should look sad and disappointed; and at the end of the second year's, he should have a vague and unreliant look.

20. The practice in Kû–lü of calling the (spirits of the dead[1]) back with arrows took its rise from the battle of Shang–hsing[2]. That in Lû of the women making their visits of condolence (simply) with a band of sackcloth round their hair took its rise from the defeat at Ha–thâi[3].

21. At the mourning for her mother–in–law, the Master instructed (his niece), the wife of Nan–kung Thâo[4], about the way in which she should tie up her hair with sackcloth, saying, 'Do not make it very high, nor very broad. Have the hair–pin of hazel–wood, and the hair–knots (hanging down) eight inches.'

22. Mang Hsien–dze, after the service which ended

[1. See p. 108, par. 32; p. 112, par. 15; and often, farther on.

2. In B.C. 638. See the Zo Kwan of that year.

3. See in the Zo Kwan, under B.C. 569.

4. This must have been the Nan Yung of the Analects, V, 1, 2.]

the mourning rites, had his instruments of music hung on their stands,. but did not use them; and when he might have approached the inmates of his harem, he did not enter it. The Master said, 'Hsien–dze is a degree above other men[1].'

23. Confucius, after the service at the close of the one year's mourning, in five days more (began

to) handle his lute, but brought no perfect sounds from it; in ten days he played on the organ and sang to it[2].

2.4. Yû–dze, it appears, after the service of the same period of mourning, wore shoes of (white) silk, and had ribbons of (white) silk for his cap–strings[3].

[1. The sacrificial service on the final putting off of the mourning dress; and to which reference is here made, was called than. It will come several times before us hereafter. It is celebrated at the end of the 'three years' mourning' for a parent; that is, at the end of twenty–seven months from the death: see the Introduction, p. 49. Wang Sû of the Wei dynasty contended that the mourning was put off at the end of twenty–five months, and the editors of the Khang–hsî dictionary rather approve of his decision: see their note under the character than. I do not think the controversy as to the exact time when the mourning ceased can be entirely cleared up. Confucius praised Hsien–dze, because he could not forget his grief, when the outward sign of it was put off.

2. The sacrificial service here is called by a different name from than; it is hsiang; and in mourning for parents there was 'the small hsiang,' at the end of the first year, and 'the great hsiang,' at the end of the second. The character here probably denotes the mourning for one year, which is not continued beyond that time. Music was not used during any of the period of mourning; and it is doing violence to the text to take hsiang here as equivalent to than.

3. In condemnation of Yû-dze (see Analects, 1, 2), as quick to forget his grief.]

25. There are three deaths on which no condolence should be offered:—from cowardice; from being crushed (through heedlessness); and from drowning[1].

26. When Dze-lû might have ended his mourning for his eldest sister, he still did not do so. Confucius said to him, 'Why do you not leave off your mourning?' He replied, 'I have but few brothers, and I cannot bear to do so.' Confucius said, 'When the ancient kings framed their rules, (they might have said that) they could not bear (to cease mourning) even for (ordinary) men on the roads.' When Dze-lû heard this, he forthwith left off his mourning.

27. Thâi-kung was invested with his state, (and had his capital) in Ying-khiû; but for five generations (his descendants, the marquises of Khî) were all taken back and buried in Kâu. A superior man has said, 'For music, we use that of him from whom we sprang; in ceremonies, we do not forget him to whom we trace our root.' The ancients had a saying, that a fox, when dying, adjusts its head in the direction of the mound (where it was whelped); manifesting thereby (how it shares in the feeling of) humanity.

28. When the mother of Po-yü died, he kept on wailing for her after the year. Confucius heard him, and said, 'Who is it that is thus wailing?' The disciples said, 'It is Lî.' The Master said, 'Ah! (such a demonstration) is excessive.' When Po-yü heard it, he forthwith gave up wailing[2].

[1. The third death here must be supplemented, as I have done the second.

2. Compare paragraph 4, and the note on it. Lî, designated Po-yü, was the son of Confucius, and it has been supposed that his mother had been divorced, so that his protracted wailing for her gave occasion to the rebuke of his father. But while his father was alive, a son did not wail for his mother beyond the year. The passage does not prove that Confucius had divorced his wife, but the contrary; though he might have shown more sympathy with his son's sorrow.]

29. Shun was buried in the wilderness of Zhang-wû, and it would thus appear that the three ladies of his harem were not buried in the same grave with him[1]. Kî Wû-dze said, 'Burying (husband and wife) in the same grave appears to have originated with the duke of Kâu.'

PART II.

1. At the mourning rites for Zang-dze, his body was washed in the cook-room[2].

2. During the mourning for nine months[3] one should suspend his (musical) studies. Some one has said, 'It is permissible during that time to croon over the words (of the pieces).'

3. When Dze-kang was ill, he called (his son), Shan-hsiang, and addressed him, saying, 'We speak of the end of a superior man, and of the death of

[1. From the first part of the Shû King we know that Shun married the two daughters of Yao. The mention of 'three' wives here has greatly perplexed the commentators. Where Zhang-wû was is also much disputed.

2. The proper place for the operation was the principal chamber. There is only conjecture to account for the different place in the case of Zang-dze.

3. In relationships of the third degree: as by a man for a married aunt or sister, a brother's wife, a first cousin, &c.; by a wife, for her husband's grand-parents, uncles, &c.; by a married woman, for her uncle and uncle's wife, a spinster aunt, brothers, sisters, &c. See Appendix at the end of this Book.]

a small man. I am to–day, perhaps, drawing near to my end (as a superior man).'

4. Zang–dze said, 'May not what remains in the cupboard suffice to set down (as the offerings) by (the corpse of) one who has just died?'

5. Zang–dze said, 'Not to have places (for wailing) in cases of the five months' mourning[1] is a rule which sprang from the ways in small lanes.' When, Dze–sze wailed for his sister–in–law, he made such places, and his wife took the lead in the stamping. When Shan–hsiang wailed for Yen–sze, he also did the same.

6. Anciently, (all) caps were (made) with the seams going up and down them; now the (mourning cap) is made with the seams going round. Hence to have the mourning cap different from that worn on felicitous occasions is not the way of antiquity[2].

7. Zang–dze said to Dze–sze, 'Khî, when I was engaged in the mourning for my parents, no water or other liquid entered my mouth for seven days.' Sze–sze said, 'With regard to the rules of ceremony framed by the ancient kings, those who would go beyond them should stoop down to them, and those who do not reach them should stand on tip–toe to do so. Hence, when a superior man is engaged in mourning for his parents, no water or other liquid

[1. In relationships of the fourth degree: as by a man for his grand–uncle and his wife, a spinster grand–aunt, a second cousin, &c.; by a wife for her husband's aunt, brother or sister, &c.; by a married woman, for her spinster aunt, married sister, &c. See Appendix.

2. This paragraph does not seem to contain any lessons of censure or approval, but simply to relate a fact.]

enters his mouth for three days, and with the aid of his staff he is still able to rise.'

8. Zang–dze said, 'If, in cases coming under the five months' mourning, none be worn when the death is not heard of till after the lapse of that time, then when brethren are far apart there would be no wearing of mourning for them at all; and would this be right?'

9. On the mourning rites for Po–kâo, before the messenger from Confucius could arrive, Zan–dze had taken it on him, as his substitute, to present a parcel of silks and a team of

four horses. Confucius said, 'Strange! He has only made me fail in showing my sincerity in the case of Po–kâo[1].'

10. Po–kâo died in Wei, and news of the event was sent to Confucius. He said, 'Where shall I wail for him? For brethren, I wail in the ancestral temple; for a friend of my father, outside the gate of the temple; for a teacher, in my chamber; for a friend, outside the door of the chamber; for an acquaintance, in the open country, (some distance off). (To wail) in the open country would in this case be too slight (an expression of grief), and to do so in the bed–chamber would be too great a one. But it was by Zhze that he was introduced to me. I will wail for him in Zhze's.' Accordingly he ordered Dze–kung to act as presiding mourner on the occasion,

[1. We know almost nothing of the Po–kâo (the eldest son, Kâo) here. From the next paragraph it does not appear that his intimacy with Confucius had been great. Zan–dze had taken too much on himself. Perhaps the gift was too great, and sympathy cannot well be expressed by proxy. The parcel of silks contained five pieces.]

saying to him, 'Bow to those who come because you have a wailing in your house, but do not bow to those who come (simply) because they knew Po–kâo.'

11. Zang–dze said, 'When one during his mourning rites falls ill, and has to eat meat and drink spirits, there must be added the strengthening flavours from vegetables and trees;' meaning thereby ginger and cinnamon.

12. When Dze–hsiâ was mourning for his son, he lost his eyesight. Zang–dze went to condole with him, and said, 'I have heard that when a friend loses his eyesight, we should wail for him.' Thereupon he wailed, and Dze–hsiâ also wailed, and said, 'O Heaven, and I have no guilt!' Zan–dze was angry, and said, 'Shang, how can you say that you have no guilt?'

'I and you served the Master between the Kû and the Sze'; and (after his death) you retired, and grew old in the neighbourhood of the Western Ho, where you made the people compare you with the Master. This was one offence.

'When you mourned for your parents, you did so in such a way that the people heard nothing of it. This was a second offence.

'When you mourned for your son, you did it in such a way that you have lost your eyesight. This is a third offence. And how do you say that you have no guilt?'

[1. These were two streams of Lû, near which was the home of Confucius. I thought of this passage when I crossed at least one of them on my way to Khü–fû, 'the city of Confucius,' about twelve years ago.]

Dze–hsiâ threw down his staff, and bowed, saying, 'I was wrong, I was wrong. It is a long time since I left the herd, and lived apart here.'

13. When a man stops during the daytime in his inner (chamber), it is allowable to come and ask about his illness. When he stops outside during the night, it is allowable to come and condole with him. Hence a superior man, except for some great cause[1], does not pass the night outside (his chamber); and unless he is carrying out a fast or is ill, he does not day and night stop inside.

14. When Kâo Dze–kâo was engaged with the mourning for his parents, his tears flowed (silently) like blood for three years, and he never (laughed) so as to show his teeth. Superior men considered that he did a difficult thing.

15. It is better not to wear mourning at all than not to have it of the proper materials and fashion. When wearing the sackcloth with the edges even (for a mother), one should not sit unevenly or to one side, nor should he do any toilsome labour, (even) in the nine months' mourning[2].

16. When Confucius went to Wei, he found the mourning rites going on for a man with whom he had formerly lodged. Entering the house, he wailed for him bitterly; and when he came out, he told Dze–kung to take out the outside horses of his carriage, and present them as his gift. Dze–kung said, 'At the mourning for any of your disciples, you have

[1. 'A great cause:'—such as danger from enemies, or death and the consequent mourning, which, especially in the case of a father's death, required the son thus to 'afflict himself.'

2. The whole of this paragraph seems overstrained and trivial.]

never taken out those horses (for such a purpose); is it not excessive to do so for a man with whom you (merely) lodged?' The Master said, 'I entered a little ago, and wailed for him; and I found (the mourner) so dissolved in grief that my tears flowed (with his). I should hate it, if those tears were not (properly) followed. Do it, my child[1].'

17. When Confucius was in Wei, there was (a son) following his (father's) coffin to the grave. After Confucius had looked at him, he said, 'How admirably did he manage this mourning rite! He is fit to be a pattern. Remember it, my little children.' Dze-kung said, 'What did you, Master, see in him so admirable?' 'He went,' was the reply, 'as if he were full of eager affection. He came back (looking) as if he were in doubt.' 'Would it not have been better, if he had come back hastily, to present the offering of repose?' The Master said, 'Remember it, my children. I have not been able to attain to it.'

18. At the mourning rites for Yen Yüan, some of the flesh of the sacrifice at the end of (? two) years was sent to Confucius, who went out and received it, On re-entering he played on his lute, and afterwards ate it[2].

19. Confucius was standing (once) with his disciples,

[1. We are willing to believe this paragraph, because it shows how the depths of Confucius' sympathy could be stirred in him. He was not in general easily moved.

2. This paragraph has occasioned a good deal of discussion. The text does not make it clear whether the sacrifice was that at the end of one, or that at the end of two years. Why did Confucius play on his lute? and was he right in doing so?]

having his hands joined across his breast, and the right hand uppermost. They also all placed their right hands uppermost. He said to them, 'You do so from your wish to imitate me, but I place my hands so, because I am mourning for an elder sister.' On this they all placed their left hands uppermost (according to the usual fashion).

20. Confucius rose early (one day), and with his hands behind him, and trailing his staff, moved slowly about near the door, singing—

The great mountain must crumble;
The strong beam must break;

The wise man must wither away like a plant.'

Having thus sung, he entered and sat down opposite the door. Dze–kung had heard him, and said, 'If the great mountain crumble, to what shall I look up? If the strong beam break, (on what shall I lean)[1]? If the wise man wither like a plant, whom, shall I imitate? The Master, I am afraid, is going to be ill.' He then hastened into the house. The Master said, Zhze, what makes you so late? Under the sovereigns of Hsiâ, the body was dressed and coffined at the top of the steps on the east, so that it was where the deceased used to go up (as master of the house). The people of Yin performed the same ceremony between the two pillars, so that the steps for the host were on one side of the corpse, and those for

[1. The original of this supplement has dropt out of the text. it is found in the 'Narratives of the School;' and in a Corean edition of the Lî Kî.]

the guest on the other. The people of Kâu perform it at the top of the western steps, treating the deceased as if he were a guest. I am a man (descended from the house) of Yin[1], and last night I dreamt that I was sitting with the offerings to the dead by my side between the two pillars. Intelligent kings do not arise; and what one under heaven s able to take me as his Master? I apprehend I am about to die.' With this he took to his bed, was ill for seven days, and died.

21. At the mourning rites for Confucius, the disciples were in perplexity as to what dress they should wear. Dze–kung said, 'Formerly, when the Master was mourning for Yen Yüan, he acted in other respects as if he were mourning for a son, but wore no mourning dress. He did the same in the case of Dze–lû. Let us mourn for the Master, as if we were mourning for a father, but wear no mourning dress[2].'

22. At the mourning for Confucius, Kung–hsî Khih made the ornaments of commemoration. As the adornments of the coffin, there –were the wall–like curtains, the fan–like screens, and the cords at its sides, after the manner of Kâu. There were the flags with their toothed edges, after the manner of Yin; and there were the flag–staffs bound with white silk, and

[1. It is well known that the Khung family was a branch of the ducal house of Sung, the lords of which were the representatives of the royal house of Shang. The Khungs were obliged to flee from Sung, and take refuge in Lû in the time of the great–grandfather of Confucius.

2. It is doubtful whether this advice was entirely followed as regards the matter of the dress.]

long streamers pendent from them, after the manner of Hsiâ[1].

23. At the mourning for Dze–kang, Kung–ming made the ornaments of commemoration. There was a tent–like pall, made of plain silk of a carnation colour, with clusters of ants at the four corners, (as if he had been) an officer of Yin[2].

24. Dze–hsiâ asked Confucius, saying, 'How should (a son) conduct himself with reference to the man who has killed his father or mother?' The Master said, 'He should sleep on straw, with his shield for a pillow; he should not take office; he must be determined not to live with the slayer under the same heaven. If he meet with him in the market–place or the court, he should not have to go back for his weapon, but (instantly) fight with him.'

'Allow me to ask,' said (the other), 'how one should do with reference to the man who has slain his brother?' 'He may take office,' was the reply, 'but not in the same state with the slayer; if he be sent on a mission by his ruler's orders, though he may then meet with the man, he should not fight with him.'

'And how should one do,' continued Dze–hsiâ, 'in the case of a man who has slain one of his paternal cousins?' Confucius said, 'He should not take the lead (in the avenging). If he whom it chiefly concerns is able to do that, he should support him from behind, with his weapon in his hand.'

[1. See the full description of a coffin and hearse with all its ornaments in Book XIX.

2. In honour of the Master, though Dze–hang himself could not claim to be descended from the kings of Yin.]

25. At the mourning rites for Confucius, his disciples all wore their head–bands of sackcloth, when they went out. For one of their own number, they wore them in the house

(when condoling), but not when they went out.

26. Keeping (the ground about) their graves clear of grass was not a practice of antiquity[1].

27. Dze–lû said, 'I heard the Master say that in the rites of mourning, exceeding grief with deficient rites is better than little demonstration of grief with superabounding rites; and that in those of sacrifice, exceeding reverence with deficient rites is better than an excess of rites with but little reverence.'

28. Zang–dze having gone on a visit of condolence to Fû–hsiâ, the chief mourner had already presented the sacrifice of departure, and removed the offerings. He caused the bier, however, to be pushed back to its former place, and made the women come down (again), after which (the visitor) went through his ceremony. The disciples who accompanied Zang–dze asked him if this proceeding were according to rule, and he said, 'The sacrifice at starting is an unimportant matter, And why might he not bring (the bier) back, and 'let it rest (for a while)?'

The disciples further asked the same question of Dze–yû, who said, 'The rice and precious shell are put into the mouth of the corpse under the window (of the western chamber); the slighter dressing is

[1. Some would interpret this sentence as if it were—'changing the grave' (and not); but the Khien–lung editors say that this practice, originating in geomancy, arose in the time of Sin, and was unknown during the Han dynasty.]

done inside the door, and the more complete one at (the top of) the eastern steps; the coffining takes place at the guests' place; the sacrifice at starting in the courtyard; and the interment at the grave. The proceedings go on in this way to what is more remote, and hence in the details of mourning there is a constant advance and no receding.' When Zang–dze heard of this reply, he said, 'This is a much better account than I gave of the going forth to offer the sacrifice of departure.'

29. Zang–dze went an a visit of condolence, wearing his fur robe over the silk one, while Dze–yû went, wearing the silk one over his fur. Zang–dze, pointing to him, and calling the attention of others, said, 'That man has the reputation of being well versed in

ceremonies, how is it that he comes to condole with his silk robe displayed over his fur one?' (By–and–by), when the chief mourner had finished the slighter dressing of the corpse, he bared his breast and tied up his hair with sackcloth, on which Dze–yû hastened out, and (soon) came back, wearing his fur robe over the silk, and with a girdle of sackcloth. Zang–dze on this said, 'I was wrong, I was wrong. That man was right.'

20. When Dze–hsiâ was introduced (to the Master) after he had put off the mourning (for his parents), a lute was given to him. He tried to tune it, but could hardly do so; he touched it, but brought no melody from it. He rose up and said, 'I have not yet forgotten my grief. The ancient kings framed the rules of ceremony, and I dare not go beyond them?' When a lute was given to Dze–kang in the same circumstances, he tried to tune it, and easily did so; he touched it, and brought melody from it. He rose up and said, 'The ancient kings framed the rules of ceremony, and I do not dare not to come up to them.'

31. At the mourning rites for Hui–dze, who had been minister of Crime, Dze–yû (went to condole), wearing for him a robe of sackcloth, and a headband made of the product of the male plant. Wan–dze (the brother of Hui–dze), wishing to decline the honour, said, 'You condescended to be the associate of my younger brother, and now further condescend to wear this mourning; I venture to decline the honour.' Dze–yû said, 'It is in, rule;' on which Wan–dze returned and continued his wailing. Dze–yû then hastened and took his place among the officers (of the family); but Wan–dze also declined this honour, and said, 'You condescended to be the associate of my younger brother, and now further condescend to wear for him this mourning, and to come and take part in the mourning rites I venture to decline the honour.' Dze–yû said, 'I beg firmly to request you to allow me (to remain here).'

Wan–dze then returned, and supporting the rightful son to take his position with his face to the south, said, 'You condescended to be the associate of my younger brother, and now you further condescend to wear this mourning for him, and to come and take part in the rites; dare Hû but return to his (proper) place?' Dze–yû on this hastened to take his position among the guests'.

[1. The object of Dze–yû in all the movements detailed here is supposed to have been to correct some irregularity in the proceedings on the occasion. Kang Hsüan thinks that Wan–dze was supporting a grandson, instead of Hû, his deceased brother's rightful son, to be the principal mourner, and consequently to succeed Hui–dze as his representative and successor. Hui–dze and Wan–dze (called Mei–mâu) were of the state of Wei.]

32. At the mourning rites for the general Wan–dze, when the first year's mourning was at an end, there came a man from Yüeh[1] on a visit of condolence. The chief mourner, wearing the long robe (assumed on the completion of the first year's mourning), and the cap worn before that, wailed for him in the ancestral temple, with the tears running from his eyes and the rheum from his nose. Dze–yû saw it, and said, 'The son of the general Wan is not far from being (a master of ceremonies). In his observances at this time, for which there is no special rule, his proceeding is correct.'

33. The giving of the name in childhood[2], of the designation at the capping, of the title of elder uncle or younger uncle at fifty, and of the honorary title after death, was the practice of the Kâu dynasty.

The wearing of the sackcloth head–bands and girdles, to express the real (feeling of the heart); the digging a hole in the middle of the apartment (over which) to wash (the corpse); taking down the (tiles of the) furnace, and placing them at the feet (of it)[3]; and at the interment pulling down (part of the wall on the west of the door of) the ancestral temple, so as to pass by the upper side (of the altar to the spirit)

[1. A distant state, south of Wû, on the seaboard.

2 Three months after birth.

3. To show the deceased had no more occasion for food, and to keep the feet straight, so that the shoes might be put on at the dressing of the corpse.]

of the way, and issue by the great gate;—these were the practices of the Yin dynasty, and the learners (in the school of Confucius) followed them.

34. When the mother of Dze–liû died, (his younger brother) Dze–shih asked for the means (to provide what was necessary for the mourning rites). Dze–liû said, 'How shall we get them?' 'Let us sell (the concubines), the mothers of our half–brothers,' said the other. 'How can we sell the mothers of other men to bury our mother?' was the reply; 'that cannot be done.'

After the burial, Dze-shih wished to take what remained of the money and other things contributed towards their expenses, to provide sacrificial vessels; but Dze-liû said, 'Neither can that be done. I have heard that a superior man will not enrich his family by means of his mourning. Let us distribute it among the poor of our brethren.'

35. A superior man said, 'He who has given counsel to another about his army should die with it when it is defeated. He who has given counsel about the country or its capital should perish with it when it comes into peril.'

36. Kung-shû Wan-dze ascended the mound of Hsiâ, with, Kü Po-yü following him. Wan-dze said, 'How pleasant is this mound! I should like to be buried here when I die.' Kü Po-yü said, 'You may find pleasure in such a thought, but allow me (to go home) before (you say any more about it)

37. There was a man of Pien who wept like a

[1. Was there anything more than a joke in this reply of Po-yü? The commentators make it out to be a reproof of Wan-dze for wishing to appropriate for his grave the pleasant ground of another.]

child on the death of his mother. Confucius said, 'This is grief indeed, but it would be difficult to continue it. Now the rules of ceremony require to be handed down, and to be perpetuated. Hence the wailing and leaping are subject to fixed regulations.'

38. When the mother of Shu-sun Wû-shû died, and the slighter dressing had been completed, the bearers went out at the door (of the apartment) with the corpse. When he had himself gone out at the door, he bared his arms, throwing down also his cap, and binding his hair with sackcloth, Dze-yû said (in derision), 'He knows the rules[1]!'

39. (When a ruler was ill), the high chamberlain supported him on the right, and the assigner of positions at audiences did so on the left. When he died these two officers lifted (the corpse)[2].

4o. There are the husband of a maternal cousin and the wife of a maternal uncle;-that these two should wear mourning for each other has not been said by any superior man. Some one says, 'If they have eaten together from the same fireplace, the three months' mourning [3] should be worn.'

41. It is desirable that affairs of mourning should be gone about with urgency, and festive affairs in a

[1. He should have made his preparations before, and not have had to throw down his cap on the ground.

2 The text of this paragraph would make the assisting parties to be the chief diviner and the chief archer. The translation is according to an emendation of it from the Kâu Lû.

3 Worn in relationships of the fifth degree: as by a man for his great–grand–uncle and his wife, a spinster great–grand–aunt, the son of a mother's brother or sister, &c.; by a wife for her husband's great–great–grand–parents, &c. See Appendix.]

leisurely way. Hence, though affairs of mourning require urgency, they should not go beyond the prescribed rules; and though festive affairs may be delayed, they should not be transacted negligently. Hurry therefore (in the former) becomes rudeness, and too much ease (in the latter) shows a small man. The superior man will conduct himself in them as they severally require.

42. A superior man is ashamed[1] to prepare (beforehand) all that he may require in discharging his mourning rites. What can be made in one or two days, he does not prepare (beforehand).

43. The mourning worn for the son of a brother should be the same as for one's own son: the object being to bring him still nearer to one's self. An elder brother's wife and his younger brother do not wear mourning for each other: the object being to maintain the distance between them. Slight mourning is worn for an aunt, and an elder or younger sister, (when they have been married); the reason being that there are those who received them from us, and will render to them the full measure of observance.

PART III.

1. When (the Master) was eating by the side of one who had mourning rites in hand, he

never ate to the full.

2. Zang–dze was standing with (another) visitor by the side of the door (of their house of entertainment), when a companion (of the other) came hurrying out.

[1. Lest he should seem not to be wishing individuals to live long.]

'Where are you going?' said Zang–dze; and the man replied, 'My father is dead, and I am going to wail for him in the lane.' 'Return to your apartment,' was the reply, 'and wail for him there.' (The man did so), and Zang–dze made him a visit of condolence, standing with his face to the north.

3. Confucius said, 'In dealing with the dead, if we treat them as if they were entirely dead, that would show a want of affection, and should not be done; or, if we treat them as if they were entirely alive, that would show a want of wisdom, and should not be done. On this account the vessels of bamboo (used in connexion with the burial of the dead) are not fit for actual use; those of earthenware cannot be used to wash in; those of wood are incapable of being carved; the lutes are strung, but not evenly; the pandean pipes are complete, but not in tune; the bells and musical stones are there, but they have no stands. They are called vessels to the eye of fancy; that is, (the dead) are thus treated as if they were spiritual intelligences[1].'

[1. The Khien–lung editors say on this:—'To serve the dead as he served the living is the highest reach of a son's feeling. But there is a difference, it is to be presumed, between the ways of spirits and those of men. In the offerings put down immediately after death, there is an approach to treating the deceased as if he were still a (living) man. But at the burial the treatment of him approaches to that due to a (disembodied) spirit, Therefore the dealing with the dead may be spoken of generally as something between that due to a man and that due to a spirit,—a manifestation of the utmost respect without any familiar liberty.' We should like to have something still more definite. Evidently the subject was difficult to those editors, versed in all Chinese lore, and not distracted by views from foreign habits and ways of thinking. How much more difficult must it be for a foreigner to place himself 'en rapport' with the thoughts and ways of men, so far removed from him in time and in mental training! The subject of these vessels, which yet were no vessels, will come up again.]

4. Yû-dze asked Zang-dze if he had ever questioned the Master about (an officer's) losing his place. 'I heard from him,' was the reply, 'that the officer in such a case should wish to become poor quickly, Oust as) we should wish to decay away quickly when we have died.' Yû-dze said, 'These are not the words of a superior man.' 'I heard them from the Master,' returned Zang-dze. Yû-dze repeated that they were not the words of a superior man, and the other affirmed that both he and, Dze-yû had heard them. 'Yes, yes,' said Yû-dze, 'but the Master must have spoken them with a special reference.' Zang-dze reported Yû-dze's words to Dze-yû, who said, 'How very like his words are to those of the Master! Formerly, when the Master was staying in Sung, he saw that Hwan, the minister of War, had been for three years having a stone coffin made for himself without its being finished, and said, "What extravagance! It would be better that when dead he should quickly decay away." It was with reference to Hwan, the minister of War, that he said, "We should wish to decay away quickly when we die." When Nan-kung King-shû returned (to the state), he made it a point to carry his treasures with him in his carriage when he went to court, on which the Master said, "Such an amount of property! It would have been better for him, when he lost his office, to make haste to become poor." It was with reference to Nan-kung King-shû that he said that we should work to become poor quickly, when we have lost office."'

3. Zang-dze reported these words of Dze-yû to Yû-dze, who said, 'Yes, I did say that these were not the words of the Master.' When the other asked him how he knew it, he said, 'The Master made an ordinance in Kung-tû that the inner coffin should be four inches thick, and the outer five. By this I knew that he did not wish that the dead should decay away quickly. And formerly, when he had lost the office of minister of Crime in Lû, and was about to go to King, he first sent Dze-hsiâ there, and afterwards Zan Yû. By this, I knew that he did not wish to become poor quickly[1].'

5. When Kwang-dze of Khin died, announcement of the event was sent to Lû. They did not want to wail for him there, but duke Mû[2] called Hsien-dze, and consulted him. He said, 'In old times, no messages from Great officers, not even such as -were accompanied by a bundle of pieces of dried meat, went out beyond the boundaries of their states. Though it had been wished to wail for them, how could it have been done? Nowadays the Great officers share in the measures of government throughout the middle states. Though it may be wished not to wail for one, how can it be avoided? I have heard, moreover, that there are two grounds for the wailing; one from love, and one from fear.' The duke said, 'Very well; but how is the thing to be managed in this

[1. Confucius sent those two disciples, that he might get their report of King (or Khû), and know whether he might himself go and take office there as be wished to do.

2. B.C. 409–377.]

case?' Hsien–dze said, 'I would ask you to wail for him in the temple of (a family of) a different surname;' and hereon the duke and he wailed for Kwang–dze in (the temple of) the Hsien family.

6. Kung Hsien said to Zang–dze, 'Under the sovereigns of the Hsiâ dynasty, they used (at burials) the vessels which were such only to the eye of fancy, intimating to the people that (the dead) had no knowledge. Under the Yin they used the (ordinary) sacrificial vessels, intimating to the people that (the dead) had knowledge. Under the Kâu we use both, intimating to the people that the thing is doubtful.' Zang–dze replied, ' It is not so! What are vessels (only) to the eye of fancy are for the shades (of the departed); the vessels of sacrifice are those of men; how should those ancients have treated their parents as if they were dead?'

7. An elder brother of Kung–shû Mû, by the same mother but a different father, having died, he asked, Dze–yû (whether he should go into mourning for him), and was answered, 'Perhaps you should do so for the period of nine months.'

A brother, similarly related to Tî Î, having died, he consulted Dze–hsiâ in the same way, and was answered, 'I have not heard anything about it before, but the people of Lû wear the one year's mourning in such a case.' Tî Î did so, and the present practice of wearing that mourning arose from his question'.

8. When Dze–sze's mother died in Wei, Liû Zo said to him, 'You, Sir, are the descendant of a sage.

[1. Confucius gives a decision against mourning at all in such a case, excepting it were exceptional,—in the 'Narratives of the School,' chapter 10, article 1.]

From all quarters they look to you for an example in ceremonies; let me advise you to be careful in the matter.' Dze–sze said, 'Of what have I to be careful? I have heard that when there are certain ceremonies to be observed, and he has not the necessary means for them, a superior man does not observe them', and that neither does he do so, when there are the ceremonies, and he has the means, but the time is not suitable; of what have I to be careful[1]?'

9. Hsien–dze So said, 'I have heard that the ancients made no diminution (in the degrees of mourning on any other ground); but mourned for every one above and below them according to his relationship. Thus Wan, the earl of Thang, wore the year's mourning for Mang–hû, who was his uncle, and the same for Mang Phî, whose uncle he was.'

10. Hâu Mû said, 'I heard Hsien–dze say about the rites of mourning, that (a son) should certainly think deeply and long about them all, and that (for instance) in buying the coffin he should see that, inside and outside, it be (equally) well completed. When I die, let it be so also with me[2].'

11. Zang–dze said, 'Until the corpse has its ornaments put on it, they curtain off the hall; and after the slighter dressing the curtain is removed.' Kung–liang–dze said, 'Husband and wife are at first all in

[1. Dze–sze's mother, after his father's death, had married again into the Shû family of Wei. What mourning was Dze–sze now to wear for her? Liû Zo seems to have apprehended that he would be carried away by his feelings and would do more than was according to rule in such a case. Dze–sze's reply to him is not at all explicit.

2. This record is supposed to be intended to ridicule Hâu Mû for troubling himself as he did.]

confusion[1], and therefore the hall is curtained off. After the slighter dressing, the curtain is removed.'

12. With regard to the offerings to the dead at the time of the slighter dressing, Dze–yû said that they should be placed on the east (of the corpse). Zang–dze said, 'They should be placed on the west, on the mat there at the time of the dressing.' The placing the offerings on the west at the time of the slighter dressing was an error of the later times of Lû.

13. Hsien–dze said, 'To have the mourning robe of coarse dolichos cloth, and the lower garment of fine linen with a wide texture, was not (the way of) antiquity.'

14. When Dze–phû died, the wailers called out his name Mieh[2]. Dze–kâo said, 'So rude and uncultivated are they!' On this they changed their style.

15. At the mourning rites for the mother of Tû Khiâo no one was employed in the house to assist (the son in the ceremonics), which was accounted a careless omission.

16. The Master said, 'As soon as a death occurs, (the members of the family) should change their lambskin furs and dark–coloured caps, though they may do nothing more.' The Master did not pay a visit of condolence in these articles of dress.

17. Dze–yû asked about the articles to be provided for the mourning rites, and the Master said, 'They should be according to the means of the family.'

[1. Settling places for the wailers, &c. But this explanation is deemed unsatisfactory.

2. The name was used only in calling the spirit back immediately after death; the wailing was a subsequent thing.]

Dze–yû urged, 'How can a family that has means and one that has not have things done in the same way?' 'Where there are means,' was the reply, 'let there be no exceeding the prescribed rites. If there be a want of means, let the body be lightly covered from head to foot, and forthwith buried, the coffin being simply let down by means of ropes. Who in such a case will blame the procedure?'

18. Pan, superintendent of officers' registries, informed Dze–yû of his wish to dress his dead on the couch. 'You may,' said Dze–yû. When Hsien–dze heard of this, he said, 'How arrogant is the old gentleman! He takes it on himself to allow men in what is the proper rule[1].'

19. At the burial of his wife, duke Hsiang of Sung[2] placed (in the grave) a hundred jars of vinegar and pickles. Zang–dze said, 'They are called "vessels only to the eye of fancy," and yet he filled them!'

20. After the mourning rites for Mang Hsien–dze, the chief minister of his family made his subordinates return their money–offerings to all the donors. The Master said that such a thing was allowable.

21. About the reading of the list of the material contributions (towards the service of a funeral), Zang–dze

[1. On death, the body was lifted from the couch, and laid on the ground. When there was no response to the recalling of the spirit, it was returned to the couch and dressed. A practice seems to have arisen of slightly dressing it on the ground, which Pin did not wish to follow. Dze–ya ought to have told him that his proposal was according to rule; whereas he expressed his permission of it,–a piece of arrogance, which Hsien–dze condemned.

2. Hsiang died in B.C. 637.]

said, 'It is not an ancient practice; it is a second announcement (to the departed)[1]!'

22. When Kang–dze Kâo was lying ill, Khang went in to see him, and asked his (parting) commands, saying, 'Your disease, Sir, is severe. If it should go on to be the great illness, what are we to do?' Dze–kâo said, 'I have heard that in life we should be of use to others, and in death should do them no harm. Although I may have been of no use to others during my life, shall I do them any harm by my death? When I am dead, choose a piece of barren ground, and bury me there.'

23. Dze–hsiâ asked the Master (how one should deport himself) during the mourning for the ruler's mother or wife, (and the reply was), 'In sitting and stopping with others, in his conversation, and when eating and drinking, he should appear to be at ease[2].

24. When a stranger–visitor arrived, and had nowhere to lodge, the Master would say, 'While he is alive, let him lodge with me. Should he die, I will see to his coffining[3].'

25. Kwo–dze kâo[4] said, 'Burying means hiding

[1. The contributions had been announced by the bier, as if to the departed, and a record of them made. To read the list, as is here supposed, as the procession was about to set forth, was a vain–glorious proceeding, which Zang–dze thus derided.

2. The supplements in this paragraph are from the 'Narratives of the School.' Some contend that the whole should be read as what Dze–hsiâ said, and that the Master gave him no reply, disapproving of his sentiments.

3. This paragraph, like the preceding, appears in rather a different form in the 'Narratives of the School.'

4. Kwo–dze Kâo was the same as the Khang–dze Kâo of par. 22. Kwo was the surname, and Khang the posthumous title. It is difficult to decide between Kwo–dze Kâo and Kwo Dze–kâo.]

away; and that hiding (of the body) is from a wish that men should not see it. Hence there are the clothes sufficient for an elegant covering; the coffin all round about the clothes; the shell all round about the coffin; and the earth all round about the shell. And shall we farther raise a mound over the grave and plant it with trees?'

26. At the mourning for Confucius, there came a man from Yen to see (what was done), and lodged at Dze–hsiâ's. Dze–hsiâ said to him, 'If it had been for the sage's conducting a burial, (there would have been something worthy to see); but what is there to see in our burying of the sage? Formerly the Master made some remarks to me, saying, "I have seen some mounds made like a raised hall; others like a dyke on a river's bank; others like the roof of a large house; and others in the shape of an axe–head." We have followed the axe–shape, making what is called the horse–mane mound. In one day we thrice shifted the frame–boards, and completed the mound. I hope we have carried out the wish of the Master.'

27. Women (in mourning) do not (change) the girdle made of dolichos fibre.

28. When new offerings (of grain or fruits) are presented (beside the body in the coffin), they should be (abundant), like the offerings on the first day of the moon.

29. When the interment has taken place, everyone should make a change in his mourning dress.

30. The gutters of the tent–like frame over the coffin should be like the double gutters of a house.

31. When a ruler succeeds to his state, he makes his coffin, and thereafter varnishes it once a year, keeping it deposited away.

32. Calling the departed back; plugging the teeth open; keeping the feet straight; filling the mouth; dressing the corpse; and curtaining the hall: these things are set about together, The uncles and elder cousins give their charges to those who are to communicate the death (to friends).

33. The (soul of a deceased) ruler is called back in his smaller chambers, and the large chamber; in the smaller ancestral temples and in the great one: and at the gate leading to the court of the external audience, and in the suburbs all round.

34. Why do they leave the offerings of the mourning rites uncovered? May they do so with the flesh of sacrifice[1]?

35. When the coffining has taken place, in ten days after, provision should be made for the materials (for the shell), and for the vessels to the eye of fancy.

36. The morning offerings should be set forth (beside the body) at sunrise; the evening when the sun is about to set.

37. In mourning for a parent, there is no restriction to (set) times for wailing. If one be sent on a mission, he must announce his return (to the spirits of his departed).

38. After the twelfth month of mourning, the (inner) garment should be of white silk, with a yellow

[1. This short paragraph is difficult to construe. The Khien–lung editors seem to approve of another interpretation of it; but even that is not without its difficulties. The flesh of sacrifice, it is said, left uncovered, would become unfit for use or to be sold.]

lining, and having the collar and the edges of the cuffs of a light purple. The waist–band should be of dolichos cloth; the shoes of hempen string, without the usual ornaments at the points; and the ear-plugs of horn. The lining of the deer's-fur (for winter) should be made broader and with longer cuffs, and a robe of thin silk may be worn over it[1].

39. When (a parent's) corpse has been coffined, if the son hear of mourning going on for a cousin at a distance, he must go (to condole), though the relationship would only require the three months' mourning. If the mourning be for a neighbour, who is not a relative, he does not go.

At (the mourning) for an acquaintance, he must pay visits of condolence to all his brethren, though they might not have lived with him.

40, The coffin of the son of Heaven is fourfold. The hides of a water-buffalo and a rhinoceros, overlapping each other, (form the first), three inches in thickness. Then there is a coffin of Î wood[2], and there are two of the Rottlera. The four are all complete enclosures. The bands for the (composite) coffin are (five); two straight, and three cross; with a double wedge under each band (where it is on the edge).

[1. The outer sackcloth remained unchanged; but inside it was now worn this robe of white silk, a good deal ornamented. Inside this and over the deer's-fur in winter might be worn another robe of thin silk, through which the fur was seen. Inside the fur was what we should call the shirt, always worn.

2 Tracing the Î tree, through the dictionaries from synonym to synonym, we come at last to identify it with the 'white aspen;' whether correctly or not I do not know.]

The shell is of cypress wood, in pieces six cubits long, from the trunk near the root.

41. When the son of Heaven is wailing for a feudal prince, he wears the bird's-(head) cap[1], a headband of sackcloth, and black robes. Some one says, 'He employs an officer to wail for him.' While so engaged, he has no music at his meals.

42. When the son of Heaven is put into his coffin it is surrounded with boards plastered over, and (rests on the hearse), on whose shafts are painted dragons, so as to form a (kind of) shell. Then over the coffin is placed a pall with the axe-heads figured on it. This being done, it forms a plastered house. Such is the rule for (the coffining of) the son of Heaven[2].

43. It is only at the mourning rites for the son of Heaven that the feudal princes are arranged for the wailing according to their different surnames.

44. Duke Âi of Lû eulogised Khung Khiû in the words, 'Heaven has not left the old man, and there is no one to assist me in my place. Oh! Alas! Nî–fû[3]!'

45– When a state had lost a large tract of territory

[1. This cap, it is said, was of leather, of the dark, colour of a male sparrow's head. Hence its name.

2 See Book XIX.

3. Confucius' death took place on the 18th of the fourth month of duke Âi's 16th year, B.C. 479. The eulogy is given somewhat differently in the Zo Kwan under that year: 'Compassionate Heaven vouchsafes me no comfort, and has not left me the aged man, to support me, the One man, on my seat. Dispirited I am, and full of distress. Woe is me! Alas! O Nî–fû. There is no one now to be a rule to me!' Khiû was Confucius' name, and Kung–nî his designation.' After this eulogy, Nî–fû was for a time his posthumous title.]

with its cities, the highest and other ministers, and the Great and other officers, all wailed in the grand ancestral temple, in mourning caps, for three days; and the ruler (for the same time) had no full meal with music. Some one says, 'The ruler has his full meals and music, but wails at the altar to the spirit of the land.'

46. Confucius disliked those who wailed in the open fields[1].

47. (A son) who has not been in office should not presume to give away anything belonging to the family. If he should have to do so[2], he ought to have the order of his father or elder brother for the act.

48. When the (ordinary) officers[3] are all entered, then (the chief mourner and all the others) fall to their leaping, morning and evening.

49. After the service on the conclusion of the twenty–fourth month of mourning, the plain white cap is assumed. In that month the service on leaving off mourning is

performed, and after another month (the mourners) may take to their music[4].

50. The ruler may confer on any officer the small curtain (as a pall for his father's coffin).

[1. It was the rule to mourn in the open country for an acquaintance. See p. 134. There must have been some irregularity in the practice adverted to.

2. That is, supposing him to have been in office; though some suppose that the necessity might arise, even in the case of a son who had not been in office.

3. Of course the higher officers must also be. there. This refers to the mourning rites for a ruler.

4. See the note on page 130. It is difficult, notwithstanding all the references to it, to say definitely in what month the than sacrifice was performed.]

SECTION II. PART I.

I. (At the funeral of) a ruler's eldest son by his acknowledged wife, who has died under age, there are three (small) carriages (with the flesh of sacrifice to be put in the grave). At that of an eldest son by one of his concubines, dying under age, there is one such carriage; as at the funeral of the eldest rightful son of a Great officer in the same circumstances[1].

2. At the mourning rites for a feudal lord, his chief officers who had received their appointments. directly from him, carried their staffs.

3. When a Great officer of a state was about to be buried, its ruler (went to) condole with (his son) in the hall where the coffin was. When it was

[1. This refers to a strange custom which was practised at the burial of men of rank, or of others who were treated as such, as in the cases here. 'The carriages employed in it,' says Ying–tâ, 'were very small. When the funeral car was about to set off from the temple, and all to be done at the grave was arranged, they took portions of the bodies which had supplied the offerings put down by the coffin, broke them in small pieces, wrapped them up, and placed them in these carriages, to be conveyed after the car. At the grave the little bundles were placed one by one, inside the outer shell at its four corners.' The number of these small carriages varied according to the rank of the deceased. We shall find the practice mentioned again and again. It is not easy for a foreigner fully to understand it, and I have found great haziness in the attempts of native scholars to explain it. 'The eldest sons' would have died between sixteen and nineteen.]

being taken out, he ordered some one to draw the (bier–carriage) for him This moved on for three paces and stopped; in all for three times; afterwhich the ruler retired. The same proceeding was gone through, when the bier entered the ancestral temple, and also at the place of (special) grief[1].

4. Men of fifty, who had no carriage, did not make visits of condolence beyond the boundaries (of their states).

5. When Kî Wû–dze was lying ill in his chamber, Kiâo Kû entered and appeared before him without taking off the mourning with its even edges (which he happened to wear). 'This practice,' said he, 'has nearly fallen into disuse. But it is only at the gate of the ruler that an officer should take off such mourning as I have on.' Wû–dze replied, 'Is it not good that you should act thus[2]? A superior man illustrates the smallest points (of propriety).'

At the mourning rites for Wû–dze, Zang Tien leant against his gate and sang[3].

6. If a Great officer pay a visit of condolence

[1. Where visitors had been lodged during the mourning rites, outside the great gate.

2. Wû–dze was the posthumous title of Ki–sun Suh, the principal minister of Lû in the time of duke Hsiang (D.C. 572–543). He was arrogant, and made other officers pay to him the same observances as to the ruler; but he was constrained to express his approval of the bold rectitude of Kiâo.

3. This is added by the writer, and implies a condemnation of Zang Tien, who did not know how to temper his censure of the minister, as Kiâo Kû had done. But there must be an error in the passage. Tien (the father of Zang Shan) could have been but a boy when

Wû–dze died.]

(to an ordinary officer), and he arrive when (the latter) is occupied with the business of the occasion, an apology is made (for not coming to the gate to receive him).

7. When one has paid a visit of condolence, he should not on the same day show manifestations of joy[1].

8. A wife should not go beyond the boundaries of the state on a visit of condolence.

9. On the day when he has made a visit of condolence, one should not drink spirits nor eat flesh.

10. When one pays a visit of condolence, and the arrangements for the funeral are going on, he should take hold of the ropes (attached to the car). Those who follow to the grave should take hold of those attached to the coffin.

11. During the mourning rites, if the ruler send a message of condolence, there must be some one to acknowledge it, by bowing to the messenger. A friend, or neighbour, or even a temporary resident in the house, may perform the duty. The message is announced in the words:—'Our unworthy ruler wishes to take part in your (sad) business.' The chief mourner responds:—'We acknowledge your presence with his message[2].'

12. When a ruler meets a bier on the way, he must send some one to present his condolences (to the chief mourner).

[1. Or it may be, 'should not have music;' toning one of the characters differently.

2. It is supposed that the deceased had left no son to preside at the mourning rites.]

13. At the mourning rites for a Great officer, a son by an inferior wife should not receive the condolences[1].

14. On the death of his wife's brother who was the successor of their father, (the husband) should wail for him in (the court of) the principal chamber[2]. He should appoint his (own) son to preside (on the occasion). With breast unbared and wearing the cincture

instead of the cap, he wails and leaps. When he enters on the right side of the gate, he should make some one stand outside it, to inform comers of the occasion of the wailing; and those who were intimate (with the deceased) will enter and wail. If his own father be in the house, the wailing should take place (before) his wife's chamber. If (the deceased) were not the successor of his father, the wailing should take place before a different chamber.

15. If a man have the coffin of a parent in his hall, and hear of mourning going on for a cousin of the same surname at a distance, he wails for him in a side apartment. If there be no such apartment, he should wail in the court on the right of the gate. If the deceased's body be in the same state, he should go to the place, and wail for him there.

16. When Dze–kang died, Zang–dze was in mourning for his mother, and went in his mourning dress

[1. But if there be no son by the wife proper, the oldest son by an inferior wife may receive the condolences. See the Khien–lung editors, in loc.

2. For some reason or other he has not gone to the house of the deceased, to wail for him there.]

to wail for him. Some one said, 'That dress of sackcloth with its even edges is not proper. for a visit of condolence.' Zang–dze replied, 'Am I condoling (with the living)?'

17. At the mourning rites for Yû Zo, duke Tâo[1] came to condole. Dze–yû received him, and introduced him by (the steps on) the left[2].

18. When the news was sent from Khî of the mourning for the king's daughter who had been married to the marquis, duke Kwang of Lû wore the nine months' mourning for her. Some have said, 'She was married from Lû[3]; therefore he wore the same mourning for her as for a sister of his own.' Others have said, 'She was his mother's mother, and therefore he wore it.'

19. At the mourning rites for duke Hsien of Zin, duke Mû of Khin sent a messenger to present his condolences to Hsien's son Khung–r (who was then an exile), and to add this message:—'I have heard that a time like this is specially adapted to the

[1. B.C. 467–431. Yû Zo had been a disciple of Confucius, and here we find the greater follower of the sage, Dze–yû, present and assisting at the mourning rites for him.

2. That is, the prince went up to the hall by the steps on the east, set apart for the use of the master and father of the house. But the ruler was master everywhere in his state, as the king was in his kingdom. An error prevailed on this matter, and Dze–yû took the opportunity to correct it.

3. That is, she had gone from the royal court to Lû, and been married thence under the superintendence of the marquis of that state, who also was of the royal surname. This was a usual practice in the marriage of kings' daughters; and it was on this account the lord of the officiating state wore mourning for them. The relationship assigned in the next clause is wrong; and so would have been the mourning mentioned, if it had been correct.]

losing of a state, or the gaining of a state. Though you, my son, are quiet here, in sorrow and in mourning, your exile should not be allowed to continue long, and the opportunity should not be lost. Think of it and take your measures, my young son.' Khung–r reported the words to his maternal uncle Fan, who said,' My son, decline the proffer. An exile as you are, nothing precious remains to you; but a loving regard for your father is to be considered precious. How shall the death of a father be told? And if you take advantage of it to seek your own profit, who under heaven will be able to give a good account of your conduct? Decline the proffer, my son.

On this the prince replied to his visitor:—'The ruler has kindly (sent you) to condole with his exiled servant. My person in banishment, and my father dead, so that I cannot take any share in the sad services of wailing and weeping for him;—this has awakened the sympathy of the ruler. But how shall the death of a father be described? Shall I presume (on occasion of it) to think of any other thing, and prove myself unworthy of your ruler's righteous regard?' With this he laid his head to the ground, but did not bow (to the visitor); wailed and then arose, and after he had risen did not enter into any private conversation with him.

Dze–hsien reported the execution of his commission to duke Mû, who said, 'Truly virtuous is this prince Khung–r. In laying his forehead on the ground and not bowing (to the messenger), he acknowledged that he was not his father's successor, and therefore he did not complete the giving of thanks. In wailing before he rose, he showed how he loved his father. In having no private conversation after he arose, he showed how he put from him the thought of gain[1].'

20. The keeping the curtain up before the coffin with the corpse in it was not a custom of antiquity. It originated with the wailing of King Kiang for Mû–po[2].

21. The rites of mourning are the extreme expression of grief and sorrow. The graduated reduction of that expression in accordance with the natural changes (of time and feeling) was made by the superior men, mindful of those to whom we owe our being[3].

22. Calling (the soul) back is the way in which love receives its consummation, and has in it the mind which is expressed by prayer. The looking for it to return from the dark region is a way of seeking for it among the spiritual beings. The turning the face to the north springs from the idea of its being in the dark region.

2S. Bowing to the (condoling) visitor, and laying the forehead on the ground are the most painful demonstrations of grief and sorrow. The laying the forehead in the ground is the greatest expression of the pain (from the bereavement).

[1. Fully to understand this paragraph, one must know more particulars of the history of Khung–r, and his relations with his father and the duke of Khin, than can be given here in a note. He became the ablest of the five chiefs of the Khun Khiû period.

2. This was a prudish action of the young widow, but it changed an old custom and introduced a new one.

3. This has respect to the modifications adopted in regulating the mourning rites for parents.]

24. Filling the mouth with rice uncooked and fine shells arises from a feeling which cannot bear that it should be empty. The idea is not that of giving food; and therefore these fine things are used.

25. The inscription[1] forms a banner to the eye of fancy. Because (the person of) the deceased, can no longer be distinguished, therefore (the son) by this flag maintains the remembrance of him. From his love for him he makes this record. His reverence for him

finds in this its utmost expression.

26. The first tablet for the spirit (with this inscription on it) serves the same purpose as that (subsequently) placed in the temple, at the conclusion of the mourning rites. Under the Yin dynasty the former was still kept. Under the Kâu, it was removed[1].

27. The offerings to the unburied dead are placed in plain unornamented vessels, because the hearts

[1. This inscription contained the surname, name, and rank of the deceased. It was at first written, I suppose, on a strip of silk, and fastened up under the eaves above the steps on the cast. In the meantime a tablet of wood called Khung, the first character in the next paragraph, and for which I have given 'The first tablet for the spirit,' was prepared. The inscription was transferred to it, and it was set up on or by the coffin, now having the body in it, and by and by it was removed to the east of the coffin pit, where it remained till after the interment.

The observances in this paragraph and the next remain substantially the same at the present day. 'The bier,' writes Wang Thâo, 'is placed in the apartment, and the tablet with the inscription, as a resting–place for the spirit, is set up, while the offerings are set forth near it morning and evening. After the interment this tablet is burned, and the permanent tablet is made, before which the offerings are presented at the family sacrifices from generation to generation. Thus "the dead are served as the living have been."']

of the living are full of unaffected sorrow. It is only in the sacrifices (subsequent to the interment), that the principal mourner does his utmost (in the way of ornament). Does he know that the spirit will enjoy (his offerings)? He is guided only by his pure and reverent heart.

28. Beating the breast (by the women), and leaping (by the men) are extreme expressions of grief. But the number of such acts is limited. There are graduated rules for them.

29. Baring the shoulders and binding up the hair (with the band of sackcloth) are changes, (showing) the excited feeling which is a change in the grief. The removal of the (usual) ornaments and elegancies (of dress) has manifold expression, but this baring of the shoulders and the sackcloth band are the chief. But now the shoulders are quite bared,

and anon they are covered (with a thin garment);—marking gradations in the grief

30. At the interment they used the cap of plain white (silk), and the headband of dolichos fibre; thinking these more suitable for their intercourse with (the departed) now in their spirit–state. The feeling of reverence had now arisen. The people of Kiu use the pien cap at interments; those of Yin used the hsü[1].

[1. The 'Three Rituals Explained'), ch. 238, give the figures of these caps thus:—

The hsü {illustration}. The pien {illustration}.]

31. The gruel of the chief mourner (the son), the presiding wife[1], and the steward of the family (of a Great officer) is taken by them at the order of the ruler lest they should get ill.

32. On returning (from the grave) to wail, (the son) should ascend the hall (of the ancestral temple);—returning to the place where (the deceased) performed his rites. The presiding wife should enter the chamber;—returning to the place where he received his nourishment.

33. Condolences should be presented (to the son) when he returns (from the grave) and is wailing, at which time his grief is at its height. He has returned, and (his father) is not to be seen; he feels that he has lost him. (His grief is) then most intense. Under the Yin, they presented condolences immediately at the grave; under the Kâu, when the son had returned and was wailing. Confucius said, 'Yin was too blunt; I follow Kâu.'

34. To bury on the north (of the city), and with the head (of the dead) turned to the north, was the common practice of the three dynasties:—because (the dead) go to the dark region.

35. When the coffin has been let down into the grave, the chief mourner presents the (ruler's) gifts (to the dead in the grave[2]), and the officer of prayer (returns beforehand) to give notice of the sacrifice of repose[3] to him who is to personate the departed.

[1. This would be the wife of the deceased, or the wife of his son.

2. These were some rolls of purplish silks, sent by the ruler as, his parting gifts, when the hearse–car reached the city gate on its way to the grave.

3. Where was the spirit of the departed now? The bones and flesh had returned to the dust, but the soul–spirit might be anywhere. To afford it a resting–place, the permanent tablet was now put in the shrine, and this sacrifice of repose was offered, so that the son might be able to think that his father was never far from him. For a father of course the personator was a male; for a mother, a female; but there are doubts on this point.]

36. When he has returned and wailed, the chief mourner with the (proper) officer inspects the victim. (In the meantime other) officers have set out a stool and mat with the necessary offerings on the left of the grave[1]. They return, and at midday the sacrifice of repose is offered[2].

37. The sacrifice is offered on the day of interment; they cannot bear that the departed should be left a single day (without a place to rest in).

38. On that day the offerings, (previously) set forth (by the coffin), are exchanged for the sacrifice of repose. The (continuous) wailing is ended, and they say, 'The business is finished.'

39. On that day the sacrifices of mourning were exchanged for one of joy. The next day the service of placing the spirit–tablet of the departed next to that of his grandfather was performed.

40. The change to an auspicious sacrifice took place on that day, and the placing the tablet in its place on the day succeeding:—(the son) was unable

[1. For the spirit of the ground.

2. If the grave were too far distant to allow all this to be transacted before midday, then the sacrifice was performed in the chamber where the coffin had rested. So says Wang Thâo on the authority of Zan Yî–shang ({}).]

to bear that (the spirit of the departed) should be a single day without a resting–place.

41. Under the Yin, the tablet was put in its place on the change of the mourning at the end of twelve months; under the Kâu, when the (continuous) wailing was over. Confucius approved the practice of Yin.

42. When a ruler went to the mourning rites for a minister, he took with him a sorcerer with a peach–wand, an officer of prayer with his reed–(brush), and a lance–bearer,—disliking (the presence of death), and to make his appearance different from (what it was at any affair of) life[1]. In the mourning rites it is death that is dealt with, and the ancient kings felt it difficult to speak of this[2].

43. The ceremony in the mourning rites of (the coffined corpse) appearing in the court (of the ancestral temple) is in accordance with the filial heart of the deceased. He is (supposed to be) grieved at leaving his chamber, and therefore he is brought to the temple of his fathers, and then (the coffin) goes on its way.

Under the Yin, the body was thus presented and then coffined in the temple; under the Kâu the interment followed immediately after its presentation (in the coffin).

44. Confucius said, 'He who made the vessels

[1. When visiting a minister when alive, the ruler was accompanied by the lance–bearer, but not by those other officers;–there was the difference between life and death.

2. I suspect that the sorcerer and exorcist were ancient superstitions, not established by the former kings, but with which they did not care to interfere by saying anything about them.]

which are so (only) in imagination, knew the principles underlying the mourning rites. They were complete (to all appearance), and yet could not be used. Alas! if for the dead they had used the vessels of the living, would there not have been a danger of this leading to the interment of the living with the dead?'

45. They were called 'vessels in imagination,' (the dead) being thus treated as spiritual intelligences, From of old there were the carriages of clay and the figures of straw,—in accordance with the idea in these vessels in imagination. Confucius said that the making of the straw figures was good, and that the making of the (wooden) automaton was not

benevolent.—Was there not a danger of its leading to the use of (living) men?

PART II.

1. Duke Mû[1] asked Dze-sze whether it was the way of antiquity for a retired officer still to wear the mourning for his old ruler. 'Princes of old,' was the reply, 'advanced men and dismissed them equally according to the rules of propriety; and hence there was that rule about still wearing mourning for the old ruler. But nowadays princes advance men as if they were going to take them on their knees, and dismiss them as if they were going to push them into an abyss. Is it not good if (men so treated) do not head rebellion? How should there be the observance of that rule about still wearing mourning (for old rulers)?'

[1. Of Lû, B.C. 409-377.]

2. At the mourning rites for duke Tâo[1]. Kî Kâo-dze asked Mang King-dze what they should eat (to show their grief) for the ruler. King-dze replied, 'To eat gruel is the general rule for all the kingdom.' (The other said), 'It is known throughout the four quarters that we three ministers[2] have not been able to live in harmony with the ducal house. I could by an effort make myself emaciated; but would it not make men doubt whether I was doing so in sincerity? I will eat rice as usual.'

3. When Sze-thû King-dze of Wei died, Dze-hsiâ made a visit of condolence (to his house); and, though the chief mourner had not completed the slight dressing (of the corpse), he went in the headband and robe of mourning. Dze-ya paid a similar visit; and, when the chief mourner had completed the slight dressing, he went out, put on the bands, returned and wailed. Dze-hsiâ said to him, 'Did you ever hear (that) that (was the proper method to observe)? I heard the Master say,' was the reply, 'that until the chief mourner had changed his dress, one should not assume the mourning bands'.'

4. Zang-dze said, 'An-dze may be said to have known well the rules of propriety;-he was humble and reverent! Yû Zo said, 'An-dze wore the same (robe of) fox-fur for thirty years. (At the burial of

[1. B.C. 467-431.

2. The heads of the Kung-sun, Shû-sun, and Ki-sun families; whose power Confucius had tried in vain to break.

3. In this case Dze-yû was correct, according to rule, following the example of the chief mourner. Sze-thû was a name of office,—the ministry of Instruction; but it had become in this case the family name; from some ancestor of King-dze, who had been minister of Instruction.]

his father), he had only one small carriage (with the offerings to be put into the grave[1]); and he returned immediately from the grave (without showing the usual attentions to his guests). The ruler of a state has seven bundles of the offerings, and seven such small carriages for them, and a Great officer five. How can it be said that An-dze knew propriety?' Zang-dze replied, 'When a state is not well governed, the superior man is ashamed to observe all ceremonies to the full. Where there is extravagance in the administration of the state, he shows an example of economy. If the administration be economical, he shows an example of (the strict) observance' of all rules.'

5. On the death of the mother of Kwo Kâo-dze, he asked Dze-kang, saying, 'At the interment, when (all) are at the grave, what should be the places of the men and of the women?' Dze-kang said, 'At the mourning rites for Sze-thû King-dze, when the Master directed the ceremonies, the men stood with their faces to the west and the women stood with theirs to the east.' 'Ah!' said the other, 'that will not do;' adding, 'All will be here to see these mourning rites of mine. Do you take the sole charge of them. Let the guests be the guests, while I (alone) act as the host. Let the women take their places behind the men, and all have their faces towards the west[2].'

[1. See the note on paragraph 1, page 161. An-Sze was the chief minister of Khî.

[2. 'The master' here would seem to be Confucius; and yet he died before Sze-thû King-dze. There are other difficulties in parts of the paragraph.]

6. At the mourning for Mû-po (her husband), King Kiang wailed for him in the daytime, and at that for Wan-po (her son), she wailed for him both in the daytime and the night. Confucius said, 'She knows the rules of propriety[1].'

At the mourning for Wan–po, King Kiang (once) put her hand on the couch (where his body lay), and without wailing said, 'Formerly, when I had this son, I thought that he would be a man of worth. (But) I never went with him to the court (to see his conduct there); and now that he is dead, of all his friends, the other ministers, there is no one that has shed tears for him, while the members of his harem all wail till they lose their voices. This son must have committed many lapses in his observance of the rules of propriety!'

7. When the mother of Kî Khang–dze died, (her body was laid out with) her private clothes displayed. King Kiang (Khang–dze's grand–uncle's wife) said, 'A wife does not dare to see her husband's parents without the ornament (of her upper robes); and there will be the guests from all quarters coming;—why are her under–clothes displayed here?' With this she ordered them to be removed.

8. Yû–dze and Dze–yû were standing together when they saw (a mourner) giving all a child's demonstrations of affection. Yû–dze said, 'I have never understood this leaping in mourning, and have long wished to do away with it. The sincere feeling (of sorrow) which appears here is right, (and

[1. It is said, 'She mourned for her husband according to propriety; for her son according to her feelings.']

should be sufficient).' Dze–yû. replied, 'In the rules of propriety, there are some intended to lessen the (display of) feeling, and there are others which purposely introduce things (to excite it). To give direct vent to the feeling and act it out as by a short cut is the way of the rude Zung and Tî. The method of the rules is not so. When a man rejoices, he looks pleased; when pleased, he thereon sings; when singing, he sways himself about; swaying himself about, he proceeds to dancing; from dancing, he gets into a state of wild excitement[1]; that excitement goes on to distress; distress expresses itself in sighing; sighing is followed by beating the breast; and beating the breast by leaping. The observances to regulate all this are what are called the rules of propriety.

'When a man dies, there arises a feeling of disgust (at the corpse). Its impotency goes on to make us revolt from it. On this account, there is the wrapping it in the shroud, and there are the curtains, plumes (and other ornaments of the coffin), to preserve men from that feeling of disgust. Immediately after death, the dried flesh and pickled meats are set out (by the side of the corpse), When the interment is about to take place, there are the things sent and offered (at the grave); and after the interment, there is the food presented (in the sacrifices of repose). The dead have never been seen to partake of these things. But from

[1. Evidently there is a lacuna in the text here; there should be some mention of stamping. Many of the critics have seen this, especially the Khien–lung editors; and various additions have been proposed by way of correction and supplement.]

the highest ages to the present they have never been neglected;—all to cause men not to revolt (from their dead). Thus it is that what you blame in the rules of propriety is really nothing that is wrong in them.'

9. Wû made an incursion into Khan, destroying the (places of) sacrifice, and putting to death those who were suffering from a pestilence (which prevailed). When the army retired, and had left the territory, Phî, the Grand–administrator of Khan, was sent to the army (of Wû). Fû Khâi (king of Wû) said to his internuncius Î, 'This fellow has much to say. Let us ask him a question.' (Then, turning to the visitor), he said, 'A campaign must have a name. What name do men give to this expedition?' The Grand–administrator said, 'Anciently, armies in their incursions and attacks did not hew down (trees about the) places of sacrifice; did not slay sufferers from pestilence; did not make captives of those whose hair was turning. But now, have not you in this campaign slain the sufferers from pestilence? Do they not call it the sick–killing expedition?' The king rejoined, ' If we give back your territory, and return our captives, what will you call it?' The reply was, 'O ruler and king, you came and punished the offences of our poor state. If the result of the campaign be that you now compassionate and forgive it, will the campaign be without its (proper) name[1]?'

[1. This incursion must be that mentioned in the Zo Kwan under B.C. 494. Various corruptions and disruptions of the text of the paragraph have to be rectified, however; and the interpretation is otherwise difficult.]

10. Yen Ting[1] deported himself skilfully during his mourning. Immediately after the death (of his father), he looked grave and restless, as if he were seeking for something, and could not find it. When the coffining had taken place, he looked expectant, as if he were following some one and could not get up with him. After the interment he looked sad, and as if, not getting his father to return (with him), he would wait for him[2].

11. Dze-kang asked, saying, 'The Book of History says, that Kâo Zung for three-years did not speak; and that when he did his words were received with joy[3]. Was it so?' Kung-ni replied, 'Why should it not have been so? Anciently, on the demise of the son of Heaven, the king, his heir, left everything to the chief minister for three years.'

12. When Kih Tâo-dze died[4], before he was buried, duke Phing was (one day) drinking along with the music-master Kwang and Lî Thiâo. The bells struck up; and when Tû Khwâi, who was coming in from outside, heard them, he said, 'Where is the music?' Being told that it was in the (principal) apartment, he entered it; and having ascended the steps one by one, he poured out a cup of spirits, and said, 'Kwang, drink this.' He then poured out another, and said, Thiâo, drink this.' He poured out a third cup; and kneeling in the hall, with his face to the north, he drank it himself, went down the steps, and hurried out.

[1. An officer of Lû.

2. Compare above, paragraph 17, p. 137 et al.

3. See vol. iii, p. 113. The Shû is not quoted exactly.

This was in B.C. 533. Kih Tâo-dze was a great officer of Zin. See the story in the Zo Kwan under that year.]

Duke Phing called him in again, and said, 'Khwâi, just now I thought you had something in mind to enlighten me about, and therefore I did not speak to you. Why did you give the cup to Kwang?' 'On the days (Kiâ-)dze and (Kî-)mâo,' was the reply, 'there should be no music; and now Kih Tâo-dze is (in his coffin) in his hall, and this should be a great dze or mâo day. Kwang is the grand music-master, and did not remind you of this. It was on this account that I made him drink.'

'And why did you give a cup to Thiâo?' Tû Khwâi said, 'Thiâo is your lordship's favourite officer; and for this drinking and eating he forgot the fault you were committing. It was on this account I made him drink.'

'And why did you drink a cup yourself?' Khwâi replied, 'I am (only) the cook; and neglecting my (proper work of) supplying you with knives and spoons, I also presumed to take my part in showing my knowledge of what should be prohibited. It was on this account that I drank a cup myself.'

Duke Phing said,' I also have been in fault. Pour out a cup and give it to me.' Tû Khwâi then rinsed the cup, and presented it. The duke said to the attendants, 'When I die, you must take care that this cup is not lost.' Down to the present day, (at feasts in Sin), when the cups have been presented all round, they then raise up this cup, and say, 'It is that which Tû presented.'

13. When Kung–shû Wan–dze died, his son Shû begged the ruler (of the state) to fix his honorary title, saying, 'The sun and moon have brought the time;—we are about to bury him. I beg that you will fix the title, for which we shall change his name.' The ruler said, 'Formerly when our state of Wei was suffering from a severe famine, your father had gruel made, and gave it to the famishing;—was not this a roof of how kind he was? Moreover, in a time of trouble[1], he protected me at the risk of his own life;—was not this a proof of how faithful he was? And while he administered the government of Wei, he so maintained the regulations for the different classes, and conducted its intercourse with the neighbouring states all round, that its altars sustained no disgrace;—was not this a proof of how accomplished he was? Therefore let us call him "The Faithful, Kind, and Accomplished."'

14: Shih Tâi–kung died, leaving no son by his wife proper, and six sons by concubines. The tortoise–shell being consulted as to which of them should be the father's successor, it was said that by their bathing and wearing of their girdle–pendants the indication would be given. Five of them accordingly bathed and put on the girdle–pendants with their gems. Shih Khî–dze, however, said, 'Whoever, being engaged with the mourning rites for a parent, bathed his head or his body, and put on his girdle–pendants?' and he declined to do either, and this was considered to be the indication. The people of Wei considered that the tortoise–shell had shown a (true) knowledge.

15. Khan Dze–kü having died in Wei, his wife and the principal officer of the family consulted together

[1. This was in B.C. 512. Twice in the Analects (XIV, 14, 19) Kung–shuh Wan–dze, 'Kung–shu, the accomplished,' is mentioned. Whether he received the long honorary title given in the conclusion of this paragraph is considered doubtful.]

about burying some living persons (to follow him). When they had decided to do so, (his brother), Khan Dze-khang arrived[1], and they informed him about their plan, saying, 'When the master was ill, (he was far away) and there was no provision for his nourishment in the lower world; let us bury some persons alive (to supply it).' Dze-khang said, 'To bury living persons (for the sake of the dead) is contrary to what is proper. Nevertheless, in the event of his being ill, and requiring to be nourished, who are so fit for that purpose as his wife and steward? If the thing can be done without, I wish it to be so. If it cannot be done without, I wish you two to be the parties for it.' On this the proposal was not carried into effect.

16. Dze-lû said, 'Alas for the poor! While (their parents) are alive, they have not the means to nourish them; and when they are dead, they have not the means to perform the mourning rites for them.' Confucius said, 'Bean soup, and water to drink, while the parents are made happy, may be pronounced filial piety. If (a son) can only wrap the body round from head to foot, and inter it immediately, without a shell, that being all which his means allow, he may be said to discharge (all) the rites of mourning.'

17. Duke Hsien of Wei having (been obliged to) flee from the state, when he returned[2], and had

[1. Khan Dze-khang was one of the disciples of Confucius, mentioned in the Analects I, 10; VII, 25. It is difficult to follow the reasoning of the wife and steward in justification of their proposals.

2 Duke Hsien fled from Wei in B.C. 559, and returned to it in 547.]

reached the suburbs (of the capital), he was about to grant certain towns and lands to those who had attended him in his exile before entering. Liû Kwang said, 'If all had (remained at home) to guard the altars for you, who would have been able to follow you with halter and bridle? And if all had followed you, who would have guarded the altars? Your lordship has now returned to the state, and will -it not be wrong for you to show a partial feeling?' The intended allotment did not take place.

18. There was the grand historiographer of Wei, called Liû Kwang, lying ill. The duke said[1], 'If the illness prove fatal, though I may be engaged at the time in sacrificing, you must let me know.' (It happened accordingly, and, on hearing the news), the duke bowed

twice, laying his head to the ground, and begged permission from the personator of the dead, saying, 'There was the minister Liû Kwang,—not a minister of mine (merely), but a minister of the altars of the state. I have heard that he is dead, and beg leave to go (to his house).' On this, without putting off his robes, he went; and on the occasion presented them as his contribution (to the mourning rites). He also gave the deceased the towns of Khiû–shih and Hsien–fan–shih by a writing of assignment which was put into the coffin, containing the words:—'For the myriads of his descendants, to hold from generation to generation without change.'

19. When Khan Kan–hsî was lying ill, he assembled his brethren, and charged his son Zun–kî,

[1. The same duke Hsien of Wei. Khan Hâo and others condemn his action in this case. Readers may not agree with them.]

saying,—When I am dead, you must make my coffin large, and make my two concubines lie in it with me, one on each side.' When he died, his son said, 'To bury the living with the dead is contrary to propriety; how much more must it be so to bury them in the same coffin!' Accordingly he did not put the two ladies to death.

20. Kung Sui died in Khui; and on the next day, which was Zan–wû, the sacrifice of the previous day was notwithstanding repeated (in the capital of Lû.). When the pantomimes entered, however, they put away their flutes. Kung–nî said, 'It was contrary to rule. When a high minister dies, the sacrifice of the day before should not be repeated[1].'

21. When the mother of Kî Khang–dze died, Kung–shû Zo was still young. After the dressing[2], Pan asked leave to let the coffin down into the grave by a mechanical contrivance. They were about to accede, when Kung–kien Kiâ said, 'No. According to the early practice in Lu, the ducal house used (for this purpose) the arrangement looking like large stone pillars, and the three families that like large wooden columns. Pan, you would, in the case of another man's mother, make trial of your ingenuity;–could you not in the case of your own mother do so? Would that distress you? Bah!' They did not allow him to carry out his plan[3].

[1. See this incident in the Chinese Classics, V, i, pp. 301, 302, where the account of it is discussed in a note.

2. This must be the greater dressing.

3. Pan and Zo were probably the same man; but we know that Pan lived at a later period. The incident in this paragraph therefore is doubted.]

22. During the fight at Lang[1], Kung–shu Zu–zan saw (many of) the men, carrying their clubs on their shoulders, entering behind the shelter of the small wall, and said, 'Although the services required of them are distressing, and the burdens laid on them heavy, (they ought to fight): but though our superiors do not form (good) plans, it is not right that soldiers should not be prepared to die. This is what I say.' On this along with Wang Î, a youth, (the son) of a neighbour, he went forward, and both of them met their death.

The people of Lû wished to bury the lad Wang not as one who had died prematurely, and asked Kung–ni about the point. He said, 'As he was able to bear his shield and spear in the defence of our altars, may you not do as you wish, and bury him as one who has not died prematurely?'

23. When Dze–lû was going away from Lû, he said to Yen Yüan, 'What have you to send me away with?' 'I have heard,' was the reply, 'that, when one is leaving his state, he wails at the graves (of his fathers), and then takes his journey, while on his return to it, he does not wail, but goes to look at the graves, and (then) enters (the city).' He then said to Dze–lû, 'And what have you to leave with me here?' 'I have heard,' was the reply, 'that, when you pass by a grave, you should bow forward to the cross–bar, and, when you pass a place of sacrifice, you should dismount.'

24. Shang Yang, director of Works (in Khû), and

[1. The fight at Lang is mentioned in the Khun Khiû under B.C. 484. Zo's description of the battle gives the incident mentioned here, but somewhat differently.]

Kan Khî–kî[1] were pursuing the army of Wu, and came up with it. The latter said to Shang Yang, 'It is the king's' business. It will be well for you to take your bow in hand.' He did so, and Khî–kî told him to shoot, which he did, killing a man, and returning immediately the bow to its case. They came up with the enemy again, and being told as before to shoot, he killed other two men; whenever he killed a man, he covered his eyes. Then stopping the chariot, he said, 'I have no place at the audiences; nor do I take part in the feasts. The death of three men will be sufficient for me to report.' Confucius said, 'Amidst his killing of men, he was still observant of the rules of propriety[3].'

25. The princes were engaged in an invasion of Khin, when duke Hwan of Zhâo died at their meeting[4]. The others asked leave to (see) the plugging of his teeth with the jade, and they were made to enshroud (his corpse)[5].

Duke Hsiang being in attendance at the court of King, king Khang died[6] . The people of King said to him, 'We must beg you to cover (the corpse

[1. Khî–kî was a son of the king of Khû, and afterwards became king Phing. Khû, in B.C. 534, reduced Khan to be a dependency of itself, and put it under Khî–kî, who became known as Khî–kî of Khan.

2. The king's business;' that is, the business of the count of Khû, who had usurped the title of king.

3. It is not easy to discover the point of Confucius' reply. Even Dze–lû questioned him about it (as related in the Narratives of the School), and got an answer which does not make it any clearer.

4. In B.C. 578.

5. Probably by the marquis of Zin—duke Wan—as 'lord of Meetings and Covenants.'

6. In B.C. 545.]

with your gift of a robe).' The men of Lû (who were with him) said, 'The thing is contrary to propriety.' They of Khû, however, obliged him to do what they asked; and he first employed a sorcerer with his reed–brush to brush (and purify) the bier. The people of King then regretted what they had done'.

26. At the mourning rites for duke Khang of Thang[2], Dze–shû King–shû was sent (from Lû) on a mission of condolence, and to present a letter (from duke Âi), Sze–fû Hui–po being assistant–commissioner. When they arrived at the suburbs (of the capital of Thang), because it was the anniversary of the death, of Î–po, (Hui–po's uncle), King–shû

hesitated to enter the city. Hui–po, however, said, 'We are on government business, and should not for the private affair of my uncle's (death) neglect the duke's affairs.' They forthwith entered.

PART III.

1. Duke Âi sent a message of condolence to Khwâi Shang, and the messenger met him (on the way to the grave). They withdrew to the way–side, where Khwâi drew the figure of his house, (with the coffin in it), and there received the condolences[3].

Zang–dze said, 'Khwâi Shang's knowledge of the

[1. King was another name for Khû. Duke Hsiang went from Lû in B.C. 545; and it was in the spring of the next year, probably, that the incident occurred. The sorcerer and his reed–brush were used when a ruler went to the mourning for a minister (see Part i. 42), so that Khû intending to humiliate Lû was itself humiliated.

2 Duke Khang of Thang died in B.C. 539.

3. This must have been a case for which the rule is given in Part i. 12.]

rules of ceremony was not equal to that of the wife of Khî Liang. When duke Kwang fell on Kû by surprise at Thui, Khî Liang met his death. His wife met his bier on the way, and wailed for him bitterly. Duke Kwang sent a person to convey his condolences to her; but she said, 'If his lordship's officer had been guilty of any offence, then his body should have been exposed in the court or the market–place, and his wife and concubines apprehended. If he were not chargeable with any offence, there is the poor cottage of his father. This is not the place where the ruler should demean himself to send me a message[1].'

2. At the mourning rites for his young son Tun, duke Âi wished to employ the (elm–juice) sprinklers, and asked Yû Zo about the matter, who said that it might be done, for his three ministers even used them. Yen Liû said, 'For the son of Heaven dragons are painted on (the shafts of) the funeral carriage, and the boards surrounding the coffin, like the shell, have a covering over them. For the feudal princes there is a similar carriage

(without the painted dragons), and the covering above. (In both cases) they prepare the elm–juice, and therefore employ sprinklers. The three ministers, not employing (such a carriage), and yet employing the sprinklers, thus appropriate a ceremony which is not suitable for them; and why should your lordship imitate them[2]?'

[1. See the Zo Kwan, under B.C. 550, the twenty–third year of duke Hsiang. The name of the place in the text (To, read Thui by Kang Hsüan) seems to be a mistake. See the Khang–hsi dictionary on the character To.

2. There is a good deal of difficulty and difference of opinion in the interpretation of this paragraph. According to the common view, the funeral carriage used by the king and princes was very heavy, and difficult to drag along. To ease its transit, a juice was prepared from the elm bark, and sprinkled on the ground to make it slippery. But this practice was because of the heaviness of the carriage; and was not required in the case of lighter conveyances.]

3. After the death of the mother of (his son, who became) duke Tâo, duke Âi wore for her the one year's mourning with its unfrayed edges. Yû Zo asked him, if it was in rule. for him to wear that mourning for a concubine. 'Can I help it?' replied the duke. 'The people of Lû will have it that she, was my wife.'

4. When Kî Dze–kâo buried his wife, some injury was done to the standing corn, which Shan–hsiang told him of, begging him to make the damage good. Dze–kâo said, 'The Mang has not blamed me for this, and my friends have not cast me off. I am here the commandant of the city. To buy (in this manner a right of) way in order to bury (my dead) would be a precedent difficult to follow[1].'

5. When one receives no salary for the official duties which he performs[2], and what the ruler sends to him is called 'an offering,' while the messenger charged with it uses the style of our unworthy ruler;' if such an one leave the state, and afterwards the ruler dies, he does not wear mourning for him.

6. At the sacrifice of Repose a personator of the

[1. This Kî Dze–kâo was Kâo Khâi, one of the disciples of Confucius. Shan–hsiang was the son of Dze–kang; see paragraph 3, page 132.

2. Such was Dze-sze in Lû, and Mencius in Khî. They were 'guests,' not ministers. Declining salary, they avoided the obligations incurred by receiving it.]

dead is appointed, and a stool, with a mat and viands on it, is placed (for him). When the wailing is over, the name of the deceased is avoided. The service of him as living is over, and that for him in his ghostly state has begun. When the wailing is over, the cook, with a bell having a wooden clapper, issues an order throughout the palace, saying, 'Give up disusing the names of the former rulers, and henceforth disuse (only) the name of him who is newly deceased.' This was done from the door leading to the chambers to the outer gate.

7. When a name was composed of two characters they were not avoided when used singly. The name of the Master's mother was Kang-Zâi. When he used Zâi, he did not at the same time use Kang; nor Zâi, when he used Kang.

8. When any sad disaster occurred to an army, (the ruler) in plain white robes wailed for it outside the Khû gate[1]. A carriage conveying the news of such disaster carried no cover for buff-coats nor case for bows.

9. When the (shrine-)apartment of his father was burned, (the ruler) wailed for it three days. Hence it is said, 'The new temple took fire;' and also, 'There was a wailing for three days[2].'

10. In passing by the side of mount Thâi, Confucius came on a woman who was wailing bitterly by a grave. The Master bowed forward to the cross-bar, and hastened to her; and then sent

[1. The Khû (arsenal or treasury gate) was the second of the palace gates, and near the ancestral temple. Hence the position selected for the wailing.

2. See the Khun Khiû, under B.C. 588.]

Dze-lû to question her. 'Your wailing,' said he, 'is altogether like that of one who has suffered sorrow upon sorrow.' She replied, ' It is so. Formerly, my husband's father was killed here by a tiger. My husband was also killed (by another), and now my son has died in the same way.' The Master said, 'Why do you not leave the place?' The answer was,

'There is no oppressive government here.' The Master then said (to the disciples), 'Remember this, my little children. Oppressive government is more terrible than tigers.'

11. In Lû there was one Kâu Fang[1], to whom duke Âi went, carrying an introductory present, and requesting an interview, which, however, the other refused. The duke said, 'I must give it up then.' And he sent a messenger with the following questions:—'(Shun), the lord of Yü, had not shown his good faith, to the people, and yet they put confidence in him. The sovereign of Hsiâ had not shown his reverence for the people, and yet the people revered him:—what shall I exhibit that I may obtain such things from the people?' The reply was:—'Ruins and graves express no mournfulness to the people, and yet the people mourn (amidst them). The altars of the spirits of the land and grain and the ancestral temples express no reverence to the people, and yet the people revere them. The kings of Yin made their solemn proclamations, and yet the people began to rebel; those of Kâu made their covenants, and the people began to distrust them. If there be not the heart

[1. This Kâu Fang must have been a worthy who had withdrawn from public life.]

observant of righteousness, self-consecration, good faith, sincerity, and guilelessness, though a ruler may, try to knit. the people firmly to him, will not all bonds between them be dissolved?'

12. While mourning (for a father), one should not be concerned about (the discomfort of) his own resting-place[1], nor, in emaciating himself, should he do so to the endangering of his life. He should not be the former;—he has to be concerned that (his father's spirit-tablet) is not (yet) in the temple. He should not do the latter, lest (his father) should thereby have no posterity.

13. Kî-dze of Yen-ling[2] had gone to Khî; and his eldest son having died, on the way back (to Wû), he buried him between Ying and Po. Confucius (afterwards) said, 'Kî-dze was the one man in Wû most versed in the rules of propriety, so I went and saw his manner of interment. The grave was not so deep as to reach the water-springs. The grave-clothes were such as (the deceased) had ordinarily worn. After the interment, he raised a mound over the grave of dimensions sufficient to cover it, and high enough for the hand to be easily placed on it. When the mound was completed, he bared his left arm;

[1. Referring, I think, to the discomfort of the mourning shed. But other interpretations of the paragraph are to be found in Khan Hâo's work, and elsewhere.

2. This Ki–dze is better known as Kî Kâ, a brother of the ruler of Wû. Having declined the state of Wû, he lived in the principality of Yen–ling. He visited the northern states Lû, Khî, Zin, and the others, in B.C. 515; and his sayings and doings in them are very famous. He was a good man and able, whom Confucius could appreciate. Ying and Po were two places in Khî.]

and, moving to the right, he went round it thrice, crying out, "That the bones and flesh should return again to the earth is what is appointed. But the soul in its energy can go everywhere; it can go everywhere." And with this he went on his way.' Confucius (also) said, 'Was not Kî–dze of Yen–ling's observance of the rules of ceremony in accordance with (the idea of them)?'

14. At the mourning rites for the duke Khâo of Kû–lü[1], the ruler of Hsü sent Yung Kü with a message of condolence, and with the articles to fill the mouth of the deceased. 'My unworthy ruler,' said he, 'hath sent me to kneel and put the jade for a marquis which he has presented into your (deceased) ruler's mouth. Please allow me to kneel and do so.' The officers of Kü replied, 'When any of the princes has deigned to send or come to our poor city, the observances have been kept according to their nature, whether simple and easy, or troublesome and more difficult; but such a blending of the easy and troublesome as in your case, we have not known.' Yung Kü replied, 'I have heard that in the service of his ruler one should not forget that ruler, nor be oblivious of his ancestral (rules). Formerly, our ruler, king Kü, in his warlike operations towards the west, in which he crossed the Ho, everywhere used this style of speech. I am a plain, blunt man, and do not presume to forget his example[2].'

[1. Khâo should probably be Ting. Duke Khâo lived after the period of the Khun Khiû, during which the power of Hsü had been entirely broken.

2. Here was Yung Kü, merely a Great officer, wishing to do what only a prince could do, according to the rules of propriety. He defends himself on the ground that the lords of Hsü claimed the title of King. The language of the officers of Kû shows that they were embarrassed by his mission.]

15. When the mother of Dze-sze died in Wei, and news of the event was brought to him, he wailed in the ancestral temple. His disciples came to him. and said, 'Your mother is dead, after marrying into another family[1]; why do you wail for her in the temple of the Khung family?' He replied, 'I am wrong, I am wrong.' And thereon he wailed in one of the smaller apartments of his house.

16. When the son of Heaven died, three days afterwards, the officers of prayer[2] were the first to assume mourning. In five days the heads of official departments did so; in seven days both males and females throughout the royal domain; and in three months all in the kingdom.

The foresters examined the trees about the various altars, and cut down those which they thought suitable for the coffins and shell, If these did not come up to what was required, the sacrifices were abolished, and the men had their throats cut[3].

17. During a great dearth in Khî, Khien Âo had food prepared on the roads, to wait the approach of hungry people and give to them. (One day), there came a famished man, looking as if he could

[1. Literally, 'The mother of the Shû family is dead,' but the interpretation of the text is disputed. The Khien-lung editors and many others question the genuineness of the whole paragraph.

2. The officers of prayer were divided into five classes; the first and third of which are intended here. See the Official Book of Kâu, ch. 25.

3. Great efforts are made to explain away this last sentence.]

hardly see, his face covered with his sleeve, and dragging his feet together. Khien Âo, carrying with his left hand some rice, and holding some drink with the other, said to him, 'Poor man! come and eat.' The man, opening his eyes with a stare, and looking at him, said, 'It was because I would not eat "Poor man come here's" food, that I am come to this state.' Khien Âo immediately apologised for his words, but the man after all would not take the food and died.

When Zang-dze heard the circumstances, he said, 'Was it not a small matter? When the other expressed his pity as he did, the man might have gone away. When he apologised, the man might have taken the food.'

18. In the time of duke Ting of Kû-lü[1], there occurred the case of a man killing his father. The officers reported it; when the duke, with an appearance of dismay, left his mat and said, 'This is the crime of unworthy me!' He added, 'I have learned how to decide on such a charge. When a minister kills his ruler, all who are in office with him should kill him without mercy. When a son kills his father, all who are in the house with him should kill him without mercy. The man should be killed; his house should be destroyed; the whole place should be laid under water and reduced to a swamp. And his ruler should let a month elapse before he raises a cup to his lips.'

[1. This duke Ting became ruler of Kû in B.C. 613. Some interpret the paragraph as if it said that all the officers, as well as the whole family of a regicide or parricide, should be killed with him. But that cannot be, and need not be, the meaning.]

19. (The ruler of) Zin having congratulated Wan-dze on the completion of his residence, the Great officers of the state went to the house-warming[1]. Kang Lâo said, 'How elegant it is, and lofty! How elegant and splendid! Here will you have your songs! Here will you have your wailings! Here will you assemble the representatives of the great families of the state!' Wan-dze replied, 'If I can have my songs here, and my wailings, and assemble here the representatives of the great families of the state, (it will be enough). I will then (only) seek to preserve my waist and neck to follow the former Great officers of my family to the Nine Plains.' He then bowed twice, laying his head also on the ground.

A superior man will say (of the two), that the one was skilful in the expression of his praise and the other in his prayer.

20. The dog kept by Kung-nî having died, he employed Dze-kung to bury it, saying, 'I have heard that a worn-out curtain should not be thrown away, but may be used to bury a horse in; and that a worn-out umbrella should not be thrown away, but may be used to bury a dog in. I am poor and have no, umbrella. In putting the dog into the grave, you can use my mat; and do not

[1. It is doubtful how this first sentence should be translated. Most naturally we should render Hsien–wan–dze of Zin having completed his house, but binomial honorary titles were not yet known; and the view seems to be correct that this Wan–dze was Kâo Wû, a well–known minister of Zin. The 'Nine Plains' below must have been the name of a burying–place used by the officers of Zin. There seems to be an error in the name in the text, which is given correctly in paragraph 25.]

let its head get buried in the earth. When one of the horses of the ruler's carriage dies, it is buried in a curtain (in good condition)[1].'

21. When the mother of Kî–sun died, duke Âi paid a visit of condolence to him. (Soon after), Zang–dze and Dze–kung arrived for the same purpose; but the porter declined to admit them, because the ruler was present. On this they went into the stable, and adjusted their dress more fully. (Shortly) they entered the house, Dze–kung going first[2] . The porter said to him, 'I have already announced your arrival;' and when Zang–dze followed, he moved on one side for him. They passed on to the inner place for the droppings from the roof, the Great officers all moving out of their way, and the duke descending a step and bowing to them. A superior man has said about the case, 'So it is when the toilet is complete! Immediately its influence extends far[3].'

22. A man–at–arms at the Yang gate (of the capital of Sung) having died, Dze–han, the superintendent of Works, went to (his house), and wailed for him bitterly. The men of Zin who were in Sung as spies returned, and reported the thing to

[1. The concluding sentence is found also in the 'Narratives of the School,' and may have been added to the rest by the compiler of this Than Kung. We are not prepared for the instance which Confucius gives of his poverty; but perhaps we like him better for keeping a dog, and seeing after its burial.

2. Because he was older than Zang–dze.

3. This concluding sentence is much objected to; seeming, as it does, to attribute to their toilet what was due to the respectful demeanour of the two worthies, and their established reputation. But the text must stand as it is.]

the marquis of Zin, saying, 'A man-at-arms at the Yang gate having died, Dze-han wailed for him bitterly, and the people were pleased; (Sung), we apprehend, cannot be attacked (with success).'

When Confucius heard of the circumstances, he said, 'Skilfully did those men do their duty as spies in Sung. It is said in the Book of Poetry,—

"If there was any mourning among the people,
I did my utmost to help them."

Though there had been other enemies besides Zin, what state under the sky could have withstood one (in the condition of Sung)[1]?'

23. At the mourning rites for duke Kwang of Lû, when the interment was over, (the new ruler) did not enter the outer gate with his girdle of dolichos cloth. The ordinary and Great officers, when they had finished their wailing, also did not enter in their sackcloth[2].

24. There was an old acquaintance of Confucius, called Yüan Zang. When his mother died, the Master assisted him in preparing the shell for the coffin. Yüan (then) got up on the wood, and said, 'It is long since I sang to anything;' and (with this he struck the wood), singing:—

It is marked like a wild cat's head;
It is(smooth) as a young lady's hand which you hold.'

The Master, however, made as if he did not hear, and passed by him.

[1. The whole narrative here is doubted. See the Shih, I. iii. Ode 10. 4. The reading of the poem, but not the meaning, is different from the text. The application is far-fetched.

2. The time was one of great disorder; there may have been reasons for the violations of propriety, which we do not know.]

The disciples who were with him said, 'Can you not have done with him?' 'I have heard,' was the reply, 'that relations should not forget their relationship, nor old acquaintances their friendship[1],'

25. Kâo Wan-dze and Shû-yü were looking about them at the Nine Plains[2], when Wan-dze said, 'If these dead could arise, with whom would I associate myself?' Shû-yü asked, 'Would it be with Yang Khû-fû[3]?' 'He managed by his course,' was the reply, 'to concentrate in himself all the power of Zin, and yet he did not die a natural death. His wisdom does not deserve to be commended.'

'Would it be with uncle Fan[4]?' Wan-dze said, 'When he saw gain in prospect, he did not think of his ruler; his virtue does not deserve to be commended[4]. I think I would follow Wû-dze of Sui[5]. While seeking the advantage of his ruler, he did not forget himself; and while consulting for his own advantage, he was not forgetful of his friends.'

The people of Zin thought that Wan-dze knew men. He carried himself in a retiring way, as if he could not bear even his clothes. His speech

[1. We have another instance of Confucius's relations with Yüan Zang in the Analects, XIV, 46. He was evidently 'queer,' with a sort of craze. It gives one a new idea of Confucius to find his interest in, and kindly feeling for, such a man.

2. See paragraph 19 and note.

3. Master of duke Hsiang B.C. 627-621, and an important minister afterwards.

4. See in paragraph 19, Part i. But scant measure is dealt here to 'uncle Fan.'

5. Wû-dze of Sui had an eventful life, and played an important part in the affairs of Zin and Khin in his time. See a fine testimony to him in the Zo Kwan, under B.C. 546.]

was low and stuttering, as if he could not get his words out. The officers whom he advanced to responsible charges in the depositories of Zin were more than seventy. During his life, he had no contentions with any of them about gain, and when dying he required nothing from them for his sons.

26. Shû-kung Phî instructed (his son) Dze-liû (in the rules of ceremony); and when he died, Dze-liû's wife, who was a plain, blunt woman, wore for him the one year's

mourning and the headband with its two ends tied together. (Phî's brother), Shû-kung Khien spoke to Dze-liû about it, and requested that she should wear the three months' mourning and the simple headband; saying, 'Formerly, when I was mourning for my aunts and sisters, I wore this mourning, and no one forbade it.' When he withdrew, however, (Dze-liû) made his wife wear the three months' mourning and the simple headband[1].

27. There was a man of Khang, who did not go into mourning on the death of his elder brother. Hearing, however, that Dze-kâo was about to become governor of the city, he forthwith did so. The people of Khang said, 'The silkworm spins

[1. Shû-kung Phî was the first of a branch of the Shû-sun clan, descended from the ruling house of Lû The object of the paragraph seems to be to show, that Dze-liû's wife, though a plain simple woman, was taught what to do, by her native feeling and sense, in a matter of ceremony, more correctly than the two gentlemen, mere men of the world, her husband and his uncle. The paragraph, however, is not skilfully constructed, nor quite clear. Kang Hsüan thought that Dze-liû was Phî's son, which, the Khien-lung editors say, some think a mistake, They do not give definitely their own opinion.]

its cocoons, but the crab supplies the box for them; the bee has its cap, but the cicada supplies the strings for it. His elder brother died, but it was Dze-kâo who made the mourning for him[1].'

28. When Yo Kang, Dze-khun's mother, died, he was five days without eating. He then said, 'I am sorry for it. Since in the case of my mother's death, I could not eat according to my feelings, on what occasion shall I be able to do so?'

29. In a year of drought duke Mû[2] called to him Hsien-dze, and asked him about it. 'Heaven,' said he, 'has not sent down rain for a long time. I wish to expose a deformed person in the sun (to move its pity), what do you say to my doing so?' 'Heaven, indeed,' was the reply, 'does not send down rain; but would it not be an improper act of cruelty, on that account to expose the diseased son of some one in the sun?'

'Well then,' (said the duke), 'I wish to expose in the sun a witch; what do you say to that?' Hsien-dze said, 'Heaven, indeed, does not send down rain; but would it not be wide of the mark to hope anything from (the suffering of) a foolish woman, and by means of that to seek for rain[3]?'

[1. The Dze-kâo here was the same as Kao Khâi; see the note on paragraph 4. The incident here shows the influence of his well-known character. He is the crab whose shell forms a box for the cocoons, and the cicada whose antennae form the strings for the cap.

2. 'Duke Mû and Hsien-dze;' see Section I. Part iii. 5.

3. In the Zo Kwan, under B.C. 639, duke Hsî of Lû makes a proposal about exposing a deformed person and a witch like that which is recorded here. Nothing is said, however, about changing the site of the market. Reference is made, however, to that practice in a work of Tung Kung-shu (second century, B.C.), Of which Wang Thâo ventures to give a geomantic explanation. The narrative in the text is probably taken from the Zo Kwan, the compiler having forgotten the time and parties in the earlier account.]

'What do you say then to my moving the marketplace elsewhere?' The answer was, 'When the son of Heaven dies, the market is held in the lanes for seven days; and it is held in them for three days, when the ruler of a state dies. It will perhaps be a proper measure to move it there on account of the present distress.'

30. Confucius said, 'The people of Wei, in burying husband and wife together (in the same grave and shell), leave a space between the coffins. The people of Lû, in doing the same, place them together;—which is the better way.

APPENDIX TO BOOK II.

THE reader will have been struck by the many references in the Than Kung to the degrees and dress of mourning; and no other subject occupies so prominent a place in many of the books of the Lî Kî that follow. It is thought well, therefore, to introduce here, by way of appendix to it, the following passage from a very valuable paper on 'Marriage, Affinity, and Inheritance in China,' contributed, on February 8th, 1853, to the China Branch of the Royal Asiatic Society, by Mr. W. H. Medhurst, jun., now Sir Walter H. Medhurst. The information and subjoined illustrative tables were taken by him mainly from the Ritual and Penal Code of China, a preliminary chapter of which is devoted to the subject of 'The Dress of Mourning:'—

The ideas of the Chinese as to nearness of kin, whether by blood or marriage, differ widely from our own. They divide relationships into two classes, Nêi khin and Wâi yin, terms analogous to our "consanguinity" and "affinity," but conveying, nevertheless, other associations than those which we attach to these words. The former (Nêi khin) comprehends all kindred derived from common stock with the individual, but only by descent through the male line; the latter (Wâi yin) includes what the Chinese designate mû tang and nü tang three terms best translated, perhaps, by "mother's kin," "wife's kin," and "daughter's kin," and understood by them to mean a mother's relatives, relatives of females received into one's kindred by marriage, and members of families into which one's kinswomen marry. Thus, for example, a first cousin twice removed, lineally descended from the same great–great–grandfather through the male line, is a nêi–khin relative; but a mother's parents, wife's sister, and a sister's husband or child, are all equally wâi–yin kindred. The principle on which the distinction is drawn appears to be, that a woman alienates herself from her own kin on marriage, and becomes a part of the stock on which she is grafted; and it will be necessary to keep this principle distinctly in mind in perusing any further remarks that may be made, as otherwise it will be found impossible to reconcile the many apparent contradictions in the theory and practice of the Chinese Code.

'The indication of the prohibited degrees (in marriage) depends then upon a peculiar genealogical disposition of the several members of a family with respect to the mourning worn for deceased relatives; and this I shall now proceed to explain. The Ritual prescribes five different kinds of mourning, called wû fû, to be worn for all relatives within a definite proximity of degree, graduating the character of the habit in proportion to the nearness of kin. These habits are designated by certain names, which by a species of metonymy come to be applied to the relationships themselves, and are used somewhat as we apply the terms "1st degree," "2nd degree," and so on; and plans, similar to our genealogical tables, are laid down, showing the specific habit suitable for each kinsman. The principal one of these tables, that for a married or unmarried man, comprises cousins twice removed, that is, derived by lineal descent from a common great–great–grandfather, that ancestor himself, and all relatives included within the two lines of descent from him to them; below the individual, it comprehends his own descendants (in the male line) as far as great–great–grandchildren, his brother's as far as great–grand children, his cousin's as far as grandchildren, and the children 'of his cousin once removed. In this table nêi–khin relationships will alone be found; mourning is worn for very few of the wâi–yin, and these, though actually, that is, in our eyes, ties of consanguinity; and deserving far more consideration than many for which a deeper habit is prescribed, are classed among the very lowest degrees of mourning.

'Six tables are given in the Ritual to which the five habits are common; they prescribe the mourning to be worn by

1st, A man for his kinsmen and kinswomen;
2nd, A wife for her husband's kinsfolk;
3rd, A married female for her own kinsfolk;
4th, A man for his mother's kinsfolk;
5th, A man for his wife's kinsfolk;
6th, A concubine for her master's kinsfolk.

'A seventh table is given, exhibiting the mourning to be worn for step–fathers and fathers by adoption, and for step– and foster–mothers, &c.; but I have not thought it necessary to encumber my paper by wandering into so remote a portion of the field.

'To render these details more easily comprehensible, I shall class the relationships in each table under their appropriate degrees of mourning, and leave the reader to examine the tables at his leisure. It need only be borne in mind, that, excepting where otherwise specified, the relationship indicated is male, and only by descent through the male line, as, for example, that by "cousin" a father's brother's son alone is meant, and not a father's sister's son or daughter.

'The five kinds of mourning, the names of which serve, as has been said, to indicate the degrees of relationship to which they belong, are:—

1st, Kan–zui, nominally worn for three years, really for twenty–seven months;

2nd, Dze–zui, worn for one year, for five months, or for three months;

3rd, Tâ–kung, worn for nine months;

4th, Hsiâ–kung, worn for five months;

5th, Sze–mâ worn for three months.

'The character of each habit, and the relatives for whom it is worn, are prescribed as follows:—

'1st, Kan–Zui indicates relationships of the first degree. The prescribed habit for it is composed of the coarsest hempen fabric, and left unhemmed at the borders. It is worn:—

'By a man, for his parents; by a wife, for her husband, and husband's parents; and by a concubine, for her master.

'2nd, Dze–zui indicates relationships of the second degree. The prescribed habit for it is composed of coarse hempen fabric, with hemmed borders. It is worn for one year:—

'By a man, for his grandparents; uncle; uncle's wife; spinster aunt; brother; spinster sister; wife; son (of wife or concubine); daughter–in–law (wife of first–born); nephew; spinster niece; grandson (first–born son of first–born); by a wife, for her husband's nephew, and husband's spinster niece; by a married woman, for her parents, and grandparents; and by a concubine, for her master's wife; her master's parents; her master's sons (by wife or other concubine), and for sons. It is worn for five months:—

'By a man, for his great–grandparents; and by a married woman, for her great–grandparents. It is worn for three months:—

'By a man, for his great–great–grandparents; and by, a married woman, for her great–great–grandparents.

'3rd, Tâ–kung indicates relationships of the third degree. The prescribed habit for it is composed of coarse cotton fabric[1]. It is worn:—

'By a man, for his married aunt; married sister; brother's wife; first cousin; spinster first cousin; daughter–in–law (wife of a younger son, or of a son of a concubine); nephew's wife; married niece; and grandson (son of a younger son, or of a concubine's son); by a wife, for her husband's grandparents; husband's uncle; husband's daughter–in–law (wife of a younger son, or of a concubine's son); husband's nephew's wife; husband's married niece; and grandson; by a married woman, for her uncle; uncle's wife; spinster aunt; brother; sister; nephew; spinster niece; and by a concubine, for her grandson.

'4th, Hsiâo–kung indicates relationships of the fourth degree. The habit prescribed for it is composed of rather coarse cotton fabric. It is worn:—

'By a man, for his grand–uncle; grand–uncle's wife; spinster grand–aunt; father's first cousin; father's first cousin's wife; father's spinster first cousin married female first cousin; first cousin once removed spinster female first cousin once removed; second cousin; spinster female second cousin; grand–daughter–in–law (wife of first–born of first born son); grand–nephew; spinster grand–niece; mother's parents; mother's brother; mother's

[1. In the very brief account of this preliminary chapter in the Penal Code, given by Sir George Staunton, in his translation of the Code (page lxxv), he gives for the material 'coarse' linen cloth. The Chinese character is simply 'cloth.' I suppose the material originally was linen; but since the use of cotton, both of native and foreign manufacture, has increased in China, it is often substituted for linen. I have seen some mourners wearing linen, and others wearing cotton.]

sister'; by a wife, for her husband's aunt; husband's brother; husband's brother's wife; husband's sister; husband's second cousin; spinster female second cousin of husband; husband's grand–nephew; and spinster grandniece of husband; by a married woman, for her spinster aunt; married sister; first cousin; and married niece; and by a concubine, for her master's grandparents.

'5th, Sze–mâ indicates relationships of the fifth degree. The prescribed dress for it is composed of rather fine cotton cloth. It is worn:—

'By a man, for his great–grand–uncle; great–granduncle's wife; spinster great–grand–aunt; married grandaunt; grandfather's first cousin; grandfather's first cousin's wife; spinster first cousin of grandfather; married female first cousin of rather; father's first cousin once removed; wife of father's first cousin once removed; father's spinster first cousin once removed; first cousin's wife; married female first cousin once removed; first cousin twice removed; spinster first cousin twice removed; married female second cousin; second cousin once removed; spinster second cousin once removed; grand–daughter–in–law (wife of son of a younger son,– or of son of a concubine) grand–nephew's wife; married grand–niece; third cousin spinster third cousin; great–grandson; great–grand–nephew; spinster great–grand–niece;

great-great-grandson; aunt's son; mother's brother's son; mother's sister's son; wife's parents; son-in-law; daughter's child: by a wife, for her husband's great-great-grand-parents; husband's great-grand-parents; husband's grand-uncle; husband's spinster grand-aunt; father-in-law's first cousin; father-in-law's first cousin's wife; spinster first cousin of father-in-law; female first cousin of husband; husband's second cousin's wife; married female second cousin of husband; husband's second cousin once removed; husband's

[1. These names and others farther on, printed with spaced letters, all belong to the Wâi-yin relationships.]

spinster second cousin once removed; grand -daughter-in-law (wife of own or a concubine's grandson); husband's grand-nephew's wife; husband's married grand-niece; husband's third cousin; spinster third cousin of husband; great-grandson; great-grand-daughter-in-law; husband's great-grand-nephew; spinster great-grand-niece of husband; and great-great-grandson: and by a married woman, for her grand-uncle; spinster grand-aunt; father's first cousin; spinster first cousin of father; spinster first cousin; second cousin; spinster second cousin.'

BOOK III. THE ROYAL REGULATIONS[1]

SECTION I

1. According to the regulations of emolument and rank framed by the kings, there were the duke; the marquis; the earl; the count; and the baron [2]:—in all, five gradations (of rank). There were (also), in the feudal states, Great officers[3] of the highest grade,-the ministers; and Great officers of the lowest grade; officers of the highest, the middle, and the lowest grades:—in all, five gradations (of office).

2. The territory of the son of Heaven amounted to 1000 lî square; that of a duke or marquis to 500 lî square; that of an earl to 79 lî square; and that of a count or baron to 50 lî square[4]. (Lords) who could not number 50 lî square, were not

[1. See the Introduction, chapter iii, pages 18-20.

2. Most sinologists have adopted these names for the Chinese terms. Callery says, 'Les ducs, les marquis, les comtes, les vicomtes, et les barons.' See the note on Mencius, V, i, 2, 3, for the meaning given to the different terms.

3. 'Great officers' are in Chinese Tâ Fû, 'Great Sustainers.' The character fû is different from that for 'officer,' which follows. The latter is called shih, often translated 'scholar,' and is 'the designation of one having a special charge.' Callery generally retains the Chinese name Tâ Fû, which I have not liked to do.

4. A lî is made up of 360 paces. At present 27.8 lî = 10 English miles, and one geographical lî = 1458.53 English feet. The territories were not squares, but when properly measured, 'taking the length with the breadth,' were equal to so many lî square. The Chinese term rendered 'territory' is here, meaning 'fields;' but it is not to be supposed that that term merely denotes 'ground that could be cultivated,' as some of the commentators maintain.]

admitted directly to (the audiences of) the son of Heaven. Their territories were called 'attached,' being joined to those of one of the other princes.

3. The territory assigned to each of the ducal ministers of the son of Heaven was equal to that of a duke or marquis; that of each of his high ministers was equal to that of an earl; that of his Great officers to the territory of a count or baron; and that of his officers of the chief grade to an attached territory.

4. According to the regulations, the fields of the husbandmen were in portions of a hundred acres[1]. According to the different qualities of those acres, when they were of the highest quality, a farmer supported nine individuals; where they were of the next, eight; and so on, seven, six, and five. The pay of the common people, who were employed in government offices[2], was regulated in harmony with these distinctions among the husbandmen.

5. The officers of the lowest grade in the feudal states had an emolument equal to that of the husbandmen whose fields were of the highest quality; equal to what they would have made by tilling the fields. Those of the middle grade had double that of the lowest grade; and those of the highest grade double that of the middle. A Great officer of the lowest grade had double that of an officer of the highest. A high minister had four times that of

[1. The mâu is much less than an English acre, measuring only 733 1/3 square yards. An English acre is rather more than 6 mâu.

2. But held their appointments– only from the Head of their department, and were removable by him. at pleasure, having no commission from the king, or from the ruler of the state in which they were.]

a Great officer; and the ruler had ten times that of a high minister. In a state of the second class, the emolument of a minister was three times that of a Great officer; and that of the ruler ten times that of a minister. In small states, a high minister had twice as much as a Great officer; and the ruler ten times as much as a minister.

6. The highest minister, in a state of the second class, ranked with the one of the middle grade in a great state; the second, with the one of the lowest grade; and the lowest, with a Great officer of the highest grade. The highest minister in a small state ranked with the lowest of a great state; the second, with the highest Great officer of the other; and the lowest, with one of the lower grade.

7. Where there were officers of the middle grade and of the lowest, the number in each was three times that in the grade above it.[1]

8. Of the nine provinces embracing all within[2], the four seas, a province was 1000 lî square, and there were established in it 30 states of 100 lî (square) each.; 60 of 70 lî; 120 of 5o lî:–in all, 210 states. The famous hills and great meres were not included in the investitures[3]. The rest of the

[1. Some of the critics think that this sentence is out of place, and really belongs to paragraph 5 of next section. As the text stands, and simple as it appears, it is not easy to construe.

2 The expression 'the four seas' must have originated from an erroneous idea that the country was an insular square, with a sea or ocean on each side. The explanation of it in the R Ya as denoting the country surrounded by 'The 9 Î, the 8 Tî, the 7 Zung, and the 6 Man,' was an attempt to reconcile the early error with the more accurate knowledge acquired in the course of time. But the name of 'seas' cannot be got over.

3. That is, these hills and meres were still held to belong to all the people, and all had a right to the game on the hills and the fish of the waters. The princes could not deny to any the right of access to them; though I suppose they could levy a tax on what they caught.]

ground formed attached territories and unoccupied lands of the eight provinces (apart from that which formed the royal domain), each contained (the above) 210 states[1].

9. Within the domain[2] of the son of Heaven there were 9 states of 100 lî square; 21 of 70 lî; and 63 of 50 lî:–in all, 93 states. The famous hills and great meres were not assigned[3]. The rest of the ground served to endow the officers, and to form unoccupied lands.

10. In all, in the nine provinces, there were 1773 states, not counting in (the lands of) the officers of the chief grade of the son of Heaven, nor the attached territories in the feudal states.

SECTION II.

1. (The contributions from) the first hundred lî (square) of the son of Heaven served to supply (the needs of) the (various) public offices; (those from the rest of) the thousand lî were for his own special use[4].

2. Beyond his thousand lî, chiefs of regions were appointed. Five states formed a union, which had

[1. This statement must be in a great degree imaginary, supposing, as it does, that the provinces were all of the same size. They were not so; nor are the eighteen provinces of the present day so.

2. The character in the text here is different from that usually employed to denote the royal domain.

3. The term is different from the 'invested' of the previous paragraph. The tenures in the royal domain were not hereditary.

4. Such seems to be the view of the Khien–lung editors. Callery translates the paragraph substantially as I have done.]

a President. Ten formed a combination, which had a Leader. Thirty formed a confederation, which had a Director. Two hundred and ten formed a province, which had a Chief. In the eight provinces there were eight Chiefs, fifty–six Directors, one hundred and sixty–eight Leaders, and three hundred and thirty–six Presidents. The eight Chiefs, with those under them, were all under the two Ancients of the son of Heaven. They divided all under the sky between them, one having charge of the regions on the left and the other of those on the right, and were called the two (Great) Chiefs[1].

3. All within the thousand lî (of the royal domain) was called the Tien (or field Tenure). Outside that domain there were the Zhâi (or service territories) and the Liû (or territory for banished persons).

4. The son of Heaven had three dukes[2], nine high ministers[2], twenty–seven Great officers, and eighty–one officers of the chief grade.

5. In a great state there were three high ministers[3], all appointed by the son of Heaven; five Great

[1. Of these two great chiefs, we have an instance in the dukes of Kâu and Shâo, at the rise of the Kâu dynasty, the former having under his jurisdiction all the states west of the Shen river, and the other, all east of it. But in general, this constitution of the kingdom is imaginary.

2. Compare the Shû V, xx. The three dukes (Kung) were the Grand Tutor, Grand Assistant, and Grand Guardian. The nine ministers were the Prime Minister, the Ministers of Instruction, Religion, War, Crime, and Works, with the junior Tutor, junior Assistant, and junior Guardian added. The six ministers exist Still, substantially, in the six Boards. The titles of the three Kung and their juniors also still exist.

3. These appear to have been the Ministers of Instruction, War, and Works. The first had also the duties of Premier, the second those of minister of Religion, anti the third those of minister of Crime.]

officers of the lower grade; and twenty-seven officers of the highest grade. In a state of the second class there were three high ministers, two appointed by the son of Heaven and one by the ruler; five Great officers of the lower grade; and twenty-seven officers of the highest grade. In a small state there were two high ministers, both appointed by the ruler; five, Great officers of the lower grade; and twenty-seven officers of the highest grade.

6. The son of Heaven employed his Great officers as the Three Inspectors,—to inspect the states under the Chiefs of Regions[1]. For each state there were three Inspectors.

7. Within the domain of the son of Heaven the princes enjoyed their allowances; outside it they had their inheritances[2].

8. According to the regulations, any one of the three ducal ministers might wear one additional symbol of distinction,—that of the descending dragon[3].

[1. The Khien-lung editors think that this was a department first appointed by the Han dynasty, and that the compilers of this Book took for it the name of 'the Three Inspectors,' from king Wû's appointment of his three brothers to watch the proceedings of the son of the last sovereign of Yin, in order to give it an air of antiquity. Was it the origin of the existing Censorate?

2. Outside the royal domain, the feudal states were all hereditary. This is a fact of all early Chinese history. In the domain itself the territories were appanages rather than states. Yet they were in some sense hereditary too. The descendants of all who had served the country well, were not to be left unprovided for. Compare Mencius I, ii, 5, 3.

See the Shih, Part I, xv, Ode 6. x, with the note in my edition of 'the Chinese Classics.' The old symbols of distinction gave rise to 'the Insignia of Civil and Military Officers' of the present dynasty, called Kiu phin. See Williams' Dictionary, p. 698. This paragraph is in the expurgated edition of the Lî Kî, used by Callery, and he gives for it, unfortunately, the following version:—'Il est de règle que les trois ministres (qui d'habitude n'appartiennent qu'au 8e ordre de dignitaires), en montant un degré portent I'habit des dragons en broderie. Si, après cela, il y a lieu de leur accorder de nouvelles récompenses, on leur donne des objets de valeur, car on ne va pas au delà du 9e ordre.'

But if such an addition were made (to his eight symbols), it must be by special grant. There were only nine symbols (in all). The ruler of a state of the second class wore only seven of them, and the ruler of a small state only five.

9. The high minister of a great state could not wear more than three of the symbols, and the ministers below him only two. The high ministers of a small state, and Great officers of the lowest class, wore only one.

10. The rule was that the abilities of all put into offices over the people should first be discussed. After they had been discussed with. discrimination, the men were employed. When they had been (proved) in the conduct of affairs, their rank was assigned; and when their position was (thus) fixed, they received salary.

11. It was in the court that rank was conferred, the (already existing) officers being (thus) associated in the act[1]. It was in the market–place that punishment was inflicted; the multitude being (thus) associated in casting the criminals off. hence, neither the ruler, nor (the head of)a clan, would keep a criminal who had been punished about; him; a Great officer would not maintain him; nor would an officer, meeting

[1. The presence of the officers generally would be a safeguard against error in the appointments, as they would know the individuals.]

him on the road, speak to him. Such men were sent away to one of the four quarters, according to the sentence on each. They were not allowed to have anything to do with affairs of government, to show that there was no object in allowing them to live[1].

12. In their relation to the son of Heaven, the feudal princes were required to send every year a minor mission to the court, and every three years a greater mission; once in five years they had to appear there in person.

13. The son of Heaven, every five years, made a tour of Inspection through the fiefs[2].

14. In the second month of the year, he visited those on the East, going to the honoured mountain of Tâi. There he burnt a (great) pile of wood, and announced his arrival to Heaven; and with looks directed to them, sacrificed to the hills and rivers. He gave audience to the princes; inquired out those who were 100 years old, and went to see them:

ordered the Grand music-master to bring him the poems (current in the different states)[3] 3, that he might see the manners of the people; ordered the superintendents of markets to present (lists of prices), that he might see what the people liked and disliked, and whether they were set on extravagance and loved

[1. It has been said that these were rules of the Yin or Shang dynasty. The Khien-lung editors maintain that they were followed by all the three feudal dynasties.

2. Compare vol. iii, pp. 39, 40.

3. These would include ballads and songs. Perhaps 'Grand music-master' should be in the plural, meaning those officers of each state. Probably these would have given them to the king's Grand music-master.]

what was bad; he ordered the superintendent of rites to examine the seasons and months, and fix the days, and to make uniform the standard tubes, the various ceremonies, the (instruments of) music, all measures, and (the fashions of) clothes. (Whatever was wrong in these) was rectified.

15. Where any of the spirits of the hills and rivers had been unattended to, it was held to be an act of irreverence, and the irreverent ruler was deprived of a part of his territory. Where there had been neglect of the proper order in the observances of the ancestral temple, it was held to show a want of filial piety and the rank of the unfilial ruler was reduced. Where any ceremony had been altered, or any instrument of music changed, it was held to be an instance of disobedience, and the disobedient ruler was banished. Where the statutory measures and the (fashion of) clothes had been changed, it was held to be rebellion, and the rebellious ruler was taken off. The ruler who had done good service for the people, and shown them an example of virtue, received an addition to his territory and rank.

16. In the seventh month, (the son of Heaven) continued his tour, going to the south, to the mountain of that quarter[1], observing the same ceremonies as in the east. In the eighth month, he went on to the west, to the mountain of that quarter[2], observing the

[1. Mount Hang; in the present district of Hang-shan, dept. Hang-kâu, Hu-nan.

2. Mount Hwa; in the present district of Hwa–yin, dept. Thung–kâu, Shen–hsî.]

same ceremonies as in the south. In the eleventh month, he went on to the north, to the mountain of that quarter[1], observing the same ceremonies as in the west. (When all was done), he returned (to the capital), repaired (to the ancestral temple) and offered a bull in each of the fanes, from that of his (high) ancestor to that of his father[2].

17. When the son of Heaven was about to go forth, hc sacrificed specially, but with the usual forms., to God, offered the Î sacrifice at the altar of the earth, and the Zhâo in the fane of his father[3]. When one of the feudal princes was about to go forth, he offered the Î sacrifice to the spirits of the land, and the Zhâo in the fane of his father.

18. When the son of Heaven received the feudal princes, and there was no special affair on hand, it was (simply) called an audience. They examined their ceremonies, rectified their punishments, and made uniform what they considered virtuous; thus giving honour to the son of Heaven[4].

19. When the son of Heaven gave (an instrument of) music to a duke or marquis, the presentation was

[1. Mount Hang; in the present district of Khü–yang, dept. Ting–kâu, Kih–lî.

2. I have followed here the view of Khung Ying–tâ. It seems to me that all the seven fanes of the son of Heaven were under one roof, or composed one great building, called 'the Ancestral Temple.' See p. 224.

3. The meaning of the names of the different sacrifices here is little more than guessed at.

4. The second sentence of this paragraph is variously understood.]

preceded by a note from the signal box[1]; when giving one to an earl, count, or baron, the presentation was preceded by shaking the hand–drum. When the bow and arrows were conferred on a prince, he could proceed to execute the royal justice. When the hatchet and battle–axe were conferred, he could proceed to inflict death. When a large: libation–cup was conferred, he could make the spirits from the black millet for himself. When this cup was not conferred, be had to depend for those spirits (as a gift) from the son of Heaven.

20. 'When the son of Heaven ordered a prince to institute instruction, he proceeded to build his schools; the children's[2], to the south of his palace, on the left of it; that for adults, in the suburbs. (The college of) the son of Heaven was called (the palace of) Bright Harmony, (and had a circlet of water). (That of) the princes was called the Palace with its semicircle of water.

[1. A representation of the signal box is here given (i). The note was made by turning the upright handle, which then struck on some arrangement inside. The hand–drum is also represented (2). It was merely a sort of rattle only that the noise was made by the two little balls striking against the ends of the drum. It is constantly seen and heard in the streets of Chinese cities at the present day, in the hands of pedlers and others.

2. That; is, the children of the princes; but an impulse was thus given to the education of children of lower degree.]

21. When the son of Heaven was about to go forth on a punitive expedition, he sacrificed specially, but with the usual forms, to God; offered the Î sacrifice at the altar of the Earth, and the Zhâo in the fane of his father. He offered sacrifice also to the Father of War (on arriving) at the state which was the object of the expedition. He had received his charge from his ancestors, and the complete (plan) for the execution of it in the college. He went forth accordingly, and seized the criminals; and on his return he set forth in the college his offerings, and announced (to his ancestors) how he had questioned (his prisoners), and cut off the cars (of the slain)[1].

22. When the son of Heaven and the princes had no (special) business in hand, they had three huntings[2] in the year. The first object in them was to supply the sacrificial dishes with dried flesh; the second, to provide for guests and visitors; and the third, to supply the ruler's kitchen.

23. Not to hunt when there was no (special) business in the way was deemed an act of irreverence[3]. To hunt without observing the rules (for hunting) was deemed cruelty to the creatures of Heaven.

24. The sop of Heaven did not entirely surround (the hunting ground)[4]; and a feudal prince did not

[1. Compare paragraph 17, and vol. iii, pp. 392, 393.

2. The huntings were in spring, summer, and winter, for each of which there was its proper name. In autumn the labours of the field forbade hunting.

3. Irreverence, in not making provision for sacrifices; disrespect, in not providing properly for guests.

4. He left one opening for the game. This paragraph contains some of the rules for hunting]

take a (whole) herd by surprise. When the son of Heaven had done killing, his large flag was lowered; and when the princes had done, their smaller flag. When the Great officers had done, the auxiliary carriages were stopped[1]; and after this, the common people fell a hunting (for themselves).

25. When the otter sacrificed its fish[2], the foresters entered the meres and dams. When the wolf sacrificed its prey, the hunting commenced. When the dove changed into a hawk, they set their nets, large and small. When the plants and trees began to drop their leaves, they entered the hills and forests (with the axe). Until the insects had all withdrawn into their burrows, they did not fire the fields. They did not take fawns nor eggs. They did not kill pregnant animals, nor those which had not attained to their full growth. They did not throw down nests[3].

26. The chief minister determined the expenditure of the states, and it was the rule that he should do so at the close of the year. When the five kinds of grain had all been gathered in, he then determined the expenditure;–according to the size of each territory, as large or small, and the returns of the year, as abundant or poor. On the average of thirty years he determined the expenditure, regulating the outgoing by the income.

[1. These were light carriages used in driving and keeping the game together.

2. See the next Book, where all these regulations are separately mentioned.

3. The Chinese have a reputation for being callous in the infliction of punishment and witnessing suffering; And I think they are so. But these rules were designed evidently to foster kindness and sympathy.]

27. A tenth of the (year's) expenditure was for sacrifices. During the three years of the mourning rites (for parents), the king did not sacrifice (in person), excepting to Heaven, Earth, and the Spirits of the land and grain; and when he went to transact any business, the ropes (for his chariot) were made of hemp (and not of silk)[1]. A tithe of three years, expenditure was allowed for the rites of mourning. When there was not sufficient for the rites of sacrifice and mourning, it was owing to lavish waste; when there was more than enough, the state was described as affluent. In sacrifices there should be no extravagance in good years, and no niggardliness in bad.

28. If in a state there was not accumulated (a surplus) sufficient for nine years, its condition was called one of insufficiency; if there was not enough for six years, one of urgency. If there was not a surplus sufficient for three years, the state could not continue. The husbandry of three years was held to give an overplus of food sufficient for one year; that of nine years, an overplus sufficient for three years. Going through thirty years (in this way), though there might be bad years, drought, and inundations, the people would have no lack or be reduced to (eating merely) vegetables, and then the son of Heaven would every day have full meals and music at them.

SECTION III.

1. The son of Heaven was encoffined on the seventh day (after his death), and interred in the seventh month. The prince of a state was encoffined

[1. Such is the meaning of the text here given by the Khien–lung editors. It is found also in the Khang–hsî dictionary, under the character, called in this usage hwo.]

on the fifth day, and interred in the fifth month. A Great officer, (other) officers, and the common people were encoffined on the third day, and interred in the third month. The mourning rites of three years (for parents) extended from the son of Heaven to all.

2. The common people let the coffin down into the grave by ropes, and did not suspend

the interment because of rain. They raised no mound, nor planted trees over the grave. That no other business should interfere with the rites of mourning was a thing extending from the son of Heaven to the common people.

3. In the mourning rites they followed (the rank of) the dead; in sacrificing to them, that of the living. A son by a concubine did not (preside at) the sacrifices[1].

4. (The ancestral temple of) the son of Heaven embraced seven fanes (or smaller temples); three on the left and three on the right, and that of his great ancestor (fronting the south):—in all, seven. (The temple of) the prince of a state embraced five such fanes: those of two on the left, and two on the right, and that of his great ancestor:—in all, five. Great officers had three fanes:–one on the left, one on the right, and that of his great ancestor:—in all, three. Other officers had (only) one. The common people presented their offerings in their (principal) apartment[2]

[1. Even though he might attain to higher rank than the son of the wife proper, who represented their father.

2. The technical terms (as they may be called) in the text make it impossible to translate this paragraph concisely, so as to make it intelligible to a foreign reader unacquainted with the significance of those terms. The following ground–plan of an ancestral temple of a king of Kâu is given in the plates of the Khien–lung edition of the Lî kî:—after Kû Hsî. I introduce it here with some condensations.

Entering at the gate on the south, we have, fronting us, at the northern end, the fane of the grand ancestor to whom, in the distant past, the family traced its line. South of his fane, on the right and left, were two fanes dedicated to kings Wan and Wû, father and son, the joint founders of the dynasty. The four below them, two on each side, were dedicated to the four kings preceding the reigning king, the sacrificer. At the back of each fane was a comparatively dark apartment, called khin where the spirit tablet was kept during the intervals between the sacrifices. When a sacrifice was offered, the tablet was brought out and placed in the centre of a screen, in the middle of the fane. As the line lengthened, while the tablets of the grand ancestor and joint ancestors always remained untouched, on a death and accession, the tablet of the next oldest occupant was removed and placed in a general apartment for the keeping of all such tablets, and that of the newly deceased king was placed in the father's fane, and the other three were shifted up, care being always taken that the tablet of a son should never follow that of his father on the same side. The number of the lower fanes was maintained, as a rule, at four. Those on the east were called Kâo and on the west Mû, the names in the text here. See the Chinese Classics, I, pp. 266, 267, and the note there.]

5. The sacrifices in the ancestral temples of the son of Heaven and the feudal princes were that of spring, called Yo; that of summer, called Tî; that of autumn, called Khang; and that of winter, called Khang[1].

6. The son of Heaven sacrificed to Heaven and Earth; the princes of the states, to the (spirits of the) land and grain; Great officers offered the five sacrifices (of the house). The son of Heaven sacrificed to all the famous hills and great streams under the sky, the five mountains[2] receiving (sacrificial) honours like the honours paid (at court) to the three ducal ministers, and the four rivers[2] honours like those paid to the princes of states; the princes sacrificed to the famous hills and great streams which were in their own territories.

7. The son of Heaven and the feudal lords sacrificed to the ancient princes who had no successors to

[1. The names of some of these sacrifices and their order are sometimes given differently.

2. For four of these mountains, see pages 217, 218, notes. The fifth was that of the Centre, mount Sung, in the present district of Sung, department Ho-nan, Ho-nan. The four rivers were the Kiang, the Hwâi, the Ho, and the Kî.]

preside over the sacrifices to them, and whose possessions now formed part of the royal domain or of their respective states.

8. The son of Heaven offered the spring sacrifice apart and by itself alone, but his sacrifices of all the other seasons were conducted on a greater scale in the fane of the high ancestor. The princes of the states who offered the spring sacrifice omitted that of the summer; those who offered that of the summer omitted that of the autumn; those who sacrificed in autumn did not do so in winter; and those who sacrificed in winter did not do so in spring[1].

In spring they offered the sacrifice of the season by itself apart; in summer, in the fane of the high ancestor[2]; in autumn and winter both the sacrifices were there associated together.

9. In sacrificing at the altars to the spirits of the land and grain, the son of Heaven used in each case a bull, a ram, and a boar; the princes, (only) a ram and a boar. Great and other officers, at the sacrifices in their ancestral temples, if they had lands, sacrificed an animal; and, if they had no lands, they only presented fruits. The common people, in the spring, presented scallions; in summer, wheat; in autumn, millet; and in winter, rice unhulled. The scallions were set forth with eggs; the wheat with

[1. The princes who omitted one sacrifice in the year would probably be absent in that season, attending at the royal court. They paid that attendance in turns from the several quarters.

2. If in this summer service the seasonal and the sacrifice in the fane of the high sacrifice were associated together, the rule for the princes was the same as for the king. There was the ordinary associate sacrifice, and 'the great;' about which the discussions and different views have been endless.]

fish; the millet with a sucking–pig; and the rice with a goose.

10. Of the bulls used in sacrificing to Heaven and Earth, the horns were (not larger than) a cocoon or a chestnut[1]. Those of the one used in the ancestral temple could be grasped with the hand; those of the ox used for (feasting) guests were a foot long.

Without sufficient cause, a prince did not kill an ox, nor a Great officer a sheep, nor another officer a dog or a pig, nor a common person eat delicate food.

The various provisions (at a feast) did not go beyond the sacrificial victims killed; the private, clothes were not superior to the robes of sacrifice; the house and its apartments did not surpass the ancestral temple.

11. Anciently, the public fields were cultivated by the united labours of the farmers around them, from the produce of whose private fields nothing was levied. A rent was charged for the stances in the marketplaces, but wares were not taxed. Travellers were

examined at the different passes, but no duties were levied from them. Into the forests and plains at the foot of mountains the people went without hindrance at the proper seasons. None of the produce was levied from the fields assigned to the younger sons of a family, nor from the holy fields. Only three days' labour was required (by the state) from the people in the course of a year. Fields and residences in the hamlets, (when once assigned), could

[1. The victims must all have been young animals; 'to show,' says Wang Thâo, 'that the sincerity of the worshipper is the chief thing in the view of Heaven.']

not be sold. Ground set apart for graves could not be sought (for any other purpose)[1].

12. The minister of Works with his (various) instruments measured the ground for the settlements of the people. About the hills and rivers, the oozy ground and the meres, he determined the periods of the four seasons. He measured the distances of one spot from another, and commenced his operations in employing the labour of the people. In all his employment of them, he imposed (only) the tasks of old men (on the able-bodied), and gave (to the old) the food-allowance of the able-bodied.

13. In all their settlements, the bodily capacities of the people are sure to be according to the sky and earthly influences, as cold or hot, dry or moist. Where the valleys are wide and the rivers large, the ground was differently laid out; and the people born in them had different customs. Their temperaments,

[1. Compare Mencius III, i, 3, 6–9, et al.; II, i, 5, 2–4; I, i, 3, 3, 4; III, i, 3, 15–17; with the notes. I give here also the note of P. Callery on the first sentence of this paragraph:—'Sous les trois premières dynasties, époque éloignée où il y avait peu de terrains cultivés dans l'empire, le gouvernement concédait les terres incultes par carrés équilatères ayant 900 mâu, ou arpents, de superficie. Ces carrés, qu'on nommait Zing, d'après leur analogie de tracé avec le caractère Zing, "a well," étaient divisés en neuf carrés égaux de 100 mâu chacun, au moyen de deux lignes médianes que deux autres lignes coupaient à angle droit à des distances égales. Il résultait de cette intersection de lignes une sorte de damier de trois cases de côté, ayant huit carrés sur la circonférence, et un carré au milieu. Les huit carrés du pourtour devenaient la propriété de huit colons; mais celui du centre était un champ de réserve dont la culture restait bien à la charge des huit voisins, mais dont les produits appartenaient à 1'empereur.']

as hard or soft, light or grave, slow or rapid, were made uniform by different measures; their preferences as to flavours were differently harmonised; their implements were differently made; their clothes were differently fashioned, but always suitably. Their training was varied, without changing their customs; and the governmental arrangements were uniform, without changing the suitability (in each case).

14. The people of those five regions–the Middle states, and the Zung, Î, (and other wild tribes round them)—had all their several natures, which they could not be made to alter. The tribes on the east were called Î. They had their hair unbound, and tattooed their bodies. Some of them ate their food without its being cooked. Those on the south were called Man. They tattooed their foreheads, and had their feet turned in towards each other. Some of them (also) ate their food without its being cooked. Those on the west were called Zung. They had their hair unbound, and wore skins. Some of them did not eat grain–food. Those on the north were called Tî. They wore skins of animals and birds, and dwelt in caves. Some of them also did not eat grain–food.

The people of the Middle states, and of those Man, Zung, and Tî, all had their dwellings, where they lived at ease; their flavours which they preferred; the clothes suitable for them; their proper implements for use; and their vessels which they prepared in abundance. In those five regions, the languages of the people were not mutually intelligible, and their likings and desires were different. To make what was in their minds apprehended, and to communicate their likings and desires, (there were officers),—in the east, called transmitters; in the south, representationists; in the west, Tî–tîs[1]; and in the north, interpreters.

15. In settling the people, the ground was measured for the formation of towns, and then measured again in smaller portions for the allotments of the people. When the division of the ground, the cities, and the allotments were thus fixed in adaptation to one another, so that there was no ground unoccupied, and none of the people left to wander about idle, economical arrangements were made about food; and its proper business appointed for each season. Then the people had rest in their dwellings, did joy fully what they had to do, exhorted one another to labour, honoured their rulers, and loved their superiors. This having been secured, there ensued the institution of schools.

SECTION IV.

1. The minister of Instruction defined and set forth the six ceremonial observances[2]:—to direct and control the nature of the people; clearly illustrated the seven lessons (of morality)[3] to stimulate their virtue; inculcated uniformity in the eight objects of government[2], to guard against all excess; taught the

[1. I cannot translate Tî–tî. It was the name of a region (Williams says, 'near the Koko–nor'), the people of which had a reputation for singing.

2. See the last paragraph of these Regulations, at the end of next Section.

3. It has become the rule, apparently with all sinologists, to call the minister in the text here, Sze Thû, by the name of 'The minister of Instruction.' Callery describes him as 'Le ministre qui a dans ses attributions l'instruction publiquee et les, rites.' And this is correct according to the account of his functions here, in the Kâu Lî, and in the Shû (V, xx, 8); but the characters simply denote 'superintendent of the multitudes.' This, then, was the conception anciently of what government had to do for the multitudes,—to teach them all moral and social duties, how to discharge their obligations to men living and dead, and to spiritual beings. The name is now applied to the president and vice–president of the board of Revenue.]

sameness of the course (of duty) and virtue, to assimilate manners; nourished the aged, to secure the completion of filial piety; showed pity to orphans and solitaries, to reach those who had been bereaved; exalted men of talents and worth, to give honour to virtue; and dealt summarily with the unworthy, to discountenance wickedness.

2. He commanded that, throughout the districts[1], there should be marked and pointed out to him those who were disobedient to his lessons. (This having been done), the aged men were all assembled in the school[2], and on a good day archery was practised and places were given according to merit. (At the same time) there was a feast, when places were given according to age. The Grand minister of Instruction[3] conducted thither the eminent scholars of the state and along with them superintended the business.

[1. That is, the six districts embraced in the royal domain, each nominally containing

12,500 families.

2. The great school of the district. The aged men would be good officers retired from duty, and others of known worth.

3. Here we have 'the Grand minister of Instruction;' and it may be thought we 'should translate the name in the first paragraph in the plural. No doubt, where there is no specification of 'the grand,' it means the board or department of Education.]

If those (who had been reported to him) did not (now) change, he gave orders that they who were noted as continuing disobedient in the districts on the left should be removed to those on the right, and those noted on the right to the districts on the left. Then another examination was held in the same way, and those who had not changed were removed to the nearest outlying territory. Still continuing unchanged, they were removed, after a similar trial, to the more distant territory. There they were again examined and tried, and if still found defective, they were cast out to a remote region, and for all their lives excluded from distinction.

3. Orders were given that, throughout the districts, the youths who were decided on as of promising ability should have their names passed up to the minister of Instruction, when they were called 'select scholars.' He then decided which of them gave still greater promise, and promoted them to the (great) college[1], where they were called 'eminent scholars[2]. ' Those who were brought to the notice of the minister were exempted from services in the districts; and those who were promoted to the (great) school, from all services under his own department, and (by and by) were called 'complete scholars[2].'

4. The (board for) the direction of Music gave all honour to its four subjects of instruction[3], and

[1. This would be the college at the capital.

2. Have we not in these the prototypes of the 'Flowering Talents' (Hsiû Zhai) and Promoted Men' (Kü Zan) of to–day?

3. In the text these are called 'the four Arts' and 'the four Teachings;' but the different phrases seem to have the same meaning.]

arranged the lessons in them, following closely the poems, histories, ceremonies, and music of the former kings, in order to complete its scholars. The spring and autumn were devoted to teaching the ceremonies and music; the winter and summer to the poems and histories[1]. The eldest son of the king and his other sons, the eldest sons of all the feudal princes, the sons, by their wives proper, of the high ministers, Great officers, and officers of the highest grade, and the eminent and select scholars from (all) the states, all repaired (to their instruction), entering the schools according to their years.

5. When the time drew near for their quitting the college, the smaller and greater assistants[2], and the inferior director of the board, put down those who had not attended to their instructions, and reported them to the Grand director, who in turn reported them to the king. The king ordered the three ducal ministers, his nine (other) ministers, the Great officers, and the (other) officers, all to enter the school (and hold an examination). If this did not produce the necessary change; the king in person inspected the school; and if this also failed, for three days he took no full meal nor had music, after which the (culprits) were cast but to the remote regions. Sending them to those of the west was called 'a (temporary) expulsion;'

[1. The Khien–lung editors say that ' in spring and autumn the temperature is equable and the bodily spirits good, well adapted for the practice of ceremonies and moving in time to the music, whereas the long days of summer and long nights of winter are better adapted for the tasks of learning the poems and histories.'

2. The smaller assistants of the Grand director of Music were eighteen, and the greater four. See the Kâu Lî, XVII, 21. Their functions are described in XXII, 45–53.]

to the east, 'a temporary exile.' But all their lives they were excluded from distinction.

6. The Grand director of Music, having fully considered who were the most promising of the 'completed scholars,' reported them to the king, after which they were advanced to be under the minister of War, and called 'scholars ready for employment[1].'

7. The minister of War gave discriminating consideration (to the scholars thus submitted to him), with a view to determine the offices for which their abilities fitted them. He then reported his decisions concerning the best and ablest of them to the king, to have that judgment fixed[2]. When it was, they were put into offices. After they had discharged the

duties of these, rank was given them; and, their positions being thus fixed, they received salary.

8. When a Great officer was dismissed as incompetent from his duties, be was not (again) employed in any office to the end of his life. At his death, he was buried as an (ordinary) officer.

[1. Exactly the name to the candidates of to–day who have succeeded at the triennial examinations at the capital the; 'Metropolitan Graduates,' as Mayers (page 72) calls them.

2. It is strange to find the minister of War performing the services here mentioned, and only these. The Khien–lung editors say that the compilers of this Book had not seen the Kâu Lî nor the Shû. It has been seen in the Introduction, pages 4, 5, how the Kâu Lî came to light in the reign of Wû, perhaps fifty years after this Book was made, and even then did not take its place among the other restored monuments till the time of Liû Hsin. To make the duties here ascribed to the Minister of War (literally, 'Master of Horse,') appear less anomalous, Kang and other commentators quote from the Shû (V, xx, 14) only a part of the account of his functions.]

9. If any expedition of war were contemplated, orders were given to the Grand minister of Instruction to teach the scholars the management of the chariot and the wearing of the coat of mail.

10. In the case of all who professed any particular art, respect was bad to their strength. If they were to go to a distant quarter, the), had to display their arms and legs, and their skill in archery and charioteering was tested. All who professed particular arts for the service of their superiors, such as prayermakers, writers, archers, carriage–drivers, doctors, diviners, and artizans,—all who professed particular arts for the service of their superiors, were not allowed to practise any other thing, or to change their offices; and when they left their districts, they did not take rank with officers. Those who did service in families (also), when they left their districts, did not take rank with officers.

11. The minister of Crime adapted the punishments (to the offences for which they were inflicted), and made the laws clear in order to deal with criminal charges and litigations. He required the three references as to its justice (before the infliction of a capital punishment)[1]. If a party had the intention, but there were not evidence of the deed, the

charge was not listened to. Where a case appeared as doubtful, it was lightly dealt with; where it might be pardoned, it was (still) gravely considered.

12. In all determining on the application of any of the five punishments[2], it was required to decide

[1. See the Kâu Lî, XXXVII, 45, 46.

2. Branding; cutting off the nose; Cutting off the feet; castration; death. See vol, iii, p. 40.]

according to the judgment of Heaven. Inadvertent and redeemable offences were determined by (the circumstances of) each particular case[1].

13. When hearing a case requiring the application of any of the five punishments, (the judge) was required to have respect to the affection between father and son[2], or the righteousness between ruler and minister[3] (which might have been in the mind of the defendant), to balance his own judgment. He must consider the gravity or lightness (of the offence), and carefully try to fathom the capacity (of the offender) as shallow or deep, to determine the exact character (of his guilt). He must exert his intelligence to the utmost, and give the fullest play to his generous and loving feeling, to arrive at his final judgment, If the criminal charge appeared to him doubtful, he was to take the multitude into consultation with him; and if they also doubted, he was to pardon the defendant. At the same time he was to examine analogous cases, great and small, and then give his decision.

14. The evidence in a criminal case having thus been all taken and judgment given, the clerk reported it all to the director (of the district), who heard it and reported it to the Grand minister of Crime. He also heard it in the outer court[4], and then reported it to the king, who ordered the three ducal ministers,

[1. Vol. iii, pp. 260–263. The compilers in this part evidently had some parts of the Shû before them.

2. Which might make either party conceal the guilt of the other.

3. Which might in a similar way affect the evidence.

4. The text says, 'Under the Zizyphus trees.' These were planted in the outer court of audience, and under them the different ministers of the court had their places.]

with the minister and director, again to hear it. When they had (once more) reported it to the king, he considered it with the three mitigating conditions[1], and then only determined the punishment.

15. In all inflictions of punishments and fines, even light offenders (that were not doubtful) were not forgiven. Punishment may be compared to the body. The body is a complete thing; when once completed, there cannot be any subsequent change in it[2]. Hence the wise man will do his utmost (in deciding on all these inflictions).

16. Splitting words so as to break (the force of) the laws; confounding names so as to change what had been definitely settled; practising corrupt ways so as to throw government into confusion: all guilty of these things were put to death. Using licentious music; strange garments; wonderful contrivances and extraordinary implements, thus raising doubts among the multitudes: all who used or formed such things were put to death. Those who were persistent in hypocritical conduct and disputatious in hypocritical speeches; who studied what was wrong, and went on to do so more and more, and whoever increasingly followed what was wrong so as to bewilder the multitudes: these were put to death. Those

[1. Callery gives for this, 'qui pardonne trois fois.' The conditions were–ignorance, mistake, forgetfulness.

2. There is here a play upon the homophonous names of different Chinese characters, often employed, as will be pointed out, in the Lî Kî, and in which the scholars of Han set an example to future times. Callery frames a French example of the reasoning that results from it: 'Un saint est un ceint; or, la ceinture signifiant au figuré la continence, il s'ensuit que la vertu de continence est essentielle à la sainteté!']

who gave false reports about (appearances of) spirits, about seasons and days, about consultings of the tortoise–shell and stalks, so as to perplex the multitudes: these were put to death. These four classes were taken off, and no defence listened to.

17. All who had charge of the prohibitions for the regulation of the multitudes[1] did not forgive transgressions of them. Those who had rank–tokens, the long or the round, and gilt libation–cups were not allowed to sell them in the market–places; nor were any allowed to sell robes or chariots, the gift of the king; or vessels of an ancestral temple; or victims for sacrifice; or instruments of war; or vessels which were not according to the prescribed measurements; or chariots of war which were not according to the same; or cloth or silk, fine or coarse, not according to the prescribed quality, or broader or narrower than the proper rule; or of the illegitimate colours, confusing those that were correct[2]; or cloth, embroidered or figured; or vessels made with pearls or jade; or clothes, or food, or drink, (in any way extravagant); or grain which was not in season, or fruit which was unripe; or wood which was not fit for the axe; or birds, beasts, fishes, or reptiles, which were not fit to be killed. At the frontier gates, those in charge of the prohibitions, examined travellers, forbidding such as wore strange clothes, and taking note of such as spoke a strange language.

18. The Grand recorder had the superintendence of

[1. These would be, especially, the superintendents of the markets.

2. The five correct colours were—black, carnation, azure, white. and yellow.]

ceremonies. He was in charge of the tablets of record, and brought before the king what (names) were to be avoided', and what days were unfavourable (for the doing of particular affairs)'. The son of Heaven received his admonitions with reverence[2].

19. (The office of) the accountants[3] prepared the complete accounts of the year to be submitted to the son of Heaven which were reverently received by the chief minister. The Grand director of Music, the Grand minister of Crime, and the (chief) superintendent of the markets, these three officers, followed with the completed accounts of their departments to be submitted to the son of Heaven. The Grand minister of Instruction, the Grand minister of War, and the Grand minister of Works, reverently received the completed accounts of their several departments from their various subordinates, and examined them, then presenting them to the son of Heaven. Those subordinates then reverently received them after being so examined and adjudicated on. This being done, the aged were feasted and the royal sympathy shown to the husbandmen. The business of the year was concluded, and the expenditure of the states was determined.

[1. See pages 93, 180, et al.

2. Some of the functions here belonged to the assistant recorder, according to the Kâu Lî, but the two were of the same department.

3. This office was under the board of the chief minister, and consisted of sixty–two men of different grades under the Kâu dynasty (the Kâu Lî, I, 38; their duties are described in Book VI). It is not easy to understand all the text of the rest of the paragraph. about the final settlement of the accounts of the year.]

SECTION V.

1. In nourishing the aged, (Shun), the lord of Yü, used the ceremonies of the drinking entertainment; the sovereigns of Hsiâ, those at entertainments (after) a reverent sacrifice or offering[1]; the men of Yin, those of a (substantial) feast; and the men of Kâu cultivated and used all the three.

2. Those of fifty years received their nourishment in the (schools of the) districts; those of sixty, theirs in the (smaller school of the) state; and those of seventy, theirs in the college. This rule extended to the feudal states. An old man of eighty made his acknowledgment for the ruler's message, by kneeling once and bringing his head twice to the ground. The blind did the same. An old man of ninety employed another to receive (the message and gift for him).

3. For those of fifty the grain was (fine and) different (from that used by younger men). For those of sixty, flesh was kept in store. For those of seventy, there was a second service of savoury meat. For those of eighty, there was a constant supply of delicacies. For those of ninety, food and drink were never out of their chambers. Wherever they wandered (to another place), it was required that savoury meat and drink should follow them.

[1. The commentators make this to have been a Barmecide feast, merely to show respect for the age; and Callery, after them, gives for the text: 'La dynastie des Hsiâ faisait servir un repas qu'on ne mangeait point.' But Ying–tâ's authorities adduced to support this view do not appear to me to bear it out. See the commencing chapter of Book X, Section ii, where all this about nourishing the aged is repeated.]

4. After sixty, (the coffin and other things for the mourning rites) were seen to be in readiness, (once) in the year; after seventy, once in the season; after eighty, once in the month; and after ninety; every day they were kept in good repair. But the bandages, sheet, and coverlets and cases (for the corpse) were prepared after death,

5. At fifty, one begins to decay; at sixty, he does not feel satisfied unless he eats flesh; at seventy, he does not feel warm unless he wears silk; at eighty, he does not feel warm unless there be some one (to sleep) with him; and at ninety, he does not feel warm even with that.

6. At fifty, one kept his staff always in his hand in his family; at sixty, in his district; at seventy, in the city; at eighty, (an officer) did so in the court. If the son of Heaven wished to put questions to (all officer) of ninety, he went to his house, and had rich food carried after him.

7. At seventy, (an officer) did not wait till the court was over (before he retired); at eighty, he reported every month (to the ruler's messenger) that he was still alive; at ninety; he (had delicate food sent) regularly to him every day.

8. At fifty, a (common) man was not employed in services requiring strength; at sixty, he was discharged from bearing arms along with others; at seventy, he was exempted from the business of receiving guests and visitors; and at eighty, he was free from the abstinences and other rites of mourning.

9. When one was fifty, he received the rank (of a Great officer)[1]; at sixty, he did not go in person to the college; at seventy, he retired from the service of the government; and in mourning, he used only the dress of sackcloth (without adopting the privations of the mourning rites).

10. (Shun), the lord of Yü, nourished the aged (who had retired from the service) of the state in (the school called) the higher hsiang, and the aged of the common people (and officers who had not obtained rank) in (the school called) the lower hsiang. The sovereigns of Hsiâ nourished the former in (the school called) the hsü on the east, and the latter in (that called) the hsü on the west. The men of Yin nourished the former in the

school of the right, and the latter in that of the left. The men of Kâu entertained the former in (the school called) the eastern kiâo, and the latter in (what corresponded to) the hsiang of Yü. This was in the suburb of the capital on the west[2].

11. The lord of Yü wore the hwang cap in sacrificing

[1. See Book X, Section ii, i. This was, say the Khien-lung editors, a lesson against forwardness in seeking office and rank, as retirement at seventy was a lesson against cleaving to these too long.

2. It is wearisome to try and thread one's way through the discussions about the schools, called by all these different names. One thing is plain, that there were the lower schools which boys entered when they were eight, and the higher schools into which the passed from these. But in this paragraph these institutions are mentioned not in connexion with education,. but as they were made available for the assembling and cherishing of the aged. They served various purposes. A school-room with us may do the same, occasionally; it was the rule in ancient China that the young should be taught and the old ministered to in the same buildings.]

(in the ancestral temple), and the white robes in nourishing the aged. The sovereigns of Hsiâ used the shâu cap in sacrificing, and the upper and lower dark garments of undress in nourishing the aged. During the Yin, they used the hsü cap in sacrificing, and the tipper and lower garments, both of white thin silk, in nourishing the aged. During the Kâu dynasty, they used the mien cap in sacrificing, and the dark-coloured upper and lower garments in nourishing the aged.

12. The kings of the three dynasties[1], in nourishing the old, always had the years of those connected with them brought to their notice. Where (an officer) was eighty, one of his sons was free from all duties of government service; where he was ninety, all the members of his family were set free from them. In cases of parties who were disabled or ill, and where the attendance of others was required to wait upon them, one man was discharged from those duties (for the purpose). Parties mourning for their parents had a discharge for three years. Those mourning for one year or nine months had a discharge for three months. Where an officer was about to move to another state, he was discharged from service for three months beforehand. When one came from another state, he was not required to take active service for around year.

13. One who, while quite young, lost his father was called an orphan; an old man who had lost his sons was called a solitary. An old man who had lost his wife was called a pitiable (widower); an old woman who had lost her husband was called a poor

[1. Hsiâ, Shang or Yin, and Kâu.]

(widow). These four classes were the most forlorn of Heaven's people, and had none to whom to tell their wants; they all received regular allowances.

14. The dumb, the deaf, the lame, such as had lost a member, pigmies, and mechanics, were all fed according to what work they were able to do.

15. On the roads, men took the right side and women the left; carriages kept in the middle. A man kept behind another who had a father's years; he followed one who might be his elder brother more closely, but still keeping behind, as geese fly after one another in a row. Friends did not pass by one another, when going the same way. (In the case of an old and a young man, carrying burdens,) both were borne by the younger; and if the two were too heavy for one, he took the heavier. A man with grey hair was not allowed to carry anything, though he might do it with one hand.

16. An officer of superior rank, of the age of sixty or seventy, did not walk on foot. A common man, at that age, did not go without flesh to eat.

17. A Great officer, (having land of his own), was' not permitted to borrow the vessels for sacrifice; nor to make vessels for his own private use before he had made those for sacrifice.

I& A space of one lî square contained fields amounting to 900 mâu[1]. Ten lî square were equal to 100 spaces of one lî square, and contained 90,000 mâu. A hundred lî square were equal to 100 spaces of ten lî square, and contained 9,000,999 mâu. A

[1. See note as to the size of the mâu on page 218.]

thousand lî square were equal to 100 spaces of 100 lî square, and contained 900,000,000 mâu.

19. From mount Hang[1] to the southernmost point of the Ho was hardly 1000 lî. From that point to the Kiang was hardly I000 lî. From the Kiang to mount Hang in the south was more than 1000 lî. From the Ho on the cast to the eastern sea was more than 1000 lî. From the Ho on the east to the same river on the west was hardly 1000 lî; and from that to the Moving Sands[2] was more than 1000 lî. (The kingdom) did not pass the Moving Sands on the west, nor mount Hang on the south. On the east it did not pass the eastern sea, nor on the north did it pass (the other) mount Hang. All within the four seas, taking the length with the breadth, made up a space Of 3000 lî square, and contained eighty trillions of mâu[3].

2o. A space of 100 lî square contained ground to the amount of 9,000,000 mâu. Hills and mounds, forests and thickets, rivers and marshes, ditches and canals, city walls and suburbs., houses, roads, and

[1. See notes on pages 217, 218. I have said below '(the other) mount Hang;' but the names, or characters for the names, of the two mountains are different in Chinese.

2. What is now called the desert of Gobi.

3. As it is in the text =80 x 10000 x 10000 x 10000 x 10000 mâu. A translator, if I may speak of others from my own experience, is much perplexed in following and verifying the calculations, in this and the other paragraphs before and after it. The Khien–lung editors and Wang Thâo use many pages in pointing out the errors of earlier commentators, and establishing the correct results according to their own views, and 1 have thought it well to content myself with simply giving a translation of the text.]

lanes took up one third of it, leaving 6,000,000 mâu.

21. Anciently, according to the cubit of Kâu, eight cubits formed a pace. Now, according to the same, six cubits and four inches make a pace. One hundred ancient mâu were equal to 146 of the present day and thirty paces. One hundred ancient lî were equal to 121 of the present day, sixty paces, four cubits, two inches and two–tenths.

22. A space of 1000 lî square contained 100 spaces of 100 lî square each. In this were constituted thirty states of 100 lî square, leaving what would have been enough for other seventy of the same size. There were also constituted sixty states Of 70 lî square,

twenty-nine of 100 lî square, and forty spaces of 10 lî square; leaving enough for forty states of 100 lî square, and sixty spaces of 10 lî square. There were also constituted a hundred and twenty states of 50 lî square, and thirty of 100 lî square, leaving enough for ten of the same size, and sixty spaces of 10 lî square.

The famous hills and great meres were not included in the fiefs; and what remained was assigned for attached territories and unoccupied lands. Those unappropriated lands were taken to reward any of the princes of acknowledged merit, and what was cut off from some others (because of their demerit) became unappropriated land.

23. The territory of the son of Heaven, amounting to 1000 lî square, contained 100 spaces of 100 lî square each. There were constituted nine appanages of 100 lî square, leaving ninety-one spaces of the same size. There were also constituted twenty-one appanages of 70 lî square, ten of 100 lî, and twenty-nine spaces of 10 lî square; leaving enough for eighty of 100 lî square, and seventy-one of 10 lî There were further constituted sixty-three appanages of 50 lî square, fifteen of 100 lî, and seventy-five spaces of 10 lî, while there still remained enough for sixty-four appanages of 100 lî square, and ninety-six spaces of 10 lî each.

24. The officers of the lowest grade in the feudal states received salary sufficient to feed nine individuals; those of the second grade, enough to feed eighteen; and those of the highest, enough for thirty-six. A Great officer could feed 72 individuals; a minister, 288; and the ruler, 2880.

In a state of the second class, a minister could feed 216; and the ruler, 2160.

A minister ' of a small state could feed 144 individuals; and the ruler, 1440.

In a state of the second class, the minister who was appointed by its ruler received the same emolument as the minister of a small state.

2 5. The Great officers of the son of Heaven acted as 'the three inspectors.' When they were inspecting a state, their salary was equal to one of its ministers, and their rank was that of a ruler of a: state of the second class. Their salaries were derived from the territories under the chiefs of regions[1].

26. The chiefs of regions, on occasion of their appearing at the court of the son of Heaven, had cities assigned them for purification[2] within his domain like those of his officers of the chief grade.

[1. See page 212, paragraph 2, and note 1, page 213.

2. The text says, 'Cities for bathing and washing the hair;' but preparing by mental exercises for appearing before the king is also intimated by the phrase.]

27. The (appointed) heir–sons[1] of the feudal princes inherited their states. Great officers (in the royal domain) did not inherit their rank. They were employed as their ability and character were recognised, and received rank as their merit was proved. Till their rank was conferred (by the king), (the princes) were in the position of his officers of the chief grade, and so they ruled their states, The Great officers of the states did not inherit their rank and emoluments.

28. The six ceremonial observances were:—capping; marrying; mourning rites; sacrifices; feasts; and interviews. The seven lessons (of morality) were:—(the duties between) father and son; elder brother and younger; husband and wife; ruler and minister; old and young; friend and friend; host and guest. The eight objects of government were:–food and drink; clothes; business (or, the profession); maintenance of distinctions; measures of length; measures of capacity; and definitely assigned rules[2].

[1. A son, generally the eldest son by the wife proper, had to be recognised by the king before he could be sure of succeeding to his father.

2. See page 230, paragraph 1.]

BOOK IV. THE YÜEH LING, OR PROCEEDINGS OF GOVERNMENT IN THE DIFFERENT MONTHS.

SECTION 1. PART 1.

1. In the first month of spring the sun is in Shih, the star culminating at dusk being Zhan,

and that culminating at dawn Wei[1].

2. Its days are kiâ and yî[2].

[1. In this month the conjunction of the sun and moon took place in Shih or a Alarkab Pegasi. Zhan is a constellation embracing Betelguese, Bellatrix, Rigel, {gamma}, {delta}, {epsilon}, {zeta}, {eta}, of Orion; and Wei is {epsilon}, {mu}, of Scorpio. Shih is called in the text Ying Shih, 'the Building Shih,' because this month was the proper time at which to commence building.

2 Kiâ and yî are the first two of the 'ten heavenly stems,' which are combined with the 'twelve earthly branches,' to form the sixty binomial terms of 'the cycle of sixty,' that was devised in a remote antiquity for the registration of successive days, and was subsequently used also in the registration of successive years. The origin of the cycle and of the names of its terms is thus far shrouded in mystery; and also the application of those terms to the various purposes of divination. The five pairs of the stems correspond, in the jargon of mysterious. speculation, to the five elements of wood, fire, earth, metal, and water, and, as will be seen in his Book, to the seasons of spring, summer, the intermediate centre, autumn, and winter. Whether there be anything more in this short notice than a declaration of this fact, or any indication of the suitableness of 'the days' for certain 'undertakings' in them, as even the Khien–lung editors seem to think, I cannot say.]

3. Its divine ruler is Thâi Hâo, and the (attending) spirit is Kâu–mang[1].

4. Its creatures are the scaly[2].

5. Its musical note is Kio, and its pitch–tube is the Thâi Zhâu[3].

6. Its number is eight[4]; its take is sour; its smell is rank.

[1. Thâi Hâo, 'the Grandly Bright,' is what is called the dynastic designation' of Fû–hsî and his line. By the time that the observances described in this Book had come into use, Fû–hsî and other early personages had been deified and were supposed to preside over the seasons of the year. To him as the earliest of them was assigned the presidency of the spring and the element of wood, the phenomena of vegetation being then most striking. He was the 'divine ruler' of the spring, and sacrificed to in its months; and at the sacrifices there was associated with him, as assessor, an inferior personage called Kâu–mang (literally, 'curling fronds and spikelets'), said to have been a son of Shâo Hâo, another mythical sovereign, founder of the line of Kin Thien. But Shâo Hâo was separated from Thâi Hâo by more than 1000 years. The association at these sacrifices in the spring months of two personages so distant in time from each other as Fû–hsî and Kâu–mang, shows how slowly and irregularly the process of deification and these sacrifices had grown up.

2. The character for which I have given ' creatures' is' often translated by 'insects;' but fishes, having scales, must form a large portion of what are here intended. 'The seven (zodiacal) constellations of the east,' says Wû Khang, I make up the Azure Dragon, and hence all moving creatures that have scales belong to (the element of) wood.'

3. Kio is the name of the third of the five musical notes of the Chinese scale, corresponding to our B (?); and Thâi Zhâu is the name of one of the twelve tubes by which, from a very early date, music was regulated. The Thâi Zhâu, or ' Great Pipe,' was the second of the tubes that give the 'six upper musical accords.'

4. The 'number' of wood is three, which added to five, the number' of earth, gives eight, the 'number' of the months of spring; but this, to me at least, is only a jargon.]

7. Its sacrifice is that at the door[1], and of the parts of the victim the spleen has the foremost place[1].

8. The east winds resolve the cold. Creatures that have been torpid during the winter begin to move. The fishes rise up to the ice. Otters sacrifice fish. The wild geese make their appearance[2].

9. The son of Heaven occupies the apartment on the left of the Khing Yang (Fane); rides in the carriage with the phœnix (bells), drawn by the azure–dragon (horses), and carrying the green flag; wears the green

[1. This was one of the sacrifices of the house; see paragraph 6, page 116, and especially the seventh paragraph of Book XX. As the door is the place of exodus, it was the proper place for this sacrifice in the spring, when all the energies of nature begin to be displayed afresh. Among the five viscera,—the heart, the liver, the spleen, the lungs, and the kidneys,—the spleen corresponds to the element of earth, and therefore it was made prominent in this service, in the season when the earth seems to open its womb beneath the growing warmth of the year.

2. These are all phenomena of the spring. The third of them is differently expressed in Hwai–nan Dze, the Tâoist grandson of the founder of the Han dynasty (see Book V of his works), and in the Hsiâ Hsiâo Mang, showing that this text of the Lî Kî was taken from Lü Pû–wei, if the whole Book were not written by him. They read, which Professor Douglas renders, Fish mount (to the surface of) the water, bearing on their backs pieces of ice.' But the meaning of the longer text is simply what I have given. Ying–tâ says, 'Fishes, during the intense cold of winter, lie close at the bottom of the water, attracted by the greater warmth of the earth; but, when the sun's influence is felt, they rise and swim near to the ice.' = 'with their backs near to the ice.' What is said about the otter is simply a superstitious misinterpretation of its habit of eating only a small part of its prey, and leaving the rest on the bank. The geese come from the south on the way to their quarters during the warmer season in the north.]

robes, and the (pieces of) green jade (on his cap and at his girdle pendant). He eats wheat and mutton. The vessels which he uses are slightly carved, (to resemble) the shooting forth (of plants)[1].

[1. The Khing Yang ('Green and Bright') was one of the principal divisions in the Hall of Distinction of Book XII. We must suppose that the sovereign went there (among other purposes) to give out the first day of the month, and did so in the apartment indicated, and in the style and robes and ornaments of the text, in the first month of spring. The ancient Shun, it is said, set the example of the carriage with bells, whose tinkling was supposed to resemble the notes of the lwan, a bird at which we can only guess, and which has been called the phœnix, and the argus pheasant. Horses above eight feet high were called dragon steeds. The predominating green colour suits the season and month; but what made wheat and mutton then peculiarly suitable for the royal mat, I do not know the fancies of Tâoism sufficiently to be able to understand.

In the plates to the Khien–lung edition of our classic, the following rude ground–plan of the structure is given to illustrate the various references to it in this Book:—

{illustration}

The building is made to consist of nine large apartments or halls; three fronting the different points of the compass, and one in the centre; making nine in all. That in the centre was called 'The Grand Apartment of the Grand Fane;' south from it was 'The Ming Thang Grand Fane;' on the east 'The Khing Yang Grand Fane;' on the west 'The Zung Yang Grand Fane;' and on the north 'The Hsüan Thang Grand Fane.'

In the second month of the seasons, the king went the round of the Grand Fanes. The four corner apartments were divided into two each, each one being named from the Grand Fane on the left or right of which it was. Commencing with the half on the left of the Khing Yang Fane, the king made the circuit of all the others and of the Fanes, returning to the other half on the right of the Hsüan Thang Fane in the twelfth month. The Grand Apartment in the centre was devoted to the imaginary season of the centre, between the sixth and seventh months, or the end of summer and beginning of autumn.]

10. In this month there takes place the inauguration of spring. Three days before this ceremony, the Grand recorder informs the son of Heaven, saying, 'On such and such a day is the inauguration of the spring. The energies of the season are fully seen in wood. On this the son of Heaven devotes himself to self–purification, and on the day he leads in person the three ducal ministers, his nine high ministers, the feudal princes (who are at court), and his Great officers, to meet the spring in the eastern suburb[1];

[1. We are not told what the ceremonies in the inauguration of the spring were. The phrase li khun is the name of the first of the twenty–four terms into which the Chinese year is divided, dating now from the sun's being in the fifteenth degree of Aquarius. Kang Hsüan thought that the meeting of the spring in the eastern suburb was by a sacrifice to the first of 'the five planetary gods,' corresponding to Jupiter, 'the Azure Tî, called Ling–wei–jang' But where he found that name, and what is its significance, is a mystery; and the whole doctrine of five planetary Tîs is held to be heresy, and certainly does not come from the five King.]

and on their return, he rewards them all in the court[1].

11. He charges his assistants[2] to disseminate (lessons of) virtue, and harmonise the governmental orders, to give effect to the expressions of his satisfaction and bestow his favours; down to the millions of the people. Those expressions and gifts thereupon proceed, every one in proper (degree and direction).

12. He also orders the Grand recorder to guard the statutes and maintain the laws, and (especially) to observe the motions in the heavens of the sun and moon, and of the zodiacal stars in which the conjunctions of these bodies take place, so that there should be no error as to where they rest and what they pass over; that there should be no failure in the record of all these things, according to the regular practice of early times.

13. In this month the son of Heaven on the first (hsin)[3] day prays to God for a good year; and afterwards, the day of thc first conjunction of the sun and moon having been chosen, with the handle and share of the plough in the carriage, placed between the man–at–arms who is its third occupant and the driver, he conducts his three ducal ministers, his nine high ministers, the feudal princes and his Great officers, all with their own hands to plough the field of

[1. This rewarding, it is understood, was that mentioned in paragraph 15, p. 217.

2. These assistants are supposed to be the 'three ducal ministers.'

3. This took and takes place on the first in day, the first day commencing with that character, the eighth of the ' stems.']

God. The son of Heaven turns up three furrows, each of the ducal ministers five, and the other ministers and feudal princes nine[1]. When they return, he takes in his hand a cup in the great chamber, all the others being in attendance on him and the Great officers, and says, 'Drink this cup of comfort after your toil.'

14. In this month the vapours of heaven descend and those of the earth ascend. Heaven and earth are in harmonious co–operation. All plants bud and grow.

15. The king gives orders to set forward the business of husbandry. The inspectors of the fields are ordered to reside in the lands having an eastward exposure, and (see that) all repair the marches and divisions (of the o–round), and mark out clearly the paths and ditches. They must skilfully survey the mounds and rising grounds, the slopes and defiles, the plains and marshes, determining what the different lands are suitable for, and where the different grains will grow best. They must thus instruct and lead on the people, themselves also engaging in the tasks. The business of the fields being thus ordered, the guiding line is first put in requisition, and the husbandry is carried on without error[2].

16. In this month orders are given to the chief director of Music to enter the college, and practise the dances (with his pupils)[3].

[1. The services described here are still performed, in substance, by the emperors of China and their representatives throughout the provinces. The field is generally called 'the imperial field,' through error. The grain produced by it was employed in the sacrifices or religious services of which God (Shang Tî) was the object, and hence arose the denomination.

2. Compare vol. iii, pp. 320–322, 370–373.

3. 'The chief director of Music' would be the same as the Tî Sze Yo of the Kâu Lî, Book XXII. There were dances of war (wan), and dances of peace (wân); but neither is in the text. But either term may include both classes of dancing. Callery translates by 'faire des évolutions.']

17. The canons of sacrifice are examined and set forth, an d orders are given to sacrifice to the hills and forests, the streams and meres, care being taken not to use any female victims[1].

18. Prohibitions are issued against cutting down trees.

19. Nests should not be thrown down; unformed insects should not be killed, nor creatures in the Womb, nor very young creatures, nor birds just taking to the wing, nor fawns, nor should eggs be destroyed.

20. No congregating of multitudes should be allowed, and no setting about the rearing of fortifications and walls[2].

21. Skeletons should be covered up, and bones with the flesh attached to them buried.

22. In this month no warlike operations should be undertaken; the undertaking of such is sure to be followed by calamities from Heaven. The not undertaking warlike operations means that they should not commence on our side[3].

[1. Not to destroy the life unborn. At 'the great sacrifices,' those to Heaven and Earth, and in the ancestral temple, only male victims were used, females being deemed 'unclean.' The host of minor sacrifices is intended here.

2. Such operations would interfere with the labours of husbandry.

3. War is specially out of time in the genial season of spring; but a state, when attacked, must, and might, defend itself even then.]

23. No change in the ways of heaven is allowed; nor any extinction of the principles of earth; nor an), confounding of the bonds of men[1].

24. If in the first month of spring the governmental proceedings proper to summer were carried out, the rain would fall unseasonably, plants and trees would decay prematurely, and the states would be kept in continual fear. If the proceedings proper to autumn were carried out, there would be great pestilence among the people; boisterous winds would work their violence; rain would descend in torrents; orach, fescue, darnel, and southernwood would grow up together. If the proceedings proper to winter were carried out, pools of water would produce their destructive effects, snow and frost would prove very injurious, and the first sown seeds would not enter the ground[2].

PART II.

I. In the second month of spring, the sun is in Khwei, the star culminating at dusk being Hû, and that culminating at dawn Kien–hsing[3].

2. It s days are kiâ and yî. Its divine ruler is Thâi Hâo, the attending spirit is Kâu–mang. Its

[1. Compare what is said in the fifth Appendix to the Yî King, paragraph 4 (vol. xvi, pp. 423, 424). The next paragraph is the sequel of this.

2. Such government would be comparable to the inversion of the seasons in the course of nature. Compare Proverbs xxvi. 1.

3. The constellation Khwei contains {beta} (Mirac), {delta}, {epsilon}, {zeta}, {mu}, {nu}, {pi} of Andromeda, and, some stars of Pisces. Hû or Hû Kih contains {delta}, {epsilon}, {eta}, {kappa}, of Canis Major; and {delta}, {omega}, of Argo; and Kien–hsing, {nu}, {xi}, {pi}, {rho}, {sigma} of Sagittarius' head.]

creatures are the scaly. Its musical note is Kio, and its pitch–tube is the Kiâ Kung[1].

3. Its number is eight; its taste is sour; its smell is rank. Its sacrifice is that at the door, and of the parts of the victim the spleen has the foremost place.

4. The rain begins to fall[2]. The peach tree begins to blossom. The oriole sings. Hawks are transformed into doves[3].

5. The son of Heaven occupies the Khing Yang Grand Fane[4]; rides in the carriage with the phœnix bells, drawn by the azure dragon–(horses), and bearing the green flag. He is dressed in the green robes, and wears the azure gems. He eats wheat

[1. Kiâ Kung, 'the double tube,' is the second tube of the six lower accords.

2. Literally, 'There commence the rains.' 'The rains' is now the name of the second of the twenty–four terms (February 15 to March 4).

3. This is the converse of the phenomenon in page 277, paragraph 3. Both are absurd, but the natural rendering in the translation is the view of Kang, Ying–tâ, Kâo Yû (the glossarist of Hwâi–nan Dze), and the Khien–lung editors. Seeking for the actual phenomenon which gave rise to the superstitious fancy, Professor Douglas renders the corresponding sentence of the Hsiâ Kang by 'hawks become crested hawks,' and thinks that the notice is based on the appearance of the hawks when 'the rearing instinct becomes excessive, and birds of prey become excited.' It may be so, but this meaning cannot be brought out of the text, and should not be presented as that of the writer of the Book.

4. See the note on p. 252. The three apartments (two of them subdivided) on the east of the Hall of, Distinction, all received the general designation of Khing Yang, 'the Green and Bright,' as characteristic of the season of Spring. It was now the second month of that season, and the king takes his place in the principal or central apartment, 'the Grand

Fane.]'

and mutton. The vessels which he uses are slightly carved, (to resemble) the bursting forth (of nature).

6. In this month, they keep both the young buds and those more advanced from being disturbed; they nourish both the young animals and those not fully grown; they especially watch over all orphans.

7. The fortunate day is chosen, and orders are given to the people to sacrifice at their altars to the spirits of the ground[1].

8. Orders are given to the (proper) officers to examine the prisons; to remove fetters and handcuffs; that there shall be no unregulated infliction of the bastinado; and that efforts shall be made to stop criminal actions and litigations.

9. In this month the swallow makes its appearance[2]. On the day of its arrival, the son of Heaven sacrifices to the first match–maker with a bull, a ram, and a boar. He goes to do so in person, with his queen and help–mates, attended by his nine ladies of honour. Peculiar courtesy is shown to those whom he has (lately) approached. Bow–cases have been brought, and a bow and arrows are given to each before (the altar of) the first match–maker.

10. In this month day and night are equal[3]. Thunder utters its voice, and the lightning begins

[1. The sacrifice here was not that to Earth, which it was competent to the king alone to offer; nor to the spirits of the territories of the different states. It was offered by the people generally to the spirits presiding over their fields.

2. The swallow is, 'the dark–coloured bird,' of the third sacrificial ode of the Shang dynasty; see Vol. iii, p. 307.

3. The vernal equinox.]

to be seen. Insects in their burrows are all in motion, opening their doors and beginning to come forth.

11. Three days before the thunder[1], a bell with a wooden tongue is sounded, to give notice to all the people. 'The thunder,' it is said, 'is about to utter its voice. If any of you be not careful of your behaviour, you shall bring forth children incomplete; there are sure to be evils and calamities.'

12. At the equinox they make uniform the measures of length and capacity; the weight Of 30 catties, the steelyard, and the weight of 120 catties. They correct the peck and bushel, the steelyard weights and the bushel–scraper[2].

13. In this month few of the husbandmen remain in their houses in the towns. They repair, however, their gates and doors, both of wood and wattles; and put their sleeping apartments and temples all in good repair. No great labours, which would interfere with the work of husbandry, should be undertaken[3].

14. In this month (the fishermen) should not let the streams and meres run dry, nor drain off all the water from the dams and ponds, (in order to catch all the fish), nor should (the hunters) fire the hills and forests.

[1. We are not told how they knew this third day.

2. A catty (kin) at present = 1 1/3 lb. avoirdupois. The khün, or 30 catties, = 40 lbs. av.; and the shih, or 120 catties, = 160 lbs. av.; see Williams' Commercial Guide, pp. 278–231. The tâu (or peck, in use in the market) contains 10 catties of dry, cleaned rice, and measures 30 cubic zhun, or inches; and the hû, or bushel, = 5 tâu. The bushel–scraper is a piece of wood or roller used to level the top of the hû. But see Williams, pp. 281, 282.

3. Compare vol. iii, pp. 368–373.]

15. The son of Heaven at this time offers a lamb (to the ruler of cold), and opens the (reservoirs of) ice. Before (using it generally), they offer some in their principal apartment or in the ancestral temple[1].

16. On the first ting day[2] orders are given to the chief director of Music to exhibit the civil dances and unfold the offerings of vegetables[3] (to the inventor of music). The son of Heaven, at the head of the three ducal ministers, his nine high ministers, the feudal princes (at court), and his Great officers, goes in person to see the ceremony. On the second ting[2] day orders are given again to the same chief to enter the college, and practise music (with his pupils).

17. In this month at the (smaller) services of supplication[4] they do not use victims. They use offerings of jade, square and round, and instead (of victims) skins and pieces of silk.

18. If in this second month of spring the governmental proceedings proper to autumn were observed,

[1. Compare vol. iii, page 445. Where there was an ancestral temple, the ice would be presented there. The people who had no such temple might present it before the spirit–tablets of their deceased in their principal apartment, where these were set up.

2. The fourth and fourteenth cycle days.

3. The offerings were small and scanty in this month, fruits not yet being ready for such a use. Cress and tussel–pondweed are mentioned among the vegetables which were presented on this occasion.

4 The received text here means not 'services of supplication,' but sacrifices. That which I have adopted is, found in Zhâi Yung, and is approved by the Khien–lung editors. It is a necessary alteration, for in paragraphs 9 and 15 we have instances of victims used this month at sacrifices. The change in the text is not great in Chinese, the character for .]

there would be great floods, in the states; cold airs would be constantly coming; and plundering attacks would be frequent. If those of winter were observed, the warm and genial airs would be insufficient; the wheat would not ripen; and raids and strifes would be rife among the people. If those of summer were observed, there would be great droughts among the people; the hot airs would come too early; and caterpillars and other insects would harm the grain[1].

PART III.

1. In the last month of spring, the sun is in Wei, the constellation culminating at dusk being Khih hsing, and that culminating at dawn Khien–niû[2].

2. Its days are kiâ and yî. Its divine ruler is Thâi Hâo, and the attending spirit is Kâu–mang. Its creatures are the scaly. Its musical note is the Kio, and its pitch–tube is the Kû Hsien[3]. Its number is eight. Its taste is sour. Its smell is rank.

3. Its sacrifice is that at the door, and of the parts of the victim the spleen has the foremost place.

[1. Before this and the corresponding paragraphs in the Parts of the Book that follow, we must always understand paragraph 23 of the last Part, of which these concluding paragraphs are supposed to be the natural sequence.

2. Wei is the seventeenth of the twenty–eight Chinese constellations (longitude in 1800, 44° 81' 17" corresponding to Musca borealis. Khih–hsing is understood to be {alpha} (Alphard) of Hydra, and small stars near it. Khien–niû corresponds to certain stars ({epsilon}, {mu}, {nu}) in the neck of Aquila.

3. Kû Hsien, 'the lady bathes,' is the third of the tubes that give the six upper musical accords.]

4. The Elaeococca begins to flower[1]. Moles are transformed into quails[2] . Rainbows begin to appear. Duckweed begins to grow.

5. The son of Heaven occupies the apartment on the right of the Khing Yang (Fane); rides in the carriage with the phœnix bells, drawn by the azure dragon–(horses), and bearing the green flag. He is dressed in the green robes, and wears the azure gems. He eats wheat and mutton. The vessels which he uses are slightly carved, (to resemble) the bursting forth (of nature).

6. In this month the son of Heaven presents robes yellow as the young leaves of the mulberry tree to the ancient divine ruler (and his queen)[3].

7. Orders are given to the officer in charge of the boats to turn a boat bottom up. Five times he does so, and five times he turns it back again, after which he reports that it is ready for the son of Heaven, who

[1. This would probably be the Elaeococca vernicia, or Aleurites cordata.

2. This statement, perhaps, arose from seeing quails running about among the mole–hills. The Khien–lung editors say that the quails fly at night, and in the. day keep hidden among the grass; but they seem to admit the transformation. Professor Douglas explains the error from a want of recognition of the migration of quails.

3. Callery translates this by:—'L'empereur offre de la belle jaune de céréales (aux empereurs anciens et modernes qui l'ont précédé),' following a different reading for the article offered. The general view is what I have followed. The offering is supposed to have been in connexion with a sacrifice preparatory to the silkworm season. The rearing of silkworms was due, it was supposed, to Hsî–ling, the wife of the Yellow Tî. He is the 'Ancient Tî' intended here, I suppose. The name is not to be taken as in the plural. See the Khang–hsî, dictionary on the character khü.]

then gets into it for the first time (this spring). He offers a snouted sturgeon (which he has caught) in the rear apartment of the ancestral temple, and also prays that the wheat may yield its produce[1].

8. In this month the influences of life and growth are fully developed; and the warm and genial airs diffuse themselves. The crooked shoots are all put forth, and the buds are unfolded. Things do not admit of being restrained.

9. The son of Heaven spreads his goodness abroad, and carries out his kindly promptings. He gives orders to the proper officers to distribute from his granaries and vaults, giving their contents to the poor and friendless, and to relieve the needy and destitute; and to open his treasuries and storehouses, and to send abroad through all the nation the silks and other articles for presents, thus stimulating the princes of states to encourage the resort to them of famous scholars and show courtesy to men of ability and virtue.

10. In this month, he charges the superintendents of works, saying, 'The rains of the season will be coming down, and the waters beneath will be swelling up. Go in order

over the states and visit the towns, inspecting everywhere the low and level grounds. Put the dykes and dams in good repair, clear the ditches and larger channels, and open all paths, allowing no obstruction to exist.'

[1. The five times repeated inspection of the boat does seem rather ridiculous. We must regard the king's taking to the boat as an encouragement to the fishermen, as his ploughing was to the husbandmen. The long–snouted sturgeon has always been called 'the royal sturgeon.' How the praying for a good wheat harvest seems to be connected with this ceremony I do not know.]

11. The nets used in hunting animals and birds, hand nets, archers' disguises, and injurious baits should not (in this month) issue from (any of) the nine gates[1].

12. In this month orders are given to the foresters throughout the country not to allow the cutting down of the mulberry trees and silk–worm oaks. About these the cooing doves clap their wings, and the crested birds light on them[2] . The trays and baskets with the stands (for the worms and cocoons) are got ready. The queen, after vigil and fasting, goes in person to the eastern fields to work on the mulberry trees. She orders the wives and younger women (of the palace) not to wear their ornamental dresses, and to suspend their woman's–work, thus stimulating them to attend to their business with the worms. When this has been completed, she apportions the cocoons, weighs out (afterwards) the silk, on which they go to work, to supply the robes for the solstitial and other great religious services, and for use in the ancestral temple. Not one is allowed to be idle.

13. In this month orders are given to the chiefs of works, to charge the workmen of their various departments to inspect the materials in the five storehouses:—those of iron and other metals; of skins

[1. 'On each side of the wall of the royal city,' says Lû Tien (early in the Sung dynasty), 'there were three gates.' Wû Khang says, 'The three gates on the south were the chief gates. Generally, such things as are mentioned here might issue from the other gates, but not from these; but in this month they could not issue from any of the nine.' Other explanations of 'the nine gates' have been attempted. The 'baits' (or medicines) were used to attract and to stupefy.

2 Perhaps the hoopoe.]

and hides and sinews; of horn and ivory; of feathers, arrows and wood (for bows); and of grease, glue, cinnabar, and varnish. (They are to see) that all these things be good. The workmen then labour at their several tasks. (The chiefs) inspect their work, and daily give them their orders. They must not produce anything contrary to what the time requires; nor can they practise a licentious ingenuity, which would dissipate the minds of their superiors.

14. In the end of this month a fortunate day is chosen for a grand concert of music. The son of Heaven, at the head of the three ducal ministers, the nine high ministers, the feudal princes (at court), and his great officers, goes in person to witness it.

15. In this month they collect the large, heavy bulls, and fiery stallions, and send them forth to the females in the pasture grounds. They number and make a list of the animals fit for victims, with the foals and calves.

16. Orders are given for the ceremonies against pestilence throughout the city; at the nine gates (also) animals are torn in pieces in deprecation (of the danger):–to secure the full development of the (healthy) airs of the spring[1].

17. If, in this last month of spring, the governmental

[1. Compare Analects X, 10, 2. The ceremonies there referred to were the same as those here, carried out in the villages and, indeed, throughout the land. Diseases prevailing were attributed by superstition to the action of evil spirits, and ridiculous measures adopted to drive them away. Confucius and others, even the government itself, gave countenance to these, seeing, perhaps, that in connexion with them the natural causes of disease would be in a measure dispelled.]

proceedings proper to winter were observed, cold airs would constantly be prevailing; all plants and trees would decay; and in the states there would be great terrors. If those proper to summer were observed, many of the people would suffer from pestilential diseases; the seasonable rains would not fall; and no produce would be derived from the mountains and heights. If those proper to autumn were observed, the sky would be full of moisture and gloom; excessive rains would fall early; and warlike movements would be everywhere arising.

SECTION II. PART 1.

1. In the first month of summer, the sun is in Pî; the constellation culminating at dusk being Yî, and that culminating at dawn Wû–nü[1].

2. Its days are ping and ting[2].

3. Its divine ruler is Yen Tî, and the (attending) spirit is Kû–yung[3].

4. Its creatures are the feathered.

5. Its musical note is Kih, and its pitch–tube is the Kung Lü[4].

6. Its number is seven[5]. Its taste is acrid. Its smell is that of things burning.

[1. Pî is the name for the Hyades, or, more exactly, of six stars in Hyades, with {mu} and {nu} of Taurus; it is the nineteenth of the Chinese constellations. Yî is crater. Wû–nü is not so well identified. Williams says that it is 'a star near the middle of Capricorn,' but others say in Hercules. The R Yâ makes it the same as Hsü–nü. Probably it was a star in the constellation Nü of Aquarius.

2. The third and fourth stem characters of the cycle.

3. Yen Tî ('the blazing Tî') is the dynastic designation of Shan Nang, generally placed next to Fû–hsî in Chinese chronology, and whose date cannot be assigned later than the thirty–first century B.C. Kû–yung in one account is placed before Fû–hsî; in a second, as one of the ministers of Hwang Tî; and in a third, as a son of Khwan–hsü (B.C. 2510–2433). He was 'the Director of Fire,' and had the presidency of summer.

4 Kih is the fourth of the notes of the Chinese scale, and Kung Lü ('the middle Spine') the third of the tubes that give the six lower accords.

5. The number of fire is 2, which + 5, that of earth, = 7.]

7. Its sacrifice is that at the furnace[1]; and of the parts of the victim the lungs have the

foremost place.

8. The green frogs croak. Earth–worms come forth. The royal melons grow[2]. The sow–thistle is in seed.

9. The son of Heaven occupies the apartment on the left of the Ming Thang (Grand Fane); rides in the vermilion carriage, drawn by the red horses with black tails, and bearing the red flag. He is dressed in the red robes, and wears the carnation jade. He eats beans and fowls. The vessels which he uses are tall, (to resemble) the large growth (of things).

10. In this month there takes place the inauguration of summer. Three days before this ceremony, the Grand recorder informs the son of Heaven, saying, 'On such–and–such a day is the inauguration of summer. The energies of the season are most fully seen in fire.' On this the son of Heaven devotes himself to self–purification; and on the day, at the head of the three ducal ministers, the nine high ministers, and his Great officers, he proceeds to meet the summer in the southern suburbs. On their return, rewards are distributed. He grants to the feudal princes (an increase of) territory. Congratulations and gifts proceed, and all are joyful and pleased.

11. Orders are also given to the chief master of

[1. It was natural that they should sacrifice here in the summer. 'The lungs' is the fourth of the five viscera, and 'metal' the fourth of the five elements; but 'fire subdues metal.' This is supposed to account for the prominence given to the lungs in this sacrifice.

2. According to Williams this is the 'common cucumber.']

music to teach the practice of ceremonies and music together.

12. Orders are given to the Grand Peace–maintainer[1] to recommend men of eminence, allow the worthy and good to have free course and bring forward the tall and large. His conferring of rank and regulation of emolument must be in accordance with the position (of the individual).

13. In this month what is long should be encouraged to grow longer, and what is high to grow higher. There should be no injuring or overthrowing of anything; no commencing of works in earth; no sending forth of great multitudes (on expeditions); no cutting down of large trees.

14. In this month the son of Heaven begins to wear thin dolichos cloth.

15. Orders are given to the foresters throughout the country to go forth over the fields and plains, and, for the son of Heaven, to encourage the husbandmen, and stimulate them to work, and not let the season slip by unimproved.

Orders are (also) given to the minister of Instruction to travel in order through the districts to the borders, charging the husbandmen to work vigorously, and not to rest in the towns.

16. In this month they chase away wild animals to prevent them from doing harm to any of the

[1. The 'Grand Peace–maintainer' was a title under the Khin dynasty, and instituted by it, of the Minister of War. The functions of the latter, as described in the last Book, page 234, are in harmony with what is said here. The occurrence of the name bears out the attributing of this Book to Lü Pû–wei.]

(growing) grain; but they should not have a great hunting.

17. When the husbandmen present (the first–fruits of) their wheat, the son of Heaven tastes it along with some pork, first offering a portion in the apartment behind (the hall of the) ancestral temple.

18. In this month they collect and store up the various medicinal herbs. Delicate herbs (now) die; it is the harvest time (even) of the wheat. They decide cases for which the punishments are light; they make short work of small crimes, and liberate those who are in prison for slight offences[1].

19. When the work with the silk–worms is over, the queen presents her cocoons; and the tithe–tax of cocoons generally is collected, according to the number of mulberry trees;

for noble and mean, for old and young there is one law. The object is with such cocoons to provide materials for the robes to be used at the sacrifices in the suburbs and in the ancestral temple.

20. In this month the son of Heaven (entertains his ministers and princes) with strong drink and with (much) observance of ceremony and with music[2].

[1. There does not appear to be any connexion between the first sentence of this paragraph and the remainder of it. The medicinal herbs are collected while all their vigour is in them. For the things in the second sentence the 'summer heats' make a premature harvest; and this seems to lead to the third topic,—the saving those charged with slight offences from the effects of that heat in confinement.

2 The Khien–lung editors have a note here, which is worth quoting, to the effect that as the great solstitial sacrifices and the seasonal sacrifices of the ancestral temple do not appear in this Book, the drinking here was at court entertainments.]

21. If, in this first month of summer, the proceedings proper to autumn were observed, pitiless rains would be frequent; the five esculent plants[1] would not grow large, and in all the borders people would have to enter the places of shelter. If those proper to winter were observed, all plants and trees would wither early, and afterwards, there would be great floods, destroying city and suburban walls. If those proper to spring were observed, there would be the calamity of locusts, violent winds would come, and plants in flower would not go on to seed.

PART II.

1. In the second month of summer the sun is in the eastern Zing, the constellation culminating at dusk being Khang, and that culminating at dawn Wei[2].

2. Its days are ping and ting. Its divine ruler is Yen Tî, and the (attending) spirit is Khû–yung. Its creatures are the feathered. Its musical note is Kih, and its pitch–tube is Sui Pin[3].

3. Its number is seven. Its taste is acrid. Its smell is that of things burning. Its sacrifice is

that at the furnace; and of the parts of the victim the lungs have the foremost place.

4. The (period of) slighter heat arrives; the praying mantis is produced; the shrike begins to give its notes; the mocking–bird ceases to sing[4].

[1. Hemp or flax, millet, rice, bearded grain, and pulse.

2. Zing comprehends {gamma}, {epsilon}, {xi}, {lambda}, {mu},{nu} Gemini; Khang, {iota}, {kappa}, {lambda}, {mu}, {rho} Virgo; and Wei corresponds to {alpha}, Aquarius, and {epsilon}, {theta}, Pegasus.

3. Sui Pin, 'the flourishing Guest,' is the fourth of the tubes that give the six upper musical accords.

4. This is here 'the inverted Tongue.' The Khang–hsî dictionary says it is the same as 'the hundred Tongues;' the Chinese mocking–bird.]

5. The son of Heaven occupies the Ming Thang Grand Fane; rides in the vermilion carriage, drawn by the red horses with black tails, and bearing the red flag. He is dressed in the red robes, and wears the carnation gems. He eats beans and fowls. The vessels which he uses are tall, (to resemble) the large growth (of things).

6. They encourage the (continued) growth of what is strong and beautiful'.

7. In this month orders are given to the music–masters to put in repair the hand–drums, smaller drums, and large drums; to adjust the lutes, large and small, the double flutes, and the pan–pipes; to teach the holding of the shields, pole–axes, lances, and plumes; to tune the organs, large and small, with their pipes and tongues; and to put in order the bells, sonorous stones, the instrument to give the symbol for commencing, and the stopper[2].

8. Orders are given to the (proper) officers to pray for the people and offer sacrifice to the (spirits of the) hills, streams, and all springs. (After that) comes the great summer sacrifice for rain to God, when all

[1. Kû Hsî would remove this paragraph to the thirteenth of the last Part. It seems to me to be in its proper place.

2. See vol. iii, p. 324. The stopper is represented thus:—

{illustration}

It was made to sound by a metal rod drawn along the spinous back. I have seen a similar instrument, used for the same purpose, brought from Madras.]

the instruments of music are employed. Then orders are given throughout all the districts to sacrifice to the various princes, high ministers, and officers who benefited the people; praying that there may be a good harvest of grain[1].

9. The husbandmen present (the first–fruits of) their millet; and in this month the son of Heaven partakes of it along with pullets, and with cherries set forth beside them, first offering a portion in the apartment behind the ancestral temple.

10. The people are forbidden to cut down the indigo plant to use it in dyeing[2],

11. Or to burn wood for charcoal, or to bleach cloth in the sun.

12. The gates of cities and villages should not be shut[3], nor should vexatious inquiries be instituted at the barrier gates or in the markets.

[1. The first and last of the three sacrificial services in the paragraph were subsidiary to the second, the great praying for rain to God by the sovereign; the motive is not mentioned in the text, but only he could conduct a service to God. Callery renders:—'En même temps l'empereur invoque le ciel auec grand apparat (afin d'obtenir de la pluie), et cette cérémonie est accompagnée de grande musique.' All Chinese commentators admit that the performer was the sovereign. Kang Khang–khang says: 'For this sacrifice to God, they made an altar (or altars) by the side of the (grand altar in the) southern suburb, and sacrificed to the five essential (or elemental) gods with the former rulers as their assessors.' But the Khien–lung editors insist on the text's having ' God,' and not ' five gods,' and that the correct view is that the sacrifice was to the one God dwelling in the bright sky, or, as Williams renders the phrase, 'the Shang Tî of the glorious heaven.'

2. The plant would not yet be fully fit for use.

3. Every facility should be afforded for the circulation of air during the summer heats.]

13. Leniency should be shown to prisoners charged (even) with great crimes, and their allowance of food be increased[1].

14. Impregnated mares are collected in herds by themselves, and the fiery stallions are tied up. The rules for the rearing of horses are given out.

15. In this month the longest day arrives. The influences in nature of darkness and decay and those 'Of brightness and growth struggle together; the tendencies to death and life are divided[2]. Superior men give themselves to vigil and fasting. They keep retired in their houses, avoid all violent exercise, restrain their indulgence in music and beautiful sights, eschew the society of their wives, make their diet spare, use no piquant condiments, keep their desires under rule, and maintain their spirits free from excitement. The various magistrates keep things quiet and inflict no punishments[3];—to bring about that state of settled quiet in which the influence of darkness and decay shall obtain its full development.

16. Deer shed their horns. Cicadas begin to sing. The midsummer herb is produced. The tree hibiscus flowers[4].

17. In this month fires should not be lighted (out of doors) in the southern regions (of the country).

[1. The leniency would be seen in the lightening of their fetters for one thing,—in consequence of the exhaustion produced by the season.

2. Decay begins to set in, while growth and vigour seek to maintain their hold.

3. The Khien–lung editors approve a reading here, which means, instead of 'no punishments,' 'no rash or hurried action.'

4. The 'tree hibiscus' is the 'hibiscus syriacus.' The 'half–summer herb' is medicinal. It is 'white, with round seeds, and of a hot and pungent taste.']

18. People may live in buildings high and bright. They may enjoy distant prospects. They may ascend hills and heights. They may occupy towers and lofty pavilions[1].

19. If, in the second month of summer, the governmental proceedings of winter were observed, hail and told would injure the grain; the roads would not be passable; and violent assaults of war would come. If the proceedings proper to spring were observed, the grains would be late in ripening; all kinds of locusts would continually be appearing; and there would be famine in the states. If those proper to autumn were observed, herbs and plants would drop their leaves; fruits would ripen prematurely; and the people would be consumed by pestilence.

PART III.

I. In the third month of summer the sun is in Liû, the constellation culminating at dusk being Kwo, and that culminating at dawn Khwei[2].

2. Its days are ping and ting. Its divine ruler is Yen Tî, and the (assisting) spirit is Khû–yung. Its musical note is Kih, and its pitch–tube is Lin Kung[3].

[1. At the beginning of this paragraph there should be—'In this month.'

2. Liû comprehends {delta}, {epsilon}, {eta}, {theta}, {rho}, {sigma} and {omega} Hydræ; Hwo is the same as Hsin, the fifth of the Chinese zodiacal constellations comprehending Antares, {sigma}, {tau}, and two C. 2584, 2587, Scorpio; Khwei (as stated above, p. 257) comprehends {beta} (Mirac), {delta}, {epsilon}, {xi}, {mu}, {nu}, {pi} of Andromeda, and some stars of Pisces.

3. The fourth of the tubes that give the six lower musical accords.]

3. Its number is seven. Its taste is acrid. Its smell is that of things burning. Its sacrifice is that at the furnace; and of the parts of the victim the lungs have the foremost place.

4. Gentle winds begin to blow. The cricket takes its place in the walls. (Young) hawks learn to practise (the ways of their parents).[1] Decaying grass becomes fire–flies.

5. The son of Heaven occupies the apartment on the right of the Ming Thang (Fane); rides in the vermilion carriage, drawn by the red horses with black tails, and bearing the red flag. He is dressed in the red robes, and wears the carnation gems. He eats beans and fowls. The vessels which he uses are tall, (to resemble) the large growth (of things).

6. Orders are given to the master of the Fishermen to attack the alligator, to take the gavial, to present the tortoise, and to take the great turtle[2].

7. Orders are given to the superintendent of the Meres to collect and send in the rushes available for use.

8. In this month orders are given to the four

[1. Compare what is said about hawks in paragraph 4, page 258. 'Here,' says Wang Thao, 'we have the turtle–doves transformed back to hawks, showing that the former notice was metaphorical.' What is said about the fire–flies is, of course, a mistaken fancy.

2. The first of these animals—the kiâo—is, probably, the alligator or crocodile it was taken only after a struggle or fight. The second—the tho—had a skin used in making drums; and its flesh, as well as that of the fourth—the yûan—was used in making soup.]

inspectors[1] to make a great collection over all the districts of the different kinds of fodder to nourish the sacrificial victims; and to require all the people to do their utmost towards this end;–to supply what is necessary for (the worship of) God (who dwells in) the great Heaven, and for the spirits of the famous hills, great streams, and four quarters, and for the sacrifices to the Intelligences of the ancestral temple, and at the altars to the spirits of the land and grain; that prayer may be made for blessing to the people.

9. In this month orders are given by the officers of women's (work), on the subject of dyeing[2]. (They are to see) that the white and black, the black and green, the green and carnation, the carnation and white be all according to the ancient rules, without error or change; and that their black, yellow, azure, and carnation be all genuine and good, without any presumptuous attempts at imposition. These furnish the materials for the robes used at the sacrifices in the suburbs and the ancestral temple; for flags and their ornaments; and for marking the different degrees of rank as high or low.

10. In this month the trees are luxuriant; and orders are given to the foresters to go among the hills and examine the trees, and see that the people do not cut any down or lop their branches[3].

[1. Of hills, forests, rivers, and meres.

2. We find full details of the number and duties of the superintendents of women's work, with its tailoring, dyeing, and other things, in the Kâu Lî, Books I and VII.

3. The Khien–lung editors say that this was to let the process of growth have its full course; and, besides, that wood cut down in spring and summer will be found full of insects.]

11. There should not be any work in earth[1], (now) undertaken; nor any assembling of the princes of the states; nor any military movements, causing general excitement. There should be no undertaking of (such) great affairs, which will disturb the nourishing growth that is proceeding, nor any issuing of orders to be hereafter carried into effect. All these things will interfere with the business of husbandry, (which is specially dear to) the Spirits[2] . The floods are now great and overflow the roads; husbandry (dear to) the Spirits has to take in hand its various tasks. The curse of Heaven will come on the undertaking of great affairs (at this time).

[1. Such as building walls and fortifications, or laying out the ground.

2. The text is—'will interfere with the business of Shan Nang.' How is it that 'husbandry' has here the epithet of Shan, or 'spiritual,' 'mysterious,' applied to it? The Khien–lung editors say:–'Zhâi Yung (our second century) makes Shan Nang to be Yen Tî (the divine ruler of the summer). Kang made the name to be that of "the spirit of the ground." Kâo Yû (second century) took it as a name for the minister of Husbandry. To some extent each of these views might be admitted, but none of them is very certain. Looking carefully at the text it simply says that no great undertakings should be allowed to interfere with husbandry. That it does not plainly say husbandry, but calls it the Shan husbandry, is from a sense of its importance, and therefore making it out to be Spirit–sanctioned. Heaven produced the people, and the grain to nourish them; is not sowing and reaping the business of Heaven? When a ruler knows this, he feels that he is under the inspection of Heaven in his reverent regard of the people, and the importance

which he attaches to husbandry. He will not dare lightly to use the people's strength, so as to offend against Heaven.' I have tried to bring out their view in my version.]

12. In this month the ground lies steaming and wet beneath the heats, for great rains are (also) continually coming. They burn the grass lying cut upon the ground[1] and bring the water over it. This is as effectual to kill the roots as hot water would be; and the grass thus serves to manure the fields of grain and hemp, and to fatten the ground which has been but just marked out for cultivation.

13. If, in the last month of summer, the governmental proceedings proper to spring were observed, the produce of grain would be scanty and fail; in the states there would be many colds and coughs; and the people would remove to other places. If the proceedings proper to autumn were observed, even the high grounds would be flooded; the grain that had been sown would not ripen; and there would be many miscarriages among women. If those proper to winter were observed, the winds and cold would come out of season; the hawks and falcons would prematurely attack their prey; and all along the four borders people would enter their places of shelter.

SUPPLEMENTARY SECTION.

1. Right in the middle (between. Heaven and Earth, and the other elements) is earth.

2. Its days are wû and kî.

3. Its divine ruler is Hwang Tî, and the (attending) spirit is Hâu–thû.

[1. Compare what is said on the duties of those who cut the grass, as is here assumed to be done, in the Kâu Lî, Book XXXVII, paragraphs 80, 81.]

4. Its creature is that without any natural covering but the skin.

5. Its musical note is Kung, and its pitch–tube gives the kung note from the tube Hwang Kung.

6. Its number is five. Its taste is sweet. Its smell is fragrant.

7. Its sacrifice is that of the middle court; and of the parts of the victim the heart has the foremost place.

8. The son of Heaven occupies the Grand apartment of the Grand fane; rides in the great carriage drawn by the yellow horses with black tails, and bearing the yellow flag; is clothed in the yellow robes, and wears the yellow gems. He eats panicled millet and beef. The vessels which he uses are round, (and made to resemble) the capacity (of the earth)[1].

[1. I have called this a supplementary section. It is dropt in, in all its brevity, without mention of any proceedings of government, between the end of summer and the beginning of autumn. It has all the appearance of an after–thought, suggested by the superstitious fancies of the compiler. Callery says on it:—

'This passage can only be comprehended by help of the intimate affinities which Chinese philosophers have attributed to the different beings of nature. According to them, the four seasons are related to the four cardinal points: spring to the east, summer to the south, autumn to the west, and winter to the north. Each of the cardinal points is related to an element: the east to wood, the south to fire, the west to metal, and the north to water. But as there is a fifth element, that of earth, and the four cardinal points have no reason for being distinguished as they are, but that there is a point in the middle between them, which is still the earth, it follows from this that the earth ought to have its place in the midst of the four seasons, that is, at the point of separation between summer and autumn. Here a difficulty presented itself. The bamboo flutes to which the Chinese months are referred being but twelve, where shall be found the musical affinities of the earth? But the Chinese philosopher did not find himself embarrassed. See how he reasoned. The sound of the first flute, that is, of the longest and largest, is the strongest and most grave, and, like a bass, harmonizes with all the other sounds more acute. So the earth, likewise, is the most important of all the elements; it extends towards all the cardinal points, and intervenes in the products of each season. Hence the earth ought to correspond to the sound of the first flute! These affinities extend to colours, tastes, and a crowd of other categories.'

The Khien–lung editors say:—

Speaking from the standpoint of Heaven, then the earth is in the midst of Heaven; that is, (the element of) earth. Speaking from the standpoint of the Earth, then wood, fire, metal, and water are all supported on it. The manner in which the way of Earth is affected by that of Heaven cannot be described by reference to one point, or one month. Speaking from the standpoint of the heavenly stems, then wû and kî occupy the middle places, and are between the stems for fire and metal, to convey the system of mutual production. Speaking from the standpoint of the "earthly branches," the khan, hsü, khâu, and wi occupy the corners of the four points; wood, fire, metal, and water, all turn to earth. This is what the idea of reciprocal ending, and that of elemental flourishing, arise from. This may be exhibited in the several points, and reckoned by the periods of days. The talk about the elements takes many directions, but the underlying principle comes to be the same!'

I shall be glad if my readers can understand this.]

SECTION III. PART I.

1. In the first month of autumn, the sun is in Yî the constellation culminating at dusk being Kien–hsing, and that culminating at dawn Pî[1].

2. Its days are kang and hsin.

3. Its divine ruler is Shâo Hâo, and the (attending) spirit is Zû–shâu[2].

4. Its creatures are the hairy.

5. Its musical note is Shang; its pitch–tube is Î Zeh[3].

6. Its number is nine. Its taste is bitter. Its smell is rank.

7. Its sacrifice is that at the gate; and of the parts of the victim the liver has the foremost place.

8. Cool winds come; the white dew descends[4] the cicada of the cold chirps[5]. (Young) hawks at this

[1. Yî corresponds to Crater. Kien–hsing comprehends stars in Sagittarius (see page 257). Pî corresponds to the Hyades.

2. Shâo Hâo follows Hwang Tî, whose eldest son he was, as the fourth in the list of the five Tî, or divine rulers (B.C. 2594). His capital was at Khü–fâu, the city of Confucius; and I have seen, at a little distance from it, perhaps the only pyramid in China, which is in memory of him, and said to be on or near his grave. His personal appellation is Kin–thien or Thien–kin, the element to which he and his reign are assigned being kin, or metal. Zû–shâu was one of his sons.

3. Î Zeh, 'the equalization of the Laws,' is the tube giving the fifth of the upper musical accords.

4. White dew is a name for hoar–frost.

5. This cicada (Williams thinks the cicada viridis) is called 'the dumb.' Now it begins to chirp. Its colour is 'green and red.']

time sacrifice birds, as the first step they take to killing (and eating) them[1].

9. The son of Heaven occupies the apartment on the left of the Zung–kang (Fane); rides in the war chariot, drawn by the white horses with black manes, and bearing the white flag. He is clothed in the white robes, and wears the white jade. He eats hemp–seeds and dog's flesh. The vessels which he uses are rectangular, and going on to be deep[2].

10. In this month there takes place the inauguration of autumn. Three days before the ceremony) the Grand recorder informs the son of Heaven, saying, 'On such–and–such a day is the inauguration of the autumn. The character of the season is fully seen in metal.' On this the son of Heaven devotes himself to self–adjustment; and on the day he leads in person the three ducal ministers, the nine high ministers, the princes of states (at court), and his Great officers, to meet the autumn in the western suburb, and on their return he rewards the general–in–chief, and the military officers in the court.

11. The son of Heaven also orders the leaders and commanders to choose men and sharpen weapons, to select and exercise those of distinguished merit, and

[1. Compare what is said about the otter, page 251.

2. Zung-kang is made out to mean, 'all bright,' and the apartment was on the west; with mystical reference to the maturity and gathering of all things in the autumn, or season of the west. The vessels were rectangular, having sharp corners in harmony with the sharp weapons made of metal, to which element the season of autumn is referred; and they were deep, to resemble the deep bosom of the earth, to which things now begin to return.]

to give their entire trust only to men whose services have been proved;—thereby to correct all unrighteousness. (He instructs them also) to make enquiries about and punish the oppressive and insolent;—thereby making it clear whom he loves and whom he hates, and giving effect to (the wishes of) the people, even the most distant from court.

12. In this month orders are given to the proper officers to revise the laws and ordinances, to put the prisons in good repair, to provide handcuffs and fetters, to repress and stop villainy, to maintain a watch against crime and wickedness, and to do their endeavour to capture criminals. Orders are (also) given to the managers (of prisons) to look at wounds, examine sores, inspect broken members, and judge particularly of dislocations. The determination of cases, both criminal and civil, must be correct and just. Heaven and earth now begin to be severe; there should be no excess in copying that severity, or in the opposite indulgence[1].

13. In this month the husbandmen present their grain. The son of Heaven tastes it, while still new, first offering some in the apartment at the back of the ancestral temple.

14. Orders are given to all the officers to begin their collecting and storing the contributions (from

[1. For this last sentence Callery has:—'(Ce mois-ci) la nature commencant à devenir rigoureuse, on ne doit pas augmenter (ses rigeurs par l'application de châtiments trop sévères).' Wang Thâo takes an opposite view. I think I have got the thought that was in the compiler's mind. See the note of the Khien-lung editors with reference to the advocacy of it by commentators of 'the Brief Calendar of Hsiâ.']

the husbandmen); to finish the embankments and dykes; to look to the dams and fillings up in preparation for the floods, and also to refit all houses; to strengthen walls and enclosures; and to repair city and suburban walls.

15. In this month there should be no investing of princes, and no appointment of great ministers. There should be no dismemberment of any territory, no sending out on any great commission, and no issuing of great presents.

16. If, in this first month of autumn, the proceedings of government proper to winter were observed, then the dark and gloomy influence (of nature) would greatly prevail; the shelly insects would destroy the grain; and warlike operations would be called for. If the proceedings proper to spring were observed, there would be droughts in the states; the bright and growing influence would return; and the five kinds of grain would not yield their fruit. If the proceedings proper to summer were observed, there would be many calamities from fire in the states; the cold and the heat would be subject to no rule; and there would be many fevers among the people.

PART II.

1. In the second month of autumn the sun is in Kio, the constellation culminating at dusk being Khien–niû, and that culminating at dawn Dze–hsî,.

2. Its days are kang and hsin. Its divine ruler

[1. Kio corresponds to {alpha} (Spica) and {zeta} of Virgo; Khien–niû (see on page 262) to certain stars in the neck of Aquila; and Dze–hsî is said to be {lambda} Orion.

is Shâo Hâo, and the (attending) spirit is Zû–shâu. Its insects are the hairy. Its musical note is Shang, and its pitch–tube is Nan Lü[1].

3. Its number is nine. Its taste is bitter. Its smell is rank. Its sacrifice is that of the gate; and of the parts of the victim the liver has the foremost place.

4. Sudden and violent winds come. The wild geese arrive. The swallows return (whence they came)[2]. Tribes of birds store up provisions (for the future)[3].

5. The son of Heaven occupies the Zung–kang Grand Fane; rides in the war chariot,

drawn by the white horses with black manes, and bearing the white flag. He is clothed in the white robes, and wears the white gems. He eats hemp–seed and dog's flesh. The vessels which he uses are rectangular or cornered, and rather deep.

6. In this month they take especial care of the

[1. Nan Lü, 'the southern spine,' is the tube that gives the fifth of the lower musical accords.

2. The wild geese are now returning to their winter quarters, from which they had come in the first month of spring; see page 251. So with the swallows, who had appeared in the second month of spring; see page 259.

3 This sentence is hardly translatable or intelligible. Some would read as in paragraph 95 of 'the Brief Calendar of Hsiâ', translated by Professor Douglas: 'The red birds (i. e. fire–flies) devour the white birds (i. e. mosquitoes),' which be ingeniously supports by a reference to the habits of the fire–fly from Chambers' Encyclopædia. But his translation of hsiû by 'devour' is inadmissible. Wang Thâo says that this view is 'chisseling.' 'Sparrows and other birds,' he says, 'now collect seeds of grapes and trees, and store them in their nests and holes against the time of rain and snow.']

decaying and old; give them stools and staves, and distribute supplies of congee for food.

7. Orders are given to the superintendent of robes to have ready the upper and lower dresses with their various ornaments. For the figures and embroidery on them there are fixed patterns. Their size, length, and dimensions must all be according to the old examples. For the caps and girdles (also) there are regular rules.

8. Orders are given to the proper officers to revise with strict accuracy (the laws about) the various punishments. Beheading and (the other) capital executions must be according to (the crimes) without excess or defect. Excess or defect out of such proportion will bring on itself the judgment (of Heaven).

9. In this month orders are given to the officers of slaughter and prayer to go round among the victims for sacrifice, seeing that they are entire and complete, examining their fodder and grain, inspecting their condition as fat or thin, and judging of their looks. They

must arrange them according to their classes. In measuring their size, and looking at the length (of their horns), they must have them according to the (assigned) measures. When all these points are as they ought to be, God will accept the sacrifices[1].

10. The son of Heaven performs the ceremonies against pestilence, to secure development for the (healthy) airs of autumn.

11. He eats the hemp–seed (which is now presented)

[1. Kang says here: 'And if God accept them, of course there is no other spirit that will not do so.']

along with dog's flesh, first offering some in the apartment at the back of the ancestral temple.

12. In this month it is allowable to rear city and suburban walls, to establish cities and towns, to dig underground passages and grain–pits, and to repair granaries, round and square.

13. Orders are given to the proper officers to be urgent with the people, and (to finish) receiving their contributions and storing them. They should do their best to accumulate (large) stores of vegetables and other things.

14. They should (also) stimulate the wheat–sowing. (The husbandmen) should not be allowed to miss the proper time for the operation. Any who do so shall be punished without fail.

15. In this month day and night are equal. The thunder begins to restrain its voice. Insects stop up the entrances to their burrows. The influence to decay and death gradually increases. That of brightness and growth daily diminishes. The waters begin to dry up.

16. At the equinox, they make uniform the measures of length and capacity; equalise the steel–yards and their weights; rectify the weights of 30 and 120 catties; and adjust the pecks and bushels.

17. In this month they regulate and reduce the charges at the frontier gates and in the markets, to encourage the resort of both regular and travelling traders, and the receipt of goods and money; for the convenience of the business of the people. When merchants and others collect from all quarters, and come from the most distant parts, then the resources (of the government) do not fail. There is no want of means for its use; and all things proceed prosperously.

18. In commencing great undertakings, there should be no opposition to the great periods (for them) as defined (by the motion of the sun). They must be conformed to the times (as thereby marked out), and particular attention paid to the nature of each[1].

19. If in this second month of autumn the proceedings proper to spring were observed, the autumnal

[1. Callery translates this paragraph by: 'Toute personne ayant une chose importante à accomplir ne doit pas se mettre en opposition avec les grands principes (yin et yang); il doit se conformer au temps (propre à agir; mais il doit aussi) bien examiner la nature même de l'entreprise.' He appends to this the following note:—'Les deux principes yin et yang auxquels se rapportent tous les êtres, ayant tour–à–tour la prédominance dans certaines époques de l'année, le temps convenable pour une chose quelconque est celui auquel prédomine le principe dont cette chose dépend par son affinité naturelle. Ainsi, par exemple, les travaux de terrassement et de construction conviennent en automne, parce que le principe yin dont ils dépendent est en progrès pendant l'automne. Néanmoins, de ce que cette époque de l'année est favorable sous ce point de vue, il ne s'ensuit pas que toute entreprise de construction faite en automne soit avantageuse en elle–même; une foule de circonstances peuvent la rendre ruineuse, et c'est à l'entrepreneur de bien l'examiner, abstraction faite de la saison.'

The text rendered by Callery, 'les deux principes (yin et yang),' is simply tâ shû, 'the grand numbers,' the meaning of which I have endeavoured to bring out by the supplements in my version. The yin and yang are not mentioned in the text of the paragraph. They are simply a binomial phrase for the course of nature, with special reference to the weather and its conditions, as regulated by the action of the sun on the earth in the coarse of the seasons.]

rains would not fall; plants and trees would blossom; and in the states there would be alarms. If those proper to summer were observed, there would be droughts in the states; insects would not retire to their burrows; and the five grains would begin to grow again. If those proper to winter were observed, calamities springing from (unseasonable) winds would be constantly arising; the thunder now silent would be heard before its time; and plants and trees would die prematurely.

PART III.

1. In the last month of autumn the sun is in Fang, the constellation culminating at dusk being Hsü [1], and that culminating at dawn Liû.

2. Its days are kang and hsin. Its divine ruler is Shâo Hâo, and the (attending) spirit is 3û-shâu. Its creatures are the hairy. Its musical note is Shang, and its pitch-tube is Wû Yî[2].

3. Its number is nine. Its taste is bitter. Its smell is rank. Its sacrifice is that at the gate; and of the parts of the victim the liver has the foremost place.

4. The wild geese come, (and abide) like guests[3].

[1. Fang comprehends {beta}, {delta}, {pi}, {rho} Scorpio. Hsü corresponds to {beta} Aquarius; and Liû comprehends {delta}, {epsilon}, {zeta}, {eta}, {rho}, {sigma}, {phi} Hydra.

2. Wû Yî, 'the unwearied,' is the tube giving the sixth upper musical accord.

3. The addition of guests here is a difficulty. It is said on the previous month that 'the wild geese come;' are these here the same as those, or are they others,—the younger birds, as some suppose, which had waited after the former, and still found it necessary to remain on their passage to recruit their strength?]

Small birds enter the great water and become mollusks[1]. Chrysanthemums show their yellow flowers. The khâi sacrifice larger animals, and kill (and devour) the smaller[2].

5. The son of Heaven occupies the apartment on the right of the Zung-kang (Fane); rides in the war chariot, drawn by the white horses with black manes, and bearing the white flags; is dressed in the white robes, and wears the white jade. He eats hemp-seeds and dog's flesh. The vessels which he uses are rectangular, cornered, and rather deep.

6. In this month the orders are renewed and

[1. Professor Douglas has made it more than probable that the 'small birds' here are sand-pipers. What is said about them, however, will, not admit of his version, that they 'go into the sea or lakes for crustaceae.' His 'crustaceae' should be 'mollusks.' According to all rules of Chinese composition, what he renders 'for' must be taken verbally, = 'to become.' It is not merely the Chinese 'commentators,' who consider the sentence to mean, 'Sparrows go into the sea and become crustaceae (? mollusks);' it is what the text says. It is indeed an absurd statement, but a translator is not responsible for that. The Khien-lung editors observe that there is no mention here of the little birds being 'transformed,' as in the paragraph about the 'hawks' on page 258, and hence they argue that we cannot understand the notice here metaphorically. They accept the fact (?). The marine Ko, which is mentioned here, as figured in the plates of the Pan Zhâo Kang-mû, is the Calyptroida Trochita.

2. Compare what is said. about the otter, page 251. Professor Douglas argues that the khâi is the polecat. But this identification cannot yet be received as certain. The khâi is 'dogfooted,' 'hunts in troops,' and has 'a voice like that of the dog.' In Japanese plates it is not at all like 'the polecat.' An English naturalist, to whom I submitted a Japanese work illustrative of the Shih King, many years ago, has written over the khâi, 'a wild dog or wolf.']

strictly enjoined, charging the various, officers (to see) that noble and mean all exert themselves in the work of ingathering, in harmony with the storing of heaven and earth. They must not allow anything to remain out in the fields.

7. Orders are also given to the chief minister, after the fruits of husbandry have all been gathered in, to take in hand the registers of the produce of the different grains (from all the country), and to store up the produce that has been gathered from the acres of God in the granary of the spirits; doing this with the utmost reverence and correctness[1].

8. In this month the hoar–frost begins to fall; and all labours cease (for a season).

9. Orders are given to the proper officers, saying, 'The cold airs are all coming, and the people will not be able to endure them. Let all enter within their houses (for a time).'

10. On the first ting day orders are given to the chief Director of music to enter the college, and to practise (with his pupils) on the wind instruments.

11. In this month an announcement is made to the son of Heaven that the victims for the great sacrifice to God, and the autumnal sacrifice in the ancestral temple' are fit and ready.

[1. This,' says Hsü sze–zang (Ming dynasty), 'is the great rule of making provision for the sustenance of men and for serving spiritual beings,—two things demanding the utmost inward reverence and outward reverential vigour.' I suppose that the 'spirit–granary' contained the grain for all governmental sacrifices, as well as that gathered from 'the acres of God,' and to be used specially in sacrifices to Him.

2. This paragraph gives great trouble to the Khien–lung editors but we need not enter on their discussions.]

12. The princes of the states are assembled, and orders given to the officers of the various districts (in the royal domain). They receive the first days of the months for the coming year[1], and the laws for the taxation of the people by the princes, both light and heavy, and the amount of the regular contribution to the government, which is determined by the distance of the territories and the nature of their several productions. The object of this is to provide what is necessary for the suburban sacrifices and those in the ancestral temple. No private considerations are allowed to have place in this.

13. In this month the son of Heaven, by means of hunting, teaches how to use the five weapons of war, and the rules for the management of horses.

14. Orders are given to the charioteers and the seven (classes of) grooms[2] to see to the yoking of the several teams, to set up in the carriages the flags and various banners[3], to assign the carriages according to the rank (of those who were to occupy them), and to arrange and set up the screens outside (the royal tent). The minister of Instruction, with

his baton

[1. This last month of autumn, the ninth from the first month of spring, was the last month of the year with the dynasty of Zhin, when it was high time to give out the calendar for the months of the next year.

2. The sovereign's horses were divided into six classes, and every class had its own grooms, with one among them who had the superintendence of the rest. See a narrative in the Zo Kwan, under the eighteenth year of duke Khang.

3. Two of these insignia are mentioned in the text;—the Zing, which was only a pennant, and the Kâo, a large banner with a tortoise and serpent intertwined. No doubt the meaning is, 'the various banners,']

stuck in his girdle, addresses all before him with his face to the north.

15. Then the son of Heaven, in his martial ornaments, with his bow in one hand, and the arrows under the armpit of the other, proceeds to hunt. (Finally), he gives orders to the superintendent of Sacrifices, to offer some of the captured game to (the spirits of) the four quarters.

16. In this month the plants and trees become yellow and their leaves fall, on which the branches are cut down to make charcoal.

17. Insects in their burrows all try to push deeper, and from within plaster up the entrances. In accordance with (the season), they hurry on the decision and punishment of criminal cases, wishing not to leave them any longer undealt with. They call in emoluments that have been assigned incorrectly, and minister to those whose means are insufficient for their wants.

18. In this month the son of Heaven eats dog's flesh and rice, first presenting some in the apartment at the back of the ancestral temple.

19. If, in this last month of autumn, the proceedings proper to summer were observed, there would be great floods in the states; the winter stores would be injured and damaged; there would be many colds and catarrhs among the people. If those proper to winter were

observed, there would be many thieves and robbers in the states; the borders would be unquiet; and portions of territory would be torn from the rest. If those proper to spring were observed, the warm airs would come; the energies of the people would be relaxed and languid; and the troops would be kept moving about.

SECTION IV. PART I.

1. In the first month of winter the sun is in Wei, the constellation culminating at dusk being Wei, and the constellation culminating at dawn Khih–hsing[1].

2. Its days are the zan and kwei.

3. Its divine ruler is Kwan–hsü, and the (attending) spirit is Hsüan–ming[2].

4. Its creatures are the shell–covered.

5. Its musical note is Yu, and its pitch–tube is Ying Kung[3].

6. Its number is six. Its taste is salt. Its smell is that of things that are rotten.

7. Its sacrifice is that at (the altar of) the path, and

[1. Wei comprehends {epsilon}, {mu} Scorpio; Wei (, as on page 272) corresponds to stars in Aquarius and Pegasus. Khih Hsing (as on p. 262) corresponds to stars in Hydra.

2. Kwan–hsü is the dynastic designation of the grandson of Hwang Tî, the commencement of whose reign is, assigned in B.C. 2510. He is known also by the personal designation of Kâo–yang, from the name of his second capital. Among the elements his reign is assigned to water, and thence to the north; and hence the designation of his minister as Hsüan–ming, 'the dark and mysterious,' who was called Hsiû and Hsî (##), and is said to have been a son of Shâo Hâo.

3. Yü is the fifth of the notes of the scale; and Ying Kung, 'the responsive tube,' the name of the last of the tubes giving the six lower musical accords.]

among the parts of the victim the kidneys have the foremost place[1].

8. Water begins to congeal. The earth begins to be penetrated by the cold. Pheasants enter the great water and become large mollusks[2]. Rainbows are hidden and do not appear.

9. The son of Heaven occupies the apartment on the left of the Hsüan Thang (Fane); rides in the dark–coloured carriage, drawn by the iron black horses, and bearing the dark–coloured flag; is dressed in the black robes, and wears the dark–coloured jade. He eats millet and sucking–pig. The vessels which he uses are large and rather deep.

10. In this month there takes place the inauguration of winter. Three days before this ceremony, the Grand recorder informs the son of Heaven, saying, 'On such–and–such a day is the inauguration of winter. The character of the season is fully seen in

[1. This altar was outside the gate leading to the ancestral temple, on the, west of it. Many say that here was the 'well' supplying the water used for the temple, and would read zang for hsing.

2. The 'great water' here is said in the 'Narratives of the States' (Book XV) to be the Hwâi. The khan is said to be a large species of the ko, into which small birds are transformed (p. 292). Of course the transmutation of the pheasants into these is absurd. Professor Douglas has found in a Chinese Encyclopædia a statement that khan is sometimes an equivalent of phû lû, 'sweet flags and rushes.' The lû, however, is sometimes read lo, and said to have the same sound and meaning as 'a spiral univalve;' but the great objection to Professor Douglas' view is the meaning he puts on the as pointed out on p. 292. The text cannot be construed as he proposes.]

water.' On this the son of Heaven devotes himself to self–adjustment; and on the day of the inauguration he leads in person the three ducal ministers, the nine high ministers, and his Great officers to meet the winter in the northern suburbs. On his return he rewards (the descendants of) those who died in the service (of the kingdom), and shows his compassion to orphans and widows.

11. In this month orders are given to the Grand recorder to smear with blood the tortoise–shells and divining stalks', and by interpreting the indications of the former and examining the figures formed by the latter, to determine the good and evil of their

intimations. (In this way) all flattery and partizanship in the interpretation of them (will become clear), and the crime of the: operators be brought home. No concealment or deceit will be allowed.

12. In this month the son of Heaven sets the example of wearing furs.

13. Orders are issued to the proper officers in the words:—'The airs of heaven are ascended on high, and those of earth have descended beneath. There is no intercommunion of heaven and earth. All is shut up and winter is completely formed.'

14. Orders are given to all the officers to cover up carefully the stores (of their departments). The minister of Instruction is also ordered to go round (among the people and see) that they have formed their stores, and that nothing is left ungathered.

15. The city and suburban walls are put in good

[1. See in Mencius, I, 7, 4, on the consecration of a bell by smearing parts of it with blood.]

repair; the gates of towns and villages are looked after; bolts and nuts are put to rights; locks and keys are carefully attended to; the field–boundaries are strengthened; the frontiers are well secured; important defiles are thoroughly defended; passes and bridges are carefully seen after; and narrow ways and cross–paths are shut up.

16. The rules for mourning are revised; the distinctions of the upper and lower garments are defined; the thickness of the inner and outer coffins is decided on; with the size, height and other dimensions of graves. The measures for all these things are assigned, with the degrees and differences in them according to rank.

17. In this month orders are given to the chief Director of works to prepare a memorial on the work of the artificers; setting forth especially the sacrificial vessels with the measures and capacity (of them and all others), and seeing that there be no licentious ingenuity in the workmanship which might introduce an element of dissipation into the minds of superiors; and making the suitability of the article the first consideration. Every article should have its maker's name engraved on it, for the determination of its, genuineness. When the production is not what it ought to be, the artificer should be held guilty and an

end be thus put to deception.

18. In this month there is the great festivity when they drink together, and each of the stands bears half its animal roasted[1].

[1. Wang Thâo understands this paragraph as meaning that at this season all, both high and low, feast in expression and augmentation of their joy. The characters will bear this interpretation. The kang, of the text however, has also the meaning which appears in the translation; though on that view the statement is not so general. See the 'Narratives of the States,' I, ii. 8.]

19. The son of Heaven prays for (a blessing on) the coming year to the Honoured ones of heaven; sacrifices with an ox, a ram, and a boar at the public altar to the spirits of the land, and at the gates of towns and villages; offers the sacrifice three days after the winter solstice with the spoils of the chase to all ancestors, and at the five (household) sacrifices; –thus cheering the husbandmen and helping them to rest from their toils[1].

20. The son of Heaven orders his leaders and commanders to give instruction on military operations,

[1. The most common view seems to be that we have here the various parts of one sacrificial service, three days after the winter solstice, called kâ, in the time of Kâu, and lâ, in that of Khin. While the son of Heaven performed these services, it must have been at different places in the capital I suppose, analogous and modified services were celebrated generally throughout the kingdom.

There is no agreement as to who are intended by 'the Honoured ones of heaven.' Many hold that they are 'the six Honoured ones,' to whom Shun is said to have sacrificed in the second part of the Shû King. But the Khien–lung editors contend that the want of 'six' is a fatal objection to this view. Kâo Yû, supposing the six Honoured ones to be meant, argued that 'heaven, earth, and the four seasons' were intended by them,—those seasons co–operating with heaven and earth in the production of all things; but the same editors show, from the passages in the Shû, that heaven can in no sense be included among the six Honoured ones. They do not say, however, who or what is intended by the designation in the text. The lâ in the paragraph is taken in a pregnant sense, as if it were lieh (and not), meaning 'to sacrifice with the spoils of the chase.']

and to exercise (the soldiers) in archery and chariot–driving, and in trials of strength.

21. In this month orders are given to the superintendent of waters and the master of fishermen to collect the revenues from rivers, springs, ponds, and meres, taking care not to encroach in any way on any among the myriads of the people, so as to awaken a feeling of dissatisfaction in them against the son of Heaven. If they do this, they shall be punished for their guilt without forgiveness.

22. If, in the first month of winter, the proceedings of government proper to spring were observed, the cold that shuts up all beneath it would not do so tightly; the vapours of the earth would rise up and go abroad; many of the people would wander away and disappear. If those proper to summer were observed, there would be many violent winds in the states; winter itself would not be cold; and insects would come forth again from their burrows. If those proper to autumn were observed ' the snow and hoarfrost would come unseasonably; small military affairs would constantly be arising; and incursions and loss of territory would occur.

PART II.

1. In the second month of winter the sun is in Tâu, the constellation culminating at dusk being the eastern Pî, and that culminating at dawn Kan[1].

[1. Tâu comprehends {zeta}, {lambda}, {mu}, {sigma}, {tau}, {phi} of Sagittarius; the eastern Pî, the fourteenth of the Chinese constellations, consists of Algenib or {gamma} Pegasus, and a of Andromeda; Kan is the last of the constellations, and contains {beta}, {gamma}, {delta} and {epsilon} Corvus.]

2. Its days are zan and kwei. Its divine ruler is Kwan–hsü, and the (attending) spirit is Hsüan–ming. Its creatures are the shell–covered. Its musical note is Yü, and its pitch–tube is Hwang Kung[1].

3. Its number is six. Its taste is salt. Its smell is that of things that are rotten. Its sacrifice is that at (the altar of) the path, and of the parts of the victim the kidneys have the foremost place.

4. The ice becomes more strong. The earth begins to crack or split. The night bird ceases to sing. Tigers begin to pair[2].

5. The son of Heaven occupies the Grand Fane Hsüan Thang; rides in the dark–coloured carriage, drawn by the iron black horses, and bearing the dark–coloured flag. He is dressed in the black robes, and wears the dark–coloured gems of jade. He eats millet and sucking–pig. The vessels which he uses are large and rather deep.

6. All things relating to the dead are revised and regulated[3].

7. Orders are given to the proper officer to the following effect[4]:—'There should nothing be done in

[1. See page 281, paragraph 5.

2. The earth begins to crack;' some say from the increasing intensity of the cold; others from the warmth which has begun to return. The returning warmth is indicated by the undivided line with which Hi, the hexagram of the eleventh month, commences—

____ ___
____ ___
____ ___
____ ___
____ ___
____

'The night bird' sings during the night till the dawn; 'a hill bird, like a fowl.'

3. See paragraph 16, page 299. The paragraph may be inadvertently introduced here.

4. 'The proper officer' here is said to be 'the minister of Instruction,' or 'the officer of the People.']

works of earth; care should be taken not to expose anything that is covered, nor to throw open apartments and houses, and rouse the masses to action;—that all may be kept securely shut up. (Otherwise) the genial influences of earth will find vent, which might be called a throwing open of the house of heaven and earth. In this case all insects would die; and the people be sure to fall ill from Pestilence, and various losses would ensue.' This charge is said to be giving full development to the (idea of the) month.

8. In this month orders are given to the Director of the eunuchs to issue afresh the orders for the palace, to examine all the doors, inner and outer, and look carefully after all the apartments. They must be kept strictly shut. All woman's–work must be diminished, and none of an extravagant nature permitted. Though noble and nearly related friends should come to visit the inmates, they must all be excluded.

9. Orders are given to the Grand superintendent of the preparation of liquors to see that the rice and other glutinous grains are all complete; that the leaven–cakes are in season; that the soaking and heating are cleanly conducted; that the water be fragrant; that the vessels of pottery be good; and that the regulation of the fire be right. These six things have all to be attended to, and the Grand superintendent has the inspection of them, to secure that there be no error or mistake.

10. The son of Heaven issues orders to the proper officers to pray and sacrifice to (the spirits presiding over) the four seas, the great rivers (with their) famous sources, the deep tarns, and the meres, (all) wells and springs[1].

11. In this month) if the husbandmen have any productions in the fields, which they have not stored or collected, or if there be any horses, oxen or other animals,—which have been left at large, any one may take, them without its being inquired into.

12. If there be those who are able to take from, the hills and forests, marshes and meres. edible fruits[2], or to capture game by hunting, the wardens and foresters should give them the necessary information and guidance. If there be among them those who encroach on or rob the others, they should be punished without fail.

13. In this month the shortest day arrives. The principle of darkness and decay (in nature) struggles with that of brightness and growth[3]. The elements of life begin to move. Superior men give themselves to self–adjustment and fasting. They keep retired in their houses. They wish to be at rest in their

[1. Winter is the season in which the element of water predominates, and it was in virtue of this that the dynasty of Zhin professed to rule. The Khwan–lun mountains (Koulkun), between the desert of Gobi and Thibet, are the source of the Hwang Ho; Yüan–min, the source of the Kiang; Thung–po, that of the Hwâi; the Kî grew out of the Yen, rising from the hill of Wang–wa. See Chinese Classics, Vol. iii, pp. 127–140.

2 Hazel–nuts and chestnuts are given as examples of the former; and the water–caltrops and Euryale ferox, or 'cock's head,' of the latter.

This description of the month is well illustrated by the lines of Fû, the hexagram of it referred to above,—

____ ___
____ ___
____ ___
____ ___
____ ___
____

the lowest line representing the principle of light and growth, which just found readmission in the year, and is seeking to develop itself.]

persons; put away all indulgence in music and beautiful sights; repress their various desires; give repose to their bodies and all mental excitements. They wish all affairs to be quiet, while they wait for the settlement of those principles of darkness and decay, and brightness and growth.

14. Rice begins to grow. The broom–sedge rises up vigorously[1]. Worms curl[2]. The moose–deer shed their horns[3]. The springs of water are (all) in movement.

15. When the shortest day has arrived, they fell trees, and carry away bamboos, (especially) the small species suitable for arrows.

16. In this month–offices in which there is no business may be closed, and vessels for which there is no use may be removed.

17. They plaster (and repair) the pillars and gateways (of the palace), and the courtyard (within), and also doors and other gateways; rebuilding (also all) prisons, to co–operate with the tendency of nature to shut up and secure (the genial influences at this season).

18. If in this second month of winter the proceedings of government proper to summer were observed,

[1. This is called by Dr. Williams 'a species of iris.' The roots. are made into brooms.

2. This is a fancy. The commentators say that the worms curl and twist, with their heads turned downwards, as if seeking to return to the warmth beneath the surface.

3. The shedding of the horns in. winter shows that the mî here,, is a species of the elk or moose–deer, and different from the lû which sheds its horns in the sixth month. The mî is described as being fond of the water, and as large as a small ox.]

there would be droughts in the states; vapours and fogs would shed abroad their gloom, and thunder would utter its voice. If those proper to autumn were observed, the weather would be rainy and slushy; melons and gourds would not attain their full growth; and there would be great wars in the states. If those proper to spring were observed, locusts would work their harm; the springs would all become dry; and many of the people would suffer from leprosy and foul ulcers.

PART III.

1. In the third month of winter the sun is in Wû–nü, the constellation culminating at dusk being Lâu, and that culminating at dawn Tî[1].

2. Its days are zan and kwei. Its divine ruler is Kwan–hsü, and the (attendant) spirit is Hsüan–ming. Its creatures are the shell–covered. Its musical note is Yü, and its pitch–tube is Tâ Lü[1].

3. Its number is six. Its taste is salt. Its smell is that of things that are rotten. Its sacrifice is that at (the altar of) the path; and the part of the victim occupying the foremost place is the kidneys.

4. The wild geese go northwards. The magpie begins to build. The (cock) pheasant crows[3]. Hens hatch.

[1. Wû-nü, as in paragraph 1, Page 269. Lâu corresponds to {alpha}, {beta}, {gamma}, {iota} in the head of Aries; Tî, to {alpha}, {beta}, {delta}, {iota}, {mu}, {nu} Libra.

2. Tâ Lü is the first of the tubes giving the six lower musical accords.

3. As is said in the Shih, II, v, 3, 5:—

'Crows the pheasant at the dawn,
And his mate is to him drawn.']

5. The son of Heaven occupies the apartment on the right of the Hsüan Thang (Fane); rides in the dark-coloured carriage, drawn by the iron-black horses, and bearing the dark-coloured flag. He is dressed in the black robes, and wears the dark-coloured gems of jade. He cats millet and sucking-pig. The vessels which he uses are large and rather deep.

6. He issues orders to the proper officers to institute on a great scale all ceremonies against pestilence, to have (animals) torn in pieces on all sides, and (then) to send forth the ox of earth, to escort away the (injurious) airs of the cold[1].

7. Birds of prey fly high and rapidly[2].

8. They now offer sacrifices all round to (the spirits of) the hills and rivers, to the great ministers of the (ancient) deified sovereigns, and to the spirits of heaven (and earth)[3].

9. In this month orders are given to the master of the Fishermen to commence the fishers' work. The son of Heaven goes in person (to look on). He partakes of the fish caught, first presenting some in the apartment at the back of the ancestral temple[4].

[1. Compare par. 16, p. 266. The 'ox of earth' is still seen in China. This evidently is one of the natural phenomena of the season, and should belong to paragraph 4. The translation of the first two characters by 'Birds of prey' is sufficiently close and exact.

3 The Khien–lung editors point out the difficulties in explaining the three sacrifices here referred to, and seem to think they were practices of Khin, about which we have little information. 'The great ministers of the Tî' in the second member were probably those mentioned at the commencement of each season. They supplement the concluding member, as I have done, from Lü's Khun Khiû.

4. Compare paragraphs 7, p. 263; 17, p. 271. in paragraph 7,p. 263, the sovereign gets himself into a boat, a thing now impossible through the ice. Fish are in their prime condition in winter and spring.]

10. The ice is now abundant: thick and strong to the bottom of the waters and meres. Orders are given to collect it, which is done, and it is carried into (the ice–houses).

11. Orders are given to make announcement to the people to bring forth their seed of the five grains. The husbandmen are ordered to reckon up the pairs which they can furnish for the ploughing; to repair the handles and shares of their ploughs; and to provide all the other instruments for the fields.

12. Orders are given to the chief director of Music to institute a grand concert of wind instruments; and with this (the music of the year) is, closed[1].

13. Orders are given to the four Inspectors[2] to collect and arrange the faggots to supply the wood and torches for the suburban sacrifices, those in the ancestral temple, and all others.

14. In this month the sun has gone through all his mansions; the moon has completed the number of her conjunctions; the stars return to (their places) in the heavens. The exact length (of the year) is nearly completed, and the year will soon begin again. (It is said), 'Attend to the business of your husbandmen. Let them not be employed on anything else.'

15. The son of Heaven, along with his ducal and

[1. Compare paragraph 16, p. 261, et al. Wind instruments were supposed to suit the quiet and meditativeness of autumn and winter, better than the drums and dances of the other seasons.

2. 'The four Inspectors' Compare paragraph 8, p. 277. Some read thien for Sze, 'Inspectors of the fields.']

other high ministers and his Great officers, revises the statutes for the states, and discusses the proceedings of the different seasons; to be prepared with what is suitable for the ensuing year.

16. Orders are given to the Grand recorder to make a list of the princes of the states according to the positions severally assigned to them[1], and of the victims required from them to supply the offerings for the worship of God dwelling in the great heaven, and at the altars of (the spirits of) the land and grain. Orders were also given to the states ruled by princes of the royal surname to supply the fodder and grain for the (victims used in the worship of the) ancestral temple. Orders are given, moreover, to the chief minister to make a list of (the appanages of) the various high ministers and Great officers, with the amount of the land assigned to the common people, and assess them with the victims which they are to contribute to furnish for the sacrifices to (the spirits presiding over) the hills, forests, and famous streams. All the people under the sky, within the nine provinces, must, without exception, do their utmost to contribute to the sacrifices:–to God dwelling in the great heaven; at the altars of the (spirits of the) land and grain; in the ancestral temple and the apartment at the back of it; and of the hills, forests, and famous streams.

17. If, in the last month of winter, the governmental proceedings proper to autumn were observed, the white dews would descend too early; the shelly creatures

[1. As being of the same surname as the royal house, or otherwise; the degree of their rank; the size of their territory.]

would appear in monstrous forms[1]; throughout the four borders people would have to seek their places of shelter. If those proper to spring were observed, women with child and young children would suffer many disasters; throughout the states there would be many cases of obstinate disease; fate would appear to be adverse. If those proper to summer were observed, floods would work their ruin in the states; the seasonable snow would not fall, the ice would melt, and the cold disappear.

[1. This is the proper force of the characters. Wang Thâo interprets them as meaning that the creatures would bore through dykes and boats, so that the former would let the water through and the latter sink.]

BOOK V. THE QUESTIONS OF ZANG-DZE[1].

SECTION 1.

Zang-dze asked, 'If a ruler dies and a son and heir is born (immediately after), what course should be adopted?'

Confucius said, 'The high nobles[2], Great officers and (other) officers, following the chief (minister), who takes charge of the government for the time, (should collect) at the south of the western steps, with their faces towards the north[3]. (Then) the Grand officer of prayer, in his court robes and cap, bearing in his hands a bundle of rolls of silk, will go up to the topmost step, and (there), without ascending the hall, will order the wailing to cease. Mournfully clearing his voice three times[4], he will make announcement (to the spirit of the deceased ruler), saying, "The son of such and such a lady has been born. I venture to announce the fact." He will then go up, and place the silks on a stool on the east of the body in the coffin[5], wail, and descend. All the relatives of the deceased who are there (at the mourning), the high nobles, the Great and other

[1. See the introduction, pp. 21, 22.

2. These were also ministers; see paragraph 4, page 213.

3. The usual place was at the eastern steps.

4. To call the attention of the spirit of the deceased.

5. The rolls of silk were, I suppose, the introductory present proper on an interview with a superior.]

officers, (with the women) in the apartments, all will wail, but without the leaping. When this burst of sorrow is over, they will return to their (proper) places, and proceed forthwith to set forth the mourning offerings to the dead. The minor minister will ascend, and take away the bundle of silks[1].

2. 'On the third day, all the relatives, high nobles, Great and other officers, should take their places as before, with their faces to the north. The Grand minister, the Grand master of the ancestral temple, and the Grand officer of prayer, should all be in their court–robes and caps. The master for the child[2] will carry the child in his arms on a mat of sackcloth. The officer of prayer will precede, followed by the child, and the minister and master of the temple will come after. Thus they will enter the door (of the apartment where the coffin is), when the wailers will cease. The child has been brought up by the western steps[3], and is held in front of the coffin with his face to the north, while the officer of prayer stands at the south–east corner of it. Mournfully clearing his voice three times, he will say, "So and So, the son of such and such a lady, and we, his servants, who follow him, presume to appear before you." The boy is (then made) to do obeisance, with his forehead on the ground, and to wail. The officer of prayer, the minister, the officer of the temple, all the relatives, the high nobles, with the Great and other officers,

[1. And bury it in the court between the two flights of stairs.

2. Thus early is it made to appear that the child is put under a master; p. Zottoli translates the name by 'secundus magister.'

3. The child had been brought by the master from the women's apartments, and carried to the court, that he might thus go up again to the hall by these steps.]

will wail and leap[1], leaping three times with each burst of grief. (Those who had gone up to the hall then) descend, and go back to their proper places on the east; where all bare the left arm and shoulder. The son (in the arms of his bearer is made) to leap, and (the women) in the apartments also leap. Thrice they will do so, leaping three times each time. (The bearer for the son) will cover up his sackcloth[2], walk with a staff, (ascend and) set forth the offerings by the dead, and then quit the scene. The Grand minister will charge the officer of prayer and the recorder to announce the name all round, at the five altars of the house, and at those (to the spirits) of the hills and streams[3].'

3. Zang–dze asked, 'If the son and heir have been born after the burial (of the) ruler, what course should be followed?'

Confucius said, 'The Grand minister and the Grand master of the ancestral temple will follow the Grand officer of prayer, and announce the fact before the spirit tablet (of the deceased ruler)[4]. Three months after they will give the name in the same place, and announce it all round', and also at the altars to (the

[1. A most expressive indication of the sorrow proper to the occasion.

2. The breast and shoulder of the child had also been bared.

3. The 'five household altars' are those at which the sacrifices were offered in the palace or house, often mentioned in the last Book.

4 The characters of the text, 'in the shrine temple of the father,' denote the special shrine or smaller temple assigned to the father in the great ancestral temple; but that was not assigned till after all the rites of mourning were over. The characters here denote the spirit tablet which had been before the burial set up over the coffin, and which was now removed to a rear apartment. p. Zottoli simply has 'coram tabellâ.'

5 At the courts of the sovereign and of the other princes.]

spirits of) the land and grain, in the ancestral temple, and (at the altars of) the hills and streams.'

4. Confucius said, 'When princes of states are about to go to the (court of the) son of Heaven, they must announce (their departure) before (the shrine of) their grandfather, and lay their offerings in that of their father[1]. They then put on the court cap, and go forth to hold their own court. (At this) they charge the officer of prayer and the recorder to announce (their departure) to the (spirits of the) land and grain, in the ancestral temple, and at the (altars of the) hills and rivers. They then give (the business of) the state in charge to the five (subordinate) officers[2], and take their journey, presenting the offerings to the spirits of the road[3] as they set forth. All the announcements should be completed in five days. To go beyond this in making them is contrary to rule. In every one of them they use a victim and silks. On the return (of the princes) there are the same observances.'

5. 'When princes of states are about to visit one another, they must announce (their departure) before

[1. The characters here are the same as in the preceding paragraph, but here they have their usual force. Announcement and offerings were made at both shrines.

2. The most likely opinion is that these five officers were–two belonging to the department of the minister of Instruction, two to that of the minister of Works, and one to that of the minister of War. On them, for reasons which we may not be able to give, devolved on such occasions the superintendence of the state.

3. There seems to be no doubt of the meaning here, but this significance of not given in the Khang–hsî dictionary. The more common term is .]

the shrine of their father[1]. They will then put on their court robes, and go forth to hold their own court. (At this) they charge the officer of prayer and the recorder to announce (their departure) at the five shrines in the ancestral temple, and at the altars of the hills and rivers which they will pass. They then give (the business of) the state in charge to the five officers, and take their journey, presenting the offerings to the spirits of the road as they set forth. When they return, they will announce (the fact) in person to their grandfather and father[1], and will charge the officer of prayer and the recorder to make announcement of it at the altars where they announced (their departure). (When this has been done), they enter and give audience in the court.'

6. Zang–dze asked, 'If the funerals of both parents[2] take place together, what course is adopted? Which is first and which last?'

Confucius said, 'The rule is that the burying of the less important (mother) should have the precedence, and that of the more important (father) follow, while the offerings to them are set down in the opposite order. From the opening of the apartment and conveying out the coffin (of the mother) till its interment no offerings are put down; when the coffin is on the route to the grave, there is no wailing at the regular place for that ceremony. When they return from this interment, they set down the offerings (to the father), and afterwards announce (to his spirit) when the removal of his coffin will take

[1. There would seem. to be an omission in the former of these sentences of the announcement to the grandfathers.

2. Or grandparents.]

place, and proceed to arrange for the interment. It is the rule that the sacrifice of repose should first be offered to the more important (father), and afterwards to the less important (mother).

7. Coufucius said[1], 'The eldest son, even though seventy, should never be without a wife to take her part in presiding at the funeral rites. If there be no such eldest son, the rites may be performed without a presiding wife.'

8. Zang–dze asked, 'It has been proposed to invest a son with the cap, and the investors have arrived, and after exchanging bows and courtesies (with the master of the house), have entered. If then news should come that the death of some relative has occurred, for whom a year's mourning or that of nine months must be worn, what should be done?'

Confucius said, 'If the death has taken place within (the circle of the same surname), the ceremony should be given up[2]; but if without (that circle), it will go on, but the sweet wine will not be presented to the youth. The viands will be removed and the place swept, after which he will go to his proper position and wail. If the investors have not yet arrived, the capping will be given up (for the time)[3].

9. 'If the arrangements for the capping have been

[1. The words of Confucius are here, as in some other paragraphs, not preceded by the formula, 'Zang–dze asked.' Some say this is an omission, intentional or unintentional, of the compiler. Some commentators deride the judgment (see especially Ho Kung–yü), holding it unworthy of Confucius.

2. Because then a festal and a mourning service would come together in the ancestral temple.

3. The investors may have previously heard of the death, and not kept their appointment.]

made, but before the day arrives, an occasion for the one year's mourning, or for that of nine months, or five months, have arrived, the youth shall be capped in his mourning dress.'

10. 'When all mourning is over, may a son continue to wear the cap which he has hitherto worn[1]?'

Confucius said, 'When the son of Heaven gives to the (young) prince of a state or a Great officer his robes and the cap proper to each in the grand ancestral temple, the youth on his return home– will set forth his offering (in his own ancestral temple), wearing the robes that have been given to him, and here he will drink the cup of capping (as if) offered by his father[2], without the cup of wine at the ceremony.

11. 'When a son is (thus) capped after his father's death, he is considered to be properly capped; he will sweep the ground, and sacrifice at his father's shrine. This being done, he will present himself before his uncles, and then offer the proper courtesies to the investors.'

12. Zang–dze asked, 'Under what circumstances is it that at sacrifice they do not carry out the practice of all drinking to one another?'

Confucius said, 'I have heard that at the close of the one year's mourning, the principal concerned in it

[1. Till he was capped, a youth wore nothing on his head. But in the case supposed the youth's time for capping had arrived; and he had assumed a cap without the ceremony.

2. When a father gave orders to his son about his capping or marriage, he gave him a cup of ordinary wine. The sweet wine was given to the youth by a friend or friends who had invested him with the cap. The real answer to Zang–dze's question is in paragraph 11.]

sacrifices in his inner garment of soft silk, and there is not that drinking all round. The cup is set down beside the guests, but they do not take it up. This is the rule. Formerly duke Kâo of Lû[1], while in that silken garment, took the cup and sent it all round, but it was against the rule; and duke Hâo[2], at the end of the second year's mourning, put down the cup presented to him, and did not send it all round, but this also was against the rule.'

13. Zang-dze asked, 'In a case (of the) mourning for nine months, can (the principal) take part in contributing to the offerings (to the dead of others)?'

Confucius said, 'Why speak only of (the mourning for) nine months? In all cases from (the mourning for) three years downwards, it may be done. This is the rule.'

Zang-dze said, 'Would not this be making the mourning of little importance, and attaching (undue) importance to mutual helpfulness?'

Confucius said, 'This is not what I mean. When there is mourning for the son of Heaven or the prince of a state, (all) who wear the sackcloth with the jagged edges (will contribute to) the offerings. At the mourning of a Great officer, (all) who wear the sackcloth with the even edges will do so. At the mourner of an ordinary officer, his associates and friends will do so. If all these be not sufficient, they may receive contributions from all who should mourn for nine months downwards; and if these be still insufficient, they will repeat the process[3].'

[1. B.C. 541-510.

2. B.C. 795-769. This is going a long way back.

3. On this paragraph p. Zottoli says:—'Zang-dze petit an aliquis in novem mensium luctu constitutus possit adjuvare alterius funestae familiae oblationem. Confucius intelligit de adjuvanda proprii funeris oblatione.' There appears to be a similar misunderstanding between the two in the next paragraph.]

14. Zang-dze asked, 'In a case of the mourning for five months, may (the principal) take part in the other sacrifices (of mourning)[1]?'

Confucius said, 'Why speak only of the mourning for five months? In all cases from the mourning for three years downwards, (the principals) take part in those sacrifices.'

Zang-dze said, 'Would not this be making the mourning of little importance, and giving (undue) importance to the sacrifices?'

Confucius said, 'In the mourning sacrifices for the son of Heaven and the prince of a state, none but those who wear the sackcloth with the jagged edges take part in them. In those for a Great officer, they who wear the sackcloth with the even edges do so. In those for another officer, if the participants be insufficient, they add to them from their brethren who should wear mourning for nine months downwards.'

15. Zang–dze asked, 'When acquaintances are in mourning, may they participate in one another's sacrifices?'

Confucius said, 'When wearing the three months' mourning, one has no occasion to sacrifice (in his own ancestral temple), and how should he assist another man (out of his own line)?'

[1. Khung Ying–tâ makes this out to be the sacrifices of repose, and at the end of the wailing. I think the reference is more general.]

16. Zang–dze asked, 'When one has put off his mourning, may he take part in contributing to the offerings (for the dead of another)?'

Confucius said, 'To take part in the offerings (to another's dead), on putting off one's own sackcloth, is contrary to the rule. Possibly, he may perform the part of assisting him in receiving visitors.'

17. Zang–dze asked, 'According to the rules for marriages, the presents have been received and a fortunate day has been fixed;—if then the father or mother of the young lady die, what course should be adopted?'

Confucius said, 'The son–in–law will send some one to condole; and if it be his father or mother that has died, the family of the lady will in the same way send some to present their condolences. If the father have died, (the messenger) will name the (other) father (as having sent him); if the mother, he will name the (other) mother. If both parents be dead (on both sides), he will name the oldest uncle and his wife. When the son–in–law has buried (his dead), his oldest uncle will offer a release from the engagement to the lady, saying, "My son, being occupied with the mourning for his father or mother, and not having obtained the right to be reckoned among your brethren, has employed me to offer a release from the engagement." (In this case) it is the rule for the lady to agree to the message and not presume to (insist on) the marriage (taking place immediately). When the son–in–law has concluded his mourning, the parents of the lady will send and request (the fulfilment of the engagement). The son–in–law will not (immediately come to) carry her (to his house), but afterwards she will be married to him; this is the rule. If it be the father or mother of the lady who died, the son–in–law will follow a similar course[1].'

18. Zang–dze asked, 'The son–in–law has met the lady in person, and she is on the way with him:—if (then) his father or mother die, what course should be adopted?'

Confucius said, 'The lady will change her dress[2]; and in the long linen robe[3], with 'the cincture of white silk round her hair, will hasten to be present at the mourning rites. If, while she is on the way, it be her own father or mother who dies, she will return[4].'

19. 'If the son–in–law have met the lady in person, and before she has arrived at his house, there occur a death requiring the year's or the nine months' mourning, what course should be adopted?'

Confucius said, 'Before the gentleman enters, be will change his dress in a place outside. The lady will enter and change her dress in a place inside. They will then go to the proper positions and wail.'

Zang–dze asked, 'When the mourning is ended, will they not resume the marriage ceremonies?'

[1. Is the final marriage of the lady to the original betrothed 'son–in–law,' or bridegroom as we should say; or to another, that she may not pass the proper time for her marrying? Khung Ying–tâ, and other old commentators, advocate the latter view. Others, and especially the Khien–lung editors, maintain the former; and I have indicated in the version my agreement with them. There are difficulties with the text; but Confucius would hardly have sanctioned the other course.

2. At the house of him who was now her husband.

3. This, called 'the deep garment,' had the body and skirt sown together. See Book XXXIV.

4 This would be done, it is said, by Hsü Sze–zhang (Ming dynasty), to allow play to her filial piety, but she would live at the house of 'the son–in–law.']

Confucius said, 'It is the rule, that when the time of sacrifice has been allowed to pass by, it is not then offered. Why in this case should they go back to what must have taken place previously?'

20. Confucius said, 'The family that has married a daughter away, does not extinguish its candles for three nights, thinking of the separation that has taken place. The family that has received the (new) wife for three days has no music; thinking her bridegroom is now in the place of his parents[1]. After three months she presents herself in the ancestral temple, and is styled "The new wife that has come." A day is chosen for her to sacrifice at the shrine of her father–in–law; expressing the idea of her being (now) the established wife.'

21. Zang–dze asked, 'If the lady die before she has presented herself in the ancestral temple, what course should be adopted?'

Confucius said, '(Her coffin) should not be removed to the ancestral temple, nor should (her tablet) be placed next to that of her mother–in–law. The husband should not carry the staff; nor wear the shoes of straw; nor have a (special) place (for wailing). She should be taken back, and buried among her kindred of her own family;—showing that she had not become the established wife.'

22. Zang–dze asked, 'The fortunate day has been fixed for taking the lady (to her new home), and she dies (in the meantime):—what should be done?'

Confucius said, 'The son–in–law will come to condole, wearing the one year's mourning, which he will

[1. This and the statements that follow suppose that the bridegroom's parents are dead.]

lay aside when the interment has taken place. If it be the husband who dies, a similar course will be followed on the other side.'

23. Zang-dze asked, 'Is it according to rule "that at the mourning rites there should be two (performing the part of) the orphan son (and heir, receiving visitors)[1], or that at a temple-shrine there should be two spirit-tablets?'

Confucius said, 'In heaven there are not two suns; in a country there are not two kings[2]; in the seasonal sacrifices, and those to Heaven and Earth[3], there are not. two who occupy the highest place of honour. I do not know that what you ask about is according to rule. Formerly duke Hwan of Khî[4], going frequently to war, made fictitious tablets and took them with him on his expeditions, depositing them on his return in the ancestral temple[5]. The practice of having two tablets in a temple-shrine originated from duke Hwan. As to two (playing the part of the) orphan son, it may be thus explained:—Formerly, on occasion of a visit to Lû by duke Ling of Wei, the mourning rites of Kî Hwan-dze were in progress. The ruler of Wei requested leave to offer his condolences. Duke Âi (of Lû), declined (the ceremony), but could not

[1. The Chinese characters mean simply 'two orphans.' Neither Khang-hsî nor any English-Chinese dictionary explains the peculiar use of the term here; nor is Confucius' explanation satisfactory, or to the point.

2 Compare paragraphs 5, 8, III, iii, pages 224-226.

3 See the 'Doctrine of the Mean,' 19, 6, Chinese Classics, vol. i.

4. B.C. 685-643.

5. Literally 'the temple-shrine of his grandfather;' but I think the name must have the general meaning I have given.

6. It has been shown that the ruler of Wei here could not be duke Ling. He must have been duke Khû. But this error discredits the view of the statement having come from Confucius.]

enforce his refusal. He therefore acted as the principal (mourner), and the visitor came in to condole with him. Khang-dze stood on the right of the gate with his face to the north. The duke, after the usual bows and courtesies, ascended by the steps on the east with his face towards the west. The visitor ascended by those on the west, and paid his condolences. The duke bowed ceremoniously to him, and then rose up and wailed, while Khang–dze bowed with his forehead to the ground, in the position where he was. The superintending officers made no attempt to put the thing to rights. The having two now acting as the orphan son arose from the error of Kî Khang–dze.'

24. Zang–dze asked, 'Anciently when an army went on an expedition, was it not first necessary to carry with it the spirit–tablets that had been removed from their shrines[1]?'

Confucius said, 'When the son of Heaven went on his tours of Inspection, he took (one of) those tablets along with him, conveying it in the carriage of Reverence, thus intimating how it was felt necessary to have with him that object of honour[2]. The practice

[1. See note 2 and plan of the royal ancestral temple of Mu on pages 223–225.

2. This, it is said, was the tablet of the royal ancestor which had been last removed from its shrine, and placed in the shrine–house for all such removed tablets. The carriage of Reverence was the 'metal–guilt' carriage of the king, second to that adorned with jade, in which he rode to sacrifice. Zottoli renders:—'Imperator perlustrans custodita, cum translatitii delubri tabella peragrabat, imposita super casti curru, significatum necessariam praesentiam superioris.']

now–a–days of taking the tablets of the seven temple–shrines along with them on an expedition is an error. No shrine in all the seven (of the king), or in the five of the prince of a state, ought to be (left) empty. A shrine can only be so left without its tablet, when the son of Heaven has died, or the prince of a state deceased, or left his state, or when all the tablets are brought together at the united sacrifice, in the shrine–temple of the highest ancestor. I heard the following statement from Lâo Tan[1]:—"On the death of the son of Heaven, or of the prince of a state, it is the rule that the officer of prayer should take the tablets from all the other shrines and deposit them in that of the high ancestor[2], When the wailing was over, and the business (of placing the tablet of the deceased in its shrine) was completed, then every other tablet was restored to its shrine. When a ruler abandoned his state, it was the rule that the Grand minister should take the tablets from all the shrines and follow him. When there was the united sacrifice in the shrine of the high ancestor, the officer of prayer met (and received) the tablets from the four shrines. When they were taken from their shrines or carried back to them all were required to keep out of the way." So said Lâo Tan.'

[1. This was, most probably, Lâo–dze, though some of the commentators deny it. Kang says: 'Lâo Tan, the title of old for men of longevity, was a contemporary of Confucius;' and Khan Hâo quotes a note on this from Wang of Shih–liang, that 'This was not the author of the "Five thousand words,"' i.e. of the Tâo Teh King.

2. While the special sacrifices and other funeral rites were going on, the other sacrifices, which belonged to a different category of rites, were suspended.]

25. Zang–dze asked, 'Anciently, when they marched on an expedition, and carried no displaced tablets with them, what did they make their chief consideration?'

Confucius said, 'They made the instructions from the tablet their chief consideration[1].'

'What does that mean?' asked the other.

Confucius said, 'When the son of Heaven or the prince of a state was about to go forth, he would, with gifts of silk, skins, and jade–tokens, announce his purpose at the shrines of his grandfather and father. He then took those gifts with him, conveying them on the march in the carriage of Reverence. At every stage (of the march), he would place offerings of food by them, and afterwards occupy the station. On returning, they would make announcement (at the same shrines), and when they had set forth (again) their offerings, they would collect the silk and jade, and bury them between the steps (leading) up to the fane of the high ancestor; after which they left the temple. This was how they made the instructions they received their chief consideration.'

26. Dze–yû asked, 'Is it the rule to mourn for a foster–mother' as for a mother?'

[1. Zottoli gives for this phrase simply 'adhaerebant numini,' subjoining no note on it. The parties spoken of put down their offerings before the shrines, announcing that they were about to undertake such an expedition; and taking it for granted that their progenitors approved of their object, proceeded to carry it out, as if they had received a charge from them to do so, carrying the offerings with them in token of that charge from the spirits in the tablets of the shrines. This view is distinctly set forth by Hwang Khan (end of early Sung dynasty) and others.

2. This foster–mother was not what we call 'a nurse;' but a lady of the harem to whom the care of an orphan boy was entrusted;—it may have been after he ceased to be suckled. The reasoning of Confucius goes on the assumption that mourning should be worn only in cases of consanguinity or affinity; and it may be inferred from this that concubinage was not the most ancient rule in China.]

Confucius said, 'It is not the rule. Anciently, outside the palace, a boy had his master, and at home his foster–mother; they were those whom the ruler employed to teach his son;–what ground should these be for wearing mourning for them? Formerly duke Kâo of Lû having lost his mother when he was little, had a foster–mother, who was good; and when she died, he could not bear (not) to mourn for her, and wished to do so. The proper officer on hearing of it, said, "According to the ancient rule, there is no mourning for a foster–mother. If you wear this mourning, you will act contrary to that ancient rule, and introduce confusion into the laws of the state. If you will after all do it, then we will put it on record, and transmit the act to the future;—will not that be undesirable?" The duke said, "Anciently the son of Heaven, when unoccupied and at ease, wore the soft inner garment, assumed after the year's mourning, and the cap." The duke could not bear not to wear mourning, and on this he mourned for his foster–mother in this garb. The mourning for a foster–mother originated with duke Kâo of Lû[1].'

[1. See the eleventh article in the forty–third chapter of the 'Narratives of the School,' where a similar, probably the same, conversation, with some variations, is found. The duke of Lû in it, however, is not Kâo, but Hâo; see paragraph 12, page 315.]

SECTION II.

1. Zang–dze asked, 'The princes are assembled in a body to appear before the son of Heaven; they have entered the gate, but are not able to go through with the rites (of audience);—how many occurrences will make these be discontinued?'

Confucius said, 'Four.' 'May I ask what they are?' said the other. The reply was:—'The grand ancestral temple taking fire; an eclipse of the sun; funeral rites of the queen; their robes all unsightly through soaking rain. If, when the princes are all there, an eclipse of the sun take place, they follow the son of Heaven to save it[1]; each one dressed in the colour of his quarter, and with the weapon proper to it[2]. If there be a fire in the grand ancestral temple, they follow him to extinguish it without those robes and weapons.

2. Zang-dze said, 'Princes are visiting one another. (The strangers) have entered the gate after the customary bowings and courtesies, but they are not able to go through with the rites (of audience);how many occurrences will make these be discontinued?'

Confucius said, 'Six;' and, in answer to the question

[1. The phenomenon of an eclipse suggested the idea of some enemy or adverse influence devouring the sun's disk.

2. The colour appropriate to the east was green, and the weapon the spear with two hooks; the colour of the south was red, and the weapon the spear with one hook and two points; the colour of the west was white, and the weapon the bow; the colour of the north was black, and the weapon the shield; the colour of the centre was yellow, and the weapon the drum.]

as to what they were, replied:—'The death of the son of Heaven; the grand ancestral temple taking fire; an eclipse of the sun; the funeral rites of the queen or of the princess of the state; and their robes all unsightly through soaking rain.'

3. Zang-dze said, 'At the seasonal sacrifices of the son of Heaven, at those to Heaven and Earth, and at (any of) the five sacrifices of the house, after the vessels, round and square, with their contents have been set forth, if there occur the death of the son of Heaven or mourning rites for the queen, what should be done?'

Confucius, said, 'The sacrifice should be stopped.' The other asked, 'If, during the sacrifice, there occur an eclipse of the sun, or the grand ancestral temple take fire ' what should be done?' The reply was, 'The steps of the sacrifice should be hurried on. If the victim have arrived, but has not yet been slain, the sacrifice should be discontinued.

4. 'When the son of Heaven has died and is not yet coffined, the sacrifices of the house are not offered. When he is coffined, they are resumed; but at any one of them the representative of the dead takes (only) three mouthfuls (of the food), and is not urged (to take more). He is then presented with a cup, but does not respond by presenting another, and there is an end (of the ceremony). From the removal of the coffin to the return (from

the burial) and the subsequent wailing, those sacrifices (again) cease. After the burial they are offered, but when the officer of prayer has finished the cup presented to him, they stop.'

5. Zang–dze asked, 'At the sacrifices to the spirits of the land and grain proper to the feudal princes, if, after the stands and vessels, with their contents, have been arranged, news arrive of the death of the son of Heaven or of the mourning rites for his queen, or if the ruler die or there be mourning rites for his consort, what should be done?'

Confucius said, 'The sacrifice should be discontinued. From the ruler's death to the coffining, and from the removal of the coffin to the return (from the burial) and the (subsequent) wailing, they will follow the example set by the son of Heaven[1].'

6. Zang–dze asked, 'At the sacrifices of a Great officer[2], when the tripods and stands have been arranged, and the dishes of bamboo and wood, with their contents, have been set forth, but they are not able to go through with the rites, how many occurrences will cause them to be discontinued?'

Confucius said, 'Nine;' and when asked what they were, he added:—'The death of the son of Heaven; funeral rites for his queen; the death of the ruler (of the state); funeral rites for his consort; the ruler's grand ancestral temple taking fire; an eclipse of the sun; (a call to) the three years' mourning; to that of one year; or to that of nine months. In all these cases the sacrifice should be given up. If the mourning be merely for relatives by affinity, from all degrees of it up to the twelve months, the sacrifice will go on. At one where the mourning is worn for twelve months, the representative of the dead, after entering, will take (only) three mouthfuls (of the food), and not be urged to take (any more).

[1. As given in the preceding paragraphs.

2. In his ancestral temple.]

He will be presented with a cup, but will not respond by presenting one in return, and there will be an end (of the ceremony). Where the mourning is for nine months, after he has presented the responsive cup, the thing will end. Where it is for five or for three months, it will not end till all the observances in the apartment are gone through. What distinguishes the proceedings of an ordinary officer is, that he does not sacrifice when wearing the three months' mourning. He sacrifices, however, if the dead to whom he does so had no relationship with him requiring him to wear mourning.'

7. Zang–dze asked, 'May one, wearing the three years' mourning for a parent, go to condole with others?'

Confucius said, 'On the completion of the first of the three years, one should not be seen standing with others, or going along in a crowd. With a superior man the use of ceremonies is to give proper and elegant expression to the feelings. Would it not be an empty form[1] to go and condole and wail with others, while wearing the three years' mourning?'

8. Zang–dze asked, 'If a Great officer or ordinary officer be in mourning for a parent[2] he may put it off[3]; and if he be in mourning for his ruler, under what conditions will he put that off?'

Confucius said, 'If he have the mourning for his

[1. How could he, occupied with his own sorrow, offer anything but an empty form of condolence to others?

2. Literally 'private mourning,' as below; but evidently the master and disciple both had the mourning for a parent in mind.

3. On his having to go into mourning for his ruler.]

ruler on his person, he will not venture to wear any private mourning;—what putting off can there be? In this case, even if the time be passed (for any observances which the private mourning would require), he will not put it off. When the mourning for the ruler is put off, he will then perform the great sacrifices (of his private mourning)[1]. This is the rule.'

9. Zang–dze asked, 'But is it allowable thus to give up all the mourning rites for a parent through this keeping on of the mourning (for a ruler)?'

Confucius said, 'According to the ceremonies as determined by the ancient kings, it is the rule that when the time has passed (for the observance of any ceremony), there should be no attempt to perform it. It is not that one could not keep from not putting off the mourning; but the evil would be in his going beyond the definite statute. Therefore it is that a superior man does not offer a sacrifice, when the proper time for doing so has passed.'

I0. Zang-dze said, 'If, when the ruler has died, and is now lying in his coffin, the minister be called to the funeral rites for his father or mother, what course will he pursue?'

Confucius said, 'He should go home and remain there; going indeed to the ruler's for the great

[1. That is, the rightful son and heir may then perform the sacrifice marking the close of the first year's mourning for a parent, and that marking the close of the second year's mourning in the month after. But Khan Hâo argues that it was only the rightful son who could thus go back and offer the sacrifices proper to the mourning rites for parents, and that the other sons could not do so. This is the case underlying the next paragraph.]

services (to the departed), but not for those of every morning and evening[1].'

11. (Zang-dze asked), 'If, when they have begun to remove the coffin, the minister be called to the funeral rites for his father or mother, how should he do?'

Confucius said, 'He should go home and wail, and then return and accompany the funeral of the ruler.'

12. 'If,' said (Zang-dze), 'before the ruler has been coffined, a minister be called to the funeral rites for his father or mother, what should be his course?'

Confucius said, 'He should go home, and have the deceased put into the coffin, returning (then) to the ruler's. On occasion of the great services, he will go home, but not for those of every morning and evening. In the case of a Great officer, the chief servant of the household will attend to matters'; in the case of an ordinary officer, a son or grandson. When there are the great services at the ruler's, the wife of the Great officer will also go there, but not for those of every morning and evening.'

13. One in a low position should not pronounce the eulogy of another in a high, nor a younger man that of one older than himself. In the case of the son of Heaven, they refer to Heaven as giving his

[1. It has been seen that morning and evening offerings to the dead were placed near the coffin. On the first and fifteenth of the month these were on a great scale, and with special observances,—at the new and full moon. They were 'the great services.' The practice still continues.]

eulogy. It is not the rule for princes of states to deliver the eulogy of one another[1].

14. Zang–dze asked, 'When a ruler goes across the boundary of his own state, he takes with him his inner coffin as a precaution for the preparations against the three years'(mourning rites) for him[2]. If he die (abroad), what are the proceedings on his being brought back?'

Confucius said, 'The clothes to be put on him after the coffining having been provided, the son in the linen cap, with the sackcloth band round it, wearing coarse sackcloth and the shoes of straw, and carrying a staff, will enter by the opening made in the wall of the apartment for the coffin, having ascended by the western steps. If the slighter dressing (preparatory to the coffining) have still (to be made), the son will follow the bier without a cap, enter by the gate, and ascend by the steps on the east. There is one and the same rule for a ruler, a Great officer, and an ordinary officer.'

15. Zang–dze asked, 'If one is occupied in drawing (the carriage with the bier on it) at the funeral rites of his ruler, and is then called to the funeral rites of his father or mother, what should he do?'

[1. The eulogy has in China for more than a thousand years taken the form of inscriptions on tombs and sacrificial compositions; of which there are many elegant and eloquent specimens. It should be summed up in the honorary title. Truth, however, might require that that should be the reverse of eulogistic; and perhaps this led to its being conferred, as a rule, by one superior in rank and position. The honorary title of a deceased sovereign was first proclaimed at the great sacrifice to Heaven at the winter solstice; and hence it is referred to in the text as coming from Heaven.'

2 That is, I think, simply, as a precaution against his dying while abroad.' Zottoli renders:—'Regulus excedens confinia, ut in tres annos praecaveatur, habit sandapilam sequacem.']

Confucius said, 'He should complete what he is engaged in; and when the coffin has been let down into the grave, return home, without waiting for the departure of the (ruler's) son.'

16. Zang–dze asked, 'If one, occupied with the, funeral rites of a parent, has (assisted in) drawing the bier to the path (to the grave), and there hear of the death of his ruler, what should he do?'

Confucius said, 'He should complete the burial; and, when the coffin has been let down, he should change his dress, and go to (the ruler's).'

17. Zang–dze asked, 'If the eldest son by the proper wife be (only) an officer, and a son by a secondary wife be a Great officer, how will the latter proceed in his sacrificing?'

Confucius said, 'He will sacrifice, with the victims belonging to his higher rank, in the house of the eldest son., The officer of prayer will say, "So and So, the filial son, in behalf of So and So, the attendant son, presents his regular offering[1]."'

18. 'If the eldest son, now the head of the family, be residing, in consequence of some charge of guilt, in another state, and a son by a secondary wife be a Great officer, when (the latter) is offering a sacrifice (for the other), the officer of prayer will say, "So

[1. Here two things were in collision. The oldest son by the proper wife was the representative of the father, and only he could preside at the service in the ancestral temple of the family. But here an inferior son has been advanced to a higher rank than his older brother. As a Great officer he is entitled to have three shrine temples; but it would be contrary to the solidarity of the family for him to erect an ancestral temple for himself. The difficulty is met in the way described, the sacrifice being ascribed to the elder brother, as head of the family.]

and So, the filial son, employs the attendant son, So and So, to perform for him the regular service." (In this case, however), the principal in this vicarious service will not conduct the sacrifice so as to see that the spirit of the deceased is satisfied to the full; nor send the cup round among all who are present, nor receive the blessing (at the close); nor lay on the ground the portions of the sacrifice as thank–offerings; nor have with him (the wife of the elder brother) who should appear before the spirit–tablet of her mother–in–law, the wife of the deceased. He will put down the cup before the (principal) guests, but they will put it down (in another place), and not send it round. He will not send to them portions of the flesh. In his address to the guests (at the beginning of the service), he will say, "My honoured brother, the honoured son (of our father), being in another state, has employed me, So and So, to make announcement to you[1].'"

19. Zang–dze asked, 'If the eldest son have gone and is in another state, while a son by a secondary

[1. This paragraph continues the case in the preceding, with the additional circumstances that the head of the family is a fugitive from it, and that the sacrifice referred to in it is performed by the inferior brother remaining in the state, in lieu of him. It is difficult to translate without amplification so as to be intelligible, because of what may be called the technical terms in it. The five points in which the service was deficient, different from what it would have been, if performed by the proper brother, are given in the reverse order of their regular occurrence; whether designedly or not, we cannot tell. For that portion of the paragraph p. Zottoli gives:—'Sed vicarius dominus vacabit satisfactionis sacrificio; vacabit universali propinatione; vacabit benedictione; vacabit consternationis sacrificio; vacabit copulatione;' appending a note to explain the terms.]

wife, and without rank, remains at home, may the latter offer the sacrifice?'

Confucius said, 'Yes, certainly.' 'And how will he sacrifice?' 'He will rear an altar in front of the (family–)grave, and there he will sacrifice at the different seasons. If the oldest son die, he will announce the event at the grave, and afterwards sacrifice in the house, calling himself, however, only by his name, and abstaining from the epithet "filial." This abstinence will cease after his death.' The disciples of Dze–yû, in the case of sons by inferior wives sacrificing, held that this practice was in accordance with what was right. Those of them who sacrifice now–a–days do not ground their practice on this principle of right;—they have no truthful ground for their sacrifices[1].

20. Zang-dze asked, 'Is it necessary that there should be a representative of the dead in sacrifice? or may he be dispensed with as when the satisfying offerings are made to the dead?'

Confucius said, 'In sacrificing to a full-grown man for whom there have been the funeral rites, there must be such a representative, who should be a grandson; and if the grandson be too young, some one, must be employed to carry him in his arms. If there be no grandson, some one of the same surname should be selected for the occasion. In sacrificing to one who has died prematurely, there are (only) the satisfying offerings, for he was not

[1. These last two sentences evidently should not be ascribed to Confucius. It was only after his death that Dze-yû would have a school of his own. They must have been written moreover after the death of Dze-yû.]

full-grown. To sacrifice to a full-grown man, for whom there have been the funeral rites without a representative, would be to treat him as if he had died prematurely.'

21. Confucius said, 'There is the offering of satisfaction made in the dark chamber, and that made in the brighter place.'

Zang-dze answered with a question, 'But to one who has died prematurely there is not made a complete sacrifice; what do you mean by speaking of two satisfying offerings, the dark and the bright?'

Confucius said, 'When the oldest son, who would take the father's place, dies prematurely, no brother by an inferior wife can be his successor. At the auspicious sacrifice to him', there is a single bullock; but the service being to one who died prematurely, there is no presentation (of the lungs), no stand with the heart and tongue, no dark-coloured spirits[2], no announcement of the nourishment being completed. This is what is called the dark satisfying offering. In regard to all others who have died prematurely and have left no offspring, the sacrifice is offered to them in the house of the oldest son, where the apartment is most light, with the vases in the chamber on the east. This is what is called the bright satisfying offering.'

22. Zang-dze asked, 'At a burial, when the bier has been drawn to the path (leading to the place), if there happen an eclipse of the sun, is any change made or not?'

[1. The first auspicious sacrifice took place when the ceremony of wailing was over.

2. A name for water.]

Confucius said, 'Formerly, along with Lâo Tan[1], I was assisting at a burial in the village of Hsiang, and when we had got to the path, the sun was eclipsed. Lâo Tan said to me, "Khiû, let the bier be stopped on the left of the road[2]; and then let us wail and wait till the eclipse pass away. When it is light again, we will proceed." He said that this was the rule. When we had returned and completed the burial, I said to him, "In the progress of a bier there should be no returning. When there is an eclipse of the sun, we do not know whether it will pass away quickly or not, would it not have been better to go on?" Lâo Tan said, "When the prince of a state is going to the court of the son of Heaven, he travels while he can see the sun. At sun-down he halts, and presents his offerings (to the spirit of the way). When a Great officer is on a mission, he travels while he can see the sun, and at sun-down he halts. Now a bier does not set forth in the early morning, nor does it rest anywhere at night; but those who travel by star-light are only criminals and those who are hastening to the funeral rites of a parent. When there is an eclipse of the sun, how do we know that we shall not see the stars? And moreover, a superior man, in his performance of rites, will not expose his relatives to the risk of distress or evil." This is what I heard from Lâo Tan.'

23. Zang-dze asked, 'In the case of one dying where he is stopping, when discharging a mission for

[1. This was Lâo-dze, 'the old master.' It seems better to keep Lâo as if it had been the surname. See paragraph 24, p. 325.

2. The east of the road. Graves were north of the towns.]

his ruler, the rules say[1] that, (if he die) in a government hotel his spirit shall be recalled; but not, (if he die) in a private one[2]. But to whatever state a commissioner may be sent, the lodging which may be assigned to him by the proper officer becomes a public hotel;—what is the meaning of his spirit not being recalled, (if he die) in a private one?'

Confucius said, 'You have asked well. The houses of a high minister, a Great officer, or an ordinary officer, may be called private hotels. The government hotel, and any other which the government may appoint, may be called a public hotel. In this you have the meaning of that saying that the spirit is recalled at a public hotel.'

24. Zang–dze asked, 'Children dying prematurely, between eight and eleven, should be buried in the garden in a brick grave, and carried thither on a contrivance serving the purpose of a carriage, the place being near; but now if the grave is chosen at a distance, what do you say about their being buried there?'

Confucius said, 'I have heard this account from Lâo Tan:—"Formerly," he said, "the recorder Yî had a son who died thus prematurely, and the grave was distant. The duke of Shâo said to him, 'Why not shroud and coffin him in your palace?' The recorder said, 'Dare I do so?' The

[1. Where these rules are to be found I do not know.

2. I use 'hotel' here in the French meaning of the term. We must suppose that 'the private hotel' about which Zang–dze asked was one to which the commissioner had gone without the instructions of the state; and, as the Khien–lung editors say, 'the rites were therefore so far diminished.']

duke of Shâo spoke about it to the duke of Kâu, who said, 'Why may it not be done?' and the recorder did it. The practice of coffins for boys who have died so prematurely, and shrouding them, began with the recorder Yî."

25. Zang–dze asked, 'A minister or a Great officer is about to act the part of a personator of the dead for his ruler; If, when he has received (orders) to pass the night in solemn vigil, there occur in his own family an occasion for him to wear the robe of hemmed sackcloth, what should he do?'

Confucius said, 'The rule is for him to leave (his house) and lodge in a state hotel, and wait till (the ruler's) business is accomplished.'

26. Confucius said, 'When one who has represented the dead comes forth in the (officer's) leathern cap, or the (Great officer's) tasseled cap (which he has worn), ministers, Great

officers, and other officers, all will descend from their carriages (when his passes). He will bow forward to them, and he will also have a forerunner (to notify his approach).'

27. Dze–hsiâ asked, 'There is such a thing as no longer declining military service, after the wailing in the three years I mourning has come to an end. Is this the rule? or was it at first required by the officers (of the state)?'

Confucius said, 'Under the sovereigns of Hsiâ, as soon as the coffining in the three year's mourning was completed, they resigned all their public duties. Under Yin they did so as soon as the interment was over. Is not this the meaning of what we find in the record, that "the ruler does not take from men their affection to their parents, nor do men take from their parents their filial duty?"'

28. Dze–hsiâ asked, 'Is then not declining military service (during mourning) to be condemned?'

'Confucius said, 'I heard from Lâo Tan that duke Po–khin engaged once in such service, when there was occasion for it; but I do, not know if I should allow it in those who seek (by it) their own advantage during the period of the three years' mourning[1].'

[1. Po–khin was the son of the duke of Kâu, and the first marquis of Lû. The time of his entering on the rule of that state was a very critical one in the kingdom; and though it was then, it would appear, the period of his mourning for his mother's death, he discharged his public duty in the time of his own grief.]

BOOK VI. WAN WANG SHIH SZE

OR

KING WAN AS SON AND HEIR[1].

SECTION 1.

1. Thus did king Wan act when he was eldest son and heir:—Thrice a day he made a visit

in due form to king Kî. When the cock first crowed he dressed himself, and going to the outside of the bedroom, asked one of the servants of the interior who was in attendance how the king was and if he were well. When told that he was well, the prince was glad. At midday he repeated the visit in the same way; and so he did again in the evening[2]. If the king were not so well as usual, the servant would tell the prince, and then his sorrow appeared in his countenance, and his walk was affected and disturbed. When king Kî took his food again, Wan recovered his former appearance. When the food went up (to the king), he would examine it and see if it were cold and hot as it ought to be[3]. When it came down, he asked of what dishes the king had eaten. He gave orders to the cook that none of the dishes should go up again, and withdrew on receiving the cook's assurance accordingly[4].

[1. See the introduction, pages 22, 23.

2 If was the duty of a son to wait on his father twice a day,–at morning and night. King Win showed his filial duty by paying king Kî a third visit.

3. According to the season.

4. According to the ordinary dates in Chinese chronology, king Wan was born in B.C. 1258, and named Khang. King Ki died in 1185, when he was in his seventy–fourth year.]

2. King Wû acted according to the example (of Wan), not presuming to go (in anything) beyond it. When king Wan was ill, Wû nursed him without taking off his cap or girdle. When king Wan took a meal, he also took a meal; and when king Wan took a second, he did the same. It was not till after twelve days that he intermitted his attentions.

King Wan said to Wû, 'What have you been dreaming?' 'I dreamt,' was the reply, 'that God gave me nine ling?' 'And what do you think was the meaning?' King Wû said, 'There are nine states in the west;—may it not mean that you will yet bring them all under your happy sway?' Wan said, 'That was not the meaning. Anciently they called a year ling. The age is also called ling. I am 100; and you are go. I give you three years.' King Wan was 97 when he died, and king Wû was 93[1].

3. King Khang, being quite young, could not perform his part at the eastern steps[2]. The duke of Kâu acted as regent, trod those steps, and administered

[1. It is difficult to understand and interpret the latter half of this paragraph. The Khien–lung editors say that, according to the ordinary accounts, king Wû was born when wan was fifteen years old, and there was an elder son, Yî–khâo, who died prematurely; whereas king Wû died at 93, leaving his son Sung (king Khang) only seven years old. 'Wan,' they said, 'must have married very early, and Wû very late.' They say also that they cannot understand the text that Wan gave to his son 'three years,' &c., and suppose that some erroneous tradition has here been introduced.

2 The king received his nobles at the top of the eastern steps. The phrase = 'in the government of the kingdom.']

the government. He illustrated the rules for the behaviour of a young heir in his treatment of Po–khin, that king Khang might thereby know the courses to be pursued by father and son, ruler and minister, old and young. When he committed an error, the duke punished Po–khin. This was the way in which he showed king Khang his duty as the son and heir.

4. So much on the way in which king Wan acted as son and heir.

5. In teaching the heir–sons (of the king and feudal princes), and young men (chosen from their aptitude) for' learning', the subjects were different at different seasons. In spring and summer they were taught the use of the shield and spear; in autumn and winter that of the feather and flute:—all in the eastern school. The inferior directors of music[2] taught the use of the shield aided by the great assistants. The flute masters taught the use of the spear, aided by the subdirectors, while the assistants regulated by the drum (the chanting of) the Nan[3].

In spring they recited (the pieces), and in summer

[1. These 'scholars' no doubt, were those of whose selection for the higher instruction we have an account in the fourth and other paragraphs of Section IV, Book III.

2. These are mentioned in the 'Royal Regulations, though the title does not occur in the Kâu Lî. They are supposed to be the same as its 'music masters' (Yo Sze, Book XXII).

3 This clause about the 'drum' is perplexing to a translator. It destroys the symmetry of the paragraph, What we are to understand by the 'Nan' is also much disputed. I suppose

the term should embrace the two Nan, or two first Books of the Shih, Part I. Compare the Shih II, vi, 4. 4.]

they played on the guitar,—being taught by the grand master in the Hall of the Blind[1]. In autumn they learned ceremonies,—being instructed by the masters of ceremonies. In winter they read the book of History,—being instructed by the guardians of it. Ceremonies were taught in the Hall of the Blind; the book in the upper school.

[1. The names of these different schools are also very perplexing; and I here give a note about them by Liû Khang of our eleventh century. 'Under the Kiu dynasty they had its own schools and those of the three former dynasties; four buildings, all erected in proximity to one another. Alost in the centre was the Pî Yung of Kâu itself. On the north of it was the school of Shun (the lord Yü); on the east that of Hsiâ; and on the west that of Shang. Those who were learning the use (in dancing) of the shield and spear, and of the plume and flute, went to the eastern school; those who were learning ceremonies went to that of Shang; and those who were learning history, to that of Shun. In the Pî Yung the son of Heaven nourished the old, sent forth his armies, matured his plans, received prisoners, and practised archery. When he came to the Pî Yung, they came from all the other three schools, and stood round the encircling water to look at him. There were also schools on the plan of Shun—the hsiang—in the large districts (the, containing 12500 families); others on the plan of Hsiâ—the hsü in the Kâu, or smaller districts (the, containing 2500 families); and others still on the plan of Shang—the hsiâo–in the Tang or those still smaller (containing 500 families). These were all schools for young boys. The most promising scholars (in the family schools) were removed to the hsiang; the best in the hsiang, again to the hsü; and the best in the hsü, to the hsiâo. The best in these were removed finally to the great school (or college) in the suburbs (of the capital).' Such is the account of Liû Khang. Other scholars differ from him in some points; but there is a general agreement as to the existence of a system of graduated training.]

6. All the rules about sacrificial offerings[1] and at the nourishing of the old begging them to speak (their wise counsels)[2] and the conversation at general reunions, were taught by the lower directors of Music in the eastern school.

7. The Grand director of Music taught how to brandish the shield and axe. He also delivered the graduated rules relating to conversations and the charges about begging the old to speak. The Grand perfecter (of Instruction)[3] discussed all about (these matters) in

the eastern school.

8. Whenever a pupil was sitting with the Grand completer (of Instruction), there was required to be between them the width of three mats. He might put questions to him; and when he had finished, sit back on the mat near to the wall. While the instructor had not finished all he had to say on any one point, he did not ask about another.

9. In all the schools, the officer (in charge), in spring set forth offerings to the master who first, taught (the subjects); and in autumn and winter he did the same[4].

10. In every case of the first establishment of a school the offerings must be set forth to the earlier

[1. Probably, not sacrifices in general, but offerings to sages, distinguished old men, &c.

2. This asking the old men to speak was a part of the festal nourishment of them.

3. I do not think this officer appears in the lists of the Kâu Lî. He seems to be named as giving the finishing touch to the training of the young princes.

4. No mention is made of summer; but, no doubt, there were then the same observances as in the other seasons,—a tribute to the merit of the past, and a stimulus to the students.]

sages and the earlier teachers; and in the doing of this, pieces of silk must be used.

11. In all the cases of setting forth the offerings, it was required to have the accompaniments (of dancing and singing). When there were any events of engrossing interest in a state (at the time), these were omitted.

12. When there was the accompaniment of music on a great scale, they proceeded immediately to feast the aged.

13. At all examinations in the suburban schools, the rule was to select the best and mark out the most talented. The pupils might be advanced for their virtue, or commended for something they had accomplished, or distinguished for their eloquence[1]. Those who had studied minor arts were encouraged and told to expect a second examination[2]. If

they (then) had one of the three things (above mentioned), they were advanced to a higher grade, according to their several orders, and were styled 'Men of the schools.' They were (still, however,) kept out of the royal college[3], and could not receive the cup from the vase restricted to the superior students.

14. On the first establishment of schools (in any state), when the instruments of music were

[1. See paragraphs 2–4, pp. 231–233.

2. These minor arts, it is understood, were such as medicine and divination.

3. The name for this college here perhaps indicates that on reaching it, all from the other schools were 'on the same level.' The youths would appear to have passed into it with a festive ceremony. The 'suburban schools' were those in the note on p. 346, with the addition of the 'Eastern Kiâo', which it is not easy to distinguish from 'the eastern school,' already mentioned.]

completed[1], offerings of silk were set forth; and afterwards those of vegetables[2]. But there was no dancing and (consequently) no giving out of the spears and other things used in it. They simply retired and received visitors in the eastern school. Only one cup was passed round. The ceremony might pass without (parade of) attendants or conversation.

15. (All these things) belonged to the education of the young princes.

16. In the education of the crown princes adopted by the founders of the three dynasties the subjects were the rules of propriety and music. Music served to give the interior cultivation; the rules to give the external. The two, operating reciprocally within, had their outward manifestation, and the result was a peaceful serenity,—reverence of inward feeling and mild elegance of manners.

17. The Grand tutor and the assistant tutor were appointed for their training, to make them acquainted with the duties of father and son, and of ruler and minister. The former made himself perfectly master of those duties in order to exhibit them; the latter guided the princes to observe the virtuous ways of the other and fully instructed him about them.

The Grand tutor went before them, and the assistant came

[1. 'Were completed,' should be, according to Khang-khang, were consecrated.' For the character in the text he would substitute that which we find in Mencius, I. i, 7, 4, applied to the consecration of a bell. Compare vol. iii, p. 323.

2. The ordinary offerings (see above, paragraph 9); but now a sequel to the offerings of silk. These two offerings, it is understood, were in the school on the west (the hsiang), and thence the parties officiating adjourned to that on the east (the hsü).]

after them. In the palace was the guardian, outside it was the master; and thus by this training and instruction the virtue (of the princes) was completed. The master taught them by means of occurring things, and made them understand what was virtuous. The guardian watched over their persons, and was as a stay and wings to them, leading them in the right way. The history says, 'Under the dynasties of Yü, Hsiâ, Shang, and Kâu, there were the master, the guardian, the Î, and the Khang, and there were appointed the four aides and the three ducal ministers. That these offices should all be filled was not so necessary as that there should be the men for them;'—showing how the object was to employ the able[1].

18. When we speak of 'a superior man' we intend chiefly his virtue. The virtue perfect and his instructions honoured; his instructions honoured and the (various) officers correct; the officers correct and order maintained in the state:—these things give the ideal of a ruler[2].

[1. The Khien-lung editors seem to say that 'the Grand tutor' and 'the assistant tutor,' who had the charge of the young prince from his infancy, must have been ladies of the harem; so that, in fact, the government of a ruler's household was regulated after the model of the government of the state in his maturer years. There are no materials to illustrate the duties of the ministers who are called 'the Î and the Khang.'

2 Wû Khang thinks that the first three characters here should be translated—'The superior man (Kün-dze) says;' a sequel to 'The history says' of the preceding paragraph. He then proposes to suppress one of the virtues that follow. But the structure of the whole will not admit this way of dealing with it. There is a play on the characters rendered 'a superior man' and 'a ruler,'—Kün-dze and Kun; like our English 'a noble man' and 'a noble,' 'a

princely man' and 'a prince.']

19. Kung-nî said, 'Formerly, when the duke of Kâu was administering the government, he did so while he (continued to) go up by the eastern steps. He (also) set forth the rules for a crown prince in (his dealing with) Po-khin, and it was thus that he secured the excellence of king Khang. I have heard it said, "A minister will sacrifice himself to benefit his ruler, and how much more will he swerve from the ordinary course to secure his excellence!" This was what the duke of Kâu did with ease and unconcern.

20. 'Therefore he who knows how to show himself what a son should be can afterwards show himself what a father should be; he who knows how to show himself what a minister should be can afterwards show himself what a ruler should be; he who knows how to serve others can afterwards employ them. King Khang, being quite young, could not discharge the duties of the government. He had no means of learning how to show himself what the crown prince should be[1]. On this account the rules for a crown prince were exhibited in (the treatment of) Po-khin, and he was made to live with the young king that the latter might thus understand all that was right between father and son, ruler and minister, elders and youngers[2].'

[1. His father being dead.

2. With reference to this paragraph, which, he thinks, appears here as from Confucius, Wû Khang says:-,When king Wû died, Khang was quite young. (His uncles of) Kwan and Zhâi sent their reports abroad, and the people of Yin planned their rebellion. Then the duke of Kâu left the capital, and dwelt in the east, and Po-khin went to his jurisdiction, and defeated the people of Hsü and the Zung. Three years afterwards the duke of Kâu returned, took the regency and made his expedition to the east,-it was impossible for Khang and Po-khin to be always together. Perhaps the duke made them keep so, while king Wû was alive; and the account in the text was an erroneous tradition.' To this the Khien-lung editors reply:—'Immediately on the death of king Wû, the duke of Kâu must have adopted the method described in the text. Thâi Kung was Grand master; the duke of Shâo, Grand guardian; and the duke of Kâu himself Grand tutor. They, no doubt, made Po-khin, Kün Khan, Lü Ki, Wang-sun Mâu, and others associate with the young king. In the winter of his first year, the duke removed to the eastern capital, while the other two continued in their places, and Po-khin was daily with Khang, and there was no change in the rules for a son and heir. Next year happened the storm which changed the king's

views about the duke, who returned to the court. The third year saw the removal of the people of Yen, and Po–khin proceeded to his jurisdiction in Lû. But by this time king Khang's virtue and ability were matured. Wû's objections to the ordinary view of the text are without foundation.']

21. Take the case of the sovereign and his son and heir. Looked at from the standpoint of affection, the former is father; from that of honour, he is ruler. If the son can give the affection due to the father, and the honour due to the ruler, hereafter he 'will (be fit to) be the lord of all under the sky. On this account the training of crown princes ought to be most carefully attended to.

22. It is only in the case of the crown prince that by the doing of one thing three excellent things are realised; and it is with reference to his taking his place in the schools according to his age that this is spoken. Thus it is that when he takes his place in them in this way, the people observing it, one will say, 'He is to be our ruler, how is it that he gives place to us in the matter of years?' and it will be replied, 'While his father is alive, it is the rule that he should do so.' Thus all will understand the right course as between father and son. A second will make the same remark, and put the same question; and it will be replied, 'While the ruler is alive, it is the rule that he should do so;' and thus all will understand the righteousness that should obtain between ruler and minister. To a third putting the same question it will be said, 'He is giving to his elders what is due to their age;' and thus all will understand the observances that should rule between young and old. Therefore, while his father is alive, he is but a son; and, while his ruler is alive, he may be called merely a minister. Occupying aright the position of son and Minister is the way in which he shows the honour due to a ruler and the affection due to a father. He is thus taught the duties between father and son, between ruler and minister, between old and young; and when he has become master of all these, the state will be well governed. The saying,

'Music's Director the foundation lays;
The Master this doth to perfection raise.
Let him but once the great and good be taught,
And all the states are to correctness brought,'

finds its application in the case of the heir–son.

23. So much for the duke of Kâu's going up by the eastern steps.

SECTION II.

1. The Shû-dze[1], who had the direction of the (other) members of the royal and princely families,

[1. See Book XLIV, paragraph 1, and note. The Shû-dze or Kû-dze belonged to the department of the Sze-mâ. They were two Great officers of the third grade; and under them thirty assistants,—officers and employés. The superintendents of the Lists in {the} next paragraph belonged to the same department;-also two of the same rank as the Shû-dze, and under them sixty-eight others. The functions of both are described in the Kâu Lî, Book XXXI.]

inculcated on them filial piety and fraternal duty, harmony and friendship, and kindly consideration; illustrating the righteousness that should prevail between father and son, and the order to be observed between elders and juniors.

2. When they appeared at court, if it were at a reception in the innermost (courtyard of the palace), they took their places, facing the east, those of the most honourable rank among them, as ministers, being to the north (of the others); but they were arranged according to their age. If it were a reception in the outer (and second courtyard), they were arranged according to their offices;—(as in the former case), by the superintendents of the official lists.

3. When they were in the ancestral temple, they took their places as at the reception in the outer (and second courtyard); and the superintendent of the temple[1] assigned his business to each according to rank and office. In their ascending (to the hall), partaking of what had been left (by the personator of the dead), presenting (the cup to him), and receiving it (from him)[2], the eldest son by the wife took the precedence. The proceedings were regulated by the Shû-dze. Although one might have received three of the gifts of distinction, he did not take precedence of an uncle or elder cousin.

4. At the funeral rites for rulers, they were arranged according to the character of their mourning-dress

[1. See the Kâu Lî, Book XXVII.

2. These ceremonies do not appear to be mentioned here in the order of their occurrence.]

in the fineness or coarseness of the material. In case of such rites among themselves, the same order was observed, the principal mourner, however, always taking precedence of all others.

5. If the ruler were feasting with his kindred, then all of a different kindred were received as guests. The cook acted as master of the ceremonies[1]. The ruler took place among his uncles and cousins according to age. Each generation of kindred took a lower place as it was a degree removed from the parent-stem.

6. When with the army, the kindred guarded the spirit-tablets that had been brought from their shrines. If any public duties called the ruler beyond the limits of the state, those officers of the kindred employed the members of it, who had not other duties, to guard the ancestral temple and the apartments of the palace, the eldest sons by the proper wives guarding the temple of the Grand ancestor; the various uncles, the most honoured temple-shrines and apartments; the other sons and grandsons, the inferior shrines and apartments.

7. All descended from any of the five rulers to whom the temple-shrines were dedicated, even those who were now classed among the common people, were required to announce the events of capping and marriage, so long as the temple-shrine of the (Grand ancestor) had not been removed. Their deaths had to be announced; and also their sacrifices during the

[1. We have here an instance of the important part which the cook played in the establishments of the kings and princes of those days; see vol. iii, pp. 356, 422. The ruler was too dignified to drink with the guests.]

period of mourning. In the relations of the kindred among themselves, the proper officers punished any neglect of the regulations for condoling and not condoling, leaving off and not leaving off the cap (in mourning). There were the correct rules for the mourning gifts of articles, money, robes, and jade to put into the mouth (of the deceased).

8. When one of the ruler's kindred was found guilty of a capital offence, he was hanged by some one of the foresters' department. If the punishment for his offence were corporal

infliction or dismemberment, it was also handed over to the same department. No one of the ruler's kindred was punished with castration.

When the trial was concluded, the proper officer reported the sentence to the ruler. If the penalty were death, he would say, 'The offence of So and So is a capital crime.' If the penalty were less, he would say, 'The offence of So and So has received a lighter sentence.' The ruler would say', 'Let the sentence be remitted for another;' and the officer would say, 'That is the sentence.' This was repeated till the third time, when the officer would make no answer, but hurry off and put the execution into the hands of the appointed forester. Still the ruler would send some one after him, and say, 'Yes, but grant forgiveness,' to which there would be the reply, 'It is too late.' When the execution was reported to the ruler, he put on white clothes, and did not have a full meal or music, thus changing his usual habits. Though the kinsman might be within the degree for which there should be mourning rites, the ruler did not wear mourning, but wailed for him himself (in some family of a different surname).

9. That the rulers kindred appeared at the reception in the innermost (court) showed how (the ruler) would honour the relatives of his own surname. That they took places according to their age, even those among them of high rank, showed the relation to be maintained between father and son. That they took places at the reception in the outer court according to their offices, showed how (the ruler) would show that they formed one body with (the officers of) other surnames[1].

10. Their taking their places in the ancestral temple according to rank served to exalt the sense of virtue. That the superintendent of the temple assigned to them their several services according to their offices was a tribute of honour to worth. That the eldest son by the proper wife was employed to ascend, take precedence in partaking of what had been left, and in receiving the cup, was to do honour to their ancestor.

11. That the distinctions at the funeral rites were arranged according to the fineness or coarseness of their mourning robes was not to take from any one the degree of his relationship[3].

12. The ruler, when feasting with his kindred, took his place among them according to age, and thus development was given to filial piety and fraternal duty. That each generation took a lower place as it was removed a degree from the parent–stem showed

the graduation of affection among relatives[4].

[1. See paragraph 2, above.

2 See paragraph 3, above.

3. See paragraph 4, above.

4 See paragraph 5, above.]

13. The guard maintained during war over the spirit–tablets in the army showed the deep sense of filial piety and love. When the eldest son by the proper wife guarded the temple of the Grand ancestor, honour was done to the temple by the most honoured, and the rule as between ruler and minister was exhibited. When the uncles guarded the most honoured shrines and apartments, and the cousins those that were inferior, the principles of subordination and deference were displayed[1].

14. That the descendants of the five rulers, to whom the temple–shrines were dedicated, were required, so long as the shrine of the Grand ancestor had not been removed, to announce their cappings and marriages, and their death was also required to be announced, showed how kinship was to be kept in mind[2]. While the kinship was yet maintained, that some were classed among the common people showed how mean position followed on want of ability. The reverent observance of condoling, wailing, and of presenting contributions to the funeral rites in articles and money, Was the way taken to maintain harmony and friendliness[3].

15. Anciently, when the duties of these officers of the royal or princely kindred were well discharged, there was a constant model for the regions and states; and when this model was maintained, all knew to what to direct their views and aims[4].

[1. See paragraph 6, above.

2. See paragraph 12, above.

3. See paragraph 7, above,

4. This paragraph is evidently out of place, and should follow the next. Some of the critics endeavour very ingeniously to account for its having been designedly placed where it stands.]

16. When any of the ruler's kindred were guilty of offences, notwithstanding their kinship, they were not allowed to transgress with impunity, but the proper officers had their methods of dealing with them:—this showed the regard cherished for the people. That the offender was punished in secret[1], and not associated with common people, showed (the ruler's) concern for his brethren. That he offered no condolence, wore no mourning, and wailed for the criminal in the temple of a different surname, showed how he kept aloof from him as having disgraced their ancestors. That he wore white, occupied a chamber outside, and did not listen to music, was a private mourning for him, and showed how the feeling of kinship was not extinguished. That one of the ruler's kindred was not subjected to castration, showed how he shrank from cutting off the perpetuation of their family.

17. When the son of Heaven was about to visit the college, the drum was beaten at early dawn to arouse all (the students). When all were come together, the son of Heaven then arrived and ordered the proper officers to discharge their business, proceeding in the regular order, and sacrificing to the former masters and former Sages. When

[1. This refers to the statement in paragraph 8, that members of the ruler's kindred, instead of being executed or exposed in the court or market–place, were handed over to be dealt with in the country, by the foresters' department. On that department and the duties and members of it, see the Kâu Lî, Book I, II; IV, 64–69.]

they reported to him that everything had been done, he then began to go to the nourishing (of the aged).

18. Proceeding to the school on the east, he unfolded and set forth the offerings to the aged of former times, and immediately afterwards arranged the mats and places for the three (classes of the) old, and the five (classes of the) experienced, for all the aged (indeed who were present),.

19. He (then) went to look at the food and examine the liquor. When the delicacies for the nourishment of the aged were all ready, he caused the song to be raised (as a signal for

the aged to come). After this he retired and thus it was that he provided for (the aged) his filial nourishment.

20. When (the aged) had returned (to their seats after partaking of the feast), the musicians went up and sang the Khang Miâo[2], after which there was

[1. There is great difference of opinion about ' the three old' and 'the five experienced.' A common view is that the former name denotes the old men of 80, 90, and 100; which appears to have been first propounded by Tû Yü (A. D. 222–284). The Khien–lung editors speak contemptuously of it, and ask what analogous division is to be made of the five classes of the experienced. Callery has a note on the paragraph, to the effect that there were two old men, one called 'the san–lâo,' and the other 'the wû–kang.' The emperor of the Khien–lung period, he tells us, because of the great age at which he had himself arrived, wished to restore the ancient practices in honour of old age. His proposal, however, was so vigorously opposed in council, especially by a Chinese minister, that he was obliged to abandon it. 'Many volumes,' he says, 'have been written on the origin and meaning of the denominations in the text, but nothing certain is known on the subject.'

2. 'Khing Miâo' is the name of the first of 'The Sacrificial Odes of Kâu;' see vol. iii, pp. 313, 314.]

conversation to bring out fully its meaning. They spoke of the duties between father and son, ruler and minister, elders and juniors. This union (of the conversation) with the highest description of virtue in the piece constituted the greatest feature of the ceremony.

21. Below (in the court–yard), the flute–players played the tune of the Hsiang[1], while the Tâ–wei was danced, all uniting in the grand concert according to their parts, giving full development to the spirit (of the music), and stimulating the sense of virtue. The positions of ruler and minister, and the gradations of noble and mean were correctly exhibited, and the respective duties of high and low took their proper course.

22. The officers having announced that the music was over, the king then charged the dukes, marquises, earls, counts, and barons, with all the officers, saying, 'Return, and nourish the aged and the young[2] in your eastern schools.' Thus did he end (the ceremony) with (the manifestation of) benevolence.

23. The above statements show how the sage (sovereign) bore in mind the various steps (of this ceremony)[3]. He anxiously thought of it as its greatness deserved; his love for the aged was blended

[1. 'Hsiang' was the name of a piece of music played to the dance Tâ–wû, in memory of the kings wan and Wû. It is hardly possible to give any more detailed description either of the piece or of the dance.

2. 'The young' is supposed to be an interpolation.

3. This sentence is difficult. Callery translates it:—'En vue de tout cela l'empereur vertueux repasse dans sa mémoire ce que (les anciens) ont fait (pour honorer la vieillesse, afin de les imiter).']

with reverence; he carried the thing through with attention to propriety; he adorned it with his filial nourishing; he connected with it the exhibition of the legitimate distinctions (of rank); and concluded it with (the manifestation of) benevolence. In this way the ancients, in the exhibition of this one ceremony, made all know how complete was their virtue. Among them, when they undertook any great affair, they were sure to carry it through carefully from beginning to end, so that it was impossible for any not to understand them. As it is said in the Yüeh Ming', 'The thoughts from first to last should be fixed on (this) learning.'

24. The Record of (king Wan's) son and heir says, 'Morning and evening he went to the outside of the door of the great chamber, and asked the attendant of the interior whether his father were well, and how he was. If told that he was well, his joy appeared in his countenance. If his father were not so well, the attendant would tell him so, and then his sorrow and anxiety appeared, and his demeanour was disturbed. When the attendant told him that his father was better, he resumed his former appearance. Morning and evening when the food went up, he would examine it and see if it were hot or cold as it ought to be. When it came down, he asked what his father had eaten. He made it a point to know what viands went in, and to give his orders to the cook; and then he retired.

'If the attendant reported that his father was ill, then he himself fasted and waited on him in his dark–coloured dress. He inspected with reverence the

[1. See the 'Charge to Yueh,' in vol. iii, p. ix 7.]

food prepared by the cook, and tasted himself the medicine for the patient. If his father ate well of the food, then he was able to eat. If his father ate but little, then he could not take a full meal. When his father had recovered, then he resumed his former ways[1].'

[1. This is evidently an unskilful reproduction of the first paragraph of Section i. We try in vain to discover why the compiler inserted it here.]

BOOK VII. THE, LÎ YUN

OR

CEREMONIAL USAGES; THEIR ORIGIN, DEVELOPMENT, AND INTENTION[1].

SECTION I.

1. Formerly Kung-nî was present as one of the guests at the Kâ sacrifice[2]; and when it was over, he went out and walked backwards and forwards on the terrace over the gate of Proclamations[3], looking sad and sighing. What made him sigh was the state of Lû[4]. Yen Yen was by his side, and said to him, 'Master, what are you sighing about?' Confucius replied, 'I never saw the practice of the Grand course[5], and the eminent men of the three dynasties[6]; but I have my object (in harmony with theirs).

.2. 'When the Grand course was pursued, a public and common spirit ruled all under the sky; they

[1. See the introduction, pages 23, 24.

2. Offered in the end of the year, in thanksgiving for all the crops that had been reaped. See in Book IX, ii, paragraphs 9, 10.

3. The gateway where illustrated copies of the laws and punishments were suspended, It belonged of right only to the royal palace, but it was among the things which Lû had usurped, or was privileged to use.

4. As usurping royal rites, and in disorder.

5. This sounds Tâoistic. It is explained of the time of the five Tîs.

6. The founders of the Hsiâ, Shang, and Kâu, and their great ministers.]

chose[1] men of talents, virtue, and ability; their words were sincere, and what they cultivated was harmony. Thus men did not love their parents only, nor treat as children only their own sons. A competent provision was secured for the aged till their death, employment for the able-bodied, and the means of growing up to the young. They showed kindness and compassion to widows, orphans, childless men, and those who were disabled by disease, so that they were all sufficiently maintained. Males had their proper work, and females had their homes. (They accumulated) articles (of value), disliking that they should be thrown away upon the ground, but not wishing to keep them for their own gratification[2]. (The), laboured) with their strength, disliking that it should not be exerted, but not exerting it (only) with a view to their own advantage[3]. In this way (selfish) schemings were repressed and found no development. Robbers, filchers, and

[1. 'They chose;' who are intended by the 'they?' Shall we find them in the 'all under the sky' of the preceding clause? Callery has:—'Sous le grand régne de la vertu, l'empire était la chose publique. On choisissait pour le gouverneur les hommes éminents,' &c. Khung Ying-tâ explains the clause by 'They made no hereditary princes., Perhaps it would be well to translate passively,—'Men of virtue and ability were chosen (to govern).' The writer has before him the Tâoistic period of the primitive simplicity, when there was no necessity for organised government as in after ages.

2 It is rather difficult to construe and translate these two sentences. Callery gives for them, not very successfully:—'Quant aux objets matériels, ceux qu'on n'aimait pas, on les abandonnait (aux personnes qui en avaient besoin), sans les mettre en réserve pour soi. Les choses dont on était capable, on regardait comme fort mauvais de ne pas les faire, lors même que cc n'était pas pour soi.']

rebellious traitors did not show themselves, and hence the outer doors remained open, and were not shut. This was (the period of) what we call the Grand Union.

3. 'Now that the Grand course has fallen into disuse and obscurity, the kingdom is a family inheritance. Every one loves (above all others) his own parents and cherishes (as) children (only) his own sons. People accumulate articles and exert their strength for their own advantage. Great men imagine it is the rule that their states should descend in their own families. Their object is to make the walls of their cities and suburbs strong and their ditches and moats secure. The rules of propriety and of what is right are regarded as the threads by which they seek to maintain in its correctness the relation between ruler and minister; in its generous regard that between father and son; in its harmony that between elder brother and younger; and in a community of sentiment that between husband and wife; and in accordance with them they frame buildings and measures; lay out the fields and hamlets (for the dwellings of the husbandmen); adjudge the superiority to men of valour and knowledge; and regulate their achievements with a view to their own advantage. Thus it is that (selfish) schemes and enterprises are constantly taking their rise, and recourse is had to arms; and thus it was (also) that Yü, Thang, Wan and Wû, king Khang, and the duke of Kâu obtained their distinction. Of these six great men every one was very attentive to the rules of propriety, thus to secure the display of righteousness, the realisation of sincerity, the exhibition of errors, the exemplification of benevolence, and the discussion of courtesy, showing the people all the normal virtues. Any rulers who did not follow this course were driven away by those who possessed power and position, and all regarded them as pests. This is the period of what we call Small Tranquillity[1].'

4. Yen Yen again asked, 'Are the rules of Propriety indeed of such urgent importance?' Confucius said, 'It was by those rules that the ancient kings sought to represent the ways of Heaven, and to regulate the feelings of men. Therefore he who neglects or violates them may be (spoken of) as dead, and he who observes them, as alive. It is said in the Book of Poetry,

Look at a rat–how small its limbs and fine!
Then mark the course that scorns the proper line.
Propriety's neglect may well provoke
A wish the man would quickly court death's stroke"

Therefore those rules are rooted in heaven, have their correspondencies in earth, and are applicable to spiritual beings. They extend to funeral rites, sacrifices, archery, chariot–driving, capping, marriage, audiences, and friendly missions. Thus the sages made known these rules, and it became possible for the kingdom, with its states and clans, to reach its correct condition.'

5. Yen Yen again asked, 'May I be allowed to hear, Master, the full account that you would give of

[1. The Tâoism in this and the preceding paragraph is evident, and we need not be surprised that Wang of Shih–liang should say that they ought not to be ascribed to Confucius. The Khien–lung editors try to weaken the force of his judgment by a theory of misplaced tablets and spurious additions to the text.

The Shih, I, iv, 8; metrical version, page 99.]

these rules?' Confucius said, 'I wished to see the ways of Hsiâ, and for that purpose went to Khî. But it was not able to attest my words, though I found there "The seasons of Hsiâ." I wished to see the ways of Yin, and for that purpose went to Sung. But it was not able to attest my words, though I found there "The Khwan Khien." In this way I got to see the meanings in the Khwan Khien, and the different steps in the seasons of Hsiâ[1].

6. 'At the first use of ceremonies, they began with meat and drink. They roasted millet and pieces of pork[2]; they excavated the ground in the form of a jar, and scooped the water from it with their two hands; they fashioned a handle of clay, and struck with it an earthen drum. (Simple as these arrangements were), they yet seemed to be able to express by them their reverence for Spiritual Beings.

7. '(By–and–by)[3], when one died, they went upon

[1. Compare with this paragraph the ninth in the third Book of the Analects. In that Confucius tells of his visits to Khî and Sung; but says nothing of his finding any book or fragment of a book in either, dwelling instead on the insufficiency of their records. 'The seasons of Hsü,' which it is said here 'he got in Khî,' is supposed to be the 'small calendar of Hsiâ,' preserved by the Greater Tai, and 'the Khwan Khien' to have been the 'Kwei Zhang Yî,' attributed by many to the Shang dynasty. But all this is very uncertain.

2. In an unartificial manner, we are told, 'by placing them on heated stones.' It is only the last sentence of the paragraph which makes us think that the previous parts have anything to do with sacrifice or religion.

3. Khung Ying–t–â thinks that this describes the practices of the period of 'the five Tîs.' The north is the quarter of darkness and decay, the south that of brightness and life. 'The paragraph teaches us,' says Hsu Shih–zang, 'that the burial and other mourning ceremonies were not inventions of later sages, but grew from the natural feelings and sorrow of the earliest men.']

the housetop, and called out his name in a prolonged note, saying, "Come back, So and So." After this they filled the mouth (of the dead) with uncooked rice, and (set forth as offerings to him) packets of raw flesh. Thus they looked up to heaven (whither the spirit was gone), and buried (the body) in the earth. The body and the animal soul go downwards; and the intelligent spirit is on high.

Thus (also) the dead are placed with their heads to the north, while the living look towards the south. In all these matters the earliest practice is followed.

8. 'Formerly the ancient kings' had no houses. In winter they lived in caves which they had excavated, and in summer in nests which they had framed. They knew not yet the transforming power of fire, but ate the fruits of plants and trees, and the flesh of birds and beasts, drinking their blood, and swallowing (also) the hair and feathers. They knew not yet the use of flax and silk, but clothed themselves with feathers and skins.

9. 'The later sages then arose, and men (learned) to take advantage of the benefits of fire. They moulded the metals and fashioned clay, so as to rear towers with structures on them, and houses with windows and doors. They toasted, grilled, boiled, and roasted. They produced must and sauces. They dealt with the flax and silk so as to form linen and silken fabrics. They were thus able to nourish the living, and to make offerings to the dead; to serve

[1. This was, says King, 'the time of the highest antiquity;' 'the time,' says Ying–Lâ, 'before the five Tîs.']

the spirits of the departed and God[1]. In all these things we follow the example of that early time.

10. 'Thus it is that the dark-coloured liquor is in the apartment (where the representative of the dead is entertained)[2]; that the vessel of must is near its (entrance) door; that the reddish liquor is in the hall; and the clear, in the (court) below. The victims (also) are displayed, and the tripods and stands are prepared. The lutes and citherns are put in their places, with the flutes, sonorous stones, bells, and drums. The prayers (of the principal in the sacrifice to the spirits) and the benedictions (of the representatives of the departed) are carefully framed. The

[1. According to Ying-tâ, 'this is descriptive of the times of Shan Nang in middle antiquity, of the five Tîs, and of the three kings.' This would extend it over a very long space of time. When it is said that men in their advancing civilisation were able to serve the spirits of the departed and God, the peculiarity of style by which those spirits (literally, the Kwei Shan) are placed before God (Shang Tî) does not fail to attract the notice of the student. The explanation of it was given ingeniously, and I believe correctly, by Dr. Medhurst (Theology of the Chinese, page 78), who says, I it was done, probably, in order to distinguish the one from the other, and to prevent the reader from imagining that the Kwei Shans belonged to the Shang Tî, which mistake might have occurred had the characters been differently arranged! I translate the last sentence in the present tense, the, speaker having, I think, his own times in mind.

2. The 'dark-coloured' liquor was water, which was employed in the earliest times, before there was any preparation of liquor made from grain, either by fermentation or distillation, and the use of it was continued in the subsequent times of which this paragraph speaks, in honour of the practice of antiquity; and is continued, probably, to the present day. The other liquors are mentioned in the order of their invention, following one another in the historical line of their discovery, the older always having a nearer and more honourable place.]

object of all the ceremonies is to bring down the spirits from above, even their ancestors[1]; serving (also) to rectify the relations between ruler and ministers; to maintain the generous feeling between father and son, and the harmony between elder and younger brother; to adjust the relations between high and low; and to give their proper places to husband and wife. The whole may be said to secure the blessing of

Heaven.

11. 'They proceed to their invocations, using in each the appropriate terms. The dark-coloured liquor is employed in (every) sacrifice. The blood with the hair and feathers (of the victim) is presented. The flesh, uncooked, is set forth on the stands[2]. The bones with the flesh on them are sodden; and rush mats and coarse cloth are placed underneath and over the vases and cups. The robes of dyed silk are put on. The must and clarified liquor are presented. The flesh, roasted and grilled, is brought forward[3]. The ruler and his wife take alternate parts in presenting these offerings, all being done to please the souls of the departed, and constituting a union (of the living) with the disembodied and unseen.

[1. Dr. Medhurst rendered this—'to bring down the Shans of the upper world, together with the manes of their first ancestors.' In giving to the two phrases one and the same reference I am following Ying–tâ and others.

2. The last three observances were in imitation of what was done in the earliest antiquity.

3. In these six things the ways of ' middle antiquity' were observed. The whole paragraph is descriptive of a sacrifice in the ancestral temple under Kâu, where an effort was made to reproduce all sacrificial customs from the earliest times.]

12. 'These services having been completed, they retire, and cook again all that was insufficiently done. The dogs, pigs, bullocks, and sheep are dismembered. The shorter dishes (round and square), the taller ones of bamboo and wood, and the soup vessels are all filled. There are the prayers which express the filial piety (of the worshipper), and the benediction announcing the favour (of his ancestors). This may be called the greatest omen of prosperity; and in this the ceremony obtains its grand completion[1].'

SECTION II.

1. Confucius said, 'Ah! Alas! I look at the ways of Kâu. (The kings) Yû[2] and Lî[3] corrupted them indeed, but if I leave Lû, where shall I go (to find them better)? The border sacrifice of Lû, (however,) and (the association with it of) the founder of the line (of Kâu) is contrary to propriety;—how have (the institutions of) the duke of Kâu fallen

into decay[4]! At the border sacrifice in Khî, Yü was the assessor, and at that in Sung, Hsieh; but these were observances

[1. This last paragraph appears to me to give a very condensed account of the banquet to a ruler's kindred, with which a service in the ancestral temple concluded. Paragraphs 10, 11, 12 are all descriptive of the parts of such a service. Compare the accounts of it in the Shih II, vi, ode 5, and other pieces.

2 B.C. 791–771.

3. B.C. 878–828.

4. That the sacrificial ceremonies of Lû were in many things corrupted in Lû in the time of Confucius is plain to the reader of the Analects. How the corruption first began is a subject of endless controversy. it seems to be established that special privileges were granted in this respect to the duke of Kâu and his son, Po–khin. Guarded at first and innocent, encroachments were made by successive princes, as the vigour, of the royal authority declined; and by–and–by as those princes became themselves more and more weak, their ministers followed in their wake, and usurped the same ceremonies in their own services.

The commentators throw little light on the special corruption selected here for condemnation by Confucius. I have interpreted it by the analogy of the cases of Khî and Sung. The lords of those states were descended from the sovereigns of Hsiâ and Shang respectively, and were invested with them at the rise of the Kâu dynasty, that they might continue in them the sacrifices of their royal ancestors. They did so not as the lords of Khî and Sung, but as representing the lines of Hsiâ and Shang. But the case was different with the lords of Lû, belonging to the time of Kâu, but not representing it. Its kings were still reigning. Whether the words of Confucius should be extended over all the paragraph is a doubtful point.]

of the sons of Heaven, preserved (in those states by their descendants). The rule is that (only) the son of Heaven sacrifices to heaven and earth, and the princes of states sacrifice at the altars to the spirits of the land and grain.'

2. When no change is presumptuously made from the constant practice from the oldest times between the prayer and blessing (at the beginning of the sacrifice)[1], and the benediction (at the end of it)[1], we have what might be called a great and happy service.

3. For the words of prayer and blessing and those of benediction to be kept hidden away by the officers of prayer of the ancestral temple, and the sorcerers and recorders, is a violation of the rules of propriety. This may be called keeping a state in darkness[2].

[1. See paragraph 12 of the last section.

2. In this way new forms of prayer and benediction came into use, and the old forms were forgotten. The sorcerers; see page 172, paragraph 42.]

4. (The use of) the kan cup (of Hsiâ) and the kiâ cup (of Yin), and (the pledging in them) between the representative of the dead and the ruler are contrary to propriety;–these things constitute 'a usurping ruler[1].'

5. (For ministers and Great officers to) keep the cap with pendents and the leathern cap, or military weapons, in their own houses is contrary to propriety. To do so constitutes 'restraint of the ruler[2].'

6. For Great officers to maintain a full staff of employés, to have so many sacrificial vessels that they do not need to borrow any; and have singers and musical instruments all complete, is contrary to propriety. For them to do so leads to 'disorder in a state'.[3]

7. Thus, one sustaining office under the ruler is called a minister, and one sustaining office under the head of a clan is called a servant. Either of these, who is in mourning for a parent, or has newly married, is not sent on any mission for a year[4].

[1. It would be of little use to give representations of those cups, as they are ordinarily figured. Only in Khî, Sung, and Lû could they be used with any degree of propriety. In the times referred to in these paragraphs they were used by other states; which was an act of usurpation.

2. Certain styles of these caps were peculiar to the king, and of course could not be used by inferiors. Others might be used by them, but were kept in public offices, and given out

when required. Sometimes they were conferred by special gift; but none could make them for themselves.

3. A Great officer, if he had land, might have a ruler or steward, to whom everything was entrusted; and he might have some sacrificial vessels, but not a complete set. He did not have music at his sacrifices, unless it were by special permission.

4. Compare Deuteronomy xxiv. 5.]

To enter court in decayed robes, or to live promiscuously with his servants, taking place among them according to age:—all these things are contrary to propriety. Where we have them, we have what is called 'ruler and minister sharing the state.'

8. Thus, the son of Heaven has his domain that he may settle there his sons and grandsons; and the feudal princes have their states; and Great officers their appanages that they may do the same for theirs. This constitutes 'the statutory arrangement.'

9. Thus, when the son of Heaven goes to visit a feudal prince, the rule is that he shall lodge in the ancestral temple, and that he do not enter it without having with him all the rules to be observed. If he act otherwise, we have an instance of 'The son of Heaven perverting the laws, and throwing the regulations into confusion.' A prince, unless it be to ask about the sick or to condole with a mourner, does not enter the house of a minister. If he act otherwise, we have the case of 'ruler and minister playing with each other.'

10. Therefore, ceremonies form a great instrument in the hands of a ruler. It is by them that he resolves what is doubtful and brings to light what is abstruse; that he conducts his intercourse with spiritual beings, examines all statutory arrangements, and distinguishes benevolence from righteousness; it is by them, in short, that government is rightly ordered, and his own tranquillity secured.

11. When government is not correct, the ruler's seat is insecure. When the ruler's seat is insecure, the great ministers revolt, and smaller ones begin pilfering. Punishments (then) are made severe, and manners deteriorate. Thus the laws become irregular, and the rules of ceremony uncertain. When these are uncertain, officers do not perform their duties; and when punishments become severe, and manners deteriorate, the people do not turn (to what is right). We have that condition which may be described as 'an infirm state.'

12. In this way government is the means by which the ruler keeps and protects his person, and therefore it must have a fundamental connection with Heaven. This uses a variety of ways in sending down the intimations of Its will. As learned from the altars of the land, these are (receptivity and docility) imparted to the earth. As learned from the ancestral temple, they are benevolence and righteousness. As learned from the altars of the hills and streams, they are movement and activity. As learned from the five sacrifices of the house, they are the statutes (of their various spirits). It is in this way that the sage rulers made provision for the safe keeping of their persons[1].

[1. On this paragraph M. Callery has the following note:—'Très difficile à comprendre dans nos idées, ce passage offre un sens tout simple et naturel aux Chinois, dont la bizarre métaphysique va chercher dans la nature une analogie essentielle entre les accidents divers des êtres, et les phénomènes rationnels ou psychologiques. Ainsi, suivant les philosophes Chinois, tant anciens que modernes, la société présente des inégalités dans ses classes d'individus, comme la terre présente à sa surface des montagnes et des vallées; telle loi provoque l'action et le mouvement, comme les rivières pleines de poissons et les montagnes couvertes de forêts sont des foyers de vie et de développement; telle autre loi impose des obligations humanitaires, comme les temples inspirent la piété filiale envers les ancêtres, ou le respect envers les Dieux. Ces analogies sont quelquefois poussées jusqu'au dernier ridicule; mais les Chinois ne les trouvent jamais forcées, et semblent faire très peu de cas de la logique Européenne, qui ne les admire pas.'

The Khien–lung editors say on it:–'Hsiâo gives the idea of distribution. All the principles under the sky are simply expressive of the mind of the one Heaven. Heaven is everywhere, and its distributions from which we see its ordinations are also everywhere. Khien 'great and originating,' contains all the meaning belonging to the name Heaven. Earth obediently receives the influences of heaven. Consequently, when we see how earth supports all things, we know how the ordination of Heaven has descended on it. Heaven is the author of all things. It produced men, and men go on to produce one another, in succession. From this we see that every man has his ancestor, and know how the ordination of Heaven has descended on the ancestral temple. Hills and streams are also the productions of Heaven, but every one of them is also able to produce other things; and when we see their productiveness, we know that the ordination of Heaven to that effect has descended on them. The productive power of Heaven is distributed in the five elements, and their results, which are most important to men, are exhibited in the five sacrifices of the house, so that we see those results in these, and know that the ordination of Heaven has descended on them. Now the ancestral temples, the hills and streams, and those five altars of the house, are all distributed on the earth, but in reality have their root in Heaven. And so it is that the sages after the pattern of Heaven made their ordinations; and their filial piety and righteousness, and all the duties enjoined by them, effective, though unseen, secure the issues of government.']

13. Hence the sage forms a ternion with Heaven and Earth, and stands side by side with spiritual beings, in order to the right ordering of government. Taking his place on the ground of the principles inherent in them, he devised ceremonies in their order; calling them to the happy exercise of that in which they find pleasure, he secured the success of the government of the people.

14. Heaven produces the seasons. Earth produces all the sources of wealth. Man is begotten by his father, and instructed by his teacher. The ruler correctly uses these four agencies, and therefore he stands in the place where there is no error[1].

15. Hence the ruler is he to whose brightness men look; he does not seek to brighten men. It is he whom men support; he does not seek to support men. It is he whom men serve; he does not seek to serve men. If the ruler were to seek to brighten men, he would fall into errors. If he were to seek to nourish men, he would be unequal to the task. If he were to seek to serve men, he would be giving up his position. Therefore the people imitate the ruler, and we have their self–government; they nourish their ruler, and they find their security in doing so; they serve the ruler, and find their distinction in doing so. Thus it is by the universal application of the rules of propriety, that the lot and duty (of different classes) are fixed; thus it is that men (acting contrary to those rules,) would all have to account death a boon, and life an evil.

16. Therefore (the ruler), making use of the wisdom of others, will put away the cunning to which that wisdom might lead him; using their courage, he will (in the same way) put away

[1. 'If the ruler,' says Khung Ying–tâ, 'were to undertake to do all the work of these agencies himself, he would commit many errors. Employing them according to the natural operation of each, the work is easily performed, and without error.']

passion; and using their benevolence, he will put away covetousness[1].

17. Therefore, when calamity comes on a state, for the ruler to die for its altars is to be regarded as right; but for a Great officer to die for the ancestral temple is to be regarded as a change (of the duty required from him)[2].

18. Therefore when it is said that (the ruler being) a sage can look on all under the sky as one family, and on all in the Middle states as one man, this does not mean that he will do so on premeditation and purpose. He must know men's feelings, lay open to them what they consider right, show clearly to them what is advantageous, and comprehend what are their calamities. Being so furnished, he is then able to effect the thing.

19. What are the feelings of men? They are joy, anger, sadness, fear, love, disliking, and liking. These seven feelings belong to men without their learning them. What are 'the things which men consider right?' Kindness on the part of the father, and filial duty on that of the son; gentleness on the part of the elder brother, and obedience on that of

[1. I have here followed the Khien–lung editors in preference to Kang Khang–khang and others. The latter consider that the cunning, passion, and covetousness are those of the men whom the ruler employs,–vices generally found, along with the good qualities belonging to them.

2. It is not easy to see the ground of the reprehension of the devotion of a Great officer which is here implied. 'The care of the state is a trust committed to the ruler by the sovereign,–he should die in maintaining it. An officer has services to discharge, and not trusts to maintain. When the services can no longer be discharged, hc may leave them and save himself'(?).]

the younger; righteousness on the part of the husband, and submission on that of the wife; kindness on the part of elders, and deference on that of juniors; with benevolence on the part of the ruler, and loyalty on that of the minister;—these ten are the things which –men consider to be right. Truthfulness in speech and the cultivation of harmony constitute what are called 'the things advantageous to men.' Quarrels, plundering, and murders are 'the things disastrous to men.' Hence, when a sage (ruler) would regulate the seven feelings of men, cultivate the ten virtues that are right; promote truthfulness of speech, and the maintenance of harmony; show his value for kindly consideration and complaisant courtesy; and put away quarrelling and plundering, if he neglect the rules of propriety, how shall he succeed?

20. The things which men greatly desire are comprehended in meat and drink and sexual pleasure; those which they greatly dislike are comprehended in death, exile, poverty, and suffering. Thus liking and disliking are the great elements in men's minds. But men keep them hidden in their minds, where they cannot be fathomed or measured. The good and the bad of them being in their minds, and no outward manifestation of them being visible, if it be wished to determine these qualities in one uniform way, how can it be done without the use of the rules of propriety (implied in the ceremonial usages)?

SECTION III.

1. Man is (the product of) the attributes of Heaven and Earth, (by) the interaction of the dual forces of nature, the union of the animal and intelligent (souls), and the finest subtile matter of the five elements[1].

2. Heaven exercises the control of the strong and light force, and hangs out the sun and stars. Earth exercises the control of the dark and weaker force, and gives vent to it in the hills and streams. The five elements are distributed through the four seasons, and it is by their harmonious action that the moon is produced, which therefore keeps waxing for fifteen days and waning for fifteen[2].

[1. Callery's translation of this paragraph is the following:—'L'homme émane, (pour le moral), de la vertu du Ciel et de la Terre; (pour le physique il émane) de la combinaison des (deux principes) Yin et Yang; (pour la partie spirituelle, il émane) de la réunion des esprits et des Dieux; et pour la forme qui lui est propre, il émane de l'essence la plus subtile des cinq éléments.' To this be subjoins the following note:—'Il m'est difficile de croire que les Chinois eux–mêmes aient jamais rien compris à ces théories androgénésiques, dont tout le mérite gît dans le vague de l'énoncé.' The Khien–lung editors say:—'The characteristic attributes of Heaven and Earth are blended and hid in the two forces of nature; and this is called the truth that is unlimited. If we speak of those forces in their fundamental character, we call them the Yin and Yang. If we speak of them as they develop their power, we call them Kwei and Shan. If we speak of them as they become substantial, we call them the five elements. And this is what is called the essence of what is meant by the second and fifth lines of the Khien hexagram,' &c. &c.

2. Callery says here:–' Cest toujours l'application de la théorie des affinités naturelles

dont nous avons parlé (see note, p. 281) et dont il importe de bien se pénétrer lorsqu'on veut comprendre quelque chose aux dissertations philosophiques des Chinois.' But after the student has done his best to get hold of the theory, he will often be baffled in trying to follow the applications of it. For example, I cannot get hold of what is said here about the genesis of the moon. Much of the next four paragraphs is very obscure. A little light seems to flash on them from parts of different sections of Book IV, but it is neither bright nor steady.]

3. The five elements in their movements alternately displace and exhaust one another. Each one of them, in the revolving course of the twelve months of the four seasons, comes to be in its turn the fundamental one for the time.

4. The five notes of harmony, with their six upper musical accords, and the twelve pitch-tubes, come each, in their revolutions among themselves, to be the first note of the scale.

5. The five flavours, with the six condiments, and the twelve articles of diet, come each one, in their revolutions (in the course of the year), to give its character to the food.

6. The five colours, with the six elegant figures, which they form on the two robes, come each one, in their revolutions among themselves, to give the character of the dress that is worn.

7. Therefore Man is the heart and mind of Heaven and Earth, and the visible embodiment of the five elements. He lives in the enjoyment of all flavours, the discriminating of all notes (of harmony), and the enrobing of all colours[1].

[1. For this paragraph M. Callery gives:—'L'homme est donc le cœur du Ciel et de la Terre, la fine essence des cinq éléments, et vit en mangeant des choses sapides, en distinguant les sons, et en s'habillant de différentes couleurs (contrairement à la brute, dont les goûts sont grossiers, et les instincts sans raison).' Of course the first predicate about man, and, we might almost say, the second also, are metaphorical. 'La fine essence' is not a correct translation of the text in the second predicate, the Chinese character so rendered is different from the two characters in paragraph 1. On the former predicate Hsiang An-shih (Sung dynasty) says:—'The heart of Heaven and Earth is simply benevolence. The perfect benevolence of Heaven and Earth is lodged in man. Given the human body, and forthwith there is the benevolent heart. Hence it is said (Mencius VII, ii, 16), "Man is benevolence;" "Benevolence is the heart of man." Moreover, the heart of Heaven and Earth is seen in the very idea of life, so that the heart (or kernel) of all fruits is called Zan or benevolence, which is again a name for man.']

8. Thus it was that when the sages would make rules (for men), they felt it necessary to find the origin (of all things) in heaven and earth; to make the two forces (of nature) the commencement (of all); to use the four seasons as the handle (of their arrangements); to adopt the sun and stars as the recorders (of time), the moon as the measurer (of work to be done), the spirits breathing (in nature) as associates[1], the five elements as giving substance (to things), rules of propriety and righteousness as (their) instruments, the feelings of men as the field (to be cultivated), and the four intelligent creatures as domestic animals (to be reared)[2].

9. The origin of all things being found in heaven and earth, they could be taken in hand, one after the other. The commencement of these being found in the two forces (of nature), their character and tendencies could be observed. The four seasons being used as a handle, (the people) could be stimulated to the business (of each). The sun and stars being constituted the measures of time,

[1. Callery has for this:—'Les Esprits et les Dieux pour compagnons;' Medhurst, 'the Kwei Shins, as the associates.' Kang and Khung say that by Kwei Shan are to be understood 'the hills and streams of last section,' paragraph 12, for 'those help the respiration of the earth.'

2 See paragraph 10.]

that business could be laid out in order. The moon being taken as the measure (of work to be done), that work could be accomplished successfully. The spirits breathing (in nature) being considered as associates, what is done will be maintained permanently. The five elements being considered as giving substance (to things), what has been done could be repeated. Rules of propriety and righteousness being viewed as the instruments, whatever was done would be completed. The feelings of men being the field to be cultivated, men would look up (to the sages) as to their lords. The four intelligent creatures being made to become domestic animals, there would be constant sources of food and drink.

10. What were the four intelligent creatures[1]? They were the Khî–lin, the phœnix, the tortoise, and the dragon. When the dragon becomes a domestic animal, (all other) fishes and the sturgeon do not lie hidden from men (in the mud). When the phœnix becomes so, the birds do not fly from them in terror. When the Khî–lin does so, the beasts do not scamper away. When the tortoise does so, the feelings of men take no erroneous course.

[1. Callery calls these four creatures 'le cerf, l'aigle, la tortue, et le dragon;' and says:—'D'après la mythologie historique des Chinois, ces quatre animaux ne se montrent sur la terre que sous le règne des empereurs d'une vertu extraordinaire. Alors, la plus grande paix règne dans l'univers; tous les hommes sont heureux; personne ne manque de rien:—C'est l'âge d'or, moins les idées poétiques des Grecs et des Latins.' All the four excepting the tortoise are fabulous animals, and even Confucius believed in them (Ana. IX, 8). The lesson drawn from the text by many is that men's goodness is the pledge of, and the way to, all prosperity.]

SECTION IV.

1. The ancient kings made use of the stalks and the tortoise–shell; arranged their sacrifices; buried their offerings of silk; recited their words of supplication and benediction; and made their statutes and measures. In this way arose the ceremonial usages of the states, the official departments with their administrators, each separate business with its own duties, and the rules of ceremony in their orderly arrangements.

2. Thus it was that the ancient kings were troubled lest the ceremonial usages should not be generally understood by all below them. They therefore sacrificed to God in the suburb (of the capital), and thus the place of heaven was established. They sacrificed at the altar of the earth inside the capital, and thus they intimated the benefits derived from the earth. Their sacrifices in the ancestral temple gave their fundamental place to the sentiments of humanity. Those at the altars of the hills and streams served to mark their intercourse with the spirits breathing (in nature). Their five sacrifices (of the house) were a recognition of the various business which was to be done.

For the same reason, there are the officers of prayer in the ancestral temple; the three ducal ministers in the court; and the three classes of old men in the college. In front of the king there were the sorcerers, and behind him the recorders; the diviners by the tortoise–shell and by the stalks, the blind musicians and their helpers were all on his left and right. He himself was in the centre. His mind had nothing to do, but to maintain what was entirely correct.

3. By means of the ceremonies performed in the suburb, all the spirits receive their offices. By means of those performed at the altar of the earth, all the things yielded (by the earth) receive their fullest development. By means of those in the ancestral temple, the services of filial duty and of kindly affection come to be discharged. By means of those at the five sacrifices of the house, the laws and rules of life are correctly exhibited. Hence when the ideas in these sacrifices in the suburb, at the altar of the earth, in the ancestral temple, at the altars of the hills and streams, and of the five sacrifices of the house are fully apprehended, the ceremonies used are found to be lodged in them[1].

4. From all this it follows that rules of ceremony Must be traced to their origin in the Grand Unity[2].

[1. Mang explains 'all the spirits' in the first sentence of this paragraph by 'all the constellations.' Khung agrees with him. Khan Hâo (Yüan dynasty) explains it of 'wind, rain, cold, and heat.' The Khien–lung editors say that the two explanations must be united. But why are these phenomena described as all or 'the hundred spirits?' Is it by personification? or a kind of pantheism?

2. Medhurst translated this name by 'the Supreme One;' Callery, as I do, by 'la Grande Unité,' adding in parentheses, 'principe de toutes choses.' Does the name denote what we are to consider an Immaterial Being, acting with wisdom, intention, and goodness? Medhurst came to this conclusion. He says:—'Thâi Yî must mean the Supreme One, or the infinitely great and undivided one. Bearing in mind also that this paragraph follows another in which Tî the ruling Power, is honoured .With the highest adoration, and that this ruling, Power is the same with the being here called the Supreme One, there can be no doubt that the reference in the whole passage is to the Almighty One who rules over all things' (Dissertation on the Theology of the Chinese, p. 85). He goes on to say that 'the Critical Commentary makes this still more plain by saying that this Supreme One is the source of all others, and that he existed before the powers of nature were divided, and before the myriad things were produced, the one only being. The operations ascribed to him ' of dividing heaven and earth, of revolving light and darkness, of changing the four seasons, and of appointing the various Kwei Shins to their several offices, are all

indicative of that omnipotent power which must be ascribed to him alone.' But the operations referred to in this last sentence are mentioned in the text, not as performed by the Supreme One, but as undergone by the Grand Unity. And, moreover, 'the Critical Commentary' yields a testimony different from what Dr. Medhurst supposed. Khung Ying–tâ says:—'The name Thâi Yî means the original vapoury matter of chaos, before the separation of heaven and earth, and there is nothing in any of the other commentators contrary to this. But the concluding sentence of the paragraph, that 'The law and authority (of all the lessons in the rules of ceremony) is in Heaven,' seems to me to imply 'a recognition (indistinct it may be) of a Power or Being anterior to and independent of the Grand Unity.' Wû Khang says:—'The character Thien (Heaven) is used to cover the five things–the Grand Unity, heaven and earth, the (dual force of) Yin and Yang, the four seasons, and the Kwei Shan.' The attempt, apparent in the whole treatise, to give Tâoistic views a place in the old philosophy of the nation, is prominent here. Medhurst is not correct in saying that the Tî in paragraph 2 is the same as the Thâi Yî in this paragraph, but It, or rather He, is the same as the Thien with which it concludes. The earliest Chinese adopted Thien or Heaven as, the name for the supreme Power, which arose in their minds on the contemplation of the order of 'nature, and the principles of love and righteousness developed in the constitution of man and the course of providence, and proceeded to devise the personal name of Tî or God, as the appellation of this; and neither Tâoism, nor any other form of materialistic philosophising, has succeeded in eradicating the precious inheritance of those two terms from the mind of peasant or scholar.

Callery has misconstrued the paragraph by making 'Les Rites,' or the 'toutes choses' of his gloss, the subject of all the predicates in it:—'Les rites ont pour origine essentielle la Grande Unité (principe de toutes choses). Ils se divisent ensuite, les uns pour le Ciel, les autres pour la Terre,' &c.]

This separated and became heaven and earth. It revolved and became the dual force (in nature).

It changed and became the four seasons. It was distributed and became the breathings (thrilling in the universal frame). Its (lessons) transmitted (to men) are called its orders; the law and authority of them is in Heaven.

5. While the rules of ceremony have their origin in heaven, the movement of them reaches to earth. The distribution of them extends to all the business (of life). They

change with the seasons; they agree in reference to the (variations of) lot and condition. In regard to man, they serve to nurture (his nature). They are practised by means of offerings, acts of strength, words and postures of courtesy, in eating and drinking, in the observances of capping, marriage, mourning, sacrificing, archery, chariot–driving, audiences, and friendly missions.

6. Thus propriety and righteousness are the great elements for man's (character); it is by means of them that his speech is the expression of truth and his intercourse (with others) the promotion of harmony; they are (like) the union of the cuticle and cutis, and the binding together of the muscles and bones in strengthening (the body). They constitute the great methods by which we nourish the living, bury the dead, and serve the spirits of the departed. They supply the channels by which we can apprehend the ways of Heaven and act as the feelings of men require. It was on this account that the sages knew that the rules of ceremony could not be dispensed with, while the ruin of states, the destruction of families, and the perishing of individuals are always preceded by their abandonment of the rules of propriety,

7. Therefore the rules of propriety are for man what the yeast is for liquor[1]. The superior man by (his use of them) becomes better and greater. The small man by his neglect of them becomes meaner and worse.

8. Therefore the sage kings cultivated and fashioned the lever of righteousness and the ordering of ceremonial usages, in order to regulate the feelings of men. Those feelings were the field (to be cultivated by) the sage kings. They fashioned the rules of ceremony to plough it. They set forth the principles of righteousness with which to plant it. They instituted the lessons of the school to weed it. They made love the fundamental subject by which to gather all its fruits, and they employed the training in music to give repose (to the minds of learners).

[1. On this comparison Callery says:—'Ce que les Chinois appellent du vin n'étant une autre chose qu'une eau de vie de grains obtenue par la distillation, plus il y a de ferment dans la macération primitive, plus la fermentation vineuse est forte, et plus il y a d'alcool quand on la passe par l'alambic. Dè là cette comparaison entre le degré d'urbanité chez le sage et le degré de force dans le vin.']

9. Thus, rules of ceremony are the embodied expression of what is right. If an observance stand the test of being judged by the standard of what is right, although it may not have been among the usages of the ancient kings, it may be adopted on the ground of its being right.

10. (The idea of) right makes the distinction between things, and serves to regulate (the manifestation of) humanity. When it is found in anything and its relation to humanity has been discussed, the possessor of it will be strong.

11. Humanity is the root of right, and the embodying of deferential consideration. The possessor of it is honoured.

12. Therefore to govern a state without the rules of propriety would be to plough a field without a share. To make those rules without laying their foundation in right would be to plough the ground and not sow the seed. To think to practise the right without enforcing it in the school would be to sow the seed and not weed the plants. To enforce the lessons in the schools, and insist on their agreement with humanity, would be to weed and not to reap. To insist on the agreement of the lessons with humanity, and not give repose to (the minds of) the learners by music, would be to reap, and not eat (the product). To supply the repose of music and not proceed to the result of deferential consideration would be to eat the product and get no fattening from it.

13. When the four limbs are all well proportioned, and the skin is smooth and full, the individual is in good condition. When there is generous affection between father and son, harmony between brothers, and happy union between husband and wife, the family is in good condition. When the great ministers are observant of the laws, the smaller ministers pure, officers and their duties kept in their regular relations and the ruler and his ministers are correctly helpful to one another, the state is in good condition. When the son of Heaven moves in his virtue as a chariot, with music as his driver, while all the princes conduct their mutual intercourse according to the rules of propriety, the Great officers maintain the order between them according to the laws, inferior officers complete one another by their good faith, and the common people guard one another with a spirit of harmony, all under the sky is in good condition. All this produces what we call (the state of) great mutual consideration (and harmony).

14. This great mutual consideration and harmony would ensure the constant nourishment of the living, the burial of the dead, and the service of the spirits (of the departed). However greatly things might accumulate, there would be no entanglement among them. They would move on together without error, and the smallest matters would proceed without failure. However deep some might be, they would be comprehended. However thick and close their array, there would be spaces between them. They would follow one another without coming into contact. They would move about without doing any hurt to one another. This would be the perfection of such a state of mutual harmony.

15. Therefore the clear understanding of this state will lead to the securing of safety in the midst of danger. Hence the different usages of ceremony, and the maintenance of them in their relative proportions as many or few, are means of keeping hold of the feelings of men, and of uniting (high and low, and saving them from) peril.

16. The sage kings showed their sense of this state of harmony in the following way:—They did not make the occupants of the hills (remove and) live by the streams, nor the occupants of the islands (remove and live) in the plains; and thus the (people) complained of no hardship. They used water, fire, metal, wood, and the different articles of food and drink, each in its proper season. They promoted the marriages of men and women, and distributed rank and office, according to the years and virtues of the parties. They employed the people with due regard to their duties and wishes. Thus it was that there were no plagues of flood, drought, or insects, and the people did not suffer from bad grass or famine, from untimely deaths or irregular births. On account of all this heaven did not grudge its methods; earth did not grudge its treasures; men did not grudge (the regulation of) their feelings. Heaven sent down its fattening dews[1]; earth sent forth its springs of sweet wine[1]; hills produced implements and chariots[2]; the Ho sent forth the horse with the map (on, his

[1. Kâo Yî in his Filial Miscellanies, Book III, art. 9, contends that these are only different names for the same phenomenon. Few readers will agree with him, though the language means no more than that 'the dews were abundant, and the water of the springs delicious!

2. There must have been some legend which would have explained this language, but I have not succeeded in finding any trace of it.]

back)'. Phœnixes and Khî–lins were among the trees of the suburbs, tortoises and dragons in the ponds of the palaces, while the other birds and beasts could be seen at a glance in their nests and breeding places. All this resulted from no other cause but that the ancient kings were able to fashion their ceremonial usages so as to convey the underlying ideas of right, and embody their truthfulness so as to secure the universal and mutual harmony. This was the realisation of it.

[1. The famous 'River Map' from which, it has been fabled, Fû–hsî fashioned his eight trigrams. See vol. xvi, pp. 14–16.]

BOOK VIII. THE LÎ KHÎ OR RITES IN THE FORMATION OF CHARACTER[1].

SECTION I.

1. The rules of propriety serve as instruments to form men's characters, and they are therefore prepared on a great scale. Being so, the value of them is very high. They remove from a man all perversity, and increase what is beautiful in his nature. They make him correct, when employed in the ordering of himself; they ensure for him free course, when employed towards others. They are to him what their outer coating is to bamboos, and what its heart is to a pine or cypress[2]. These two are the best of all the productions of the (vegetable) world. They endure through all the four seasons, without altering a branch or changing a leaf. The superior man observes these rules of propriety, so that all in a wider circle are harmonious with him, and those in his narrower circle have no dissatisfactions with him. Men acknowledge and are affected by his goodness, and spirits enjoy his virtue.

2. The rules as instituted by the ancient kings had their radical element and their outward and

[1. See the introductory notice, p. 25.

2. The author evidently knew the different conditions of their structure on which the growth and vigour of Endogens (the monocotyledonous plants) and Exogens

(dicotyledons) respectively depend.]

elegant form. A true heart and good faith are their radical element. The characteristics of each according to the idea of what is right in it are its outward and elegant form: Without the radical element, they could not have been established; without the elegant form, they could not have been put in practice[1].

3. (The things used in performing) the rites should be suitable to the season, taken from the resources supplied by the ground, in accordance with (the requirements of) the spirits[2], and agreeable to the minds of men;–according to the characteristics of all things. Thus each season has its productions, each soil its appropriate produce, each sense its peculiar power, and each thing its advantageousness. Therefore what any season does not produce, what any soil does not nourish, will not be used by a superior man in performing his rites, nor be enjoyed by the spirits. If mountaineers were to (seek to) use fish and turtles in their rites, or the dwellers

[1. Callery gives for this short paragraph—'Les rites établis par les anciens rois ont leur essence intimé et leur dehors; la droiture est l'essence des rites; leur accord patent avec la raison en est le dehors. Sans essence, ils ne peuvent exister; sans dehors ils ne peuvent fonctionner.' He appends a long note on the difficulty of translation occasioned by the character (wan), which he renders by 'le dehors,' and I by 'the outward, elegant form;' and concludes by saying, 'Traduise mieux qui pourra.' I can only say that I have done the best I could (at the time) with this and every other paragraph.

2. Khung Ying–tâ says here that 'the spirits were men who, when alive, had done good service, and were therefore sacrificed to when dead. From which it follows that what was agreeable to the minds of men would be in accordance with (the requirements of) the spirits.']

near lakes, deer and pigs, the superior man would say of them that they did not know (the nature of) those usages.

4. Therefore it is necessary to take the established revenues of a state as the great rule for its ceremonial (expenditure). Important for the determination of this is the size of its territory. The amount of the offerings (also) should have regard to the character of the year as good or bad. In this way, though the harvest of a year may be very defective, the

masses will not be afraid, and the ceremonies as appointed by the superiors will be economically regulated.

5. In (judging of) rites the time[1] should be the great consideration. (Their relation to) natural duties, their material substance, their appropriateness to circumstances, and their proportioning are all secondary.

Yâo's resignation of the throne to Shun, and Shun's resignation of it to Yü; Thang's dethronement of Kieh; and the overthrow of Kâu by Wan and Wû:—all these are to be judged of by the time. As the Book of Poetry says,

It was not that he was in haste to gratify his wishes;
It was to show the filial duty that had come down to him.'

[1. 'The time' comes about by the ordering of heaven. The instances given of it are all great events in the changing of dynasties. But such changes can hardly be regarded as rites. Perhaps the writer thought that the abdication in some cases, and the violent dethroning in others, were precedents, which might be regarded as having that character. For the quotation from the Shih, which is not very happy, see Part III, ode 10, 2.]

The sacrifices to heaven and earth; the services of the ancestral temple; the courses for father and son; and the righteousness between ruler and minister:—these are to be judged of as natural duties.

The services at the altars of the land and grain and of the hills and streams; and the sacrifices t6 spirits:—these are to be judged of by the material substance of the offerings. The use of the funeral rites and sacrifices; and the reciprocities of host and guest:—these are to be judged of by their appropriateness to circumstances.

Sacrificing with a lamb and a sucking pig, by the multitude of officers, when yet there was enough; and sacrificing with an ox, a ram, and a boar, when yet there was nothing to spare:—in these we have an instance of the proportioning.

6. The princes set great store by the tortoise, and consider their jade-tokens as the insignia of their rank, while the (chiefs of) clans have not the tortoises that are so precious, nor the jade-tokens to keep (by themselves), nor the towered gateways:—these

(also) are instances of the proportioning.

7. In some ceremonial usages the multitude of things formed the mark of distinction, The son of Heaven had 7 shrines in his ancestral temple; the prince of a state, 5; Great officers, 3; and other officers, 1. The dishes of the son of Heaven on stands were 26; of a duke, 16; of another prince, 12; of a Great officer of the upper class, 8; of one of the lower class, 6, To a prince there were given 7 attendants and 7 oxen; and to a Great officer, 5 of each, The son of Heaven sat on 5 mats placed over one another; a prince, on 3; and a Great officer, on 2. When the son of Heaven died, he was buried after 7 months, in a fivefold coffin, with 8 plumes; a prince was buried after 5 months, in a threefold coffin, with 6 plumes; a Great officer after 3 months, in a twofold coffin, with 4 Plumes. In these cases, the multitude of things was the mark of distinction[1].

8. In other usages, the paucity of things formed the mark of distinction. To the son of Heaven there were given no attendants[2], and he sacrificed to Heaven with a single victim; when he visited the princes (on his tours of inspection), he was feasted with a single bullock. When princes went to the courts of one another, fragrant spirits were used in libations, and there were no dishes on stands, either of wood or bamboo. At friendly missions by Great officers, the ceremonial offerings were slices of dried meat and pickles. The son of Heaven declared himself satisfied after 1 dish; a prince, after 2; a Great officer and other officers, after 3; while no limit was set to the eating of people who lived by their labour. (The horses of) the Great carriage had 1 ornamental tassel at their breast–bands; those of the other carriages had 7 (pieces of) jade for rank–tokens; and libation cups were presented singly; as also the tiger–shaped and yellow cups. In sacrificing to spirits a single mat was used; when princes were giving audience to their ministers, they (bowed to) the Great officers one by one, but to all the other officers

[1. The different views in attempting to verify all the numbers and other points in the specifications here are endless.

2. The attendants waited on the visitors. But the son of Heaven was lord of all under the sky. He was at home everywhere; and could not be received as a visitor.]

together. In these cases the fewness of the things formed the mark of distinction.

9. In others, greatness of size formed the mark. The dimensions of palaces and apartments; the measurements of dishes and (other) articles; the thickness of the inner and outer coffins; the greatness of eminences and mounds[1]:—these were cases in which the greatness of size was the mark.

10. In others, smallness of size formed the mark. At the sacrifices of the ancestral temple, the highest in rank presented a cup (of spirits to the representative of the dead), and the low, a san (containing five times as much): (at some other sacrifices), the honourable took a khih (containing 3 cups), and the low a horn (containing 4). (At the feasts of viscounts and barons), when the vase went round 5 times, outside the door was the earthenware fâu (of supply), and inside, the hû; while the ruler's vase was an earthenware wei:—these were cases in which the smallness of size was the mark of distinction[2].

11. In others, the height formed the mark of

[1. Both these names refer, probably, to mounds raised over the dead. Those over the emperors of the Ming dynasty, about midway between Peking and the Great Wall, and that over Confucius at Khü-fû in Shan-tung, are the best specimens of these which I have seen.

2. It is difficult to explain fully and verify all the statements in this paragraph, for want of evidence. The unit in them is the shang, or 'pint,' now = 1.031 litre; the cup, (zio,) contained one shang; the khih, three; the kio four; and the san, five. The hû contained one 'stone' = 10.310 litre; and the wû 51.55. The size of the fâu is unknown.]

distinction. The hall of the son of Heaven was ascended by 9 steps[1]; that of a prince, by 7; that of a Great officer, by 5; and that of an ordinary officer, by 3. The son of Heaven and the princes had (also) the towered gateway. In these cases height was the mark.

12. In others, the lowness formed the mark. In sacrificing, the highest reverence was not shown on the raised altar, but on the ground beneath, which, had been swept. The vases of the son of Heaven and the princes were set on a tray without feet[2]; those of Great and other officers on one with feet (3 inches high). In these cases the lowness was the mark of distinction.

13. In others, ornament formed the mark. The son of Heaven wore his upper robe with the dragons figured on it; princes, the lower robe with the axes' embroidered on it; Great officers, their lower robe with the symbol of distinction; and other officers, the dark–coloured upper robe, and the lower one red. The cap of the soil of Heaven had 12 pendents of jade beads set on strings hanging–down of red and green silk; that of princes, 9; that of Great officers of the highest grade, 7; and if they were of the lowest grade, 5; and that of other officers, in these cases the ornament was the mark of distinction.

14. In others, plainness formed the mark. Acts of the greatest reverence admit of no ornament.

[1. This literally is 'nine cubits;' each step, it is said, was a cubit high.

2. This tray was four cubits long, two cubits four inches wide, and five inches deep.]

The relatives of a father do not put themselves into postures (like other visitors). The Grand jade–token has no engraving on it. The Grand soup has no condiments. The Grand carriage is plain, and the mats in it are of rushes. The goblet with the victim–ox carved on it is covered with a plain white cloth. The ladle is made of white–veined wood. These are cases in which plainness is the mark.

15. Confucius said,' Ceremonial usages should be most carefully considered.' This is the meaning of the remark that 'while usages are different, the relations between them as many or few should be maintained[1].' His words had reference to the proportioning of rites.

16. That in the (instituting of) rites the multitude of things was considered a mark of distinction, arose from the minds (of the framers) being directed outwards. The energy (of nature) shoots forth and is displayed everywhere in all things, with a great discriminating control over their vast multitude. In such a case, how could they keep from making multitude a mark of distinction in rites? Hence the superior men, (the framers), rejoiced in displaying (their discrimination).

But that in (the instituting of) rites the paucity of things was (also) considered a mark of distinction, arose from the minds (of the framers) being directed inwards. Extreme as is the energy (of nature) in production, it is exquisite and minute. When we look at all the things under the sky, they do not

[1. See page 392, paragraph 15. We may conclude that the Lî Yun was compiled and published before the Lî Khî; or it may be that the sentences common to them both had long been in use.]

seem to be in proportion to that energy, In such a case, how could they keep from considering paucity a mark of distinction? Hence the superior men, (the framers), watched carefully over the solitude (of their own thoughts)[1].

17. The ancient sages (thus) gave honour to what was internal, and sought pleasure in what was external; found a mark of distinction in paucity, and one of what was admirable in multitude; and therefore in the ceremonial usages instituted by the ancient kings we should look neither for multitude nor for paucity, but for the due relative proportion.

18. Therefore, when a man of rank uses a large victim in sacrifice, we say he acts according to propriety, but when an ordinary officer does so, we say be commits an act of usurpation.

19. Kwan Kung had his sacrificial dishes of grain carved, and red bands to his cap; fashioned hills on the capitals of his pillars, and pondweed on the small pillars above the beams[2]:—the superior man considered it wild extravagance.

:2o. An Phing-kung, in sacrificing to his father, used a sucking-pig which did not fill the dish, and went to court in an (old) washed robe and cap:—the superior man considered it was niggardliness[3].

[1. Callery thinks that the theory about rites underlying this paragraph is 'éminemment obscure.' One difficulty with me is to discover any connection between its parts and what is said in paragraphs 7 and 8 about the 'multitude and paucity of rites.'

2. See the Analects, V, xvii, and the note there. In that passage the extravagance is charged on the Zang Win-kung of paragraph 23.

3. An Phing-kung was a Great officer of Khî, and ought not to have been so niggardly.]

21 Therefore the superior man thinks it necessary to use the utmost care in his practice of ceremonies. They are the bond that holds the multitudes together; and if the bond be removed, those multitude's fall into confusion. Confucius said, 'If I fight, I overcome; when I sacrifice, I receive blessing[1].' He said so, because he had the right way (of doing everything).

22. A superior man will say[2], 'The object in sacrifices is not to pray; the time of them should not be hastened on; a great apparatus is not required at them; ornamental matters are not to be approved; the victims need not be fat and large; a profusion of the other offerings is not to be admired.'

23. Confucius said, 'How can it be said that Zang Wan–kung was acquainted with the rules of propriety? When Hsiâ Fû–khî went right in the teeth of sacrificial order[3], he did not stop him, (nor could he

[1. It is understood that the 'I' is not used by Confucius of himself, but as personating one who knew the true nature of ceremonial usages. See the language again in the next Book, Sect. i, 22; it is found also in the 'Narratives of the School.'

2 Khan Hâo remarks that the compiler of the Book intends himself by 'the superior man.' Thus the compiler delivers his own judgment in an indirect way. Most of what he says will be admitted. It is to the general effect that simple offerings and sincere worship are acceptable, more acceptable than rich offerings and a formal service. But is he right in saying that in sacrificing we should not 'pray?' So long as men feel their own weakness and needs, they will not fail to pray at their religious services. So it has been in China in all the past as much as elsewhere.

3 Hsiâ Fû–khî was the keeper, or minister in charge, of the ancestral temple of Lû, and contemporary with Zang Wan–kung during the marquisates of Kwang, Wan, and Hsî. He introduced at least one great irregularity in the ancestral temple, placing the tablet of Hsî above that of wan; and Win–kung made no protest. Of the other irregularity mentioned in the text we have not much information; and I need not try to explain it. It seems to me that it must have been greater than the other.]

prevent) his burning a pile of firewood in sacrificing to the spirit of the furnace. Now that sacrifice is paid to an old wife. The materials for it might be contained in a tub, and the vase is the (common) wine–jar.'

SECTION II.

I. The rules of propriety may be compared to the human body. When the parts of one's body are not complete, the beholder' will call him 'An imperfect man;' and so a rule which has been made unsuitably may be denominated 'incomplete.'

Some ceremonies are great, and some small; some are manifest, and some minute. The great should not be diminished, nor the small increased. The manifest should not be hidden, nor the minute made great. But while the important rules are 300, and the smaller rules 3000, the result to which they all lead is one and the same[2]. No one can enter an apartment but by the door.

2. A superior man in his observance of the rules, where he does his utmost and uses the greatest care, is extreme in his reverence and the manifestation of sincerity. Where they excite admiration and an

[1. The text has here 'the superior man,' for which Callery has 'au dire du sage.'

2 See Book XXVIII, ii, paragraph 38. What the 300 and 3000 rules are is very much disputed. The 'one and the same result' 'is, according to most, 'reverence and sincerity;' according to some, 'suitability.']

elegant attractiveness, there is (still) that manifestation of sincerity.

3. A superior man, in his consideration of the rules, finds those which are carried directly into practice; those in which one has to bend and make some modification; those which are regular and the same for all classes; those which are diminished in a certain order; those in which (a kind of) transplantation takes place, and (the ceremony) is distributed; those in which individuals are pushed forward and take part in the rules of a higher grade; those in which there are ornamental imitations (of natural objects); those in which the ornamental imitations are not carried out so fully; and those where appropriation (of higher observances) is not deemed usurpation[1].

4. The usages of the three dynasties had one and the same object, and the people all observed them. In such matters as colour, whether it should be white or dark, Hsiâ instituted and Yin adopted (its choice, or did not do So)[2].

5. Under the Kâu dynasty the representatives of

[1. Nine peculiarities in ceremonial usages are here indicated. It would be possible to illustrate them fully after the most approved commentators; but there would be little advantage in thus recalling the past which has for the most part passed away,—even in China.

2 Callery takes a different view of the second sentence in this paragraph, and translates it:—'(Si quelque chose a subi des modifications, ce n'a été que) la couleur blanche ou la couleur verte (caractéristique de telle ou telle autre dynastie; en dehors de ces choses peu importantes, pour tout ce qui est essentiel) la dynastie des Yin s'est scrupuleusement conformée à ce qui a été établi par les Hsiâ.' His view of the whole paragraph, however, comes to much the same as mine.]

the dead sat. Their monitors and cup–suppliers observed no regular rules, The usages were the same (as those of Yin), and the underlying principle was one. Under the Hsiâ dynasty, the personators had stood till the sacrifice was ended, (whereas) under Yin they sat. Under Kâu, when the cup went round among all, there were six personators'. Zang–dze said, 'The usages of Kâu might be compared to those of a subscription club[2].'

6. A superior man will say, 'The usages of ceremony that come closest to our human feelings are not those of the highest sacrifices; (as may be seen in) the blood of the border sacrifice; the raw flesh in the great offering (to all the royal ancestors) of the ancestral temple; the sodden flesh, where the spirits are presented thrice; and the roast meat, where they are presented once[3].'

7. And so those usages were not devised by

[1. This would be on occasion of the united sacrifice to all the ancestors; the personator of Hâu Kî being left out of the enumeration, as more honourable than the others.

That is, all stand equally as if each had paid his contribution to the expenses.

3 The greatest of all sacrifices was that to Heaven in a suburb of the capital; the next was the great triennial or quinquennial sacrifice in the ancestral temple; the third was that at the altars of the land and grain, and of the hills and rivers, which is supposed to be described here as that at which ' the cup' was thrice presented; and the last in order and importance were small sacrifices to individual spirits. The four offerings in the text were presented at the first three; but not in the same order. That to Heaven began with blood; that in the ancestral temple with raw flesh. Those farthest from our human feelings had the place of honour in the greatest services. We must seek for a higher and deeper origin of them than our ordinary feelings.]

superior men in order to give expression to their feelings. There was a beginning of them from (the oldest times); as when (two princes) have an interview, there are seven attendants to wait on them and direct them. Without these the interview would be too plain and dull. They reach (the ancestral temple) after the visitor has thrice declined the welcome of the host, and the host has thrice tried to give precedence to the other. Without these courtesies the interview would be too hurried and abrupt.

In the same way, when in Lû they were about to perform the service to God (in the suburb), they felt it necessary first to have a service in the college with its semicircular pool. When they were about in Zin to sacrifice to the Ho, they would first do so to the pool of Wû. When in Khî they were about to sacrifice to mount Thâi, they would do so first in the forest of Phei.

Moreover, the keeping the victims (for the altar of Heaven) for three months (in the stable); the abstinence (of the worshippers) for seven days; and the vigil of three days:–all showed the extreme degree of (preparatory) care (for the service).

The ritual arrangements, further, of the reception (of guests) and communication between them and the host, and for assisting and guiding the steps of the (blind) musicians, showed the extreme degree of kindly (provision)[1].

[1. It is not easy to construe this paragraph, nor to discover and indicate the connexion between its different parts. Generally we may say that it illustrates the previous statement about the rites as not simply the expression of natural feeling, but of that feeling wisely guided and embodied so as to be most beneficial to the individual and society, The auxiliary services in the first part of it were all preparatory to the great services that followed. That in the great college of Lû was concerned with Hâu Kî, the ancestor of the House of Kâu and all its branches, and preliminary to the place he was to occupy at the great sacrifice to Heaven.

The remaining two paragraphs show how the natural feeling was quietly nourished, guided, and modified.]

8. In ceremonial usages we should go back to the root of them (in the mind), and maintain the old (arrangements of them), not forgetting what they were at first. Hence there is no (need to be) calling attention to the demonstrations expressive of grief[1]; and those which (more particularly) belong to the court are accompanied by music. There is the use of sweet spirits, and the value set on water; there is the use of the (ordinary) knife, and the honour expressed by that furnished with (small) bells; there is the comfort afforded by the rush and fine bamboo mats, and the (special) employment of those which are made of straw. Therefore the ancient kings in their institution of the rules of propriety had a ruling idea, and thus it is that they were capable of being transmitted, and might be learned, however many they were.

9. The superior man will say, 'If a man do not have in himself the distinctions (embodied in ceremonies), he will contemplate that embodiment without any intelligent discrimination; if he wish to exercise that discrimination, and not follow the guidance of the rules, he will not succeed in his object. Hence if his practice of ceremonies be not according to the rules, men will not respect them;

[1. Yet much is said in the Than Kung about those demonstrations of grief in the mourning rites.]

and if his words be not according to those rules, men will not believe them. Accordingly it is said, "The rules of ceremony are the highest expression of (the truth of) things."'

10. Hence it was that in old times, when the ancient kings instituted ceremonies, they conveyed their idea by means of the qualities of the articles and observances which they employed. In their great undertakings, they were sure to act in accordance with the seasons; in their doings morning and evening, they imitated the sun and moon; in what required a high situation, they took advantage of mounds and hillocks, and in what required a low situation, of the (banks of the) rivers and lakes. Hence each season has its

rains and benefits, and those wise men sought to make use of them with intelligence with all the earnestness they could command[1].

11. The ancient kings valued (men's) possession of virtue, honoured those who pursued the right course, and employed those who displayed ability. They selected men of talents and virtue, and

[1. See Caller 's translation of this paragraph. He says on it:—'Cette période offre, par son incohérence, des difficultés sérieuses qui me font supposer une grave altération du texte primitif;' and justifies his own version by the remark, 'Je me suis dit qu'après tout il vaut mieux embellir que défigurer.' He takes the whole, like Kang, as referring to the ceremonies of different sacrifices. Ying Yung (Sung dynasty; earlier than Kû Hsî) understood it more generally of other royal and imperial doings. The Khien–lung editors say that the two views must be united. They remark on the last sentence that, as I every season has its appropriate productions and every situation its own suitabilities, we must examine them in order to use things appropriately.']

appointed them. They assembled the whole of them and solemnly addressed them[1].

12. Then in accordance with (the height of) heaven they did service to Heaven, in accordance with (the lower position of) earth they did service to Earth; taking advantage of the famous hills they ascended them, and announced to Heaven the good government (of the princes). When thus at the felicitous spot (chosen for their capitals) they presented their offerings to God in the suburb and announced to Heaven (the general good government from the famous hills), the phœnix descended, and tortoises and dragons made their appearance[2]. When they presented their offerings to God in the suburb the winds and rains were duly regulated, and the cold and heat came each in its proper time, so that the sage (king) had only to stand with his face to the south, and order prevailed all under the sky.

13. The courses of the heavenly (bodies) supply the most perfect lessons, and the sages possessed the highest degree of virtue. Above, in the hall of the ancestral temple, there was the jar, with clouds and hills represented on it on the east, and that with the victim represented on it on the west. Below the hall the larger drums were suspended on the west, and the smaller drums answering to them on the east. The ruler appeared at the (top of the) steps on the cast; his wife was in the apartment on the west. The great luminary

makes his appearance in

[1. The 'selection' here, it is understood, was of the functionaries to take part in the sacrificial ceremonies, and the solemn address was on the duties they had to perform.

2. See pp. 392, 393, paragraph 16.]

the east; the moon makes her appearance in the west. Such are the different ways in which the processes of darkness and light are distributed in nature, and such are the arrangements for the positions (corresponding thereto) of husband and wife. The ruler fills his cup from the jar with an elephant represented on it; his wife fills hers from that with clouds and hills. With such reciprocation do the ceremonies proceed above, while the music responds in the same way below;—there is the perfection of harmony.

14. It is the object of ceremonies to go back to the circumstances from which they sprang, and of music to express pleasure in the results which first gave occasion to it. Thus it was that the ancient kings, in their institution of ceremonies, sought to express their regulation of circumstances, and, in their cultivation of music, to express the aims they had in mind. Hence by an examination of their ceremonies and music, the conditions of order and disorder in which they originated can be known. Kü Po-yü[1] said, 'A wise man, by his intelligence, from the sight of any article, knows the skill of the artificer, and from the contemplation of an action knows the wisdom of its performer.' Hence there is the saying, 'The superior man watches over the manner in which he maintains his intercourse with other men.'

15. Within the ancestral temple reverence prevailed. The ruler himself led the victim forward,

[1. A friend, and perhaps a disciple of Confucius, an officer of the state of Wei. He is mentioned in the Confucian Analects and in Mencius.]

while the Great officers assisted and followed, bearing the offerings of silk. The ruler himself cut out (the liver) for (the preliminary) offering, while his wife bore the dish in which it should be presented. The ruler himself cut up the victim, while his wife presented the spirits.

The high ministers and Great officers followed the ruler; their wives followed his wife. How grave and still was their reverence! How were they absorbed in their sincerity! How earnest was their wish that their offerings should be accepted! The arrival of the victim was announced (to the spirits) in the courtyard; on the presentation of the blood and the flesh with the hair on it, announcement was made in the chamber; on the presentation of the soup and boiled meat, in the hall. The announcement was made thrice, each time in a different place; indicating how they were seeking for the spirits, and had not yet found them. When the sacrifice was set forth in the hall, it was repeated next day outside (the gate of the temple); and hence arose the saying, ' Are they there? Are they here?'

16. One offering of the cup showed the simplicity of the service; three offerings served to ornament it; five, to mark discriminating care; and seven, to show (the reverence for) the spirits[1].

17. Was not the great quinquennial sacrifice a service belonging to the king? The three animal victims, the fish, and flesh, were the richest tributes for the

[1. The sacrifices where only one cup was presented were, it is said, the smallest; three cups belonged to the altars of the land and grain; five, to those of the hills and rivers; and seven, to those in the ancestral temple. All this is quite uncertain.]

palate from all within the four seas and the nine provinces. The fruits and grain presented in the high dishes of wood and bamboo were the product of the harmonious influences of the four seasons, The tribute of metal showed the harmonious submission (of the princes). The rolls of silk with the round pieces of jade placed on them showed the honour they rendered to virtue. The tortoise was placed in front of all the other offerings, because of its knowledge of the future; the tribute of metal succeeded to it, showing the (hold it has on) human feelings. The vermilion, the varnish, the silk, the floss, the large bamboos and the smaller for arrows–the articles which all the states contribute; with the other uncommon articles, which each state contributed according to its resources, even to those from the remote regions:–(these followed the former). When the Visitors left they were escorted with the music of the Sze Hsiâ[1]. All these things showed how important was the sacrifice.

18. In the sacrifice to God in the suburb, we have the utmost expression of reverence. In the sacrifices of the ancestral temple, we have the utmost expression of humanity. In the

rites d mourning, we have the utmost expression of leal–heartedness. In the preparation of the robes and vessels for the dead, we have the utmost expression of affection. In

[1. We are told in the Kâu Lî, Book XXIII, art. 32, that the bell master, with bells and drums, performed the nine Hsiâ pieces, on the occasions appropriate to them. The second of them was 'the Sze Hsiâ,' as here, but the occasion for it in the text would be inappropriate. The eighth, or Kâi Hsiâ, would be appropriate here, and hence Mang said that sze was a mistake for kâu.]

the use of gifts and offerings between host and guest, we have the utmost expression of what is right. Therefore when the superior man would see the ways of humanity and righteousness, he finds them rooted in these ceremonial usages.

19. A superior man has said, 'What is sweet may be tempered; what is white may be coloured. So the man who is right in heart and sincere can learn the (meaning of the) rites.' The rites should not be perfunctorily performed by the man who is not right in heart and sincere. Hence it is all important (in the performance of them) to get the proper men.

20. Confucius said, 'One may repeat the three hundred odes, and not be fit to offer the sacrifice where there is (but) one offering of the cup. He may offer that sacrifice, and not be fit to join in a great sacrifice. He may join in such a sacrifice, and not be fit to offer a great sacrifice to the hills. He may perform that fully, and yet not be able to join in the sacrifice to God, Let no one lightly discuss the subject of rites[1].'

[1. It is not easy to trace satisfactorily the progress of thought here from one sacrificial service to another. 'The great sacrifice' is understood to be the triennial or quinquennial sacrifice to all the ancestors of the ruling House. It is a great step to that from a small sacrifice where only one cup was presented, What 'the great sacrifice to the hills was' is uncertain. It is in the text Tâ Lü. The meaning of Lü as a sacrifice to the spirit of a hill is well established from the Analects III, 6. Once the phrase Tâ Lü appears as used in the Kâu Lî, Book V, 91, of the royal sacrifice to God (Lorsque 1'empereur offre un grand sacrifice au Seigneur Suprême,' Biot); but it cannot have that meaning here, because the text goes on to speak of that sacrifice as superior to this. Mang Hsüan made Tâ Lü to be the sacrifice to the 'five Tîs,' or the five Planetary Gods, which view, as the Khien–lung editors point out, cannot be adopted. And how any sacrifice to the hills, however great, could be represented as greater than the quinquennial sacrifice in the ancestral temple, I cannot understand. I must leave the paragraph in the obscurity that belongs to it.]

21. When Dze–lû was steward to the House of Kî, its chief had been accustomed to commence his sacrifices before it was light, and when the day was insufficient for them, to continue them by torchlight. All engaged in them, however strong they might appear, and however reverent they might be, were worn out and tired. The officers limped and leaned, wherever they could, in performing their parts, and the want of reverence was great. Afterwards, when Dze–lû took the direction of them, the sacrifices proceeded differently. For the services in the chamber, he had parties communicating outside and inside the door; and for those in the hall, he had parties communicating at the steps. As soon as it was light, the services began, and by the time of the evening audience all were ready to retire. When Confucius heard of this management, he said, 'Who will say that this Yû does not understand ceremonies[1]?'

[1. The Khien–lung editors say:—'Dze–lû was a leal–hearted and sincere man, and the Book ends with this account of him. From the mention of the preparation of the rites on a great scale and of their high value at the beginning of the Book down to this tribute to Dze–lû as understanding ceremonies, its whole contents show that what is valuable in the rites is the combination of the idea of what is Tight with the elegant and outward form as sufficient to remove from a man all perversity and increase what is good in his nature, without a multiplicity of forms which would injure the natural goodness and sincerity, and lead their practiser to a crooked perversity. Deep and far–reaching is the idea of it!']

BOOK IX. THE KIÂO THEH SANG, OR THE SINGLE VICTIM AT THE BORDER SACRIFICES.

SECTION I.

1. At the border sacrifices a single victim was used, and at the altars to (the spirits of) the land and grain there was (the full complement of) three Victims[2]. When the son of Heaven went on his

[1. See the introductory notice, p. 26.

2. The object of the statements here and some other paragraphs is to show that the degree of honour was expressed by the 'paucity' of the articles; compare last Book, Sect. i, paragraph 8. Perhaps the name Kiâo in the title should be translated in the plural as the name for all the border sacrifices, or those offered in the suburbs of the capital. There were several of them, of which the greatest was that at the winter solstice, on the round hillock in the southern suburb. Besides this, there was in the first month the border sacrifice for 'grain,'—to pray for the blessing of Heaven on the agricultural labours of the year, in which Hâu Kî, the father of the line of Kâu, and its 'Father of Husbandry,' was associated by that dynasty. There were also the five seasonal border sacrifices, of which we have mention in the different parts of Book IV, though, so far as what is said in them goes, the idea of Heaven falls into the background, and the five deified ancient sovereigns come forward as so many Tîs. In the first month of summer there was, further, a great border sacrifice for rain, and in the last month of autumn a great border sacrifice of thanks giving. 'Of all these border sacrifices,' say the Khien–lung editors, there is clear evidence in classical texts.' Into the discussions growing out of them about 'one Heaven,' or 'five Heavens,' and about their origin, it is not necessary that I should enter; it would be foreign, indeed, to my object in this translation to do so. The border sacrifices were the greatest religious or ceremonial services of the ancient Chinese; and the fact to which our attention is called in this Book, is that at them there was used only a single victim.]

inspecting tours to the princes, the viands of the feast to him were composed of a (single) calf; and when they visited him, the rites with which he received them showed the three regular animals. (The feasting of him in such a manner) was to do honour to the idea of sincerity[1]. Therefore if the animal happened to be pregnant, the son of Heaven did not eat of it, nor did he use such a victim in sacrificing to God[2].

2. The horses of the Grand carriage had one ornamental tassel at the breast; those of the carriages that preceded had three; and those of the carriages that followed had five[3]. There were the blood at the border sacrifice; the raw flesh in the great offering of the ancestral temple; the sodden flesh where spirits are presented thrice; and the roast meat where they are presented once[3]:—these were expressive of the greatest reverence, but the taste was not valued; what was held in honour was the scent of the air[4]. When the princes appeared as guests,

[1. Why 'a calf? Because of its guileless simplicity,' says Kâu Hsü of our eleventh century; earlier than Kû Hsî, who adopted his explanation. The calf, whether male or female, has not yet felt the appetency of sex, and is unconscious of any 'dissipation.' This is a refinement on the Hebrew idea of the victim lamb, 'without blemish.'

2. This might be referred to his unwillingness, to take life unnecessarily, but for what has just been said about the calf.

3. See last Book, Sect. i, 8; and Sect. ii, 6.

4. Little is said on the meaning of this statement, which appears to say that the most subtle and ethereal thing in sacrifices, the 'sweet savour' of the offerings, was the most important, and should excite the worshippers to add to their sincerity and reverence all other graces of character. The same lesson was given to the feudal princes when they were entertained as visitors at the royal court.]

they were presented with herb–flavoured spirits, because of their fragrance; at the great entertainment to them the value was given to (the preliminary) pieces of flesh prepared with cinnamon and nothing more.

3. At a great feast (to the ruler of another state), the ruler (who was the host) received the cup seated on his three mats. (On occasion of a visit through a minister or Great officer) when the cup was thrice presented, the ruler received it on a single mat:—so did he descend from the privilege of his more honourable rank, and assume the lower distinction (of his visitor).

4. In feasting (the orphaned young in spring) and at the vernal sacrifice in the ancestral temple they had music; but in feeding (the aged) and at the autumnal sacrifice they had no music:–these were based in the developing and receding influences (prevalent in nature). All drinking serves to nourish the developing influence; all eating to nourish the receding influence. Hence came the different character of the vernal and autumnal sacrifices; the feasting the orphaned young in spring, and the feeding the aged in autumn:–the idea was the same. But in the feeding and at the autumnal sacrifice there was no music. Drinking serves to nourish the developing influence and therefore is accompanied with music. Eating serves to nourish the receding influence, and therefore is not accompanied with music. All modulation of sound partakes of the character of development.

5. The number of tripods and meat-stands was odd, and that of the tall dishes of wood and bamboo was even[1]; this also was based in the numbers belonging to the developing and receding influences. The stands were filled with the products of the water and the land. They did not dare to use for them things of extraordinary flavours[2] or to attach a value to the multitude and variety of their contents, and it was thus that they maintained their intercourse with spiritual intelligences.

6. When the guests had entered the great door[3], the music struck up the Sze Hsiâ[4], showing the blended ease and respect (of the king). (While feasting), at the end of (every) cup the music stopped (for a moment), a practice of which Confucius often indicated his admiration. When the last cup had been put down, the performers ascended the hall, and sang;—exhibiting the virtues (of host and guests). The singers were (in the hall) above, and the organists were (in the court) below;—the honour being thus

[1. Every Chinese scholar knows that odd numbers all belong to the category of Yang (————–), and even numbers to that of Yin (—— ——).

2. The meaning of this clause is uncertain, and I have not found it anywhere sufficiently explained, considering what the characters are.

3. This paragraph and the next describe ceremonies on occasion of the king's reception of the great nobles, when they appeared in great force at court. With this the expurgated Lî Kî begins.

4 See note 1, page 413.]

given to the human voice. Music comes from the expanding influence (that operates in nature); ceremonies from the contracting. When the two are in harmony, all things obtain (their full development).

7. There were no fixed rules for the various articles of tribute. They were the different products of the different territories according to their several suitabilities, and were regulated by their distances (from the royal domain). The tortoises were placed in front of all the other offerings;–because (the shell.) gave the knowledge of the future. The bells succeeded to them;–because of their harmony, they were a symbol of the union of feeling that should prevail'. Then there were the skins of tigers and leopards;–emblems of the

fierce energy with which insubordination would be repressed; and there were the bundles of silks with disks of jade on them, showing how (the princes) came to (admire and experience) the virtue (of the king).

8. (The use of) a hundred torches in his courtyard began with duke Hwan of Khî. The playing of the Sze Hsiâ (at receptions) of Great officers began with Kâo Wan–dze[2].

9. When appearing at another court, for a Great officer to have a private audience was contrary to propriety. If he were there as a commissioner, bearing

[1. As we have no account anywhere of bells, made, being sent as tribute, many understand the name as merely = 'metal.'

2 This and the five paragraphs that follow seem the work of another hand, and are not in the expurgated Kî. Duke Hwan was the first and greatest of 'the five presiding princes' of the Khun Khiû period. He died B.C. 643. Kâo Wan–dze was a Great officer and chief minister of Zin about a century after. The king alone might have a hundred torches in his courtyard.]

his own prince's token of rank, this served as his credentials. That he did not dare to seek a private audience showed the reverence of his loyalty. What had he to do with the tribute–offerings in the court of the other prince that he should seek a private audience? The minister of a prince had no intercourse outside his own state, thereby showing how he did not dare to serve two rulers.

10. For a Great officer to receive his ruler to an entertainment was contrary to propriety. For a ruler to put to death a Great officer who had violently exercised his power was (held) an act of righteousness; and it was first seen in the case of the three Hwan[1].

The son of Heaven did not observe any of the rules for a visitor or guest;–no one could presume to be his host. When a ruler visited one of his ministers, he went up to the hall by the steps proper to the master;–the minister did not presume in such a case to consider the house to be his own. According to the rules for audiences, the son of Heaven did not go down from the hall and meet the princes. To descend from the hall and meet the princes, was an error on the part of the son of Heaven, which began with king Î [2], and was afterwards observed.

[1. The 'three Hwan' intended here were three sons of duke Hwan' of Lû, known as Khing–fû, Yâ, and Kî–yû; see the Zo Kwan, and Kung–yang, on the last year of duke Kwang. Instances of the execution of strong and insubordinate officers in different states, more to the point, bad occurred before; but the writer had in mind only the history of Lû.

2. I was the ninth of the sovereigns of Kâu (B.C. 894–879); with him appeared the first symptoms of decline in the dynasty.]

11. For the princes to suspend (their drums and bells) in four rows like the walls of an apartment (after the fashion of the king), and to use a white bull in sacrificing[1]; to strike the sonorous jade; to use the red shields with their metal fronts and the cap with descending tassels in dancing the Tâ–wû; and to ride in the grand chariot:—these were usages which they usurped. The towered gateway with the screen across the path, and the stand to receive the emptied cups; the axes embroidered on the inner garment with its vermilion colour:—these were usurpations of the Great officers. Thus, when the son of Heaven was small and weak, the princes pushed their usurpations; and when the Great officers were strong, the princes were oppressed by them, In this state (those officers) gave honour to one another as if they had been of (high) degree; had interviews with one another and made offerings; and bribed one another for their individual benefit: and thus all usages of ceremony were thrown into disorder. It was not lawful for the princes to sacrifice to the king to whom they traced their ancestry, nor for the Great officers to do so to the rulers from whom they sprang. The practice of having a temple to such rulers in their private families, was contrary to propriety. It originated with the three Hwan[2].

12. The son of Heaven[3] preserved the descendants

[1. That a white bull was used in Lû in sacrificing to the duke of Kâu, appears from the fourth of the Praise Odes of Lû. See vol. iii, p. 343.

2 These must be the three families of Lû, so powerful in the time of Confucius, all descended from duke Hwan. The expression in this (state) shows that the writer was a man of Lû.

3. We must think of this 'son of Heaven' as the founder of a new dynasty. Thus it was that king Wû of Kâu enfeoffed the duke of Sung as representing the kings of Shang, and the rulers of Kü as representing those of Hsiâ.]

of (the sovereigns of) the two (previous) dynasties, still honouring the worth (of their founders). But this honouring the (ancient) worthies did not extend beyond the two dynasties.

13. Princes did not employ as ministers refugee rulers[1]. Hence anciently refugee rulers left no son who continued their title.

14. A ruler stood with his face towards the south, to show that he would be (in his sphere) what the influence of light and heat was (in nature). His ministers stood with their faces to the north, in response to him. The minister of a Great officer did not bow his face to the ground before him, not from any honour paid to the minister, but that the officer might avoid receiving the homage which he had paid himself to the ruler.

15. When a Great officer was presenting (anything to his ruler), he did not do so in his own person; when the ruler was making him a gift, he did not go to bow in acknowledgment to him:–that the ruler might not (have the trouble of) responding to him.

16. When the villagers were driving away pestilential influences, Confucius would stand at the top of his eastern steps, in his court robes, to keep the spirits (of his departed) undisturbed in their shrines[2].

[1. Rulers expelled from their own state. But the princes might employ their sons as ministers, who ceased to be named from their former dignity.

2. See the Confucian Analects X, 10, 2, and note. Dr. Williams (on) says that the ceremony is now performed by the Board of Rites ten days before the new year.]

17. Confucius said, 'The practice of archery to the notes of music (is difficult). How shall the archer listen, and how shall he shoot, (that the two things shall be in harmony)?'

Confucius said, 'When an officer is required to shoot, if he be not able, he declines on the ground of being ill, with reference to the bow suspended at the left of the door (at his birth)[1].'

18. Confucius said, 'There are three days' fasting on hand., If one fast for the first day, he should still be afraid of not being (sufficiently) reverent. What are we to think of it, if on

the second day he beat his drums[2]?'

19. Confucius said, 'The repetition of the sacrifice next day inside the Khû gate; the searching for the spirits in the eastern quarter; and the holding the market in the morning in the western quarter:—these all are errors.'

20. At the Shû, they sacrificed to (the spirits of) the land, and on the tablet rested the power of the darker and retiring influence of nature. The ruler stands (in sacrificing) with his face to the south at the foot of the wall on the north, responding to the idea of that influence as coming from the north. A kiâ day is used (for the sacrifice),—to employ a commencing day (in the Cycle)[3].

[1. Every gentleman was supposed to learn archery as one of the six liberal arts;' and a bow was suspended near the door on the birth of a boy in recognition of this. The excuse in the paragraph is a lame one. See the 'Narratives of the School,' article 28; and Book XLIII, 19.

2. 'Narratives of the School,' XLIV, 9.

3. There are of course six decades of days in the Cycle, each beginning with a kiâ day.]

The great Shê altar of the son of Heaven was open to receive the hoarfrost, dew, wind, and rain, and allow the influences of heaven and earth to have full development upon it. For this reason the Shê altar of a state that had perished was roofed in, so that it was not touched by the brightness and warmth of Heaven. The altar (of Yin) at Po[1] had an opening in the wall on the north, so that the dim and cold (moon) might shine into it.

21. In the sacrifice at the Shê altars they dealt with the earth as if it were a spirit. The earth supported all things, while heaven hung out its brilliant signs. They derived their material resources from the earth; they derived rules (for their courses of labour) from the heavens. Thus they were led to give honour to heaven and their affection to the earth, and therefore they taught the people to render a good return (to the earth). (The Heads of) families provided (for the sacrifice to it) at the altar in the open court (of their houses); in the kingdom and the states they did so at the Shê altars; showing how it was the source (of their prosperity).

When there was a sacrifice at the Shê altar of a village[2], some one went out to it from every house. When there was such a sacrifice in preparation for a hunt, the men of the state all engaged in it. When there was such a sacrifice, from the towns, small and large, they contributed their vessels of rice, thereby

[1. Po had been the capital of the Shang dynasty. The site was in the present Ho–nan; changed more than once, but always retaining the name. We have the Northern, the Southern, and the Western Po.

2. See page 259, Paragraph 7.]

expressing their gratitude to the source (of their prosperity) and going back in their thoughts to the beginning (of all being).

22. In the last month of spring[1], 'the fire star having appeared, they set fire to (the grass and brushwood). When this was done, they reviewed the chariots and men, numbering the companies, of a hundred and of five. Then the ruler in person addressed them in front of the Shê altar, and proceeded to exercise their squadrons, now wheeling to the left, now wheeling to the right, now making them lie down, now making them rise up; and observing how they practised these evolutions. When the game came in sight and the desire of capturing it was exerted, (he watched) to see that (the hunters) did not break any of the rules (for their proceedings). It was thus sought to bring their wills into subjection, and make them not pursue the animals (in an irregular way). In this way such men conquered in fight, and such sacrificing obtained blessing.

SECTION II.

1. The son of Heaven, in his tours (of Inspection) to the four quarters (of the kingdom), as the first thing (on his arrival at each) reared the pile of wood (and set fire to it)[2].

[1. Perhaps 'the last month' should be 'the second month.' There is much contention on the point.

2. This paragraph is not in the expurgated Lî. It does seem out of place, for the book goes on to speak of the border or suburban sacrifices presented in the vicinity of the capital,

and having nothing to do with the tours of Inspection, of which we first read in the Canon of Shun, in the Shû. Those tours, however, were understood to be under the direction of Heaven, and the lighting of the pile of wood, on reaching the mountain of each quarter, is taken as having been an announcement to Heaven of the king's arrival.]

2. At the (Great) border sacrifice, he welcomed the arrival of the longest day. It was a great act of thanksgiving to Heaven, and the sun was the chief object considered in it'. The space marked off for it was in the southern suburb;—the place most open to the brightness and warmth (of the heavenly

[1. P. Callery has here the following note:—'Il résulte de ce passage et de plusieurs autres des chapitres suivants, que dès les temps les plus anciens, les Chinois rendaient au soleil un véritable culte, sans même y supposer un esprit ou génie dont il fût la demeure, ainsi qu'ils le faisaient pour les montagnes, les rivières et tous les autres lieux auxquels ils offraient des sacrifices. De nos jours encore on sacrifie au soleil et h la lune; mais c'est plutôt un acte officiel de la part des autorités, qu'une pratique de conviction, car le peuple Chinois n'a pas, comme les Japonais, une grande dévotion pour l'astre du jour. Voyez la fin du chapitre XVIII.'

The text conveys no idea to me of such an ancient worship, but I call the attention of the reader to Callery's view. The other passages to which he refers will be noticed as they occur. For my, 'and the sun was the principal object regarded in it,' he says, 'C'est le soleil qui est le principal objet (des adorations).' The original text is simply . I let my translation stand as I first made it; but on a prolonged consideration, I think, it would be more accurate to say, 'and the sun was considered (for the occasion) as the residence of (the spirit of) Heaven.' Such an acceptation of is quite legitimate. The sun became for the time the 'spirit–tablet' of Heaven. Fang Küeh says:—'(The Son of Heaven) was welcoming the arrival of the longest day, and therefore he regarded the sun as the residence (for the time) of the spirit of Heaven. That spirit could not be seen; what could be looked up to and beheld were only the sun, moon, and stars.']

influence). The sacrifice was offered on the ground which had been swept for the purpose;—to mark the simplicity (of the ceremony). The vessels used were of earthenware and of gourds;—to emblem the natural (productive power of) heaven and earth. The place was the suburb, and therefore the sacrifice was called the suburban or border. The victim was red, that being the colour preferred by the (Kâu) dynasty; and it was a calf;—to show the estimation of simple sincerity.

3. For (all) sacrifices in the border they used a hsin day[1]; because when Kâu first offered the border sacrifice, it was the longest day, and its name began with hsin.

4. When divining about the border sacrifice, (the king) received the reply in the fane of his (great) ancestor, and the tortoise-shell was operated on in that of his father;-honour being thus done to his ancestor, and affection shown to his father. On the day of divination, he stood by the lake[2], and listened himself to the declarations and orders which were

[1. The mention of the 'hsin day' requires that we should understand kiâo here of other sacrifices so called, and not merely of the great one at the winter solstice. The Khien-lung editors say:—'The border sacrifices for which they used the hsin days were those at which they prayed for a good year. They used such a day, because when king Wû offered his great sacrifice after the battle of Mû-yêh, and announced the completion of his enterprise, the day was hsin-hâi, and from it dated Kâu's possession of the kingdom, and the hsin days became sacred days for the dynasty.' There were of course three hsin days in every month.

2 The 'lake' here must be a name for the royal college with the water round it. So Lû Tien and others explain it and Yüan Yüan's dictionary with reference to this paragraph, defines it as 'the place where they practised ceremonies.']

delivered[1],—showing an example of receiving lessons and reproof. (The officers) having communicated to him the orders (to be issued), he gives warning notice of them to all the officers (of a different surname from himself), inside the Khû gate (of the palace), and to those of the same surname, in the Grand temple.

5. On the day of the sacrifice, the king in his skin cap waits for the news that all is ready,-showing the people how they ought to venerate their superiors. Those who were engaged in mourning rites did not wail nor venture to put on their mourning dress. (The people) watered and swept the road, and turned it up afresh with the spade; at (the top of) the fields in the neighbourhood they kept torches burning,—thus without special orders complying with (the wish of) the king[2].

6. On that day, the king assumed the robe with the ascending dragons on it as an emblem of the heavens[3]. He wore the cap with the pendants of jade–pearls, to the number of twelve[4], which is the

[1. By the officers as the result of the divination.

2. It was an established custom that they should do so.

3. The robe with the dragons on it,'—Kwan,—is thus described in the dictionary. But there must have been also some emblazonry of the heavenly figures on it also; otherwise it would not have emblemed the heavens. But I have not been able to find this in any dictionary.

4. Having now changed the skin cap mentioned in the preceding paragraph.]

number of heaven[1]. He rode in the plain carriage, because of its simplicity. From the flag hung twelve pendants, and on it was the emblazonry of dragons, and the figures of the sun and moon, in imitation of the heavens. Heaven hangs out its brilliant figures, and the sages imitated them. This border sacrifice is the illustration of the way of Heaven.

7. If there appeared anything infelicitous about the victim intended for God, it was used for that intended for Kî[2]. That intended for God required to be kept in its clean stall for three months. That intended for Kî simply required to be perfect in its parts. This was the way in which they made a distinction between the spirits of Heaven and the manes of a man[3].

8. All things originate from Heaven; man originates from his (great) ancestor. This is the reason

[1. 'The heavenly number;'—with reference, I suppose, to the twelve months of the year.

2. Kî, better known as Hâu Kî, the prince, the minister of agriculture,' appears in the Shû as Shun's minister of agriculture (Khî, vol. iii, pp. 42), and one of the principal assistants of Yü, in his more than Herculean achievement (vol. iii, pp. 56–58); and in the Shih as the father of agriculture (vol. iii, pp. 396–399). To him the kings of Kâu traced their lineage, and they associated him with God at the Great border sacrifice. See the ode to

him, so associated, vol. iii, p. 320. In that service there was thus the expression of reverence for God and of filial piety, the second virtue coming in as the complement of the other. It would seem to be implied that they used the ox for Kî for the blemished one.

3 By ' spirit' and 'manes' I have endeavoured to come as near as I could to the different significance of the characters shan and kwei.]

why Kî was associated with God (at this sacrifice). In the sacrifices at the border there was an expression of gratitude to the source (of their prosperity and a going back in their thoughts to the beginning of (all being).

9. The great kâ sacrifice of the son of Heaven consisted of eight (sacrifices). This sacrifice was first instituted by Yin Khî[1]. (The word) kâ expresses the idea of searching out. In the twelfth month of a year, they brought together (some of) all the productions (of the harvest), and sought out (the authors of them) to present them to them as offerings.

10. In the kâ sacrifice, the principal object contemplated was the Father of Husbandry. They also presented offerings to (ancient) superintendents of husbandry, and to the (discoverers of the) various grains, to express thanks for the crops which had been reaped.

They presented offerings (also) to the (representatives of the ancient inventors of the overseers of the) husbandmen, and of the buildings marking out the boundaries of the fields, and of the birds and beasts. The service showed the highest sentiments of benevolence and of righteousness.

The ancient wise men had appointed all these agencies, and it was felt necessary to make this

[1. Who this Yin Khî was is unknown. Mang thought he was an ancient sovereign. The Khien–lung editors seem to prove in opposition to him and others that he was the minister of some ancient sovereign. His descendants were subordinate ministers under Mu, having to do with sacrifice. They are mentioned at the end of the 37th Book of the Kâu Lî.]

return to them. They met the (representatives of the) cats, because they devoured the rats and mice (which injured the fruits) of the fields, and (those of) the tigers, because they devoured the (wild) boars (which destroyed them). They met them and made offerings to them. They offered also to (the ancient Inventors of) the dykes and water-channels;—(all these were) provisions for the husbandry[1].

11. They said,—

'May the ground no sliding show,
Water in its channels flow,
Insects to keep quiet know;
Only in the fens weeds grow!'

They presented their offerings in skin caps and white robes;–in white robes to escort the closing year (to its grave). They wore sashes of dolychos cloth, and carried staffs of hazel,—as being reduced forms of mourning. In the kâ were expressed the highest sentiments of benevolence and righteousness.

[1. This and the other paragraphs down to 13 about the kâ sacrifice are not in the expurgated copies. It is difficult to understand what it really was. What is said of it leads us to think of it as a Chinese Saturnalia at the end of the year, when all the crops had been gathered in, and the people abandoned themselves to license and revel under the form of sacrificial services. 'The Father of Husbandry' was probably Shan Nang, the successor of Fû–hsî; see vol. iii, pp. 371, 372. 'The Superintendents of Husbandry' would be Hâu Kî and others, though Hâu Kî appears in the Shih as really the father of agriculture. 'The overseer' occurs in the Shih (vol. iii, p. 371 et al.) as 'the surveyor of the fields.' The commentators, so far as I have read, are very chary of giving us any information about the offerings to 'the cats and tigers.' Kiang Kâo–hsî says, 'They met the cats and tigers, that is, their spirits.']

(After this)[1] they proceeded to sacrifice in yellow robes and yellow caps,—releasing the field–labourers from the toils (of the year). Countrymen wore yellow hats, which were made of straw.

12. The Great Netter[2] was the officer who had the management for the son of Heaven of his birds and (captured) beasts, and to his department belonged (all such creatures)

sent by the princes as tribute. (Those who brought them)[3] wore hats of straw or bamboo splints, appearing, by way of honour to it, in that country dress. The Netter declined the deer and women (which they brought)[4], and announced to the visitors the message (of the king) to this effect, that they might warn the princes with it:—

'He who loves hunting and women,
Brings his state to ruin.'

The son of Heaven planted gourds and flowering plants; not such things as might be reaped and stored[5].

[1. This seems to introduce another service, following that of the kâ. It is understood to be the lâ sacrifice of Khin, described on page 300, paragraph 19.

2. We find 'the Netter' called Lo as if Lo had become the surname of the family in which the office was hereditary, as the last but one of the departments described in the 30th Book of the Kâu Lî.

3. Those would be 'Great officers' from the various states, personating for the occasion hunters or labouring men.

4. The 'deer' would be taken in the chase; the 'women,' attractive captives, taken in war, But they would not have such to present from year to year. We can say nothing more about this article of tribute.

5. Many take this concluding sentence as part of the king's message. The Khien–lung editors decide against that view; its meaning is that the king never farmed for his own gain.]

13. The kâ with its eight sacrifices served to record (the condition of the people) throughout all the quarters (of the country). If in any quarter the year had not been good, it did not contribute to those services,—out of a careful regard to the resources of the people. Where–. the labours of a good year had been successfully completed, they took part in them,—to give them pleasure and satisfaction. Alt the harvest having by this time been gathered, the people had nothing to do but to rest, and therefore after the kâ wise (rulers) commenced no new work[1].

14. The pickled contents of the ordinary dishes were water–plants produced by the harmonious powers (of nature); the brine used with them was from productions of the land. The additional dishes contained productions of the land with the brine from productions of the water.

The things in the dishes on stands were from both the water and land'. They did not venture to use in them the flavours of ordinary domestic use, but variety was considered admirable. It was in this way that they sought to have communion with the spirits; it was not intended to imitate the flavours of food[2].

15. The things set before the ancient kings served as food, but did not minister to the pleasures of the palate. The dragon–robe, the tasseled cap, and

[1. This paragraph treats of the kâ as celebrated in the states.

2. The conclusion of this paragraph leads us to take all the dishes spoken of in it as containing sacrificial offerings. It would take too long to discuss all that is said about the 'regular' and the 'additional' dishes in the first part.]

the great carriage served for display, but did not awaken a fondness for their use.

The various dances displayed the gravity of the performers, but did not awaken the emotion of delight. The ancestral temple produced the impression of majesty, but did not dispose one to rest in it. Its vessels might be employed (for their purposes in it), but could not be conveniently used for any other. The idea which leads to intercourse with spiritual Beings is not interchangeable with that which finds its realisation in rest and pleasure.

16. Admirable as are the spirits and sweet spirits, a higher value is attached to the dark spirit and the bright water[1],—in order to honour that which is the source of the five flavours. Beautiful as is the elegant embroidery of robes, a higher value is set on plain, coarse cloth,—going back to the commencement of woman's work. Inviting as is the rest afforded by the mats of fine rushes and bamboos, the preference is given to the coarse ones of reeds and straw,—distinguishing the (character of the service in which they were employed). The Grand soup is unseasoned,–in honour of its simplicity. The Grand symbols of jade have no engraving on them,—in admiration of their simple plainness. There is the beauty of the red varnish and carved border

[1. We have seen, before, that 'the dark spirit' is water. Was there a difference between this and 'the bright water?' The Khien lung editors think so, and refer to the functions of the Sze Hsüan officer (, Kâu Lî, Book XXXVII. 41–44), who by means of a mirror drew the bright water from the moon. How be did so, I do not understand. The object of the writer in this part of the section is to exhibit the value of simple sincerity in all religious services.]

(of a carriage), but (the king) rides in a plain one, doing honour to its plainness. In all these things it is simply the idea of the simplicity that is the occasion of the preference and honour. In. maintaining intercourse with spiritual and intelligent Beings, there should be nothing like an extreme desire for rest and ease in our personal gratification. It is this which makes the above usages suitable for their purpose.

17. The number of the tripods and meat–stands was odd, but that of the tall dishes of wood and bamboo was even,—having regard to the numbers belonging to the developing and receding influences of nature[1]. The vase with the yellow eyes[2] was the most valued of all, and contained the spirit with the fragrant herbs. Yellow is the colour (of earth) which occupies the central places[3]. In the eye the energy (of nature) appears most purely and brilliantly. Thus the spirit to be poured out is in that cup, the (emblem of the) centre, and (the symbol of) what is Most pure and bright appears outside[4].

[1. See the fifth paragraph of Section i, and the note. It may be added here, after Khung Ying–tâ, that 'the tripod and stand contained the body of the victim, which, as belonging to an animal that moved, was of the category of Yang, but the dishes contained the products of trees and vegetables,—which were of the category of Yin.'

2. In pictures, this vase was figured with two eyes. They were carved on the substance of the vessel and then gilt, so as to appear yellow.

3. On the central place assigned to the element of earth and its yellow colour, see the supplementary section appended to Book IV, Section ii, Part iii.

4. P. Callery characterises the reasoning of this paragraph as 'puéril et grotesque;' and concludes a long note on it with the sentence:—'Je laisse à ceux qui peuvent suivre ce logogriphe dans le texte Chinois, le soin d'en saisir toutes les finesses; car, mon sens, ce n'est qu'une ineptie.']

18. When Sacrificing to Heaven, the earth is swept, and the sacrifice presented on the ground,—from a regard to the simplicity of such an unartificial altar. Admirable as are the vinegar and pickles, suet boiled and produced through evaporation is preferred,—to do honour to the natural product of heaven. An ordinary knife might be employed (to kill the victim), but that fitted with bells is preferred,—giving honour to the idea thereby indicated; there is the harmony of sound, and then the cutting work is done.

SECTION III.

1. (As to) the meaning of (the ceremony of) capping[1]:—The cap used for the first act of the service was of black cloth,—the cap of the highest antiquity. It was originally of (white) cloth, but the colour when it was used in fasting was dyed black. As to its strings, Confucius said, 'I have not heard anything about them.' This cap, after it had been once put upon (the young man), might be disused.,

2. The son by the wife proper was capped by the eastern stairs (appropriate to the use of the master), to show how he was in their line of succession

[1. These paragraphs about capping are not in the expurgated copy of the Lî, and many commentators, especially Wang of Shih–liang, would relegate them to Book XI. And they are not all easy to be understood. The capping was thrice repeated, and each time with a different cap. So much is clear. The names and forms of the caps in paragraph 3 have given rise to much speculation, from which I purposely abstain; nor do I clearly comprehend its relation to the threefold capping in the ceremony'.]

to him. The father handed him a cup in the guests' place (without receiving one in return). The capping showed that he had reached maturity. The using of three caps was to give greater importance (to the ceremony), and show its object more clearly. The giving the name of maturity in connexion with the ceremony was to show the reverence due to that name.

3. The wei–mâo was the fashion of Kâu; the kang–fû, that of Yin; and the mâu–tui, that of the sovereigns of Hsiâ. Kâu used the pien; Yin, the hsü; and Hsiâ, the shâu. The three dynasties all used the skin cap, with the skirt–of–white gathered up at the waist.

4. There were no observances peculiar to the capping (in the families) of Great officers, though there were (peculiar) marriage ceremonies. Anciently a man was fifty when he took the rank of a Great officer; how should there have been peculiar ceremonies at his cappings? The peculiar ceremonies at the cappings as used by the princes arose in the end of the Hsiâ dynasty.

5. The eldest son of the son of Heaven by his proper queen (was capped only as) an ordinary officer. There was nowhere such a thing as being born noble. Princes received their appointments on the hereditary principle, (to teach them) to imitate the virtue of their predecessors. Men received office and rank according to the degree of their virtue. There was the conferring of an honourable designation after death; but that is a modern institution. Anciently, there was no rank on birth, and no honorary title after death.

6. That which is most important in ceremonies is to understand the idea intended in them. While the idea is missed, the number of things and observances in them may be correctly exhibited, as that is the business of the officers of prayer and the recorders. Hence that may all be exhibited, but it is difficult to know the idea. The knowledge of that idea, and the reverent maintenance of it was the way by which the sons of Heaven secured the good government of the kingdom.

7. By the united action of heaven and earth all things spring up. Thus the ceremony of marriage is the beginning of a (line that shall last for a) myriad ages. The parties are of different surnames; thus those who are distant are brought together, and the separation (to be maintained between those who are of the same surname) is emphasised[1]. There must be sincerity in the marriage presents; and all communications (to the woman) must be good. She should be admonished to be upright and sincere. Faithfulness is requisite in all service of others, and faithfulness is (specially) the virtue of a wife. Once mated with her husband, all her life she will not change (her feeling of duty to him) and hence, when the husband dies she will not marry (again)[2].

[1. I do not see how Callery translates here:—'On rapproche ce qui était éloigné, et on unit ce qui était distinct.' He says, however, in a note:—'Ceci se rapporte à l'antique loi, encore en vigueur, qui interdit le mariage entre personnes d'un même nom, parce que lors même qu'il n'existe entre elles aucune trace de parenté, il est possible qu'elles proviennent de la même souche, et se trouvent ainsi sur la ligne directe, où les Chinois admettent une parenté sans fin.'

2 This brief sentence about a woman not marrying again is not in the expurgated copies. Callery, however, says upon it:—'Dans certains textes du Lî Kî, on trouve à la suite de ce passage une phrase qui restreint à la femme cette immutabilité perpétuelle dans le mariage. En effet, les lois Chinoises ont de tout temps permis à l'homme de se remarier après la mort de sa première femme, tandis que pour les veuves, les secondes noces ont toujours été plus ou moins flétries, ou par la loi, ou par l'usage.']

8. The gentleman went in person to meet the bride, the man taking the initiative and not the woman, according to the idea that regulates the relation between the strong and the weak (in all nature). It is according to this same idea that heaven takes precedence of earth, and the ruler of the subject.

9. Presents are interchanged before (the parties) see each other[1];—this reverence serving to illustrate the distinction (that should be observed between man and woman). When this distinction (between husband and wife) is exhibited, affection comes to prevail between father and son. When there is this affection, the idea of righteousness arises in the mind, and to this idea of righteousness succeeds (the observance of) ceremonies. Through those ceremonies there ensues universal repose. The absence of such distinction and righteousness is characteristic of the way of beasts.

10. The bridegroom himself stands by (the carriage of the bride), and hands to her the strap (to assist her in mounting[2]),—showing his affection. Having

[1. Callery has for this:—'Les présents que porte l'époux dans ses visites.' But the young people did not see each other till the day of the marriage.

2. On the 'strap' to help in mounting the carriage, see p. 45, et al. Callery has here 'les rênes.' The text would seem to say that the bridegroom. was himself driving, and handed the strap to help the other up; but that would have been contrary to all etiquette; and they appear immediately, not sitting together, but follow in each other.]

that affection, he seeks to bring her near to him. It was by such reverence and affection for their wives that the ancient kings obtained the kingdom. In passing out from the great gate (of her father's house), he precedes, and she follows, and with this the right relation between husband and wife commences. The woman follows (and obeys) the man:–in her youth, she follows her father and elder brother; when married, she follows her husband;

when her husband is dead, she follows her son. 'Man' denotes supporter. A man by his wisdom should (be able to) lead others.

11. The dark-coloured cap, and the (preceding) fasting and vigil, (with which the bridegroom meets the bride, makes the ceremony like the service of) spiritual beings, and (the meeting of) the bright and developing and receding influences (in nature). The result of it will be to give the lord for the altars to the spirits of the land and grain, and the successors of the forefathers of the past;—is not the utmost reverence appropriate in it? Husband and wife ate, together of the same victim,—thus declaring that they were of the same rank. Hence while the wife had (herself) no rank, she was held to be of the rank of her husband, and she took her seat according to the position belonging to him[1].

[1. It is exceedingly difficult to construe this sentence, nor do the commentators give a translator much help. Rendering ad verbum, all that we have is this:—'The dark-coloured cap, self-purification (and) abstinence; spiritual beings, Yin (and) Yang.' Kang s explanation is very brief:—'The dark-coloured cap (was) the dress in sacrificing: Yin (and) Yang mean husband and wife.' I have tried to catch and indicate the ideas in the mind of the writer. Taken as I have done, the passage is a most emphatic declaration of the religious meaning which was attached to marriage. Dr. Medhurst (Theology of the Chinese, pp. 88, 89) has translated the greater part of the paragraph, but not very successfully, thus:—'A black crown, with fasting and watching, is the way to serve the Kwei Shins, as well as the male and female principle of nature. The same is the case also (with regard to marriages which are contracted) with the view of obtaining some one to perpetuate the lares domestici and principally respect obtaining successors for our ancestors:—can they therefore be conducted without reverence?']

12. The old rule at sacrifices was to have the vessels (only) of earthenware and gourds; and when the kings of the three dynasties instituted the (partaking of the) victim, those were the vessels employed. On the day after the marriage, the wife, having washed her hands, prepared and presented (a sucking-pig) to her husband's parents; and when they had done eating, she ate what was left,—as a mark of their special regard. They descended from the hall by the steps on the west, while she did so by those on the east;—so was she established in the wife's (or mistress's) place.

13. At the marriage ceremony, they did not employ music,—having reference to the feeling of solitariness and darkness (natural to the separation from parents). Music

expresses the energy of the bright and expanding influence. There was no congratulation on marriage;–it indicates how (one generation of) men succeeds to another[1].

[1. See p. 322, paragraph 20; where Confucius says that in a certain case the bridegroom's family has no music for three days, on the ground that the bridegroom had lost his parents, and sorrow was more suitable than mirth as he thought of their being gone. This statement was generalised by the writer; but in the Shih, as in ordinary– life, music is an accompaniment of in marriage. See the paraphrase of the 'Amplification of the fourth of the Khang–hsî precepts.']

14. At the sacrifices in the time of the lord of Yü the smell was thought most important. There were the offerings of blood, of raw flesh, and of sodden flesh;—all these were employed for the sake of the smell.

15. Under the Yin, sound was thought most important. Before there was any smell or flavour, the music was made to resound clearly. It was not till there had been three performances of it that they went out to meet (and bring in) the victim. The noise of the music was a summons addressed to all between heaven and earth.

16. Under the Kâu, a pungent odour was thought most important. In libations they employed the smell of millet–spirits in which fragrant herbs had been infused. The fragrance, partaking of the nature of the receding influence, penetrates to the deep springs below. The libations were poured from cups with long handles of jade, (as if) to employ (also) the smell of the mineral. After the liquor was poured, they met (and brought in) the victim, having first diffused the smell into the unseen realm. Artemisia along with millet and rice having then been burned (with the fat of the victim), the fragrance penetrates through all the building. It was for this reason that, after the cup had been put down, they burnt the fat with the southernwood and millet and rice.

17. So careful were they on all occasions of sacrifice. The intelligent spirit returns to heaven the body and the animal soul return to the earth; and hence arose the idea of seeking (for the deceased) in sacrifice in the unseen darkness and in the bright region above. Under the Yin, they first sought for them in the bright region; tinder Kâu, they first sought for them in the dark.

18. They informed the officer of prayer in the apartment; they seated the representative of the departed in the hall; they killed the victim in the courtyard. The head of the victim was taken up to the apartment. This was at the regular sacrifice, when the officer of prayer addressed himself to the spirit–tablet of the departed. If it were (merely) the offering of search, the minister of prayer takes his place at the inside of the gate of the temple. They knew not whether the spirit were here, or whether it were there, or far off, away from all men. Might not that offering inside the gate be said to be a searching for the spirit in its distant place?

19. That service at the gate was expressive of the energy of the search. The stand with the heart and tongue of the victim (set forth before the personator) was expressive of reverence. (The wish of the principal) for wealth (to those assisting him) included all happiness. The (presentation of the) head was (intended as) a direct (communication with the departed). The presence (of the representative) was that the spirit might enjoy (the offerings). The blessing (pronounced by him) was for long continuance, and comprehensive. The personator (seemed) to display (the departed).

20. The (examination of the) hair and the (taking of the) blood was an announcement that the victim was complete within and without. This announcement showed the value set on its being perfect'. The offering of the blood was because of the breath which is contained in it. They offered (specially) the lungs,, the liver, and the heart, doing honour to those parts as the home of the breath.

21. In offering the millet and the glutinous millet, they presented the lungs along with it. In offering the various prepared liquors, they presented the bright water;—in both cases acknowledging their obligations to the dark and receding influence (in nature). In taking the fat of the inwards and burning it, and in taking the head up (to the hall), they made their acknowledgments to the bright and active influence.

22. In the bright water and the clear liquor the thing valued was their newness. All clarifying is a sort of making new. The water was called 'bright' because the principal in the service had purified it.

23. When the ruler bowed twice with his head to the ground, and, with breast bared, himself applied

[1. From the middle of paragraph 10 to 18 inclusive is not in the expurgated edition, which closes with the nineteenth paragraph and the half of the twenty-first. I need not quote Callery's translation of this portion, but he says on it:—'Ce passage est un de ceux qui se refusent le plus à la traduction, et qui renferment, au fond, le moins d'idées claires et raisonnables. L'auteur a voulu, ce me semble, dormer une explication mystique à des mots et à des coutumes, qui n'en étaient point susceptibles, et il lui est arrivé, comme à certains commentateurs bibliques du moyen age, de faire un galimatias, auquel lui même, sans doute, ne comprenait rien."—On what the author says about the hair and blood, compare vol. iii, page 370.]

the knife, this expressed his extreme reverence. Yes, his extreme reverence, for there was submission in it. The bowing showed his submission; the laying the head on the ground did that emphatically; and the baring his breast was the greatest (outward) exhibition of the feeling.

24. When the sacrificer styled himself 'the filial son,' or 'the filial grandson,' he did so (in all cases) according to the meaning of the name. When he styled himself 'So and So, the distant descendant,' that style was used of (the ruler of) a state or (the Head of) a clan. (Though) there were the assistants at the service, the principal himself gave every demonstration of reverence and performed all his admirable service without yielding anything to any one.

25. The flesh of the victim might be presented raw and as a whole, or cut up in pieces, or sodden, or thoroughly cooked; but how could they know whether the spirit enjoyed it? The sacrificer simply showed his reverence to the utmost of his power.

26. (When the representative of the departed) had made the libation with the kiâ cup, or the horn, (the sacrificer) was told (to bow to him) and put him at ease. Anciently, the representative stood when nothing was being done; when anything was being done, he sat. He personated the spirit; the officer of prayer was the medium of communication between him and the sacrificer.

27. In straining (the new liquor) for the cup, they used the white (mâo) grass and obtained a clear cup. The liquor beginning to clear itself was further clarified by means of pure liquor. The juice obtained by boiling aromatics (with the extract of millet) was clarified by mingling with it the liquor which had begun to clear itself:–in the same way as old and

strong spirits are qualified by the brilliantly pure liquor or that which has begun to clear itself[1].

[1. He would be a bold man who would say that he had given a translation of this paragraph, which he was sure represented exactly the mind of the author. The interpretation given of it even by Kang Hsüan is now called in question in a variety of points by most scholars; and the Khien–lung editors refrain from concluding the many pages of various commentators, which they adduce on it, with a summary and exposition of their own judgement. Until some sinologist has made himself acquainted with all the processes in the preparation of their drinks at the present day by the Chinese, and has thereby, and from his own knowledge of the general subject, attained to a knowledge of the similar preparations of antiquity, a translator can only do the best in his power with such a passage, without being sure that it is the best that might be done.

In the Kâu Li, Book V, 23–36, we have an account of the duties of the Director of Wines (; Biot, 'Intendant des Vins'). Mention is made of 'the three wines' which were employed as common beverages, and called shih kiû, hsî kiû and khing kiû; in Biot, 'vin d'affaire, vin âgé, and vin clair.' Consul Gingell, in his useful translation of 'The Institutes of the Kin Dynasty Strung as Pearls' (London: Smith, Elder, and Co., 1852), calls them—'wine made specially for any particular occasion; wine which has become ripe; and old, clear, and fine wine.'

In addition to these three kiû, the Director had to do with the five kî (; Biot, 'les cinque sorts de vins sacrés'), and called fan kî, ang kî, thî kî, and khan kî in Biot, after Kang Hsüan, 'vin surnageant, vin doux, vin qui se clarifie, vin substantiel, vin reposé;' in Gingell, 'rice–water which has undergone fermentation, wine in which dregs have formed, wine in which the dregs have risen t6 the surface, wine in which the dregs have congealed, and of which the colour has become reddish, and pure clear wine in which the dregs are subsiding.' Whether Biot be correct or not in translating kî (perhaps should be read kâi =) vin sacré,' the five preparations so called were for use at sacrifices. 'They were' say the Khien–lung editors, 'for use at sacrifices, and not as ordinary drinks.' 'They were all thin, and unpalatable; for the cup, and not for the mouth.']

28. Sacrifices were for the purpose of prayer, or of thanksgiving, or of deprecation.

29. The dark–coloured robes worn during vigil and purification had reference to the occupation of the thoughts with the dark and unseen. Hence after the three days of purification, the superior man was sure (to seem) to see those to whom his sacrifice was to be offered[1].

[1. The Khien–lung editors say that from paragraph 14 to this, the compiler mentions promiscuously a great many particulars about the ancient sacrifices, the different places in which the services at them were performed, the things used in them, &c., showing how sincere and earnest those engaged in them must be to attain to the result mentioned in this last paragraph; and that this is the fundamental object of the whole treatise.

I have called attention to this promiscuous nature of the contents of many of the Books towards the end of them, in the introduction, page 34, as a characteristic of the collection.]

BOOK X. THE NÊI ZEH, OR THE PATTERN OF THE FAMILY[1].

SECTION L

1. The sovereign and king orders the chief minister to send down his (lessons of) virtue to the millions of the people.

2. Sons[2], in serving their parents, on the first crowing of the cock, should all wash their hands and rinse their mouths, comb their hair, draw over it the covering of silk, fix this with the hair–pin, bind the hair at the roots with the fillet, brush the dust from that which is left free, and then put on their caps, leaving the ends of the strings hanging down. They should then put on their squarely made black jackets, knee–covers, and girdles, fixing in the last their tablets. From the left and right of the girdle they should hang their articles for use:—on the left side, the duster and handkerchief, the knife and whetstone, the small spike, and the metal speculum for getting fire from the sun; on the right, the archer's thimble. for the thumb and the armlet, the tube for writing instruments, the knife–case, the larger spike, and the borer for getting fire from wood. They should put on their leggings, and adjust their shoe–strings.

[1. See the introductory notice, pp. 26, 27.

2 The 'sons' here are young gentlemen of good families, shih who might be employed as ordinary officers.]

3. (Sons') wives should serve their parents-in-law as they served their own. At the first crowing of the cock, they should wash their hands, and rinse their mouths; comb their hair, draw over it the covering of silk, fix this with the hair-pin, and tie the hair at the roots with the fillet. They should then put on the jacket, and over it the sash. On the left side they should hang the duster and handkerchief, the knife and whetstone, the small spike, and the metal speculum to get fire with; and on the right, the needle-case, thread, and floss, all bestowed in the satchel, the great spike, and the borer to get fire with from wood. They will also fasten on their necklaces[1], and adjust their shoe-strings.

4. Thus dressed, they should go to their parents and parents-in-law. On getting to where they are, with bated breath and gentle voice, they should ask if their clothes are (too) warm or (too) cold, whether they are ill or pained, or uncomfortable in any part; and if they be so, they should proceed reverently to stroke and scratch the place. They should in the same way, going before or following after, help and support their parents in quitting or entering (the apartment). In bringing in the basin for them to wash, the younger will carry the stand and the elder the water; they will beg to be allowed to pour out

[1. Necklaces' is only a guess at the meaning. Khan Hâo and others make the character to mean 'scent bags.' But this also is only a guess. There is nothing in its form to suggest such a meaning; and as many other critics point out, it is inconsistent with the usage in paragraph 5. These acknowledge that they do not understand the phrase . See I, i, 3, 34, but the use of ying there is considered inappropriate here.]

the water, and when the washing is concluded, they Will hand the towel. They will ask whether they want anything, and then respectfully bring it. All this they will do with an appearance of pleasure to make their parents feel at ease. (They should bring) gruel, thick or thin, spirits or must, soup with vegetables, beans, wheat, spinach, rice, millet, maize, and glutinous millet,—whatever they wish, in fact; with dates, chestnuts, sugar and honey, to sweeten their dishes; with the ordinary or the large-leaved violets, leaves of elm-trees, fresh or dry, and the most soothing rice-water to lubricate them; and with fat and oil to enrich them. The parents will be sure to taste them, and when they have done so, the young people should withdraw[1].

5. Youths who have not yet been capped, and maidens who have not yet assumed the hair–pin, at the first crowing of the cock, should wash their hands, rinse their mouths, comb their hair, draw over it the covering of silk, brush the dust from that which is left free, bind it up in the shape of a horn, and put on their necklaces. They should all bang at their girdles[2] the ornamental (bags of) perfume; and as soon as it is daybreak, they should (go to) pay their respects (to their parents) and ask what they will eat

[1. The structure of this and the preceding sentences is easy enough, but it is not easy for a translator to assure himself that he is rendering every Chinese character by its correct equivalent in his own language.

2. They hang on these instead of the useful appendages mentioned in paragraphs 2 and 3, as being too young to employ these. This determines the meaning of in the last clause as I have given it. Zottoli's rendering is:—'Si nondum comederint, tunc adjuturi majores inspectabunt praeparata.']

and drink. If they have eaten already, they should retire; if they have not eaten, they will (remain to) assist their elder (brothers and sisters) and see what has been prepared.

6. All charged with the care of the inner and outer parts (of the house), at the first crowing of the cock, should wash their hands and mouths, gather up their pillows and fine mats, sprinkle and sweep out the apartments, hall, and courtyard, and spread the mats, each doing his proper work. The children go earlier to bed, and get up later, according to their pleasure. There is no fixed time for their meals.

7. From the time that sons receive an official appointment, they and their father occupy different parts of their residence. But at the dawn, the son will pay his respects, and express his affection by (the offer of) pleasant delicacies. At sunrise he will retire, and he and his father will attend to their different duties. At sundown, the son will pay his evening visit in the same way.

8. When the parents wish to sit (anywhere), the sons and their wives should carry their mats, and ask in what direction they shall lay them. When they wish to lie down, the eldest among them should carry the mats, and ask where they wish to place their feet,

while the youngest will carry a (small) bench for them to lean on while they stretch out their legs. (At the same time) an attendant will place a stool by them. They should take up the mat on which they had been lying and the fine mat over it, bang up the coverlet, put the pillow in its case, and roll up the fine mat and put it in its cover.

9. (Sons and their wives) should not move the clothes, coverlets, fine mats, or undermats, pillows, and stools of their parents[1]; they should reverently regard their staffs and shoes, but not presume to approach them; they should not presume to use their vessels for grain, liquor, and water, unless some of the contents be left in them; nor to eat or drink any of their ordinary food or drink, unless in the same case.

10. While the parents are both alive, at their regular meals, morning and evening, the (eldest) son and his wife will encourage them to eat everything, and what is left after all, they will themselves eat[2]. When the father is dead, and the mother still alive, the eldest son should wait upon her at her meals; and the wives of the other sons will do with what is left as in the former case. The children should have the sweet, soft', and unctuous things that are left.

11. When with their parents, (sons and their wives), when ordered to do anything, should immediately respond and reverently proceed to do it, In going forwards or backwards, or turning round, they should be careful and grave; while going out or coming in, while bowing or walking, they should not presume to eructate, sneeze, or cough, to yawn or stretch themselves, to stand on one foot, or to lean against anything, or to look askance. They should not dare to spit or snivel, nor, if it be cold, to put on more clothes, nor, if they itch anywhere, to scratch

[1. That is, the parents of the husband, and parents–in–law of the wife.

2. 'That nothing,' says Khung Ying–tâ, 'may be served up again.']

themselves. Unless for reverent attention to something[1], they should not presume to unbare their shoulders or chest. Unless it be in wading, they should not hold up their clothes. Of their private dress and coverlet, they should not display the inside. They should not allow the spittle or snivel of their parents to be seen[2]. They should ask leave to rinse away any dirt on their caps or girdles, and to wash their clothes that are dirty with lye that has been prepared for the purpose; and to stitch together, with needle and thread, any rent.

Every five days they should prepare tepid water, and ask them to take a bath, and every three days prepare water for them to wash their heads. If in the meantime their faces appear dirty, they should heat the wafer in which the rice has been cleaned, and ask them to wash with it; if their feet be dirty, they should prepare hot water, and ask them to wash them with it. Elders in serving their youngers, and the low in serving the noble, should all observe these rules.

12. The men should not speak of what belongs to the inside (of the house), nor the women of what belongs to the outside. Except at sacrifices and funeral rites, they should not hand vessels to one another. In all other cases when they have occasion to give and receive anything, the woman should receive it in a basket. If she have no basket, they should both sit down, and the other put the thing on

[1. As for archery. The meaning is, I suppose, that none of the things mentioned should be seen or known, while they are waiting on their parents.

2. But instantly wipe it off, according to Khan Hâo.]

the ground, and she then take it up. Outside or inside[1], they should not go to the same well, nor to, the same bathing–house. They should not share the same mat in lying down; they should not ask or borrow anything from one another; they should not wear similar upper or lower garments. Things spoken inside should not go out, words spoken outside should not come in. When a man goes into the interior of the house, he should not whistle nor point. If he have occasion to move in the night, he should, use a light; and if he have no light, he should not stir. When a woman goes out at the door, she must keep her face covered. She should walk at night (only) with a light; and if she have no light, she should not stir. On the road, a man should take the right side, and a woman the left.

13. Sons and sons' wives, who are filial and reverential, when they receive an order from their parents should not refuse, nor be dilatory, to execute it[2]. When (their parents) give them anything to eat or drink, which they do not like, they will notwithstanding taste it and wait (for their further orders); when they give them clothes, which are not to their mind, they will put them on, and wait (in the same way)[3]. If (their parents) give them anything to do, and then employ another to take their place,

[1. Zottoli has for this—'viri mulieresque.' The writer is speaking of men and women, indeed; but the characters have reference to place, and = 'out of the house or in it.'

2 That is, they will not presume on any indulgence which they might expect from the impression made by their general character and behaviour.

3 'Orders,' consequent on their parents' seeing that the food or garment is not to their mind.]

although they do not like the arrangement, they will in the meantime give it into his hands and let him do it, doing it again, if it be not done well.

14. When the sons and their wives are engaged with laborious tasks, although (their parents) very much love them, yet they should let them go on with them for the time;—it is better that they take other occasions frequently to give them ease.

When sons and their wives have not been filial and reverential, (the parents) should not be angry and resentful with them, but endeavour to instruct them. If they will not receive instruction, they should then be angry with them. If that anger do no good, they can then drive out the son, and send the wife away, yet not publicly showing why they have so treated them[1].

15. If a parent have a fault, (the son) should with bated breath, and bland aspect, and gentle voice, admonish him. If the admonition do not take effect, he will be the more reverential and the more filial; and when the father seems pleased, he will repeat the admonition. If he should be displeased with this, rather than allow him to commit an offence against any one in the neighbourhood or countryside, (the son) should strongly remonstrate. If the parent be angry and (more) displeased, and beat him till the blood

[1. This last sentence is enigmatical in the original text. Zottoli says:—'Si non possint coerceri, filium ejice nurum exclude, quin tamen patefacius agendi morem;' adding as an explanation of that 'agendi morem,' 'siquidem eos haud certe in finem sic ejectos voles.' Different views of the Chinese have been given by different critics; and it would not be difficult to add to their number.]

flows, he should not presume to be angry and resentful, but be (still) more reverential and more filial.

16. If parents have a boy born (to the father) by a handmaid, or the son or grandson of one of his concubines, of whom they are very fond, their sons should after their death, not allow their regard for him to decay so long as they live.

If a son have two concubines, one of whom is loved by his parents, while he himself loves the other, yet he should not dare to make this one equal to the former whom his parents love, in dress, or food, or the duties which she discharges, nor should he lessen his attentions to her after their death. If he very much approves of his wife, and his parents do not like her, he should divorce her'. If he do not approve of his wife, and his parents say, 'she serves us well,' he should behave to her in all respects as his wife,—without fail even to the end of her life.

17. Although his parents be dead, when a son is inclined to do what is good, he should think that he will thereby transmit the good name of his parents, and carry his wish into effect. When he is inclined to do what is not good, he should think that he will thereby bring disgrace on the name of his parents, and in no wise carry his wish into effect.

18. When her father-in-law is dead, her mother-in-law takes the place of the old lady[2]; but the wife of the eldest son, on all occasions of sacrificing and receiving guests. must ask her directions in everything,

[1. Khan Hâo quotes here from the Lî of the elder Tâi (Book XIII, chapter 26) the 'seven grounds of divorce,' the first of them being the wife's 'want of accordance with her husband's parents.'

2. Who now retires from the open headship of the family.]

while the other sons' wives must ask directions from her. When her parents-in-law employ the eldest son's wife, she should not be dilatory, unfriendly, or unpolite to the wives of his brothers (for their not helping her). When the parents-in-law employ any of them, they should not presume to consider themselves on an. equality with the other; walking side by side with her, or giving their orders in the same way, or sitting in the same position as she.

19. No daughter–in–law, without being told to go to her own apartment, should venture to withdraw from that (of her parents–in–law). Whatever she is about to do, she should ask leave from them. A son and his wife should have no private goods, nor animals, nor vessels; they should not presume to borrow from, or give anything to, another person. If any one give the wife an article of food or dress, a piece of cloth or silk, a handkerchief for her girdle, an iris or orchid, she should receive and offer it to her parents–in–law. If they accept it, she will be glad as if she were receiving it afresh. If they return it to her, she should decline it, and if they do not allow her to do so, she will take it as if it were a second gift, and lay it by to wait till they may want it. If she want to give it to some of her own cousins, she must ask leave to do so, and that being granted, she will give it.

20. Eldest cousins in the legitimate line of descent and their brothers should do reverent service to the son, who is the representative chief of the family and his wife[1]. Though they may be richer and

[1. These are all legitimate members of the same surname or clan, but the honoured cousin is the chief of it in the direct line. He is the chieftain of the clan. They are heads of subordinate branches of it. They may have become more wealthy and attained to higher rank in the service of their common ruler, but–within the limits of the clan, he is their superior, and has duties of sacrifice to the ancestors of it, with which they cannot of themselves intermeddle.]

higher in official rank than he, they should not presume to enter his house with (the demonstrations of) their wealth and dignity. Although they may have in attendance many chariots and footmen, these should stop outside, and they enter it in more simple style with a few followers.

If to any of the younger cousins there have been given vessels, robes, furs, coverlets, carriages and horses, he must offer the best of them (to his chief), and then use those that are inferior to this himself. If what he should thus offer be not proper for the chief, he will not presume to enter with it at his gate, not daring to appear with his wealth and dignity, to be above him who is the head of all the clan with its uncles and elder cousins.

A wealthy cousin should prepare two victims, and present the better of them to his chief. He and his wife should together, after self–purification, reverently assist at his sacrifice in the ancestral temple. When the business of that is over, they may venture to offer their own private sacrifice.

21. Of grain food, there were millet,—the glutinous rice, rice, maize, the white millet, and the yellow maize, cut when ripe, or when green.

Of prepared meats, there were beef soup, mutton soup, pork soup, and roast beef; pickle, slices of beef, pickle and minced beef; roast mutton, slices of mutton, pickle, and roast pork; pickle, slices of pork, mustard sauce, and minced fish; pheasant, hare, quail, and partridge[1].

22. Of drinks, there was must in two vessels, one strained, the other unstrained, made of rice, of millet, or of maize. In some cases, thin preparations were used as beverages, as millet gruel, pickle, with water syrup of prunes, and of steeped rice; clear wine and white[2].

Of confections, there were dried cakes, and rice–flour scones.

23. For relishes, snail–juice and a condiment of the broad–leaved water–squash were used with pheasant soup; a condiment of wheat with soups of dried slices and of fowl; broken glutinous rice with dog soup and hare soup; the rice–balls mixed with these soups had no smart–weed in them.

A sucking–pig was stewed, wrapped up in sonchus leaves and stuffed with smart–weed; a fowl, with the same stuffing, and along with pickle sauce; a fish, with the same stuffing and egg sauce; a tortoise, with the same stuffing and pickle sauce.

For meat spiced and dried they placed the brine of ants; for soup made of sliced meat, that of hare; for a ragout of elk, that of fish; for minced fish, mustard sauce; for raw elk flesh, pickle sauce; for preserved peaches and plums, egg–like suet.

24. All condiments for grain food were of a

[1. In all, four rows of prepared meats, consisting of four dishes each.

2. Both the old wine and occasional wine, mentioned in the note on page 447, were 'white.' The kiû here, probably, were the three kiû there.]

character corresponding to the spring; for soup, to the summer; for sauces, to the autumn; and for beverages, to the winter.

In all attempering ingredients, sour predominated in the spring; bitter, in the summer; acrid, in the autumn; and salt, in the winter:—with the due proportioning of the unctuous and sweet.

The glutinous rice (was thought) to suit beef; millet, to suit mutton; glutinous millet, to suit pork; maize, to suit dog; wheat, to suit goose; and the broad–leaved squash, to suit fish.

25. Lamb and sucking–pig were (thought to be) good in spring, fried with odorous (beef) suet; dried pheasant and fish, in summer, fried with the strong–smelling suet (of dog); veal and fawn, in autumn, fried with strong suet (of fowl); fresh fish and goose,' in winter, fried with the frouzy suet (of goat).

26. There were dried beef, and dried stalks of deer's flesh, of wild pig's, of elk's, and of the muntjac's. Elk's flesh, deer's, wild pig's, and muntjac's, was (also eaten uncooked; and) cut in large leaflike slices. Pheasants and hares were (made into soup) with the duckweed. There were sparrows and finches, partridges, cicadas, bees, lichens, small chestnuts, the water–caltrops, the hovenia dulcis, the zizyphus, chestnuts, hazel–nuts, persimmons, cucumbers, peaches, plums, ballaces, almonds, haws, pears, ginger, and cinnamon[1].

[1. In this there are the names of more than thirty condiments or relishes, which, according to most commentators, were, or might be, served up at the meals of the rulers of states. But from paragraph 21 we have a list of viands, drinks, and their accompaniments with no information as to when and by whom they were used. To descend to further particulars about them would be troublesome.]

27. If a Great officer, at his ordinary meals, had mince, he did not have, at the same time, dried slices of meat; and if he had the latter, he did not have the former. An ordinary officer did not have two kinds of soup, or sliced flesh. (But) old men of the common people, did not eat their meat alone without accompaniments.

28. Mince was made in spring, with onions; in autumn, with the mustard plant. Sucking–pig was used in spring, with scallions; in autumn, with smartweed. With lard they used onions; with fat, chives. With the three victim–animals they used pepper, and employed pickle as an accompaniment. For wild animals' flesh they used plums. In quail soup, fowl soup, and with the curlew, the condiment was smartweed. Bream and tench were steamed; pullets, roasted; and pheasants, (boiled), with fragrant herbs and no smart–weed.

29. Things not eaten were the turtle, when hatching; the intestines of the wolf, which were removed, as also the kidneys of the dog; the straight spine of the wild cat; the rump of the hare; the head of the fox; the brains of the sucking–pig; the yî–like bowels of fish[1]; and the perforated openings of the turtle[1].

30. (Bones and sinews) were taken from the flesh; the scales were scraped from fish; dates were made to appear as new; chestnuts were

[1. It is uncertain what some of these forbidden articles really were.]

selected; peaches were made smooth; kâ and pears had the insects drilled out of them[1].

31. When an ox lowed at night, its flesh was (considered) to be rank; that of a sheep, whose long hair showed a tendency to, get matted, to be frouzy; that of a dog which was uneasy and with (the inside of) its thighs red, to be coarse; that of birds when moulting and with their voices hoarse, to be fetid; that of pigs, when they looked upwards and closed their eyes, to be measly; that of a horse, black along the spine and with piebald fore–legs, to smell unpleasantly.

A pullet, whose tail could not be grasped by the hand, was not eaten, nor the rump of a tame goose, nor the ribs of a swan or owl, nor the rump of a tame duck, nor the liver of a I fowl, nor the kidneys of a wild goose, nor the gizzard of the wild goose without the hind–toe, nor the stomach of the deer.

32. Flesh cut small was made into mince; cut into slices it was made into hash. Some say that the flesh of elks, deer, and fish was pickled; that of muntjacs also, being cut in small pieces; that of fowls and wild pigs, in larger pieces; of hares, the stomach was pickled. Onions and scallions were mixed with the brine to soften the meat[2].

[1. The explanation of these brief notes is also perplexing. Zottoli makes the kâ to have been a kind of medlar (azarolus). Medhurst calls it, after the Khang–hsî dictionary, 'a kind of pear.' Williams, explaining it under a synonym (of the same sound), 'a sour red fruit of the size of a cherry, a kind of hawthorn.'

2. The manner of these preparations has not been definitely explained. The meaning is uncertain. So also is what is said of the cupboards in the next paragraph.]

33. Soup and boiled grain were. used by all, from the princes down to the common people, without distinction of degree. Great officers did not regularly have savoury meat, but when seventy they had their cupboards. The cupboards of the son of Heaven were five on the right (of the dining hall), and five on the left; those of dukes, marquises, and earls were five, all in one room; those of Great officers three (in a side chamber), and other officers had one on their buffet.

SECTION II.

1. In nourishing the aged[1], (Shun), the lord of Yü, used the ceremonies of a drinking entertainment; the sovereigns of Hsiâ, those (at entertainments after) a reverent sacrifice or offering; the men of Yin, those of a (substantial) feast; and the men of Kâu cultivated and used all the three[2].

Those of fifty years were entertained in the schools of the districts; those of sixty, in the school of the capital; and those of seventy, in the college. This rule extended to the feudal states. An old man of eighty made his acknowledgment for the ruler's invitation by kneeling once and bringing his head to the ground twice. The blind did the same. An

[1. Khan Hâo says:—The nourishment of the aged took place in four cases: 1st, in the case of the three classes of ancients; 2nd, in that of the father and grandfather of one who had died in the of the country; 3rd, in that of officers who had retired from age; and 4th, in that of the aged of the common people. On seven occasions of the year it was done formally.

2. On the different designations of the dynasties, see on Confucian Analects, III, 21.]

old man of ninety employed another to receive (the message and gift for him).

For those of fifty, the grain was (fine and) different (from that used by younger men). For those of sixty, there was meat kept in store (from the day before). For those of seventy, there was a second service of savoury meat. Those of eighty were supplied regularly with delicacies. For those of ninety, food and drink were never out of their chambers; wherever they wandered, it was deemed right that savoury meat and drink should follow them.

After sixty (the coffin and other things for the funeral) were seen to be in readiness (once) a year; after seventy, once a season; after eighty, once a month; and after ninety, they were every day kept in good repair. The bandages, however, the sheet, the larger coverlets, and the cases were prepared after death[1].

At fifty, one was supposed to begin to decay; at sixty, not to feel satisfied unless he had flesh to eat. At seventy, he was thought to require silk in order to make him feel warm; at eighty, to need some one (to sleep) with him, to keep him warm; and at ninety, not to feel warm even with that.

At fifty, one kept his staff in his hand in the family; at sixty, in his district; at seventy, in the city; at eighty, (an officer) did so in the court. If the son of Heaven wished to put questions to (an officer of) ninety, he went to his house, and had rich food carried after him.

[1. The sheet was for the slighter dressing of the corpse immediately after death; the coverlets for the fuller dressing at the coffining; the cases were for the upper part of the corpse and for the legs.]

At seventy, (an officer) did not wait till the court was over (before he retired). At eighty, he reported every month (to the ruler's messenger) that he was still alive; at ninety, he had (delicate food) sent to him regularly every day.

At fifty, one was not employed in services requiring strength; at sixty, he was discharged from bearing arms along with others; at seventy, he was exempted from the business of receiving guests and visitors; at eighty, he was free from the abstinences and other rites of mourning.

When one received at fifty the rank (of a Great officer), at sixty he did not go in person to the school[1]. At seventy he resigned office; and then and afterwards, in mourning he used only the unhemmed dress of sackcloth (without adopting the privations of the mourning rites)[1].

The kings of the three dynasties, in nourishing the old, always caused the members of families who were advanced in years to be brought to their notice[2]. Where an officer was eighty, one of his friends was free from all service of government; where he was ninety, all the members of his family were exempted from them. So also it was in the case of the blind.

(Shun), the lord of Yü, entertained the aged (who had retired from the service) of the state in (the school called) the higher hsiang, and the aged of the common people in (the school called) the lower

[1. Does this intimate, that if he had learned better at school, when young, he might have become a Great officer earlier? He was now too old to learn.

2. The government could not attend to all the aged; but it wished to bear of all cases of remarkable age, and would then do what it could for them.]

hsiang. The sovereigns of the line of Hsiâ entertained the former in (the school called) the hsü on the east, and the latter in (that called) the hsü on the west. The men of Yin entertained the former in the School of the Right, and the latter in that of the Left. The men of Kâu entertained the former in the kiâo on the east, and the latter in the Yü hsiang. This was in the suburb of the capital on the west.

The lord of Yu wore the hwang cap in sacrificing (in the ancestral temple), and the white robes in entertaining the aged. The sovereigns of Hsiâ sacrificed in the shin cap, and entertained the aged in the dark garments of undress. Those of Yin sacrificed in the hsü cap, and entertained in the garments of white thin silk. Those of Kâu sacrificed in the mien cap, and entertained the aged in the dark upper garment (and the lower white one)[1].

2. Zang-dze said, 'A filial son, in nourishing his aged, (seeks to) make their hearts glad, and not to go against their wishes; to promote their comfort in their bed-chambers and

the whole house; and with leal heart to supply them with their food and drink:—such is the filial son to the end of life. By "the end of life," I mean not the end of parents' lives, but the end of his own life. Thus what his parents loved he will love, and what they reverenced he will reverence. He will do so even in regard to all their

[1. The above long paragraph constitutes, with very little difference, the first twelve paragraphs of Section V of Book III. Kû Hsî says that in this Book we have 'old text,' whereas Book III is a compilation of the Han dynasty; and that the authors of it incorporated this passage. I am willing to allow that they did so; but it may be doubted if this Book in its present form be older than the time of Han.]

dogs and horses, and how much more in regard to the men (whom they valued)!'

3. In all their nourishment of the aged, (the object of) the five Tîs was to imitate (their virtue), while the kings of the three dynasties also begged them to speak (their lessons). The five Tîs taking them as models, sought to nourish their bodily vigour, and did not beg them to speak; but what good lessons they did speak were taken down by the faithful recorders. The three (lines of) kings also took them as models, and after nourishing their age begged them to speak. If they (seemed to) diminish the ceremonies (of entertainment), they all had their faithful recorders as well (to narrate their virtue).

4. For the Rich Fry, they put the pickled meat fried over rice that had been grown on a dry soil, and then enriched it with melted fat. This was called the Rich Fry.

5. For the Similar Fry, they put the pickled meat fried over the millet grains, and enriched it with melted fat. This was called the Similar Fry.

6. For the Bake, they took a sucking–pig or a (young) ram, and having cut it open and removed the entrails, filled the belly with dates. They then wrapped it round with straw and reeds, which they plastered with clay, and baked it. When the clay was all dry, they broke it off. Having washed their hands for the manipulation, they removed the crackling and macerated it along With rice–flour, so as to form a kind of gruel which they added to the pig. They then fried the whole in such a quantity of melted fat as to cover it. Having prepared a large pan of hot water, they placed in it a small tripod, and the slices of which was filled with fragrant herbs, he creature which was being prepared. They took care that the hot water did not cover this tripod, but kept up the fire without intermission for three

days and nights. After this, the whole was served up with the addition of pickled meat and vinegar.

7. For the Pounded Delicacy, they took the flesh of ox, sheep, elk, deer and muntjac, a part of that which lay along the spine, the same in quantity of each, and beat it now as it lay flat, and then turning it on its side; after that they extracted all the nerves. (Next), when it was sufficiently cooked, they brought it (from the pan), took away the outside crust, and softened the meat (by the addition of pickle and vinegar).

8. For the Steeped Delicacy, they took the beef, which was required to be that of a newly killed animal, and cut it into small pieces, taking care to obliterate all the lines in it. It was then steeped from one morning to the next in good wine, when it was eaten with pickle, vinegar, or the juice of prunes.

9. To make the Grill, they beat the beef and removed the skinny parts. They then laid it on a frame of reeds, sprinkled on it pieces of cinnamon and ginger, and added salt. It could be eaten thus when dried. Mutton was treated in the same way as beef, and also the flesh of elk, deer, and muntjac. If they wished the flesh wet, they added water and fried it with pickled meat. If they wished it dry, they ate it as eaten (at first).

10. For the (Soup) Balls, they took equal quantities of beef, mutton and pork, and cut them small. Then they took grains of rice, which they mixed with the finely cut meat, two parts of rice to one of meat, and formed cakes or balls, which they fried.

11. For the Liver and Fat, they took a dog's liver, and wrapped it round with its own fat. They then wet it and roasted it, and took it in this condition and scorched it. No smartweed was mixed with the fat.

12. They took the grains of rice and steeped. them in prepared rice–water. They then cut small the fat from a wolfs breast, and with it and the grains of rice made a fry[1].

13. The observances of propriety commence with a careful attention to the relations between husband and wife. They built the mansion and its apartments, distinguishing between the exterior and interior parts. The men occupied the exterior; the women the interior. The mansion was deep, and the doors were strong, guarded by porter and eunuch. The men did not enter the interior; the women did not come out into the exterior.

14. Males and females did not use the same stand or rack for their clothes. The wife did not presume to hang up anything on the pegs or stand of her husband; nor to put anything in his boxes or satchels; nor to share his bathing–house. When her husband had gone out (from their apartment), she put his pillow in its case, rolled up his upper and under mats, put them in their covers, and laid. them away in their proper receptacles. The young served the old; the low served the noble;–also in this way.

[1. This and the other paragraphs from 4 are understood to describe the eight delicacies which were specially prepared for the old. See the Kâu Lî, Book IV, par. 18.]

15. As between husband and wife, it was not until they were seventy, that they deposited these things in the same place without separation. Hence though a concubine were old, until she had completed her fiftieth year, it was the rule that she should be with the husband (once) in five days. When she was to do so, she purified herself, rinsed her mouth and washed, carefully adjusted her dress, combed her hair, drew over it the covering of silk, fixed her hair–pins, tied up the hair in the shape of a horn, brushed the dust from the rest of her hair, put on her necklace, and adjusted her shoe–strings. Even a favourite concubine was required in dress and diet to come after her superior. If the wife were not with the husband, a concubine waiting on him, would not venture to remain the whole night[1].

16. When a wife was about to have a child, and the month of her confinement had arrived, she occupied one of the side apartments, where her husband sent twice a day to ask for her. If he were moved and came himself to ask about her[2], she did not presume to see him, but made her governess dress herself and reply to him.

When the child was born, the husband again sent twice a day to inquire for her. He fasted now, and did not enter the door of the side apartment. If the child were a boy, a bow was placed on the left of the door; and if a girl, a handkerchief on the

[1. This paragraph has given rise to a great deal of discussion and writing among the commentators, into which it is not desirable to enter.

2. The first character in this clause occasions difficulty to a translator. Zottoli has:—'Negotiisque ipsemet interrogabit illam.' Wang Tâo understands it as I have done.]

right of it. After three days the child began to be carried, and some archery was practised for a boy, but not for a girl.

17. When a son and heir to the ruler of a state was born, and information of the fact was carried to him, he made arrangements to receive him at a feast where the three animals should all be provided; and the cook took in hand the (necessary) preparations. On the third day the tortoise–shell was consulted for a good man to carry the child; and he who was the lucky choice, kept a vigil over night, and then in his court robes, received him in his arms outside the chamber. The master of the archers then took a bow of mulberry wood, and six arrows of the wild rubus, and shot towards heaven, earth, and the four cardinal points. After this the nurse received the child and carried it in her arms. The cook (at the same time) gave (a cup of) sweet wine to the man who had carried the child, and presented him with a bundle of silks, and the tortoise–shell was again employed to determine the wife of an officer, or the concubine of a Great officer, who should be nurse.

18. In all cases of receiving a son, a day was chosen; and if it were the eldest son of the king, the three animals were killed (for the occasion). For the son of a common man, a sucking–pig was killed; for the son of an officer, a single pig; for the son of a Great officer, the two smaller animals; and for the son of the ruler of a state, all the three. If it were not the eldest son, the provision was diminished in every case one degree.

19. A special apartment was prepared in the palace for the child, and from all the concubines and other likely individuals there was sought one distinguished for her generosity of mind, her gentle kindness, her mild integrity, her respectful bearing, her carefulness and freedom from talkativeness, who should be appointed the boy's teacher; one was next chosen who should be his indulgent mother, and a third who should be his guardian mother. These all lived in his apartment, which others did not enter unless on some (special) business.

20. At the end of the third month a day was chosen for shaving off the hair of the child, excepting certain portions,—the horn–like tufts of a boy, and the circlet on the crown of a girl. If another fashion were adopted, a portion was left on the left of the boy's head, and on the right of the girl's. On that day the wife with the son appeared before the father. If they were of noble families, they were both in full dress. From the commissioned officer downwards, all rinsed their mouths and washed their heads. Husband and wife rose early,

bathed and dressed as for the feast of the first day of the month. The husband entered the door, going up by the steps on the cast, and stood at the top of them with his face to the west. The wife with the boy in her arms came forth from her room and stood beneath the lintel with her face to the east.

21. The governess then went forward and said for the lady, 'The mother, So and So, ventures to–day reverently to present to you the child!' The husband replied, 'Reverently (teach him to) follow the right way.' He then took hold of the right hand of his son, and named him with the smile and voice of a child. The wife responded, 'We will remember. May your words be fulfilled!' She then turned to the left, and delivered the child to his teacher, who on her part told the name all round to the wives of the relatives of all ranks who were present. The wife forthwith proceeded to the (festal) chamber.

22. The husband informed his principal officer of the name, and he in turn informed all the (young) males (of the same surname) of it. A record was made to the effect—' In such a year, in such, a month, on such a day, So and So was born,' and deposited. The officer also informed the secretaries of the hamlets, who made out two copies of it. One of these was deposited in the office of the village, and the other was presented to the secretary of the larger circuit, who showed it to the chief of the circuit; he again ordered it to be deposited in the office of the circuit. The husband meanwhile had gone into (the festal chamber), and a feast was celebrated with the ceremonies of that with which a wife first entertains her parents–in–law.

23. When an heir–son has been born, the ruler washed his head and whole body, and put on his court robes. His wife did the same, and then they both took their station at the top of the stairs on the east with their faces towards the west. One of the ladies of quality, with the child in her arms ascended by the steps on the west. The ruler then named the child; and (the lady) went down with it.

24. A (second) son or any other son by the wife proper was presented in the outer chamber[1], when

[1. It seems plain that the sons in this paragraph were all by the proper wife or chief lady of the harem, for it is not till paragraph 26 that sons by inferior members of it are spoken of. The Khien–lung editors clearly establish this point. Kang Hsüan took a different view, saying that '"the (second) son" was a brother of the heir–son (in paragraph 23), and "any other son" a son by a concubine,' and p. Zottoli adopts this view:—'Reguli haeres, ejus germanus frater, a subnuba filius;' adding, 'Regulus excipiebat primum in praecipua diaeta secundum in postica diaeta quae hic exterior dicitur relate ad adjacentes aedes, quibus nobilis puerpera morari solebat tertium excipiebat in adjacentibus aedibus,' But these 'side apartments' are not mentioned till paragraph 27.]

(the ruler) laid his hand on its head, and with gentle voice named it. The other observances were as before, but without any words.

25. In naming a son, the name should not be that of a day or a month or of any state, or of any hidden ailment[1]. Sons of Great and other officers must not be called by the same name as the heir–son of the ruler.

26. When a concubine was about to have a child, and the month of her confinement had arrived, the husband sent once a day to ask for her. When the son was born:, at the end of three months, she washed her mouth and feet, adjusted herself early in the morning and appeared in the inner chamber (belonging to the wife proper). There she was received with the ceremonies of her first entrance into the harem. When the husband had eaten, a special portion of what was left was given to her by herself; and forthwith she entered on her duties of attendance.

27. When the child of an inferior member of the ruler's harem was about to be born, the mother went to one of the side apartments, and at the end of three months, having washed her head and person, and

[1. See page 78, paragraph 42.]

put on her court robes, she appeared before the ruler. (One of) her waiting women (also) appeared with the child in her arms. If (the mother) was one to whom the ruler had given special favours, he himself named the son. In the case of such children generally, an officer was employed to name them.

28. Among the common people who had no side chambers, when the month of confinement was come, the husband left his bed–chamber, and occupied a common apartment. In his inquiries for his wife, however, and on his son's being presented to him, there was no difference (from the observances that have been detailed).

29. In all cases though the father is alive, the grandson is presented to the grandfather, who also names him. The ceremonies are the same as when the son is presented to the father; but there is no (interchange of) words (between the mother and him).

30. The nurse of the ruler's boy[1] quitted the palace after three years, and, when she appeared before the ruler, was rewarded for her toilsome work. The son of a Great officer had a nurse. The wife of an ordinary officer nourished her child herself.

31. The son of a commissioned officer and others above him on to the Great officer was presented (to the father once) in ten days. The eldest son of a ruler was presented to him before he had eaten, when he took him by the right hand; his second or any other son by the wife proper[2] was presented after he had eaten, when he laid his hand on his head.

32. When the child was able to take its own food,

[1. See above, par. 17.

2. See above, par. 24.]

it was taught to use the right hand. When it was able to speak, a boy (was taught to) respond boldly and clearly; a girl, submissively and low. The former was fitted with a girdle of leather; the latter, with one of silk[1].

[1. The account which follows this of the teaching and training of the brothers and sisters is interesting; and we may compare it with what is said in volume iii, p. 350, of the different reception given to sons and daughters in the royal family, though the distinction between them is not accentuated here so strongly. The passage treats of the children in a family of the higher classes, but those of the common people would be dealt with in a corresponding manner according to their circumstances. And even in the early feudal times the way was open for talent and character to rise from the lower ranks in the social scale, and be admitted to official employment. The system of competitive examinations was even then casting a shadow before. To number the days was, and is, a more complicated affair in China than with us, requiring an acquaintance with all the terms of the cycle of sixty, as well as the more compendious method by decades for each month. The education of a boy, it will be seen, comprehended much more than what we call the three R s. The conclusion of paragraph 33 gives the translator some difficulty. Zottoli has—'et petet exerceri lectionibus sermonisque veritate,' and my own first draft was—'he would ask to be exercised in (reading) the tablets, and in truthful speaking.' But it is making too much of the boys of ancient China to represent them as anxious to be taught to speak the truth. The meaning of the concluding characters, as given in the text, is that assigned to them by Kang Hsüan.

There is nothing in what is said of the daughters to indicate that they received any literary training. They were taught simply the household duties that would devolve on them in their state of society; though among them, be it observed, were the forms and provision for sacrifice and worship. It will be observed, also, at how early an age all close intercourse between them and their brothers came to an end, and that at ten they ceased to go out from the women's apartments. On what is said about the young men marrying at the age of thirty I have spoken in a note on page 65.]

33. At six years, they were taught the numbers and the names of the cardinal points; at the age of seven, boys and girls did not occupy the same mat nor eat together; at eight, when going out or coming in at a gate or door, and going to their mats to eat and drink, they were required to follow their elders:—the teaching of yielding to others was now begun; at nine, they were taught how to number the days.

At ten, (the boy) went to a master outside, and stayed with him (even) over the night. He learned the (different classes of) characters and calculation; he did not wear his jacket or trousers of silk; in his manners he followed his early lessons; morning and evening he learned the behaviour of a youth; he would ask to be exercised in (reading) the tablets, and in the forms of polite conversation.

34. At thirteen, he learned music, and to repeat the odes, and to dance the ko (of the duke of Kâu)[1]. When a full-grown lad, he danced the hsiang (of king Wû)[1]. He learned archery and chariot-driving. At twenty, he was capped, and first learned the (different classes of) ceremonies, and might wear furs and silk. He danced the tâ hsiâ (of Yü)[1] and attended sedulously to filial and fraternal duties. He might become very learned, but did not teach others;—(his object being still) to receive and not to give out.

35. At thirty, he had a wife, and began to attend

[1. It is difficult to describe exactly, amid the conflict of different views, these several dances. Dances were of two kinds, the civil and military. The ko was, perhaps, the first of the civil dances, ascribed to the duke of Kâu (vol. iii, p. 334); and the hsiang, the first of the martial. The two are said to have been combined in the tâ hsiâ.]

to the business proper to a man. He extended his learning without confining it to particular subjects. He was deferential to his friends, having regard to the aims (which they displayed). At forty, he was first appointed to office; and according to the business of it brought out his plans and communicated his thoughts. If the ways (which he proposed) were suitable, he followed them out; if they were not, he abandoned them. At fifty, he was appointed a Great officer, and laboured in the administration of his department. At seventy, he retired from his duties. In all salutations of males, the upper place was given to the left hand.

36. A girl at the age of ten ceased to go out (from the women's apartments). Her governess taught her (the arts of pleasing speech and manners, to be docile and obedient, to handle the hempen fibres, to deal with the cocoons, to weave silks and form fillets, to learn (all) woman's work, how to furnish garments, to watch the sacrifices, to supply the liquors and sauces, to fill the various stands and dishes with pickles and brine, and to assist in setting forth the appurtenances for the ceremonies.

37. At fifteen, she assumed the hair–pin; at twenty, she was married, or, if there were occasion (for the delay), at twenty–three. If there were the betrothal rites, she became a wife; and if she went without these, a concubine. In all salutations of females, the upper place was given to the right hand.

xxxxxxxxxx THE LÎ KÎ Translated by JAMES LEGGE Volume II xxxxxxxxxxxxx

BOOK XI. YÜ ZÂO

OR

THE JADE-BEAD PENDANTS OF THE ROYAL CAP[1]

SECTION I.

1. The son of Heaven, when sacrificing[2], wore (the cap) with the twelve long pendants of beads of jade hanging down from its top before and behind, and the robe embroidered with dragons.

2. When saluting the appearance of the sun[3] outside the eastern gate[4], he wore the dark-coloured square-cut robes; and (also) when listening to the notification of the first day of the month[5] outside the southern gate.

[1. See introductory notice, Vol. xxvii, pp. 27, 28.

2. Probably, to Heaven;. Kang thought it was to the former kings. Many try to unite both views.

3. At the vernal equinox. Callery has 'Quand de bon matin il sacrifie au soleil.' Probably there was a sacrifice on the occasion. but the text does not say so. The character (*khiâo*) means 'to appear at audience.'

4. Probably, of the city; many say, of the Hall of Distinction.

5. This announcement was to the spirits of his royal ancestors in the first place. Compare Analects III, 16.]

3. If the month were intercalary, he caused the left leaf of the door to be shut, and stood in the middle of that (which remained open)[1].

4. He wore the skin cap at the daily audience in the court, after which he proceeded to take the morning meal in it. At midday he partook of what was left in the morning. He had music at his meals. Every day a sheep and a pig were killed and cooked; and on the first day of the month an ox in addition. There were five beverages:—water, which was the principal; rice-water, spirits, must, and millet-water.

5. When he had done eating, he remained at ease in the dark–coloured square–cut robes[2]. His actions were written down by the recorder of the Left, and his utterances by the recorder of the Right. The blind musician in attendance judged whether the music were too high or too low[3].

6. If the year were not good and fruitful, the son of Heaven wore white and plain robes, rode in the Plain and unadorned carriage, and had no music at his meals.

[1. This is not easy to understand, nor easy to make intelligible. An intercalary month was an irregular arrangement of the year. it and the previous month formed one double month. The shutting half the door showed that one half of the time was passed. There remained the other leaf to be given—in the temple or in the palace—to the king for all the ceremonies or acts of government appropriate in such a position for the whole intercalary month. Something like this is sketched out as the meaning by the Khien–lung editors.

2. These were so named from the form in which they were made, the cloth being cut straight and square.

3. And judged, it is said, of the character of the measures of government; but this is being 'over–exquisite' to account for the custom.]

7. The princes of states, in sacrificing, wore their dark–coloured square–cut robes. At court–audiences (of the king), they wore the cap of the next inferior degree of rank to their own[1]. They wore the skin–cap, when listening to the notification of the first day of the month in the Grand temples; and their court robes when holding their daily audience in the inner court–yard.

8. (Their ministers and officers) entered (the palace) as soon as they could distinguish the dawning light[2], and the ruler came out daily (to the first court, inside the Khû gate), and received them. (After this audience), he retired, and went to the great chamber, there to listen to their proposals about the measures of government. He employed men to see whether the Great officers (were all withdrawn)[3]; and when they had left, he repaired to the smaller chamber, and put off his (court) robes.

9. He resumed his court robes, when he was about to eat. There was a single animal, with three (other) dishes of meat, the lungs forming the sacrificial offering. In the evening he

wore the long robe in one piece, and offered some of the flesh of the animal. On the first day of the moon,

[1. So it seems to be said; but why it was done so, does not clearly appear.

2. Several pieces in the Shih allude to this early attendance at court. See Book II, ii, 8; iii, 8, et al.

3. They sat or waited, not inside the chamber, but outside. Some Great officer might wish to bring a matter before the ruler which he had not ventured to mention in public. The ruler, therefore, would give him a private audience; and did not feel himself free from business till all had withdrawn.]

a sheep and a pig were killed, and there were five (other) dishes of meat, and four of grain. On Dze and Mâo days[1] there were only the glutinous rice and vegetable soup. His wife used the same kitchen as the ruler[2].

10. Without some cause for it, a ruler did not kill an ox, nor a Great officer a sheep, nor a lower officer a pig or a dog. A superior man had his shambles and kitchen at a distance (from the) house; he did not tread wherever there was such a thing as blood or (tainted) air[3].

11. When the eighth month came without rain, the ruler did not have full meals nor music. If the year were not abundant, he wore linen, and stuck in his girdle the tablet of an officer[4]. Duties were not levied at the barrier–gates and dams; the prohibitions of the hills and meres were enforced, but no contributions were required (from hunters and fishermen). No earthworks were undertaken, and Great officers did not make (any new) carriages for themselves.

12. The officer of divination by the tortoise–shell fixed the shell (to be used); the recorder applied the ink; and the ruler determined the figures (produced by the fire)[5].

[1. See vol. xxvii, p. 180.

2. That is, the wife was supplied with what was left from the ruler's meals.

3. Lû Tien says, 'He would not tread on ants.' The Khien–lung editors characterise this as 'a womanish remark.'

4. A ruler's tablet was of ivory; an officer's only of bamboo, tipt with ivory.

5. See the Kâu Lit, Book XXII, 25. The Khien–lung editors say that the methods of this divination are lost.]

13. (The cross–board in front of) the ruler was covered with lambskin, edged with tiger's fur; for his sacred carriage and court–carriage a Great officer had a covering of deer skin, edged with leopard's fur; as also had an ordinary officer for his sacred carriage[1].

14. The regular place for a gentleman was exactly opposite the door, (facing the light). He slept with his head to the east. When there came violent wind, or rapid thunder, or a great rain, he changed (countenance). It was the rule for him then, even in the night, to get up, dress himself, put on his cap, and take his seat.

15. He washed his hands five times a day. He used millet–water in washing his head, and maize–water in washing his face. For his hair (when wet) he used a comb of white–grained wood, and an ivory comb for it when dry. (After his toilet), there were brought to him the (usual) cup and some delicacy; and the musicians came up[2] and sang.

In bathing he used two towels; a fine one for the upper part (of his body), and a coarser for the lower part. When he got out of the tub, he stepped on a straw mat; and having next washed his feet with hot water, he stepped on the rush one. Then in his (bathing) robe of cloth, he dried his body (again), and put on his shoes; and a drink was then brought into him.

16. When he had arranged to go to the ruler's,

[1. 'The sacred carriage' was one used for going in to some temple service that required previous fasting. The paragraph is strangely constructed. It is supposed that the ruler's carriage at the beginning of it was also a sacred one.

2. Came up on the raised hall, that is.]

he passed the night in vigil and fasting, occupying an apartment outside his usual one. After he had washed his head and bathed, his secretary brought him the ivory tablet, on which were written his thoughts (which he should communicate to the ruler), and how he should respond to orders (that he might receive). When he was dressed he practised deportment and listened to the sounds of the gems (at his girdle pendant). When he went forth, he bowed to all in his own private court elegantly, and proceeded to mount his carriage (to go to the ruler's) in brilliant style.

17. The son of Heaven carried in his girdle the thing tablet, showing how exact and correct he should be in his relations with all under heaven. The feudal lords had the shû, rounded at the top and straight at the bottom, showing how they should give place to the son of Heaven. The tablet of the Great officers was rounded both at the top and the bottom; showing how they should be prepared to give place in all positions[1].

18. When (a minister) is sitting in attendance on his ruler, the rule was that he should occupy a mat somewhat behind him on one side. If he did not occupy such a mat, he had to draw the one assigned to him back and keep aloof from the ruler's kindred who were near him[2].

One did not take his place on his mat from the

[1. It is not clear what the tablets of this paragraph were, and whether they were carried in the hand or inserted in the girdle. The character (Zin) seems to imply the latter.

2. The Khien–lung editors say that after these two sentences the subject of the rest of the paragraph is a student before his teacher.]

front, to avoid seeming to step over it, When seated and unoccupied he did not take up the–whole of the mat by at least a cubit. If he were to read any writings or to eat, he sat forward to the edge. The dishes were put down a cubit from the mat[1].

19. If food were given (to a visitor), and the ruler proceeded to treat him as a guest, he would order him to present the offering, and the visitor would do so. If he took the precedence in eating, he would take a little of all the viands, drink a mouthful, and wait (for the ruler to eat)[2]. If there were one in attendance to taste the viands, he would wait till the ruler ate, and then eat himself After this eating, he would drink (a mouthful), and

wait (again).

20. If the ruler ordered him to partake of the delicacies, he took of that which was nearest to him. If he were told to take of all, he took of whatever he liked. In all cases, in tasting of what was some way off, they began with what was near.

(The visitor) did not dare to add the liquid to his rice till the ruler had touched the corners of his mouth with his hands and put them down[3]. When the ruler had done eating, he also took of the rice in this fashion, repeating the process three times. When the ruler had the things removed, he took his rice and sauces, and went out and gave them to his attendants.

21. Whenever pressed (by his host) to eat, one should not eat largely; when eating at another's.

[1. And also any tablets or other things to be referred to.

2. Tasting the things before the ruler to see that they were good and safe.

3. That is, touched those parts with his fingers to see that no grains were sticking to them.]

one should not eat to satiety. It was only of the water and sauces that some was not put down as an offering;—they were accounted too trivial for such a purpose.

22. If the ruler gave a cup (of drink) to an officer, he crossed over from his mat, bowed twice, laid his head to the ground and received it. Resuming his place, he poured a portion of it as an offering, drank it off, and waited. When the ruler had finished his cup, he then returned his empty.

The rule for a superior man in drinking (with the ruler) was this:—When he received the first cup, he wore a grave look; when he received the second, he looked pleased and respectful. With this the ceremony stopped. At the third cup, he looked self–possessed and prepared to withdraw. Having withdrawn, he knelt down and took his shoes, retired out of the ruler's (sight) and put them on. Kneeling on his left knee, he put on the right shoe; kneeling on the right knee, he put on the left one[1].

23. (At festive entertainments), of all the vases that with the dark-coloured liquor (of water) was considered the most honourable[2]; and only the ruler sat with his face towards it. For the uncultivated people in the country districts, the vases all contained

[1. The subject in the two parts of this paragraph does not appear to be the same. The officer in the former was merely an attendant we may suppose; in the latter, one of a superior rank. The cup in the one case was of special favour; in the second the cups were such as were drunk with the ruler at certain times, but were always confined to three.

2. 'Mindful,' says Kang, 'of the ways of antiquity.' See Book VII, i, 10, 11, et al. on the honour paid to water at sacrifices and feasts, and the reasons for it.]

prepared liquors[1]. Great officers had the vase on one side of them upon a tray without feet; other officers had it in a similar position on a tray with feet[2].

SECTION II.

1. At the ceremony of capping, the first cap put on was one of black linen. The use of this extended from the feudal lords downwards. It might, after having been thus employed, be put away or disused[3].

2. The dark-coloured cap, with red strings and tassels descending to the breast, was used at the capping of the son of Heaven. The cap of black linen, with strings and tassels of various colours, was used at the capping of a feudal prince. A dark-coloured cap with scarlet strings an,] tassels was worn by a feudal lord, when fasting. A dark-coloured cap with gray strings and tassels was worn by officers when similarly engaged.

3. A cap of white silk with the border or roll of a dark colour was worn (? at his capping) by a son or grandson (when in a certain stage of mourning)[4]. A similar cap with a plain white edging, was worn after the sacrifice at the end of the year's mourning. (The same cap) with strings hanging down five inches,

[1. The gratification of their taste was the principal thing at festive entertainments of the common people.

2. On the two trays mentioned here,—the yü (composed of and on the right of it)and the kin,—see Book VIII, i, 12.

3. Such a cap had been used anciently; and it was used in the ceremony, though subsequently disused, out of respect to the ancient custom.

4. When his grandfather was dead, and his father (still alive) was in deep mourning for him.]

served to mark the idle and listless officer[1]. A dark–coloured cap with the roll round it of white silk was worn by one excluded from the ranks of his compeers[2].

4. The cap worn in private, with the roll or border attached to it, was used by all from the son of Heaven downwards. When business called them, the strings were tied and their ends allowed to hang down.

5. At fifty, one did not accompany a funeral with his sackcloth hanging loose. When his parents were dead, (a son) did not have his hair dressed in tufts (any more). With the large white (cap) they did not use strings hanging down. The purple strings with the dark–coloured cap began with duke Hwan of Lû[3].

6. In the morning they wore the dark–coloured square–cut dress; in the evening, the long dress in one piece. That dress at the waist was thrice the width of the sleeve; and at the bottom twice as wide as at the waist. It was gathered in at each side (of the body). The sleeve could be turned back to the elbow.

7. The outer or under garment joined on to the sleeve and covered a cubit of it[4] . The collar was 2 inches wide; the cuff, a cubit and 2 inches long; the border, 1½ inch broad. To wear silk under or inside linen was contrary to rule.

8. An (ordinary) officer did not wear anything woven of silk that had been first dyed[5]. One who had left the service of his ruler wore no two articles of different colours.

[1. By way of punishment or disgrace.

2. Also in punishment. See Book III, iv, 2–5.

3. B.C. 711–694.

4. If we could see one dressed as in those early days, we should understand this better than we do.

5 Because of its expensiveness.]

if the upper garment were of one of the correct colours, the lower garment was of the (corresponding) intermediate one[1].

9. One did not enter the ruler's gate without the proper colours in his dress; nor in a single robe of grass–cloth, fine or coarse; nor with his fur robe either displayed outside, or entirely covered.

10. A garment wadded with new floss was called kien; with old, phâo. One unlined was called kiung; one lined, but not wadded, tieh.

11. The use of thin white silk in court–robes .began with Kî Khang–dze. Confucius said, 'For the audience they use the (regular) court–robes, which are put on after the announcement of the first day of the month (in the temple).' He (also) said, 'When good order does not prevail in the states and clans, (the officers) should not use the full dress (as prescribed)[2].'

12. Only a ruler wore the chequered fur robes in addressing (his troops or the multitudes), and at the autumnal hunts[4], (For him) to wear the Great fur robe was contrary to ancient practice.

13. When a ruler wore the robe of white fox–fur, he wore one of embroidered silk over it to display[5].

[1. The five 'correct' colours were azure (, of varying shade), scarlet (; carnation, the colour of the flesh, white, black, and yellow. The 'intermediate' were green, red, jade–green, purple and bay–yellow.

2. See the concluding article in the 'Narratives of the School.' The words of Confucius are understood to intimate a condemnation of Ki Khang–dze.

3. Made of black lamb's fur and white fox-fur.

4. Or, according to many, in giving charges about agriculture.

5. Of one colour, worn by the king, at a border sacrifice.]

When (the guards on) the right of the ruler wore tigers' fur, those on the left wore wolves' fur. An (ordinary) officer did not wear the fur of the white fox.

14. (Great and other) officers wore the fur of the blue fox, with sleeves of leopard's fur, and over it a jacket of dark-coloured silk to display it; which fawn's fur they used cuffs of the black wild dog[1], with a jacket of bluish yellow silk, to display it; with lamb's fur, ornaments of leopard's fur, and a jacket of black silk to display it; with fox-fur, a jacket of yellow silk to display it. A jacket of embroidered silk with fox-fur was worn by the feudal lords.

15. With dog's fur or sheep's fur[2], they did not wear any jacket of silk over it. Where there was no ornamentation, they did not use the jacket. The wearing the jacket was to show its beauty.

When condoling, they kept the jacket covered, and did now show all its ornamental character; in the presence of the ruler, they showed all this.

The covering of the dress was to hide its beauty. Hence, personators of the deceased covered their jackets of silk. Officers holding a piece of jade or a tortoise-shell (to present it) covered it; but if they had no (such official) business in hand, they displayed the silken garment, and did not presume to cover it.

16. For his memorandum-tablet, the son of Heaven used a piece of sonorous jade; the prince of a state, a piece of ivory; a Great officer, a piece of bamboo, ornamented with fishbone[3]; ordinary

[1. Or foreign dog. An animal like the tapir or rhinoceros is called by the same name, but cannot be meant here.

2. 'The dress,' says Kang, 'worn by the common people.'

The bone seems to be specified; read pan. What bone and of what fish, I do not know.]

officers might use bamboo, adorned with ivory at the bottom.

17. When appearing before the son of Heaven, and at trials of archery, there was no such thing as being without this tablet. It was contrary to rule to enter the Grand temple without it. During the five months' mourning, it was not laid aside. When engaged in the performance of some business, and wearing the cincture, one laid it aside. When he had put it in his girdle, the bearer of it was required to wash his hands; but afterwards, though he had something to do in the court, he did not wash them (again).

When one had occasion to point to or draw anything before the ruler, he used the tablet. When he went before him and received a charge, he wrote it down on it. For all these purposes the tablet was used, and therefore it was ornamental.

18. The tablet was 2 cubits and 6 inches long. Its width at the middle was 3 inches; and it tapered away to 2½ inches (at the ends).

19. (A ruler) wore a plain white girdle of silk, with ornamented ends; a Great officer, a similar girdle, with the ends hanging down; an ordinary officer, one of dyed silk, with the edges tucked in, and the ends hanging down; a scholar waiting to be employed, one of embroidered silk; and young lads, one of white silk[1].

[1. From this paragraph to the end of the part, the text is in great confusion; with characters missing here and there, and sentences thrown together without natural connexion. Khan Hâo has endeavoured to readjust them; but I have preferred to follow the order of the imperial and other editions. The Khien–lung editors advise the reader to do so, and make the best he can of them by means of Kang Hsüan's notes. Khan Hâo's order is paragraphs—25, 19, 20, 27, 23, 21, 22, 24, 26, 28, 29. By this arrangement something like a train of thought can be made out.]

20. For all these the buttons and loops were made of silk cords.

21. The knee–covers of a ruler were of vermilion colour; those of a Great officer, white; and of another officer, purple:—all of leather; and might be rounded, slanting, and straight. Those of the son of Heaven were straight (and pointed at all the corners); of the

prince of a state, square both at bottom and top; of a Great officer, square at the bottom, with the corners at the top rounded off; and of another officer, straight both at bottom and top.

22. The width of these covers was 2 cubits at bottom, and 1 at top. Their length was 3 cubits. On each side of (what was called) the neck were 5 inches, reaching to the shoulders or corners. From the shoulders to the leathern band were 2 inches[1].

23. The great girdle of a Great officer was 4

[1. The knee–covers of the prince of a state are represented thus—and of a Great officer,.

The middle suspender joined on to the top strap at the neck; the two others at the shoulders. On the central portions of the cover were represented certain of the emblems of distinction, according to the rank of the wearer:—dragons on the king's; flames on a prince's; and mountains on a Great officer's. But I do not think the makers of these figures had distinct ideas of the articles which they intended to represent. They certainly fail in giving the student such ideas. The colours, &c., moreover, appear to have varied with the occasions on which they were worn.]

inches (wide)[1]. In variegated girdles, the colours for a ruler were vermilion and green; for a Great officer, cerulean and yellow; for an (ordinary) officer, a black border Of 2 inches, and this, when carried round the body a second time, appeared to be 4 inches. On all girdles which were tucked in there was no needlework.

24. (An officer) who had received his first commission wore a cover of reddish–purple, with a black supporter for his girdle–pendant. One who had received the second commission wore a scarlet cover, (also) with a black supporter for the pendant; and one who had received the third commission, a scarlet cover, with an onion–green supporter for the pendant[2].

25. The son of Heaven wore a girdle of plain white silk, with vermilion lining, and ornamented ends.

26. The queen wore a robe with white pheasants embroidered on it; (a prince's) wife, one with green pheasants[3].

27. (The cords that formed the loops and buttons) were 3 inches long, equal to the breadth of the girdle. The rule for the length of the sash (descending from the girdle) was, that, for an officer, it should

[1. This, according to the Khien–lung editors, was the girdle or sash of 'correct dress,' and white. The variegated girdles, they say, were worn in private and when at leisure.

2. The character for a knee–cover here (fû) is different from that in paragraph 21 (, pî); but the Khien–lung editors say their significance is exactly the same. How the knee–covers and supporter or balance–yard (, hang) girdle pendant are spoken of together, I do not know.

3. The pheasants here referred to are described as I have done in the R–Ya. The 'wife' is supposed also to include the ladies called the king's 'three helpmates' in Book I, ii, Part ii, i.]

be 3 cubits; for one discharging a special service, 2½. Dze–yû said, 'Divide all below the girdle into three parts, and the sash will be equal to two of them., The sash, the knee–covers, and the ties are all of equal length[1].'

28. (The wife of a count or baron) who had received a degree of honour from the ruler[2] wore a pheasant cut out in silk on her robe; (the wife of the Great officer of a count or baron), who had received two degrees, wore a robe of fresh yellow; (the wife of a Great officer), who had received one degree, a robe of white; and the wife of an ordinary officer, a robe of black.

29. Only the ladies of honour[3] received their degree of appointment, when they presented their cocoons. The others all wore the dresses proper to them as the wives of their husbands.

[1. Khan Hâo says, 'Man's length is 8 cubits; below the waist 4½ (= 45 inches). A third of this is 15 inches. 2 x 15 = 30 or 3 cubits, the length of the sash, and of the covers in par. 22.' The cubit must have been shorter than the name now indicates. I do not know what the 'ties' were.

2. Kang Hsüan took the ruler here to be feminine, and to mean 'the queen;' and, notwithstanding the protest of the Khien–lung editors, I think he was right. This paragraph and the next speak of the queen and ladies who were brought around her by their work in silk. Why may we not suppose that in her department she could confer distinction on the deserving as the king did in his? This passage seems to show that she did so.

3. These ladies—'hereditary wives'—occur also in Bk. I, ii, Part ii, 1. It is commonly said that there were twenty–seven members of the royal harem, who had each that title; but there is much vagueness and uncertainty about all such statements. 'The others' must refer to the ladies, wives of the feudal lords and Great officers, whose rank gave them the privilege to co–operate with the queen in her direction of the nourishing of the silkworms and preparation of silk.]

SECTION III.

1. All (officers) in attendance on the ruler let the sash hang down till their feet seemed to tread on the lower edge (of their skirt)[1]. Their chins projected like–the eaves of a house, and their hands were clasped before them low down. Their eyes were directed downwards, and their ears were higher than the eyes. They saw (the ruler) from his girdle up to his 'Collar. They listened to him with their ears turned to the left[2].

2. When the ruler called (an officer) to his presence, he might send three tokens. If two of them came to him, he ran (to answer the message); if (only) one, he yet walked quickly. If in his office, he did not wait for his shoes; if he were outside elsewhere, he did not wait for his carriage.

3. When an officer received a visit from a Great officer, he did not venture to bow (when he went) to meet him[3]; but be did so when escorting him on his departure. When he went to visit one of higher rank than himself, he first bowed (at the gate) and then went into his presence. If the other bowed to him in replying, he hurried on one side to avoid (the honour).

4. When an officer was speaking before the ruler, if he had occasion to speak of a Great officer who was dead, he called him by his posthumous epithet, or by the designation of

his maturity; if of an officer

[1. See vol. xxvii, page 100, note 1.

2. They were on the right of the ruler, and turned their ears to the left to hear him.

3. That the more honourable visitor might not have the trouble of responding with a bow.]

(who was similarly dead), he called him by his name. When speaking with a Great officer, he mentioned officers by their name, and (other) Great officers by their designation.

5. In speaking at a Great officer's, he avoided using the name of the (former) ruler, but not that of any of his own dead. At all sacrifices and in the ancestral temple, there was no avoiding of names. In school there was no avoiding of any character in the text.

6. Anciently, men of rank did not fail to wear their girdle–pendants with their precious stones, those on the right giving the notes Kih and Kio, and those on the left Kung and Yü[1].

When (the king or ruler) was walking quickly (to the court of audience), he did so to the music of the Zhâi Khî; when walking more quickly (back to the reception–hall), they played the Sze hsiâ[2]. When turning round, he made a complete circle; when turning in another direction, he did so at a right angle. When advancing, he inclined forward a little; he held himself up straight; and in all these movements, the pieces of jade emitted their tinklings. So also the man of rank, when in his carriage, heard the harmonious sounds of its bells; and, when walking, those of his pendant jade–stones; and in this way evil and depraved thoughts found no entrance into his mind.

7. When the ruler was present, (his son and heir)

[1. Kih and Kio were the fourth and third notes of the musical scale, corresponding to our D and B; Kung and Yü, the first and fifth, corresponding to G and E. Seethe Chinese Classics, vol. iii, p. 84, note.

2 Zhâi Khî is taken as another name for the Khû Zhze, Chinese Classics, vol. iii, p. 317–318.]

did not wear the pendant of jade–stones. He tied it up on the left of his girdle, and left free the pendant (of useful things) on the right. When seated at ease, he wore the (jade) pendant; but in court, he tied it up[1].

in fasting and vigil they wore it, but the strings were turned round, and fastened at the girdle. They wore then the purple knee–covers[1].

8. All wore the jade–stone pendant at the girdle, excepting during the mourning rites. (At the end of the middle string) in it was the tooth–like piece, colliding with the others. A man of rank was never without this pendant, excepting for some sufficient reason; he regarded the pieces of jade as emblematic of the virtues (which he should cultivate).

9. The son of Heaven had his pendant composed of beads of white jade, hung on dark–coloured strings; a duke or marquis, his of jade–beads of hill–azure, on vermilion strings; a Great officer, his of beads of aqua–marine, on black strings; an heir–son, his of beads of Yü jade, on variegated strings; an ordinary officer, his of beads of jade–like quartz, on orange–coloured strings.

Confucius wore at his pendant balls of ivory[2], five inches (round), on gray strings.

10. According to the regulations for (the dress of) a lad[3], his upper garment was of black linen,

[1. There were three pendants from the girdle:—the jade–stone in the middle, called the pendant of 'virtue;' and two others of useful things on the left and right, of which we shall read by and by. The subject of the first two sentences is said, correctly as I think, to be the heir–son of a ruler; while the last two have a more general application.

2. Or 'an ivory ring.'

3. One who had not yet been capped.]

with an embroidered edging. His sash was embroidered, and (also) the strings for the button–loops (of his girdle). With such a string he bound up his hair. The embroidered border and strings were all red.

11. When the ends of fastening strings reached to the girdle, if they had any toilsome business to do, they put them aside. If they were running, they thrust them in the breast[1].

12. A lad did not wear furs, nor silk, nor the ornamental points on his shoes. He did not wear the three months' mourning. He did not wear the hempen band, when receiving any orders. When he had nothing to do (in mourning rites), he stood on the north of the principal mourner, with his face to the south. When going to see a teacher, he followed in the suite of others, and entered his apartment.

13. When one was sitting at a meal with another older than himself, or of a different (and higher) rank, he was the last to put down the offering', but the first to taste the food. When the guest put down the offering, the host apologised, saying that the food was not worthy of such a tribute. When the guest was enjoying the viands, the host apologised for their being scanty and poor. When the host himself put down the pickle (for the guest), the guest himself removed it. When the members of a household ate together, not being host and guests, one of them removed the dishes; and the same was done When a company had eaten together. At all festival meals, the women (of the house) did not remove the dishes.

[1. This paragraph seems to be out of place. Kang thought should follow the first sentence of paragraph 27 in the last part.

2. By way of thanksgiving to the father of Cookery.]

14. When eating dates, peaches, or plums, they did not cast the stones away (on the ground)[1]. They put down the first slice of a melon as an offering, ate the other slices, and threw away the part by which they held it. When others were eating fruits with a man of rank, they ate them after him; cooked viands they ate before him[2]. At meetings of rejoicing, if there were not some gift from the ruler, they did not congratulate one another; at meetings of sorrow[3], ...

15. If one had any toilsome business to do, he took them in his hand. If he were running, he thrust them in his breast[4].

16. When Confucius was eating with (the head of) the Kî family, he made no attempt to decline anything, but finished his meal with the rice and liquid added to it, without eating any of the flesh[5].

17. When the ruler sent (to an officer) the gift of a carriage and horses, he used them in going to give thanks for them. When the gift was of clothes, he wore them on the same occasion. (In the case of similar gifts to a commissioner from the king), until his (own) ruler had given him orders to use them, he did not dare at once to do so[6]. When the ruler's

[1. Compare vol. xxvii, page 81, paragraph 62.

2. Fruits were the productions of nature, and there could be no poison in them. Cooked food might have been tampered with, and these in attendance on a superior man first tasted it as a precaution for his safety.

3. The conclusion is evidently lost.

4. A mistaken and meaningless repetition of part of paragraph 11.

5. To express, it is supposed, his dissatisfaction with some want of courtesy in his host.

6. This sentence is perplexing, and there are different views in interpreting it. I have followed Kang Hsüan.]

gift reached him, he bowed his head to the ground with his two hands also, laying one of them over the other. A gift of liquor and flesh did not require the second expression of thanks (by the visit).

18. Whenever a gift was conferred on a man of rank, nothing was given to a small man on the same day.

19. In all cases of presenting offerings to a ruler, a Great officer sent his steward with them, and an. ordinary officer went with them himself. In both cases they did obeisance twice, with their heads to the ground as they sent the things away; and again the steward and the officer did the same at the ruler's[1]. If the offerings were of prepared food for the ruler, there were the accompaniments of ginger and other pungent vegetables, of a peach–wood and a sedge–broom[2]. A Great officer dispensed with the broom, and the officer with the pungent vegetables. (The bearers) went in with all the articles to the cook. The Great officer did not go in person to make obeisance, lest the ruler should come to respond to him.

20. When a Great officer went (next day) to do obeisance for the ruler's gift, he retired after performing the ceremony. An officer, (doing the same), waited to receive the ruler's acknowledgment (of his visit), and then retired, bowing again as he did so; but (the ruler) did not respond to his obeisance.

When a Great officer gave anything in person to an ordinary officer, the latter bowed on receiving

[1. This translation seems to make too much out of the text; but it is after Khung Ying–tâ, Khan Hâo, and others.

2. Such presents might decompose or become offensive, and therefore these accompaniments were sent with them.]

it; and also went to his house to repeat the obeisance. He did not, however, wear the clothes (which might have been the gift), in going to make that obeisance.

in interchanges between) equals, if (the recipient) were in the house (when the gift arrived), he went and made his obeisance in the house (of the donor).

21. When any one presented an offering to his superior in rank, he did not dare to say directly that it was for him[1].

An ordinary officer did not presume to receive the congratulations of a Great officer; but a Great officer of the lowest grade did so from one of the highest.

When one was exchanging courtesies with another, if his father were alive, he would appeal to his authority; if the other gave him a gift, he would say, in making obeisance for it, that he did so for his father.

22. If the ceremony were not very great, the (beauty of the) dress was not concealed. In accordance with this, when the great robe of fur was worn, it was without the appendage of one of thin silk to display it, and when (the king) rode in the grand carriage, he did not bend forward to the cross–bar (to show his reverence for any one beyond the service he was engaged on)[2].

[1. He would say, for instance, that it was for some member of his household.

2. There are only fifteen characters in this paragraph, nor is there any intricacy in its structure, but few passages in the collection perplex a translator more. If we leave out the negatives in the former sentence, the meaning becomes clear. The grand carriage and grand fur–robe were used at the greatest of all ceremonies, the solstitial sacrifice to Heaven, which itself so occupied the mind of the sovereign that he was supposed to think of nothing else. The paragraph might have had a more appropriate place in the seventh Book or the ninth.]

23. When a father's summons came to him, a son reverently obeyed it without any delay. Whatever work he had in hand, he laid aside. He ejected the meat that was in his mouth, and ran, not contenting himself with a measured, though rapid pace. When his parents were old and he had gone away, he did not go to a second place, nor delay his return beyond the time agreed on; when they were ailing, his looks and manner appeared troubled:—these were less–important observances of a filial son.

24. When his father died, he could not (bear to) read his books;—the touch of his hand seemed still to be on them. When his mother died, he could not (bear to) drink from the cups and bowls that she had used;—the breath of her mouth seemed still to be on them.

25. When a ruler, (visiting another ruler), was about to enter the gate, the attendant dusted the low post (at the middle of the threshold). The Great officers stood midway between the side–posts and this short post (behind their respective rulers). An officer, acting as an attendant, brushed the side–posts.

(A Great officer) on a mission from another court, did not enter at the middle of (either half of) the gate, nor tread on the threshold. If he were come on public business, he entered on the west of the short post; if on his own business, on the east of it.

26. A ruler and a representative of the dead brought their feet together step by step when they walked; a Great officer stepped along, one foot after the other; an ordinary officer kept the length of his foot between his steps. In walking slowly, they all observed these rules. In walking rapidly, while they wished to push on (and did so), they were not allowed to alter the motion either of hands or feet. In turning their feet inwards or outwards, they did not lift them up, and the edge of the lower garment dragged along, like the water of a stream. In walking on the mats it was the same.

When walking erect, (the body was yet bent, and) the chin projected like the eaves of a house, and their advance was straight as an arrow. When walking rapidly, the body had the appearance of rising constantly with an elevation of the feet. When carrying a tortoise–shell or (a symbol of) jade, they raised their toes and trailed their heels, presenting an appearance of carefulness.

27. In walking (on the road), the carriage of the body was straight and smart; in the ancestral temple, it was reverent and grave; in the court, it was exact and easy.

28. The carriage of a man of rank was easy, but somewhat slow;–grave and reserved, when he saw any one whom he wished to honour. He did not move his feet lightly, nor his hands irreverently. His eyes looked straightforward, and his mouth was kept quiet and composed. No sound from him broke the stillness, and his head was carried upright. His breath came without panting or stoppage, and his standing gave (the beholder) an impression of virtue. His looks were grave, and he sat like a personator of the dead[1]. When at leisure and at ease, and in conversation, he looked mild and bland.

[1. See vol. xxvii, page 62, paragraph 6, and note 2.]

29. At all sacrifices, the bearing and appearance (of the worshippers) made it appear as if they saw those to whom they were sacrificing.

30. When engaged with the mourning rites, they had a wearied look, and an aspect of sorrow and unrest. Their eyes looked startled and dim, and their speech was drawling and

low.

31. The carriage of a martialist was bold and daring; his speech had a tone of decision and command; his face was stern and determined; and his eyes were clear and bright.

32. He stood with an appearance of lowliness, but with no indication of subserviency. His head rose straight up from the centre of the neck. He stood (firm) as a mountain, and his movements were well timed. His body was well filled with the volume of his breath, which came forth powerfully like that of nature. His complexion showed (the beauty and strength of) a piece of jade[1].

33. When they spoke of themselves, the style of the son of Heaven was, 'I, the One man;' a chief of regions described himself as 'The strong minister

[1. On the translation of this, and many of the paragraphs immediately preceding, Callery says:—'The Chinese text contains dissyllabic expressions very difficult to translate, because they are a sort of onomatopœias, which have nothing in common with the nature of the things to which the are applied. We could do nothing better with them than adopt the sense given by the commentators.' But these binomial combinations, which are often repetitions Of the same character, are only onomatopoietic in the sense in which a all words, sensuously descriptive at first, are applied by the mind to express its own concepts; metaphorical rather than onomatopoietic. They are very common in the Shih, or Book of Poetry, and in all passionate, descriptive composition. So it is in other languages as well as Chinese.]

of the son of Heaven;[1] the relation of a feudal lord expressed itself by 'So and So, the guardian of such and such a territory.' If the fief were on the borders, he used the style—'So and So, the minister in such and such a screen.' Among his equals and those below him, he called himself 'The man of little virtue.' The ruler of a small state called himself 'The orphan.' The officer who answered for him (at a higher court) also styled him so[1].

34. A Great officer of the highest grade (at his own court), called himself 'Your inferior minister;' (at another court), his attendant who answered for him, described him as 'The ancient of our poor ruler.' A Great officer of the lowest grade (at his own court), called himself by his name; (at another court), his attendant described him as 'Our unworthy

Great officer.' The son and heir of a feudal prince (at his own court), called himself by his name; (at another court), his attendant described him as 'The rightful son of our unworthy ruler.'

35. A ruler's son (by an inferior lady) called himself 'Your minister, the shoot from the stock.' An (ordinary) officer styled himself 'Your minister, the fleet courier;' to a Great officer, he described himself as 'The outside commoner.' When a Great officer went on a mission about private affairs, a man of his private establishment went with him as his spokesman, and called him by his name.

36. When an officer belonging to the ruler's establishment acted (at another court for a Great officer), he spoke of him as 'Our unworthy Great officer,' or 'The ancient of our unworthy ruler.'

[1. So, most commentators; but this last sentence is not clear.]

When a Great officer went on any mission, it was the rule that he should have such an officer from the ruler's establishment with him, to answer for him.

BOOK XII. MING THANG WEI, OR THE PLACES IN THE HALL OF DISTINCTION[1].

1. Formerly, when the duke of Kâu gave audience to the feudal princes in their several places. in the Hall of Distinction, the son of Heaven stood with his back to the axe–embroidered screen [2], and his face towards the south[3].

2. The three dukes[4] were in front of the steps, in the middle, with their faces to the north, inclining to the east as the most honourable position[5]. The places of the marquises were at the east of the

[1. See introductory notice, vol. xxvii, p . 28–30. On the opposite page there is the plan of the Hall, as given in Morrison's Dictionary, vol. i, part i, page 512. Compare it with the less complicated figure in vol. xxvii, page 252.

2. See vol. xxvii, page 111, paragraph 11.

3. Many chronological and other perplexing questions arise in connexion with the great audience described in this and the paragraphs that immediately follow. The time should be referred, I think to the inauguration of Lo as the eastern capital of Kâu, probably in B.C. 1109, at the close of the duke of Kâu's regency for the young king Khang; see the Shû, V, xiii. That 'the son of Heaven' must be understood of king Khang himself, and not of the duke of Kâu, is a point, it seems to me, that no Chinese commentator should ever have called in question.

2. The three Kung, I suppose, mentioned in vol. iii, page 227, paragraph 3. The duke of Kâu was himself one of them; but perhaps, during his regency, another had been appointed in his place.

3. The text here simply = 'the east the upper.' The nearer one was to the king, the more honourable was his position.]

eastern steps, with their faces to the west, inclining to the north as the most honourable position. The lords of the earldoms were at the west of the western steps, with their faces to the east, inclining also and for the same reason to the north. The counts were on the east of the gate, with their faces to the north, inclining to the east as the more honourable position. The barons were on the west of the gate, with their faces to the north, inclining also and for the same reason to the east.

3. The chiefs of the nine Î [1] were outside the eastern door, with their faces to the west, inclining to the north as the position of honour; those of the eight Mân were outside the door on the south, with their faces to the north, inclining for the same reason to the cast; those of the six Zung were outside the door on the west, with their faces to the east, inclining for the same reason to the south; and those of the five Tî were outside the door on the north, with their faces to the south, inclining for the same reason to the east.

4. The chiefs of the nine Zhâi were outside the Ying gate, with their faces to the north, inclining to the east as the position of honour for them; those of the four Sâi (also) came, who had only once in their time to announce their arrival (at the court). These were the places of the lords in the Hall of Distinction (when they appeared before) the duke of Kâu[2].

[1. Î was the general name for the wild tribes of the east; Mân, for those of the south; Zung, for those of the west; and Tî, for those of the north.

2. It is so difficult to explain what is meant by 'the nine Zhâi,' and again by 'the four Sâi,' that I am inclined to doubt, with Wang Yen and others, the genuineness of this paragraph.]

5. The Hall of Distinction was so called, because in it the rank of the princes was clearly shown as high or low[1].

6. Formerly, when Kâu of Yin was throwing the whole kingdom into confusion, he made dried slices of (the flesh of) the marquis of Kwei[2], and used them in feasting the princes. On this account the duke of Kâu assisted king Wû in attacking Kâu. When king Wû died, king Khang being young and weak, the duke took the seat of the son of Heaven[3], and governed the kingdom. During six years he gave audience to all the princes in the Hall of Distinction; instituted ceremonies, made his instruments of music, gave out his (standard) weights and measures[4], and there was a grand submission throughout the kingdom.

7. In the seventh year, he resigned the government to king Khang; and he, in consideration of the duke's services to the kingdom, invested him with (the territory about) Khü-fû[5], seven hundred lî square, and sending forth a thousand chariots of

[1. See the introduction, vol. xxvii, page 28.

2. 'The marquis of Kwei' appears in Sze-mâ Khien's history of Yin (near the end), as the marquis of Khiû, and is made into pickle. The reference, no doubt, is to some act of atrocious and wanton cruelty on the part of Kâu.

3. This can only mean that the duke, as regent, administered the government, though the compiler of the Book wanted to exalt his personality beyond the bounds of truth.

4. The text is—measures of length and of capacity.

5. Khü-fû is still a district city in the department of Yen-kâu, Shan-tung. It was the capital of Lû; and is called by foreigners 'the city of Confucius.' It contains the great

temple of the sage, and is the residence of his representative–descendant, with thousands of other Khungs.]

war[1]. He (also) gave charge that (the princes of) Lû, from generation to generation, should sacrifice to the duke of Kâu with the ceremonies and music proper at a sacrifice by the son of Heaven.

8. Thus it was that the rulers of Lû, in the first month of spring, rode in a grand carriage, displaying the banner, suspended from its bow–like arm, with the twelve streamers, and having the sun and moon emblazoned on it, to sacrifice to God in the suburb of their metropolis, associating Hâu Kî as his assessor in the service;—according to the ceremonies used by the son of Heaven[2].

9. In the last month of summer, the sixth month, they used the ceremonies of the great sacrifice in sacrificing to the duke of Kâu in the great ancestral temple, employing for the victim to him a white bull. The cups were those with the figure of a victim bull, of an elephant, and of hills and clouds; that for the fragrant spirits was the one with gilt eyes on it. For libations they used the cup of jade with the handle made of a long rank–symbol. The dishes with the offerings were on stands of wood, adorned with jade and carved. The cups for the personator were of jade carved in the same way. There were also the plain cups and those of horn, adorned with round pieces of jade; and for the meat–stands, they used those with four feet and the cross–binders.

10. (The singers) went up to the hall (or stage),

[1. This is one of the gross exaggerations in the Book. The marquisate of Lû was only a hundred lî square on its first constitution.

2. Of this and many of the statements in the paragraphs that follow, see the fourth of the 'Praise Odes of Lû,' in the Shih, Metrical version, pp. 379–383.]

and sang the Khing Miâo; (in the court) below, (the pantomimes) performed the Hsiang dance[1], to the accompaniment of the wind instruments. With their red shields and jade–adorned axes, and in their caps with pendants, they danced to the music of the Tâ Wû[2]; in their skin caps, and large white skirts gathered at the waist, and jacket of silk, they danced the Tâ Hsiâ[3]. There (were also) the Mei, or music of the wild tribes of the

East; and the Zan, or music of those of the South. The introduction of these two in the grand temple was to signalise the distinction of Lû all over the kingdom.

11. The ruler, in his dragon–figured robe and cap with pendants, stood at the eastern steps; and his wife, in her head–dress and embroidered robe, stood in her room. The ruler, with shoulder bared, met the victim at the gate; his wife brought in the stands for the dishes. The ministers and Great officers assisted the ruler; their wives[4] assisted his wife. Each one discharged the duty proper to him or her. Any officer who neglected his duty was severely punished; and throughout the kingdom there was a great acknowledgment of, and submission to, (the worth of the duke of Kâu).

12. (In Lû) they offered (also) the sacrifices of summer, autumn, and winter (in the ancestral temple); with those at the altars of the land and grain in spring, and that at the autumnal hunt, going on to the great sacrifice of thanksgiving at

[1. See vol. xxvii, page 361, paragraph 21.

2. Attributed to king Wû.

3. Said to be of the Hsiâ dynasty.

4. 'The commissioned wives;' including, according to Khan Hâo, the ruler's 'ladies of honour,' as well as the wives of his ministers and Great officers.]

the end of the year:—all (after the pattern of) the sacrifices of the son of Heaven.

13. The grand temple (of Lû) corresponded to the Hall of Distinction of the son of Heaven, the Khû gate of the (marquis's palace) to the Kâo (or outer) gate of the king's, and the Kih gate to the Ying[1]. They shook the bell with the wooden clapper in the court as was done in the royal court, in announcing governmental orders.

14. The capitals of the pillars with hills carved on them, and the pond–weed carving on the small pillars above the beams; the second storey and the great beams projecting under the eaves; the polished pillars and the windows opposite to one another; the earthen stand on which the cups, after being used, were placed; the high stand on which the jade tokens were displayed aloft; and the slightly carved screen:—all these were ornaments of the

temple of the son of Heaven[2].

15. (The princes of Lû) had, as carriages, that of (Shun), the lord of Yü, furnished with bells; that of the sovereign of Hsiâ, with its carved front; the Great carriage (of wood), or that of Yin; and the carriage (adorned with jade), or that of Kâu.

16. They had, as flags or banners, that of (Shun), the lord of Yü; the yak's tail of the sovereign of Hsiâ; the great white flag of Yin; and the corresponding red one of Kâu.

[1. The five gates of the royal palace, beginning with the outermost, were the Kâo, the Khû, the Kih, the Ying, and the Lû; the palaces of the princes wanted the Kâo and Ying gates. The grand temples appear to have been constructed on a similar plan, to the east of the palace.

2. And in the temple of Lû, also, it is implied.]

17. They had the white horses of the sovereign of Hsiâ, with their black manes; the white horses of Yin, with their black heads; and the bay horses of Kâu, with red manes. The sovereigns of Hsiâ preferred black victims; those of Yin, white; and those of Kâu, victims which were red and strong.

18. Of jugs for liquor, they had the earthenware jug of the lord of Yü; the jug of Hsiâ, with clouds and hills figured on it; the ko of Yin, with no base, which rested directly on the ground; and the jugs of Kâu, with a victim–bull or an elephant on them.

19. For bowls or cups they had the kân[1] of Hsiâ; the kiâ of Yin; and the kiâ of Kâu[3].

20. For libations they had the jug of Hsiâ, with a cock on it; the kiâ of Yin; and that of Kâu, with gilt eyes on it.

For ladles they had that of Hsiâ, with the handle ending in a dragon's head; that of Yin, slightly carved all over; and that of Kâu, with the handle like plaited rushes.

21. They had the earthen drum, with clods for the drumstick and the reed pipe,—producing the music of Î–khî[4]; the pillow–like bundles of chaff,

[1. Made of jade, or adorned with it.

2. With plants of grain figured on it.

3. Also made of, or adorned with, jade.

4. Î–khî is said by Kang to be 'the dynastic title of an ancient son of Heaven.' Many identify him with Shan Nang, who generally follows Fû–hsî in the chronology, and who cannot be placed later than the thirty–first century B.C., if we can speak at all of so distant dates. Evidently the compiler is putting down the names of the most ancient instruments which he had heard of. There is in the Khien–lung edition of our collection, chapter 81, Page 5, a representation of the drum and its handle; with a collection of the views about them, contradictory and fantastical, so that it is not worth while to reproduce them here. There is a figure also of the reed pipe, which can only have been something a little superior to the early 'oaten pipe ' of the west.]

which were struck[1]; the sounding stone of jade; the instruments rubbed or struck, (to regulate the commencement and close of the music)[2]; the great lute and great cithern; the medium lute and little citherns[3]: the musical instruments of the four dynasties.

22. The temple of the duke of Lû was maintained from generation to generation like that of (king) Wan (in the capital of Kâu), and the temple of duke Wû in the same way like that of (king) Wû[4].

23. They had the hsiang (school) of the lord of Yü, in connexion with which were kept the stores of (sacrificial) rice[5]; the hsü school of the sovereign of Hsiâ; the school of Yin, in which the blind were

[1. This also is represented in the Khien–lung edition; but how anything like music could be brought from the pillows I do not know. The two characters, supposed to give the name, are found, perhaps, the Shû, II, iv, 9, used with verbal force of playing on the lute.

2. The Kû and Yü; see vol. xxvii, pages 219 and 273.

3. The invention of the lute and cithern is ascribed to Fû–hsî. They are represented thus—.

4. The duke of Lû here is the first duke, Po-khin (B.C. 1115-1063). Duke Wû was the ninth duke (B.C. 826-817).

5. As a lesson, it is said, of filial duty.]

honoured[1]; and the college of Kâu, with its semicircle of water.

24. They had the tripods of Khung[2] and Kwan[2]; the great jade hemisphere; and the tortoise-shell of Fang-fû[3]:—all articles (properly) belonging to the son of Heaven. They (also) had the lance of Yüeh[3]; and the great bow,—military weapons of the son of Heaven.

25. They had the drum of Hsiâ supported on four legs; that of Yin supported on a single pillar; the drums of Kâu, pendent from a stand; the peal of bells of Sui[4]; the differently toned khing (sonorous stones) of Shû[5]; and the organ of Nü-kwâ[6], with its tongues.

26. They had the music-stand of Hsiâ, with its face-board and posts, on which dragons were carved; that of Yin, with the high-toothed face-board; and that of Kâu, with its round ornaments of jade, and feathers (hung from the corners).

[1. The father of Music, it is said, was here sacrificed to, or had offerings presented to him. All this is very uncertain. Blind men were used as musicians.

2. These are names of states mentioned in the Shû, with which we find king Wan at war.

3. Fang-fû must also be the name of an ancient state; but where it was I do not know. Yüeh was a great state, south of Wû, on the seaboard.

4. See the Shû, II, i, 21, and note.

5. Shû was also called Wû-kâu.

6. Nü-kwâ is placed between Fû-hsî and Shan Nang. Various fabulous marvels are related of him or her (for many hold the name to be that of a female) in the account of the five Tîs, prefixed to Sze-mâ Khien's histories. The organ is represented-thus—.]

27. They had the two tui of the lord of Yü (for holding the grain at sacrifices); the four lien of Hsiâ; the six hû of Yin; and the eight kwei of Kâu[1].

28. They had for stands (on which to set forth the flesh of the victims), the khwan of Shun; the küeh of Hsiâ; the kü of Yin; and the room–like stand of Kâu. For the tall supports of the dishes, they used those of Hsiâ of unadorned wood; those of Yin, adorned with jade; and those of Kâu, with feathers carved on them.

29. They had the plain leather knee–covers of Shun; those of Hsiâ, with hills represented on them; those of Yin, with flames; and those of Kâu, with dragons.

30. They used for their sacrificial offerings (to the father of Cookery), like the lord of Yü, (portions of) the head; like the sovereigns of Hsiâ, (portions of) the heart; as they did under Yin, (portions of) the liver; and as they did under Kâu, (portions of) the lungs[2].

31. They used the bright water preferred by Hsiâ; the unfermented liquor preferred by Yin; and the completed liquor preferred by Kâu[3].

[1. Figures of all these are given. The number of the vessels in the different dynasties is thought to have been regulated by the number of the kinds of grain; but most of this is conjecture.

2 Kang Hsüan, in explanation of these practices, has only three characters, which I confess I do not fully comprehend. Khung Ying–tâ says nothing about them, nor the Khien–lung editors. Fang Küeh writes, on the relation between the five elements and the five colours, and the symbolical colours adopted by the different dynasties, and of the different members of the victims; very mystically and darkly, and failing to elucidate the passage.

3. There have been various references to these points already, and there will be more hereafter.]

32. They used (the names) of the 50 officers of the lord of Yü; of the 100 of thc sovereigns of Hsiâ; of the 200 of Yin; and of the 300 Of Kâu[1].

33. (At their funerals) they used the feathery ornaments of the lord of Yü; the wrappings of white silk (about the flag–staffs) of the sovereigns of Hsiâ; (the flags) with their toothed edges of Yin; and the round pieces of jade and plumes Of Kâu[2].

34. Lû (thus) used the robes, vessels and officers of all the four dynasties, and so it observed the royal ceremonies. It long transmitted them everywhere. Its rulers and ministers never killed one another, Its rites, music, punishments, laws, governmental proceedings, manners and customs never changed. Throughout the kingdom it was considered the state which exhibited the right ways; and therefore dependence, was placed on it in the matters of ceremonies and music[3].

[1. Compare the Shû, V, xx, 3. Various attempts are made to reconcile the statements there and those of this paragraph; 'all,' says Khan Hâo, 'mere conjectures.'

2. Compare paragraph 22, page 139, vol. xxvii.

BOOK XIII. SANG FÛ HSIÂO KÎ, OR RECORD OF SMALLER MATTERS IN THE DRESS OF MOURNING[1].

SECTION I.

1. When wearing the unhemmed sackcloth (for a father), (the son) tied up his hair with a hempen (band), and also when wearing it for a mother. When he exchanged this band for the cincture (in the case of mourning for his mother)[2], this was made of linen cloth.

(A wife)[3], when wearing the (one year's mourning) of sackcloth with the edges even, had the girdle (of the same), and the inferior hair–pin (of hazel–wood), and wore these to the end of the mourning.

2. (Ordinarily) men wore the cap, and women the hair–pin; (in mourning) men wore the cincture, and women the same after the female fashion.

[1. See the introductory notice, vol. xxvii, page 30.

2. This was done after the slighter dressing of the corpse. The cincture (wan,) is mentioned in the first paragraph of the Than Kung (vol. xxvii, page 120). The hempen band being removed, one of linen cloth, about the breadth of which there are different accounts, was put round the hair on the crown, taken forward to the forehead, there crossed, taken back again, and knotted at the back of the hair.

3. The text does not mention 'the wife' here; but a comparison of different passages shows that this sentence is only applicable to her.]

The idea was (simply) to maintain in this way a distinction between them[1].

3. The dark–coloured staff was of bamboo; that paired and fashioned (at the end) was of eleococca wood[2].

4. When the grandfather was dead, and afterwards (the grandson) had to go into mourning for his grandmother, he, being the representative of the family (through the death of his father), did so for three years.

5. The eldest son (at the mourning rites) for his father or mother, (before bowing to a visitor who had come to condole with him), first laid his forehead to the ground (as an expression of his sorrow).

When a Great officer came to condole (with an ordinary officer), though it might be (only) in a case of the three months' mourning (the latter first) laid his forehead to the ground[3].

A wife, at the rites for her husband or eldest son, bowed her head to the ground before she saluted

[1. Anciently, it is said, there was no distinction between these two cinctures, but in the name. There probably came to be some difference between them; but what it was I cannot discover.

2 This is found also in the Î Lî, XXXII, 5; but the interpretation there is as difficult as here. The translation of the first character (, zhü) by 'dark–coloured' is from Khung Ying–tâ. 3. The paring away the end of the dryandria branch was to make it square. The

round bamboo was carried in mourning for a father, and was supposed to symbolise heaven; the other was carried in mourning for a mother, and its square end symbolised earth. What heaven and earth were to nature that the father and mother were to a child. I can make nothing more or better of the passage.

3. We do not see how this instance coheres with the former one; nor why the two are brought together.]

a visitor; but in mourning for others, she did not do so[1].

6. The man employed to preside (at the mourning rites) was required to be of the same surname (as the deceased parent); the wife so employed, of a different surname[2].

7. The son who was his father's successor (as now head of the family) did not wear mourning for his mother who had been divorced.

8. In counting kindred (and the mourning to be worn of them), the three closest degrees become expanded into five, and those five again into nine. The mourning diminished as the degrees ascended or descended, and the collateral branches also were correspondingly less mourned for; and the mourning for kindred thus came to an end[3].

9. At the great royal sacrifice to all ancestors, the first place was given to him from whom the founder of the line sprang, and that founder had the place of assessor to him. There came thus to be established four ancestral shrines[4]. In the

[1. The 'others,' according to Kang, must be understood of her own parents. She was now identified with a family of another surname; and her husband's relatives were more to her than her own.

2. The son and his wife who should have presided are supposed to be dead. The wife elected for the office would be the wife of some other member of the family, herself therefore of a different surname.

3. The three closest degrees are 'father, son, and son's son.' Add the grandfather and grandson (counting from the son), and we have five; great-grandfather and great-grandson (here omitted), and we have seven. Then great-great-grandfather and

great–great–grandson, make nine; and the circle of kindred, for whom mourning should be worn, is complete. See Appendix, Book II, vol. xxvii.

4. This statement about the four shrines has given occasion to much writing.]

case of a son by another than the queen coming to be king, the same course was observed.

10. When a son other than (the eldest) became the ancestor (of a branch of the same line), his successor was its Honoured Head, and he who followed him (in the line) was its smaller Honoured Head. After five generations there was a change again of the Honoured Head; but all in continuation of the High Ancestor.

11. Hence the removal of the ancestor took place high up (in the line), and the change of the Honoured Head low down (in it). Because they honoured the ancestor, they reverenced the Honoured Head; their reverencing the Honoured Head was the way in which they expressed the honour which they paid to the ancestor and his immediate successor[1].

12. That any other son but the eldest did not sacrifice to his grandfather showed that (only he was in the direct line from) the Honoured Head (of their branch of the family). So, no son but he wore the (three years) unhemmed sackcloth for his eldest son, because the eldest son of no other continued (the direct line) of the grandfather and father[2].

13. None of the other sons sacrificed to a son

[1. The subject imperfectly described in these two paragraphs,—the manner in which a family, ever lengthening its line and multiplying its numbers, was divided into collateral branches, will come before the reader again in the next Book.

2. It is difficult to catch exactly the thought in the writer of these, and several of the adjacent, sentences. Even the native critics, down to the Khien–lung editors, seem to experience the difficulty.]

(of his own) who had died prematurely, or one who had left no posterity. (The tablet of) such an one was placed along with that of his grandfather, and shared in the offerings made to him.

14. Nor could any of them sacrifice to their father; showing that (the eldest son was the representative of) the Honoured Head.

15. (In the distinctions of the mourning) for the kindred who are the nearest, the honoured ones to whom honour is paid, the elders who are venerated for their age, and as the different tributes to males and females; there are seen the greatest manifestations of the course which is right for men.

16. Where mourning would be worn from one's relation with another for parties simply on the ground of that affinity, when that other was dead, the mourning ceased. Where it would have been worn for them on the ground of consanguinity, even though that other were dead, it was still worn[1].

When a concubine had followed a ruler's wife to the harem, and the wife came to be divorced, the concubine, (following her out of the harem), did not wear mourning for her son[2].

17. According to the rules, no one but the king offered the united sacrifice to all ancestors[3].

[1. Khung Ying–tâ specifies six cases coming under the former of these cases,' and four under the second. It is not necessary to set them forth. The Khien–lung editors say that the paragraph has reference only to the practice of the officer; for a Great officer did not wear mourning either for his wife or mother's kin.

2. This concubine would be either of the near relatives of the wife, who had gone with her on her marriage.

3. This paragraph is out of place. It should have formed part, probably, of paragraph 9.]

18. The heir–son (of the king or a feudal lord) did not diminish the mourning for the parents of his wife. For his wife he wore the mourning which the eldest and rightful son of a Great officer did for his[1].

19. When the father was an officer, and the son came to be king or a feudal prince, the father was sacrificed to with the rites of a king or a lord; but the personator wore the dress of an officer. When the father had been the son of Heaven, or a feudal lord, and the son was (only) an officer, the father was sacrificed to with the rites of an officer, but his personator wore only the dress of an officer[2].

20. If a wife were divorced while wearing the mourning (for her father or mother–in–law), she put it off. If the thing took place while she was wearing the mourning for her own parents, and before she had completed the first year's mourning, she continued to wear it for the three years; but if that term had been completed, she did not resume the mourning.

If she were called back before the completion of the year, she wore it to the end of that term; but if that term had been completed before she was called back, she went on wearing it to the regular term of mourning for parents.

21. The mourning which lasted for two complete years was (held to be) for three years; and that

[1. The sackcloth for one year, without carrying the staff.

2. Both the cases in this paragraph can hardly be taken as anything more than hypothetical. On the concluding statement, the Khien–lung editors ask how the robes of a king could be exhibited in the ancestral temple of an officer.]

which lasted for one complete year for two years[1]. The mourning for nine months and that for seven months[2] was held to be for three seasons; that for five months for two; and that for three months for one. Hence the sacrifice at the end of the completed year was according, to the prescribed rule; but the putting off the mourning (or a part of it) then was the course (prompted by natural feeling). The sacrifice was not on account of the putting off of the mourning[3].

22. When the interment (for some reason) did not take place till after the three years, it was the rule that the two sacrifices (proper at the end of the first and second years) should then be offered. Between them, but not all at the same time, the mourning was put off[4].

23. If a relative who had himself to wear only the nine months' mourning for the deceased took the direction of the mourning rites in the case of any who must continue their mourning for three years, it was the rule that he should offer for them the two annual terminal sacrifices. If one who was merely a friend took that direction, he only offered

[1. See the introduction on Book XXXV, vol. xxvii, page 49.

2. We have not met before with this mourning term of seven months. It occurs in the Î Lî, Book XXIV, 6, as to be worn for those who had died in the second degree of prematurity between the age of twelve and fifteen inclusive.

3. 'This remark is made by the compiler,' say the Khien–lung editors, 'to guard against the sudden abandonment of their grief by the mourners, as if they had done with the deceased when the mourning was concluded.'

4. After the first, it is said, men put off the mourning headband, and women that of the girdle. After the second they both put off their sackcloth.]

the sacrifice of Repose, and that at the placing of the tablet in the shrine[1].

24. When the concubine of an officer had a son, he wore the three months' mourning for her. If she had no son, he did not do so[2].

25. When one had been born (in another state), and had had no intercourse with his grand–uncles and aunts, uncles and cousins, and his father, on hearing of the death of any of them, proceeded to wear mourning, he did not do so.

26. If one did not (through being abroad) hear of the death of his ruler's father or mother, wife or eldest son, till the ruler had put off his mourning, he did not proceed to wear any.

27. If it were a case, however, where the mourning was reduced to that of three months, he wore it[3].

28. (Small) servants in attendance on the ruler, (who had followed him abroad), when he assumed mourning (on his return, for relatives who had died when he was away), also put it on. Other and (higher officers in his train) also did so; but if the proper term for the

mourning in the case were past, they did not do so. (Those who had remained at home), though the ruler could not know of their doing so, had worn the (regular) mourning.

[1. Because of the youth of the son, or of some other reason existing in the case. The director would himself be a cousin.

2. But Great officers wore the three months' mourning for the relatives who had accompanied their wives to the harem, though they might have had no son. No such relatives accompanied the wife of an officer.

3. This, it is supposed, should follow paragraph 25. There are doubts as to the interpretation of it.]

SECTION II.

1. (The presiding mourner), after the sacrifice of Repose, did not carry his staff in proceeding to his apartment; after the placing of the tablet of the deceased (in the shrine of the grandfather), he did not carry it in going up to the hall[1].

2. The (son of another lady of the harem), who had been adopted as the child of the (childless) wife of the ruler, when that wife died, did not go into mourning for her kindred[2].

3. The sash was shorter (than the headband), by one–fifth of the length (of the latter). The staff was of the same length as the sash[3].

4. For the ruler's eldest son a concubine wore

[1. See vol. xxvii, p. 170. I have met with 'the Pacifying sacrifice,' instead of ' the sacrifice of Repose,' which I prefer for in this application. The character is explained by, the symbol of 'being at rest.' The mourners had done all they could for the body of the deceased. It had been laid in the grave; and this sacrifice of Repose was equivalent to our wish for a departed friend, 'Requiescat in Pace.' It was offered in the principal apartment of the house. It remained only to place with an appropriate service the tablet of the deceased in its proper shrine in the ancestral temple next day. The staff was discarded by the mourner, it is said, to show that his grief was beginning to be assuaged. He and the others would pass from the principal apartment to others more private; and on leaving the temple, would have to mount the steps to the hall.

2. The Khien–lung editors argue, and, I think, correctly, that this paragraph should say the opposite of what it does. They think it has been mutilated.

3. The purely native staff in China is very long. At temples in the interior of the country I have often been asked to buy choice specimens as long as a shepherd's crook, or an alpenstock.]

mourning for the same time as his wife, (the son's mother).

5. In putting off the mourning attire, they commenced with what was considered most important. In changing it, they commenced with what was considered least important.

6. When there was not the (regular) occasion for it, they did not open the door of the temple[1]. All wailed in the (mourning) shed (at other times).

7. In calling the dead back, and writing the inscription (to be exhibited over the coffin), the language was the same for all, from the son of Heaven to the ordinary officer. A man was called by his name. For a wife they wrote her surname, and her place among her sisters. If they did not know her surname, they wrote the branch–name of her family.

8. The girdle of dolychos cloth assumed with the unhemmed sackcloth (at the end of the wailing), and the hempen girdle worn when one (first) put on the hemmed sackcloth (of one year's mourning), were of the same size. The girdle of dolychos cloth assumed (as a change) in the hemmed sackcloth mourning, and that of hempen cloth at the (beginning of the) nine months' mourning, were of the same size. When the occasion for assuming the girdle of the lighter mourning occurred, a man wore both it and the other together[2].

[1. This is not the ancestral temple; but the apartment where the body was kept in the coffin, entered regularly for wailing in the morning and evening.

2. So far as I can understand this paragraph, it describes the practice of a man (not of a woman), when, while he was wearing deep mourning, a fresh death in his circle required

him to add to it something of a lighter mourning.]

9. An early interment was followed by an early sacrifice of repose. But they did not end their wailing till the three months were completed.

10. When the mourning rites for both parents occurred at the same time, the sacrifices of repose and of the enshrining of the tablet, for the (mother) who was buried first, did not take place till after the burial of the father. The sackcloth worn at her interment was the unhemmed and jagged[1].

11. A Great officer reduced the (period of) mourning for a son by a concubine[2]; but his grandson, (the son of that son), did not reduce his mourning for his father.

12. A Great officer did not preside at the mourning rites for an (ordinary) officer.

13. For the parents of his nurse[3] a man did not wear mourning.

14. When the husband had become the successor and representative of some other man (than his own father), his wife wore the nine months' mourning for his parents–in–law[4].

15. When the tablet of an (ordinary) officer was placed in the shrine of (his grandfather who had been) a Great officer, the victim due to him (as an officer) was changed (for that due to a Great officer).

16. A son who had not lived with his step–father (did not wear mourning for him). (They) must

[1. Compare vol. xxvii, page 315, paragraph 6.

2. To nine months.

3. A concubine of his father's.

4. Her husband's own parents. But the paragraph is a difficult one; nor have the commentators elucidated it clearly.]

have lived together and both be without sons to preside at their mourning rites; and (the stepfather moreover) must have shared his resources with the son, and enabled him to sacrifice to his grandfather and father, (in order to his wearing mourning for him);—under these conditions they were said to live together. If they had sons to preside at the mourning rites for them, they lived apart.

17. When people wailed for a friend, they did so outside the door (of the principal apartment), on the left of it, with their faces towards the south[1].

18. When one was buried in a grave already occupied, there was no divination about the site (in the second case).

19. The tablet of an (ordinary) officer or of a Great officer could not be placed in the shrine of a grandfather who had been the lord of a state; it was placed in that of a brother of the grandfather who had been an (ordinary) officer or a Great officer, The tablet of his wife was placed by the tablet of that brother's wife, and that of his concubine by the tablet of that brother's concubine.

If there had been no such concubine, it was placed by the tablet of that brother's grandfather; for in all such places respect was had to the rules concerning the relative positions assigned to the tablets of father and son[2]. The tablet of a feudal lord could not be placed in the shrine of the son of Heaven (from whom he was born or descended); but that of the son of Heaven, of a feudal lord, or

[1. See vol. xxvii, page 134, paragraph 10.

2. See vol. xxvii, page 223, paragraph 4, and note.]

of a Great officer, could be placed in the shrine of an (ordinary) officer (from whom he was descended)[1].

20. For his mother's mother, who had been the wife proper of her father, if his mother were dead, a son did not wear mourning[2].

21. The son who was the lineal Head of his new branch of the surname, even though his mother were alive, (his father being dead), completed the full period of mourning for his

wife[3].

22. A concubine's son who had been reared by another, might act as son to that other; and she might be any concubine of his father or of his grandfather[4].

23. The mourning went on to the than ceremony for a parent, a wife, and the eldest son[5].

24. To a nursing mother, or any concubine who was a mother, sacrifice was not maintained for a second generation.

25. When a grown–up youth had been capped, (and died), though his death could not be considered premature; and a (young) wife, after having worn

[1. A descendant in a low position could not presume on the dignity of his ancestors; but those who had become distinguished glorified their meaner ancestors.

2. It is difficult to say exactly what is the significance of the in the text here.

3. Meaning, say some, performed the than sacrifice at the end of twenty–seven months for her. I cannot think this is the meaning. Even for such a wife there could not be the 'three years' mourning.' According to Wang Yüan, the mourning for one year terminated with a than sacrifice in the fifteenth month. This must be what is here intended.

4. This is the best I can do for this paragraph, over which there is much conflict of opinion.

5. Here is the same difficulty as in paragraph 21.]

the hair–pin, (died), though neither could her death be said to be premature; yet, (if they died childless), those who would have presided at their rites, if they had died prematurely, wore the mourning for them which they would then have done[1].

26. If an interment were delayed (by circumstances) for a long time, he who was presiding over the mourning rites was the only one who did not put off his mourning. The others having worn the hempen (band) for the number of months (proper in their relation

to the deceased), put off their mourning, and made an end of it[2].

27. The hair-pin of the arrow-bamboo was worn by (an unmarried daughter for her father) to the end of the three years' mourning[3].

28. That in which those who wore the sackcloth with even edges for three months, and those who wore (it) for all the nine months' mourning agreed, was the shoes made of strings (of hemp).

29. When the time was come for the sacrifice at the end of the first year's mourning, they consulted the divining stalks about the day for it, and the individual who was to act as personator of the deceased. They looked that everything was clean, and that all wore the proper girdle, carried their staffs, and had on the shoes of hempen-string. When the officers charged with this announced that all was ready, (the son) laid aside his staff, and assisted at the divinations for the day and for the

[1. Another difficult paragraph, about the interpretation of which there seem to be as many minds as there are commentators.

2. Yet they would keep it by them till the interment took place, and then put it on again for the occasion.

3. Should form part of the first paragraph of Section i.]

personator. The officers having announced that these were over, he resumed his staff, bowed to the guests (who had arrived in the meantime), and escorted them away. At the sacrifice for the end of the second year, (the son) wore his auspicious (court) robes, and divined about the personator.

30. The son of a concubine, living in the same house with his father, did not observe the sacrifice at the end of the mourning for his mother.

Nor did such a son carry his staff in proceeding to his place for wailing.

As the father did not preside at the mourning rites for the son of a concubine, that son's son might carry his staff in going to his place for wailing. Even while the father was present, the son of a concubine, in mourning for his wife, might carry his staff in going to that place.

31. When a feudal prince went to condole on the death of a minister of another state[1], (being himself there on a visit), the ruler of that state received him and acted as the presiding mourner. The rule was that he should wear the skin cap and the starched sackcloth. Though the deceased on account of whom he paid his condolences had been interred, the presiding mourner wore the mourning cincture. If he had not yet assumed the full mourning dress, the visitor also did not wear that starched sackcloth.

32. One who was ministering to another who was ill did not do so in the mourning clothes (which he might be wearing); and (if the patient died), he might go on to preside at the mourning rites for him. But if another relative, who had not ministered

[1. That is, if the visit were made before the removal of the coffin.]

to the deceased in his illness, came in to preside at the rites for him, he did not change the mourning which he might be wearing. In ministering to one more honourable than himself, the rule required a person to change the mourning he might be wearing, but not if the other were of lower position[1].

33. If there had been no concubine of her husband's grandmother by whose tablet that of a deceased concubine might be placed, it might be placed by that of the grandmother, the victim offered on the occasion being changed.

34. In the mourning rites for a wife, at the sacrifices of repose and on the ending of the wailing, her husband or son presided; when her tablet was put in its place, her father–in–law presided.

35. An (ordinary) officer did not take the place of presiding (at the mourning rites) for a Great officer. It was only when he was the direct descendant of the Honoured Head of their branch of the surname that he could do so.

36. If a cousin arrived from another state (to take part in the rites), before the presiding mourner had put off his mourning, the latter received him in the part of host, but without the mourning cincture[2].

37. The course pursued in displaying the articles, (vessels to the eye of fancy, to be put into the grave)[3], was this:—If they were (too) many as displayed,

[1. If the other, it is said, in the former case were elder, an uncle or elder cousin; in the latter, a younger cousin.

2. If the ruler came to condole after the interment, the presiding mourner would resume his cincture to receive him, out of respect to his rank; but this was not required on the late arrival of a relative.

3. These articles were the contributions of friends and those prepared by the family. They were displayed inside the gate of the temple on the east of it when the body was being moved, and in front of the grave, on the east of the path leading to it.]

a portion of them might be put into the grave; if they were comparatively few as displayed, they might all be put into it.

38. Parties hurrying to the mourning rites for a brother or cousin (whose burial had taken place) first went to the grave and afterwards to the house, selecting places at which to perform their wailing. If the deceased had (only) been an acquaintance, they (first) wailed in the apartment (where the coffin had been), and afterwards went to the grave.

39. A father (at the mourning rites) for any of his other sons did not pass the night in the shed outside (the middle door, as for his eldest son by his wife).

40. The brothers and cousins of a feudal prince wore the unhemmed sackcloth (in mourning for him)[1].

41. In the five months' mourning for one who had died in the lowest stage of immaturity, the sash was of bleached hemp from which the roots were not cut away. These were turned back and tucked in.

42. When the tablet of a wife was to be placed by that of her husband's grandmother, if there were three (who could be so denominated), it was placed by that of her who' was the mother of her husband's father[2].

43. In the case of a wife dying while her husband

[1. Even though they might not be in the same state with him.

2. We must suppose that the grandfather had had three wives; not at the same time, but married one after another's death. Some suppose the three to be a mistake for two. 'The mother of her husband's father' is simply 'the nearest' in the text.]

was a Great officer, and his ceasing, after her death, to be of that rank; if his tablet were placed (on his death) by that of his wife, the victim on the occasion was not changed (from that due to an ordinary officer). But if her husband (who had been an officer) became a Great officer after her death, then the victim at the placing of his tablet by hers was that due to a Great officer[1].

44. A son who was or would be his fathers successor did not wear mourning for his divorced mother. He did not wear such mourning, because one engaged in mourning rites could not offer sacrifice[2].

45. When a wife did not preside at the mourning rites and yet carried the staff, it was when her mother-in-law was alive, and she did so for her husband. A mother carried the eleococca staff with its end cut square for the oldest son. A daughter, who was still in her apartment unmarried, carried a staff for her father or mother. If the relative superintending the rites did not carry the staff, then this one child did so[3].

[1. We must suppose that the appointment of the husband, whether as officer or Great officer, had been so recent that there had been no time for any tablets of an elder generation to get into his ancestral temple. His wife's had been the first to be placed in it.

2 That is, he might have to preside at the sacrifices in the ancestral temple of his own family, and would be incapacitated for doing so, if he were mourning for her. The reader should bear in mind that there were seven justifiable causes for the divorce of a wife, without her being guilty of infidelity, or of any criminal act.

3. It is supposed there was no brother in the family to preside at the rites, and a relative of the same surname was called in to do so. But it was not in rule for him to carry the staff, and this daughter therefore did so, as if she had been a son.]

46. In the mourning for three months and five months, at the sacrifice of repose and the ending of the wailing, they wore the mourning cincture.

After the interment, if they did not immediately go to perform the sacrifice of repose, they all, even the presiding mourner, wore their caps; but when they came to the sacrifice of repose, they all assumed the cincture.

When they had put off the mourning for a relative, on the arrival of his interment, they resumed it; and when they came to the sacrifice of repose and the ending of the wailing, they put on the cincture. If they did not immediately perform the sacrifice, they put it off.

When they had been burying at a distance, and were returning to wail, they put on their caps. On arriving at the suburbs, they put on the cincture, and came back to wail.

47. If the ruler came to condole with mourners, though it might not be the time for wearing the cincture, even the president of the rites assumed it, and did not allow the ends of his hempen girdle to hang loose. Even in the case of a visit from the ruler of another state, they assumed the cincture. The relatives all did so.

48. When they put off the mourning for one who had died prematurely, the rule was that at the (accompanying sacrifice, the dress should be dark–coloured. When they put off the mourning for one fully grown, they wore their court robes, with the cap of white, plain, silk.

49. A son, who had hurried to the mourning rites of his father (from a distance), bound up his hair in the raised hall, bared his chest, descended to the court, and there performed his leaping. (The leaping over, he reascended), covered his chest, and put on his sash in an apartment on the east.

If the rites were for his mother, he did not bind up his hair. He bared his chest, however, in the hall, descended to the court, and went through his leaping. (Reascending then), he covered his chest, and put on the cincture in the apartment on the east. In the girdle (or the cincture), he proceeded to the appointed place, and completed the leaping. He then went out from the door (of the coffin–room), and went to (the mourning shed). The wailing commencing at death had by this time ceased. In three days he wailed five times, and thrice bared his chest for the leaping.

50. When an eldest son and his wife could not take the place hereafter of his parents, then, (in the event of her death), her mother–in–law wore for her (only) the five months' mourning[1].

BOOK XIV. TÂ KWAN, OR THE GREAT TREATISE[1].

According to the rules, only the king offered the united sacrifice to all ancestors. The chief place was then given to him from whom the founder of the line sprang, and that founder had the place of assessor to him[2].

The sacrifices of the princes of states reached to their highest ancestor. Great officers and other officers, who had performed great services, when these were examined (and approved) by the ruler, were able to carry their sacrifices up to their high ancestor.

2. The field of Mû–yeh was the great achievement of king Wû. When he withdrew after the victory, he reared a burning pile to God; prayed at the altar of the earth; and set forth his offerings in the house of Mû[3]. He then led all the princes of the kingdom, bearing his offerings in their various stands, and hurrying about, and carried the title of king back to Thâi who was Than–fû, Kî–lî, and king Wan who was Khang;—he would not approach his honourable ancestors with their former humbler titles.

[1. See the introductory notice, vol. xxvii, pages 30, 31.

2. See the last Book, I, paragraphs 9, 17, et al.

3. I suppose that all which is here described was done by king Wû after his victory at Mû, under the advice of his brother, known to us as the duke of Kâu; see the Kung Yung, paragraphs 54, 55. 'The house of Mû' would be a building converted for the occasion into a temple.]

3. Thus he regulated the services to be rendered to his father and grandfather before him;—giving honour to the most honourable. He regulated the places to be given to his sons and grandsons below him;—showing his affection to his kindred. He regulated (also) the observances for the collateral branches of his cousins;–associating all their

members in the feasting. He defined their places according to their order of descent; and his every distinction was in harmony with what was proper and right. In this way the procedure of human duty was made complete.

4. When a sage sovereign stood with his face to the south, and all the affairs of the kingdom came before him, there were five things which for the time claimed his first care, and the people were not reckoned among them. The first was the regulating what was due to his kindred (as above) the second, the reward of merit; the third, the promotion of worth; the fourth, the employment of ability; and the fifth, the maintenance of a loving vigilance. When these five things were all fully realised, the people had all their necessities satisfied, all that they wanted supplied. If one of them were defective, the people could not complete their lives in comfort.

It was necessary for a sage on the throne of government to begin with the (above) procedure of human duty.

5. The appointment of the measures of weight, length, and capacity; the fixing the elegancies (of ceremony); the changing the commencement of the year and month; alterations in the colour of dress; differences of flags and their blazonry; changes in vessels and weapons, and distinctions in dress: these were things, changes in which could be enjoined on the people. But no changes could be enjoined upon them in what concerned affection for kin, the honour paid to the honourable, the respect due to the aged, and the different positions and functions of male and female.

6. Members of the same surname were united together in the various ramifications of their kinship, under the Heads of their different branches[1]. Those of a different surname[2] had their mutual relations regulated principally by the names assigned to them. Those names being clearly set forth, the different positions of males and females were determined.

When the husband belonged to the class of fathers [or uncles][3], the wife was placed in that of mothers [or aunts]; when he belonged to the class of sons [or cousins], the wife was placed in that of (junior) wives[4]. Since the wife of a younger brother was (thus) styled (junior) wife, could the wife of his elder brother be at the same time styled mother [or aunt]? The name or appellation is of the greatest

[1. That is the males all called by the surname of the family.

2. That is: the females, married into the family from other families of different surnames, and receiving different names or appellations from the places of their husbands in the family roll.

3. 'Fathers' and 'mothers' here are really uncles and aunts, the for the former being equivalent to ; and the for the latter to . The uncles were of the same category as the father in respect to age, and the aunts in the same category as the mother.

4 Fû, the character here for wife, does not in itself contain the idea of this inferiority in point of age. That idea was in the mind of the writer, arising from the subject of which he was treating.]

importance in the regulation of the family:—was not anxious care required in the declaration of it?

7. For parties four generations removed (from the same common ancestor) the mourning was reduced to that worn for three months, and this was the limit of wearing the hempen cloth. If the generations were five, the shoulders were bared and the cincture assumed; and in this way the mourning within the circle of the same was gradually reduced. After the sixth generation the bond of kinship was held to be at an end.

8. As the branch–surnames which arose separated the members of them from their relatives of a former time, and the kinship disappeared as time went on, (so far as wearing mourning was concerned), could marriage be contracted. between parties (so wide apart)[1]? But there was that original surname tying all the members together without distinction, and the maintenance of the connexion by means of the common feast[2];—while there were these conditions, there could be no intermarriage, even after a hundred generations. Such was the rule of Kâo[3].

9. The considerations which regulated the mourning worn were six:—first., the nearness of the kinship[4];

[1. Khan Hâo says that under the Yin dynasty intermarriages were allowed after the fifth generation in a family of the same surname. The same statement is referred to by Khung

Ying–tâ, from whom Khan, probably, took it; but the Khien–lung editors discard it, as being 'without proof.'

2. 'The feast' given to all the kindred after the seasonal sacrifices in the ancestral temple.

3. Khan Hâo refers to this prohibition of intermarriages by Kau as the grand distinction of the dynasty, marking clearly 'for the first time the distinction between man and beast.'

4. As between parents and children.]

second, the honour due to the honourable[1]; third, the names (as expressing the position in the relative circle)[2]; fourth, the cases of women still unmarried in the paternal home, and of those who had married and left it[3]; fifth, age[4]; and sixth, affinity, and external relationship[5].

10. Of the considerations of affinity and external relationship there were six cases:—those arising from inter–relationship[6]; those in which there was no inter–relationship[7]; those where mourning should be worn, and yet was not, those where it should not be worn, and yet was; those where it should be deep, and yet was light; and those where it should be light, and yet was deep.

11. Where the starting–point was affection, it began from the father. Going up from him by degrees it reached to the (high) ancestor, and was said to diminish. Where the starting–point was the consideration of what is right, it began with the ancestor. Coming down by natural degrees from him, it reached to the father, and was said to increase. In the diminution and the increase, the considerations of affection and right acted thus.

12. It was the way for the ruler to assemble and feast all the members of his kindred. None of

[1. As to the ruler, Great officers, and ministers.

2. See paragraph 6.

3. Spinsters and married aunts, cousins, sisters, &c.

4. Relatives dying as minors, and after maturity.

5. See next paragraph.

6. Mother's kin; husband's kin; wife's kin.

7. As when a minister wore mourning for his ruler's kindred; a concubine for the kindred of the wife, &c. The reader must task himself to imagine cases in which the other four conditions would apply.]

them could, because of their mutual kinship, claim a nearer kinship with him than what was expressed by the places (assigned to them).

13. Any son but the eldest, (though all sons of the wife proper), did not sacrifice to his grandfather,—to show there was the Honoured Head (who should do so). Nor could he wear mourning for his eldest son for three years, because he was not the continuator of his grandfather[1].

14. When any other son but the eldest became an ancestor of a line, he who succeeded him became the Honoured Head (of the branch); and his successor again became the smaller Head[1].

15. There was the (great) Honoured Head whose tablet was not removed for a hundred generations. There were the (smaller) Honoured Heads whose tablets were removed after five generations. He whose tablet was not removed for a hundred generations was the successor and representative of the other than the eldest son (who became an ancestor of a line); and he was so honoured (by the members of his line) because he continued the (High) ancestor from whom (both) he and they sprang; this was why his tablet was not removed for a hundred generations. He who honoured the continuator of the High ancestor was he whose tablet was removed after five generations. They honoured the Ancestor, and therefore they reverenced the Head. The reverence showed the significance of that honour.

16. There might be cases in which there was a smaller Honoured Head, and no Greater Head (of

[1. See the last Book, I, paragraphs 10–12.]

a branch family); cases in which there was a Greater Honoured Head, and no smaller Head; and cases in which there was an Honoured Head, with none to honour him. All these might exist in the instance of the son of the ruler of a state[1].

The course to be adopted for the headship of such a son was this; that the ruler,. himself the proper representative of former rulers, should for all his half–brothers who were officers and Great officers appoint a full brother, also an officer or a Great officer, to be the Honoured Head. Such was the regular course.

17. When the kinship was no longer counted, there was no further wearing of mourning. The kinship was the bond of connexion (expressed in the degree of mourning).

18. Where the starting–point was in affection, it began with the father, and ascended by steps to the ancestor. Where it was in a consideration of what was right, it began with the ancestor, and descended in natural order to the deceased father. Thus the course of humanity (in this matter of mourning) was all comprehended in the love for kindred.

19. From the affection for parents came the honouring of ancestors; from the honouring of the

[1. Suppose a ruler bad no brother by his father's wife, and appointed one of his brothers by another lady of the harem, to take the headship of all the others, this would represent the first case. If he appointed a full brother to the position, but could not appoint a half–brother to the inferior position, this would represent the second; and if the younger brothers of the ruling house were reduced to one man, he would represent the third case, having merely the name and nothing more. Such is the explanation of the text, so far as I can apprehend it.]

ancestor came the respect and attention shown to the Heads (of the family branches). By that respect and attention to those Heads all the members of the kindred were kept together. Through their being kept together came the dignity of the ancestral temple. From that dignity arose the importance attached to the altars of the land and grain. From that importance there ensued the love of all the (people with their) hundred surnames. From that love came the right administration of punishments and penalties. Through that administration the people had the feeling of repose. Through that restfulness all resources for expenditure became, sufficient. Through the sufficiency of these, what all desired was realised. The realisation led to all courteous usages and good customs; and from these, in fine, came all happiness and enjoyment:—affording an illustration of what is said in the ode:—

'Glory and honour follow Wan's great name,
And ne'er will men be weary of his fame[1].'

BOOK XV. SHÂO Î OR SMALLER RULES OF DEMEANOUR[1].

1. I have heard (the following things):—

When one wished to see for the first time another of character and position, his language was, so and so, earnestly wish my name to be reported to the officer of communication[2].' He could not go up the steps directly to the host. If the visitor were of equal rank with the host, he said, 'I, so and so, earnestly wish to see him.' If he were an infrequent visitor, he asked his name to be reported. If he were a frequent visitor, he added, 'this morning or evening.' If he were blind[3], he asked his name to be reported.

2. If it were on an occasion of mourning, the visitor said he had come as a servant and helper; if he were a youth, that he had come to perform whatever might be required of him. If the visit were at the mourning rites for a ruler or high minister, the language was, 'I am come to be employed by the chief minister of the household[4].'

[1. See the introductory notice, vol. xxvii, pages 31, 32.

2. The visitor did not dare to send even a message directly to the master of the establishment where he was calling.

3. That is, an officer of music, high or low.

4. The name of the minister here is generally translated by 'Minister of Instruction.' But that can hardly be its meaning here; and there were officers so called also in the

establishments of Great officers; see vol. xxvii, page 154, paragraph 20.]

3. When a ruler was about to go out of his own state[1], if a minister were presenting to him money or pieces of jade, or any other article, the language was, 'I present this to the officer for the expenses of his horses.' To an equal in a similar case it was said, 'This is presented for the use of your followers.'

4. When a minister contributed a shroud to his ruler, he said, 'I send this laid–aside garment to the valuers[2].' An equal, sending such a gift to another equal, simply said, 'a shroud.' Relatives, such as brothers, did not go in with the shrouds which they presented.

5. When a minister was contributing articles or their value to his ruler who had mourning rites on hand for the previous ruler, he said, 'I present these products of my fields to the officers[3].'

6. A carriage and horses presented for a funeral, entered the gate of the ancestral temple. Contributions of money and horses with the accompanying presents of silk, the white flag (of a mourning carriage) and war chariots, did not enter the gate of the temple[4].

7. When the hearer of the contribution had

[1. About to proceed to the royal court.

2. In the Kâu Lî, Book I, 35, we find that among the functionaries attached to the 'Treasury of Jade,' there were eight men thus denominated 'valuers.' There were officers, probably, performing a similar duty in the department to which the charge of the offering in this paragraph would be consigned.

3. The things presented here are called articles (coarse), shells', the meaning being, I think, what I have given. The things were not the produce of the donor's land; but that land being held by him from the ruler, he so expressed himself.

4. It is difficult for us to appreciate the reasons given for the distinction made between these contributions.]

delivered his message, he knelt down and left the things on the ground. The officer of communication took them up. The presiding mourner did not himself receive them.

8. When the receiver stood, the giver stood; neither knelt. Parties of a straightforward character might, perhaps, do so.

9. When (the guest was) first entering, and it was proper to give the precedence to him, the officer of communication said (to the host), 'Give precedence.' When they proceeded to their mats, he said to them, 'Yes; be seated.'

When the leaves of the door were opened, only one man could take off his shoes inside the door. If there were already an honourable and elderly visitor, parties coming later could not do so.

10. When asking about the various dishes (of a feast), they said, 'Have you enjoyed such and such a dish?'

When asking one another about their (various) courses[1] and accomplishments[2] they said, 'Have you practised such and such a course? Are you skilful at such and such an accomplishment?'

11. (A man sought to) give no occasion for doubt about himself, nor to pass his judgment on the articles of others. He did not desire the (possessions of) great families, nor speak injuriously of the things which they valued.

12. Sweeping in general was called sâo. Sweeping

[1. There was the threefold course of aim, diligence, and filial duty, in filialness, friendship, and obedience.

2. The accomplishments were six:—ceremonies, music, archery, charioteering, writing, mathematics.]

up in front of a mat was called phân. In sweeping a mat they did not use a common broom[1]. The sweeper held the dust–pan with its tongue towards himself.

13. There was no divining (twice about the same thing) with a double mind. In asking about what had been referred to the tortoise–shell or the stalks, two things were to be considered, whether the thing asked, about were right, and what was the diviner's own mind. On the matter of right he might be questioned, but not on what was in his own mind.

14. When others more honourable and older than one's self took precedence of him, he did not presume to ask their age. When they came to feast with him, he did not send to them any (formal) message. When he met them on the road, if they saw him, he went up to them, but did not ask to know where they were going. At funeral rites for them, he waited to observe the movements (of the presiding mourner), and did not offer his special condolences. When seated by them, he did not, unless ordered to do so, produce his lutes. He did not draw lines on the ground; that would have been an improper use of his hand. He did not use a fan. If they were asleep, and he had any message to communicate to them, he knelt in doing so.

15. At the game of archery, the inferior carried his four arrows in his hand. At that of throwing darts, he carried the four together in his breast. If he conquered, he washed the cup and gave it to the other, asking him to drink. If he were defeated, the elder went through the same process with him. They

[1. It might be dirty, having been used to sweep the ground.]

did not use the (large) horn; they did not remove the (figure of a) horse (for marking the numbers)[1].

16. When holding the reins of the ruler's horses, the driver knelt. He wore his sword on his right side with his back to the best strap (for the ruler.). When handing this to him, he faced him and then drew the strap towards the cross–bar. He used the second or inferior strap to help himself in mounting. He then took the reins in hand, and began to move on.

17. One asked permission to appear at court, but not to withdraw.

One was said to withdraw from court; to return home from a feast or a ramble; to close the toils of a campaign.

18. When sitting by a person of rank, if he began to yawn and stretch himself, to turn round his tablet, to play with the head of his sword, to move his shoes about, or to ask about the time of day, one might ask leave to retire.

19. For one who (wished to) serve his ruler, (the rule was) first to measure (his abilities and duties), and then enter (on the responsibilities); he did not enter on these, and then measure those. There was the same rule for all who begged or borrowed from others, or sought to engage in their service. In this way superiors had no ground for offence, and inferiors; avoided all risk of guilt.

20. They did not spy into privacies nor form intimacies on matters aside from their proper business. They did not speak of old affairs, nor wear an appearance of being in sport.

[1. See in Book XXXVII.]

21. One in the position of a minister and inferior might remonstrate (with his ruler), but not speak ill of him; might withdraw (from the state), but not (remain and) hate (its Head); might praise him, but not flatter; might remonstrate, but not give himself haughty airs (when his advice was followed). (If the ruler were) idle and indifferent, he might arouse and assist him; if (the government) were going to wreck, he might sweep it away, and institute a new one. Such a minister would be pronounced as doing service for the altars (of the state).

22. Do not commence or abandon anything hastily. Do not take liberties with or weary spiritual Beings. Do not try to defend or cover over what was wrong in the past, or to, fathom what has not yet arrived. A scholar should constantly pursue what is virtuous, and amuse himself with the accomplishments.

A workman should follow the rules (of his art), and amuse himself with the discussion (of their application). One should not think about the clothes and elegant articles (of others), nor try to make good in himself what is doubtful in words (which he has heard)[1].

23. The style prized in conversation required that it should be grave and distinct. The demeanour prized in the court required that it should be

[1. These cautions are expressed enigmatically in the text. The expurgated edition gives only the third and fourth, which P. Callery translates thus:—'L'homme de lettres s'applique à la vertu pardessus tout, et ne s'adonne que d'une façon secondaire à la culture des arts libéraux, semblable en cela à l'ouvrier qui suit d'abord les procédés fondamentaux de son art, et ne discute qu'apès les changements à introduire dans leur application.']

well regulated and urbane; that at sacrifices was to be grave, with an appearance 6f anxiety. The horses of the chariot were to be well-paced and matched. The beauty of their bells was that they intimated dignity and harmony[1].

24. To a question about the age of a ruler's son, if he were grown up, it was said, 'He is able to attend to the business of the altars.' If he were still young, it was said, 'He is able to driver' or 'He is not yet able to drive.' To the same question about a Great officer's son, if he were grown up, it was said, 'He is able to take his part in music;' if still young, it was said, 'He is able to take lessons from the music-master,' or 'He is not yet able to do so.' To the same question about the son of an ordinary officer, if he were grown up, it was said, 'He is able to guide the plough;' if he were still young, it was said, 'He is able to carry firewood,' or 'He is not yet able to do so[2].'

25. When carrying a symbol of jade, a tortoiseshell, or the divining stalks, one did not walk hastily. Nor did he do so in the raised hall, or on a city wall. In a war chariot he did not bow forward to the cross-bar. A man in his mail did not try to bow[3].

26. A wife, on festive occasions, even though it were on receiving a gift from the ruler, (only) made

[1. This paragraph is in the expurgated edition, in the commentary to which, however, the whole is understood with reference to the heir-son of the kingdom or a state; and P. Callery translates accordingly:—'(L'héritier présomptif du trône) doit avoir,' &c.

2. Compare vol. xxvii, page 115, paragraph 4.

3. Compare vol. xxvii, page 72, paragraph 30; page 96, paragraph 39; et al.]

a curtsy[1]. When seated as a personatrix (of the deceased grandmother of her husband), she did not bow with her head to her hands, but made the curtsy[2]. When presiding at the mourning rites, she did not bow with her head to her hands lowered to the ground.

27. (After the sacrifice of repose), her head–band was of dolychos cloth, and her girdle of hempen.

28. When taking meat from a stand or putting meat on it, they did not kneel.

29. An empty vessel was carried (with the same care) as a full one, and an empty apartment entered (with the same reverence) as if there were people in it.

30. At all sacrifices, whether in the apartment or in the hall, they did not have their feet bare. At a feast they might.

31. Till they had offered a portion in the temple, they did not eat of a new crop.

32. In the case of a charioteer and the gentleman whom he was driving, when the latter mounted or descended, the other handed him the strap. When the driver first mounted, he bowed towards the cross–bar. When the gentleman descended to walk, (he also descended), but (immediately) returned to the carriage and stood.

33. The riders in an attendant carriage (to court or temple), bowed forward to the bar, but not if it were to battle or hunt. Of such attendant carriages, the ruler of a state had seven; a Great officer of

[1. In Chinese fashion, an inclination of the head towards the hands.

2. Some interpret this as saying that she did not even make the curtsy.]

the highest grade, five; and one of the lowest grade, three[1].

34. People did not speak of the age of the horses or of the carriages of those who possessed such attendant carriages; nor did they put a value on the dress, or sword, or horses of a gentleman whom they saw before them.

35. In giving (to an inferior) or offering to a superior, four pots of spirits, a bundle of dried meat, and a dog, (the messenger) put down the .liquor, and carried (only) the dried meat in his hand, when discharging his commission, but he also said that he was the bearer of four pots of spirits, a bundle of dried meat, and a dog. In presenting a tripod of flesh, he carried (one piece) in his hand. In presenting birds, if there were more than a couple, he carried a couple in his hand, leaving the others outside.

36. The dog was held by a rope. A watch dog or a hunting dog was given to the officer who was the medium of communication; and on receiving it, he asked its name. An ox was held by the tether, and a horse by the bridle. They were both kept on the right of him who led them; but a prisoner or captive, who was being presented, was kept on the left.

37. In presenting a carriage, the strap was taken off and carried in the hand of the messenger. In presenting a coat of mail, if there were other things to be carried before it, the messenger bore them. If there were no such things, he took off its covering, and bore the helmet in his hands. In the case of a

[1. Compare vol. xxvii, page 125, Paragraph 4.]

vessel, he carried its cover. In the case of a bow, with his left hand he stript off the case, and took hold of the middle of the back. In the case of a sword, he opened the cover of its case, and placed it underneath. Then he put into the case a silken cloth, on which he placed the sword.

38. Official tablets; writings; stalks of dried flesh; parcels wrapped in reeds; bows; cushions; mats; pillows; stools; spikes; staffs; lutes, large and small; sharp–edged lances in sheaths; divining stalks; and flutes:—these all were borne with the left hand upwards. Of sharp–pointed weapons, the point was kept behind, and the ring presented; of sharp–edged weapons, the handle was presented. In the case of all sharp–pointed and sharp–edged weapons, the point was turned away in handing them to others.

39. When leaving the city, in mounting a war–chariot, the weapon was carried with the point in front; when returning and entering it again, the end. The left was the place for the general and officers of an army; the right, for the soldiers.

40. For visitors and guests the principal thing was a courteous humility; at sacrifices, reverence; at mourning rites, sorrow; at meetings and reunions, an active interest. In the operations of war, the dangers had to be thought of. One concealed his own feelings in order to judge the better of those of others.

41. When feasting with a man of superior rank and character, the guest first tasted the dishes and then stopt. He should not bolt the food, nor swill down the liquor. He should take small and frequent mouthfuls. While chewing quickly, he did not make faces with his mouth. When he proceeded to remove the dishes, and the host declined that service from him, he stopt[1].

42. The cup with which the guest was pledged was placed on the left; those which had been drunk (by the others) on the right. Those of the guest's attendant, of the host himself, and of the host's assistant;—these all were placed on the right[2].

43. In putting down a boiled fish to be eaten, the tail was laid in front. In winter it was placed with the fat belly on the right; in summer with the back. The slices offered in sacrifice (to the father of the fish–diet were thus more easily cut[3]).

44. All condiments were taken up with the right (hand), and were therefore placed on the left.

45. He who received the presents offered (to the ruler) was on his left; he who transmitted his words, on the right.

46. A cup was poured out for the driver of a personator of the dead as for the driver of the ruler. In the carriage, and holding the reins in his left hand, he received the cup with his right; offered a little in sacrifice at the end of the axle and crossbar

[1. Compare vol. xxvii, pages 80, 81, paragraphs 54, 57, et al The writer passes in this paragraph from the indicative to the imperative mood.

2. The guest sat facing the south, so that the east and west were on his left and right respectively. The cups were set where they could be taken up and put down most conveniently.

3. The fish, as a sacrificial offering and on great occasions, was placed lengthways on the stand. As placed in this paragraph, it was more convenient for the guest. It may be correct that the belly is the best part of a fish in winter, and the back in summer. Let gastronomers and those who are fond of pisciculture decide and explain the point.]

on the right and left (to the father of charioteering), and then drank off the cup.

47. Of all viands which were placed on the stands, the o ring was put down inside the stand.

A gentleman did not eat the entrails of grain–fed animals[1].

A boy[2] ran, but did not walk quickly with measured steps. When he took up his cup, he knelt in offering (some of the contents) in sacrifice, and then stood up and drank (the rest). Before rinsing a cup, they washed their hands. In separating the lungs of oxen and sheep, they did not cut out the central portion of them[3]; when viands were served up with sauce, they did not add condiments to it.

In selecting an onion or scallion for a gentleman, they cut off both the root and top.

When the head was presented among the viands, the snout was put forward, to be used as the offering.

48. He who set forth the jugs considered the left of the cup–bearer to be the place for the topmost one. The jugs and jars were placed with their spouts towards the arranger.

The drinkers at the ceremonies of washing the head and cupping, in presence of the stand with the divided victims on it, did not kneel. Before the common cup had gone round, they did not taste the viands.

[1. Dogs (bred to be eaten) and pigs. The reason for not eating their entrails can hardly be stated.

2. A waiting–boy.

3. That it might easily be taken in hand and put down as an offering of thanksgiving.]

49. The flesh of oxen, sheep, and fish was cut small, and made into mince. 'That of elks and deer was pickled; that of the wild pig was hashed: these were all sliced, but not cut small. The flesh of the muntjac was alone pickled, and that of fowls and hares, being sliced and cut small. Onions and shalots were sliced, and added to the brine to soften the meat.

50. When the pieces of the divided body were on the stand, in taking one of them to offer and in returning it[1], they did not kneel. So it was when they made an offering of roast meat. If the offerer, however, were a personator of the dead, he knelt.

51. When a man had his robes on his person, and did not know their names (or the meaning of their names), he was ignorant indeed.

52. If one came late and yet arrived before the torches were lighted, it was announced to him that the guests were all there, and who they were. The same things were intimated to a blind musician by the one who bid him. At a drinking entertainment, when the host carried a light, or bore a torch before them, the guests rise and decline the honour done to them. On this he gave the torch to a torchbearer, who did not move from his place, nor say a word, nor sing[2].

53. When one was carrying in water or liquor and food to a superior or elder, the rule was not to

[1. The lungs.

2. In the Zo Kwân we have many accounts of these entertainments. The singing was almost always of a few lines from one of the pieces of the Shih King, expressing a sentiment appropriate to the occasion. The custom was like our after–dinner speeches and toasts.]

breathe on it; and if a question was asked, to turn the mouth on one side.

54. When one conducted sacrifice for another (and was sending to others the flesh of the victim), the message was, 'Herewith (the flesh of) blessing.' When sending of the flesh of his own sacrifice to a superior man, the party simply announced what it was.

If it were flesh of the sacrifice on placing the tablet of the deceased in the temple, or at the close of the first year's mourning, the fact was announced. The principal mourner spread out the portions, and gave them to. his messenger on the south of the eastern steps, bowing twice, and laying his head to the ground as he sent him away; when he returned and reported the execution of his commission, the mourner again bowed twice and laid his head to the ground.

If the sacrifice were a great one, consisting of the three victims, then the portion sent was the left quarter of the ox, divided–into nine pieces from the shoulder. If the sacrifice were the smaller, the portion sent was the left quarter, divided into seven pieces. If there were but a single pig, the portion was the left quarter, divided into five portions.

BOOK XVI. HSIO KÎ, OR RECORD ON THE SUBJECT OF EDUCATION[1].

1. When a ruler is concerned that his measures should be in accordance with law, and seeks for the (assistance of the) good and upright, this is sufficient to secure him a considerable reputation, but not to move the multitudes.

When he cultivates the society of the worthy, and tries to embody the views of those who are remote (from the court), this is sufficient to move the multitudes, but not to transform the people.

If he wish to transform the people and to perfect their manners and customs, must he not start from the lessons of the school?

2. The jade uncut will not form a vessel for use; and if men do not learn, they do not know the way (in which they should go). On this account the ancient kings, when establishing states and governing the people, made instruction and schools a primary object;—as it is said in the Charge to Yüeh, 'The thoughts from first to last should be fixed on learning[2].'

3. However fine the viands be, if one do not eat, he does not know their taste; however perfect the course may be, if one do not learn it, be does not know its goodness. Therefore when he learns, one

[1. See the introductory notice, vol. xxvii, page 32.

2. Vol. iii, page 117.]

knows his own deficiencies; when he teaches, he knows the difficulties of learning. After he knows his deficiencies, one is able to turn round and examine himself; after he knows the difficulties, he is able to stimulate himself to effort. Hence it is said, 'Teaching and learning help each other;' as it is said in the Charge to Yüeh, 'Teaching is the half of learning[1].'

4. According to the system of ancient teaching, for the families of (a hamlet)[2] there was the village school; for a neighbourhood[2] there was the hsiang; for the larger districts there was the hsü; and in the capitals there was the college.

5. Every year some entered the college, and every second year there was a comparative examination. In the first year it was seen whether they could read the texts intelligently, and what was the meaning of each; in the third year, whether they were reverently attentive to their work, and what companionship was most pleasant to them; in the fifth year, how they extended their studies and sought the company of their teachers; in the seventh year, how they could discuss the subjects of their studies and select their friends. They were now said to have made some small attainments. In the ninth year, when they knew the different classes of subjects and had gained a general intelligence, were firmly established and would not fall back, they

[1. Vol. iii, page 117.

2 The hamlet was supposed to contain twenty-five families; the neighbourhood 500; and the district 2,500. For the four institutions, P. Callery adopts the names of. school, college, academy, and university. It would be tedious to give the various explanations of the names Hsiang and-Hsü.]

were said to have made grand attainments. After this the training was sufficient to transform the people, and to change (anything bad in) manners and customs. Those who lived near at hand submitted with delight, and those who were far off thought (of the teaching) with longing desire. Such was the method of the Great learning; as is said in the Record, 'The little ant continually exercises the art (of amassing)[1].'

6. At the commencement of the teaching in the Great college, (the masters) in their skin caps presented the offerings of vegetables (to the ancient sages), to show their pupils the principle of reverence for them; and made them sing (at the same time) the (first) three pieces of the Minor Odes of the Kingdom, as their first lesson in the duties of officers[2]. When they entered the college, the drum was beaten and the satchels were produced, that they might begin their work reverently. The cane and the thorns[3] were there to secure in them a proper awe. It was not till the time for the summer sacrifice[4] was divined for, that the testing examination was held;—to give composure to their minds. They were continually under inspection, but not spoken to,—to keep their minds undisturbed. They listened, but they did not ask questions; and

[1. See the note of Callery in loc. The quotation is from some old Record; it is not known what.

2. The three pieces were the Lû Ming, the Dze Mâu, and the Hwang–hwang Kê hwâ, the first three pieces in the first decade of the Shih, Part II; showing the harmony and earnestness of officers.

3. Callery calls these 'la latte et la baguette.'

4. Khung Ying–tâ thought this was the quinquennial sacrifice. See the Khien–lung editors on the point.]

they could not transgress the order of study (imposed on them). These seven things were the chief regulations in the teaching. As it is expressed in the Record, 'In all learning, for him who would in be an officer the first thing is (the knowledge of) business; for scholars the first thing is the directing of the mind.'

7. In the system of teaching at the Great college, every season had its appropriate subject; and when the pupils withdrew, and gave up their lessons (for the day), they were required to continue their study at home.

8. If a student do not learn (at college) to play in tune, he cannot quietly enjoy his lutes; if he do not learn extensively the figures of poetry, he cannot quietly enjoy the odes; if he do not learn the varieties of dress, he cannot quietly take part in the different ceremonies; if he do not acquire the various accomplishments, he cannot take delight in learning.

9. Therefore a student of talents and virtue pursues his studies, withdrawn in college from all besides, and devoted to their cultivation, or occupied with them when retired from it, and enjoying himself. Having attained to this, he rests quietly in his studies and seeks the company of his teachers; he finds pleasure in his friends, and has all confidence in their course. Although he should be separated from his teachers and helpers, he will not act contrary to the course;—as it is said in the Charge to Yüeh, 'Maintain a reverent humility, and strive to be constantly earnest. In such a case the cultivation will surely come

[1. Vol. iii, P. Il 7. But the quotation is a little different from the text of the Shû.]

10. According to the system of teaching now–a–days, (the masters) hum over the tablets which they see before them, multiplying their questions. They speak of the learners' making rapid advances, and pay no regard to their reposing (in what they have acquired). In what they lay on their learners they are not sincere, nor do they put forth all their ability in teaching them. What they inculcate is contrary to what is right, and the learners are disappointed in what they seek for. In such a case, the latter are distressed by their studies and hate their masters; they are embittered by the difficulties, and do not find any advantage from their (labour). They may seem to finish their work, but they quickly give up its lessons. That no results are seen from their instructions:–is it not owing to these defects?

11. The rules aimed at in the Great college were the prevention of evil before it was manifested; the timeliness of instruction just when it was required; the suitability of the lessons in adaptation to circumstances; and the good influence of example to parties observing one another. It was from these four things that the teaching was so effectual and flourishing.

12. Prohibition of evil after it has been manifested meets with opposition, and is not successful. Instruction given after the time for it is past is done with toil, and carried out with difficulty. The communication of lessons in an undiscriminating manner and without suitability produces injury and disorder, and fails in its object. Learning alone and without friends makes one feel solitary and uncultivated, with but little information. Friendships of festivity lead to opposition to one's master. Friendships with the dissolute lead to the neglect of one's learning. These six things all tend to make teaching vain.

13. When a superior man knows the causes which make instruction successful, and those which make it of no effect, he can become a teacher of others. Thus in his teaching, he leads and does not drag; he strengthens and does not discourage; he opens the way but does not conduct to the end (without the learner's own efforts). Leading and not dragging produces harmony. Strengthening and not discouraging makes attainment easy. Opening the way and not conducting to the end makes (the learner) thoughtful. He who produces such harmony, easy attainment, and thoughtfulness may be pronounced a skilful teacher.

14. Among learners there are four defects with which the teacher must make himself acquainted. Some err in the multitude of their studies; some, in their fewness; some, in the feeling of ease (with which they proceed); and some, in the readiness with which they stop. These four defects arise from the difference of their minds. When a teacher knows the character of his mind, he can save the learner from the defect to which hp is liable. Teaching should be directed to develop that in which the pupil excels, and correct the defects to which he is prone.

15. The good singer makes men (able) to continue his notes, and (so) the good teacher make. them able to carry out his ideas. His words are brief, but far–reaching; unpretentious, but deep; with few illustrations, but instructive. In this way he may be said to perpetuate his ideas.

16. When a man of talents and virtue knows the difficulty (on the one hand) and the facility (on the other) in the attainment of learning, and knows (also) the good and the bad qualities (of his pupils), he can vary his methods of teaching. When he can vary his methods of teaching, he can be a master indeed. When he can be a teacher indeed, he can be the Head (of an official department). When he can be such a Head, he can be the Ruler (of a state). Hence it is from the teacher indeed, that one learns to be a ruler, and the choice of a teacher demands the greatest care; as it is said in the Record, 'The three kings and the four dynasties were what they were by their teachers[1].'

17. In pursuing the course of learning, the difficulty is in securing the proper reverence for the master. When that is done, the course (which he inculcates) is regarded with honour. When that is done, the people know how to respect learning. Thus it is that there are two among his subjects whom the ruler does not treat as subjects. When one is personating (his ancestor), he does not treat him as such, nor does he treat his master as such. According to the rules of the Great college, the master, though communicating

anything to the son of Heaven, did not stand with his face to the north. This was the way in which honour was done to him.

[1. 'The three kings' are of course the Great Yü, founder of the Hsiâ dynasty; Thang the Successful, founder of the Shang; and Wan and Wû, Considered as one, founders of Kâu. The four dynasties is an unusual expression, though we shall meet with it again, as we have met with it already. They are said to be those of Yü (the dynasty of Shun), Hsiâ, Shang, and Kâu. But how then have we only I the three kings?' I should rather take them to be Hsiâ, Shang (considered as two, Shang and Yin), and Kâu.]

18. The skilful learner, while the master seems indifferent, yet makes double the attainments of another, and in the sequel ascribes the merit (to the master). The unskilful learner, while the master is diligent with him, yet makes (only) half the attainments (of the former), and in the sequel is dissatisfied with the master. The skilful questioner is like a workman addressing himself to deal with a hard tree. First he attacks the easy parts, and then the knotty. After a long time, the pupil and master talk together, and the subject is explained. The unskilful questioner takes the opposite course. The master who skilfully waits to be questioned, may be compared to a bell when it is struck. Struck with a small hammer, it gives a small sound. Struck with a great one, it gives a great sound. But let it be struck leisurely and properly, and it gives out all the sound of which it is capable[1]. He who is not skilful in replying to questions is the opposite of this. This all describes the method of making progress in learning.

19. He who gives (only) the learning supplied by

[1. P. Callery makes this sentence refer to the master, and not to the bell, and translates it:—'(Mais quelle que soit la nature des questions qu'on lui adresse, le maître) attend que l'élève ait fait à loisir toutes ses demandes, pour y faire ensuite une réponse complète.' He appends a note on the difficulty of the passage, saying in conclusion that the translation which he has adopted was suggested by a citation of the passage in the Pei-wan Yun-fû where there is a different reading of, 'instruction,' for, 'sound.' I have not been able to find the Citation in the great Thesaurus, to which he refers. Yen Yüan does not mention any different reading in his examination of the text (, Chapter 917); and I do not see any reason for altering the translation which I first made.]

his memory in conversations is not fit to be a master. Is it not necessary that he should hear the questions (of his pupils)? Yes, but if they are not able to put questions, he should put subjects before them. If he do so, and then they do not show any knowledge of the subjects, he may let them alone.

20. The son of a good founder is sure to learn how to make a fur–robe. The son of a good maker of bows is sure to learn how to make a sieve. Those who first yoke a (young) horse place it behind, with the carriage going on in front of it. The superior man who examines these cases can by them instruct himself in (the method of) learning[1].

21. The ancients in prosecuting their learning compared different' things and traced the analogies between them. The drum has no special relation to any of the musical notes; but without it they cannot be harmonised. Water has no particular relation to any of the five colours; but without it they cannot be displayed[2]. Learning has no particular relation to any of the five senses; but without it they cannot be regulated. A teacher has no

[1. The Khien–lung editors say that this paragraph is intended to show that the course of learning must proceed gradually. So far is clear; but the illustrations employed and their application to the subject in hand are not readily understood. In his fifth Book (towards the end), Lieh–dze gives the first two illustrations as from an old poem, but rather differently from the text:—'The son of a good maker of bows must first learn to make a sieve; and the son of a good potter must first learn to make a fur–robe.' In this form they would more suitably have their place in paragraph 18.

2. That is, in painting. The Chinese only paint in water colours. 'Water itself' says Khung Ying–tâ, 'has no colour, but the paint requires to be laid on with water, in order to its display.' I cannot follow the text so easily in what it says on the other illustrations.]

special relation to the five degrees of mourning; but without his help they cannot be worn as they ought to be.

22. A wise man has said, 'The Great virtue need not be confined to one office; Great power of method need not be restricted to the production of one article; Great truth need not be limited to the confirmation of oaths; Great seasonableness accomplishes all things, and each in its proper time.' By examining these four cases, we are taught to direct our aims to what is fundamental.

BOOK XVII. YO KÎ, OR RECORD OF MUSIC[1]

SECTION I.

1. All the modulations of the voice arise from the mind, and the various affections of the mind are produced by things (external to it). The affections thus produced are manifested in the sounds that are uttered. Changes are produced by the way in which those sounds respond to one another; and those changes constitute what we call the modulations of the voice. The combination' of those modulated sounds, so as to give pleasure, and the (direction in harmony with them of the) shields and axes[2[, and of the plumes and ox–tails[2], constitutes what we call music.

2. Music is (thus) the production of the modulations of the voice, and its source is in the affections of the mind as it is influenced by (external) things.

[1. See the introductory notice, vol. xxvii, pages p. 34.

2. There was a pantomimic exhibition of scenes of war, in which the performers brandished shields and axes; and another of scenes of peace, in which they waved plumes and ox–tails. What I have rendered by 'the modulations of the voice' is in the text the one Chinese character yin for which Callery gives 'air musical,' and which Kang Hsüan explains as meaning 'the five full notes of the scale.' See the long note of Callery prefixed to this record, concluding:—'La musique Chinoise, telle que l'ont entendue les anciens, avait tous les caractères d'une représentation théatrale ayant pour but de parler tout à la fois aux yeux, aux oreilles, à l'esprit, et au cœur.']

when the mind is moved to sorrow, the sound is sharp and fading away; when it is moved to pleasure, the sound is slow and gentle; when it is moved to joy, the sound is exclamatory and soon disappears; when it is moved to anger, the sound is coarse and fierce; when it is moved to reverence, the sound is straightforward, with an indication of humility; when it is moved to love, the sound is harmonious and soft. These six peculiarities of sound are not natural[1]'; they indicate the impressions produced by (external) things. On this account the ancient kings were watchful in regard to the things by which the mind was affected.

3. And so (they instituted) ceremonies to direct men's aims aright; music to give harmony to their voices; laws to unify their conduct; and punishments to guard against their tendencies to evil. The end to which ceremonies, music, punishments, and laws conduct is one; they are the instruments by which the minds of the people are assimilated, and good order in government is made to appear.

4. All modulations of the voice spring from the minds of men. When the feelings are moved within, they are manifested in the sounds of the voice–; and when those sounds are combined so as to form compositions, we have what are called airs. Hence, the airs of an age of good order indicate composure and enjoyment. The airs of an age of disorder indicate dissatisfaction and anger, and its government is perversely

[1. Or, 'are not the nature;' that is, the voice does not naturally, when the mind is not moved, from without itself, give such peculiar expressions of feeling. What belongs to man by his nature is simply the faculty of articulate speech, slumbering until he is awakened by his sensations and perceptions.]

bad. The airs of a state going to ruin are expressive of sorrow and (troubled) thought. There is an interaction between the words and airs (of the people) and the character of their government.

5. (The note) kung represents the ruler; shang, the ministers; kio, the people; kih, affairs; and yü, things. If there be no disorder or irregularity in these five notes, there will be no want of harmony in the state. If kung be irregular, (the air) is wild and broken; the ruler of the state is haughty. If shang be irregular, (the air) is jerky; the offices of the state are decayed. If kio be irregular, (the air) expresses anxiety; the people are dissatisfied. If kih be irregular, (the air) expresses sorrow; affairs are strained. If yü be irregular, (the air) is expressive of impending ruin; the resources (of the state) are exhausted. If the five notes are all irregular, and injuriously interfere with one another, they indicate a state of insolent disorder; and the state where this is the case will at no distant day meet with extinction and ruin[1].

6. The airs of Kang[2] and Wei were those of an age of disorder, showing that those states were near such an abandoned condition. The airs near the river Pû, at the mulberry forest, were those of a state going to ruin[3]. The government (of Wei) was in a state of dissipation, and the people were unsettled, calumniating their superiors, and pursuing

their private aims beyond the possibility of restraint.

[1. On those notes, see Chinese Classics, vol. iii, page 48.

2. See Confucian Analects, XV, 10, 6.

3. This place was in the state of Wei. See the ridiculous incident which gave rise to this account of the airs in Sze–mâ Khien's monograph on music, pages 13, 14.]

7. All modulations of sound take their rise from the mind of man; and music is the intercommunication of them in their relations and differences. Hence, even beasts know sound, but not its modulations, and the masses of the common people know the modulations, but they do not know music. It is only the superior man who can (really) know music.

8. On this account we must discriminate sounds in order to know the airs; the airs in order to know the music; and the music in order to know (the character of) the government. Having attained to this, we are fully provided with the methods of good order. Hence with him who does not know the sounds we cannot speak about the airs, and with him who does not know the airs we cannot speak about the music. The knowledge of music leads to the subtle springs that underlie the rules of ceremony. He who has apprehended both ceremonies and music may be pronounced to be a possessor of virtue. Virtue means realisation (in one's self)[1].

9. Hence the greatest achievements of music were not in the perfection of the airs; the (efficacy) of the ceremonies in the sacrificial offerings was not in the exquisiteness of the flavours. In the lute's for the Khing Miâo the strings were of red (boiled) silk, and the holes were wide apart; one lute began, and

[1. Virtue and getting or realising have the same name or pronunciation (teh) in Chinese. This concluding sentence, as Callery points out, is only a sort of pun on that common name. And yet 'virtue' is the 'realisation' in one's self 'of what is good.' The next paragraph expands the writer's thought. The greatest achievement of music in its ancient perfection was the softening and refining of the character, and that of the services of the temple was the making men reverent, filial, and brotherly.]

(only) three others joined it; there was much melody not brought out. In the ceremonies of the great sacrifices, the dark–coloured liquor took precedence, and on the stands were uncooked fish, while the grand soup had no condiments: there was much flavour left undeveloped.

10. Thus we see that the ancient kings, in their institution of ceremonies and music, did not seek how fully they could satisfy the desires of the appetite and of the ears and eyes; but they intended to teach the people to regulate their likings and dislikings, and to bring them back to the normal course of humanity.

11. It belongs to the nature of man, as from Heaven, to be still at his birth. His activity shows itself as he is acted on by external things, and developes the desires incident to his nature. Things come to him more and more, and his knowledge is increased. Then arise the manifestations of liking and disliking. When these are not regulated by anything within, and growing knowledge leads more astray without, he cannot come back to himself, and his Heavenly principle is extinguished.

12. Now there is no end of the things by which man is affected; and when his likings and dislikings are not subject to regulation (from within), he is changed into the nature of things as they come before him; that is, he stifles the voice of Heavenly principle within, and gives the utmost indulgence to the desires by which men may be possessed. On this we have the rebellious and deceitful heart, with licentious and violent disorder. The strong press upon the weak; the many are cruel to the few; the knowing impose upon the dull; the bold make it bitter for the timid; the diseased are not nursed; the old and young, orphans and solitaries are neglected:—such is the great disorder that ensues.

13. Therefore the ancient kings, when they instituted their ceremonies and music, regulated them by consideration of the requirements of humanity. By the sackcloth worn for parents, the wailings, and the weepings, they defined the terms of the mourning rites. By the bells, drums, shields, and axes, they introduced harmony into their seasons of rest and enjoyment. By marriage, capping, and the assumption of the hair–pin, they maintained the separation that should exist between male and female. By the archery gatherings in the districts, and the feastings at the meetings of princes, they provided for the correct maintenance of friendly intercourse.

14. Ceremonies afforded the defined expression for the (affections of the) people's minds; music secured the harmonious utterance of their voices; the laws of government were designed to promote the performance (of the ceremonies and music); and punishments, to guard against the violation of them. When ceremonies, music, laws, and punishments had everywhere full course, without irregularity or collision, the method of kingly rule was complete[1].

[1. With this paragraph ends the first portion of the treatise on music, called Yo Pan (##), or 'Fundamental Principles in Music.' The Khien–lung editors divide it into four chapters:—the first setting forth that music takes its character as good or bad from the mind of man, as affected by what is external to it; the second, that the character of the external things affecting the mind is determined by government as good or bad; the third, that the ceremonies and music of the ancient kings were designed to regulate the minds of men in their likings and dislikings; and the fourth, that that regulation was in harmony with the will of Heaven, as indicated in the nature of man.]

15. Similarity and union are the aim of music; difference and distinction, that of ceremony. From union comes mutual affection; from difference, mutual respect. Where music prevails, we find a weak coalescence; where ceremony prevails, a tendency to separation. It is the business of the two to blend people's feelings and give elegance to their outward manifestations.

16. Through the perception of right produced by ceremony, came the degrees of the noble and the mean; through the union of culture arising from music, harmony between high and low. By the exhibition of what was to be liked and what was to be disliked, a distinction was made between the worthy and unworthy. When violence was prevented by punishments, and the worthy were raised to rank, the operation of government was made impartial. Then came benevolence in the love (of the people), and righteousness in the correction (of their errors); and in this way good government held its course.

17. Music comes from within, and ceremonies from without. Music, coming from within, produces the stillness (of the mind); ceremonies, coming from without, produce the elegancies (of manner). The highest style of music is sure to be distinguished by its ease; the highest style of elegance, by its undemonstrativeness.

18. Let music attain its full results, and there would be no dissatisfactions (in the mind); let ceremony do so, and there would be no quarrels. When bowings and courtesies marked the government of the kingdom, there would be what might be described as music and ceremony indeed. Violent oppression of the people would not arise; the princes would appear submissively at court as guests; there would be no occasion for the weapons of war, and no employment of the five punishments[1]; the common people would have no distresses, and the son of Heaven no need to be angry:—such a state of things would be an universal music. When the son of Heaven could secure affection between father and son, could illustrate the orderly relation between old and young, and make mutual respect prevail all within the four seas, then indeed would ceremony (be seen) as power.

19. In music of the grandest style there is the same harmony that prevails between heaven and earth; in ceremonies of the grandest form there is the same graduation that exists between heaven and earth. Through the harmony, things do not fail (to fulfil their ends); through the graduation we have the sacrifices to heaven and those to earth. In the visible sphere there are ceremonies and music; in the invisible, the spiritual agencies. These things being so, in all within the four seas, there must be mutual respect and love.

20. The occasions and forms of ceremonies are different, but it is the same feeling of respect (which they express). The styles of musical pieces are different, but it is the same feeling of love (which they

[1. The 'five punishments' where branding on the forehead, cutting off the nose, other various dismemberments, castration, and death; see Mayers' 'Chinese Readers' Manual,' page 313. But the one word 'punishment' would sufficiently express the writer's meaning.]

promote). The essential nature of ceremonies and music being the same, the intelligent kings, one after another, continued them as they found them. The occasions and forms were according to the times when they were made; the names agreed with the merit which they commemorated.

21. Hence the bell, the drum, the flute, and the sounding-stone; the plume, the fife, the shield, and the axe are the instruments of music; the curvings and stretchings (of the body), the bending down and lifting up (of the head); and the evolutions and numbers (of

the performers), with the slowness or rapidity (of their movements), are its elegant accompaniments. The dishes, round and square, the stands, the standing dishes, the prescribed rules and their elegant variations, are the instruments of ceremonies; the ascending and descending, the positions high and low, the wheelings about, and the changing of robes, are their elegant accompaniments.

22. Therefore they who knew the essential nature of ceremonies and music could frame them; and they who had learned their elegant accompaniments could hand them down. The framers may be pronounced sage; the transmitters, intelligent. Intelligence and sagehood are other names for transmitting and inventing.

23, Music is (an echo of) the harmony between heaven and earth; ceremonies reflect the orderly distinctions (in the operations of) heaven and earth. From that harmony all things receive their being; to those orderly distinctions they owe the differences between them. Music has its origin from heaven; ceremonies take their form from the appearances of earth. If the imitation of those appearances were carried to excess, confusion (of ceremonies) would appear; if the framing of music were carried to excess, it would be too vehement. Let there be an intelligent understanding of the nature and interaction of (heaven and earth), and there will be the ability to practise well both ceremonies and music.

24. The blending together without any mutual injuriousness (of the sentiments and the airs on the different instruments) forms the essence of music; and the exhilaration of joy and the glow of affection are its business. Exactitude and correctness, without any inflection or deviation, form the substance of ceremonies, while gravity, respectfulness, and a humble consideration are the rules for their discharge.

25. As to the employment of instruments of metal and stone in connexion with these ceremonies and this music, the manifestation of them by the voice and its modulations, the use of them in the ancestral temple, and at the altars to the spirits of the land and grain, and in sacrificing to (the spirits of) the hills and streams, and to the general spiritual agencies (in nature);–these are (external demonstrations), natural even to the people[1].

26. When the (ancient) kings had accomplished their undertakings, they made their music (to commemorate them); when they had established their

[1. The eleven Paragraphs ending with this form the second chapter of the Book, called by Liû Hsiang Yo Lun, while the third chapter, extending to the end of the section, is called Yo Lî as if the two were an expansion of the statement in the seventh paragraph, that music is 'the intercommunication of the modulated sounds and the mind in their relations and differences.']

government, they framed their ceremonies. The excellence of their music was according to the greatness of their undertakings; and the completeness of their ceremonies was according to the comprehensiveness of their government. The dances with shields and axes did not belong to the most excellent music[1], nor did the sacrifices with cooked flesh mark the highest ceremonies[1].

27. The times of the five Tîs were different, and therefore they did not each adopt the music of his predecessor. The three kings belonged to different ages, and so they did not each follow the ceremonies of his predecessor. Music carried to an extreme degree leads to sorrow, and coarseness in ceremonies indicates something one–sided. To make the grandest music, which should bring with it no element of sorrow, and frame the completest ceremonies which yet should show no one–sidedness, could be the work only of the great sage.

28. There are heaven above and earth below, and between them are distributed all the (various) beings with their different (natures and qualities):—in accordance with this proceeded the framing of ceremonies. (The influences of) heaven and earth flow forth and never cease; and by their united action (the phenomena of) production and change ensue:—in accordance with this music arose. The processes of growth in spring, and of maturing in summer (suggest the idea of) benevolence; those of in–gathering in autumn and of storing in winter, suggest

[1. As being, I suppose, commemorative of the achievements of war, and not the victories of peace; and as marking a progress of society, and a departure from the primitive era of innocent simplicity and reverence.]

righteousness. Benevolence is akin to music, and righteousness to ceremonies.

29. Harmony is the thing principally sought in music:—it therein follows heaven, and manifests the spirit–like expansive influence characteristic of it. Normal distinction is the

thing aimed at in ceremonies:–they therein follow earth, and exhibit the spirit–like retractive influence characteristic of it. Hence the sages made music in response to heaven, and framed ceremonies in correspondence with earth. In the wisdom and–completeness of their ceremonies and music we see the directing power of heaven and earth[1].

30. (The relation) between ruler and minister was determined from a consideration of heaven (conceived of as) honourable, and earth (conceived of as) mean. The positions of noble and mean were fixed with a reference to the heights and depths displayed by the surface (of the earth). The regularity with which movement and repose follow each other (in the course of nature) led to the consideration of affairs as small

[1. On the first of these two paragraphs, P. Callery says:—'The celebrated Encyclopædist, Mâ Twan–lin (Book 181), says that this passage is one of the most marvellous that ever were written, and he draws, from it the proof that the work could not have been written later than the Han, "because reckoning from that dynasty there did not appear any author capable of conceiving ideas so profound, and expressing them in language so elevated."' P. Callery adds, As regards the origin of the Li Ki, the reasoning of the Encyclopædist appears to me passably (passablement) false; as to the intrinsic worth of the passage, I leave it to the reader to form his Judgment from the translation, which I have endeavoured to render as faithful as possible.'

2. In the passage of Mâ Twan–lin, however, that author is simply quoting the words of Kû Hsî (Tâ Kwan, Book 37), and expresses no opinion of his own.]

and great. The different quarters (of the heavens) are grouped together, and the things (of the earth) are distinguished by their separate characteristics; and this gave rise to (the conception of) natures and their attributes and functions. In heaven there are formed its visible signs, and earth produces its (endless variety of) things; and thus it was that ceremonies were framed after the distinction, between heaven and earth.

31. The breath (or influence) of earth ascends on high, and that of heaven descends below. These in their repressive and expansive powers come into mutual contact, and heaven and earth act on each other. (The susceptibilities of nature) are roused by the thunder, excited by the wind and rain, moved by the four seasons, and warmed by the sun and moon; and all the processes of change and growth vigorously proceed. Thus it was

that music was framed to indicate the harmonious action of heaven and earth.

32. If these processes took place out of season, there would be no (vigorous) life; and if no distinction were observed between males and females, disorder would arise and grow:—such is the nature of the (different qualities of) heaven and earth.

33. When we think of ceremonies and music, how they reach to the height of heaven and embrace the earth; how there are in them the phenomena of retrogression and expansion, and a communication with the spirit–like (operations of nature), we must pronounce their height the highest, their reach the farthest, their depth the most profound, and their breadth the greatest.

34. Music appeared in the Grand Beginning (of all things), and ceremonies had their place on the completion of them. Their manifestation, being ceaseless, gives (the idea of) heaven; and again, being motionless, gives (the idea of) earth. Through the movement and repose (of their interaction) come all things between heaven and earth. Hence the sages simply spoke of ceremonies and music.

SECTION II.

1. Anciently, Shun made the lute with five strings, and used it in singing the Nan Fang. Khwei was the first who composed (the pieces of) music to be employed by the feudal lords as an expression of (the royal) approbation of them[1].

2. Thus the employment of music by the son of Heaven was intended to reward the most virtuous among the feudal lords. When their virtue was very great, and their instructions were honoured, and all the cereals ripened in their season, then they were rewarded by (being permitted) the use of the music. Hence, those of them whose toils in the government of the people were conspicuous, had their rows of pantomimes extended far; and those of them who bad been indifferent to the government of the people

[1. Nan Fang, 'the South wind,' was the name of a poetical piece made by Shun, and celebrating the beneficent influence of rulers and parents as being like that of the south wind. Four lines of it are found in the Narratives of the School (Article 35):—

'The south wind's genial balm
Gives to my people's sorrows ease;
Its breath amidst the season's calm,
Brings to their wealth a large increase?'

The invention of the khin or lute, here ascribed to Shun, is also attributed to the more ancient Tîs, Shin Nang and Fû-hsî. Perhaps Shun was the first to make it with five strings. Khwei was his minister of music; see vol. iii, pages 44, 45.]

had those rows made short. On seeing their pantomimes, one knew what was (the degree of) their virtue, (just as) on hearing their posthumous designations, we know what had been (the character of) their conduct.

3. The Tâ Kang expressed the brilliance (of its author's virtue); the Hsien Kih, the completeness (of its author's); the Shâo showed how (its author) continued (the virtue of his predecessor); the Hsiâ, the greatness (of its author's virtue); the music of Yin and Kâu embraced every admirable quality[1].

4. In the interaction of heaven and earth, if cold and heat do not come at the proper seasons, illnesses arise (among the people); if wind and rain do not come in their due proportions, famine ensues. The instructions (of their superiors) are the people's cold and heat; if they are not what the time requires, an injury is done to society. The affairs (of their superiors) are the people's wind and rain; if they are not properly regulated, they have no success. In accordance with this, the object of the ancient kings in their practice of music was to bring their government into harmony with those laws (of heaven and earth). If it was good, then the conduct (of the people) was like the virtue (of their superiors).

5. (The feast on) grain-fed animals, with the adjunct of drinking, was not intended to produce evil, and yet cases of litigation are more numerous in consequence of it:—it is the excessive drinking which produces the evil. Therefore the former kings framed

[1. Tâ Kang was the name of Yâo's music; Hsien Kih, that of Hwang Tî's; Shâo, that of Shun's; and Hsiâ, that of Yü's. Pages would be required to condense what is said about the pieces and their names.]

the rules to regulate the drinking. Where there is (but) one presentation of the cup (at one time), guest and host may bow to each other a hundred times, and drink together all the day without getting drunk. This was the way in which those kings provided against evil consequences.

Such feasts served for the enjoyment of the parties at them. The music was intended to illustrate virtue; the ceremonies to restrain excess.

6. Hence the former kings, on occasions of great sorrow, had their rules according to which they expressed their grief; and on occasions of great happiness, they had their rules by which they expressed their pleasure. The manifestations, whether of grief or joy, were all bounded by the limits of these rules[1].

7. In music the sages found pleasure, and (saw that) it could be used to make the hearts of the people good. Because of the deep influence which it exerts on a man, and the change which it produces in manners and customs, the ancient kings appointed it as one of the subjects of instruction.

8. Now, in the nature of men there are both the energy of their physical powers and the intelligence of the mind; but for their (affections of) grief, pleasure, joy, and anger there are no invariable rules. They are moved according to the external objects which excite them, and then there ensues the manifestation of the various faculties of the mind.

9. Hence, when a (ruler's) aims are small, notes

[1. With this paragraph ends the fourth division of the Book, called Yo Shih, meaning 'The grant of Music,' or the Principles on which the ancient kings permitted their music to be used by the feudal princes, to signify their approval of what was good, and stimulate all to virtue.]

that quickly die away characterise the music, and the people's thoughts are sad; when he is generous, harmonious, and of a placid and easy temper, the notes are varied and elegant, with frequent changes, and the people are satisfied and pleased; when he is coarse, violent, and excitable, the notes, vehement at first and distinct in the end, are full and bold throughout the piece, and the people are resolute and daring; when he is pure and straightforward, strong and correct, the notes are grave and expressive of sincerity, and the people are self–controlled and respectful; when he is magnanimous, placid, and kind, the notes are natural, full, and harmonious, and the people are affectionate and loving; when he is careless, disorderly, perverse, and dissipated, the notes are tedious and ill–regulated, and the people proceed to excesses and disorder.

10. Therefore the ancient kings (in framing their music), laid its foundations in the feelings and nature of men; they examined (the notes) by the measures (for the length and quality of each); and adapted it to express the meaning of the ceremonies (in which it was to be used). They (thus) brought it into harmony with the energy that produces life, and to give expression to the performance of the five regular constituents of moral worth. They made it indicate that energy in its Yang or phase of vigour, without any dissipation of its power, and also in its Yin or phase of remission, without the vanishing of its power. The strong phase showed no excess like that of anger, and the weak no shrinking like that of pusillanimity. These four characteristics blended harmoniously in the minds of men, and were similarly manifested in their conduct. Each occupied quietly in its proper place, and one did not interfere injuriously with another.

11. After this they established schools for (teaching their music), and different grades (for the learners). They marked most fully the divisions of the pieces, and condensed into small compass the parts and variations giving beauty and elegance, in order to regulate and increase the inward virtue (of the learners). They gave laws for the great and small notes according to their names, and harmonised the order of the beginning and the end, to represent the doing of things. Thus they made the underlying principles of the relations between the near and distant relatives, the noble and mean, the old and young, males and females, all to appear manifestly in the music. Hence it is said that 'in music we must endeavour to see its depths.'

12. When the soil is worn out, the grass and trees on it do. not grow well. When water is often troubled, the fish and tortoises in it do not become large. When the energy (of nature) is decayed, its production of things does not proceed freely. In an age of disorder, ceremonies are forgotten and neglected, and music becomes licentious.

13. In such a case the notes are melancholy but without gravity, or joyous without repose. There is remissness (in ceremonies) and the violation of them is easy. One falls into such a state of dissoluteness that he forgets the virtue properly belonging to his nature. In great matters he is capable of treachery and villainy; in small matters he becomes greedy and

covetous. There is a diminution in him of the enduring, genial forces of nature, and an extinction of the virtue of satisfaction and harmony. On this account the Superior man despises such (a style of music and ceremonies)[1].

14. Whenever notes that are evil and depraved affect men, a corresponding evil spirit responds to them (from within); and when this evil spirit accomplishes its manifestations, licentious music is the result. Whenever notes that are correct affect men, a corresponding correct spirit responds to them (from within); and when this correct spirit accomplishes its manifestations, harmonious music is the result. The initiating cause and the result correspond to each other. The round and the deflected, the crooked and the straight, have each its own category; and such is the character of all things, that they affect one another severally according to their class.

15. Hence the superior man returns to the (good) affections (proper to his nature) in order to bring h is will into harmony with them, and compares the different qualities (of actions) in order to perfect his conduct. Notes that are evil and depraved, and sights leading to disorder, and licentiousness, are not allowed to affect his ears or eyes. Licentious music and corrupted ceremonies are not admitted into the mind to affect its powers. The spirit of idleness, indifference, depravity, and perversity finds no exhibition in his person. And thus he makes his ears, eyes, nose, and mouth, the apprehensions of his mind, and the movements of all the parts of his body, all follow the course that is correct, and do that which is right.

[1. This and the six previous paragraphs form the fifth division of the Book, and are called Yo Yen, 'Words about Music.' The Khien–lung editors, however, propose changing the Yen into Hsing, so that the meaning would be Manifestations of Music.']

16. After this there ensues the manifestation (of the inward thoughts) by the modulations of note and tone, the elegant accompaniments of the lutes, small and large, the movements with the shield and battleaxe, the ornaments of the plumes and ox–tails, and the concluding with the pipes and flutes[1]. All this has the effect of exhibiting the brilliance of complete virtue, stirring up the harmonious action of the four (seasonal) energies; and displaying the true natures and qualities of all things.

17. Hence in the fine and distinct notes we have an image of heaven; in the ample and grand, an image of earth; in their beginning and ending, an image of the four seasons; in

the wheelings and revolutions (of the pantomimes), an image of the wind and rain. (The five notes, like) the five colours, form a complete and elegant whole, without any confusion. (The eight instruments of different materials, like) the eight winds, follow the musical accords, without any irregular deviation. The lengths of all the different notes have their definite measurements, without any uncertainty. The small and the great complete one another. The end leads on to the beginning, and the beginning to the end. The key notes and those harmonising with them, the sharp and the bass, succeed one another in their regular order.

18. Therefore, when the music has full course, the different relations are clearly defined by it; the perceptions of the ears and eyes become sharp and distinct; the action of the blood and physical energies is harmonious and calm; (bad) influences are removed, and manners changed; and all under heaven there is entire repose.

19. Hence we have the saying, 'Where there is music there is joy.' Superior men rejoice in attaining to the course (which they wish to pursue); and smaller men in obtaining the things which the), desire. When the objects of desire are regulated by a consideration of the course to be pursued, there is joy without any disorder. When those objects lead to the forgetfulness of that course, there is delusion, and no joy.

20. It is for this purpose that the superior man returns to the (good) affections (proper to his nature), in order to bring his will into harmony with them, and makes extensive use of music in order to perfect his instructions. When the music has free course, the people direct themselves to the quarter (to which they should proceed), and we can see (the power of) his virtue.

21. Virtue is the strong stein of (man's) nature, and music is the blossoming of virtue. Metal, stone, silk, and bamboo are (the materials of which) the instruments of music (are made). Poetry gives expression to the thoughts; singing prolongs the notes (of the voice); pantomimic movements put the body into action (in harmony with the sentiments). These three things originate in the mind, and the instruments of the music accompany them.

22. In this way the affections (from which comes the music) are deeply seated, and the elegant display of them is brilliant. All the energies (of the nature) are abundantly employed, and their transforming power is mysterious and spirit–like. A harmonious conformity (to virtue) is realised within, and the blossoming display of it is conspicuous

without, for in music, more than other things, there should be nothing that is pretentious or hypocritical.

23. Music springs from the movement of the mind; the notes are the manifestation of the music; the elegant colours and various parts are the ornaments of the notes. The superior man puts its fundamental cause in movement, makes its manifesting notes into music, and regulates its ornaments.

24. Thus they first strike the drum to warn (the performers) to be in readiness, and (the pantomimes) take three steps to show the nature of the dance. This is done a second time and they begin to move forward; and when they have completed their evolutions, they return and dress their ranks. However rapid their movements may be, there is nothing violent in them; however mysterious they may be, they are not beyond the power of being understood. One, studying them alone, finds pleasure in the object of them, and does not tire in his endeavours to understand them. When he has fully understood them, he does not keep what he desires to himself. Thus the affections (of joy) are displayed; the (ideal) of righteousness is established; and when the music is ended, the (due) honour has been paid to virtue. Superior men by it nourish their love of what is good; small men in it hear the (correction of) their errors. Hence it is said, that 'for the courses to be pursued by men the influence of music is great.'

25. In music we have the outcome and bestowal (of what its framers felt); in ceremonies a return (for what their performers had received). Music expresses the delight in what produces it, and ceremonies lead the mind back to (the favours) which originate them. Music displays the virtue (of the framer); ceremonies are a return of the feelings (which led to them), as carrying the mind back to what originated them.

26. What is called 'a Grand carriage' is one which is (the gift) of the son of Heaven; the flag with dragons, and a nine–scolloped border, was the banner (conferred by) the son of Heaven; that with the azure and black edging exhibited the precious tortoises, and was (also the gift of) the son of Heaven; and when these were followed by herds of oxen and sheep, they were the gifts bestowed on the feudal lords[1].

SECTION III.

1. In music we have the expression of feelings which do not admit of any change; in ceremonies that of principles which do not admit of any alteration. Music embraces what all equally share; ceremony distinguishes the things in which men differ. Hence the theory of music and ceremonies embraces the whole nature of man.

2. To go to the very root (of our feelings) and know the changes (which they undergo) is the province of music; to display sincerity and put away all that is hypocritical is the grand law of ceremonies. Ceremonies and music resemble the nature of Heaven and Earth, penetrate to the virtues of the spiritual Intelligences, bring down the spirits from above, and

[1. With this ends the sixth chapter of the Book, called Yo Hsiang, meaning the natural symbols of music.]

raise up those whose seat is below. They give a sort of substantial embodiment of what is most subtle as well as material, and regulate the duties between father and son, ruler and subject.

3. Therefore, when the Great man uses and exhibits his ceremonies and music, Heaven and Earth will in response to him display their brilliant influences. They will act in happy union, and the energies (of nature), now expanding, now contracting, will proceed harmoniously. The genial airs from above and the responsive action below will overspread and nourish all things. Then plants and trees will grow luxuriantly; curling sprouts and buds will expand; the feathered and winged tribes will be active; horns and antlers will grow; insects will come to the light and revive; birds will breed and brood; the hairy tribes will mate and bring forth; the mammalia will have no abortions, and no eggs will be broken or addled,—and all will have to be ascribed to the power of music[1].

4. When we speak of music we do not mean the notes emitted by the Hwang Kung, Tâ Lü, (and the other musical pipes), the stringed instruments and the singing, or the (brandishing of the) shields and axes. These are but the small accessories of the music; and hence lads act as the pantomimes. (In

[1. There is extravagance in this description. The Great man is the sage upon the throne. The imagination of the eloquent writer runs riot as he dwells on the article of his creed, that 'Heaven, Earth, and Man' are the 'Three Powers,' intended by their harmonious co-operation to make a happy and flourishing world. That would indeed be wonderful music which should bring about such a result. Compare the words of the Hebrew prophet in Hosea ii. 21, 22. Callery's translation of the concluding clause is:—'Tout cela n'est autre chose que l'harmonie de la musique rejaillissant (sous tous les êtres de la nature).']

the same way), the spreading of the mats, the disposing of the vases, and the arranging of the stands and dishes, with the movements in ascending and descending, are but the small accessories of ceremonies; and hence there are the (smaller) officers who direct them. The music-masters decide on the tunes and the pieces of poetry; and hence they have their places with their stringed instruments, and their faces directed to the north. The prayer-officers of the ancestral temple decide on the various ceremonies in it, and hence they keep behind the representatives of the deceased. Those who direct the mourning rites after the manner of the Shang dynasty[1], have their places (for the same reason) behind the presiding mourner.

5. It is for this reason that the practice of virtue is held to be of superior worth, and the practice of any art of inferior; that complete virtue takes the first place, and the doing of anything, (however ingenious, only) the second. Therefore the ancient kings had their distinctions of superior and inferior, of first and last; and so they could frame their music and ceremonies for the whole kingdom[2].

6., The marquis Wan of Wei[3] asked Dze-hsiâ, saying, 'When in my square-cut dark robes and cap I listen to the ancient music, I am only afraid that I shall go to sleep. When I listen to the music of

[1. Which was distinguished for the plain simplicity of its observances.

2. With this ends the seventh chapter, called Yo Khing, 'The attributes of Music.'

3. The marquis Wan ruled in Wei from B.C. 425 to 387. He is said to have received the classical books from Dze-hsiâ, when that disciple of Confucius must have been a hundred years old, and was blind, in B.C. 407.]

Kang and Wei, I do not feel tired; let me ask why I should feel so differently under the old and the new music.'

7. Dze–hsiâ replied, 'In the old music, (the performers) advance and retire all together; the music is harmonious, correct, and in large volume; the stringed instruments (above) and those made from gourd shells with the organs and their metal tongues (below), are all kept waiting for the striking of the drum. The music first strikes up at the sound of the drum; and when it ends, it is at the sound of the cymbals. The close of each part of the performance is regulated by the Hsiang[1], and the rapidity of the motions by the Yâ[1]. In (all) this the superior man speaks of, and follows, the way of antiquity. The character is cultivated; the family is regulated; and peace and order are secured throughout the kingdom. This is the manner of the ancient music.

8. 'But now, in the new music, (the performers) advance and retire without any regular order; the music is corrupt to excess; there is no end to its vileness. Among the players there are dwarfs like monkeys, while boys and girls are mixed together, and there is no distinction between father and son. Such music can never be talked about, and cannot be said to be after the manner of antiquity. This is the fashion of the new music.

9. 'What you ask about is music; and what you like is sound. Now music and sound are akin, but they are not the same.'

[1. These are names of musical instruments, of which figures are given in the plates to the Khien–lung edition; but there is much uncertainty about them.]

10. The marquis asked him to explain, and Dze–hsiâ replied, 'In antiquity, Heaven and Earth acted according to their several natures, and the four seasons were what they ought to be. The people were virtuous, and all the cereals produced abundantly. There were no fevers or other diseases, and no apparitions or other prodigies. This was what we call "the period of great order." After this arose the sages, and set forth the duties between father and son, and between ruler and subject, for the guidance of society. When these guiding rules were thus correctly adjusted, all under heaven, there was a great tranquillity; after which they framed with exactness the six accords (upper and lower), and gave harmony to the five notes (of the scale), and the singing to the lutes of the odes and praise–songs; constituting what we call "the virtuous airs." Such virtuous airs constituted what we call "Music," as is declared in the Book of Poetry (III, i, ode 7, 4),

'Silently grew the fame of his virtue,
His virtue was highly intelligent;
Highly intelligent, and of rare discrimination;
Able to lead, able to rule,—
To rule over this great country,
Rendering a cordial submission, effecting a cordial union.
When (the sway) came to king Wan,
His virtue left nothing to be dissatisfied with.
He received the blessing of God,
And it was extended to his descendants."

11. 'May I not say that what you love are the vile airs?' The marquis said, "Let me ask where the vile airs come from?' Dze–hsiâ replied, 'The airs of Kang go to a wild excess, and debauch the mind; those of Sung tell of slothful indulgence and women, and drown the mind; those of Wei are vehement and rapid, and perplex the mind; and those of Khî are violent and depraved, and make the mind arrogant. The airs of those four states all stimulate libidinous desire, and are injurious to virtue;—they should therefore not be used at sacrifices.

12. 'It is said in the Book of Poetry (IV, i [Part ii], ode 5),

"In solemn unison (the instruments) give forth their notes;
Our ancestors will hearken to them."

That solemn unison denotes the grave reverence and harmony of their notes:—with reverence, blended with harmony, what is there that cannot be done?

13. 'A ruler has only to be careful of what he likes and dislikes. What the ruler likes, his ministers will practise; and what superiors do, their inferiors follow. This is the sentiment in the Book of Poetry (III, ii, ode 10, 6),

"To lead the people is very easy."

14. 'Seeing this, and after (the repose of the people was secured), the sages made hand–drums and drums, the stopper and the starter, the earthen whistle and the bamboo flute,—the six instruments which produced the sounds of their virtuous airs. After these

came the bell, the sounding-stone, the organ with thirty-six pipes, and the large lute, to be played in harmony with them; the shields, axes, ox-tails, and plumes, brandished by the pantomimes in time and tune. These they employed at the sacrifices in the temple of the former kings, at festivals in offering and receiving the pledge cup; in arranging the services of officers (in the temple) according to the rank due to each, as noble or mean, and in showing to future ages how they observed the order due to rank and to age.

15. 'The bells give out a clanging sound as a signal. The signal is recognised by all, and that recognition produces a martial enthusiasm. When the ruler hears the sound of the bell, he thinks of his officers of war.

'The sounding-stones give out a tinkling sound, as a summons to the exercise of discrimination. That discrimination may lead to the encountering of death. When the ruler hears the sounding-stone, he thinks of his officers who die in defence of his frontiers.

'The stringed instruments give out a melancholy sound, which produces the thought of purity and fidelity, and awakens the determination of the mind. When the ruler hears the sound of the lute and cithern, he thinks of his officers who are bent on righteousness.

'The instruments of bamboo give out a sound like that of overflowing waters, which suggests the idea of an assembly, the object of which is to collect the multitudes together. When the ruler hears the sound of his organs, pipes, and flutes, he thinks of his officers who gather the people together.

'The drums and tambours give out their loud volume of sound, which excites the idea of movement, and tends to the advancing of the host. When the ruler hears the sounds of his drums and tambours, he thinks of his leaders and commanders. When a superior man thus hears his musical instruments, he does not hear only the sounds which they emit. There are associated ideas which accompany these[1].'

16. Pin-mâu Kiâ[2] was sitting with Confucius. Confucius talked with him about music, and said, 'At (the performance of) the Wû, how is it that the preliminary warning (of the drum) continues so long?' The answer was, 'To show (the king's) anxiety that all his multitudes should be of one mind with him.'

'How is it that (when the performance has commenced) the singers drawl their notes so long, and the pantomimes move about till they perspire?' The answer was, 'To show his apprehension that some (princes) might not come up in time for the engagement.'

'How is it that the violent movement of the arms and stamping fiercely with the feet begin so soon?' The answer was, ' To show that the time for the engagement had arrived.'

'How is it that, (in the performance of the Wû,) the pantomimes kneel on the ground with the right

[1. With this fifteenth paragraph ends the eighth chapter of the Book called simply 'Marquis Wan of Wei's Chapter'; and the Khien–lung editors say nothing more about it.

2. Pin–mâu Kiâ must have been a scholar of Confucius' time, a master of music; but, so far as I have read, nothing is known about him beyond what appears here. The Khang Hung at the end of the paragraph was a historiographer of Kâu, with whom Confucius is said to have studied music. The Wû was the dance and music which king Wû is said to have made after his conquest of Shang or Yin.]

knee, while the left is kept up?' The answer was, 'There should be no kneeling in the Wû.'

'How is it that the words of the singers go on to speak eagerly of Shang?' The answer was, 'There should be no such sounds in the Wû.'

'But if there should be no such sound in the Wû, where does it come from?' The answer was, 'The officers (of the music) failed to hand it down correctly. If they did not do so, the aim of king Wû would have been reckless and wrong.'

The Master said, 'Yes, what I heard from Khang Hung was to the same effect as what you now say.'

17. Pin–mâu Kiâ rose up, left his mat, and addressed Confucius, saying, 'On the long–continued warning (of the drum) in the Wû, I have heard your instructions; but let me ask how it is that after that first delay there is another, and that a long one?'

The Master said, 'Sit down, and I will tell you. Music is a representation of accomplished facts. The pantomimes stand with their shields, each erect and firm as a hill, representing the attitude of king Wû. The violent movements of the arms and fierce stamping represent the enthusiasm of Thâi–kung. The kneeling of all at the conclusion of the performance represents the government (of peace, instituted) by (the dukes of) Kâu and Shâo.

18. 'Moreover, the pantomimes in the first movement proceed towards the north (to imitate the marching of king Wû against Shang); in the second, they show the extinction of Shang; in the third, they show the return march to the south; in the fourth, they show the laying out of the Southern states; in the fifth, they show how (the dukes of) Kâu and Shâo were severally put in charge of the states on the left and right; in the sixth, they again unite at the point of starting to offer their homage to the son of Heaven. Two men, one on each side of the performers, excite them with bells, and four times they stop and strike and thrust, showing the great awe with which (king Wû) inspired the Middle states. Their advancing with these men on each side shows his eagerness to complete his helpful undertaking. The performers standing long together show bow he waited for the arrival of the princes.

19. 'And have you alone not heard the accounts of Mû–yeh? King Wû, after the victory over Yin, proceeded to (the capital of) Shang; and before he descended from his chariot he invested the descendants of Hwang Tî with Kî; those of the Tî Yâo with Kû; and those of the Tî Shun with Khan. When he had descended from it, he invested the descendant of the sovereign of Hsiâ with Kî; appointed the descendants of Yin to Sung; raised a mound over the grave of the king's son, Pî–kan; released the count of Khî from his imprisonment, and employed him to restore to their places the officers who were acquainted with the ceremonial usages of Shang. The common people were relieved from (the pressure) of the (bad) government which they had endured, and the emoluments of the multitude of (smaller) officers were doubled.

'(The king then) crossed the Ho, and proceeded to the West. His horses were set free on the south of mount Hwâ, not to be yoked again. His oxen were dispersed in the wild of the Peach forest, not to be put to the carriages again. His chariots and coats of mail were smeared with blood, and despatched to his arsenals, not to be used again. The shields and spears were turned upside down and conveyed away, wrapped in tiger skins, which were styled "the appointed cases." The leaders and commanders were then constituted feudal lords; and it was known throughout the kingdom that king Wû would have recourse to weapons of war no more[1].

20. 'The army having been disbanded (the king commanded) a practice of archery at the colleges in the suburbs. At the college on the left (or east) they shot to the music of the Lî–shâu[2]; at that on the right (or west) they shot to the music of the Zâu–yü; and (from this time) the archery which consisted in going through (so many) buffcoats ceased. They wore (only) their civil robes and caps, with their ivory tokens of rank stuck in their girdles; and the officers of the guard put off their swords. (The king) offered sacrifice in the Hall of Distinction, and the people learned to be filial. He gave audiences at court, and the feudal lords knew how they ought to demean themselves. He ploughed in the field set apart for that purpose, and the lords learned what should be the object of reverence to them (in their states), These five things constituted great lessons for the whole kingdom.'

21. In feasting the three (classes of the) old and the five (classes of the) experienced in the Great college, he himself (the son of Heaven) had his

[1. See the account of all these proceedings after the victory of Mû in the Shû, V, iii, 9, though it is difficult to reconcile the two accounts in some of their details.

2. See the Kâu Lî, Book 22, 32. The ode Lî–shâu. was used at the archery celebrations of the feudal lords, and is now lost. The Zâu–yü is the last ode in the second Book of the Shih, Part I. It was used at contests where the king presided.]

breast bared and cut up the animals. He (also) presented to them the condiments and the cups. He wore the royal cap, and stood with a shield before him. In this way he taught the lords their brotherly duties.

22. 'In this manner the ways of Kâu penetrated everywhere, and the interaction of ceremonies and music was established;—is it not right that in the performance of the Wû there should be that gradual and long–continuing action[1]?'

23. A superior man says: 'Ceremonies and music should not for a moment be neglected by any one. When one has mastered completely (the principles of) music, and regulates his heart and mind accordingly, the natural, correct, gentle, and honest heart is easily

developed, and with this development of the heart comes joy. This joy goes on to a feeling of repose. This repose is long–continued. The man in this constant repose becomes (a sort of) Heaven. Heaven–like, (his action) is spirit–like. Heaven–like, he is believed without the use of words. Spirit–like, he is regarded with awe, without any display of rage. So it is, when one by his mastering of music regulates his mind and heart.

24. 'When one has mastered completely (the principle of) ceremonies so as to regulate his person accordingly, he becomes grave and reverential. Grave and reverential, he comes to be regarded with awe. If the heart be for a moment without the feeling of harmony and joy, meanness and deceitfulness enter

[1. The preceding seven paragraphs form the ninth chapter, which, like the former, simply bears the name of one of the parties in it, and is called 'The chapter of Pin–mâu Kiâ.']

it. If the outward demeanour be for a moment without gravity and respectfulness, indifference and rudeness show themselves.

25. 'Therefore the sphere in which music acts is the interior of man, and that of ceremonies is his exterior. The result of music is a perfect harmony, and that of ceremonies a perfect observance (of propriety). When one's inner man is (thus) harmonious, and his outer man thus docile, the people behold his countenance and do not strive with him; they look to his demeanour, and no feeling of indifference or rudeness arises in them. Thus it is that when virtue shines and acts within (a superior), the people are sure to accept (his rule), and hearken to him; and when the principles (of propriety) are displayed in his conduct, the people are sure (in the same way) to accept and obey him. Hence it is said, "Carry out perfectly ceremonies and music, and give them their outward manifestation and application, and under heaven nothing difficult to manage will appear."'

26. Music springs from the inward movements (of the soul); ceremonies appear in the outward movements (of the body). Hence it is the rule to make ceremonies as few and brief as possible, and to give to music its fullest development. This rule for ceremonies leads to the forward exhibition of them, and therein their beauty resides; that for music leads to the introspective consideration of it, and therein its beauty resides. If ceremonies demanding this condensation were not performed with this forward exhibition of them,

they would almost disappear altogether; if music, demanding this full development, were not accompanied with this introspection, it would produce a dissipation of the mind. Thus it is that to every ceremony there is its proper response, and for music there is its introspection. When ceremonies are responded to, there arises pleasure; and when music is accompanied with the right introspection, there arises the (feeling of) repose. The responses of ceremony and the introspection of music spring from one and the same idea, and have one and the same object.

27. Now music produces pleasure;—what the nature of man cannot be without. That pleasure must arise from the modulation of the sounds, and have its embodiment in the movements (of the body);—such is the rule of humanity. These modulations and movements are the changes required by the nature, and they are found complete in music. Thus men will not be without the ministration of pleasure, and pleasure will not be without its embodiment, but if that embodiment be not suitably conducted, it is impossible that disorder should not arise. The ancient kings, feeling that they would feel ashamed (in the event of such disorder arising), appointed the tunes and words of the Yâ and the Sung to guide (in the music), so that its notes should give sufficient pleasure, without any intermixture of what was bad, while the words should afford sufficient material for consideration without causing weariness; and the bends and straight courses, the swell and diminution, the sharp angles, and soft melody throughout all its parts, should be sufficient to stir up in the minds of the hearers what was good in them, without inducing any looseness of thought or depraved air to be suggested. Such was the plan of the ancient kings when they framed their music.

28. Therefore in the ancestral temple, rulers and ministers, high and low, listen together to the music, and all is harmony and reverence; at the district and village meetings of the heads of clans, old and young listen together to it, and all is harmony and deference. Within the gate of the family, fathers and sons, brothers and cousins, listen together to it, and all is harmony and affection. Thus in music there is a careful discrimination (of the voices) to blend them in unison so as to bring out their harmony; there is a union of the (various) instruments to give ornamental effect to its different parts; and these parts are combined and performed so as to complete its elegance. In this way fathers and sons, rulers and subjects are united in harmony, and the people of the .myriad states are associated in love. Such was the method of the ancient kings when they framed their music.

29. In listening to the singing of the Yâ and the Sung, the aims and thoughts receive an expansion. From the manner in which the shields and axes are held and brandished, and from the movements of the body in the practice with them, now turned up, now bent down, now retiring, now stretching forward, the carriage of the person receives gravity. From the way in which (the pantomimes) move to their several places, and adapt themselves to the several parts (of the performance), the arrangement of their ranks is made correct, and their order in advancing and re tiring is secured. In this way music becomes the lesson of Heaven and Earth, the regulator of true harmony, and what the nature of man cannot dispense with.

30. It was by music that the ancient kings gave elegant expression to their joy; by their armies and axes that they gave the same to their anger. Hence their joy and anger always received their appropriate response. When they were joyful, all under heaven were joyful with them; when they were angry, the oppressive and disorderly feared them. In the ways of the ancient kings, ceremonies and music may be said to have attained perfection[1].

31. (Once), when Dze-kung had an interview with the music-master Yî, he asked him, saying, 'I have heard that in the music and words belonging to it there is that which is specially appropriate to every man; what songs are specially appropriate to me?' The other replied, 'I am but a poor musician, and am not worthy to be asked what songs arc appropriate for particular individuals;-allow me to repeat to you what I have heard, and you can select for yourself (what is appropriate to you). The generous and calm, the mild and correct, should sing the Sung; the magnanimous and calm, and those of wide penetration and sincere, the Tâ Yâ (Major Odes of the Kingdom); the courteous and self-restraining, the lovers of the rules of propriety, the Hsiâo Yâ (Minor Odes of the Kingdom); the correct, upright, and calm, the discriminating and humble, the Fang, (Airs of the States); the determinedly upright, but yet gentle and loving, the Shang; and the mild and honest, but yet capable of decision, the Khî The object of this singing is for one to make himself right, and then to display his virtue. When he has thus put

[1. From paragraph 23 to this forms the tenth chapter of the Book, which has the name of Yo Hwâ, 'The Transforming Operation of Music,' supplementing and summarising all the previous chapters.]

himself in a condition to act, Heaven and Earth respond to him, the four seasons revolve in harmony with him, the stars and constellations observe their proper laws, and all things are nourished and thrive.

32. 'What are called the Shang[1] were the airs and words transmitted from the five Tîs; and having been remembered by the people of Shang, we call them the Shang. What are called the Khî were transmitted from the three dynasties; and having been remembered by the people of Khî, we call them the Khî. He who is versed in the airs of the Shang Will generally be found to manifest decision in the conduct of affairs. He who is versed in the airs of the Khî, when he is attracted by the prospect of profit, will yet give place to others. To manifest decision in the conduct of affairs is bravery; to give. place to others in the prospect of gain is righteousness. Who, without singing these songs, can assure himself that he will always preserve such bravery and righteousness?

33. 'In singing, the high notes rise as if they were borne aloft; the low descend as if they were falling to the ground; the turns resemble a thing broken off; and the finale resembles the breaking) of a willow tree; emphatical notes seem made by the

[1. All the other pieces of song, mentioned in the preceding paragraph are well known, as the divisions under which the odes of the Shih King are arranged. What are called the Shang and Khî are lost, but some account of them is given in this paragraph. When it is said that the people of Shang remembered the airs and poetry of the five Tîs, we must understand by Shang the duchy of Sung which was ruled by the representation of the line of the Shang kings. Why the state of Khî should have remembered the airs and songs of 'the three dynasties' more than any other state, I cannot tell.]

square; quavers are like the hook (of a spear); and those prolonged on the same key are like pearls strung together. Hence, singing means the prolonged expression of the words; there is the utterance of the words, and when the simple utterance is not sufficient, the prolonged expression of them. When that prolonged expression is not sufficient, there come the sigh and exclamation. When these are insufficient, unconsciously there come the motions of the hands and the stamping of the feet[1].'

(Such was the answer to) Dze–kung's question about music[2].

[1. On this passage, P. Callery says:—'Quoique, à la rigueur, on puisse comparer des airs à des objets, ou à des accidents matériels, comme nous disons de tel motif musical qu'il est "Large," "Sec," "Dur," etc., il faut avouer que les comparaisons adoptées par l'artiste

Chinois sont, en général, fort mauvaises, c'est une amplification gâtée de ce qu'il a dit plus haut.'

BOOK XVIII. ZÂ KÎ, OR MISCELLANEOUS RECORDS[1].

SECTION I.

PART I.

1. When a feudal lord was on the march and died in his lodging[2], they called back his soul in the same way as in his state. If he died on the road, (one) got up on the nave of the left wheel of the chariot in which he had been riding, and called it, waving the pennon of his flag.

(For the carriage with the bier) there was a pall, and attached to it a fringe made of black cloth, like a lower garment, serving as a curtain (to the temporary coffin), and the whole was made into a sort of house by a covering of white brocade. With this they travelled (back to his state), and on arriving at the gate of the temple, without removing the (curtain) wall, they entered and went straight to the place where the coffining was to take place. The pall was removed at the outside of the door.

2. When a Great officer or an ordinary officer died on the road, (one) got up on the left end of the nave of his carriage, and called back his soul, waving his pennon. If he died in his lodging, they called the soul back in the same manner as if he had died in his house.

[1. See the introductory notice, vol. xxvii, page 34.

2. The public lodging assigned to him in the state where he was.]

In the case of a Great officer they made a pall of cloth, and so proceeded homewards. On arriving at the house, they removed the pall, took the (temporary) coffin on a handbarrow, entered the gate, and proceeding to the eastern steps, there halted and removed the barrow, after which they took the body up the steps, right to the place where it was to be coffined.

The pall–house made over the body of an ordinary officer was made of the phragmites rush; and the fringe for a curtain below of the typha.

4. In every announcement of a death to the ruler it was said, 'Your lordship's minister, so and so, has died. When the announcement was from a parent, a wife, or an eldest son, it was said, 'Your lordship's minister, my ——–, has died.' In an announcement of the death of a ruler to the ruler of another state, it was said, 'My unworthy ruler has ceased to receive his emoluments. I venture to announce it to your officers[1].' If the announcement were about the death of his wife, it was said, 'The inferior partner of my poor ruler has ceased to receive her emoluments.' On the death of a ruler's eldest son, the announcement ran, 'The heir–Son of my unworthy ruler, so and so, has died.'

5. When an announcement of the death of a Great officer was sent to another of the same grade, in the same state, it was said, 'So and so has ceased to receive his emoluments.' The same terms were employed when the announcement was to an ordinary officer. When it was sent to the ruler of another state, it ran, 'Your lordship's outside minister,

[1. Not daring to communicate the evil tidings directly to the ruler.]

my poor Great officer, so and so, has died.' If it were to one of equal degree (in the other state), it was said, 'Sir, your outside servant, our poor Great officer, has ceased to receive his emoluments, and I am sent here to inform you.' If it were to an ordinary officer, the announcement was made in the same terms.

6. In the announcement of the death of an ordinary officer to the same parties, it was made in the same–style, only that 'So and so has died,' was employed in all the cases.

7. A Great officer had his place in the lodgings about the palace, till the end of the mourning rites (for a ruler), while another officer returned to his home on the completion of a year. An ordinary officer had his place in the same lodgings. A Great officer occupied the mourning shed; another officer, the unplastered apartment[1].

8. In the mourning for a cousin, either paternal or maternal, who had not attained to the rank of a Great officer, a Great officer wore the mourning appropriate

[1. Two places of lodging about the palace are mentioned, here the mourning shed, and the unplastered apartment. Both these appear to have been in the courtyard, outside the palace itself; the former, a hut, formed by trees and branches of trees, placed against the wall on the east, with the most slender provision for accommodation and comfort; the latter, an apartment in some other place, made of unburnt bricks, and unplastered, more commodious, but nearly as destitute of comfort. In the former, the chief mourners 'afflicted themselves,' while those whose mourning was not so intense occupied the other.

The ordinary officer, who returned home at the end of a year, is supposed to hive had his charge in some town at a distance from court, where his presence could no longer be dispensed with; and the other, who occupies the unplastered apartment to the end of the rites, to have been employed at the court.]

for an ordinary officer; and an ordinary officer, in mourning similarly for a cousin on either side who had been a Great officer, wore the same mourning.

9. The son of a Great officer by his wife proper wore the mourning appropriate for a Great officer.

10. The son of a Great officer by any other member of his harem, who was himself a Great officer wore for his father or mother the mourning of a Great officer; but his Place was only the same as that of a son by the proper wife who was not a Great officer.

11. When the son of an ordinary officer had become a Great officer, his parents could not preside at his mourning rites. They made his son do so; and if he had no son, they appointed some one to perform that part, and be the representative of the deceased.

12. When they were divining by the tortoise-shell about the grave and the day of interment of a Great officer, the officer superintending (the operation) wore an upper robe of sackcloth, with (strips of) coarser cloth (across the chest), and a girdle of the same and the usual mourning shoes. His cap was of black material, without any fringe. The diviner wore a skin cap.

13. If the stalks were employed, then the manipulator wore a cap of plain silk, and the long robe. The reader of the result wore his court robes.

14. At the mourning rites for a Great officer (preparatory to the interment), the horses were brought out. The man who brought them wailed, stamped, and went out. After this (the son) folded up the offerings, and read the list (of the gifts that had been sent).

15. At the mourning rites for a Great officer, one from the department of the chief superintendent of the ancestral temple assisted (the presiding mourner), and one from that of the assistant superintendent put the question to the tortoise–shell, which was then manipulated in the proper form by the diviner.

16. In calling back (the soul of) a feudal lord, they used the robe which had first been conferred on him, with the cap and corresponding robes, varying according to the order of his nobility.

17. (In calling back the soul of) a friends wife, they used the black upper robe with a purple border, or that with pheasants embroidered on it in various colours; both of them lined with white crape.

18. (In calling back that of) the wife of a high noble, they used the upper robe of light green, worn on her first appointment to that position, and lined with white crape; (in calling back that of the wife of) a Great officer of the lowest grade, the upper robe of plain white. (The souls of other wives were called back) by parties with the same robe as in the case of an ordinary officer.

19. In the calling back, they stood (with their faces to the north), inclining to the west[1].

20. (To the pall over the coffin of a Great officer) there was not attached the (curtain of) yellow silk with pheasants on it, descending below the (bamboo) catch for water.

21. (The tablet of a grandson who had been) a Great officer was placed (in the shrine of his grandfather who had (only) been an officer; but not if he

[1. Paragraph 18 in the ordinary editions is before 16. The tablets must have been confused, and were, perhaps, defective.]

had only been an officer, and the grandfather a Great officer. In that case, the tablet was placed in the shrine of a brother of the grandfather (who had only been an officer). If there were no such brother, (it was placed in the shrine of their high ancestor), according to the regular order of relationship. Even if his grand–parents were alive, it was so.

22. The (tablet of a) wife was placed after that of the wife (of the principal of the shrine), in which her husband's tablet was placed. If there had been no such wife, it was placed in the shrine of the wife of the high ancestor, according to the regular order of relationship. The (tablet of a) concubine was placed in the shrine of her husband's grandmother (concubine). If there had been no such concubine, then (it was placed in that of the concubine of the high ancestor) according to the regular order of relationship.

23. (The tablet of) an unmarried son was placed in the shrine of his grandfather, and was used at sacrifices. That of an unmarried daughter was placed in the shrine of her grandmother, but was not used at sacrifices. The (tablet of) the son of a ruler was placed in the shrine of (one of) the sons (of his grandfather), that grandfather having also been a ruler.

24. When a ruler died, his eldest son was simply styled son (for that year), but he was treated (by other rulers) as the ruler.

25. If one, after wearing for a year the mourning and cap proper to the three years for a parent, met with the death of a relative for whom he had to wear the mourning of nine months, he changed it for the hempen–cloth proper to the nine months; but he did not change the staff and shoes.

26. In mourning for a parent, (after a year) the sackcloth of the nine months' mourning is preferred; but if there occurred the placing in its shrine of the tablet of a brother who had died prematurely, the cap and other mourning worn during that first year was worn in doing so. The youth who had died prematurely was called 'The Bright Lad,' and (the mourner said), 'My so and so,' without naming him. This was treating him with reference to his being in the spirit–state.

27. In the case of brothers living in different houses, when one first heard of the death of another, he might reply to the messenger simply with a wail. His first step then was to put on the sackcloth, and the girdle with dishevelled edges. If, before he had put on the sackcloth, he hurried off to the mourning rites, and the presiding mourner had not yet adjusted his head–band and girdle, in the case of the deceased being one for whom he

had to mourn for five months, he completed that term along with the presiding. mourner. If nine months were due to the deceased, he included the time that had elapsed since he assumed the sackcloth and girdle.

28. The master, presiding at the mourning rites for a concubine, himself conducted the placing of her tablet (in its proper shrine). At the sacrifices at the end of the first and second years, he employed her son to preside at them. The sacrifice at her offering did not take place in the principal apartment.

29. A ruler did not stroke the corpse of a servant or a concubine.

30. Even after the wife of a ruler was dead, the concubines (of the harem) wore mourning for her relatives. If one of them took her place (and acted as mistress of the establishment), she did not wear mourning for the relatives[1].

PART II.

1. If one heard of the mourning rites for a cousin for whom he had to wear mourning for nine months or more, when he looked in the direction of the place where those rites were going on, he wailed. If he were going to accompany the funeral to the grave, but did not get to the house in time, though he met the presiding mourner returning, he himself went on to the grave. The president at the mourning rites for a cousin, though the relationship might not have been near, also presented the sacrifice of Repose.

2. On all occasions of mourning, if, before the mourning robes had all been completed, any one arrived to offer condolences, (the president) took the proper place, wailed, bowed to the visitor, and leaped.

3. At the wailing for a Great officer, another of the same rank, wore the conical cap, with a sackcloth band round it. He wore the same also when engaged with the coffining.

If he had on the cap of dolichos–cloth in mourning for his own wife or son, and were called away to the lighter mourning for a distant relative, he put on the conical cap and band.

4. (In wailing for) an eldest son, he carried a staff, but not for that son's son; he went without it

[1. This lady took the deceased wife's place, and performed many of the duties; but she bad not the position of wife. Anciently, a feudal ruler could only, in all his life, have one wife, one lady, that is, to be called by that name.]

to the place of wailing. (An eldest son), going to wail for his wife, if his parents were alive, did not carry a staff, nor bow so as to lay his forehead on the ground. If (only) his mother were alive, he did not lay his forehead to the ground. Where such a prostration should have taken place, as in the case of one who brought a gift with his condolence, an ordinary bow was made.

5. (An officer) who had left a feudal prince and gone into the service of a Great officer did not on the lord's death return and wear mourning for him; nor did one who had left a Great officer to serve a prince, return to mourn on the death of the former.

6. The strings of the mourning cap served to distinguish it from one used on a festive occasion. The silk cap worn after a year's mourning, and belonging to that for three years, had such strings, and the seam of it was on the right. That worn in the mourning of five months, and a still shorter time, was seamed on the left. The cap of the shortest mourning had a tassel of reddish silk. The ends of the girdle in the mourning of nine months and upward hung loose.

7. Court robes were made with fifteen skeins (1200 threads) in the warp. Half that number made the coarse cloth for the shortest mourning, which then was glazed by being steeped with ashes.

8. In sending presents to one another for the use of the dead, the princes of the states sent their carriages of the second class with caps and robes. They did not send their carriages of the first class, nor the robes which they had themselves received (from the king).

9. The number of (small) carriages sent (to the grave) was according to that of the parcels of flesh to be Conveyed. Each one had a pall of coarse cloth. All round were ornamental figures. These parcels were placed at the four corners of the coffin.

10. (Sometimes) rice was sent, but Yû–dze said that such an offering was contrary to rule. The food put down (by the dead) in mourning was only dried meat and pickled.

11. At the sacrifices (after the sacrifice of Repose), the mourner styled himself 'The filial son,' or 'The filial grandson;' at the previous rites, 'The grieving son,' or 'The grieving grandson.'

12. In the square upper garment of the mourner and the sackcloth over it, and in the carriage in which he rode to the grave, there was no difference of degree.

13. The white cap of high (antiquity) and the cap of black cloth were both without any ornamental fringe. The azure–coloured and that of white silk with turned–up rim had such a fringe.

14. A Great officer wore the cap with the square top when assisting at a sacrifice of his ruler; but that of skin when sacrificing at his own shrines. An ordinary officer used the latter in his ruler's temple, and the cap (of dark cloth) in his own. As an officer wore the skin cap, when going in person to meet his bride, he might also use it at his own shrines.

15. The mortar for the fragrant herbs, in making sacrificial spirits, was made of cypress wood, and the pestle of dryandria. The ladle (for lifting out the flesh) was of mulberry wood, three, some say five, cubits long. The scoop used in addition was of mulberry, three cubits long, with its handle and end carved.

16. The girdle over the shroud used for a prince or a Great officer was of five colours; that used for another officer, only of two.

17. The must (put into the grave) was made from the malt of rice. There were the jars (for it and other liquids), the baskets (for the millet), and the boxes (in which these were placed). These were placed outside the covering of the coffin; and then the tray for the mats was put in.

18. The spirit–tablet (which had been set up over the coffin) was buried after the sacrifice of Repose.

19. (The mourning rites for) all wives were according to the rank of their husbands.

20. (Visitors who had arrived) during the slighter dressing of the corpse, the more complete dressing, or the opening (the enclosure where the coffin was), were all saluted and bowed to (after these operations were finished).

21. At the wailing morning and evening, (the coffin) was not screened from view. When the bier had been removed, the curtain was no more suspended.

22. When the ruler came to condole, after the carriage with its coffin (had reached the gate of the temple), the presiding mourner bowed towards him with his face towards the east, and moving to the right of the gate, leaped there, with his face towards the north. Going outside, he waited till the ruler took his departure and bade him go back, after which he put down (by the bier the gifts which the ruler had brought).

23. When Dze–kâo was fully dressed after his death, first, there were the upper and lower garments both wadded with floss silk, and over them a suit of black with a purple border below; next, there was a. suit of white made square and straight, (the suit belonging to) the skin cap; next, that belonging to the skin cap like the colour of a sparrow's head; and next, (that belonging to) the dark–coloured cap, with the square top. Zang–dze said, 'In such a dressing there should be nothing of woman's dress.'

24. When an officer died on some commission, upon which he had gone for his ruler, if the death took place in a public hotel, they called his soul back; if in a private hotel, they did not do so. By a public hotel was meant a ruler's palace, or some other building, erected by him, and by a private hotel, the house of a noble, a Great officer, or an officer below that rank[1].

25. (On the death of) a ruler, there is the leaping for him for seven days in succession; and on that of a Great officer, it lasts for five days. The women take their share in this expression of grief at intervals, between the presiding mourner and his visitors. On the death of an ordinary officer, it lasts for three days; the women taking their part in the same way.

26. In dressing the corpse of a ruler, there is first put on it the upper robe with the dragon; next, a dark–coloured square–cut suit; next, his court–robes; next, the white lower garment with gathers; next, a purple–coloured lower garment; next, a sparrow–head

[1. It is generally supposed that the Dze–kâo here was the disciple of Confucius, so styled, and also known as Mo Khâi; but the dressing here is that of the corpse of a Great officer, and there is no evidence that the disciple ever attained to that rank; and I am inclined to doubt, with Kiang Kâo–hsî and others, whether the party in the text may not have been another Dze–kâo. The caps of the last three suits are understood to be used for the suits themselves, with which they were generally worn. Zang–dze's condemnation of the dressing was grounded on the purple border of one of the articles in the first suit. See Analects X, 4.]

skin cap; next, the dark–coloured cap with the square top; next, the robe given on his first investiture; next, a girdle of red and green; over which was laid out the great girdle.

27. At the slight dressing of the corpse the son (or the presiding mourner) wore the band of sackcloth about his head. Rulers, Great officers, and ordinary officers agreed in this.

28. When the ruler came to see the great dressing of the corpse, as he was ascending to the hall, the Shang priest spread the mat (afresh), and proceeded to the dressing.

29. The gifts (for the dead, and to be placed in the grave), contributed by the people of Lo, consisted of three rolls of dark–coloured silk, and two of light red, but they were (only) a cubit in width, and completing the length of (one) roll[1].

30. When one came (from another ruler) with a message of condolence, he took his place outside, on the west of the gate, with his face to the east. The chief officer attending him was on the south–east of him, with his face to the north, inclining to the west, and west from the gate. The orphan mourner, with his face to the west, gave his instructions to the officer waiting on him, who then went to the visitor and said, 'My orphaned master has sent me to ask why you have given yourself this trouble,' to which the visitor replies, 'Our ruler has sent me to ask for your master in his trouble.' With this reply the officer returned to the mourner and reported it,

[1. This paragraph, which it is not easy to construe or interpret, is understood to be condemnatory of a stinginess in the matter spoken of, which had begun in the Lû. The rule had been that such pieces of silk should be twenty–five cubits wide, and eighteen cubits long.]

returning and saying, 'My orphaned master is waiting for you.' On this the visitor advanced. The mourning host then went up to the reception hall by the steps on the east, and the visitor by those on the west. The latter, with his face to the east, communicated his message, saying, 'Our ruler has heard of the bereavement you have sustained, and has sent me to ask for you in your sorrows.' The mourning son then bowed to him, kneeling with his forehead to the ground. The messenger then descended the steps, and returned to his place.

31. The attendant charged with the jade for the mouth of the deceased, and holding it in his hands flat round piece of jade—communicated his instructions, saying, 'Our ruler has sent me with the gem for the mouth.' The officer in waiting went in and reported the message, then returning and saying, 'Our orphaned master is waiting for you.' The bearer of the gem then advanced, ascended the steps, and communicated his message. The son bowed to him, with his forehead to the ground. The bearer then knelt, and placed the gem on the south–east of the coffin, upon a phragmites mat; but if the interment had taken place, on a typha mat. After this, he descended the steps, and returned to his place, The major–domo, in his court robes, but still wearing his mourning shoes, then ascended the western steps, and kneeling with his face to the west, took up the piece of jade, and descending by the same steps, went towards the east (to deposit it in the proper place).

32. The officer charged with the grave–clothes said, 'Our ruler has sent me with the grave–clothes.' The officer in waiting, having gone in and reported, returned and said, 'Our orphaned master is waiting for you.' Then the other took up first the cap with the square top and robes, with his left hand holding the neck of the upper garment, and with his right the waist. He advanced, went up to the hall, and communicated his message, saying, 'Our ruler has sent me with the grave–clothes.' The son bowed to him, with his forehead to the ground; and when the bearer laid down the things on the east of the coffin, he then went down, and received the skin cap of the sparrow's–head colour, with the clothes belonging to it inside the gate, under the eaves. These he presented with the same forms; then the skin cap and clothes which he received in the middle of the courtyard; then the court robes; then the dark–coloured, square–cut garments, which he received at the foot of the steps on the west. When all these presentations were made, five men from the department of the major–domo took the things up, and going down the steps on the west, went away with them to the–east. They all took them up with their faces towards the west.

33. The chief of the attendants (of the messenger) had charge of the carriage and horses, and with a long symbol of jade in his hand communicated his message, saying, 'Our ruler has sent me to present the carriage and horses.' The officer in waiting went in and informed the presiding mourner, and returned with the message, 'The orphan, so and so, is waiting for you.' The attendant then had the team of yellow horses and the grand carriage exhibited in the central courtyard, with the front to the north; and with the symbol in hand he communicated his message. His grooms were all below, on the west of the carriage. The son bowed to him, with his forehead to the ground. He then knelt, and placed his symbol in the corner, on the southeast of the coffin. The major–domo then took the symbol up, and proceeded with it to the east.

34, The message was always delivered with the face turned towards the coffin, and the son always bowed to the attendant charged with it, with his forehead down to the ground. The attendant then knelt with his face to the west, and deposited his gift (or its representative). The major–domo and his employés ascended by the steps on the west to take these up, and did so with their faces towards the west, descending (again) by the same steps.

The attendant charged with the carriage and horses went out, and returned to his place outside the gate.

35. The chief visitor then, (wishing) to perform the ceremony of wailing, said, 'My ruler, being engaged in the services of his own ancestral temple, could not come and take part in your rites, and has sent me, so and so, his old servant, to assist in holding the rope.' The officer in waiting (reported his request), and returned with the message, 'The orphan, so and so, is waiting for you.' The messenger then entered and took his place on the right of the gate. His attendants all followed him, and stood on his left, on the cast. The superintendent of ceremonies introduced the visitor, and went up on the hall, and received his ruler's instructions, then descending and saying, ' The orphan ventures to decline the honour which you propose, and begs you to return to your place.' The messenger, however, replied. 'My ruler charged me that I should not demean myself as a visitor or guest, and I venture to decline doing as you request.' The other then reported this reply, and returned, and told the messenger that the orphan firmly declined the honour which he proposed, and repeated the request that he would return to his place. The messenger repeated his reply, saying that he also firmly declined (to return to his place). The same message from the mourner was repeated, and the same reply to it, (after

which) the mourner said, 'Since he thus firmly declines what I request, I will venture respectfully to comply with his wish.'

The messenger then stood on the west of the gate, and his attendants on his left, facing the west. The orphaned mourner descended by the steps on the east, and bowed to him, after which they both ascended and wailed, each of them leaping three times in response to each other. The messenger then went out, escorted by the mourner outside of the gate, who then bowed to him, with his forehead down to the ground.

36. When the ruler of a state had mourning rites in hand for a parent, (any officer who was mourning for a parent) did not dare to receive visits of condolence (from another state).

37. The female relatives of the exterior kept in their apartments; the servants spread the mats; the officer of prayer, who used the Shang forms, spread out the girdle, sash, and upper coverings; the officers washed their hands, standing on the north of the vessel; they then removed the corpse to the place where it was to be dressed. When the dressing was finished, the major–domo reported it. The son then leant on the coffin and leaped. The wife with her face to the east, also leant on it, kneeling; and then she got up and leaped[1].

38. There are three things in the mourning rites for an officer which agree with those used on the death of the son of Heaven:—the torches kept burning all night (when the coffin is to be conveyed to the grave); the employment of men to draw the carriage; and the keeping of the road free from all travellers on it.

[1. See the twelfth paragraph in the second, section of next Book. it appears here, with some alteration, by mistake.]

SECTION II.

PART I.

1. When a man was wearing mourning for his father, if his mother died before the period was completed, he put off the mourning for his father (and assumed that proper for his

mother). He put on, however, the proper dress when sacrificial services required it; but when they were over[1], he returned to the mourning (for his mother).

2. When occasion occurred for wearing the mourning for uncles or cousins, if it arrived during the period of mourning for a parent, then the previous mourning was not laid aside, save when the sacrificial services in these cases required it to be so; and when they were finished, the mourning for a parent was resumed.

3. If during the three years' mourning (there occurred also another three years' mourning for the eldest son), then after the coarser girdle of the Kiung hemp had been assumed in the latter case, the sacrifices at the end of the first or second year's mourning for a parent might be proceeded with.

4. When a grandfather had died, and his grandson also died before the sacrifices at the end of the first or second year had been performed, (his spirit–tablet) was still placed next to the grandfather's.

5. When a mourner, while the coffin was in the house, heard of the death of another relative at a

[1. That is, the sacrifices regularly presented at the end of the first and second year from the death. The translation here and in the next three paragraphs, if it were from an Aryan or Semitic language, could not be said to be literal; but it correctly represents the ideas of the author.]

distance, he went to another apartment and wailed for him. (Next day), he entered where the coffin was, and put down the offerings (to the deceased), after which he went out, changed his clothes, went to the other apartment, and repeated the ceremony of the day before.

6. When a Great officer or another officer was about to take part in a sacrifice at his ruler's, if, after the inspection of the washing of the vessels to be used, his father or mother died, he still went to the sacrifice; but took his place in a different apartment. After the sacrifice he put off his (sacrificial) dress, went outside the gate of the palace, wailed, and returned to his own house. In other respects he acted as he would have done in hurrying to the mourning rites. If the parent's death took place before the inspection of

the washing, he sent a messenger to inform the ruler of his position; and when he returned, proceeded to wail (for his deceased parent).

When the death that occurred was that of an uncle, aunt, or cousin, if he had received the previous notice to fast, he went to the sacrifice; and when it was over, he went out at the ruler's gate, put off his (sacrificial) dress, and returned to his own house. In other respects he acted as if he had been hurrying to the mourning rites. If the deceased relative lived under the same roof with him, he took up his residence in other apartments[1].

[1. The Khien–lung editors doubt the genuineness of this last sentence. A commissioned officer, they say, and much more a Great officer, occupied his own residence, and had left the family at home; and they fail to see how the condition supposed could' have existed.]

7. Zang dze asked, 'When a high minister or Great officer is about to act the part of the personator of the dead at a sacrifice by his ruler, and has received instructions to pass the night previous in solemn vigil, if there occur in his own family occasion for him to wear the robe of hemmed sackcloth, what is he to do?' Confucius said, 'The rule is for him to leave his own house, and lodge in the ruler's palace till the service (for the ruler) is accomplished.

8. Confucius said, 'When the personator of the dead comes forth in his leathern cap, or that with the square top, ministers, Great officers, and other officers, all should descend from their carriages when he passes. He should bow forward to them, and he should (also) have people going before him (to notify his approach, that people may get out of the way[1]).

9. During the mourning rites for a parent, when the occasion for one of the sacrifices was at hand, if a death occurred in the family of a brother or cousin, the sacrifice was postponed till the burial of the dead had taken place. If the cousin or brother were an inmate of the same palace with himself, although the death were that of a servant or concubine, the party postponed his sacrifice in this way, At the sacrifice the mourner went up and descended the steps with only one foot on each, all assisting him, doing the same. They did so even for the sacrifice of Repose, and to put the spirit–tablet in its place.

10. From the feudal rulers down to all officers, at the sacrifice at the end of the first year's mourning

[1. See vol. xxvii, Page 341, Paragraph 26, which is here repeated.]

for a parent, when the chief mourner took the cup offered to him by the chief among the visitors, he raised it to his teeth, while the visitors, brothers, and cousins all sipped the cups presented to them. After the sacrifice at the end of the second year, the chief mourner might sip his cup, while all the visitors, brothers, and cousins might drink off their cups.

11. The attendants at the sacrifices during the funeral rites give notice to the visitors to present the offerings, of which, however, they did not afterwards partake.

12. Dze–kung asked about the rites of mourning (for parents), and the Master said, 'Reverence is the most important thing; grief is next to it; and emaciation is the last. The face should wear the appearance of the inward feeling, and the demeanour and carriage should be in accordance with the dress.'

He begged to ask about the mourning for a brother, and the Master said, 'The rites of mourning for a brother are to be found in the tablets where they are written.'

13. A superior man will not interfere with the mourning of other men to diminish it, nor will he do so with his own mourning[1].

14. Confucius said, 'Shâo–lien and Tâ–lien demeaned themselves skilfully during their mourning (for their parents). During the (first) three days they were alert; for the (first) three months they manifested no weariness; for the (first) year they were full of grief; for the (whole) three years they were

[1. The Khien–lung editors think paragraph 13 is out of place, and would place it farther on, after paragraph 43.]

sorrowful. (And yet) they belonged to one of the rude tribes on the East[1]'.

15. During the three years of mourning (for his father), (a son) might speak, but did riot discourse; might reply, but did not ask questions. In the shed or the unplastered apartment he sat (alone), nobody with him. While occupying that apartment, unless there were some occasion for him to appear before his mother, he did not enter the door (of the house). On all occasions of wearing the sackcloth with its edges even, he occupied the unplastered apartment, and not the shed. To occupy the shed was the severest form in mourning.

16. (The grief) in mourning for a wife was like that for an uncle or aunt; that for a father's sister or one's own sister was like that for a cousin; that for any of the three classes of minors dying prematurely was as if they had been full–grown.

17. The mourning for parents is taken away (at the end of three years), (but only) its external symbols; the mourning for brothers (at the end of one year), (and also) internally.

18. (The period of mourning) for ruler's mother or wife is the same as that for brothers. But (beyond) what appears in the countenance is this, that (in the latter case) the mourners do not eat and drink (as usual).

19. After a man has put off the mourning (for his father), if, when walking along the road, he sees one like (his father), his eyes look startled. If he hear one with the same name, his heart is agitated.

[1. Shâo–lien; see Analects XVIII, 8, 3, and 'Narratives of the School,' Article 43.]

In condoling with mourners on occasion of a death, and inquiring for one who is ill, there will be something in his face and distressed manner different from other men. He who is thus affected is fit to wear 'the three years' mourning. So far as other mourning is concerned, he may walk right on (without anything) having such an effect on him.

20. The sacrifice at the end of the second[1], year is signalized by the principal mourner putting off his mourning dress. The evening (before), he announces the time for it, and puts on his court robes, which he then wears at the sacrifice.

21. Dze–yû said, 'After the sacrifice at the end of the second year, although the mourner should not wear the cap of white silk, (occasions may occur when) he must do so[2]. Afterwards he resumes the proper dress.'

22. (At the mourning rites of an officer), if, when he had bared his breast, a Great officer arrived (on a visit of condolence), although he might be engaged in the leaping, he put a stop to it, and went to salute and bow to him. Returning then, he resumed his leaping and completed it, after which he readjusted his dress and covered his breast.

In the case of a visit from another officer, he went on with his leaping, completed it, readjusted his upper dress, and then went to salute and bow to him, without having occasion to resume and complete the leaping.

23. At the sacrifice of Repose for a Great officer of the highest grade, there were offered a boar and a

[1. So, Khan Kâo.

2. Such as receiving the condolences of visitors on account of some other occasion of mourning.]

ram; at the conclusion of the wailing, and at the placing of his spirit–tablet, there was, in addition, the bull. On the similar occasions for a Great officer of the lowest grade, there was in the first case a single victim, and in the others the boar and the ram.

24. In consulting the tortoise–shell about the burial and sacrifice of Repose, the style of the petition was as follows:—A son or grandson spoke of himself as 'the sorrowing,' (when divining about his father or grandfather); a husband (divining about his wife) said, 'So and so for so and so;' an elder brother about a younger brother, simply said, 'So and so;' a younger brother about an elder brother said, 'For my elder brother, so and so.'

25. Anciently, noble and mean all carried staffs. (On one occasion) Shû–sun Wû–shû[1], when going to court, saw a wheelwright put his staff through the nave of a wheel, and turn it round. After this (it was made a rule that) only men of rank should carry a staff

,26. (The custom of) making a hole in the napkin (covering the face of the dead) by which to introduce what was put into the mouth, was begun by Kung yang Kiâ[2].

27. What were the grave–clothes (contributed to the dead)? The object of them was to cover the body. From the enshrouding to the slighter dressing, they were not put on, and

the figure of the body was seen. Therefore the corpse was first enshrouded, and afterwards came the grave–clothes.

28. Some one asked Zang–dze, 'After sending

[1. A Great officer of Lû, about B.C. 500.

2. We do not find anything about this man elsewhere.]

away to the grave the offerings to the dead, we wrap up what up remains;—is this not like a man, after partaking of a meal, wrapping–what is left (to take with him)? Does a gentleman do such a thing? Zang–dze said, 'Have you not seen what is done at a great feast? At a great feast, given by a Great officer, after all have partaken, he rolls up what is left on the stands for the three animals, and sends it to the lodgings of his guests. When a son treats his parents in this way as his (honoured) guests, it is an expression of his grief (for their loss). Have you, Sir, not seen what is done at a great feast?'

29. 'Excepting at men's funeral rites, do they make such inquiries and present such gifts as they then do? At the three years' mourning, the mourner bows to his visitors in the manner appropriate to the occasion; at the mourning of a shorter period, he salutes them in the usual way

30. During the three years' mourning, if any one sent wine or flesh to the mourner, be received it after declining it thrice; he received it in his sackcloth and band. If it came from the ruler with a message from him, he did not presume to decline it;—he received it and presented it (in his ancestral temple).

One occupied with such mourning did not send any gift, but when men sent gifts to him he received them. When engaged in the mourning rites for an uncle, cousin, or brother, and others of a shorter period, after the wailing was concluded, he might send gifts to others.

31. Hsien–dze said, 'The pain occasioned by the

[1. See vol. xxvii, pp. 122–3, paragraph 5. There is probably something wanting at the beginning of this paragraph.]

mourning for three years is like that of beheading; that arising from the one year's mourning, is like the stab from a sharp weapon.'

32. During the one year's mourning, in the eleventh month, they put on the dress of silk, which was called lien; in the thirteenth month they offered the hsiang sacrifice, and in the same month that called than;—which concluded the mourning.

During the mourning for three years, even though they had occasion to assume the dress proper for the nine months' mourning, they did not go to condole (with the other mourners). From the feudal lords down to all officers, if they bad occasion to dress and go to wail (for a relative newly deceased), they did so in the dress proper to the mourning for him, After putting on the lien silk, they paid visits of condolence.

33. When one was occupied with the nine months' mourning, if the burial had been performed, he might go and condole with another mourner, retiring after he had wailed without waiting for any other part of the mourner's proceedings.

During the mourning for one year, if before the burial one went to condole with another in the same district, he withdrew after he had wailed, without waiting for the rest of the proceedings.

If condoling during the mourning for nine months, he waited to see the other proceedings, but did not take part in them.

During the mourning for five months or three months, he waited to assist at the other proceedings, but did not take part in the (principal) ceremony

[1. That is, in putting down the offerings to the deceased.]

34. When one (was condoling with) another whom he had been accustomed to pass with a hasty step[1], (at the interment of his dead relative), he retired when the bier had passed out from the gate of the temple. If they had been on bowing terms, he retired when they had reached the station for wailing. If they had been in the habit of exchanging inquiries, he retired after–the coffin was let down into the grave. if they had attended court together, he went back to the house with the other, and wailed with him. If they were intimate friends, he did not retire till after the sacrifice of Repose, and the placing of the

spirit tablet of the deceased in the shrine.

35. Condoling friends did not (merely) follow the principal mourner. Those who were forty (or less) held the ropes when the coffin was let down into the grave. Those of the same district who were fifty followed him back to the house and wailed; and those who were forty waited till the grave was filled up.

36. During mourning, though the food might be bad, the mourner was required to satisfy his hunger with it. If for hunger he had to neglect anything, this was contrary to the rules. If he through satiety forgot his sorrow, that also was contrary to the rules. It was a distress to the wise men (who made the rules) to think that a mourner should not see or hear distinctly; should not walk correctly or be unconscious of his occasion for sorrow; and therefore (they enjoined) that a mourner, when ill, should drink wine and eat flesh; that people of fifty should do nothing to bring on emaciation; that at sixty they should not be emaciated; that at seventy they should drink

[1. This was a mark of respect. Compare Analects IX, 9.]

liquor and eat flesh:—all these rules were intended as preventives against death.

37. If one, while in mourning, was invited by another to eat with him, he did not go while wearing the nine months' mourning or that of a shorter period; if the burial had taken place, he might go to another party's house. If that other party belonged to his relative circle, and wished him to eat with him, he might do so; if he did not belong to that circle, he did not eat with him.

38. While wearing the mourning of nine months, one might eat vegetables and fruits, and drink water and congee, using no salt or cream. If he could not eat dry provisions, he might use salt or cream with them.

39. Confucius said, 'If a man have a sore on his body, he should bathe. If he have a wound on his head, he should wash it. If he be ill, he should drink liquor and eat flesh. A superior man will not emaciate himself so as to be ill. If one die from such emaciation, a superior man will say of him that he has failed in the duty of a son.'

40. Excepting when following the carriage with the bier to the grave, and returning from it, one was not seen on. the road with the mourning cap, which was used instead of the ordinary one.

41. During the course of mourning, from that worn for five months and more, the mourner did not wash his head or bathe, excepting for the sacrifice of Repose, the placing the spirit–tablet in the shrine, the assuming the dress of lien silk, and the sacrifice at the end of a year.

42. During mourning rites, when the sackcloth with the edges even was worn, after the burial, if one asked an interview with the mourner, he saw him, but he himself did not ask to see any person. He might do so when wearing the mourning of five months. When wearing that for nine months, he did not carry the introductory present in his hand (when seeking an interview). It was only when wearing the mourning for a parent that the mourner did not avoid seeing any one, (even) while the teats were running from him.

43. A man while wearing the mourning for three years might execute any orders of government after the sacrifice at the end of a year. One mourning for a year, might do so when the wailing was ended; one mourning for nine months, after the burial; one mourning for five months or three, after the encoffining and dressing.

44. .Zang Shen asked Zang–dze, saying, 'In wailing for a parent, should one do so always in the same voice?' The answer was, 'When a child has lost its mother on the road, is it possible for it to think about the regular and proper voice?'

PART II.

1. After the wailing was ended, there commenced the avoiding of certain names. (An officer) did not use the name of his (paternal) grandfather or grandmother, of his father's brothers or uncles; of his father's aunts or sisters. Father and son agreed in avoiding all these names. The names avoided by his mother the son avoided in the house. Those avoided by his wife he did not use when at. her side. If among them there were names which had been borne by his own paternal great–grandfather or great–grand–uncles, he avoided them (in all places).

2. When (the time for) capping (a young man) came during the time of the mourning rites, though they were those for a parent, the ceremony might be performed. After being capped in the proper place, the subject went in, wailed and leaped,—three times each bout, and then came out again.

3. At the end of the nine months' mourning, it was allowable to cap a son or to marry a daughter. A father at the end of the five months' mourning, might cap a son, or marry a daughter, or take a wife (for a son). Although one himself were occupied with the five months' mourning, yet when he had ended the wailing, he might be capped, or take a wife. If it were the five months' mourning for one who had died in the lowest degree of immaturity, he could not do so[1].

4. Whenever one wore the cap of skin with a sackcloth band (in paying a visit of condolence), his upper garment of mourning had the large sleeves.

5. When the father was wearing mourning, a son, who lived in the same house with him, kept away from all music. When the mother was wearing it, the son might listen to music, but not play himself When a wife was wearing it, the son, (her husband), did not play music by her side. When an occasion for the nine months' mourning was about to occur, the lute and cithern were laid aside. If it were only an occasion for the five months' mourning, music was not stopped.

6. When an aunt or sister died (leaving no son), if her husband (also) were dead, and there were no

[1. This paragraph seems to me, as to many of the Chinese critics, irretrievably corrupt or defective.]

brother or cousin in his relative circle, some other of her husband's more distant relatives was employed to preside at her mourning rites. None of a wife's relatives, however near, could preside at them. If no distant relative even of her husband could be found, then a neighbour, on the east or the west, was employed. If no such person (suitable) could be found, then the head man of the neighbourhood presided. Some say, 'One (of her relatives) might preside, but her tablet was placed by that of the (proper) relative of her husband.'

7. The girdle was not used along with the sackcloth band. That band could not be used by one who carried in his hand his jade–token; nor could it be used along with a dress of various colours.

8. On occasions of prohibitions issued by the state (in connexion with the great sacrifices), the wailing ceased; as to the offerings deposited by the coffin, morning and evening, and the repairing to their proper positions, mourners proceeded as usual[1].

9. A lad, when wailing, did not sob or quaver; did not leap; did not carry a staff; did not wear the straw sandals; and did not occupy the mourning shed.

10. Confucius said, 'For grand–aunts the mourning with the edges even is worn, but the feet in leaping are not lifted from the ground. For aunts and sisters the mourning for nine months is worn, but the feet in leaping are lifted from the ground. If a man understands these things, will he not (always) follow, the right forms of ceremonies? Will he not do so?'

[1. The punctuation and place of this short paragraph vary. Its integrity is also doubted.]

11. When the mother of Î Liû died, his assistants in the rites stood on his left; when Î Liû died, they stood on his right. The practice of the assistants (at funeral rites) giving their aid on the right, originated from the case of Î Liû.[1].

12. The mouth of the son of Heaven was stuffed after death with nine shells; that of a feudal lord, with seven; that of a Great officer, with five; and that of an ordinary officer, with three[2].

13. An officer was interred after three months, and the same month the wailing was ended. A Great officer was interred (also) after three months, and after five months the wailing was ended. A prince was interred after five months, and after seven the wailing was ended.

For an officer the sacrifice of Repose was offered three times; for a Great officer, five times; and for a feudal prince, seven times.

14. A feudal lord sent a messenger to offer his condolences; and after that, his contributions for the mouth, the grave–clothes, and the carriage. All these things were transacted on the same day, and in the order thus indicated.

15. When a high minister or Great officer was ill, the ruler inquired about him many times. When an ordinary officer was ill, he inquired about him once. When a Great officer or high minister was buried, the ruler did not eat flesh; when the wailing was finished, he did not have music. When an officer was encoffined, he did not have music.

16. After they had gone up, and made the bier

[1. A minister of duke Mû of Lû, B.C. 409–377.

2. This was not the practice in the Kâu dynasty.]

ready, in the case of the burial of a feudal lord, there were 500 men to draw the ropes. At each of the four ropes they were all gagged. The minister of War superintended the clappers; eight men with these walking on each side of the bier. The chief artizan, carrying a shade of feathers, guided the progress (of the procession). At the burial of a Great officer, after they had gone up and made the bier ready, 300 men drew the ropes; four men with their clappers walked on each side of the bier; and its progress was guided (by the chief artizan) with a reed of white grass in his hand.

17. Confucius said, 'Kwan Kung had carving on the square vessels for holding the grain of his offerings, and red ornaments for his cap; he set up a screen where he lodged on the way, and had a stand of earth on which the cups he had used, in giving a feast, were replaced; he had hills carved on the capitals of his pillars, and. pondweed on the lower pillars supporting the rafters'. He was a worthy Great officer, but made it difficult for his superiors (to distinguish themselves from him).

'An Phing–kung[2], in sacrificing to his father and other progenitors, used only the shoulders of a pig, not large enough to cover the dish. He was a worthy Great officer, but made it difficult for his inferiors (to distinguish themselves from him).

'A superior man will not encroach on (the observances of) those above him, nor put difficulties in the way of those below him.'

[1. See Confucian Analects Ill, 22, and V, 17.

2. A minister of Khî, contemporary with Confucius, distinguished for his simple, and perhaps parsimonious, ways.]

18. Excepting on the death of her father or mother, the wife (of a feudal lord) did not cross the boundaries of the state to pay a visit of condolence. On that occasion she did so, and went back to her original home, where she used the ceremonies of condolence proper to a feudal lord, and she was treated as one. When she arrived, she entered by the women's gate, and went up (to the reception hall) by steps at the side (of the principal steps), the ruler receiving her at the top of the steps on the east. The other ceremonies were the same as those of a guest who hastened to attend the funeral rites.

19. A sister-in-law did not lay the soothing hand on the corpse of her brother-in-law; and vice versâ.

20. There are three things that occasion sorrow to a superior man (who is devoted to learning):—If there be any subject of which he has not heard, and he cannot get to hear of it; if he hear of it, and cannot get to learn it; if he have learned it, and cannot get to carry it out in practice. There are five things that occasion shame to a superior man (who is engaged in governmental duties):—If he occupy an office, and have not well described its duties; if he describe its duties well, but do not carry them into practice; if he have got his office, and lost it again; if he be charged with the care of a large territory, and the people be not correspondingly numerous; if another, in a charge like his own, have more merit than he.

21. Confucius said, 'In bad years they used in their carriages their poorest horses, and in their sacrifices the victims lowest (in the classes belonging to them).'

22. At the mourning rites for Hsü Yû, duke Âi sent Zû Pî to Confucius to learn the rites proper at the mourning for the officer. Those rites were thus committed at that time to writing.

23. Dze-kung having gone to see the agricultural sacrifice at the end of the year, Confucius said to him, 'Zhze, did it give you pleasure?' The answer was, 'The people of the whole state appeared to be mad; I do not know in what I could find pleasure.' The

Master said, 'For their hundred days' labour in the field, (the husbandmen) receive this one day's enjoyment (from the state);—this is what you do not understand. (Even) Wan and Wû could not keep a bow (in good condition), if it were always drawn and never relaxed; nor did they leave it always relaxed and never drawn. To keep it now strung and now unstrung was the way of Wan and Wû.'

24. Mang Hsien–dze said, 'If in the first month at the (winter) solstice it be allowable to offer the (border) sacrifice to God, in the seventh month, at the summer solstice, we may offer the sacrifice in the temple of the ancestor (of our ruling House).' Accordingly Hsien–dze offered that sacrifice to all the progenitors (of the line of Lû) in the seventh month'.

25. The practice of not obtaining from the son of Heaven the confirmation of her dignity for the wife (of the ruler of Lû) began with duke Kâo[2].

[1. Hsien–dze was the honorary title of Kung–sun Mieh, a good officer of Lû, under dukes Wan, Hsüan, Khang, and Hsiang. He must understand him as speaking of the sacrifices of the state, and not of his own.

2. See Confucian Analects VII. 30. Duke Kâo married a lady of Wû, of the same surname with himself, and therefore had not announced the marriage to the king.]

26. The mourning of a ruler and his wife were regulated by the same rules for the ladies of his family married in other states and for those married in his own[1].

27. When the stables of Confucius were burned, and the friends of his district came (to offer their condolences) on account of the fire, he bowed once to the ordinary officers, and twice to the Greater officers;—according to the rule on occasions of mutual condolence.

28. Confucius said, 'Kwan Kung selected two men from among (certain) thieves with whom he was dealing, and appointed them to offices in the state, saying, "They were led astray by bad men with whom they bad associated, but they are proper men themselves." When he died, duke Hwan made these two wear mourning for him. The practice of old servants of a Great officer wearing mourning for him, thus arose from Kwan Kung. But these two men only mourned for him by the duke's orders.'

29. When an officer, in a mistake, used a name to his ruler which should be avoided, he rose to his feet. If he were speaking to any one who had the name that should be avoided with the ruler, he called him by the name given to him on his maturity.

30. (A Great officer) took no part in any seditious movements within his state, and did not try to avoid calamities coming from without.

31. The treatise on the duties of the Chief Internuncius says, 'The length of the long symbol of rank was for a duke, nine inches; for a marquis or

[1. There are differences of opinion as to the meaning of this paragraph, between which it is not easy to decide. It would be tedious to go into an exhibition and discussion of them.]

earl, seven; for a count or baron, five. The width in each case was three inches; and the thickness, half an inch. They tapered to the point for one inch and a half. They were all of jade. The mats for them were made with three different colours, (two rows of each,) six in all.'

32. Duke Âi asked Dze-kâo, 'When did members of your family first begin to be in office?' The answer was) 'My ancestor held a small office under duke Wan[1].'

33. When a temple was completed, they proceeded to consecrate it with the following ceremony:—The officer of prayer, the cook, and the butcher, all wore the cap of leather of the colour of a sparrow's head, and the dark-coloured dress with the purple border. The butcher rubbed the sheep clean, the officer of prayer blessed it, and the cook with his face to the north took it to the pillar and placed it on the south-east of it. Then the butcher took it in his arms, went up on the roof at the middle point between the east and west, and with his face to the south stabbed it, so that the blood ran down in front; and then he descended. At the gate of the temple, and of each of the two side apartments, they used a fowl, one at the gate of each (going up as before and stabbing them). The hair and feathers about the ears were first pulled out under the roof (before the victims were killed). When the fowls were cut at the gates of the temple, and the apartments on each side of it, officers stood, opposite to each gate on the north. When the thing was over, the officer of prayer announced that it

[1. This paragraph is supposed to be defective. Duke Wan was marquis of Lû from B.C. 626 to 609.]

was so, and they all retired, after which he announced it to the ruler, saying, 'The blood–consecration has been performed.' This announcement was made at the door of the back apartment of the temple, inside which the ruler stood in his court–robes, looking towards the south. This concluded the ceremony, and all withdrew[1].

When the great apartment (of the palace) was completed, it was inaugurated (by a feast), but there was no shedding of blood. The consecration by blood of the temple building was the method taken to show how intercourse with the spirits was sought. All the more distinguished vessels of the ancestral temple were consecrated, when completed, by the blood of a young boar.

34. When a feudal lord sent his wife away, she proceeded on her journey to her own state, and was received there with the observances due to a lord's wife. The messenger, accompanying her, then discharged his commission, saying, 'My poor ruler, from his want of ability, was not able to follow her, and take part in the services at your altars and in your ancestral temple. He has, therefore, sent me, so and so, and I venture to inform your officer appointed for the purpose of what he has done.' The officer presiding (on the occasion) replied, 'My poor ruler in his former communication did not lay (her defects) before you, and he does not presume to do anything but respectfully receive your lord's message.' The officers in attendance on the commissioner

[1. This ceremony is also described in the 'Rites of the greater Tâi,' Book X, with some difference in the details. It is difficult, even from the two accounts, to bring the ceremony fully before the mind's eye.]

then set forth the various articles sent with the other the lady on her marriage, and those on side received them.

35. When the wife went away from her husband, she sent a messenger and took leave of him, saying, 'So and so, through her want of ability, is not able to keep on supplying the vessels of grain for your sacrifices, and has sent me, so and so, to, presume to announce this to your attendants.' The principal party (on the other side) replied, 'My son, in his inferiority, does not presume to avoid you punishing him, and dares not but respectfully

receive your orders.' The messenger then retired, the principal party bowing to him, and escorting him. If the father–in–law were alive, then he named him self; if he were dead, an elder brother of the husband acted for him, and the message was given as from him; if there were no elder brother, then it ran as from the husband himself. The message, as given above, was) 'The son of me, so and so, in his inferiority.' (At the other end of the transaction), if the lady were an aunt, an elder sister, or a younger, she was mentioned as such.

36. Confucius said, 'When I was at a meal at Shâo–shih's, I ate to the full. He entertained me courteously, according to the rules. When I was about to offer some in sacrifice, he got up and wished to stop me, saying, "My poor food is not worth being offered in sacrifice." When I was about to take the concluding portions, he got up and wished to stop me, saying, "I would not injure you with my poor provisions[1]."

[1. See pages 20, 21, paragraph 13.]

37. A bundle of silk (in a marriage treaty) contained live double rolls, each double roll being forty cubits in length.

38. At the (first) interview of a wife with her father and mother–in–law, (her husband's) unmarried aunts and sisters all stood below the reception hall, with their faces towards the west, the north being the place of honour. After this interview, she visited all the married uncles of her husband, each in his own apartment.

Although not engaged to be married, the rule was for a young lady to wear the hair–pin;—she was thus treated with the honours of maturity. The (principal) wife managed the ceremony. When she was unoccupied and at ease, she wore her hair without the pin, on each side of her head.

BOOK XIX. SANG TÂ KÎ, OR THE GREATER RECORD OF MOURNING RITES[1]

SECTION I.

1. When the illness was extreme, all about the establishment was swept clean, inside and out. In the case of a ruler or Great officer, the stands, with the martial instruments suspended from them, were removed; in that of an officer, his lute and cithern. The sufferer lay with his head to the east, under the window on the north. His couch was removed (and he was laid on the ground). The clothes ordinarily worn at home were removed, and new clothes substituted for them. (In moving the body) one person took hold of each limb. Males and females changed their dress[2]. Some fine floss was put (on the mouth and nostrils), to make sure that the breath was gone. A man was not permitted to die in the hands of the women, or a woman in the hands of the men.

2. A ruler and his wife both died in the Great chamber, a Great officer and his acknowledged wife in the Proper chamber[3]; the not yet acknowledged

[1. See introductory notice, vol., xxvii, pages 34, 35.

2. The clothes of the dying master and friend were changed; it was right that all about them should also change their dress. The court or best robes were put on, moreover, that inquiring visitors might be properly received.

3. This proper, or 'legitimate' chamber corresponded in the mansion of a Great officer to the Grand chamber in the palace. Connected with the Grand chamber were two smaller apartments. It is mentioned in the Zo Kwan, under B.C. 627, that duke Hsî of Lû died 'in the small apartment;' which has always been understood as discreditable to him.]

wife of a high minister, in an inferior chamber, but the corpse was then removed to the higher chamber. The wives of officers died in their chambers.

3. At (the ceremony of) calling back the soul, if (the deceased were a lord on whose territory) there were forests and copses, the forester arranged the steps (by which to go up on the roof); and if there were no forests, one of the salvage men (employed about the court in menial offices) did so. An officer of low rank performed the ceremony. All who did so employed some of the court robes (of the deceased):—for a ruler, the robe with the descending dragon; for the wife, that with the descending pheasant; for a Great officer,

the dark robe and red skirt; for his recognised wife, the robe of fresh yellow; for an officer, that worn with the cap of deep purple leather; and for his wife, the dark dress with the red border. In all cases they ascended from the east wing to the middle of the roof, where the footing was perilous. Facing the north, they gave three loud calls for the deceased, after which they rolled up the garment they had employed, and cast it down in front, where the curator of the robes received it, and then they themselves descended by the wing on the north–west.

If the deceased were a visitor, and in a public lodging, his soul was called back; if the lodging were private, it was not called back. If he were in the open country, one got up on the left end of the nave of the carriage in which he had been riding, and called it back.

4. The garment which had been used in calling not employed to cover the corpse, the soul back was nor in dressing it. In calling back the soul of a wife, the upper robe with the purple border in which she had been married was not employed. In all cases of calling back the soul, a man was called by his name, and a woman by her designation. Nothing but the wailing preceded the calling the soul back. After that calling they did what was requisite on an occasion of death.

5. Immediately after death, the principal mourners sobbed[1]; brothers and cousins (of the deceased) wailed; his female relatives wailed and leaped.

6. When the dead body (of a ruler) had been placed properly (beneath the window with the head to the south), his son sat (or knelt) on the east; his ministers, Great officers, uncles, cousins, their sons and grandsons, stood (also) on the cast; the multitude of ordinary officers, who had the charge of the different departments, wailed below the hall, facing the north. His wife knelt on the west; the wives, aunts, sisters, their daughters and grand–daughters, whose husbands were of the same surname as he, stood (behind her) on the west; and the wives, his relatives of the same surname, whose position had been confirmed in their relation to their husbands, at the head of all the others married similarly to husbands of other surnames, wailed above in the hall, facing the north.

7. At the mourning rites (immediately after death) of a Great officer, the (son), presiding, knelt on the east, and the wife, presiding, on the west. The

[1. They were too much affected, it is said, to give loud expression to their grief.]

husbands and wives (among the relations) whose positions had been officially confirmed, sat (or knelt); others who had not that confirmation, stood.

At the rites for a deceased officer, the son presiding, uncles, brothers, and cousins, with their sons and grandsons, all sat (or knelt) on the east; the wife presiding, aunts, sisters, and cousins, with their female children and grandchildren, all sat (or knelt) on the west.

Whenever they wailed by the corpse in the apartment, the presiding mourner did so, holding up the shroud with his two hands at the same time.

8. At the mourning rites of a ruler, before the slighter dressing was completed, the principal mourner came out to receive the visit of a refugee ruler, or a visitor from another state.

At those for a Great officer, at the same period, he came out to receive a message from his ruler. At those for an ordinary officer, also at the same period, he came out to receive a Great officer, if he were not engaged in the dressing.

9. Whenever the presiding mourner went forth (to meet visitors), he had his feet bare, his skirt tucked under his girdle, and his hands across his chest over his heart. Having gone down by the steps on the west, if a ruler, he bowed to a refugee ruler, or a minister commissioned from another state, each in his proper place. When a message from his ruler came to a Great officer, he came to the outside of the door of the apartment (where the dead was), to receive the messenger who had ascended to the hall and communicated his instructions. (They then went down together), and the mourner bowed to the messenger below.

When a Great officer came himself to condole with an ordinary officer, the latter wailed along with him, but did not meet him outside the gate.

10. The wife of a ruler went out (of her apartment) on a visit from the wife of a refugee ruler.

The confirmed wife (of a Great officer) went out (in the same way) on the arrival of a message from the ruler's wife.

The wife of an officer, if not engaged in the dressing, (also) went out to receive the confirmed wife (of a Great officer).

11. At the slighter dressing, the presiding mourner took his place inside the door (on the east of it), and the presiding wife had her face to the east. When the dressing was ended, both of them made as if they leant on the body, and leaped. The mourner unbared his breast, took off the tufts of juvenility, and bound up his hair with sackcloth. The wife knotted up her hair, and put on her sackcloth girdle in her room.

12. When the curtain (which screened the body) was removed, the men and women carried it and put it down in the hall, (the eldest son) going down the step's and bowing (to the visitors).

13. The (young) ruler (who was mourning) bowed to refugee lords, and to ministers, commissioners from other states. Great officers and other officers bowed to ministers and Great officers in their respective places. In the case of (the three grades of) officers, they received three side bows[1], one for each grade. The ruler's wife also bowed to the wife of a refugee

[1. The side–bows were somehow made, without the ruler's turning directly towards the officers.]

lord, above in the hall. With regard to the wives of Great officers and of other officers, she bowed specially to each whose position had received the official appointment; to the others she gave a general bow;—all above in the hall.

14. When the mourner had gone to his own place (after bowing to his visitors), he closed the robe which was drawn on one side, covering his breast, put on his girdle and head–band, and leapt. When the mourning was for his mother, he went to his place, and tied up his hair, after which he put down the offerings by the body. The visitors who had come to condole, covered their fur robes, put the roll at the back of their caps, assumed their girdles and head–bands, and leapt in correspondence with the mourner.

15. At the funeral rites for a ruler, the chief forester supplied wood and horns; the chief of the salvage–men supplied the vases for water; the chief of the slaughtering department supplied boilers; and (an officer from the department of) the minister of War (saw to the)

hanging of these. Thus they secured the succession of wailers. Some of those in the department took their part in the wailing. If they did not hang up the vases, and the Great officers were sufficient to take the wailing in turns, then they did not use those others[1].

In the hall of the ruler there were two lights above and two below; for that of a Great officer, one above

[1. The object of the arrangements in this obscure paragraph was evidently to maintain the wailing uninterrupted, and to provide, by means of the clepsydra, a regular marking of the time for that purpose. See, in the Kâu Kwan XXX, 51–52, the duties of the officer of the department of the minister of War who had charge of the vase.]

and two below; for that of an ordinary officer, one above and one below[1].

16. When the guests went out, the curtain was removed[2].

17. When they were wailing the corpse above in the hall, the principal mourner was at the east; visitors coming from without, took their place at the west, and the women stood facing the south.

18. The wife (presiding), in receiving guests and escorting them, did not go down from the hall with them. If she did go down (as with the wife of the ruler), she bowed to her, but did not wail.

If the son (presiding), had occasion to go outside the door of the apartment, and saw the guest (whom he so went to meet), he did not wail.

When there was no female to preside, a son did so, and bowed to the female visitors inside the door of the apartment. If there were no son to preside, a daughter did so, and bowed to the male visitors at the foot of the steps on the east.

If the son were a child, then he was carried in his sackcloth in the arms, and his bearer bowed for him.

If the successor of the deceased were not present, and wag a man of rank, an apology was made to the guests; if he were not a man of rank, some other one bowed to them for him.

If he were anywhere in the state, they waited for him; if he had gone beyond it, the encoffining and burial might go on. The funeral rites might proceed without the presence of the successor of the deceased, but not without one to preside over them.

[1. This must have been towards morning. During the night torches were kept burning.

2. This should be at the end of paragraph 14.]

19. At the mourning rites for a ruler, on the third day his son and his wife assumed the staff. On the fifth day, when the corpse was put into the coffin, his daughters who had become the wives of Great officers were allowed to use it. His (eldest) son and Great officers used it outside the door of the apartment (where the coffin was); inside the door they carried it in their hands (but did not use it). The wife and his daughters, the wives of Great officers, used the staff in their rooms; when they went to their places (in the apartment where the coffin was), people were employed to hold it for them.

When a message came from the king, (the son presiding) put away his staff; when one came from the ruler of another state, he only held it in his hand. When attending to any consultation of the tortoise–shell about the corpse, he put away his staff.

A Great officer, in the place of the ruler, carried his staff in his hand; at another Great officer's, he used it.

20. At the mourning rites for a Great officer, on the morning of the third day, when the body was put into the coffin, his son presiding, his wife presiding, and the steward of the House, all assumed the staff. On a message from the ruler, the (new) Great officer put away his staff; on a message from another Great officer, he carried it in his hand. His wife, on a message from the wife of the ruler, put her staff away; on a message from the confirmed wife (of another Great officer), she gave it to some one to hold for her.

21. At the mourning rites for an officer, the body on the second day was put into the coffin. On the morning of the third day, the presiding mourner assumed the staff, and his wife also. The same observances as in the rites fur a Great officer were observed on messages arriving from the ruler or his wife, or from a Great officer and his confirmed wife.

22. All the sons assumed the staff, but only the eldest son used it when they were going to their places (in the apartment where the coffin was). Great officers and other officers, when wailing by the coffin, used the staff; when wailing by the bier, they carried it in their hands. When the staff (used in mourning) was thrown away, it was broken and thrown away in secret.

23. As soon as death took place, the corpse was transferred to the couch[1], and covered with a large sheet. The clothes in which the deceased had died were removed. A servant plugged the mouth open with the spoon of horn; and to keep the feet from contracting, an easy stool was employed[2]. These observances were the same for a ruler, a Great officer, and an ordinary officer[3].

24. The servant in charge of the apartments drew the water, and without removing the well–rope from the bucket gathered it up, and carried the whole up to the top of the steps. There, without going on the hall, he gave it to the attendants in waiting on the body. These then went in to wash the corpse, four

[1. When death seemed to be imminent, the body was removed from the couch and laid on the ground;—if, perhaps, contact with 'mother' earth might revive it. When death had taken place, it was replaced on the couch.

2. I do not quite understand how this stool was applied so as to accomplish its purpose.

3. This paragraph is the 24th in We Khien–lung edition. See below, paragraph 26.]

lower servants holding up the sheet, and two performing the washing; having put the water in basins, to which they took it with ladles. In washing they used napkins of fine linen, and in drying the body the ordinary bathing clothes. Another servant then pared the nails of the feet, after which they threw away the rest of the water into the pit. At the funeral rites for a mother (or other female), the female attendants in waiting in the inner room held up the sheet and washed the body.

25. The servant in charge of the apartments, having drawn water and given it to the attendants in waiting on the body, these prepared the wash for the head, above in the hall:—for a ruler, made from maize–water; for a Great officer, from that of the glutinous millet; and for an ordinary officer, that from maize–water. After this, some of the

forester's department made a sort of furnace at the foot of the wall on the west; and the potter brought out a large boiler, in which the servant in charge of the apartments should boil the water. The servants of the forester's department brought the fuel which he had removed from the crypt in the north-west of the apartment, now converted into a shrine, to use for that purpose. When the water was heated, he gave it to the attendants, who proceeded to wash the head, and poured the water into an earthenware basin, using the napkin as on ordinary occasions to dry the head. Another servant then clipped the nails of the fingers, and wiped the beard. The water was then thrown into the pit.

26. For a ruler they put down a large vessel, full of ice; for a Great officer, a middle-sized one, full of ice; and for an ordinary officer, only one of earthenware, without any ice in it. Over these they placed the couch with a single sheet and pillow on it; another couch on which the jade should be put into the mouth; and another still, where the fuller dressing should be done. Then the corpse was removed to a couch in the hall, on which was a pillow and mat. The same forms were observed for a ruler, a Great officer, and an ordinary officer[1].

27. At the mourning rites for a ruler, his (eldest) son, Great officers, his other sons and all the (other) officers (employed about the court), ate nothing for three days, but confined themselves to gruel. (Afterwards) for their consumption they received in the morning a handful of rice, and another in the evening; which they ate without any observance of stated times. Officers (at a distance) were restricted to coarse rice and water for their drink, without regard to any stated times. The wife (of the new ruler), the confirmed wives (of the Great officers), and all the members of their harems, had coarse rice and drank water, having no regard in their eating to stated times.

28. At the mourning rites for a Great officer, the presiding mourner, the steward, and grandsons, all were confined to gruel. All the inferior officers were restricted to coarse rice, and water to drink. Wives and concubines took coarse rice, and water to drink. At the rites for an ordinary officer the same rules were observed.

29. After the burial, the presiding mourner had (only) coarse rice and water to drink;—he did not

[1. This paragraph is the 23rd in the Khien-lung edition, confessedly out of place.]

eat vegetables or fruits. His wife observed the same rule. So it was in the case of rulers, Great officers, and other officers.

After the change of mourning, towards the end of the year, they ate vegetables and fruit; and after the subsequent sacrifice, they ate flesh.

30. They took their gruel in bowls, and did not wash their bands (before doing so). When they took their rice from the basket, they washed their hands. They ate their vegetables along with pickles and sauces. When they first ate flesh, it was dry flesh; when they first drank liquor, it was that newly made.

31. During the mourning of a year, on three occasions they abstained from eating. When eating coarse rice, with water to drink, they did not eat vegetables or fruits. After the burial, at the end of three months, they ate flesh and drank liquor. When the year's mourning was ended, they did not eat flesh nor drink liquor. When the father was alive, in the mourning of nine months, the rules were the same as in that for a year, on account of the mother or of the wife. Though they ate flesh and drank liquor, they could not take the enjoyment of these things in company with others[1].

32. During the mourning for five months, and that for three months, it was allowable to abstain from eating once or twice. Between the coffining and burial[2], when eating flesh and drinking liquor,

[1. The statements in this paragraph, and those in the next, might certainly be stated more distinctly.

2. Such is the meaning of the text here, as fully defined by a Fang Pâo.]

they did not take the enjoyment of these things in company with others. While mourning for an aunt, the confirmed wife of an uncle, one's old ruler, or the head of a clan, they ate flesh and drank liquor.

If a mourner could not eat the gruel, he might eat soup of vegetables. If he were ill, he might eat flesh and drink liquor. At fifty, one did not go through all the observances of mourning. At seventy, he simply wore the sackcloth on his person.

33. After the burial, if his ruler feasted a mourner, he partook of the viands; if a Great officer or a friend of his father did so, he partook in the same way. He, did not even decline the grain and flesh that might be set before him, but wine and new wine he declined.

SECTION II.

1. The slighter dressing was performed inside the door (of the apartment where the body was); the fuller dressing (at the top of) the steps (leading up to the reception hall) on the east. The body of a ruler was laid on a mat of fine bamboo; of a Great officer, on one of typha grass; and of an ordinary officer, on one of phragmites grass.

2. At the slighter dressing one band of cloth was laid straight, and, there were three bands laid cross-wise. The sheet for a ruler's body was embroidered; for a Great officer's? white; for an ordinary officer's, black:—each had one sheet.

There were nineteen suits of clothes[1]; those for

[1. So in all our dictionaries; as in Medhurst,, 'a suit of clothes.' But why nineteen suits? King and Ying-ta make up ten, the concluding number of heaven; and nine, that of earth.' But how shall we account for the hundred, fifty, and thirty suits at the greater dressing, in next paragraph? These suits were set forth, I suppose, for display; they could hardly be for use.]

the ruler, displayed in the corridor on the east; and those for a Great officer, or a common officer, inside the apartments:—all with their collars towards the west, those in the north being the best. The sash and sheet were not reckoned among them.

3. At the fuller dressing there were three bands of cloth laid straight, and five laid cross-wise. There were (also) strings of cloth, and two sheets:—equally for a ruler, a Great officer, and a common officer. The clothes for a ruler consisted of one hundred suits, displayed in the courtyard, having their collars towards the north, those on the west being the best; those of a Great officer were fifty suits, displayed in the corridor on the east, having the collars towards the west, those on the south being the best; those of a common officer were thirty suits, displayed also in the corridor on the east, with their

collars towards the west, the best on the south. The bands and strings were of the same quality as the court robes. One strip of the band–cloth was divided into three, but at the ends was not further divided. The sheets were made of five pieces, without strings or buttons.

4. Among the clothes at the slighter dressing, the sacrificial robes were not placed below the others. For the ruler no clothes were used that were presented. For a Great officer and a common officer, the sacrificial (and other) robes belonging to the principal mourner were all used, and then they used those contributed by their relatives; but these were not displayed along with the others.

At the slighter dressing, for a ruler, a Great officer, and a common officer, they used wadded upper robes and sheets.

At the greater dressing, the number of sacrificial (and other) robes put on a ruler, a Great officer, or another officer', was not definitely fixed; but the upper robes and sheets for a ruler had only a thin lining, (instead of being wadded); for a Great officer and a common officer, they were as at the slighter dressing.

5. The long robe (worn in private) had a shorter one placed over it;—it was not displayed alone. It was the rule that with the upper garment the lower one should also be shown. So only could they be called a suit.

6. All who set forth the clothes took them from the chests in which they had been deposited; and those who received. the clothes brought (as contributions) placed them in (similar) chests. In going up to the hall and descending from it, they did so by the steps on the west. They displayed the clothes without rumpling them. They did not admit any that were not correct; nor any of fine or coarse dolychos fibre[2] or of coarse flax.

7. All engaged in dressing the corpse hag their arms bared; those who moved it into the coffin, had their breasts covered. At the funeral rites for a ruler, the Great officer of prayer performed the dressing, assisted by all the members of his department; at those for a Great officer, the same officer stood by, and saw all the others dress the body; at those of a common officer, the members of that department stood by, while other officers (his friends) performed the dressing.

8. At both the dressings the sacrificial robes were not placed below the others. They were all placed with the lappel to lie on the left side. The bands were tied firmly, and not in a bow–knot.

9. The rule was that the dressers should wail, when they had completed their work. But in the case of an officer, as the dressing was performed by those who had served in office along with him, they, after the work was done, omitted a meal. In all cases the dressers were six.

10. The body cases (used before the dressing) were made:—for a ruler, the upper one embroidered, and the lower one striped black and white, with seven strings on the open side; for a Great officer, the upper one dark blue, and the lower one striped black and white, with five tie–strings on the side; for a common officer, the upper one black, and the lower one red, with three tie–strings at the side. The upper case came down to the end of the hands, and the lower case was three feet long. At the smaller dressing and afterwards, they used coverlets laid on the body (instead of these cases), their size being the same as that of the cases.

11. When the great dressing of a ruler's body was about to commence, his son, with the sackcloth band about his cap, went to his place at the (south) end of the (eastern) corridor, while the ministers and Great officers took theirs at the corner of the hall, with the pillar on their west, their faces to the north, and their row ascending to the east. The uncles, brothers, and cousins were below the hall, with their faces to the north, The (son's) wife, and other wives whose position had been confirmed were on the west of the body, with their faces to other states the east. The female relations from the other states were in their apartments with their faces to the south. Inferior officers spread the mats. The Shang officers of prayer spread the strings, the coverlet, and clothes. The officers had their hands over the vessels. They then lifted the corpse and removed it to the place for the dressing. When the dressing was finished, the superintendent announced the fact. The son then (seemed to) lean on it, and leaped while his wife did the same, with her face to the east.

2. At the mourning rites of a Great officer, they were about to proceed to the great dressing, and the tie–strings, coverlets, and clothes had all been spread out, the ruler arrived, and was met by (the son), the principal mourner. The son entered before him, (and stood) at the right of the gate, outside which the exorcist stopped. The ruler having

put down the vegetables (as an offering to the spirit of the gate), and the blesser entered preceding him, entered and went up to the hall. He then repaired to his place at the end of the corridor, while the ministers, and Great officers took theirs at the corner of the hall on the west of the pillar, looking to the north, their row ascending to the east. The presiding mourner was outside the apartment (where the corpse was), facing the south. His wife presiding was on the west of the body, facing the east. When they had moved the corpse, and finished the dressing, the steward reported that they had done so, and the presiding mourner went down below the hall, with his face to the north. There the ruler laid on him the soothing hand, and he bowed with his forehead, to the ground. The ruler signified to him to go up, and lean on the body, and also requested his wife, presiding, to lean on it.

13. At the mourning rites for a common officer, when they were about to proceed to the great dressing, the ruler was not present. In other respects the observances were the same as in the case of a Great officer.

14. They also leaped at the spreading out of the ties and strings; of the sheet; of the clothes; at the moving of the corpse; at the putting on of the clothes; of the coverlet; and of the adjusting of the ties and bands.

15. The ruler laid his hand on the body of a Great officer, and on that of the most honourable ladies of his own harem. A Great officer laid his hand on the body of the steward of his house, and on that of his niece and the sister of his wife, who had accompanied her to the harem.

The ruler and a Great officer leant closely with their breasts over the bodies of their parents, wives, and eldest sons, but not over those of their other sons.

A common officer, however, did so also to all his other sons.

If a son by a concubine had a son, the parents did not perform this ceremony over him. When it was performed, the parents did it first, and then the wife and son.

A ruler laid his hand on the body of a minister; parents, while bending over that of a son, also took hold of his hand. A son bent over his parents, bringing his breast near to theirs. A wife seemed as if she would place her two arms beneath the bodies of her patents–in–law; while they (simply) laid their hands on her. A wife made as if she would cling to her husband's body; while the husband held her hand as he did that of a brother or cousin. When others brought the breast near the body of a corpse, they avoided the point at which the ruler had touched it. After every such mark of sorrow, the mourner rose up and leaped.

16. At the mourning rites for a parent, (the son) occupied the slanting shed, unplastered; slept on straw, with a clod of earth for his pillow. He spoke of nothing but what related to the rites. A ruler enclosed this hut; but Great and common officers left it exposed.

After the burial, the inclined posts were set up on lintels, and the hut was plastered, but not on the outside which could be seen. Rulers, Great and common officers, all had it enclosed.

All the other sons, but the eldest by the proper wife, even before the burial had huts made for themselves in out–of–the–way places.

17. After the burial, the son would stand with others. If a ruler, he would speak of the king's affairs, but not of those of his own state. If a Great officer, or a common officer, he would speak of the ruler's affairs, but not of those of his own clan or family.

18. When the ruler was buried, the royal ordinances came into the state. After the wailing was finished, the new ruler engaged in the king's affairs.

When a Great officer or a common officer was buried, the ordinances of the state came to his family. After the wailing was finished, while continuing the sackcloth band round his cap, and the girdle, he might don his armour and go into the field.

19. After the mourning was changed at the end of a year, (the sons) occupied the unplastered apartment, and did not occupy one along with others. Then the ruler consulted about the government of the state; and Great officers and common officers about the affairs of their clan and families. After the sacrifice at the end of two years, the ground of the apartment was made of a dark green, and the walls were whitened. After this, they no longer wailed outside; and after the sacrifice at the end of twenty–seven months, they did not do so inside; for, after it, music began to be heard.

20. After that sacrifice, at the end of twenty–seven months, (the son) attended to all his duties; and after the felicitous sacrifice (of re–arranging the tablets in his ancestral temple), he returned to his (usual) chamber.

At the one year's mourning, he occupied the hut; and when it was completed, the occasions on which he did not seek the nuptial chamber were:–when his father was alive, and he had been wearing the hemmed sackcloth of a year for his mother or his wife, and when he had been wearing the cloth mourning of nine months; on these occasions, for three months he did not seek the intercourse of the inner chamber.

A wife did not occupy the hut, nor sleep on the straw. At the mourning for her father or mother, when she had changed the mourning at the end of a year, she returned to her husband; when the mourning was that of nine months, she returned after the burial.

21. At the mourning rites for a duke (of the royal domain), his Great officers continued till the change of mourning at the end of a year, and then returned to their own residences. A common officer returned at the conclusion of the wailing.

22. At the mourning rites for their parents, (the other sons who were) Great officers or common officers, returned to their own residences after the change of the mourning at the end of the year; but on the first day of the month and at full moon, and on the return of the death–day, they came back and wailed in the house of him who was now the Head of their family.

At the mourning for uncles and cousins, they returned to their own residences at the conclusion of the wailing.

23. A father did not take up his quarters (during the mourning) at a son's, nor an elder brother at a younger's.

24. At the mourning rites for a Great officer or his acknowledged wife, a ruler (went to see) the greater dressing; but if he wished to show special favour, he attended the slighter dressing.

The ruler, in the case of an acknowledged wife, married to a Great officer of a different surname from his own, arrived after the lid was put on the coffin.

He went to an officer's, when the body was put into the coffin.; but if he wanted to show special favour, he attended at the greater dressing.

The ruler's wife, at the mourning for a (Great officer's) acknowledged wife, attended at the greater dressing; but if she wished to show special favour, at the slighter. In the case of his other wives, if she wished to show special favour, she attended at the greater dressing in the case of a Great officer's acknowledged wife, who was of a different surname from her own, she appeared after the coffining had taken place.

25. When the ruler went to a Great officer's or a common officer's, after the coffining had taken place, he sent word beforehand of his coming. The chief mourner provided all the offerings to be set down for the dead in the fullest measure, and waited outside the gate, till he saw the heads of the horses. He then led the way in by the right side of the gate. The exorcist stopped outside, and the blesser took his place, and preceded the ruler, who put down the offerings of vegetables (for the spirit of the gate) inside it. The blesser then preceded him up the eastern steps, and took his place with his back to the wall, facing the south. The ruler took his place at (thc top of) the steps; two men with spears standing before him, and two behind. The officer of reception then advanced. The chief mourner bowed, laying his forehead to the ground. The ruler then said what he had to say; looked towards the blesser and leaped. The chief mourner then (also) leaped.

26. If the visit were paid to a Great officer, the offerings might at this point be put down by the coffin. If it were to a common officer, he went out to wait outside the gate. Being requested to return and put down the offerings, he did so. When this was done, he preceded the ruler, and waited for him outside the gate. When the ruler retired, the chief mourner escorted him outside the gate, and bowed to him, with his forehead to the ground.

27. When a Great officer was ill, the ruler thrice inquired for him; and when his body was coffined, visited (his son) thrice. When a common officer was ill, he inquired for him once; and when his body was coffined, visited (his son) once.

When the ruler came to condole (after the coffining), the (son) put on again the clothes he had worn at the coffining.

28. When the ruler's wife went lo condole at a Great officer's or a common officer's, the chief mourner went out to meet her outside the gate, and, when he saw her horses heads, went in before her by the right side of the gate. She then entered, went up to the hall, and took her place. The wife presiding went down by the steps on the west, and bowed with her head to the ground below (the hall). The ruler's wife looked towards her eldest son (who had accompanied her), and leaped.

The offerings were put down according to the rules for them on the visit of the ruler. When she retired, the wife presiding went with her to the inside of the door of the apartment, and bowed to her with her head to the ground. The chief mourner escorted her to the outside of the great gate, but did not bow.

29. When a Great officer came to the mourning rites of one of his officers to whom he stood in the relation of ruler, the officer did not meet him outside the gate. He entered and took his place below the hall. The chief mourner (stood on the south of his place), with his face to the north, though the general rule for chief mourners was to face the south. The wife took her place in the room.

If, at this juncture, there came a message from the ruler of the state, or one from a confirmed (Great) officer or his confirmed wife, or visitors from, the neighbouring states, the Great officer–ruler, having the chief mourner behind him, performed the bow of ceremony to each visitor.

30. When a ruler, on a visit of condolence, saw the bier for the corpse, he leaped.

If a ruler had not given notice beforehand of his coining to a Great officer or a common officer, and he had not prepared the various offerings to be put down by the coffin on the occasion, when the ruler withdrew, the rule was that they should then be put down.

31. The largest (or outermost) coffin of the ruler of a state was eight inches thick; the next, six inches; and the innermost, four inches. The larger coffin of a Great officer of the highest grade was eight inches thick; and the inner, six inches; for one of the lowest grade, the dimensions were six inches and four. The coffin of a common officer was six inches thick.

32. The (inner) coffin of a ruler was lined with red (silk), fixed in its place with nails of various metals; that of a Great officer with (silk of a) dark blue, fixed with nails of ox–bone; that of a common officer was lined, but had no nails.

33. The lid of a ruler's coffin was varnished, with three double wedges (at the edges) over which were three bands; that of a Great officer's was (also) varnished, with two double wedges and two bands; that of a common officer was not varnished, but it had two double wedges and two bands.

34. The (accumulated) hair and nails of a ruler and Great officer were placed (in bags) at the four corners of the coffin; those of an officer were buried (without being put in the coffin).

The coffin of a ruler was placed upon a bier, which was surrounded with high stakes, inclined over it till, when all was finished and plastered, there was the appearance of a house. That of a Great officer, having been covered with a pall, was placed in the did not western corridor and staked, but the plastering did not reach all over the coffin. That of a common officer was placed so that the double wedges could be seen; above that it was plastered. All were screened.

36. Of scorched grain there were put by the coffin of a ruler eight baskets, containing four different kinds; by that of a Great officer, six baskets, containing three kinds; by that of a common officer, four baskets, containing two kinds. Besides these, there were (dried) fish and flesh.

37. Ornamenting the coffin (on its way to the grave), there were for a ruler:—the curtains with dragons (figured on them), and over them three gutter–Spouts; the fluttering ornaments (with pheasants figured on them and the ends of the curtains); above (on the sloping roof of the catafalque) were figures of axe–heads, of the symbol of discrimination, thrice repeated, and of flames, thrice repeated. These occupied the pall–like roof of white silk, as embroidery, and above it was the false covering attached to it by six purple ties, and rising up with ornaments in five, colours and five rows of shells. There were (at the corners) two streamers of feathers, suspended from a frame with the axes on it; two from another, bearing the symbol of discrimination; two from another, variously figured; all the frames on staffs, showing jade–symbols at the top. Fishes were made as if leaping at the ends of the gutters, The whole of the catafalque was

kept together by six supports rising from the coffin, and wound round with purple silk, and six sustaining ropes, also purple, (drawn through the curtains).

For the catafalque of a Great officer there were painted curtains, with two gutter–spouts (above them); there were not the fluttering ornaments; above (on the sloping roof) there were flames painted, thrice repeated; and three symbols of discrimination, These formed the pall–like roof, and there were two purple ties, and two of deep blue. At the very top there were ornaments in three colours, and three rows of shells. There were two feather–streamers from a frame with axes, and two from a painted frame; all the frames on staffs with plumage at the tops. Figures of fishes were made at the ends of the gutters. The front supports of a Great officer's catafalque were purple, and those behind deep blue. So also were the sustaining ropes.

For the catafalque of a common officer, the curtains were of (plain) linen, and there was the sloping roof. There was (but) one gutter–spout. There were the fluttering pheasants on the bands. The purple ties were two, and the black also two. At the very top the ornaments were of three colours, and there was only one row of shells. The streamers of feathers from a painted frame were two, the staffs of which had plumage at their tops. The front supports of the catafalque were purple, and those behind black. The sustaining ropes were purple.

38. In burying the coffin of a ruler, they used a bier, four ropes, and two pillars. Those guiding the course of the coffin carried the shade with pendent feathers.

In burying a Great officer, they used two ropes and two pillars. Those who guided the coffin used a reed of white grass.

In burying a common officer, they used a carriage of the state. They employed two ropes and no post. As soon as they left the residence, those who directed the coffin used the shade of merit.

39. In letting down the coffin into the grave, they removed the ropes from the posts, and pulled at them with their. backs to the posts. For a ruler's coffin, they also used levers, and for a Great officer's or a common officer's, ropes attached to the sides of the coffin. Orders were given that they should not cry out in letting down that of the ruler. They let it down as guided by the sound of a drum. in letting down a Great officer's, they were

commanded not to wail. In letting down a common officer's, those who began to wail stopped one another.

40. The outer shell of the coffin of a ruler was of pine; of a Great officer, of cypress; of another officer, of various kinds of wood.

41. The surface between the coffin and shell of a ruler was sufficient to contain a music stopper; in the case of the coffin and shell of a Great officer, a vase for water; in that of the coffin and shell of a common officer, a jar of liquor.

42. In the rites of a ruler, the shell was lined, and there were baskets of yü; in those of a Great officer, the shell was not lined; in those of a common officer, there were no baskets of yü[1].

[1. We cannot tell what these baskets were. Kang says he did not know, and the Khien–lung editors think they may have contained the grain mentioned in paragraph 36. Otherwise, the paragraph is obscure.

On the next page there is given a figure of the catafalque over the coffin as borne to the grave, copied from the second volume of P. Zottoli's work. A larger one, more fully illustrating the details of the text, forms the last plate in the Khien–lung edition of the Classic; but it is so rough and complicated that the friend who has assisted me with most of the figures that I have ventured to introduce shrank from attempting to reproduce it on a smaller scale.]

BOOK XX. KÎ FÂ, OR THE LAW OF SACRIFICES

According to the law of sacrifices, (Shun), the sovereign of the line of Yü, at the great associate sacrifice, gave the place of honour to Hwang Tî, and at the border sacrifice made Khû the correlate of Heaven; he sacrificed (also) to Kwan–hsü as his ancestor (on the throne) and to Yâo as his honoured predecessor.

[1. See the introduction) vol., xxvii, pp. 35, 36. It is there said that in the idea of sacrifices (kî), which is here given, there is no indication of deprecation by means of them, and much less of atonement, but that they were merely expressions of gratitude. The character kî is one of them formed by combination of the ideas in its several parts. The Shwo–wan, the earliest Chinese dictionary, says that it is made up of two ideograms:, the symbol for spiritual beings; and another, composed of and, representing a right hand and a piece of flesh. Offerings of flesh must have been a common when the character was formed, which then itself entered, as the phonetic element, into the formation of between twenty and thirty other characters. The explanations of it given by Morrison (Dict., part i), taken from the Khang–hsî dictionary, are:—'To carry human affairs before the gods [i.e., spirits]. That which is the medium between, or brings together men and gods [spirits]. To offer flesh in the rites of worship; to sacrifice with worship.' There is nothing, however, in the Khang–hsî corresponding to this last sentence; and I suppose that Morrison gave it from the analysis of the character in the Shwo–wan. The general idea symbolised by it is—an offering by which communication and spiritual beings is effected.]

The sovereigns of Hsiâ, at the corresponding sacrifice, gave the place of honour also to Hwang Tî, and made Khwan the correlate at the border sacrifice; they sacrificed to Kwan–hsü as their ancestor, and to Yü as their honoured predecessor.

Under Yin, they gave the place of honour to Khû, and made Ming the correlate at the border sacrifice; they sacrificed to Hsieh as their ancestor, and to Thang as their honoured predecessor.

Under Kâu they gave the place of honour to Khû, and made Kî the correlate at the border sacrifice, they sacrificed to king Wan as their ancestor, and to king Wân as their honoured predecessor[1].

2. With a blazing pile of wood on the Grand altar they sacrificed to Heaven[2]; by burying (the victim)

[1. This and other portions of the Book are taken mainly from the seventh article in the second section of the 'Narratives of the States,' part i. The statements have much perplexed the commentators, and are held to be of doubtful authority. Some of them, indeed, are said by Khan Hâo to be inexplicable. Khwan, 'the correlate in the sacrifices of Hsiâ, was the father of Yü,' of whom we receive a bad impression from the references to him in the Shû King; and Ming, who occupied the same position in those of Yin, was the fifth in descent from Hsieh, the ancestor of that dynasty, a minister of Works, who died somehow in his labours on a flood. P. Zottoli thinks that of the four sacrifices here mentioned, the first was to the Supreme Deity (Supremo Numini), and the second, to the Highest Heaven (Summo Coelo). My own view is different, and agrees with that of the Khien–lung editors. They discuss the different questions that have been agitated on the subject, and their conclusions may be taken as the orthodoxy of Chinese scholars on the subject; into the exhibition of which it is not necessary to go at greater length.

2. On the blazing pile were placed the victim and pieces of jade; in the square mound were buried the victim and pieces of silk. For,which follow, Zottoli gives solenni angulari, and I have met with 'the great pit' as a translation of them. Of course a 'pit' was formed in the mound to receive the offerings; but in the Khang–hsî dictionary is specially defined with reference to this passage as 'a mound of earth as a place of sacrifice;' though we do not find this account of the character in Morrison, Medhurst, or Williams.]

in the Grand mound, they sacrificed to the Earth. (In both cases) they used a red victim[1].

3. By burying a sheep and a pig at the (altar of) Great brightness, they sacrificed to the seasons. (With similar) victims they sacrificed to (the spirits of cold and heat, at the pit and the altar, using prayers of deprecation and petition[2]; to the sun, at the (altar called the) royal palace; to the moon, at the (pit called the) light of the night; to the stars at the honoured place of gloom; to (the spirits of) flood and drought at the honoured altar of rain; to the (spirits of the) four quarters at the place of the four pits and altars; mountains, forests, streams, valleys, hills, and mounds, which are able to produce clouds, and occasion winds and rain, were all regarded as (dominated by) spirits.

He by whom all under the sky was held sacrificed to all spirits. The princes of states sacrificed to those which were in their own territories; to those which were not in their territories, they did not sacrifice.

4. Generally speaking, all born between heaven and earth were said to have their allotted times; the death of all creatures is spoken of as their dissolution; but man when dead is said to be in the ghostly

[1. This was specially the colour of the victims under the Kâu dynasty.

2. Such is the meaning given by Ying–tâ and others to which they think should be .]

state. There was no change in regard to these points in the five[1] dynasties. What, the seven[2] dynasties made changes in, were the assessors at the Great associate and the border sacrifices, and the parties sacrificed to in the ancestral temple;—they made no other changes.

5. The sovereigns, coming to the possession of the kingdom, divided the land and established the feudal principalities; they assigned (great) cities (to their nobles), and smaller towns (to their chiefs); they made ancestral temples, and the arrangements for altering the order of the spirit-tablets; they raised altars, and they cleared the ground around them for the performance of their sacrifices. In all these arrangements they made provision for the sacrifices according to the nearer or more remote kinship, and for the assignment of lands of greater or less amount.

Thus the king made for himself seven ancestral temples, with a raised altar and the surrounding area for each. The temples were-his father's; his grandfather's; his great-grandfather's; his great-great-grandfather's; and the temple of his (high) ancestor. At all of these a sacrifice was offered every month. The temples of the more remote ancestors formed the receptacles for the tablets as they were displaced; they were two, and at these only the seasonal sacrifices were offered. For the removed tablet of one more remote, an altar was

[1. Those of Yâo, Shun, Hsiâ, Shang or Yin, and Kâu.

2. What these 'seven' dynasties were is doubtful. Add to the preceding five, the names of Kwan-hsü and Khû, and we get the number, all descended from Hwang Tî. The writer must have regarded him as the founder of the Chinese kingdom.]

raised and its corresponding area; and on occasions of prayer at this altar and area, a sacrifice was offered, but if there were no prayer, there was no sacrifice. In the case of one still more remote, (there was no sacrifice);—he was left in his ghostly state.

A feudal prince made for himself five ancestral temples, with an altar and a cleared area about it for each. The temples were—his father's; his grandfather's; and his great-grandfather's; in all of which a sacrifice was offered every month. In the temples of the great-great-grandfather, and that of the (high) ancestor only, the seasonal sacrifices were offered. For one beyond the high ancestor a special altar was raised, and for one still more remote, an area was prepared. If there were prayer at these, a sacrifice was offered; but if there were no prayer, there was no sacrifice. In the case of one still more remote, (there was no service);—he was left in his ghostly state.

A Great officer made for himself three ancestral temples and two altars. The temples were–his father's; his grandfather's; and his great–grandfather's. In this only the seasonal sacrifices were offered. To the great–great–grandfather and the (high) ancestor there were no temples. If there were occasion for prayer to them, altars were raised, and sacrifices offered on them. An ancestor still more remote was left in his ghostly state.

An officer of the highest grade had two ancestral temples and one altar;—the temples of his father and grandfather, at which only the seasonal sacrifices were presented. There was no temple for his great–grandfather. If there were occasion to pray to him, an altar was raised, and a sacrifice offered to him. Ancestors more remote were left in their ghostly state.

An officer in charge merely of one department had one ancestral temple; that, namely, of his father. There was no temple for his grandfather, but he was sacrificed to (in the father's temple.) Ancestors beyond the grandfather were left in their ghostly state.

The mass of ordinary officers and the common people had no ancestral temple. Their dead were left in their ghostly state, (to have offerings presented to them in the back apartment, as occasion required).

6. The king, for all the people, erected an altar to (the spirit of) the ground, called the Grand altar, and one for himself, called the Royal altar.

A feudal prince, for all his people, erected one called the altar of the state, and one for himself called the altar of the prince.

Great officers and all below them in association erected such an altar, called the Appointed altar.

7. The king, for all the people, appointed (seven altars for) the seven sacrifices:—one to the superintendent of the lot; one in the central court, for the admission of light and the rain from the roofs; one at the gates of the city wall; one in the roads leading from the

city; one for the discontented ghosts of kings who had died without posterity; one for the guardian of the door; and one for the guardian of the furnace. He also had seven corresponding altars for himself.

A feudal prince, for his state, appointed (five altars for) the five sacrifices:—one for the superintendent of the lot; one in the central court, for the admission of light and rain; one at the gates of the city wall; one in the roads leading from the city; one for the discontented ghosts of princes who had died without posterity. He also had five corresponding altars for himself.

A Great officer appointed (three altars for) the three sacrifice:—one for the discontented ghosts of his predecessors who had died without posterity; one at the gates of his city; and one on the roads leading from it.

An officer of the first grade appointed (two altars for) the two sacrifices:—one at the gates; and one on the roads (outside the gates).

Other officers and the common people had one (altar and one) sacrifice. Some raised one altar for the guardian of the door; and others, one for the guardian of the furnace.

8. The king, carrying down (his favour), sacrificed to five classes of those who had died prematurely:—namely, to the rightful eldest sons (of former kings); to rightful grandsons; to rightful great–grandsons; to rightful great–great–grandsons; and to the rightful sons of these last.

A feudal prince, carrying down (his favour), sacrificed to three classes; a Great officer similarly to two; another officer of the first grade and the common people sacrificed only to the son who had died prematurely[1],

9. According to the institutes of the sage kings about sacrifices, sacrifice should be offered to him who had given (good) laws to the people to him

[1. From paragraph 1 down to this is absent from the expurgated edition of Fan Dze–tang, which P. Callery translated, so that the book contains in it only the one long paragraph that follows.]

who had laboured to the death in the discharge of his duties; to him who had strengthened the state by his laborious toil; to him who had boldly and successfully met great calamities; and to him who had warded off great evils.

Such were the following:—Nang, the son of the lord of Lî–shan[1], who possessed the kingdom, and showed how to cultivate all the cereals; and Khî (the progenitor) of Kâu, who continued his work after the decay of Hsiâ, and was sacrificed to under the name of Kî[2]; Hâu–thû, a son of the line of Kung–kung[3], that swayed the nine provinces, who was able to reduce them all to order, and was sacrificed to as the spirit of the ground; the Tî Khû, who could define all the zodiacal stars, and exhibit their times to the people; Yâo, who rewarded (the worthy), made the penal laws impartial, and the end of whose course was distinguished by his righteousness; Shun, who, toiling amid all his affairs, died in the country (far from his capital); Yü, (the son of) Khwan, who was kept a prisoner till death for trying to dam up the waters of the flood, while Yü completed the work, and atoned for his father's failure; Hwang Tî, who gave everything its right name, thereby showing the people how to avail themselves of its qualities; Kwan–hsü, who completed this work

[1. Li–shan is generally mentioned as Lieh–shan, and sometimes Lien–shan. Where the country so–called was, we do not know. Nang, or Shan Nang, is generally accepted as the first of the line, about B.C. 3072.

2 This account of Kî is given confusedly.

3 It is difficult to find a place in chronology for this Kung–kung. An article in the Zo Kwan (under duke Kao's seventeenth year, paragraph 3) places him between Fû–hsî and Shan Nang.]

of Hwang Tî; Hsieh, who was minister of Instruction, and perfected the (condition and manners of the) people; Ming, who, through his attention to the duties of his office, died in the waters; Thang, who ruled the people with a benignant sway and cut off their oppressor; and king Wan, who by his peaceful rule, and king Wû, who by his martial achievements, delivered the people from their afflictions. All these rendered distinguished services to the people.

BOOK XXI. KÎ Î, OR THE MEANING OF SACRIFICES[1].

SECTION I.

1. Sacrifices should not be frequently repeated. Such frequency is indicative of importunateness; and importunateness is inconsistent with reverence. Nor should they be at distant intervals. Such infrequency is indicative of indifference; and indifference leads to forgetting them altogether. Therefore the superior man, in harmony with the course of Heaven, offers the sacrifices of spring[2] and autumn. When he treads on the dew which has descended as hoar–frost he cannot help a feeling of sadness, which arises in his mind, and cannot be ascribed to the cold. In spring, when he treads on the ground, wet with the rains and dews that have fallen heavily, he cannot avoid being moved by a feeling as if he were seeing his departed friends. We meet the approach of our friends with music, and escort them away with sadness, and hence at the sacrifice in spring we use music, but not at the sacrifice in autumn.

2. The severest vigil and purification is maintained and carried on inwardly; while a looser vigil

[1. See the introduction, vol. xxvii, pages 36, 37.

2. The spring sacrifice is here called tî, probably by mistake for yo, the proper name for it.]

is maintained externally. During the days of such vigil, the mourner thinks of his departed, how and where they sat, how they smiled and spoke, what were their aims and views, what they delighted in, and what things they desired and enjoyed. On the third day of such exercise he will see those for whom it is employed.

3. On the day of sacrifice, when he enters the apartment (of the temple), he will seem to see (the deceased) in the place (where his spirit–tablet is). After he has moved about (and performed his operations), and is leaving at the door, he will seem to be arrested by hearing the sound of his movements, and will sigh as he seems to hear the sound of his

sighing.

4. Thus the filial piety taught by the ancient kings required that the eyes of the son should not forget the looks (of his parents), nor his ears their voices; and that he should retain the memory of their aims, likings, and wishes. As he gave full play to his love, they seemed to live again; and to his reverence, they seemed to stand out before him. So seeming to live and stand out, so unforgotten by him, how could his sacrifices be without the accompaniment of reverence?

5. The superior man, while (his parents) are alive, reverently nourishes them; and, when–they are dead, he reverently sacrifices to them;—his (chief) thought is how to the end of life not to disgrace them. The saying that the superior man mourns all his life for his parents has reference to the recurrence of the day of their death. That he does not do his ordinary work on that day does not mean that it would be unpropitious to do so; it means that on that day his thoughts are occupied with them, and he does not dare to occupy himself as on other days with his private and personal affairs.

6. It is only the sage[1] who can sacrifice to God, and (only) the filial son who can sacrifice to his parents. Sacrificing means directing one's self to, The son directs his thoughts (to his parents), and then he can offer his sacrifice (so that they shall enjoy it). Hence the filial son approaches the personator of the departed without having occasion to blush; the ruler leads the victim forward, while his wife puts down the bowls; the ruler presents the offerings to the personator, while his wife sets forth the various dishes; his ministers and Great officers assist the ruler, while their acknowledged wives assist his wife. How well sustained was their reverence! How complete was the expression of their loyal devotion! How earnest was their wish that the departed should enjoy the service!

7. King Wan, in sacrificing, served the dead as if he were serving the living. He thought of them dead as if he did not wish to live (any longer himself)[2]. On the recurrence of their death–day, he was sad; in calling his father by the name elsewhere forbidden, he looked as if he saw him. So sincere was he in sacrificing that he looked as if he saw the things which his father loved, and the

[1. According to rule, and in fact, only. the sovereign sacrifices to God. He may be 'a sage,' but more frequently is not. But the ritual of China should impress on him, as on no other person, the truth in the words 'noblesse oblige.'

2. Khan Hâo says here:—'As if he wished to die himself and follow them.']

pleased expression of his face:–such was king Wan! The lines of the ode (II, v, ode 2),

'When early dawn unseals my eyes,
Before my mind my parents rise,'

might be applied to king Win. On the day after the sacrifice, when the day broke, he did not sleep, but hastened to repeat it; and after it was finished, he still thought of his parents. On the day of sacrifice his joy and sorrow were blended together. He could not but rejoice in the opportunity of offering the sacrifice; and when it was over, he could not but be sad.

8. At the autumnal sacrifice, when Kung–nî advanced, bearing the offerings, his general appearance was indicative of simple sincerity, but his steps were short and oft repeated. When the sacrifice was over, Dze–kung questioned him, saying, 'Your account of sacrificing was that it should be marked by the dignity and intense absorption of all engaged in it; and now how is it that in your sacrificing there has been no such dignity and absorption?'

The Master said, 'That dignity of demeanour should belong to those who are only distantly connected (with him who is sacrificed to), and that absorbed demeanour to one whose thoughts are turned in on himself (lest he should make any mistake). But how should such demeanour consist with communion with the spirits (sacrificed to)? How should such unity and absorption be seen in my sacrifice? (At the sacrifices of the king and rulers) there is the return of the personator to his apartment, and the offering of food to him there; there are the performances of the music, and the setting forth of the stands with the victims on them; there are the ordering of the various ceremonies and the music; and there is the complete array of the officers for all the services. When they are engaged in the maintenance of that dignity and absorption in their duties, how can they be lost in their abandonment to intercourse with the spiritual presences? Should words be understood only in one way? Each saying has its own appropriate application.'

9. When a filial son is about to sacrifice, he is anxious that all preparations should be made beforehand; and when the time arrives, that everything necessary should be found complete; and then, with a mind free from all pre–occupation, he should address himself

to the performance of his sacrifice.

The temple and its apartments having been repaired, the walls and roofs having been put in order, and all the assisting officers having been provided, husband and wife, after vigil and footing, bathe their heads and persons, and array themselves in full dress. In coming in with the things which they carry, how grave and still are they! how absorbed in what they do! as if they were not able to sustain their weight, as if they would let them fall:—Is not theirs the highest filial reverence? He sets forth the stands with the victims on them; arranges all the ceremonies and music; provides the officers for, the various ministries. These aid in sustaining and bringing in the things, and thus he declares his mind and wish, and in his lost abstraction of mind seeks to have communion with the dead in their spiritual state, if peradventure they will enjoy his offerings, if peradventure they will do so. Such is the aim of the filial son (in his sacrifices)!

10. The filial son, in sacrificing, seems never able to exhaust his earnest purpose, his sincerity, and reverence. He observes every rule, without transgression or short–coming. His reverence appears in his movements of advancing and retiring, as if he were hearing the orders (of his parents), or as if they were perhaps directing him.

11. What the sacrifice of a filial son should be can be known. While he is standing (waiting for the service to commence), he should be reverent, with his body somewhat bent; while he is. engaged in carrying forward the service, he should be reverent, with an expression of pleasure; when he is presenting the offerings, he should be reverent, with an expression of desire. He should then retire and stand, as if he were about to receive orders; when he has removed the offerings and (finally) retires, the expression of reverent gravity should continue to be worn on his face. Such is the sacrifice of a filial son.

To stand without any inclination of the body would show insensibility; to carry the service forward without an expression of pleasure would show indifference; to present the offerings without an expression of desire (that they may be enjoyed) would show a want of love; to retire and stand without seeming to expect to receive orders would show pride; to retire and stand, after the removal of the offerings, without an expression of reverent gravity would show a forgetfulness of the parent to whom he owes his being. A sacrifice so conducted would be wanting in its proper characteristics.

12. A filial son, cherishing a deep love (for his parents), is sure to have a bland air; having a bland air, he will have a look of pleasure; having a look of pleasure, his demeanour will be mild and compliant. A filial son will move as if he were carrying a jade symbol, or bearing a full vessel. Still and grave, absorbed in what he is doing, he will seem as if he were unable to sustain the burden, and in danger of letting it fall. A severe gravity and austere manner are not proper to the service of parents;—such is the manner of a full-grown man.

13. There were five things by means of which the ancient kings secured the good government of the whole kingdom:—the honour which they paid to the virtuous; to the noble; and to the old; the reverence which they showed to the aged; and their kindness to the young. It was by these five things that they maintained the stability of the kingdom.

Why did they give honour to the virtuous? Because of their approximation to the course of duty[1]. They did so to the noble because of their approximation to the position of the ruler; and to the old because of their approximation to that of parents. They showed reverence to the aged, because of their approximation to the position of elder brothers; and kindness to the young, because of their approximation to the position of sons.

[1. P. Callery translates this by—'Parce qu'ils sont proche de la vérité,' saying in a note:—'According to the Chinese philosophers, they understand by teh that which man has obtained by his own efforts or the virtue he has acquired, and by tâo that which all men should be striving to reach, what is suitable, what is in order, or virtue in the abstract. Now, as I think, there is nothing but truth which satisfies these conditions, for, according to the Christian philosophy, God Himself is the truth,' &c. Zottoli's translation is, 'Quia hi appropinquant ad perfectionem.']

14. Therefore he who is perfectly filial approximates to be king, and he who is perfectly fraternal approximates to being presiding chieftain. He who is perfectly filial approximates to being king, for even the son of Heaven had the father (whom he must revere); and he who is perfectly fraternal approximates to being presiding chieftain, for even a feudal lord bad his elder brothers (or cousins), (whom he must obey). The observance of the lessons of the ancient kings, without admitting any change in them, was the way by which they united and kept together the kingdom with its states and families[1].

15. The Master said, 'The laying the foundation of (all) love in the love of parents teaches people concord. The laying the foundation of (all) reverence in the reverence of elders teaches the people obedience. When taught loving harmony, the people set the (proper) value on their parents; when taught to reverence their superiors, the people set the (Proper) value in obeying the orders given to them. Filial piety in the service of parents, and obedience in the discharge of orders can be displayed throughout the kingdom, and they will everywhere take effect.

16. At (the time of) the border sacrifice (to Heaven), those who are engaged in funeral rites do not dare to wail, and those who are wearing mourning do not dare to enter the gate of the capital;—this is the highest expression of reverence.

17. On the day of sacrifice, the ruler led the victim forward, along with and assisted by his son on

[1. The sequence in the writer's mind in this paragraph almost eludes my discovery; it does so still more in the translation of it by Callery and Zottoli.]

the opposite side; while the Great officers followed in order. When they had entered the gate of the temple, they fastened the victim to the stone pillar. The ministers and Great officers then bared their arms, and proceeded to inspect the hair, paying particular attention to that of the ears. They then with the knife with the bells attached to it, cut it open, took out the fat about the inwards, and withdrew (for a time[1]). Afterwards they offered some of the flesh boiled, and some raw, then (finally) withdrawing. There was the highest reverence about everything.

18. The sacrifice in the suburb of the capital was the great expression of gratitude to Heaven, and it was specially addressed to the sun, with which the moon was associated[2]. The sovereigns of Hsiâ presented it in the dark. Under the Yin dynasty they did so

[1. They withdrew for a time, 'to offer the hair and blood.'

This sentence is translated by Zottoli:—'Coeli sacrificio summe rependitur coelum sed potissimum intenditur Sol, consociatus cum luna.' Callery says:—'Le sacrifice qu'on offre dans la campagne est un acte de grande reconnaissance envers le ciel, et principalement envers le soleil, auquel on associe la lune.'

Here, again, nature–worship seems to crop up. Khan Hâo says on the passage:—'Heaven is the great source of tâo (the course of nature and duty), and of all the visible bodies which it hangs out, there are none greater than the sun and moon. Therefore, while the object of the suburban sacrifice was a grateful acknowledgment of Heaven, the sun was chosen as the resting place for its spirit (or spirits). The idea in the institution of the rite was deep and far–reaching.' It must be borne in mind that the rites described in the text are those of former dynasties, especially of that of Kâu. I cannot bring to mind any passages in which there is mention made of any sacrifice to the sun or sun–spirit in connexion with the great sacrifice to Heaven., or Shang Tî, at the service on the day of the water solstice in the southern suburb.]

at noon. Under the Kâu they sacrificed all the day, especially at daybreak, and towards evening.

19. They sacrificed to the sun on the altar, and to the moon in the hollow;—to mark the distinction between (the) gloom (of the one) and (the) brightness (of the other), and to show the difference between the high and the low. They sacrificed to the sun in the east, and to the moon in the west;—to mark the distinction between (the) forthcoming (of the former) and (the) withdrawing (of the latter), and to show the correctness of their (relative) position. The sun comes forth from the east, and the moon appears in the west; the darkness and the light are now long, now short; when the one ends, the other begins, in regular succession:–thus producing the harmony of all under the sky'

20. The rites to be observed by all under heaven were intended to promote the return (of the mind) to the beginning (= Creator of all); to promote (the honouring of) spiritual Beings; to promote the harmonious use (of all resources and appliances) of government; to promote righteousness; and to promote humility. They promote the return to the beginning, securing the due consideration, of their originator. They promote (the honouring) of spiritual Beings, securing the giving honour to superiors. They promote the (proper) use of all resources, thereby establishing the regulations (for the well–being of) the people. They promote

[1. The sacrifices in this paragraph are those at the equinoxes; that to the sun at the vernal in the eastern suburb, aid that to the moon at the autumnal in the western suburb. They are still maintained. See the ritual of the present dynasty Book VIII, where the former is called in and the latter .]

righteousness, and thus there are no oppositions and conflictings between high and low. They promote humility, in order to prevent occasions of strife. Let these five things be united through the rites for the regulation of all under heaven, and though there may be some extravagant and perverse who are not kept in order, they will be few.

SECTION II.

1. Zâi Wo said, 'I have heard the names Kwei and Shan, but I do not know what they mean[1].' The Master said, 'The (intelligent) spirit[2] is of the shin nature, and shows that in fullest measure; the animal soul is of the kwei nature, and shows that in fullest measure. It is the union of kwei and shan that forms the highest exhibition of doctrine.

'All the living must die, and dying, return to the ground; this is what is called kwei. The bones and flesh, moulder below, and, hidden away, become the earth of the fields. But the spirit issues forth, and is displayed on high in a condition of glorious brightness. The vapours and odours which produce a feeling of sadness, (and arise from the decay of their substance), are the subtle essences of all things, and (also) a manifestation of the shan nature.

[1. I am unable to give a translation of the characters kwei and shan, so as to make the meaning readily intelligible to the English reader. Callery gives for them 'L'âme et l'esprit.' Zottoli, 'Manes Spiritusque.' Evidently the question is about the application of them to the dead and gone, and the component elements of the human constitution.

2. The character in the text here is khî 'the breath.' Zottoli translates it by 'rationalis vis,' and Callery by 'la respiration de l'homme.']

'On the ground of these subtle essences of things, with an extreme decision and inventiveness, (the sages) framed distinctly (the names of) kwei and shan, to constitute a pattern for the black–haired race[1]; and all the multitudes were filled with awe, and the myriads of the people constrained to submission.'

2. 'The sages did not consider these (names) to be sufficient, and therefore. they built temples with their (different) apartments, and framed their rules for ancestors who were always to be honoured, and those whose tablets should be removed;—thus making a distinction for nearer and more distant kinship, and for ancestors the remote and the recent, and teaching the people to go back to their oldest fathers, and retrace their beginnings, not forgetting those to whom they owed their being. In consequence of this the multitude submitted to their lessons, and listened to them with a quicker readiness.

3. 'These two elements (of the human constitution) having been established (with the two names), two ceremonies were framed in accordance with them. They appointed the service of the morning, when the fat of the inwards was burned so as to bring out its fragrance, and this was mixed with the blaze of dried southern–wood. This served as a tribute to the (intelligent) spirit, and taught all to go back to their originating ancestors. They (also) presented millet and rice, and offered the delicacies of the liver, lungs, head, and heart, along with two bowls (of

[1. It is observed by many of the commentators that the characters here employed for 'black–haired race' were unused in the time of Confucius, and became current under the Khin dynasty.]

liquor) and odoriferous spirits. This served as a tribute to the animal soul, and taught the people to love one another, and high and low to cultivate good feeling between them;—such was the effect of those ceremonies.

4. 'The superior man, going back to his ancient fathers, and returning to the authors of his being, does not forget those to whom he owes his life, and therefore he calls forth all his reverence, gives free vent to his feelings, and exhausts his strength in discharging the above service;–as a tribute of gratitude to his parents he dares not but do his utmost[1].'

5. Thus it was that anciently the, son of Heaven had his field of a thousand acres, in which he himself held the plough, wearing the square–topped cap with red ties. The feudal princes also had their field of a hundred acres, in which they did the same, wearing the same cap with green ties. They did this in the service of Heaven, Earth, the Spirits of the land and grain, and their ancient fathers, to supply the new wine, cream, and vessels of grain. In this way did they procure these things;–it was a great expression of their reverence.

6. Anciently, the son of Heaven and the feudal lords had their officers who attended to their animals; and at the proper seasons, after vigil and fasting, they washed their heads, bathed, and visited them in person[2], taking from them for victims those which

[1. The above conversation with Zâi Wo is found in the 'Narratives of the School,' Article 17, headed 'Duke Âi's Questions about Government;' and the reply of Confucius ends here. I hesitate, therefore, to continue the points of quotation in what follows.

2. The first day, probably, of the last month of spring. If it were not bright, perhaps another was chosen.]

were spotless and perfect;—it was a great expression of their reverence.

The ruler ordered the oxen to be brought before him, and inspected them; he chose them by their hair, divined whether it would be fortunate to use them, and if the response were favourable, he had them cared for. In his skin cap, and the white skirt gathered up at the waist, on the first day and at the middle of the month, he inspected them. Thus did he do his utmost;—it was the height of filial piety.

7. Anciently, the son of Heaven and the feudal lords had their own mulberry trees and silkworms' house; the latter built near a river, ten cubits in height, the surrounding walls being topped with thorns, and the gates closed on the outside. In the early morning of a very bright day, the ruler, in his skin cap and the white skirt, divined for the most auspicious of the honourable ladies in the three palaces of his wife[1], who were then employed to take the silkworms into the house. They washed the seeds in the stream, gathered the leaves from the mulberry trees, and dried them in the wind to feed the worms.

When the (silkworm) year was ended, the honourable ladies had finished their work with the insects, and carried the cocoons to show them to the ruler. They then presented them to his wife, who said, 'Will not these supply the materials for the ruler's robes?' She forthwith received them, wearing her head–dress and the robe with pheasants on it, and afterwards caused a sheep and a pig to be killed and

[1. The queen had six palaces; the wife of a prince, three. The writer confines his account here to the latter.]

cooked to treat (the ladies). This probably was the ancient custom at the presentation of the cocoons.

Afterwards, on a good day, the wife rinsed some of them thrice in a vessel, beginning to unwind them, and then distributed them to the auspicious and honourable ladies of her three palaces to (complete) the unwinding. They then dyed the thread red and green, azure and yellow, to make the variously coloured figures on robes. When the robes were finished, the ruler wore them in sacrificing to the former kings and dukes;—all displayed the greatest reverence.

8. The superior man says, 'Ceremonies and music should not for a moment be neglected by any one. When one has mastered (the principles of) music, and regulates his heart and mind accordingly, the natural, correct, gentle, and honest heart is easily developed, and with this development of the heart comes joy. This joy goes on to a feeling of repose. This repose is long continued. The man in this constant repose becomes (a sort of) heaven. Heaven–like, his action is spirit–like. Heaven–like, he is believed, though he do not speak. Spirit–like, he is regarded with awe, though he display no rage. So it is when one by his mastering of music regulates his mind and heart.

[1. When one has mastered (the principle of) ceremonies, and regulates his person accordingly, he becomes grave and reverential. Grave and reverential, he is regarded with awe. If the heart be for a moment without the feeling of harmony and joy, meanness and deceitfulness enter it. If the outward demeanour be for a moment without gravity and reverentialness, indifference and rudeness show themselves.

'Therefore the sphere in which music acts is the interior of man, and that of ceremonies is his exterior. The result of music is a perfect harmony, and that of ceremonies is a perfect observance (of propriety). When one's inner man is thus harmonious, and his outer man thus docile, the people behold his countenance and do not strive with him; they look to his demeanour, and no feeling of indifference or rudeness arises in them. Thus it is that when virtue shines and moves within (a superior), the people are sure to accept (his rule) and hearken to him; and when the principles (of propriety) are displayed in his conduct, the people are all sure to accept (his rule) and obey him. Therefore it is said, 'Let ceremonies and music have their course till all under heaven is filled with them; then give them their manifestation and application, and nothing difficult to manage will appear.'

Music affects the inward movements (of the soul); ceremonies appear in the outward movements (of the body). Hence it is the rule to make ceremonies as few and brief as possible, and to give to music its fullest development. This leads to the forward exhibition of ceremonies, and therein their beauty resides; and to the introspective consideration of music, and therein its beauty resides. If ceremonies, demanding this condensation, did not receive this forward exhibition of them, they would almost disappear altogether; if music, demanding this full development, were not accompanied with the introspection, it would produce a dissipation of the mind. Thus it is that to every ceremony there is its proper response, and for music there is this introspection. When ceremonies are responded to, there arises pleasure, and when music is accompanied with the right introspection, there arises repose. The response of ceremony and the introspection of music spring from one and the same idea, and have one and the same object.

9. Zang–dze said, 'There are three degrees of filial piety. The highest is the honouring of our parents; the second is the not disgracing them; and the lowest is the being able to support them.'

10. (His disciple), Kung–ming Î, said, 'Can you, master, be considered (an example of a) filial son?' Zang–dze replied, 'What words are these? What words are these? What the superior man calls filial piety requires the anticipation of our parents' wishes, the carrying out of their aims and their instruction in the path (of duty). I am simply one who supports his parents;—how can I be considered filial?'

11. Zang–dze said, 'The 'body is that which has been transmitted to us by our parents; dare any one allow himself to be irreverent in the employment of their legacy? If a man in his own house and privacy be not grave, he is not filial; if in serving his ruler, he be not loyal, he is not filial; if in discharging the duties of office, he be not reverent, he is not filial; if with friends he be not sincere, he is not filial; if on the field of battle he be not brave, he is not filial. If he fail in these five things, the evil (of the disgrace) will reach his parents;—dare he but reverently attend to them?'

To prepare the fragrant flesh and grain which he has cooked, tasting and then presenting them before his parents, is not filial piety; it is only nourishing them. He whom the superior man pronounces filial is he whom (all) the people of (his) state praise, saying with admiration, 'Happy are the parents who have such a son as this!'—that indeed is what can be called being filial. The fundamental lesson for all is filial piety. The practice of it is seen in the support (of parents). One may be able to support them; the difficulty is in doing so with the proper reverence. One may attain to that reverence; the difficulty is to do so without self–constraint. That freedom from constraint may be realised;—the difficulty is to maintain it to the end. When his parents are dead, and the son carefully watches over his actions, so that a bad name, (involving) his parents, shall not be handed down, he may be said to be able to maintain his piety to the end. True love is the love of this; true propriety is the doing of this; true righteousness is the rightness of this; true sincerity is being sincere in this; true strength is being strong in this joy springs from conformity to this; punishments spring from the violation of this.

12. Zang–dze said, 'Set up filial piety, and it will fill the space from earth to heaven; spread it out, and it will extend over all the ground to the four seas;' hand it down to future ages, and from morning to evening it will be observed; push it on to the eastern sea, the western sea, the southern sea, and the northern sea, and it will be (everywhere) the law for men, and their obedience to it will be uniform. There will be a fulfilment of the words of the ode (III, i, ode 10, 6),

"From west to east, from south to north,
There was no unsubmissive thought."

13. Zang–dze said, 'Trees are felled and animals killed, (only) at the proper seasons. The Master said',

[1. The master here is Confucius. The record of his saying is only found only here.]

"To fell a single tree, or kill a single animal, not at the proper season, is contrary to filial piety."'

There are three degrees of filial piety:—the least, seen in the employment of one's strength (in the service of parents); the second, seen in the endurance of toil (for them); and the greatest, seen in its never failing. Thinking of the gentleness and love (of parents) and forgetting our toils (for them) may be called the employment of strength. Honouring benevolences and resting with the feeling of repose in righteousness may be called the endurance of toil; the wide dispensation of benefits and the providing of all things (necessary for the people) may be called the piety that does not fail.

When his parents love him, to rejoice, and not allow himself to forget them; when they hate him, to fear and yet feel no resentment; when they have faults, to remonstrate with them, and yet not withstand them; when they are dead, to ask (the help only of) the good to obtain the grain with which to sacrifice to them:—this is what is called the completion (by a son) of his proper services.

14. The disciple Yo-king Khun[1] injured his foot in descending from his hall, and for some months was not able to go out. Even after this he still wore a look of sorrow, and (one of the) disciples of the school said to him, 'Your foot, master, is better; and though for some months you could not go out, why should you still wear a look of sorrow?' Yo-kang Khun replied, 'It is a good question which

[1. Yo-kang Khun evidently was a disciple of Zang-dze. Mencius had a disciple of the same surname, Yo-kang Kho (I, ii, 16). Another is mentioned by him (V, ii, 3). Lieh-dze mentions a fourth. The Yo-kangs are said to have sprung from the ducal stock of Sung.]

you ask! It is a good question which you ask! I heard from Zang-dze what he had heard the Master say, that of all that Heaven produces and Earth nourishes, there is none so great as man. His parents give birth to his person all complete, and to return it, to them all complete may be called filial duty. When no member has been mutilated and no disgrace done to any part of the person, it may be called complete; and hence a superior man does not dare to take the slightest step in forgetfulness of his filial duty. But now I forgot the way of that, and therefore I wear the look of sorrow. (A son) should not forget his parents in a single lifting up of his feet, nor in the utterance of a single word. He should not forget his parents in a single lifting up of his feet, and therefore he will walk in the highway and not take a by-path, he will use a boat and not attempt to wade through a stream;—not daring, with the body left him by his parents, to go in the way of peril. He should not forget his parents in the utterance of a single word, and therefore an evil word will not issue from his mouth, and an angry word will not come back to his person. Not to disgrace his person and not to cause shame to his parents may be called filial duty.'

15. Anciently, the sovereigns of the line of Yü honoured virtue, and highly esteemed age; the sovereigns of Hsiâ honoured rank, and highly esteemed age; under Yin they honoured riches, and highly esteemed age; under Kâu, they honoured kinship, and highly esteemed age. Yü, Hsiâ, Yin, and Kâu produced the greatest kings that have appeared under Heaven, and there was not one of them who neglected age. For long has honour been paid

to years under the sky; to pay it is next to the service of parents.

16. Therefore, at court among parties of the same rank, the highest place was 'given to the oldest. Men of seventy years carried their staffs at the court. When the ruler questioned one of them, he made him sit on a mat. One of eighty years did not wait out the audience, and when the ruler would question him he went to his house. Thus the submission of a younger brother (and juniors generally) was recognised at the court.

17. A junior walking with one older (than himself), if they were walking shoulder to shoulder, yet it was not on the same line. If he did not keep transversely (a little behind), he followed the other[1]. When they saw an old man, people in carriages or walking got out of his way. Men, where the white were mingling with their black hairs, did not carry burdens on the roads. Thus the submission of juniors was recognised on the public ways.

Residents in the country took their places according to their age, and the old and poor were not neglected, nor did the strong come into collision with the weak, or members of a numerous clan do violence to those of a smaller. Thus the submission of juniors was recognised in the country districts and hamlets[2].

18. According to the ancient rule, men of fifty years were not required to serve in hunting expeditions[3]; and in the distribution of the game, a larger

[1. If the elder were a brother or cousin, the junior kept a little behind, and apart. If he were an uncle, the other followed in a line.

2. Five Kâu, translated 'districts,' made a 'hsiang,' here translated 'the country districts.'

3. Literally, 'men of the tien' The tien was a tract of considerable size; contributing to the army a chariot, three mailed men, and seventy–two foot–men. There was a levy on it also of men to serve in the hunting expeditions.]

share was given to the more aged. Thus the submission of juniors was recognised in the arrangements for the hunts. In the tens and fives of the army and its detachments, where the rank was the same, places were given according to age. Thus the submission of juniors was recognised in the army.

19. The display of filial and fraternal duty in the court; the practice of them on the road; their reaching to the districts and hamlets; their extension to the huntings; and the cultivation of them in the army, (have thus been described). All would have died for them under the constraint of righteousness, and not dared to violate them.

20. The sacrifice in the Hall of Distinction served to inculcate filial duty on the feudal lords; the feasting of the three classes of the old and five classes of the experienced in the Great college served to inculcate brotherly submission on those princes; the sacrifices to the worthies of former times in the western school served to inculcate virtue on them; the (king's) ploughing in the field set apart for him, served to teach them the duty of nourishing (the people); their appearances at court in spring and autumn served to inculcate on them their duty as subjects or ministers. Those five institutions were the great lessons for the kingdom.

21. When feasting the three classes of the old and five classes of the experienced, the son of Heaven bared his arm, cut up the bodies of the victims, and handed round the condiments; he also presented the cup with which they rinsed their mouths, wearing the square–topped cap, and carrying a shield. It was thus he inculcated brotherly submission on the princes. It was thus that in the country and villages regard was paid to age, that the old and poor were not neglected, and that the members of a numerous clan did hot oppress those of a smaller;—these things came from the Great college.

The son of Heaven appointed the four schools; and when his eldest son entered one of them, he took his place according to his age.

22. When the son of Heaven was on a tour of inspection, the princes (of each quarter) met him on their borders. The son of Heaven first visited those who were a hundred years old. If there were those of eighty or ninety, on the way to the east, he, though going to the west, did not dare to pass by (without seeing them); and so, if their route was to the west, and his to the west. If he wished to speak of matters of government, he, though ruler, might go to them.

23. Those who had received the first degree of office took places according to age (at meetings) in the country and villages; those who had received the second, took places in the same way (at meetings) of all the members of their relatives. Those who had received the third degree did not pay the same regard to age. But at meetings of all the members of

a clan no one dared to take precedence of one who was seventy years old.

Those who were seventy, did not go to court unless for some great cause. When they did so for such a cause, the ruler would bow and give place to them, afterwards going on to the parties possessed of rank.

24. Whatever good was possessed by the son of Heaven, he humbly ascribed the merit of it to Heaven; whatever good was possessed by a feudal lord, he ascribed it to the son of Heaven; whatever good was possessed by a minister or Great officer, he attributed it to the prince of his state; whatever good was possessed by an officer or a common man, he assigned the ground of it to his parents, and the preservation of it to his elders. Emolument, rank, felicitations, and rewards were (all) transacted in the ancestral temple; and it was thus that they showed (the spirit of) submissive deference.

25. Anciently, the sages, having determined the phenomena of heaven and earth in their states of rest and activity, made them the basis of the Yî (and divining by it). The diviner held the tortoise–shell in his arms, with his face towards the south, while the son of Heaven, in his dragon–robe and square–topped cap, stood with his face to the north. The latter, however intelligent might be his mind, felt it necessary to set forth and obtain a decision on what his object was;–showing that he did not dare to take his own way, and giving honour to Heaven (as the supreme Decider). What was good in him (or in his views) he ascribed to others; what was wrong, to himself; thus teaching not to boast, and giving honour to men of talents and virtue.

26. When a filial son was about to sacrifice; the

[1. Who does not see that, from the writer's point of view, divination was originally had recourse to in the search for an 'infallible' director in matters to be done? The Decider was held to be 'Heaven;' the error was in thinking that the will of Heaven could be known through any manipulation of the tortoise–shell, or the stalks.]

rule was that he should have his mind well adjusted and grave, to fit him for giving to all matters their full consideration, for providing the robes and other things, for repairing the temple and its fanes, and for regulating everything. When the day of sacrifice arrived, the rule was that his countenance should be mild, and his movements show an anxious dread, as if he feared his love were not sufficient. When he put down his offerings, it was required that his demeanour should be mild, and his body bent, as if (his parents) would speak (to him) and had not yet done so; when the officers assisting had all gone out[1], he stood lowly and still, though correct and straight, as if he were about to lose the sight (of his parents).

After the sacrifice, he looked pleased and expectant, as if they would again enter[2].

In this way his ingenuousness and goodness were never absent from his person; his ears and eyes were never withdrawn from what was in his heart; the exercises of his thoughts never left his parents. What was bound up in his heart was manifested in his countenance; and he was continually examining himself;-such was the mind of the filial son.

[1. The text here is difficult. I have followed Mang, as has Zottoli;—the interpretation of as 'assisting officers,' can otherwise be defended. Callery gives for the clause:—'Toutes les pensées étrangères (au sacrifice) il les chasse au dehors,' which it would be difficult to justify.

2. Here again translation is difficult. Zottoli gives:—'Cumque sacrificium transiverit, intendet animo, prosequetur ore, quasi mox iterum ingressuri essent.' Callery:—'Après le sacrifice il s'en va lentement, comme (s'il suivait quelqu'un pas à pas, et avait envie) de rentrer (avec lui dans le temple).']

27. The sites for the altars to the spirits of the land and grain were on the right; that for the ancestral temple on the left[1].

BOOK XXII. KÎ THUNG, OR A SUMMARY ACCOUNT OF SACRIFICES

1. Of all the methods for the good ordering of men, there is none more urgent than the use of ceremonies. Ceremonies are of five kinds[2], and there is none of them more important than sacrifices.

Sacrifice is not a thing coming to a man from without; it issues from within him, and has its birth in his heart. When the heart is deeply moved, expression is given to it by ceremonies; and hence, only men of ability and virtue can give complete exhibition to the idea of sacrifice.

2. The sacrifices of such men have their own blessing;—not indeed what the world calls blessing[3]. Blessing here means perfection;–it is the name given to the complete and natural discharge of all duties. When nothing is left incomplete or improperly discharged;—this is what we call perfection, implying the doing everything that should be done in one's internal self, and externally the performance of everything according to the proper method. There is a fundamental agreement between a loyal subject in his service of his ruler and a filial son in

[1. See the introduction, vol. xxvii, pp. 37, 38.

2. The five kinds of ceremonies are the Auspicious (including all acts of religious worship); the Mourning; those of Hospitality; the Military; and the Festive.

3. Success, longevity, the protection of spiritual Beings.]

his service of his parents. In the supernal sphere there is a compliance with (what is due to) the repose and expansion of the energies of nature[1]; in the external sphere, a compliance with (what is due) to rulers and elders; in the internal sphere, the filial service of parents;—all this constitutes what is called perfection.

It is only the able and virtuous man who can attain to this perfection; and can sacrifice when he has attained to it. Hence in the sacrifices of such a man he brings into exercise all sincerity and good faith, with all right–heartedness and reverence; he offers the (proper) things; accompanies them with the (proper) rites; employs the soothing of music; does everything suitably to the season. Thus intelligently does he offer his sacrifices, without seeking for anything to be gained by them:—such is the heart and mind of a filial son.

3. It is by sacrifice that the nourishment of parents is followed up and filial duty to them Perpetuated. The filial heart is a storehouse (of all filial duties). Compliance with everything that can mark his course, and be no violation of the relation (between parent and child):—the keeping of this is why we call it a storehouse. Therefore in three ways is a filial son's service of his parents shown:—while they are alive, by nourishing them; when they are dead, by

[1. Callery gives for these.—'Conformité avec les Esprits et les Dieux.' Zottoli:—'Ordo erga Genios Spiritusque.' Medhurst:—'Being obedient to the Kwei Shins.' If they had observed the 'three spheres' of the writer, I think they would have translated differently. I believe the idea is—'Compliance with the will of Heaven or God, as seen in the course of Nature and Providence.']

all the rites of mourning; and when the mourning is over by sacrificing to them. In his nourishing them we see his natural obedience; in his funeral rites we see his sorrow; in his sacrifices we see his reverence and observance of the (proper) seasons. In these three ways we see the practice of a filial son.

4. When a son had done everything (for his sacrifices) that he could do himself, he proceeded to seek assistance from abroad; and this came through the rites of marriage. Hence the language of a ruler, when about to marry a wife, was:—'I beg you, O ruler, to give me your elegant daughter, to share this small state with my poor self, to do service in the ancestral temple, and at the altars to (the spirits of) the land and grain.' This underlay his seeking for that assistance (from abroad).

In sacrificing, husband and wife had their several duties which they personally attended to; and on this account there was the array of officials belonging to the exterior and interior departments (of the palace). When these officers were complete, all things necessary (for the service) were made ready:—small things, such as the sourcrout of water plants and pickles from the produce of dry grounds; and fine things, such as the stands for the bodies of the three victims, and the supplies for the eight dishes. Strange insects and the fruits of plants and trees, produced under the best influences of light and shade, were all made ready. Whatever heaven produces, whatever earth developes {sic} in its growth;—all were then exhibited in the greatest abundance. Everything was there from without, and internally there was the utmost effort of the will:—such was the spirit in sacrificing.

5. For this reason, also, the son of Heaven himself guided the plough in the southern suburb, to provide the grain for the sacrificial vessels; and the queen looked after her silkworms in the northern suburb, to provide the cap and robes of silk. The princes of the states guided the plough in their eastern suburb, also to provide the grain for the sacrificial vessels, and their wives looked after their silkworms in the northern suburb, to provide the cap and robes of silk. This was not because the son of Heaven and the princes

had not men to plough for them, or 'because the queen and the princes' wives had not women to tend the silkworms for them; it was to give the exhibition of their personal sincerity. Such sincerity was what is called doing their utmost; and such doing of their utmost was what is called reverence. When they had reverently done their utmost, they could serve the spiritual Intelligences—such was the way of sacrificing.

6. When the time came for offering a sacrifice, the man wisely gave himself to the work of purification. That purification meant the production of uniformity (in all the thoughts);–it was the giving uniformity to all that was not uniform, till a uniform direction of the thoughts was realised. Hence a superior man, unless for a great occasion, and unless he were animated by a great reverence, did not attempt this purification. While it was not attained, he did not take precautions against the influence of (outward) things, nor did he cease from all (internal) desires. But when he was about to attempt it, he guarded against all things of an evil nature, and suppressed all his desires, His ears did not listen to music;—as it is said in the Record, 'People occupied with purification have no music,' meaning that they did not venture to allow its dissipation of their minds. He allowed no vain thoughts in his heart, but kept them in a strict adherence to what was right. He allowed no reckless movement of his hands or feet, but kept them firmly in the way of propriety. Thus the superior man, in his purification, devotes himself to carrying to its utmost extent his refined and intelligent virtue.

Therefore there was the looser ordering of the mind for seven days, to bring it to a state of fixed determination; and the complete ordering of it for three days, to effect the uniformity of all the thoughts. That determination is what is called purification; the final attainment is when the highest degree of refined intelligence is reached. After this it was possible to enter into communion with the spiritual Intelligences.

7. Moreover, on the eleventh day, before that appointed for the sacrifice, the governor of the palace gave warning notice to the wife of the ruler, and she also conducted that looser ordering of her thoughts for seven days, and that more complete ordering of them for three. The ruler accomplished his purification in the outer apartment, and the wife her purification in the inner. After this they met in the grand temple.

The ruler, in the dark–coloured square–topped cap, stood at the top of the steps on the cast; his wife in her head–dress and pheasant–embroidered robe stood in the eastern chamber. The ruler from his mace–handled libation–cup poured out the fragrant spirit before the personator of the dead; and the great minister in charge of the temple with his halfmace–handled cup poured the second libation (for the wife). When the victim was introduced, the ruler held it by the rope; the ministers and Great officers followed; other officers carried the dried grass (to lay on the ground when it should be killed); the wives of the ruler's surname followed the wife with the basins; she presented the purified liquid; the ruler held in his hand the knife with bells; he prepared the lungs (to be offered to the personator); and his wife put them on the dishes and presented them. All this shows what is meant in saying that husband and wife had their parts which they personally performed.

8. When they went in for the dance, the ruler, holding his shield and axe, went to the place for the performance. He took his station at the head of those on the east, and in his square–topped cap,, carrying his shield, he led on all his officers, to give pleasure to the august personator of the dead. Hence the son of Heaven in his sacrifices (gave expression to) the joy of all in the kingdom. (In the same way) the feudal princes at their sacrifices (gave expression to) the joy of all within their territories. In their square–topped caps, and carrying their shields, they led on all their officers, to give joy to the august personators:—with the idea of showing the joy of all within their territories.

9. At a sacrifice there were three things specially important. Of the offerings there was none more important than the libation; of the music there was none more important than the singing in the hall. above; of the pantomimic evolutions there was none more important than that representing (king) Wû's (army) on the night (before his battle). Such was the practice of the Kâu dynasty. All the three things were designed to increase the aim of the superior man by the use of these external representations. Hence their movements in advancing and retreating were regulated by (the degree of) that aim. If it were less intense, they were lighter; if it were more intense, they were more vehement. If the aim were less intense, and they sought to make the outward representation more vehement, even a sage could not have accomplished this.

Therefore the superior man, in sacrificing, exerted himself to the utmost in order to give clear expression to these more important things. He conducted everything according to the rules of ceremony, thereby giving prominent exhibition to them, and displaying them to the august personator:—Such was the method of the sages.

10. At sacrifices there are the provisions that are left. The dealing with these is the least important thing in sacrifices, but it is necessary to take knowledge of it. Hence there is the saying of antiquity, 'The end must be attended to even as the beginning:'—there is an illustration of it in these leavings. Hence it was the remark of a superior man of antiquity, that 'The personator also eats what the spirits have left;—it is a device of kindness, in which may be seen (the method of) government.'

Hence, when the personator rose, the ruler and his three ministers partook of what he had left. When the ruler had risen, the six Great officers partook;–the officers partook of what the ruler had left. When the Great officers rose, the eight officers partook:—the lower in rank ate what the higher had left. When these officers rose, each one took what was before him and went out, and placed it (in the court) below the hall, when all the inferior attendants entered and removed it:—the inferior class ate what the superior had left.

11. Every change in the disposal of these relics was marked by an increase in the number (of those who partook of them); and thus there was marked the distinction between the degrees of the noble and the mean, and a representation given of the dispensation of benefits (by the sovereign). Hence by means of the four vessels of millet there is shown the cultivation of this in the ancestral temple, which becomes thereby a representation of all comprised within the confines (of the state).

What is done at sacrifices afforded the greatest example of the dispensation of favours[1] Hence when the superior possessed the greatest blessing, acts of favour were sure to descend from him to those below him, the only difference being that he enjoyed the blessing first, and those below him afterwards;—there was no such thing as the superior's accumulating a great amount for himself, while the people below him might be suffering from cold and want. Therefore when the superior enjoyed his great blessing, even private individuals waited till the stream should flow down, knowing that his favours would surely come to them. This was shown by what was done with the relics at sacrifices, and hence came the saying that 'By the dealing with these was seen (the method of) government.'

[1. It is difficult to detect the mind of the writer here, and make out the train of his reasoning. Zottoli:—'Sacrificium, beneficioram maximum est.' Callery:—'Dans les sacrifices, les bien faits sont la plus grande chose.' Wylie:—'Sacrifice is tho greatest of the virtuous influences.' But is not the writer simply referring to what he has said about the admission of all classes to participate in the relics of a sacrifice?]

12. Sacrifice is the greatest of all things. Its apparatus of things employed in it is complete, but that completeness springs from all being in accordance with the requirements (of nature and reason) is it not this which enables us to find in it the basis of all the lessons of the sages? Therefore those lessons, in the external sphere, inculcated the honouring of the ruler and of elders, and, in the internal sphere, filial piety towards parents. Hence, when there was an intelligent ruler above, all his ministers submitted to and followed him. When he reverently sacrificed in his ancestral temple, and at the altars to the (spirits of the) land and grain, his sons and grandsons were filially obedient. He did all his duty in his own walk, and was correct in his righteousness; and thence grew up the lessons (of all duty).

Therefore a superior man, in the service of his ruler, should find (guidance for) all his personal conduct. What does not satisfy him in (the behaviour of) his superiors, he will not show in his employment of those below himself; and what he dislikes in the behaviour of those below him, he will not show in the service of his superiors. To disapprove of anything in another, and do the same himself, is contrary to the rule of instruction. Therefore the superior in the inculcation of his lessons, ought to proceed from the foundation (of all duty). This will show him pursuing the greatest method of what is natural and right in the highest degree; and is not this what is seen in sacrifice? Hence we have the saying that 'The first and greatest teaching is to be found in sacrifice.'

13. In sacrifice there is a recognition of what belongs to ten relationships[1]. There are seen in it the method of serving spiritual Beings; the righteousness between ruler and subject; the relation between father and son; the degrees of the noble and mean; the distance gradually increasing between relatives; the bestowment of rank and reward; the separate duties of husband and wife; impartiality in government affairs; the order to be observed between old and young; and the boundaries of high and low. These are what are called the (different duties in the) ten relationships.

14. The spreading of the mat and placing on it a stool to serve for two, was intended as a resting–place for the united spirits (of husband and wife)[2]. The instruction to the blesser in the apartment and the going out to the inside of the gate[3], was the method pursued in (seeking) communion with the spirits.

15. The ruler went to meet the victim, but not to meet the representative of the dead;–to avoid misconstruction[4]. While the representative was outside

[1. Zottoli:—'Sacrificium habet decem sensus.' Callery:—'Les sacrifices renferment dix ordres d'idées.'

2, The reason given for this practice is peculiar. 'While alive,' says Khan Hâo, 'every individual has his or her own body, and hence in the relation of husband and wife, there are the separate duties to be discharged by each; but when they are dead, there is no difference or separation between their spiritual essences (#), and one common stool for support is put down for them both.' Is there any truth that these Chinese speculators are groping after?

3. See vol. xxvii, page 444, paragraph 18.

4. It was not for the ruler to go to meet one who was still a subject, and had not yet entered on the function, which placed Urn in a position of superiority for the time and occasion.]

the gate of the temple, he was to be regarded only as a subject; inside the temple, he had the full character of a ruler. While the ruler was outside the gate of the temple, he was there the ruler; when he entered that gate (on the occasion of the sacrifice), he had the full character of a subject, or a son. Hence his not going forth (to meet the representative) made clear the right distinction between the ruler and subject.

16. According to the rule in sacrifices, a grandson acted as the representative of his grandfather. Though employed to act the part of representative, yet he was only the son of the sacrificer. When his father, with his face to the north, served him, he made clear how it is the way of a son to serve his father. Thus (sacrifice) illustrated the relation of father and son.

17. When the representative had drunk the fifth cup, the ruler washed the cup of jade, and presented it to the ministers. When he had drunk the seventh cup, that of green jasper was presented to the Great officers. When he had drunk the ninth cup, the plain one varnished was presented to the ordinary officers, and all who were taking part in the service. In all the classes the cup passed from one to another, according to age; and thus were shown

the degrees of rank as more honourable and lower.

18. At the sacrifice the parties taking part in it were arranged on the left and right, according to their order of descent from the common ancestor, and thus the distinction was maintained between the order of fathers and sons, the near and the distant, the older and the younger, the more nearly related and the more distantly, and there, was no confusion. Therefore at the services in the grand ancestral temple, all in the two lines of descent were present, and no one failed to receive his proper place in their common relationship. This was what was called (showing) the distance gradually increasing between relatives.

19. Anciently the intelligent rulers conferred rank on the virtuous, and emoluments on the meritorious; and the rule was that this should take place in the Grand temple, to show that they did not dare to do it on their own private motion. Therefore, on the day of sacrifice, after the first presenting (of the cup to the representative), the ruler descended and stood on the south of the steps on the east, with his face to the south, while those who were to receive their appointments stood facing the north. The recorder was on the right of the ruler, holding the tablets on which the appointments were written. He read these, and (each man) bowed twice, with his head to the ground, received the writing, returned (home), and presented it in his (own) ancestral temple:—such was the way in which rank and reward were given.

20. The ruler, in the dragon robe and square–topped cap, stood at the top of the steps on the east, while his wife in her head–dress and pheasant–embroidered robe, stood in the chamber on the east. When the wife presented and put down the dishes or, stands, she held them by the foot; (the officer) who held the vessels with new wine, presented them to her, holding them by the bottom; when the representative of the dead was handing, the cup to the wife, he held it by, the handle, and she gave it to him by the foot; when husband and wife were giving and receiving, the one did not touch the place where the other had held the article; in passing the pledge cup, they changed the cups:—so was the distinction to be maintained between husband and wife shown.

21. In all arrangements with the stands, the chief attention was given to the bones. Some bones were considered nobler, and some meaner. Under the Yin they preferred the thigh bone; and under the Kâu, the shoulder bone. Generally, the bones in front were thought nobler than those behind. The stands served to illustrate the rule in sacrifices of showing

favours. Hence the nobler, guests received the nobler bones, and the lower, the less noble; the nobler did not receive very much, and the lower were not left without any:—impartiality was thus shown. With impartiality of favours, government proceeded freely; with the free proceeding of government, undertakings were accomplished; with the accomplishment of undertakings, merit was established. It is necessary that the way in which merit is established should be known. The stands served to show the rule for the impartial bestowment of favours. So did the skilful administrators of government proceed, and hence it is said that (sacrifices showed the principle of) impartiality in the business of government.

22. Whenever they came to the (general) circulation of the cup, those whose place was on the left stood in one row, and also those whose place was on the right. The members of each row had places according to their age; and in the same way were arranged all the assistants at the service. This was what was called (exhibiting) the order of the old and young.

23. At sacrifices there were portions give skinners, cooks, assistants, feather–wavers, and doorkeepers,—showing how favours should descend to the lowest. Only a virtuous ruler, however, could do this; having intelligence sufficient to perceive (the wisdom of) it, and benevolence equal to the bestowment of it. Apportioning means bestowing; they were able to bestow what was left on those below them.

Skinners were the meanest of those who looked after the buff–coats; cooks' assistants, the meanest of those who looked after the flesh; feather–wavers, the meanest of those who had to do with the music; door–keepers, those who looked after the doors; for anciently they did not employ men who had suffered dismemberment to keep the doors. These four classes of keepers were the meanest of the servants; and the representative of the dead was the most honoured of all. When the most honoured, at the close of the sacrifice, did not forget those who were the most mean, but took what was left and bestowed it on them, (it may be seen how) with an intelligent ruler above, there would not be any of the people within his territory who suffered from cold and want. This is what was meant by saying that sacrifices show the relation between high and low.

24. For the sacrifices (in the ancestral temple) there were the four seasons. That in spring was called yo[1]; that in summer, tî; that in autumn, khang; and that in winter, khang. The yo and tî expressed the idea in the bright and expanding (course of nature); the khang and

khang, that in

[1. Meaning, it is said, 'meagre;' the things offered being few in the spring season; but such explanations are far-fetched.]

the sombre and contracting (course). The a showed the former in its fullest development, and the khang showed the latter in the same. Hence it is said, 'There is nothing more important than the tî and khang.' Anciently, at the tî sacrifice, they conferred rank, and bestowed robes;—acting according to the idea in the bright and expanding (course); and at the khang they gave out fields and homesteads, and issued the rules of autumn-work;—acting according to the idea in the sombre and contracting (course). Hence it is said in the Record, 'On the day of the khang sacrifice they gave forth (the stores of) the ruler's house;' showing how rewards (were then given). When the plants were cut down, the punishment of branding might be inflicted. Before the rules of autumn-work were issued, the people did not dare to cut down the grass.

25. Hence it is said that 'the ideas in the tî and khang are great, and lie at the, foundation of the government of a state; and should by all means be known.' It is for the ruler to know clearly those ideas, and for the minister to be able to execute (what they require). The ruler who does not know the ideas is not complete, and the minister who cannot carry them into execution is not complete.

Now the idea serves to direct and help the aim, and leads to the manifestation of all virtue. Hence he whose virtue is the completest, has the largest aims; and he whose aims are the largest, has the clearest idea. He whose idea is the clearest, will be most reverent in his sacrifices. When the sacrifices (of a state) are reverent, none of the sons and grandsons within its borders will dare to be irreverent. Then the superior man, when he has a sacrifice, will feel it necessary to preside at it in person. if there be a (sufficient) reason for it, he may commit the performance of it to another. But when committing the performance to another, the ruler will not fail (to think) of its meaning, because he understands the ideas in it. He whose virtue is slight, has but a small aim. He who is in doubts as to the idea in it, and will yet seek to be reverent in his sacrifice, will find it impossible to be so; and how can he, who sacrifices without reverence, be the parent of his people?

26. The tripods (at the sacrifices) had inscriptions on them. The maker of an inscription named himself, and took occasion to praise and set forth the excellent qualities of his ancestors, and clearly exhibit them to future generations. Those ancestors must have had good qualities and also bad. But the idea of an inscription is to make mention of the good qualifies and not of the bad:—such is the heart of a filial descendant; and it is only the man of ability and virtue who can attain to it.

The inscriber discourses about and panegyrises the virtues and goodness of his ancestors, their merits and zeal, their services and toils, the congratulations and rewards (given to them), their fame recognised by all under heaven; and in the discussion of these things on his spiritual vessels, he "makes himself famous; and thus he sacrifices to his ancestors. In the celebration of his ancestors he exalts his filial piety. That he himself appears after them is natural. And in the clear showing (of all this) to future generations, he is giving instruction.

27. By the one panegyric of an inscription benefit accrues to the ancestors, to their descendant and to others after them. Hence when a superior man looks at an inscription, while he admires those whom it praises, he also admires him who made it. That maker had intelligence to see (the excellences of his ancestors), virtue to associate himself with them, and wisdom to take advantage (of his position);–he may be pronounced a man of ability and virtue. Such worth without boasting may be pronounced courteous respect.

28. Thus the inscription on the tripod of Khung Khwei of Wei was:–'In the sixth month, on the day ting–hâi, the duke went to the Grand Temple, and said, "My young uncle, your ancestor Kwang Shû assisted duke Khang, who ordered him to follow him in his difficulties on the south of the Han, and afterwards to come to him in his palace (of imprisonment) in the honoured capital of Kâu; and all these hurried journeyings he endured without wearying of them. From him came the helper of duke Hsien, who charged your (later) ancestor Khang Shuh to continue the service of his ancestor. Your deceased father Wan Shû cherished and stimulated in himself the old desires and aims, roused and led on the admirable officers, and showed his own great personal interest in the state of Wei. His labours for our ducal house never wearied early or late, so that the people all testified how good he was." The duke further said, "My young uncle, I give you (this tripod with) its inscription. Carry on and out the services of your father." Khwei bowed with his head to the ground, and said, "In response to the distinction (you have conferred upon me) I will take your great and important charge, and I will put it on the

vases and tripods of my winter sacrifice."' Such was the inscription on the tripod of Khung Khwei of Wei[1].

In this way the superior men of antiquity panegyrised the excellent qualities of their ancestors, and clearly exhibited them to future generations, thereby having the opportunity to introduce their own personality and magnify their states. If descendants who maintain their ancestral temples and the altars to the spirits of the land and grain, praised their ancestors for good qualities which they did not possess, that was falsehood; if they did not take knowledge of the good qualities which they did possess, that showed their want of intelligence; if they knew them and did not transmit them (by their inscriptions), that showed a want of virtue:—these are three things of which a superior man should have been ashamed.

29. Anciently, Tan, duke of Kâu, did most meritorious service for the kingdom. After his death the kings Khang and Khang, bearing in mind all his admirable work, and wishing to honour Lû, granted to its lords the right of offering the greatest sacrifices;—those in the borders of their capital to. Heaven and Earth, in the wider sphere of sacrifice; and the great summer and autumnal sacrifices in the ancestral temple of the state. At those great summer and autumnal sacrifices, on the hall above, they sang the Khing Miâo, and in the courtyard below it they danced the Hsiang to the flute; they

[1. In the year that Confucius died, B.C. 479, this Khung Khwei was obliged to flee from Wei to Sung. The duke Kang, who is mentioned in connexion with his ancestor known as Kwang Shû, was marquis of Wei from B.C. 635 to 600. Duke Hsien ruled from B.C. 577 to 559.]

carried red shields and axes adorned with jade in performing the Tâ Wû dance; and this was the music employed by the son of Heaven. (Those kings) in acknowledgment of the great merit of the duke of Kâu, allowed (the use of those sacrifices and this music) to the (marquis of) Lû. His descendants have continued it, and down to the present day it is not abolished, thereby showing clearly the virtue of the lords of Kâu and magnifying their state[1].

BOOK XXIII. KING KIEH, OR THE DIFFERENT TEACHING OF THE DIFFERENT KINGS[1].

1. Confucius said, 'When you enter any state you can know what subjects (its people) have been taught. If they show themselves men who are mild and gentle, sincere and good, they have been taught from the Book of Poetry. If they have a wide comprehension (of things), and know what is remote and old, they have been taught from the Book of History. If they be large–hearted and generous, bland and honest, they have been taught from the Book of Music. If they be pure and still, refined and subtile, they have been taught from the Yî. If they be courteous and modest, grave and respectful, they have been taught from the Book of Rites and Ceremonies. If they suitably adapt their language to the things of which they speak, they have been taught from the Khun Khiû.

'Hence the failing that may arise in connexion with the study of the Poems is a stupid simplicity; that in connexion. with the History is duplicity; that in connexion with Music is extravagance; that in connexion with the Yî is the violation (of reason)[1]; that in connexion with the practice of Rites and Ceremonies is fussiness; and that in connexion with the Khun Khiû is insubordination[2].

[1. See the introductory notice, vol. xxvii. p. 38.

2. Callery translates the character in the text by 'l'hérésie.' I have met with 'robbery' for it.]

2. 'If they show themselves men who are mild and gentle, sincere and good, and yet free from that simple stupidity, their comprehension of the Book of Poetry is deep. If they have a wide comprehension (of things), and know what is remote and old, and yet are free from duplicity, their understanding of the Book of History is deep. If they are large–hearted and generous, bland and honest, and yet have no tendency to extravagance, their knowledge of Music is deep. If they are pure and still, refined and subtle, and yet do not violate (reason), they have made great attainments in the Yî. If they are courteous and modest, grave and reverent, and yet not fussy, their acquaintance with the Book of Rites and Ceremonies is deep. If they suitably adapt their language to the things of which they speak, and yet have no disposition to be insubordinate, their knowledge of the Khun Khiû is deep.'

3. The son of Heaven forms a ternion with heaven and earth. Hence, in power of his goodness he is their correlate, and his benefits extend at once to all things[1]. His brilliancy is equal to that of the sun and moon, and enlightens all within the four seas, not excepting anything, however minute and small. In the audiences at his court everything is done according to the orderly procedure of benevolence, wisdom, propriety, and righteousness. At his entertainments he listens to the singing of the Odes of the Kingdom and the Odes of the Temple and Altar. When he walks, there are the notes from his girdle pendant. When he rides in his chariot, there are the harmonious sounds of the bells attached to

[1. Compare vol. xxvii, pp. 377, 378.]

his horses. When he is in private at ease, there is the observance of the rules of propriety. When he advances or retires, he does so according to rule and measure. All the officers fulfil their duties rightly, and all affairs are carried on with order. It is as described in the Book of Poetry (I, xiv, 3),

'That virtuous man, the princely one,
Has nothing wrong in his deportment;
He has nothing wrong in his deportment,
And thus he rectifies the four quarters of the state.'

4. When (a ruler) issues his notices and gives forth his orders, and the people are pleased, we have what may be called the condition of harmony. When superiors and inferiors love one another, we have the condition of benevolence. When the people get what they desire without seeking for it, we have the condition of confidence. When all things in the operations of heaven and earth that might be injurious are taken out of the way, we have the condition of rightness. Rightness and confidence, harmony and benevolence are the instruments of the presiding chieftain and the king. If anyone wishes to govern the people, and does not employ these instruments, he will not be successful.

5. In the right government of a state, the Rules of Propriety serve the same purpose as the steelyard in determining what is light and what is heavy; or as the carpenter's line in determining what is crooked and what is straight; or as the circle and square in determining what is square and what is round. Hence, if the weights of the steel–yard be true, there can be no imposition in the matter of weight; if the line be truly applied, there

can be no imposition in the evenness of a surface; if the square and compass be truly employed, there can be no imposition in the shape of a figure. When a superior man (conducts, the government of his state) with a discriminating attention to these rules, he cannot be imposed on by traitors and impostors.

6. Hence he who has an exalted idea of the rules, and guides his conduct by them, is called by us a mannerly gentleman, and be who has no such exalted idea and does not guide his conduct by the rules, is called by us one of the unmannerly people. These rules (set forth) the way of reverence and courtesy; and therefore when the services in the ancestral temple are performed according to them, there is reverence; when they are observed in the court, the noble and the mean have their proper positions; when the family is regulated by them, there is affection between father and son, and harmony among brothers; and when they are honoured in the country districts and villages, there is the proper order between old and young. There is the verification of what was said by Confucius, 'For giving security to superiors and good government Of the people, there is nothing more excellent than the Rules of Propriety[1].'

7. The ceremonies at the court audiences of the different seasons were intended to illustrate the righteous relations between ruler and subject; those of friendly messages and inquiries, to secure mutual honour and respect between the feudal princes; those of mourning and sacrifice, to illustrate the kindly feelings of ministers and sons; those of social

[1. See vol. iii, page 482 (The Hsiâo King).]

meetings in the country districts, to show the order that should prevail between young and old; and those of marriage, to exhibit the separation that should be maintained between males and females. Those ceremonies prevent the rise of disorder and confusion, and are like the embankments which prevent the overflow of water. He who thinks the old embankments useless and destroys them is sure to suffer from the desolation caused by overflowing water; and he who should consider the old rules of propriety useless and abolish them would be sure to suffer from the calamities of disorder.

8. Thus if the ceremonies of marriage were discontinued, the path of husband and wife would be embittered, and there would be many offences of licentiousness and depravity. If the drinking ceremonies at country feasts were discontinued, the order between old and

young would be neglected, and quarrelsome litigations would be numerous. If the ceremonies of mourning and sacrifice were discontinued, the kindly feeling of officers and sons would become small; there would be numerous cases in which there was a revolt from the observances due to the dead, and an oblivion of (those due) to the living. If the ceremonies of friendly messages and court attendances were discontinued, the positions of ruler and subject would fall into disuse, the conduct of the feudal princes would be evil, and the ruin wrought by rebellion, encroachment, and oppression would ensue.

9. Therefore the instructive and transforming power of ceremonies is subtile; they stop depravity before it has taken form, causing men daily to move towards what is good, and keep themselves farther apart from guilt, without being themselves conscious of it. It was on this account that the ancient kings set so high a value upon them. This sentiment is found in the words of the Yî, 'The superior man is careful at the commencement; a mistake, then, of a hair's breadth, will lead to an error of a thousand lî[1].'

BOOK XXIV. ÂI KUNG WAN, OR QUESTIONS OF DUKE ÂI[1].

1. Duke Âi[1] asked Confucius, saying, 'What do you say about the great rites? How is it that superior men, in speaking about them, ascribe so much honour to them?' Confucius said, 'I, Khiû, am a small man, and unequal to a knowledge of the rites.' 'By no means,' said the ruler. 'Tell me what you think, my Master.' Then Confucius replied, 'According to what I have heard, of all things by which the people live the rites are the greatest. Without them they would have no means of regulating the services paid to the spirits of heaven and earth; without them they would have no means of distinguishing the positions proper to father and son, to high and low, to old and young; without them they would have no means of maintaining the separate character of the intimate relations between male and female, father and son, elder brother and younger, and conducting the intercourse between the contracting families in a marriage, and the frequency or infrequency (of the reciprocities between friends). These

[1. See the introduction, vol. xxvii, pp. 39, 40.

2. Âi ('The Courteous, Benevolent, and Short–lived) was the posthumous title of the marquis Ziang of Lû (B.C. 494–468), in whose sixteenth year Confucius died. He seems to have often consulted the sage on important questions, but was too weak to follow his counsels.]

are the grounds on which superior men have honoured and reverenced (the rites) as they did.

2. 'Thereafter, (having this view of the rites), they taught them to the people, on the ground of their ability (to practise them), not disregarding their general principles or the limitations (that circumstances impose in particular cases).

3. 'When their object had been accomplished (so far), they proceeded to give rules for the engraving (of the ceremonial vessels), and the embroidering in various colours (of the robes), in order to secure the transmission (of the rites).

4. 'Having obtained the concurrence (of the people in these things), they proceeded to tell them the different periods of mourning; to provide the full amount of tripods and stands; to lay down the (offerings of) pork and dried meats; to maintain in good order their ancestral temples; and then at the different seasons of the year reverently to present their sacrifices; and to arrange thereat, in order, the different branches and members of their kindred. Meanwhile (they themselves) were content to live economically, to have nothing fine about their dress; to have their houses low and poor; to eschew much carving about their carriages; to use their vessels without carving or graving; and to have the plainest diet, in order to share all their advantages in common with the people. In this manner did the superior men of antiquity practise the rites.'

5. The duke said, 'How is it that the superior men of the present day do not practise them (in this way).' Confucius said, 'The superior men of the present day are never satisfied in their fondness for wealth, and never wearied in the extravagance of their conduct. They are wild, idle, arrogant, and insolent. They determinedly exhaust the (resources of the) people, put themselves in opposition to the multitude, and seek to overthrow those who are pursuing the right way. They seek to get whatever they desire, without reference to right or reason. The former using of the people was according to the ancient rules; the using of them now–a–days is according to later rules. The superior men of the present day do not practise the rites (as they ought to be practised).'

6. Confucius was sitting beside duke Âi, when the latter said, 'I venture to ask, according to the nature of men, which is the greatest thing (to be attended to in dealing with them).' Confucius looked startled, changed countenance, and replied, 'That your lordship should put this question is a good thing for the people. How should your servant dare but express his opinion on it?' Accordingly he proceeded, and said, 'According to the nature of men, government is the greatest thing for them.'

7. The duke said, 'I venture to ask what is meant by the practice of government.' Confucius replied, 'Government is rectification. When the ruler is correct himself, all the people will follow his government. What the ruler does is what the people follow. How should they follow what he does not do?'

8. The duke said, 'I venture to ask how this practice of government is to be effected?' Confucius replied, 'Husband and wife have their separate functions; between father and son there should be affection; between ruler and minister there should be a strict adherence to their several parts. If these three relations be correctly discharged, all other things will follow.'

9. The duke said, 'Although I cannot, in my unworthiness, count myself as having attained, I should like to hear how these three things which you have mentioned can be rightly secured. May I hear it from you?' Confucius replied, 'With the ancients in their practice of government the love of men was the great point; in their regulation of this love of men, the rules of ceremony was the great point; in their regulation of those rules, reverence was the great point. For of the extreme manifestation of reverence we find the greatest illustration in the great (rite of) marriage. Yes, in the great (rite of) marriage there is the extreme manifestation of respect; and when one took place, the bridegroom in his square–topped cap went in person to meet the bride;—thus showing his affection for her. It was his doing this himself that was the demonstration of his affection. Thus it is that the superior man commences with respect as the basis of love. To neglect respect is to leave affection unprovided for. Without loving there can be no (real) union; and without respect the love will not be correct. Yes, love and respect lie at the foundation of government.'

10. The duke said, 'I wish that I could say I agree with you, but for the bridegroom in his square–topped cap to go in person to meet the bride,—is it not making too much (of the ceremony)?' Confucius looked startled, changed countenance, and said, '(Such a

marriage) is the union of (the representatives of) two different surnames in friendship and love, in order to continue the posterity of the former sages[1], and to furnish those who shall preside at the sacrifices to heaven and earth, at those in the ancestral temple, and at those at the altars to the spirits of the land and grain;—how can your lordship say that the ceremony is made too great?'

11. The duke said, 'I am stupid. But if I were not stupid, how should I have heard what you have just said? I wish to question you, but cannot find the proper words (to do so); I beg you to go on a little further.' Confucius said, 'If there were not the united action of heaven and earth, the world of things would not grow. By means of the grand rite of marriage, the generations of men are continued through myriads of ages. How can your lordship say that the ceremony in question is too great?' He immediately added, 'In their own peculiar sphere, (this marriage) serves for the regulation of the ceremonies of the ancestral temple, and is sufficient to supply the correlates to the spiritual Intelligences of heaven and earth; in the (wider) sphere abroad, it serves for the regulation of the ceremonies of the court[2], and is sufficient to establish the respect of those below him to him who is

[1. Kang takes this in the singular, 'the former sage,' meaning the duke of Kâu, so that Confucius should say that the ceremony in question was a continuation of that instituted by the duke of Kâu. I cannot construe or interpret the text so.

2. The text here seems to be corrupt. Translating it as it stands——we should have to say, 'the regulation of straightforward speech.' Khan Hâo says that he does not understand the, and mentions the conjecture of 'some one' that they should be . I have followed this conjecture, which also is followed in Callery's expurgated edition.]

above them all. If there be ground for shame on account of (a deficiency of) resources, this is sufficient to stimulate and secure them; if there be ground for shame on account of the condition of the states, this is sufficient to revive and renew them. Ceremonies are the first thing to be attended to in the practice of government. Yes, (this) ceremony (of marriage) lies at the foundation of government!'

12. Confucius continued, 'Anciently, under the government of the intelligent kings of the three dynasties, it was required of a man to show respect to his wife and son. When the path (of right government) was pursued, the wife was the hostess of the (deceased)

parents;—could any husband dare not to show her respect? And the son was the descendant of those parents;—could any father dare not to show him respect? The superior man's respect is universal. Wherein it appears the greatest is in his respect for himself. He is in his person a branch from his parents;—can any son but have this self–respect? If he is not able to respect his own person, he is wounding his parents. If he wound his parents, he is wounding his own root; and when the root is wounded, the branches will follow it in its dying. These three things are an image of what is true with the whole people (in the body politic). One's own person reaches to the persons of others; one's own son to the sons of others; one's own wife to the wives of others. If a ruler do these things, the spirit of his conduct will reach to all under the sky. If the course of the great king be thus, all the states and families will be docilely obedient.'

113. The duke said, 'I venture to ask what is meant by "respecting one's self."' Confucius replied, 'When a man who is over others[1] transgresses in his words, the people will fashion their speech accordingly; when he transgresses in his actions, the people will make him their model. If in his words he do not go beyond what should be said, nor in his actions what should be a model, then the people, without being commanded, will reverence and honour him. When this obtains, he can be said to have respected his person. Having succeeded in respecting his person, he will (at the same time) be able to do all that can be done for his parents.'

14. The duke said, 'I venture to ask what is meant by doing all that can be done for one's parents?' Confucius replied, 'Kün–dze is the completest name for a man; when the people apply the name to him, they say (in effect) that he is the son of a kün–dze; and thus he makes his parents (?father) to be a kün–dze. This is what I intend by saying that he does all that can be done for his parents[2].'

Confucius forthwith added, 'In the practice of

[1. The phrase in the text for 'a man who is high in rank' is Kün–dze (Keun–dze, in Southern mandarin, and as it is transliterated by Morrison and our older scholars), meaning 'ruler's son,' 'a princely man,' 'a superior man,' 'a wise man,' 'a sage.' In all these ways it has been translated by Chinese scholars, and I have heard it proposed to render it by 'a gentleman.' Here all the commentators say it is to be understood of a man of rank and position which is a not unfrequent application of it.

2. What I translate by 'doing all that can be done for his parents' is in the text 'completing his parents.' Callery renders it:—'Assurant (un nom honorable) à ses père et mère.' Wylie:—'Completing his duty to his parents.' It certainly is not easy to catch the mind of Confucius here and in the context.]

government in antiquity, the love of men was the great point. If (a ruler) be not able to love men he cannot possess[1] his own person; unable to possess his own person, he cannot enjoy in quiet his land; unable to enjoy in quiet his land, he cannot rejoice in Heaven; unable to rejoice in Heaven, he cannot do all that can be done for his person.'

15. The duke said, 'I venture to ask what is meant by "doing all that could be done for one's person."' Confucius replied, 'It is keeping from all transgression of what is due in all the sphere beyond one's self[2].'

16. The duke said, 'I venture to ask what it is that the superior man values in the way of Heaven.' Confucius replied, 'He values its unceasingness. There is, for instance, the succession and sequence of the sun and moon from the east and west:—that is the way of Heaven. There is the long continuance of its progress without interruption:—that is the way of Heaven. There is its making (all) things complete without doing anything:—that is the way of Heaven. There is their brilliancy when they have been completed:—that is the way of Heaven.'

17. The duke said, 'I am very stupid, unintelligent also, and occupied with many things; do you, Sir, help me that I may keep this lesson in my mind.'

18. Confucius looked grave, moved a little from his mat, and replied, 'A man of all–comprehensive

[1. Kang says that 'to possess' is equivalent to 'to preserve' adding 'men will injure him.'—So all the other commentators.

2. Callery gives for this:—'Ce n'est autre chose que de se maintenir dans le devoir.' Wylie:—'It is not to transgress the natural order of things.' The reply of Confucius appears more fully in the 'Narratives of the School.']

virtue[1] does not transgress what is due from him in all the sphere beyond himself, and it is the same with a filial son. Therefore a son of all–comprehensive virtue serves his parents as he serves Heaven, and serves Heaven as he serves his parents. 'Hence a filial son does all that can–be done for his person[2].'

19. The duke said, 'I have heard your (excellent) words;—how is it that I shall hereafter not be able to keep from the guilt (of transgressing)?' Confucius answered, 'That your lordship gives expression to such words is a happiness to me.'

[1. 'A man of all–comprehensive virtue' is in the text simply 'the benevolent man.' But that name must be to be taken in the sense of Mencius, who says that 'Benevolence is man' (vii, ii, 16); as Julien translates it, 'Humanitas homo est.' There, 'benevolence,' is a name denoting the complex of human virtues, with the implication that it is itself man's distinguishing characteristic. So 'humanity' may be used in English to denote 'the peculiar nature of man as distinguished from other beings.'

BOOK XXV. KUNG–NÎ YEN KÜ, OR KUNG–NÎ AT HOME AT EASE[1].

1. Kung–nî 'being at home at ease[1],' with Dze–kung, Dze–kung, and Yen Yû by him, their conversation went on from general matters to the subject of ceremonies.

2. The Master said, 'Sit down[2], you three, and I will discourse to you about ceremonies, so that you may rightly employ them everywhere and in all circumstances.'

3. Dze–kung crossed over (Dze–kang's) mat[3], and replied, 'Allow me to ask what you mean.' The Master said, 'Respect shown without observing the rules of propriety is called vulgarity; courtesy without observing those rules is called forwardness; and boldness without observing them is called violence.' The Master added, 'Forwardness takes away from gentleness and benevolence.'

4. The Master said, 'Sze, you err by excess, and Shang by defect.' Dze–khan might be regarded as a

[1. See the introductory notice of this Book, vol. xxvii, page 40. The Yen in Yen Kü is said by Kang to denote that the party had been to court, and was now at his ease in his own residence.

2. The three disciples must have risen from their mats on the introduction of a new topic, according to vol. xxvii, page 76, paragraph 21.

3. Substantially a violation of vol. xxvii, page 71, paragraph 26.]

mother of the people. He could feed them, but he could not teach them'.

5. Dze–kung (again) crossed the mat, and replied, 'Allow me to ask by what means it is possible to secure this due mean.' The Master said, 'By means of the ceremonial rules; by the rules. Yes, it is those rules which define and determine the due mean.'

6. Dze–kung having retired, Yen Yû advanced, and said, 'May I be allowed to ask whether the rules of ceremony do not serve to control what is bad, and to complete what is good?' The Master said, 'They do.' 'Very well, and how do they do it?' The Master said, 'The idea in the border sacrifices to Heaven and Earth is that they should give expression to the loving feeling towards the spirits; the ceremonies of the autumnal and summer services in the ancestral temple give expression to the loving feeling towards all in the circle of the kindred; the ceremony of putting down food (by the deceased) serves to express the loving feeling towards those who are dead and for whom they are mourning; the ceremonies of the archery fêtes and the drinking at them express the loving feeling towards all in the district and neighbourhood; the ceremonies of festal entertainments express the loving feeling to)yards visitors and guests.'

[1. The Khien–lung editors say that in this paragraph, the part from 'Dze–khân' has been introduced by an error in manipulating the tablets. It is found, and more fully, also in the Narratives of the School, article 41. The previous sentence of it also appears to me to be out of place. Why should Confucius address himself to Sze?—that was not the name of Dze–kung. What is said to him is found in the Analects, VI, 15, and also more fully.]

7. The Master said, 'An intelligent understanding of the idea in the border sacrifices to Heaven and Earth, and of the ceremonies of the autumnal and summer services, would make the government of a state as easy as to point to one's palm. Therefore let the

ceremonial rules be observed:–in the ordinary life at home, and there will be the (right) distinction between young and old; inside the door of the female apartments, and there will be harmony among the three branches of kin; at court, and there will be the right ordering of office and rank; in the different hunting expeditions, and skill in war will be acquired; in the army and its battalions, and military operations will be successful.

'In this way, houses and their apartments will be made of the proper dimensions; measures and tripods will have their proper figure; food will have the flavour proper to its season; music will be according to the rules for it; carriages will have their proper form; spirits will receive their proper offerings; the different periods of mourning will have their proper expression of sorrow; discussions will be conducted by those who from their position should take part in them; officers will have their proper business and functions; the business of government will be properly distributed and applied. (The duty) laid on (each) person being discharged in the matter before him (according to these rules), all his movements, and every movement will be what they ought to be.'

8. The Master said, 'What is (the object of) the ceremonial rules? It is just the ordering of affairs. The wise man who has affairs to attend to must have the right method of ordering them. (He who should attempt) to regulate a state without those rules would be like a blind man with no one to lead him;—groping about, how could he find his way? Or he would be like one searching all night in a dark room without a light;—how could he see anything?

'If one have not the ceremonial rules, he would not (know how to) dispose of his hands and feet, or how to apply his ears and eyes; and his advancing and retiring, his bowings and giving place would be without any definite rules. Hence, when the rules are thus neglected:—in the ordinary life at home, then the right distinction between old and young will be lost; in the female apartments, then the harmony among the three branches of kin will be lost; in the court, then the order of office and rank will be lost; in the different hunting expeditions, then the prescribed methods of military tactics will be lost; in the army and its battalions, then the arrangements that secure success in war will be lost. (Also), houses and apartments will want their proper dimensions; measures and tripods will want their proper figure; food will want its seasonal flavour; music will want its proper parts; Spirits will want their proper offerings; the different periods of mourning will want their proper expression of sorrow; discussions will not be conducted by the proper men for them; officers will not have their proper business; the affairs of government will fail to be properly distributed and applied; and (in the duties) laid on (each) person to be discharged in the matters before him, all his movements, every movement, will fail to be what they ought to be. In this condition of things it will be impossible to put one's self at the head of the multitudes, and secure harmony among them.'

9. The Master said, 'Listen attentively, you three, while I discourse to you about the ceremonial rules., There are still nine things (to be described), and four of them belong to the Grand festive entertainments. When you know these, though your lot may lie among the channeled fields, if you carry them into practice, you will become wise as sages.

'When one ruler is visiting another, they bow to each other, each courteously declining to take the precedence, and then enter the gate. As soon as they have done so, the instruments of music, suspended from their frames, strike up. They then bow and give place to each other again, and ascend to the hall; and when they have gone up, the music stops. In the court below, the dances Hsiang and Wû are performed to the music of the flute, and that of Hsiâ proceeds in due order with (the brandishing of feathers and) fifes. (After this), the stands with their offerings are set out, the various ceremonies and musical performances go on in regular order, and the array of officers provided discharge their functions. In this way the superior man perceives the loving regard (which directs the entertainment). They move forward in perfect circles; they return and form again the squares. The bells of the equipages are tuned to the Khâi–khî; when the guest goes out they sing the Yung; when the things are being taken away, they sing the Khan–yü; and thus the superior man (sees that) there is not a single thing for which there is not its proper ceremonial usage. The striking up of the instruments of metal, when they enter the gate, serves to indicate their good feeling; the singing of the Khing Miâo, when they have gone up to the hall, shows the virtue (they should cultivate); the performance of the Hsiang to the flute in the court below, reminds them of the events (of history). Thus the superior men of antiquity did not need to set forth their views to one another in words; it was enough for them to show them in their music and ceremonies.

10. The Master said, 'Ceremonial usages are (the prescriptions of) reason; music is the definite limitation(of harmony). The superior man makes no movement without (a ground of) reason, and does nothing without its definite limitation. He who is not versed in the odes will err in his employment of the usages, and he who is not versed in music will be but an indifferent employer of them. He whose virtue is slender will vainly perform the

usages.'

11. The Master said, 'The determinate measures are according to the rules; and the embellishments of them are also so; but the carrying them into practice depends on the men.'

12. Dze–kung crossed over the mat and replied, 'Allow me to ask whether even Khwei was ignorant (of the ceremonial usages)[1]?'

13. The Master said, 'Was he not one of the ancients? Yes, he was one of them. To be versed in the ceremonial usages, and not versed in music, we call being poorly furnished. To be versed in the usages and not versed in music, we call being one–sided. Now Khwei was noted for his acquaintance with music, and not for his acquaintance with ceremonies,

[1. Khwei was Shun's Director of Music. See the Shû, II, i, 24.]

and therefore his name has been transmitted with that account of him (which your question implies). But he was one of the men of antiquity.

14. Dze–kang asked about government. The Master said, 'Sze, did I not instruct you on that subject before? The superior man who is well acquainted with ceremonial usages and music has only to take and apply them (in order to practise government).'

15. Dze–kang again put the question, and the Master said, 'Sze, do you think that the stools and mats must be set forth, the hall ascended and descended, the cups filled and offered, the pledge–cup presented and returned, before we can speak of ceremonial usages? Do you think that there must be the movements of the performers in taking up their positions, the brandishing of the plumes and fifes, the sounding of the bells and drums before we can speak of music? To speak and to carry into execution what you have spoken is ceremony; to act and to give and receive pleasure from what you do is music. The ruler who vigorously pursues these two things may well stand with his face to the south, for thus will great peace and order be secured all under heaven; the feudal lords will come to his court; all things will obtain their proper development and character; and no single officer will dare to shrink from the discharge of his functions. Where such ceremony prevails, all government is well ordered; where it is neglected, all falls into disorder and confusion. A house made by a good (though unassisted) eye will yet have

the corner of honour, and the steps on the east for the host to ascend by; every mat have its upper and lower end; every chariot have its right side and left; walkers follow one another, and those who stand observe a certain order:—such were the right rules of antiquity. If an apartment were made without the corner of honour and the steps on the east, there would be confusion in the hall and apartment. If mats had not their upper and lower ends, there would be confusion among the occupants of them; if carriages were made without their left side and right, there would be confusion in their seats; if people did not follow one another in walking, there would be confusion on the roads; if people observed no order in standing, there would be disorder in the places they occupy. Anciently the sage Tîs and intelligent kings and the feudal lords, in making a distinction between noble and mean, old and young, remote and near, male and female, outside and inside, did not presume to allow any to transgress the regular rule they had to observe, but all proceeded in the path which has been indicated.'

BOOK XXVI. KHUNG-DZE HSIEN KU, OR CONFUCIUS AT HOME AT LEISURE[1].

1. Confucius being at home at leisure, with Dze-hsiâ by his side, the latter said, 'With reference to the lines in the Book of Poetry (III, ii, ode 8, 1),

"The happy and courteous sovereign
is the father and mother of the people;"

I beg to ask what the sovereign must be, who can be called "the parent of the people."' Confucius said, 'Ah! the parent of the people! He must have penetrated to the fundamental principles of ceremonies and music, till he has reached the five extreme points to which they conduct, and the three that have no positive existence, and be able to exhibit these all under heaven; and when evil is impending in any part of the kingdom, he must have a foreknowledge of it:—such an one is he whom we denominate 'the parent of the people.'

2. Dze-hsiâ said, 'I have thus heard (your explanation) of the name "parent of the people;" allow me to ask what " the five extreme points" (that you mention) mean.' Confucius said, 'The furthest aim of the mind has also its furthest expression in the Book of Poetry. The furthest expression of the Book of Poetry has also its furthest embodiment

in the ceremonial usages. The furthest embodiment

[1. See the introductory notice, vol. xxvii, page 41.]

in the ceremonial usages has also its furthest indication in music. The furthest indication of music has also its furthest indication in the voice of sorrow. Sorrow and joy produce, each the other; and thus it is that when we look with the directest vision of the eyes at (these extreme points) we cannot see them, and when we have bent our ears with the utmost tension we cannot hear them. The mind and spirit must embrace all within heaven and earth:—these are what we denominate "the five extreme points."'

3. Dze-hsiâ said, 'I have heard your explanation of "the five extreme points;" allow me to ask what "the three points that have no positive existence" mean.' Confucius said, 'The music that has no sound; ceremonial usages that have no embodiment; the mourning that has no garb:—these are what we denominate "the three points that have no positive existence." Dze-hsiâ said, 'I have heard what you have said on those three negations; allow me to ask in which of the odes we find the nearest expression of them.' Confucius said, 'There is that (IV, ii, ode 1, 6),

"Night and day he enlarged its foundations by his deep and silent virtue:"—

there is music without sound. And that (I, iii, ode 1, 3),

"My deportment has been dignified and good,
Without anything wrong that can be pointed out:"—

there is the ceremony that has no embodiment. And that (I, iii, ode 10, 4),

"When among any of the people there was a death,
I crawled on my knees to help them:"—

there is the mourning that has no garb.'

4. Dze-hsiâ said, 'Your words are great, admirable, and complete. Do they exhaust all that can be said on the subject? Is there nothing more?' Confucius said, 'How should it be so? When a superior man practises these things, there still arise five other points.'

5. Dze-hsiâ said, 'How is that?' Confucius said, 'When there is that music without sound, there is no movement of the spirit or will in opposition to it. When there is that ceremony without embodiment, all the demeanour is calm and gentle. When there is that mourning without garb, there is an inward reciprocity, and great pitifulness.

'When there is that music without sound, the spirit and will are mastered. When there is that ceremony without embodiment, all the demeanour is marked by courtesy. When there is that mourning without garb, it reaches to all in all quarters.

'When there is that music without sound, the spirit and will are followed. When there is that ceremony without embodiment, high and low are harmonious and united. When there is that mourning without garb, it goes on to nourish all regions.

'When there is that music without sound, it is daily heard in all the four quarters of the kingdom. When there is that ceremony without embodiment, there is a daily progress and a monthly advance. When there is that mourning, without garb, the virtue (of him who shows it) becomes pure and very bright.

'When there is that music without sound, all spirits and wills are roused by it. When there is that ceremony without embodiment, its influence extends to all within the four seas. When there is that mourning without garb, it extends to future generations.'

6. Dze-hsiâ said, '(It is said that) the virtue of the kings (who founded the) three dynasties was equal to that of heaven and earth; allow me to ask of what nature that virtue was which could be said to put its possessors on an equality with heaven and earth.' Confucius said, 'They reverently displayed the Three Impartialities, while they comforted all beneath the sky under the toils which they imposed.' Dze-hsiâ said, 'Allow me to ask what you call the "Three Impartialities."' Confucius said, 'Heaven overspreads all without partiality; Earth sustains and contains all without partiality; the Sun and Moon shine on all without partiality. Reverently displaying these three characteristics and thereby comforting all under heaven under the toils which they imposed, is what is called "the Three Impartialities." It is said in the Book of Poetry (IV, iii, ode 4, 3),

"God in His favour Thang's House would not leave,
And then Thang rose that favour to receive.
Thang's birth was not from Hsieh too far removed,

His sagely reverence daily greater proved
For long to Heaven his brilliant influence rose,
And while his acts the fear of God disclose)
God Thang as model fit for the nine regions chose:"—

such was the virtue of Thang.

7. 'To Heaven belong the four seasons, spring, autumn, winter, summer, with wind, rain, hoar–frost, and dew;—(in the action) of all and each of these there is a lesson.

'Earth contains the mysterious energy (of nature). That mysterious energy (produces) the wind and thunder–clap. By the wind and thunder–clap the (seeds of) forms are carried abroad, and the various thing's show the appearance of life:—in all and each of these things there is a lesson.

8. 'When the personal character is pure and bright, the spirit and mind are like those of a spiritual being. When what such an one desires is about to come, there are sure to be premonitions of it in advance, (as when) Heaven sends down the seasonable rains, and the hills produce the clouds. As it is said in the Book of Poetry (III, iii, ode 5, 1),

How grand and high, with hugest bulk, arise
Those southern hills whose summits touch the skies!
Down from them came a Spirit to the earth,
And to the sires of Fû and Shan gave birth.
In those two states our Kâu a bulwark has,
O'er which the southern foemen dare not pass,
And all its states they screen, and through them spread
Lessons of virtue, by themselves displayed:—

such was the virtue of (kings) Wan and Wû.

9. 'As to the kings (who founded) the three dynasties, it was necessary that they should be preceded by the fame of their forefathers. As it is said in the Book of Poetry (III, iii, ode 8, 6),

"Very intelligent were the sons of Heaven,
Their good fame was without end:"—

such was the virtue of (the founders) of the three dynasties.

'(And again),

"He displayed his civil virtues,
And they permeated all parts of the kingdom:"—

such was the virtue of king Thâi.'

BOOK XXVII. FANG KÎ, OR RECORD OF THE DYKES[1].

1. According to what the Masters said, the ways laid down by the superior men may be compared to dykes, the object of which is to conserve that in which the people may be deficient; and though they may be on a great scale, the people will yet pass over them. Therefore the superior men framed rules of ceremony for, the conservation of virtue; punishments to serve as a barrier against licentiousness; and declared the allotments (of Heaven), as a barrier against evil desires[2].

2. The Master said, 'The small man, when poor, feels the pinch of his straitened circumstances; and when rich, is liable to become proud. Under the pinch of that poverty he may proceed to steal; and when proud, he may proceed to deeds of disorder. The rules of propriety recognise these feelings of men, and lay down definite regulations for them, to serve as dykes for the people. Hence the sages dealt with riches and honours, so that riches should

[1. See the introductory notice, vol. xxvii, pp. 41, 42.

2 Any reader acquainted with Chinese will gee that the character fang is used substantively and meaning 'a dyke,' and as a verb, 'to serve as a dyke.' But a dyke has two uses:—to conserve what is inside it, preventing its flowing away; and to ward off what is without, barring its entrance and encroachment. So the character is here used in both

ways. The Khien–lung editors insist on this twofold application of it, tersely and convincingly.]

not have power to make men proud; that poverty should not induce that feeling of being pinched; and that men in positions of honour should not be intractable to those above them. In this way the causes of disorder would more and more disappear.'

3. The Master said, 'Under heaven the cases are few in which the poor yet find enjoyment', the rich yet love the rules of propriety, and a family that is numerous (and strong) yet remains quiet and at peace. As it is said in the Book of Poetry (III, iii, ode 3, 11),

"The people desire disorder,
And find enjoyment in bitter, poisonous ways."

Hence it was made the rule that no state should have more than 1000 chariots, no chief city's wall more than 100 embrasures, no family, however rich, more than 100 chariots. These regulations were intended for the protection of the people, and yet some of the lords of states rebelled against them.'

4. The Master said, 'It is by the rules of ceremony that what is doubtful is displayed, and what is minute is distinguished, that they may serve as dykes for the people. Thus it is that there are the grades of the noble and the mean, the distinctions of dress, the different places at court; and so the people (are taught to) give place to one another.'

5. The Master said, 'There are not two suns in the sky, nor two kings in a territory, nor two masters in a family, nor two superiors of equal honour; and the people are shown how the distinction between ruler and subject should be maintained.

[1. Literally, 'the poor are fond of (enjoyment);' but the 'fond of' is acknowledged to be an addition to the text.]

The Khun Khiû does not mention the funeral rites for the kings of Khû and Yüeh. According to the rules, the ruler of a state is not spoken of as "Heaven's," and a Great officer is not spoken of as "a ruler:"—lest the people should be led astray. It is said in the ode,

"Look at (that bird) which in the night calls out for the morning[1]."

Even this is still occasion for being dissatisfied with it.'

6. The Master said, 'A ruler does not ride in the same carriage with those of the same surname with himself; and when riding with those of a different surname, he wears a different dress;—to show the people that they should avoid what may give rise to suspicion. This was intended to guard the people (from incurring suspicion), and yet they found that there were those of the same surname who murdered their ruler[2].'

7. The Master said, 'The superior man will decline a position of high honour, but not one that is mean; and riches, but not poverty. In this way confusion and disorder will more and more disappear. 'Hence the superior man, rather than have his emoluments superior to his worth, will have his worth superior to his emoluments.'

8. The Master said, 'In the matter of a cup of liquor and a dish of meat, one may forego his claim and receive that which is less than his due;

[1. This is from one of the old pieces, which have been forgotten and lost. Is the bird alluded to the cock? and where is the point of the reference?

2. The Khien-lung editors labour in vain to make this paragraph clear, and say that it is 'an error of errors' to ascribe it to Confucius.]

and yet the people will try to obtain more than is due to their years. When one's mat has been spread for him in a high place, he may move and take his seat on a lower; and yet the people will try to occupy the place due to rank. From the high place due to him at court one may in his humility move to a meaner place; and yet the people shall be intrusive even in the presence of the ruler. As it is said in the Book of Poetry (II, vii, ode 9, 4),

"When men in disputations fine
To hear their consciences refuse,
Then 'gainst each other they repine,
And each maintains his special views.
If one a place of rank obtain,

And scorn humility to show,
The others view him with disdain,
And, wrangling, all to ruin go."'

9. The Master said, 'The superior man exalts others and abases himself; he gives the first place to others and takes the last himself;—and thus the people are taught to be humble and yielding. Thus when he is speaking of the ruler of another state, he calls him "The Ruler;" but when mentioning his own ruler, he calls him "Our ruler of little virtue."'

10. The Master said, 'When advantages and rewards are given to the dead first[1], and to the living afterwards, the people will not act contrarily to the (character of) the dead. When (the ruler) places those who are exiles (from and for their state) first, and those who remain in it last, the people may be

[1. The memory of the dead would be honoured, and titles given to them, while those they left behind would be supported.]

trusted with (the most arduous duties). It is said in the Book of Poetry (1, iii, ode 3, 4),

"In thinking of our deceased lord,
She stimulated worthless me."

When this dyke is set up for the people, will they still act contrarily to the dead and have to bewail their lot, with none to whom to appeal?'

11. The Master said, 'When the ruler of a state, with its clans, thinks much of the men and little of the emoluments (which he bestows on them), the people give place readily (to those men). When he thinks much of their ability, and little of the chariots (with which he rewards them), the people address themselves to elegant arts. Hence a superior man keeps his speech under control, while the small man is forward to speak.'

12. The Master said, 'If superiors consider and are guided by the words of the people, the people receive their gifts or commands as if they were from Heaven. If superiors pay no regard to the words of the people, the people put themselves in opposition to them. When inferiors do not receive the gifts of their superiors as if they were from Heaven, there ensues violent disorder. Hence, when the superior exhibits his confidence and courtesy in

the government of the people, then the usages of the people in response to him are very great. It is said in the Book of Poetry (III, ii, ode 10, 3),

"Remember what in days of old they spake,
With grass and fuel–gatherers counsel take."'

13. The Master said, 'If (the ruler) ascribe what is good to others, and what is wrong to himself, the people will not contend (among themselves). If he ascribe what is good to others, and what is wrong to himself, dissatisfactions will more and more disappear. It is said in the Book of Poetry (I, v, ode 4, 2),

"You had consulted the tortoise–shell; you had consulted the stalks;
In their responses there was nothing unfavourable."'

14. The Master said, 'If (the ruler) ascribe what is good to others and what is wrong to himself, the people will yield to others (the credit of) what is good in them. It is said in the Book of Poetry (III, i, ode 10, 7),

"He examined and divined, did the king,
About settling in the capital of Hâo.
The tortoise–shell decided the site,
And king Wû completed the city."'

15. The Master said, 'If (ministers) ascribe what is good to their ruler and what is wrong to themselves, the people will become loyal. It is said in the Book of History (V, xxi, 6),

'"When you have any good plans or counsels, enter and lay them before your ruler in the court; and thereafter, when you are acting abroad in accordance with them, say, 'This plan, or this view, is all due to the virtue of our ruler!' Oh! in this way how good and distinguished will you be!"'

16. The Master said, 'If (a ruler, being a son,) ascribe what is good to his father, and what is wrong to himself, the people will become filial. It is said in "The Great Declaration," "If I subdue Kâu, it will not be my prowess, but the faultless virtue of my deceased father Wan. If Kâu subdues me, it will not be from any fault of my deceased father Wan, but because I, who am as a little child, am not good"' (Shû, V, i, sect. 3, 6).

17. The Master said "A superior man will forget and not make much of the errors of his father, and will show his reverence for his excellence. It is said in the Lun Yü (I, xi), "He who for three years does not change from the way of his father, may be pronounced filial;" and in the Kâo Zung (Shû, III, viii, i) it is said, "For three years he kept without speaking; when he did speak, they were delighted."'

18. The Master said, 'To obey (his parents') commands without angry (complaint); to remonstrate with them gently without being weary; and not to murmur against them, though they punish him, may be pronounced filial piety. It is said in the Book of Poetry (III, ii, ode 3, 5),

"Your filial son was unceasing in his service."'

19. The Master said, 'To cultivate harmony with all the kindred of parents may be pronounced filial! It is said in the Book of Poetry (II, vii, ode 9, 3),

"Brethren whose virtue stands the test,
By bad example still unchanged,
Their generous feelings manifest,
Nor grow among themselves estranged.
But if their virtue weakly fails
The evil influence to withstand,
Then selfishness o'er love prevails,
And troubles rise on every hand."'

20. The Master said, '(A son) may ride in the chariot of an intimate friend of his father, but he should not wear his robes. By this (rule) the superior man widens (the sphere of) his filial duty.'

21. The Master said, 'Small men are all able to support their parents. If the superior man do not also reverence them, how is his supporting to be distinguished (from theirs)?'

22. The Master said, 'Father and son should not, be in the same (official) position;—to magnify the reverence (due to the father). It is said in the Book of History (Shû, III, v, sect. 1, 3), "If the sovereign do not show himself the sovereign, he disgraces his. ancestors."'

23. The Master said, 'Before his parents (a son) should not speak of himself as old; he may speak of the duty due to parents, but not of the gentle kindness due from them; inside the female apartments he may sport, but should not sigh. By these (rules) the superior man would protect the people (from evil), and still they are found slight in their acknowledgment of filial duty, and prompt in their appreciation of gentle kindness.'

24. The Master said, 'When they who are over the people show at their courts their respect for the old, the people become filial.'

25. The Master said, 'The (use of) the representatives of the deceased at sacrifices, and of one who presides (at the services) in the ancestral temple, was intended to show the people that they had still those whom they should serve. The repairing of the ancestral temple and the reverential performance of the sacrifices were intended to teach the people to follow their dead with their filial duty. These things should guard the people (from evil), and still they are prone to forget their parents.'

26. The Master said, 'When (it is wished to) show respect (to guests), the vessels of sacrifice are used[1]. Thus it is that the superior man will not in the poverty of his viands neglect the rules of ceremony, nor in their abundance and excellence make those rules disappear. Hence, according to the rules of feasting, when the host gives in person anything to a guest, the guest offers a portion in sacrifice, but he does not do so with what the host does not himself give him. Therefore, when there is no ceremony in the gift, however admirable it may be, the superior man does not partake of it. It is said in the Yî, "The ox slain in sacrifice by the neighbour on the east is not equal to the spare spring sacrifice of the neighbour on the west, (whose sincerity) receives the blessing[2]." It is said in the Book of Poetry (III, ii, ode 3, 1),

"You have made us drink to the full of your spirits,
You have satiated us with your virtue."

But though in this way the people are admonished, they will still keep striving after profit, and forget righteousness.'

27. The Master said, 'There are the seven days of fasting, and the three days of vigil and adjustment of the thoughts; there is the appointment of the one man to act as the personator of the dead, in passing whom it is required to adopt a hurried pace:—all to

teach reverence (for the departed).'

[1. This would be in the entertainment, at the close of the sacrifices, given to the relatives and others who had taken part in them.

2. This is the symbolism of the fifth line of the 63rd Hexagram (Kî Zî). See Vol. XVI, pp. 206–208.]

The sweet liquor is in the apartment (where the personator is); the reddish in the hall; and the clear in the court below:—all to teach the people not to go to excess in being greedy[1].

The personator drinks three cups, and all the guests drink one:—teaching the people that there must be the distinction of high and low.

The ruler takes the opportunity of the spirits and flesh of his sacrifice to assemble all the members of his kindred:—teaching the people to cultivate harmony.

Thus it is that on the hall above they look at what is done in the apartment, and in the court below at what is done by those in the hall (for their pattern); as it is said in the Book of Poetry (II. vi, ode 5, 3),

'Every form is according to rule;
Every smile and word is as it should be.'

28. The Master said, 'The giving place to a visitor at every stage of his advancing (from the entrance gate), according to the rules for visitors; and the repetition of the ceremonies, according to the mourning rites, in an ever–increasing distance from the apartment of the corpse; the washing of the corpse over the pit in the centre of the open court; the putting the rice into the mouth under the window; the slighter dressing of the corpse inside the door of the apartment; the greater dressing at the top of the steps on the east; the coffining in the place for guests; the sacrifice on taking the road (with the coffin) in the courtyard; and the interment in the grave:–these were intended to teach the people how the element of distance enters into the

[1. The best liquor was in the lowest place.]

usages. Under the Yin dynasty they condoled with the mourners at the grave; they do so under Kâu in the house:—showing the people that they should not neglect the custom.'

The Master said, '(These services in connexion with) death are the last duties which the people have to pay (to their departed). I follow Kâu in them. They were intended to serve as guards to the people (to keep them from error). Among the princes, however, there still were those who did not attend the burials of other princes, and take part in them[1].'

29. The Master said, 'The going up to the hall by the steps for the guests, and receiving the condolences sent to him in the guests' place, are designed to teach the filial to continue their filial duty even to the dead.

'Until the mourning rites are finished, a son is not styled "Ruler:"—showing the people that there ought to be no contention (between father and son). Hence in the Khun Khiû of Lû, recording deaths in Zin, it is said, "(Lî Kho) killed Hsî-khî, the son of his ruler, and his ruler Kho[2]:"—a barrier was thus raised to prevent the people (from doing such deeds). And yet there were sons who still murdered their fathers.'

30. The Master said, 'Filial duty may be transferred to the service of the ruler, and brotherly submission

[1. It is not easy to determine the meaning of the text in this sentence. Chinese writers differ about it among themselves. The whole paragraph, indeed, is confused; and the second 'The Master said' should probably form a paragraph by itself.

2. This forms two entries in the Khun Khiû, under the ninth and tenth years of duke Hsî. The first notice is according to the rule about a son of a feudal prince being still only called 'Son' till the mourning for his father was completed, and the second is contrary to it. The concluding remark is also away from the point.]

to the service of elders:—showing the people that they ought not to be double-minded. Hence a superior man, while his ruler is alive, should not take counsel about taking office (in another state). It is only on the day of his consulting the tortoise-shell (about such a thing) that he will mention two rulers[1].'

The mourning for a father lasts for three years, and that for a ruler the same time:—showing the people that they must not doubt (about the duty which they owe to their ruler).

'While his parents are alive, a son should not dare to consider his wealth as his own, nor to hold any of it as for his own private use:—showing the people how they should look on the relation between high and low. Hence the son of Heaven cannot be received with the ceremonies of a guest anywhere within the four seas, and no one can presume to be his host. Hence, also, when a ruler goes to a minister's (mansion) he goes up to the hall by the (host's) steps on the east and proceeds to the place (of honour) in the hall: showing the people that they should not dare to consider their houses their own.

'While his parents are alive, the gifts presented to a son should not extend to a carriage and its team:—showing the people that they should not dare to monopolise (any honours).

'All these usages were intended to keep the people from transgressing their proper bounds; and yet there are those who forget their parents, and are double–minded to their ruler.'

31. The Master said, 'The ceremony takes place before the silks (offered in connexion with it) are

[1. The translation here is according to a view appended by the Khien–lung editors to the usual notes on the sentence.]

presented:—this is intended to teach the people to make the doing of their duties the first thing, and their salaries an after consideration. If money be sought first and the usages of propriety last, then the people will be set on gain: if the mere feeling be acted on, without any expressions (of courtesy and deference), there will be contentions among the people. Hence the superior man, when presents are brought to him, if he cannot see him who offers them, does not look at the presents. It is said in the Yî, "He reaps without having ploughed that he may reap; he gathers the produce of the third year's field without having cultivated them the first year; there will be evil[1]." In this way it is sought to guard the people, and yet there are of them who value their emoluments and set little store by their practice.'

32. The Master said, 'The superior man does not take all the profit that he might do, but leaves some for the people. It is said in the Book of Poetry (II, vi, ode 8, 3),

"There shall be handfuls left on the ground,
And ears here and there left untouched;
For the benefit of the widow."

'Hence, when a superior man is in office (and enjoys its emoluments), he does not go in for farming; if he hunts, he does not (also) fish; he eats the (fruits of the) season, and is not eager for delicacies; if a Great officer, he does not sit on sheepskins; if a lower officer, he does not sit on dogskins. It is said in the Book of Poetry (I, iii, ode 10, 1),

[1. See the symbolism of line 2, of the 25th Hexagram, vol. xvi, pp. 110, 111. The last character here is not in the Yî, and a different moral seems to be drawn from the whole.]

"When we gather the mustard–plant and earth–melons,
We do not reject them because of their roots.
While I do nothing contrary to my good name,
I should live with you till our death."

In this way it was intended to guard the people against loving wrong; and still some forget righteousness and struggle for gain, even to their own ruin.'

33. The Master said, 'The ceremonial usages serve as dykes to the people against bad excesses (to which they are prone). They display the separation which should be maintained (between the sexes), that there may be no occasion for suspicion, and the relations of the people be well defined. It is said in the Book of Poetry (I, viii, ode vi, 3, 4),

How do we proceed in hewing an axe–handle?
Without another axe it cannot be done.
How do we proceed in taking a wife?
Without a go–between it cannot be done.
How do we proceed in planting hemp?
The acres must be dressed length–wise and crosswise.
How do we proceed in taking a wife?

Announcement must first be made to our parents."

In this way it was intended to guard the people (against doing wrong), and still there are some (women) among them, who offer themselves (to the male).'

34. The Master said, 'A man in taking a wife does not take one of the same surname with himself:—to show broadly the distinction (to be maintained between man and wife). Hence, when a man is buying a concubine, if he do not know her surname, he consults the tortoise-shell about it. In this way it was intended to preserve the people (from going wrong in the matter); and yet the Khun Khiû of Lû still suppresses the surname of duke Kâo's wife, simply saying "Wû," and the record of her death is "Mang (the elder) Dze died[1]."'

35. The Master said, 'According to the rules, male and female do not give the cup to one another, excepting at sacrifice. This was intended to guard the people against (undue freedom of intercourse); and yet the marquis of Yang killed the marquis of Mû, and stole away his wife[2]. Therefore the presence of the wife at the grand entertainments was disallowed.'

36. The Master said, 'With the son of a widow one does not have interviews:—this would seem to be an obstacle to friendship, but a superior man will keep apart from intercourse in such a case, in order to avoid (suspicion). Hence, in the intercourse of friends, if the master of the house be not in, a visitor, unless there is some great cause, does not enter the door. This was intended to preserve the people (from all appearance of evil); and yet there are of them who pay more regard to beauty than to virtue.'

37. The Master said, 'The love of virtue should be like the love of beauty (from an inward constraint). Princes of states should not be like fishers for beauty

[1. The latter entry is found in the Khun Khiû, under the twelfth year of duke Âi. The lady's surname is not found in that King at all; and Confucius himself probably suppressed it. Compare what is said in the Analects, VII, 30, where the sage, on the same subject, does not appear to more advantage than he does here.

2 Who these princes were, or what were the circumstances of the case, is not known.]

(in the families) below them. Hence the superior man keeps aloof from beauty, in order to constitute a rule for the people. Thus male and female, in giving and receiving, do not allow their hands to touch; in driving his wife in a carriage, a husband advances his left hand; when a young aunt, a sister, or a daughter has been married, and returns (to her father's house), no male can sit on the same mat with her; a widow should not wail at night; when a wife is ill, in asking for her, the nature of her illness should not be mentioned:–in this way it was sought to keep the people (from irregular connexions); and yet there are those who become licentious, and introduce disorder and confusion among their kindred.'

38. The Master said, 'According to the rules of marriage, the son–in–law should go in person to meet the bride. When he is introduced to her father and mother, they bring her forward, and give her to him':–being afraid things should go contrary to what is right. In this way a dyke is raised in the interest of the people; and yet there are cases in which the wife will not go (to her husband's)[2].'

[1. Warning her, at the same time, to see that she reverenced her husband.

BOOK XXVIII. KUNG YUNG, OR THE STATE OF EQUILIBRIUM AND HARMONY[1]

SECTION I.

1. What Heaven has conferred is called the Nature. An accordance with this nature is called the Path of Duty; the regulation of this path is called the System of Instruction.

2. The path should not be left for an instant; if it could be left, it would not be the path.

3. On this account the superior man does not wait till he sees things to be cautious, nor till he hears things to be apprehensive.

4. There is nothing more visible than what is secret, and nothing more manifest than what is minute. Therefore the superior man is watchful over himself when he is alone.

5. When there are no stirrings of pleasure, anger, sorrow, or joy, we call it the State of Equilibrium. When those feelings have been stirred, and all in their due measure and degree, we call it the State of Harmony. This Equilibrium is the great root (from which grow all the human actings) in the world; and this Harmony is the universal path (in which they should all proceed).

6. Let the State of Equilibrium and Harmony exist in perfection, and heaven and earth

[1. See the introductory notice, vol. xxvii, pp. 42, 43.]

would have their (right) places, (and do their proper work), and all things would be nourished (and flourish)[1].

7. Kung–nî[2] said, 'The superior man (exhibits) the state of equilibrium and harmony[3]; the small

[1. These six short paragraphs may be considered a summary of the Confucian doctrine, and a sort of text to the sermon which follows in the rest of the Treatise;–the first chapter of it. The commencing term, Heaven, gives us, vaguely, the idea of a supreme, righteous, and benevolent Power; while 'heaven and earth,' in paragraph 6, bring before us the material heaven and earth with inherent powers and capabilities, by the interaction of which all the phenomena of production, growth, and decay are produced. Midway between these is Man; and nothing is wanting to make a perfectly happy world but his moral perfection, evidenced by his perfect conformity to the right path, the path of duty. 'The superior man,' in paragraph 3, has evidently the moral signification of the name in its highest degree. He is the man 'who embodies the path.' The description of him in paragraph 4, that 'he is watchful over himself when alone,' is, literally, that 'he is watchful over his solitariness,—his aloneness,' that 'solitariness' being, I conceive, the ideal of his own nature to which every man in his best and highest moments is capable of attaining.

2. See the introductory notice of Book XXV.

3. Formerly I translated this by 'The superior man (embodies) the course of the mean.' Zottoli gives for it, 'Sapiens vir tenet medium;' Rémusat, 'Le sage tient invariablement le milieu,' and 'Sapiens medio constat.' The two characters Kung yung, however, are evidently brought on from the preceding chapter, yung being used instead of the ho in

paragraphs 5 and 6. In the Khang–hsî dictionary, we find that yung is defined by ho, among other terms, with a reference to a remark of Kang Hsüan, preserved by Lû Teh–ming, that 'the Book is named the Kung Yung, because it records the practice of the Kung Ho.' Kang was obliged to express himself so, having defined the yung of the title by another yung, meaning 'use' or 'practice.' But both kung and yung are adjectival terms used substantively.]

man presents the opposite of those states. The superior man exhibits them, because he is the superior man, and maintains himself in them; the small man presents the opposite of them, because he is the small man, and exercises no apprehensive caution.'

8. The Master said, 'Perfect is the state of equilibrium and harmony! Rare have they long been among the people who could attain to it!'

9. The Master said, 'I know how it is that the Path is not walked in. The knowing go beyond it, and the stupid do not come up to it. The worthy go beyond it, and the unworthy do not come up to it. There is nobody but eats and drinks; but they are few who can distinguish the flavours (of what they eat and drink)[1].'

10. The Master said, 'Ah! how is the path untrodden!'

11. The Master said, 'Was not Shun grandly wise? Shun loved to question others, and to study their words though they might be shallow. He concealed what was bad (in them), and displayed what was good. He laid hold of their two extremes, determined the mean[2] between them, and used it in (his government of) the people. It was this that made him Shun!'

12. The Master said, 'Men all say, "We are wise;" but being driven forward and taken in a net, a trap, or a pitfall, not one of them knows how to escape. Men all say, "We are wise;" but when they have chosen the state of equilibrium and harmony, they are not able to keep in it for a round month.'

[1. Men eat and drink without knowing why or what.

2. Here Kung has the signification of 'the mean,' the just medium between two extremes.]

13. The Master said, 'This was the character of Hui:—Having chosen the state of equilibrium and harmony, when he found any one thing that was good, he grasped it firmly, wore it on his breast, and did not let it go[1].'

14. The Master said, 'The kingdom, its states, and clans may be perfectly ruled; dignities and emoluments may be declined; but the state of equilibrium and harmony cannot be attained to.'

15. Dze–lû[2] asked about fortitude. 16. The Master said, 'Do you mean the fortitude of the South, the fortitude of the North, or your fortitude?' 17. To show forbearance and gentleness in teaching others; and not to return conduct towards one's self which is contrary to the right path:–this is the fortitude of the South, and the good man makes it his study. 18. To lie under arms, and to die without regret:—this is the bravery of the North, and the bold make it their study. 19. Therefore, the superior man cultivates a (friendly) harmony, and is not weak; how firm is he in his fortitude! He stands erect in the middle, and does not incline to either side; how firm is he in his fortitude! If right ways prevail in (the government of his state), he does not change from what he was in retirement;—how firm is he in his fortitude! If bad ways prevail, he will die sooner than change;—how firm is he in his fortitude!'

20. The Master said, 'To search for what is

[1. Dze–hui was Yen Yüan, Confucius' favourite disciple.

2. Dze–lû was Kung Yû, another celebrated disciple, famous for his bravery. 'Your fortitude,' in paragraph 16, is probably the fortitude which you ought to cultivate, that described in paragraph 19.]

mysterious[1], and practise marvellous (arts), in order to be mentioned with honour in future ages:—this is what I do not do. 21. The good man tries to proceed according to the (right) path, but when he has gone half–way, he abandons it; I am not able (so) to stop. 22. The superior man, acting in accordance with the state of equilibrium and harmony, may be all unknown and unregarded by the world, but he feels no regret:—it is only the sage who is able for this[2].

23. 'The way of the superior man reaches far and wide, and yet is secret. 24. Common men and women, however ignorant, may intermeddle with the knowledge of it; but in its utmost reaches there is that which even the sage does not know. Common men and women, however much below the ordinary standard of character, can carry it into practice; but in its utmost reaches, there is that which even the sage cannot attain to. 25. Great as heaven and earth are, men still find things in their action with which to be dissatisfied[3].

26. 'Therefore, if the superior man were to speak (of this way) in its greatness, nothing in the world would be able to contain it; and if he were to speak of it in its smallness, nothing in the world would be

[1. This is translated from a reading of the text, as old as the second Han dynasty.

2. With this ends the second chapter of the Treatise, in which the words of Confucius are so often quoted; specially it would appear, to illustrate what is meant by 'the state of equilibrium and harmony.' Yet there is a great want of definiteness and practical guidance about the utterances.

3. Who does not grumble occasionally at the weather, and disturbances apparently of regular order in the seasons?]

found able to divide it. 27. It is said in the Book of Poetry (III, i, ode 5),

"Up to heaven flies the hawk;
Fishes spring in the deep,"

telling how (the way) is seen above and below. 28. The way of the superior man may be found in its simple elements among common men and women, but in its utmost reaches it is displayed in (the operations of) heaven and earth[1].'

29. The Master said, 'The path is not far from man. When men try to pursue a path which is far from what their nature suggests, it should not be considered the Path. 30. It is said in the Book of Poetry (I, xv, ode 5),

"In hewing an axe–shaft, in hewing an axe–shaft,
The pattern is not far off."

We grasp one axe–handle to hew the other; but if we look askance at it, we still consider it far off. 31. Therefore the superior man governs men according to their humanity; and when they change (what is wrong), he stops. 32. Fidelity to one's self and the corresponding reciprocity are not far from the path. What you do not like when done to yourself, do not do to others. 33. In the way of the superior man there are four things, to not one of which have I, Khiû[2], as yet attained.—To

[1. With this chapter commences, it is commonly and correctly held, the third part of the Treatise, intended to illustrate what is said in the second paragraph of it, that 'the path cannot be left for an instant.' The author proceeds to quote sayings of Confucius to make his meaning clear, but he does so 'in a miscellaneous way,' and so as to embrace some of the widest and most difficult exercises of Chinese thought.

2. The name first given to Confucius by his parents.]

serve my father as I would require my son to serve me, am not yet able; to serve my ruler as I would require my minister to serve me, I am not yet able; to serve my elder brother as I would require a younger brother to serve me, I am not yet able; to set the example in behaving to a friend as I would require him to behave to me, I am not yet able. 34. In the practice of the ordinary virtues, and attention to his ordinary words, if (the practice) be in anything defective, (the superior man) dares not but exert himself; if (his words) be in any way excessive, he dares not allow himself in such license. His words have respect to his practice, and his practice has respect to his words. 35. Is not the superior man characterised by a perfect sincerity?

36. 'The superior man does what is proper to the position in which he is; he does not wish to go beyond it. In a position of wealth and honour, he does what is proper to a position of wealth and honour. In a position of poverty and meanness, he does what is proper to a position of poverty, and meanness. Situated among barbarous tribes, he does what is proper in such a situation. In a position of sorrow and difficulty, he does what is proper in such a position. The superior man can find himself in no position in which he is not himself 37. In a high situation, he does not insult or oppress those who are below him; in a low situation, he does not cling to or depend on those who are above him.

38. 'He rectifies himself, and seeks for nothing from others; and thus none feel dissatisfied with him. Above, he does not murmur against Heaven; below, he does not find fault with men. 39. Therefore the superior man lives quietly and calmly, waiting for the appointments (of Heaven); while the mean man does what is full of risk, looking out for the turns of luck.' 40. The Master said, 'In archery we have something like (the way of) the superior man. When the archer misses the centre of the target, he turns round and seeks for the, cause of his failure in himself.

41. 'The way of the superior man may be compared to what takes place in travelling, when to go far we must traverse the space that is near, and in ascending a height we must begin from the lower ground. 42. It is said in the Book of Poetry (II, i, ode 4, 7, 8),

"Children and wife we love;
Union with them is sweet,

As lute's soft strain, that soothes our pain.
How joyous do we meet!
But brothers more than they
Can satisfy the heart.

'Tis their accord does peace afford,
And lasting joy impart.
For ordering of your homes,
For joy with child and wife,

Consider well the truth I tell;
This is the charm of life!"'

43. The Master said, 'How complacent are parents (in such a state of things)!'

44. The Master said, 'How abundant and rich are the powers possessed and exercised by Spiritual Beings! We look for them, but do not see them; we listen for, but do not hear them; they enter into all things, and nothing is without them[1]. 45 They

[1. We hardly see the relevancy of pars. 44–47 as illustrating the statement that 'the path cannot be left.' They bear rather on the next statement of the first chapter, the manifestness of that which is most minute, and serve to introduce the subject of 'sincerity,' which is dwelt upon so much in the last part of the Treatise. But what are the Spirits or Spiritual Beings that are spoken of? In paragraphs 45, 46, they are evidently the spirits sacrificed to in the ancestral temple and spirits generally, according to our meaning of the term. The difficulty is with the name in paragraph 44, the Kwei Shan there. Rémusat renders the phrase simply by 'les esprits,' and in his Latin version by 'spiritus geniique,' as also does Zottoli. Wylie gives for it 'the Spiritual Powers.' Of course Kâu Hsî and all the Sung scholars take it, according to their philosophy, as meaning the phenomena of expansion and contraction, the displays of the Power or Powers, working under Heaven, in nature.]

cause all under Heaven to fast and purify themselves, and to array themselves in their richest dresses in order to attend at their sacrifices. Then, like overflowing water, they seem to be over the heads, and on the left and right (of their worshippers). 46. It is said in the Book of Poetry (III, iii, ode 2, 7),

"The Spirits come, but when and where,
No one beforehand can declare.
The more should we not Spirits slight,
But ever feel as in their sight."

47. 'Such is the manifestness of what is minute. Such is the impossibility of repressing the outgoings of sincerity!'

48. The Master said, 'How greatly filial was Shun! His virtue was that of a sage; his dignity was that of the son of Heaven; his riches were all within the four seas; his ancestral temple enjoyed his offerings; his descendants preserved (those to) himself. 49. Thus it was that with his great virtue he could not but obtain his position, his riches, his fame, and his long life. 50. Therefore Heaven, in producing things, is sure to be bountiful to them according to their qualities. 51. Thus it nourishes the tree that stands flourishing, and that which is ready to fall it overthrows. 52. It is said in the Book of Poetry (III, ii, ode 5, 1),

"What brilliant virtue does our king,
Whom all admire and love, display!
People and officers all sing

The praise of his impartial sway.

Heaven to his sires the kingdom gave,
And him with equal favour views,
Heaven's strength and aid will ever save
The throne whose grant it oft renews."

Hence (we may say that) he who is greatly virtuous is sure to receive the appointment (of Heaven).'

53. The Master said, 'It is only king Wan of whom it can be said that he had no cause for grief! His father was king Kî, and his son was king Wû. His father laid the foundations of his dignity, and his son transmitted it. 54. King Wû continued the line and enterprise of kings Thâi, Kî, and Wan. Once for all he buckled on his armour, and got possession of all under heaven; and all his life he did not lose the illustrious name of being that possessor. His dignity was that of the son of Heaven; his riches were all within the four seas; his ancestral temple enjoyed his offerings; and his descendants preserved those to himself 55. It was in his old age that king Wû received the appointment (to the throne), and the duke of Kâu completed the virtuous achievements of Wan and Wû.. He carried back the title of king to Thâi and Kî, sacrificing also to all the dukes before them with the ceremonies of the son of Heaven. And the practice was extended as a rule to all the feudal princes, the Great officers, all other officers, and the common people. If the father were a Great officer, and the son an inferior officer, the former was buried with the ceremonies due to a Great officer, and sacrificed to with those due by an inferior officer. If the father were an ordinary officer, and the son a Great officer, the burial was that of an ordinary officer, and the sacrifices those of a Great officer. The one year's mourning extended up to Great officers; the three years' mourning extended to the son of Heaven (himself). In the mourning, for a father or mother no difference was made between the noble and the mean;—it was one and the same for all.'

56. The Master said, 'How far–extending was the filial piety of king Wû and the duke of Kâu! Now filial piety is the skilful carrying out of the wishes of our forefathers, and the skilful carrying on of their undertakings. In spring and autumn[1] they repaired and beautified the temple–halls of their ancestors, set forth their ancestral vessels, displayed their dresses, and presented the offerings of the several seasons. 57. By means of the ceremonies of the ancestral temple, they maintained the order of their ancestors sacrificed

to, here on the left, there on the right, according as they were father or son; by arranging the parties present according to their rank, they distinguished between the more noble and the less; by the arrangement of the various services, they made a distinction of the talents and virtue of

[1. Two seasons, instead of the four, as in the title of the Khun Khiû.]

those discharging them; in the ceremony of general pledging, the inferiors presented the cup to the superiors, and thus something was given to the lowest to do; at the (concluding) feast, places were given according to the hair, and thus was made the distinction of years. 58. They occupied the places (of their forefathers); practised their ceremonies; performed their music; showed their respect for those whom they honoured; and loved those whom they regarded with affection. Thus they served the dead as they served them when alive, and served the departed as they would have served them if they had been continued among them:–all this was the perfection of filial duty.

59. 'By the ceremonies of the border sacrifices (to Heaven and Earth), they served God, and by those of the ancestral temple they sacrificed to their forefathers[1]. 60. If one understood the ceremonies of the border sacrifices and the meaning of the sacrifices of the ancestral temple, it would be as easy for him to rule a state as to look into his palms[2].'

[1. The phraseology of this paragraph and the next is to be taken in accordance with the usage of terms in the chapters on Sacrifices.

2. With this ends, according to the old division of the Treatise, followed by the Khien–lung editors, the first section of it; and with it, we may say, ends also the special quotation by the author of the words of Confucius to illustrate what is said in the first chapter about the path being never to be left. The relevancy of much of what we read from paragraph 24 downwards to the purpose which it is said to serve, it is not easy for us to appreciate. All that the Master says from paragraph 48 seems rather to belong to a Treatise on Filial Piety than to one on the States of Equilibrium and Harmony.]

SECTION II.

1. Duke Âi asked about government[1]. The Master said, 'The government of Wan and Wû is exhibited in (the Records),—the tablets of wood and bamboo. Let there be the men, and their government would (again) flourish; but without the men, their government must cease. 2. With the (right) men the growth of government is rapid, Oust as) in the earth the growth of vegetation is rapid. 3. Government is (like) an easily-growing rush[2]. 4. Therefore the exercise of government depends on (getting) the proper men. 5. (Such) men are to be got by (the ruler's) own character. That character is to be cultivated by his pursuing the right course. That course is to be cultivated by benevolence. 6. Benevolence is (the chief element in) humanity[3], and the greatest exercise of it is in the love of relatives. Righteousness is (the accordance of actions with) what is right, and the greatest exercise of it is in the honour paid to the worthy. The decreasing

[1. A considerable portion of this chapter, with variations and additions, is found in the Narratives of the School, forming the 17th article of that compilation. It may, very well stand by itself; but the author of the Kung Yung adopted it, and made it fit into his own way of thinking.

2. Literally, 'a typha or a phragmites.' Such is Kû Hsî's view of the text. The old commentators took a different view, which appears to me, and would appear to my readers, very absurd.

3. Literally, 'Benevolence is Man;' a remarkable saying, found elsewhere in the Lî Kî, and also in Mencius. The value of it is somewhat marred by what follows about 'righteousness' and 'propriety.']

measures in the love of relatives, and the steps in the honour paid to the worthy, are produced by (the principle of) propriety. 7. When those in inferior situations do not obtain (the confidence of) their superiors, the people cannot be governed successfully[1]. 8. Therefore the wise ruler should not neglect the cultivation of his character. Desiring to cultivate his character, he should not, neglect to serve his parents. Desiring to serve his parents, he should not neglect to know men. Desiring to know men, he should not neglect to know Heaven. 9. The universal path for all under heaven is fivefold, and the (virtues) by means of which it is trodden are three. There are ruler and minister; father and son;

husband and wife; elder brother and younger; and the intercourse of friend and friend:—(the duties belonging to) these five (relationships) constitute the universal path for all. Wisdom, benevolence, and fortitude:—these three are the universal virtues of all. That whereby these are carried into exercise is one thing[2]. 10. Some are born with the knowledge of these (duties); some know them by study; and some know them as the result of painful experience. But the knowledge being possessed, it comes to one and the same thing. 11. Some practise them with the ease of nature; some for the sake of their advantage; and some by

[1. This short sentence is evidently out of place. It is found again farther on in its proper place. It has slipped in here by mistake. There is a consent of opinion, ancient and modem, on this point.

2. 'One thing;' literally 'one,' which might be translated 'singleness,' meaning, probably, the 'solitariness' of chapter i, or the 'sincerity' of which we read so often in the sequel.]

dint of strong effort. But when the work of them is done, it comes to one and the same thing[1].'

12. The Master said, 'To be fond of learning is near to wisdom; to practise with vigour is near to benevolence; to know to be ashamed is near to fortitude. He who knows these three things, knows how to cultivate his own character. Knowing how to cultivate his own character, he knows how to govern other men. Knowing how to govern other men, he knows how to govern the kingdom with its states and families.

13. 'All who have the government of the kingdom with its states and families have nine standard rules to follow:—the cultivation of themselves; the honouring of the worthy; affection towards their relatives; respect towards their great ministers; kind and sympathetic treatment of the whole body of officers; dealing with the mass of the people as their children; encouraging the resort of all classes of artisans; indulgent treatment of men from a distance; and the kindly cherishing of the princes of the states.

14. 'By (the ruler's) cultivation of himself there is set up (the example of) the course (which all should pursue); by his honouring of the worthy, he will be preserved from errors of judgment; by his showing affection towards his relatives, there will be no dissatisfaction among his uncles and brethren; by respecting the great ministers he will.

be kept from mistakes; by kindly treatment of the whole body of officers, they will be led to make the most

[1. After this, it follows in the 'Narratives:—The duke said, 'Your words are admirable, are perfect; but I am really stupid and unable to fulfil them.']

grateful return for his courtesies; by dealing with the mass of the people as his children, they will be drawn to exhort one another (to what is good); by encouraging the resort of artisans, his wealth for expenditure will be rendered sufficient; by indulgent treatment of men from a distance, they will come to him from all quarters; by his kindly cherishing of the princes of the states, all under heaven will revere him. 15. 'The adjustment of all his thoughts, purification, arraying himself in his richest dresses, and the avoiding of every movement contrary to the rules of propriety;—this is the way in which (the ruler) must cultivate his own character. Discarding slanderers, keeping himself from (the seductions of) beauty, making light of riches and honouring virtue:—this is the way by which he will encourage the worthy. Giving his relatives places of honour, and large emolument, and entering into sympathy with them in their likes and dislikes:–this is the way by which he can stimulate affection towards relatives. Giving them numerous officers to discharge their functions and execute their orders:—this is the way by which he will stimulate his Great ministers. According to them a generous confidence, and making their emoluments large:–this is the way by which he will stimulate (the body of) his officers. Employing them (only) at the regular times and making the imposts light:–this is the way by which he will stimulate the people. Daily examinations and monthly trials, and rations and allowances in proportion to the work done:—this is the way in which he will stimulate the artisans. Escorting them on their departure, and meeting them on their coming, commending the good among them and showing pity to the incompetent:—this is the way in which he will manifest his indulgent treatment of men from a distance. Continuing families whose line of succession has been broken, reviving states that have ceased to exist, reducing confusion to order, supporting where there is peril; having fixed times for receiving the princes themselves and their envoys; sending them away after liberal treatment and with liberal gifts, and requiring from them small offerings on their coming: this is the way in which he will cherish with kindness the princes of the states.

16. 'All who have the government of the kingdom with its states and families have these nine standard rules to attend to. That whereby they are carried into exercise is one thing. In all things success depends on previous preparation; without such preparation there is

failure. If what is to be spoken be determined beforehand, there will be no stumbling in the utterance. If the things to be done be determined beforehand, there will be no difficulty with them. If actions to be performed be determined beforehand, there will be no difficulty with them. If actions to be performed be determined beforehand, there will be no sorrow or distress in connexion with them. If the courses to be pursued be determined beforehand, the pursuit of them will be inexhaustible [1].

17. 'When those in inferior situations do not

[1. The 'one thing' in this paragraph carries us back to the same phrase in paragraph 9. If we confine our attention to this paragraph alone, we shall say, with King and Ying-tâ, 'the one thing' is the 'preparation beforehand,' of which it goes on to speak; and it seems to be better not to grope here for a more mysterious meaning.]

obtain (the confidence of) their superiors, the people cannot be governed successfully.

18. 'There is a way to obtain (the confidence of) the superior;—if one is not believed in by his friends, he will not obtain the confidence of his superior. There is a way to secure being believed in by his friends;–if he be not in submissive accord with his parents, he will not be believed in by his friends. There is a way to secure submissive accord with parents;—if one, on turning his thoughts in on himself, finds that he has not attained to the perfection of his nature[1], he will not be in submissive accord with his parents. There is a way to secure the perfection of the nature;—if a man have not a clear understanding of what is good, he will not attain to that perfection.

19. 'Perfection of nature is characteristic of Heaven. To attain to that perfection belongs to man. He who possesses that perfection hits what is right without any effort, and apprehends without any exercise of thought;—he is the sage [2] who

[1. Literally, 'that he is not sincere,' which is Mr. Wylie's rendering; or, as I rendered it in 1861, 'finds a want of sincerity.' But in the frequent occurrence of in the 'Sequel of the Treatise,' 'sincerity' is felt to be an inadequate rendering of it. Zottoli renders the clause by 'Si careat veritate, integritate,' and says in a note, 'est naturalis entis perfectio, quae rei convenit juxta genuinum Creatoris protypon, quaeque a creatore infunditur; proindeque est rei veritas, seu rei juxta veritatem perfectio.' it seems to me that this ideal perfection, as belonging to all things, which God made 'good,' is expressed by in the last clause; and that the realisation of that perfection by man, as belonging to his own nature, is the work of, and may be spoken of as actually and fully accomplished, or in the process of being accomplished. It is difficult with our antecedent knowledge and, opinions to place ourselves exactly in the author's point of view.

2,,—Rémusat, Zottoli, and many give for this name, 'Sanctus vir,' 'un Saint,' 'the holy man.' I prefer, after all, to adhere to the rendering, 'le sage,' 'the sage.' The sage is the ideal man; the saint is the man sanctified by the Spirit of God. Humanity predominates in the former concept; Divinity in the latter. The ideas of morality and goodness belong to both names. See Mencius, VII, ix, 25, for his graduation of the appellations of good men.]

naturally and easily embodies the right way. He who attains to perfection is he who chooses what is good, and firmly holds it fast.

20. 'He extensively studies what is good; inquires accurately about it; thinks carefully over it; clearly discriminates it; and vigorously practises it. While there is anything he has not studied, or in what he has studied there is anything he cannot (understand), he will not intermit his labour. While there is anything he has not asked about, or anything in what he has asked about that he does not know, he will not intermit his labour. While there is anything he has not thought over, or anything in what be has thought about that he does not know, he will not intermit his labour. While there is anything which he has not tried to discriminate, or anything in his discrimination that is not clear, he will not intermit his labour. While there is anything which he has not practised, or any want of vigour so far as he has practised, he will not intermit his labour.

'If another man succeed by one effort, he will use a hundred efforts; if another succeed by ten, he will use a thousand. Let a man proceed in this way, and though stupid, he is sure to become intelligent; though weak, he is sure to become strong.'

21. The understanding (of what is good), springing from moral perfection, is to be ascribed to the nature; moral perfection springing from the understanding (of what is good) is to be ascribed to instruction. But giver, the perfection, and there shall be the understanding; given the understanding, and there shall be the perfection[1].

22. It is only he of all under heaven who is entirely perfect that can give its full development to his nature. Able to give its full development to his own nature, he can also give the same to the nature of other men. Able to give its full development to the nature of other men, he can also give the same to the natures of animals and things[2]. Able to give their full development to these, he can assist the transforming and nourishing operations of heaven and earth. Capable of assisting those transforming and nourishing operations, he can form a ternion with heaven and earth.

23. Next to the above is he who cultivates to the utmost the shoots (of goodness in his nature)[3], till he becomes morally perfect. This perfection will then obtain embodiment; embodied, it will be manifested; manifested, it will become brilliant; brilliant,

[1. With this paragraph there commences the last chapter of the Treatise. Dze–sze, it is said, takes up in it the commencing utterances in paragraph 19, and variously illustrates and prosecutes them. From the words 'nature and instruction' it is evident how he had the commencing chapter of the Treatise in his mind.

2. The text is simply 'the nature of things;' but the word 'things', comprehends all beings besides man. Zottoli's 'rerum Datura' seems quite inadequate. Rémusat's Latin version is the same; his French is 'la nature des choses.' Wylie says, 'the nature of other objects.' This chapter has profoundly affected all subsequent philosophical speculation in China. The ternion of 'Heaven, Earth, and Man' is commonly called San Zhâi, 'the Three Powers.'

3. The character in the text here is a difficult one:—khû, meaning ' crooked,' often used as the antithesis of 'straight;' but the title of the first Book in this collection shows that it need not be used only of what is bad. In that case, the phrase would mean—'carries to the utmost what is bad.' Zottoli's rendering of it by 'promovere declinatam naturam' is inadmissible. Nor can we accept Rémusat's 'diriger efforts vers une seule vertu,' which Wylie follows, merely substituting 'object' for 'vertu.' See the introduction on the title of the first Book. Very much to the point is an illustration by the scholar Pâi Lü:—'Put on stone on a bamboo shoot, or where it would show itself, and it will travel round the stone and come out crookedly at its side.' So it is with the good nature, whose free and full development is repressed.]

it will go forth in action; going forth in action, it will produce changes; producing changes, it will effect transformations. It is only he of all under heaven who is entirely perfect that can transform.

24. It is characteristic of him who is entirely perfect that he can foreknow. When a state or family is about to flourish, there are sure to be lucky omens, and when it is about to perish, there are sure to be unlucky omens. They will be seen in the tortoise–shell and stalks[1]; they will affect the movements of the four limbs. When calamity or happiness is about to come, the good is sure to be foreknown by him, and the evil also. Hence, he who is entirely perfect is like a Spirit[2].

[1. These were the two principal methods of divination practised from very ancient times. The stalks were those of the Ptarmica Sibirica; of which I possess a bundle brought from the tomb of Confucius in 1873. It is difficult to say anything about 'the four limbs,' which were to Kang 'the four feet of the tortoise.'

2. 'The Spirit–man' is, according to Mencius' graduation, an advance on the Sage or Holy man, one whose action is mysterious and invisible, like the power of Heaven and Earth working in nature. Chinese predicates about him could not go farther.]

25. Perfection is seen in (its possessor's) self–completion; and the path (which is its embodiment), In its self–direction.

26. Perfection is (seen in) the beginning and end of (all) creatures and things. Without this perfection there would be no creature or thing.

27. Therefore the superior man considers perfection as the noblest of all attainments.

28. He who is perfect does not only complete himself; his perfection enables him to complete all other beings also. The completion of himself shows the complete virtue of his nature; the completion of other beings shows his Wisdom. (The two) show his nature in good operation, and the way in which the union of the external and internal is effected.

29. Hence, whenever he exercises it, (the operation) is right.

30. Thus it is that entire perfection is unresting; unresting, it continues long; continuing long, it evidences itself; evidencing itself, it reaches far; reaching far, it becomes large and substantial; large and substantial, it becomes high and brilliant.

31. By being large and substantial it contains (all) things. By being high and brilliant, it overspreads (all) things. By reaching far and continuing long, it completes (all) things. By its being so large and substantial, it makes (its possessor) the coequal of earth; by its height and brilliancy, it makes him the co–equal of heaven; by its reaching far and continuing long, it makes him infinite.

32. Such being his characteristics, without any manifestation he becomes displayed; without any movement he effects changes; without any exertion he completes. The way of heaven and earth may be completely described in one sentence:—

33. They are without any second thought, and so their production of things is inexhaustible.

34. The characteristics of heaven and earth are to be large; to be substantial; to be high; to be brilliant; to be far–reaching; to be long–continuing.

35. There now is this heaven; it is only this bright shining spot, but when viewed in its inexhaustible extent, the sun, moon, stars, and constellations of the zodiac are suspended in it, and all things are overspread by it. There is this earth; it is only a handful of soil, but when regarded in its breadth and thickness, it sustains mountains like the Hwâ and the Yo, without feeling the weight, and contains the rivers and seas without their leaking away. There is this mountain; it looks only the size of a stone, but when contemplated in all its altitude the grass and trees are produced on it, birds and beasts dwell on it, and the precious things which men treasure up are found in it. There is this water; it appears only a ladleful, but, when we think of its unfathomable depths, the largest tortoises, iguanas, iguanadons, dragons, fishes, and turtles are produced in them, and articles of value and sources of wealth abound in them.

36. It is said in the Book of Poetry (IV, i, sect. i, ode 2),

'The ordinances of Heaven,
How profound are they and unceasing!'

intimating that it is thus that Heaven is Heaven (And again):—

'Oh! how illustrious
Was the singleness of the virtue of king Wan!'

intimating that it was thus that king Wan was the accomplished (king), by his singleness unceasing.

37. How great is the course of the sage! Like an overflowing flood it sends forth and nourishes all things! It rises up to the height of heaven.

38. How complete is its greatness! It embraces the three hundred usages of ceremony, and the three thousand modes of demeanour. It waits for the right man, and then it is trodden. Hence it is said, 'If there be not perfect virtue, the perfect path cannot be exemplified.'

39. Therefore the superior man honours, the virtuous nature, and pursues the path of inquiry and study (regarding it); seeking to carry it out in its breadth and greatness, so as to omit none of the exquisite and minute points (which it embraces); raising it to its greatest height and brilliancy, so as to be found in the way of equilibrium and harmony. He cherishes his old knowledge so as (continually) to be acquiring new, and thus manifests an honest, generous, earnestness in the esteem and practice of all propriety

40. Therefore, when occupying a high situation he is not proud, and in a low situation he is not insubordinate. If the state is well-governed, his words are able to promote its prosperity; and if it be ill-governed, his silence is sufficient to secure forbearance (for himself).

41. Is not this what is said in the Book of Poetry (III, iii, ode 6, 4),

'Intelligent is he and wise,
Protecting his. own person?'

42. The Master said, 'Let a man who is ignorant be fond of using his own judgment: let one who is in a low situation be fond of arrogating a directing power; let one who is living in the present age go back to the ways of antiquity;—on all who act thus calamity

is sure to come.'

43. To no one but the son of Heaven does it belong to discuss the subject of ceremonial usages; to fix the measures; and to determine (the names of) the written characters

44. Now, throughout the whole kingdom, carriages have all wheels of the same breadth of rim, all writing is with the same characters; and for conduct there are the same rules.

45. One may occupy the throne, but if he have not the proper virtue, he should not presume to make ceremonies or music. One may have the virtue, but if he have not the throne, he in the same way should not presume to make ceremonies or music.

46. The Master said, 'I might speak of the ceremonies of Hsiâ, but Khî could not sufficiently attest (my words). I have learned the ceremonies of Yin, and they are preserved in Sung. I have learned the ceremonies of Kâu, and they are now used. I follow Kâu.'

47. If he who attains to the sovereignty of all the kingdom attach the due importance to (those) three points[1], there are likely to be few errors (among the people).

48. However excellent may have been (the regulations of) those of former times, they cannot be attested. Not being attested, they cannot command credence. Not commanding credence, the people

[1. What are those three points? The old interpretations said,—'The ceremonies of the three kings;' Kû Hsî thought they were the three things in paragraph 43;—which is more likely.]

would not follow them. However excellent might be those of one in an inferior station, they would not be honoured. Not honoured, they would not command credence. Not commanding credence, the people would not follow them.

49. Therefore the course of the superior man is rooted in his own character and conduct, and attested by the multitudes of the people. He examines (his institutions) by comparison with those of the founders of the three dynasties, and finds them without mistake. He sets them up before heaven and earth, and there is nothing in them contrary

to (their mode of operation). He presents himself with them before Spiritual Beings, and no doubts about them arise. He is prepared to wait for the rise of a sage a hundred ages hence, and has no misgivings. That he can present himself with them before Spiritual Beings, without any doubts about them arising, shows that he knows Heaven; that he is prepared to wait for the rise of a sage a hundred ages hence, without any misgivings, shows that he knows men.

50. Therefore the movements of the superior man mark out for ages the path for all under heaven; his actions are the law for ages for all under heaven; and his words are for ages the pattern for all under heaven. Those who are far from him look longingly for him, and those who are near are never weary of him.

51. It is said in the Book of Poetry (IV, i, sect. 2, ode 3),

'There in their own states are they loved,
Nor tired of are they here;
Their fame through lapse of time shall grow,
Both day and night, more clear.'

Never has a superior man obtained an early renown throughout the kingdom who did not correspond to this description.

52. Kung–nî handed down (the views of) Yâo and Shun as if they had been his ancestors, and elegantly displayed (the ways) of Wan and Wû, taking them as his model. Above, he adopted as his law the seasons of heaven; and below, he conformed to the water and land.

53. He may be compared to heaven and earth in their supporting and containing, their overshadowing and curtaining all things. He may be compared to the four seasons in their alternating progress, and to the sun and moon in their successive shining. All things are nourished together without their injuring one another; the courses (of the seasons and of the sun and moon) proceed without any collision among them. The smaller energies are like river–currents; the greater energies are seen in might transformations. It is this which makes heaven and earth so great.

54. It is only he possessed of all sagely qualities that can exist under heaven, who shows himself quick in apprehension, clear in discernment, of far–reaching intelligence and

all–embracing knowledge, fitted to exercise rule; magnanimous, generous, benign, and mild, fitted to exercise forbearance; impulsive, energetic, firm, and enduring, fitted to maintain a strong hold; self–adjusted, grave, never swerving from the mean, and correct, fitted to command respect; accomplished, distinctive, concentrative, and searching, fitted to exercise discrimination.

55. All–embracing is he and vast, deep and active as a fountain, sending forth in their due seasons these (qualities).

56. All–embracing is he and vast, like heaven. Deep and active as a fountain, he is like an abyss. He shows himself, and the people all revere him; he speaks, and the people all believe him; he acts, and the people all are pleased with him. In this way his fame overspreads the Middle kingdom, and extends to all barbarous tribes. Wherever ships and carriages reach; wherever the strength of man penetrates; wherever the heavens overshadow and the earth sustains; wherever the sun and moon shine; wherever frosts and dews fall; all who have blood and breath unfeignedly honour and love him. Hence it is said, 'He is the equal of Heaven[1].'

57. It is only he among all under heaven who is entirely perfect that can adjust and blend together the great standard duties of all under heaven, establish the great fundamental principles of all, and know the transforming and nourishing operations of heaven and earth.

58. How shall this individual have any one beyond himself on whom he depends? Call him man in his ideal, how earnest is he! Call him an abyss, how deep is he! Call him Heaven, how vast is he!

59. Who can know him but he who is indeed quick in apprehension and clear in discernment, of sagely wisdom, and all–embracing knowledge, possessing heavenly virtue?

60. It is said in the Book of Poetry (I, v, ode 3, 1),

[1. It was the old opinion that in this part of the Treatise we have his grandson's eloquent culogium of Confucius, and I agree with that opinion. Yet I have not ventured to translate the different parts of it in the past tense. Let it be read as the description of the ideal sage who found his realisation in the Master.]

'Over her embroidered robe she wears a (plain) garment;'

expressing how the wearer disliked the display of the beauty (of the robe). just so, it is the way of the superior man to prefer che concealment (of his virtue), while it daily becomes more illustrious, and it is the way of the small man to seek notoriety, while he daily goes more and more to ruin.

61. It is characteristic of the superior man, appearing insipid, yet not to produce satiety; preferring a simple negligence, yet to have his accomplishments recognised; seeming mild and simple, yet to be discriminating. He knows how what is distant lies in what is near. He knows where the wind proceeds from. he knows how what is minute becomes manifested[1]. He, we may be assured, will enter (the innermost recesses of) virtue.

62. It is said in the Book of Poetry (II, iv, ode 8, 11),

'Though they dive to the bottom, and lie there,
They are vcry clearly seen.'

Therefore the superior man internally examines his heart, that there may be nothing wrong there, and no occasion for dissatisfaction with himself.

63. That wherein the superior man cannot be equalled is simply this,—his (work) which other men do not see. It is said in the Book of Poetry (III, iii, ode 2, 7),

'When in your chamber, 'neath its light,
Maintain your conscience pure and bright.'

[1. That is how the ruler's character acts on the people as the wind on grass and plants.]

64. Therefore the superior man, even when he is not acting, has the feeling of reverence; and when he does not speak, he has the feeling of truthfulness. It is said in the Book of Poetry (IV, iii, ode 2),

'These offerings we set forth without a word,
Without contention, and with one accord,
To beg the presence of the honoured lord.'

65. Therefore the superior man does not use rewards, and the people are stimulated (to virtue); he does not show anger, and the people are awed more than by hatchets and battle–axes. It is said in the Book of Poetry (IV, i, sect. i, ode 4),

'What is most distinguished is the being virtuous;
It will secure the imitation of all the princes.'

66. Therefore the superior man being sincerely reverential, the whole kingdom is made tranquil. It is said in the Book of Poetry (III, i, ode 7, 7),

'I am pleased with your intelligent virtue,
Not loudly proclaimed, nor pourtrayed.'

67. The Master said, 'Among the appliances to transform the people, sounds and appearances (may seem to) have a trivial effect. But it is said in another ode (III, iii, ode 6, 6),

"Virtue is light as a hair."

68. 'But a hair will still admit of comparison (as to its size). in what is said in another ode (III, i, ode 17),

"The doings of high Heaven
Have neither sound nor odour,"

BOOK XXIX. PIÂO KÎ, OR THE RECORD ON EXAMPLE[1]

1. These were the words of the Master:—'Let us return[2].' The superior man, in obscurity, yet makes himself manifest; without giving himself any airs, his gravity is acknowledged; without the exercise of severity, he inspires awe; without using words, he

is believed.

2. The Master said, 'The superior man takes no erroneous step before men, nor errs in the expression of his countenance, nor in the language of his speech. Therefore his demeanour induces awe, his countenance induces fear, and his words produce confidence. It is said in The Punishments of Fû (The Shû, V, xxvii, ii): "They were all reverence and caution. They had no occasion to make choice of words in reference to their conduct."'

3. The Master said, 'The dress and the one worn over it do not take the place, the one of the other, it being intimated to the people thereby that they should not trouble or interfere with one another.'

4. The Master said, 'When a sacrifice has come to the point of greatest reverence, it should not be immediately followed by music. When the discussion

[1. See the introductory notice, vol. xxvii, pp. 44, 45.

2. Compare Analects, V, 22. When Confucius thus spoke, he was accepting his failure in the different states, and saying in effect that his principles and example would ultimately win their way, without his being immediately successful.]

of affairs at court has reached its utmost nicety, it should not be immediately followed by an idle indifference.'

5. The Master said, 'The superior man is careful (in small things), and thereby escapes calamity. His generous largeness cannot be kept in obscurity. His courtesy keeps shame at a distance.'

6. The Master said, 'The superior man, by his gravity and reverence, becomes every day stronger (for good); while indifference and want of restraint lead to a daily deterioration. The superior man does not allow any irregularity in his person, even for a single day;–how should he be like (a small man) who will not end his days (in honour)?'

7. The Master said, 'Vigil and fasting are required (as a preparation) for serving the spirits (in sacrifice); the day and month in which to appear before the ruler are chosen

beforehand:—these observances were appointed lest the people should look on these things without reverence.'

8. The Master said, '(The small man) is familiar and insolent. He may bring death on himself (by being so), and yet he stands in no fear'.'

9. The Master said, 'Without the interchange of the formal messages, there can be no reception of one party by another; without the presenting of the ceremonial (gifts), there can be no interview (with a superior):–these rules were made that the people might not take troublesome liberties with one another! It is said in the Yî, "When he shows (the sincerity that marks) the first recourse to divination, I instruct him. If he apply a second and third time,

[1. The text of this short paragraph is supposed to the defective.]

that is troublesome, and I do not instruct the troublesome[1].'"

10. These were the words of the Master:'(Humanity, of which the characteristic is) Benevolence, is the Pattern for all under Heaven; Righteousness is the Law for all under Heaven; and the Reciprocations (of ceremony) are for the Profit of all under Heaven.'

11. The Master said, 'When kindness is returned for kindness, the people are stimulated (to be kind). When injury is returned for injury, the people are warned (to refrain from wrong–doing). It is said in the Book of Poetry (III, iii, ode 26):—

"Answers to every word will leap,
Good deeds their recompense shall reap."

'It is said in the Thâi Kiâ (Shû, V, v, sect. 2, 2), "Without the sovereign, the people cannot enjoy repose with one another; without the people, the sovereign would have none to rule over in the four quarters (of the kingdom).'"

12. The Master said, 'They who return kindness for injury are such as have a regard for their own persons. They who return injury for kindness are men to be punished and put to death[2].'

13. The Master said, 'Under heaven there is, only a man (here and there) who loves what is proper to humanity without some personal object in the

[1. See the explanation of the 4th Hexagram, mang, vol. xvi, pp. 64, 65,—with this paragraph ends the first section of the Treatise. It seems to be extended to exhibit the necessity of reverence in the superior man, who is to be an example to others.

2. Comparing this utterance with the decision of Confucius in the Analects, XIV, 36, Khan Hâo thinks it doubtful that we have here the sentiment or words of the sage.]

matter, or who hates what is contrary to humanity without being apprehensive (of some evil). Therefore the superior man reasons about the path to be trodden from the standpoint of himself, and lays down his laws from the (capabilities of the) people.'

14. The Master said, '(The virtues of) humanity appear in three ways. (In some cases) the work of humanity is done, but under the influence of different feelings. In these, the (true character of the) humanity cannot be known; but where there is some abnormal manifestation of it, in those the true character can be known[1]. Those to whom it really belongs practise it easily and naturally; the wise practise it for the sake of the advantage which it brings; and those who fear the guilt of transgression practise it by constraint.

15. Humanity is the right hand; pursuing the right path is the left[2]. Humanity comprehends the (whole) man; the path pursued is the exhibition of righteousness. Those whose humanity is large, while their exhibition of righteousness is slight, are loved and not honoured. Those whose righteousness is large and their humanity slight are honoured and not loved.

16. There is the perfect path, the righteous path, and the calculated path. The perfect path conducts to sovereignty; the righteous path, to chieftaincy; and the calculated path, to freedom from error and failure[3].

[1. In illustration of this point there is always adduced the case of the duke of Kâu, who erred, under the influence of his brotherly love, in the promotion of his brothers that afterwards joined in rebellion.

2. The right hand is used most readily and with greatest effect.

3. With this paragraph ends the second section of the Treatise. It is occupied with the subject of humanity, or the whole nature of man, of which benevolence is the chief element and characteristic, as the most powerful form of example.]

17. These were the words of the Master:—'Of humanity there are various degrees; righteousness is now long, now short, now great, now small. Where there is a deep and compassionate sympathy in the heart, we have humanity evidenced in the love of others; where there is the following of (old) examples, and vigorous endeavour, we have the employment of humanity for the occasion. It is said in the Book of Poetry (III, i, ode 10, 6),

"Where the Fang–water flows,
Is the white millet grown.
So his men Wû employed,
And his merit was shown!
To his sons he would leave
His wise plans and his throne
And our Wû was a sovereign true."

'That was a humanity extending to many generations. In the Lessons from the States it is said (I, iii, ode 10, 3),

"Person slighted, life all blighted,
What can the future prove?"

'That was a humanity extending (only) to the end of the speaker's life.'

18. The Master said, 'Humanity is like a heavy vessel, and like a long road. He who tries to lift the vessel cannot sustain its weight; he who travels t e road cannot accomplish all its distance. There is nothing that has so many different degrees as (the course of) humanity; and thus he who tries to nerve himself to it finds it a difficult task. Therefore when the superior man measures men with the scale of righteousness, he finds it difficult to discover the men (whom he seeks); when he looks at men and compares them with one another, he knows who among them are the more worthy.'

19. The Master said, 'It is only one man (here and there) under heaven, who with his heart of hearts naturally rests in humanity. It is said in the Tâ Yâ, or Major Odes of the Kingdom (III, iii, ode 6, 6),

"Virtue is very light,—
Light as a hair, yet few can bear
The burden of its weight.
'Tis so; but Kung Shan, as I think,
Needs not from virtue's weight to shrink
That other men defies.
Aid from my love his strength rejects.
(if the king's measures have defects,
What's needed he supplies)."

'In the Hsiâo Yâ, or Minor Odes of the Kingdom, it is said (II, vii, ode 4, 5),

"To the high hills I looked;
The great way I pursued."'

The Master said, 'So did the poets love (the exhibition of) humanity. (They teach us how) one should pursue the path of it, not giving over in the way, forgetting his age, taking no thought that the years before him will not be sufficient (for his task), urging on his course with earnestness from day to day, and only giving up when he sinks in death.'

20. The Master said, 'Long has the attainment of a perfect humanity been difficult among men! all men err in what they love;—and hence it is easy to apologise for the errors of those who are seeking this humanity[1].'

21. The Master said, 'Courtesy is near to propriety; economy is near to humanity; good faith is near to the truth of things. When one with respect and humility practises these (virtues), though he may fall into errors, they will not be very great. Where there is courtesy, the errors are few; where there is truth, there can be good faith; where there is economy, the exercise of forbearance is easy:—will not failure be rare in the case of those who practise these things? It is said in the Book of Poetry (III. iii, ode 2, 9),

"Mildness and reverence base supply
For virtue's structure, broad and high."

22. The Master said, 'Long has the attainment of perfect humanity been difficult among men; it is only the superior man who is able to reach it. Therefore the superior man does not distress men by requiring from them that which (only) he himself can do, nor put them to shame because of what they cannot do. Hence the sage, in laying down rules for conduct, does not make himself the rule, but gives them his instructions so that they shall be able to stimulate themselves to endeavour, and have the feeling of shame if they do not put them in practice. (He enjoins) the rules of ceremony to regulate the conduct; good faith to bind it on them; right demeanour to set it off; costume to distinguish it; and friendship to perfect it:—he desires in this way to produce a uniformity of the people. It is said in the Hsiâo Yâ (V, ode 5, 3),

[1. This seems to be the meaning, about which there are various opinions.]

"Shall they unblushing break man's law?
Shall they not stand of Heaven in awe?"

23. 'Therefore, when a superior man puts on the dress (of his rank), he sets it off by the demeanour of a superior man. That demeanour he sets off with the language of a superior man; and that language he makes good by the virtues of a superior man. Hence the superior man is ashamed to wear the robes, and not have the demeanour; ashamed to have the demeanour, and not the style of speech; ashamed to have the style of speech, and not the virtues; ashamed to have the virtues, and not the conduct proper to them. Thus it is that when the superior man has on his sackcloth and other mourning, his countenance wears an air of sorrow; when he wears the square-cut dress and square-topped cap, his countenance wears an air of respect; and when he wears his mail-coat and helmet, his countenance says that he is not to be meddled with. It is said in the Book of Poetry (I, xiv, ode 2, 2),

Like pelicans, upon the dam
Which stand, and there their pouches cram,
Unwet the while their wings,
Are those who their rich dress display.
But no befitting service pay,

Intent on meanest things[1].'"

[1. With this paragraph ends the 3rd section of the Book. 'It speaks,' say the Khien–lung editors, 'of the perfect humanity, showing that to rest naturally in this is very difficult, yet it is possible by self–government to advance from the practice of it, with a view to one's advantage, to that natural resting in it; and by means of instruction to advance from the practice of it by constraint to the doing so for its advantages.']

24. These were the words of the Master:—'What the superior man calls righteousness is, that noble and mean all have the services which they discharge throughout the kingdom. The son of Heaven himself ploughs the ground for the rice with which to fill the vessels, and the black millet from which to distil the spirit to be mixed with fragrant herbs, for the services of God, and in the same way the feudal lords are diligent in discharging their services to the son of Heaven.'

25. The Master said, 'In serving (the ruler) his superior, (an officer) from his position has great opportunity to protect the people; but when he does not allow himself to have any thought of acting as the ruler of them, this shows a high degree of humanity. Therefore, the superior man is courteous and economical, seeking to exercise his benevolence, and sincere and humble in order to practise his sense of propriety. He does not himself seta high value on his services; he does not himself assert the honour due to his person. He is not ambitious of (high) position, and is very moderate in his desires. He gives place willingly to men of ability and virtue. He abases himself and gives honour to others. He is careful and in fear of doing what is not eight. His desire in all this is to serve his ruler. If he succeed in doing so (and obtaining his ruler's approbation), he feels that he has done right; if he do not so succeed, he still feels that he has done right:—prepared to accept the will of Heaven concerning himself. It is said in the Book of Poetry (III, i, ode 5, 6),

"How the creepers close twine
Round the branches and stems!
Self–possession and ease
Robed our prince as with gems.
Happiness increased unsought,
Nor by crooked ways was bought."

Might not this have been said of Shun, Yü, king Wan, or the duke of Kâu, who had the great virtues (necessary) to govern the people, and yet were (only) careful to serve their rulers? It is said again in the same Book of Poetry (III, i, ode 2, 3),

"This our king Wan in all his way
Did watchful reverence display,
With clearest wisdom serving God,
Who, pleased to see the course he trod,
Him with great favour crowned.
His virtue no deflection knew,
But always to the right was true.
The states beheld, and all approved.
With loyal ardour stirred and moved,
Wan as their head they owned."'

26. The Master said, 'The practice of the ancient kings in conferring honorary posthumous names was to do honour to the fame (of the individuals); but they limited themselves to one excellence (in the character);—they would have been ashamed if the name had been beyond the actions (of the life). An accordance with this the superior man does not himself magnify his doings, nor himself exalt his merit, seeking to be within the truth; actions of an extraordinary character he does not aim at, but seeks to occupy himself only with what is substantial and good. He displays prominently the good qualities of others, and celebrates their merits, seeking to place himself below them in the scale of worth. There fore, although the superior man abases himself, yet the people respect and honour him.'

27. The Master said, 'The meritorious services of Hâu Kî were the greatest of all under Heaven.; could his hands and feet be described as those of an ordinary man? But all which he desired was that his doings should be superior to his name, and therefore he said of himself that he was simply "a man useful to others[1]."

28. These were the words of the Master:—'Difficult is it to attain to what is called the perfect humanity of the superior man! It is said in the Book of Poetry[2],

"The happy and courteous prince
Is the father and mother of his people."

Happy, he (yet) vigorously teaches them; courteous, he makes them pleased and restful. With all their happiness, there is no wild extravagance; with all their observance of ceremonial usages, there is the feeling of affection. Notwithstanding his awing gravity, they are restful; notwithstanding his son–like gentleness, they are respectful. Thus he causes

[1. With this ends the 4th section of the Book, 'On the service of his ruler by an inferior, showing the righteousness between them, and how that righteousness completes the humanity.'

2. The ode here quoted from can hardly be any other than III, ii, 7. The first character in the former of the two lines in that ode, however, is only the phonetic part of that in the text here, and the meaning of 'force or vigour' which the writer employs seems incongruous with that belonging to it in the Shih, where it occurs several times, in combination with the character that follows it, used as a binomial adjective. I need not say more on the difficulty. The meaning of the paragraph as a whole is plain:—'The superior man,' the competent ruler, must possess, blended together, the strength of the father and the gentleness of the mother.]

them to honour him as their father, and love him as their mother. There must be all this before he is the father and mother of his people. Could any one who was not possessed of perfect virtue be able to accomplish this?

29. 'Here now is the affection of a father for his sons;—he loves the worthy among them, and places on a lower level those who do not show ability; but that of a mother for them is such, that while she loves the worthy, she pities those who do not show ability:—the mother deals with them on the ground of affection and not of showing them honour; the father, on the ground of showing them honour and not of affection. (So we may say of) water and the people, that it manifests affection to them, but does not give them honour; of fire, that it gives them honour, but does not manifest affection; of the ground, that it manifests affection, but does not give honour; of Heaven, that it gives them honour, but does not manifest affection; of the nature conferred on them, that it manifests affection, but does not give them honour; and of the manes of their departed, that they give honour, but do not manifest affection[1].'

30. 'Under the Hsiâ dynasty it was the way to give honour to the nature conferred on men; they served the manes of the departed, and respected Spiritual Beings, keeping them at a distance, while they brought the people near, and made them loyal; they put first the (attraction) of emolument, and last the terrors of power; first rewards, and then punishments; showing their affection (for the people), but

[1. The ruler–father of the previous paragraph is here contrasted with the ordinary parent; but the second half of the text is not easily translated, and is difficult to comprehend.]

not giving them honour. The bad effect on the people was, that they became stupid and ignorant, proud and clownish, and uncultivated, without any accomplishments.

'Under the Yin dynasty, they honoured Spiritual Beings, and led the people on to serve them; they put first the service of their manes, and last the usages of ceremony; first punishments, and then rewards; giving honour (to the people), but not showing affection for them. The bad effect on the people was, that they became turbulent and were restless, striving to surpass one another without any sense of shame.

'Under the Kâu dynasty, they honoured the ceremonial usages, and set a high value on bestowing (favours); they served the manes and respected Spiritual Beings, yet keeping them at a distance; they brought the people near, and made them loyal; in rewarding and punishing they used the various distinctions and arrangements of rank; showing affection (for the people), but not giving them honour. The bad effects on the people were, that they became fond of gain and crafty; were all for accomplishments, and shameless; injured one another, and had their moral sense obscured.'

31. The Master said, 'It was the method of the Hsiâ dynasty not to trouble (the people) with many notices; it did not require everything from the people, nor (indeed) look to them for great things; and they did not weary of the affection (between them and their rulers).

'Under the Yin dynasty, they did not trouble (the people) with ceremonies, and yet they required everything from them.

'Under the Kâu dynasty, they were rigorous with the people, and not troublesome in the services to the spirits; but they did all that could be done in the way of awards, conferring rank, punishments, and penalties.'

32. The Master said, 'Under the methods of (the dynasties of the line of) Yü[1] and Hsiâ, there were few dissatisfactions among the people. The methods of Yin and Kâu were not equal to the correction of their errors.'

33. The Master said, 'The plain and simple ways of (the dynasties of the line of) Yü and Hsiâ, and the multiplied forms of Yin and Kâu were both extreme. The forms of Yü and Hsiâ did not neutralise their simplicity, nor was there sufficient simplicity under Yin and Kâu to neutralise their forms.'

34. These were the words of the Master:—'Although in subsequent ages there arose (distinguished sovereigns), yet none of them succeeded in equalling the Tî of (the line of) Yü. He ruled over all under heaven, but, while he lived, he had not a selfish thought, and when he died, he did not make his son great (with the inheritance). He treated the people as his sons, as if he had been their father and mother. He had a deep and compassionate sympathy for them (like their mother); he instructed them in loyalty and what was profitable (like their father). While he showed his affection for them, he also gave them honour; in his natural restfulness, he was reverent; in the terrors of his majesty, he yet was loving; with all his riches, he was yet observant

[1. 'The line of Yü' was Shun, who succeeded to Yâo. He did not found a dynasty; but he is often spoken of as if he had done so.]

of the rules of propriety; and his kindness was yet (rightly) distributed. The superior men who stood in connexion with him gave honour to benevolence, and stood in awe of righteousness; were ashamed of lavish expenditure, and set little store by their accumulation of substance; loyal, but not coming into collision with their sovereign; righteous, and yet deferential to him; accomplished, and yet restful; generous, and yet discriminating. It is said in Fû on Punishments, "He sought to awe the people by his virtue, and all were filled with dread; he proceeded to enlighten them by his virtue, and all were enlightened." Who but the Tî of (the line of) Yü could have been able to do this[1]?' (Shû, V, xxvii, 7.)

35. These were the words of the Master:—'(A minister) in the service of his ruler will first offer his words of counsel, and (when they are accepted), he will bow and

voluntarily offer his person to make good his sincerity. Hence, whatever service a ruler requires from his minister, the minister will die in support of his words. In this way the salary which he receives is not obtained on false pretences, and the

[1. With this paragraph it is understood that the 5th section of the Book ends, 'illustrating the perfect humanity of the superior man in the government of the people.' Every fresh section thus far, however, has commenced with a—'These were the words of the Master,' and in no case ended with that phraseology. Paragraph 35 rightly begins with it. It is out of place, or rather misplaced, in this; and belongs, I believe, to another place, as we shall see. We should read here, instead of it, 'The Master said.' With regard to the greater part of the section, its genuineness is liable to suspicion, and is indeed denied by the majority of commentators, including the Khien–lung editors. The sentiments are more Tâoistic than Confucian. See the introductory notice of the Book.]

things for which he can be blamed will be more and more few.'

36. The Master said, 'In the service of a ruler, when great words are spoken to (and accepted by) him, great advantages (to the state) may be expected from them; and when words of small importance are presented to him, only small advantages are to be looked for. Therefore a superior man will not for words of small importance receive great emolument, nor for words of great importance small emolument. It is said in the Yî, "He does not enjoy his revenues in his own family, (but at court); there will be good fortune[1]."'

37. The Master said, 'In the service of a ruler, (a minister) should not descend to subjects beneath him, nor set a high value on speeches, nor accept an introduction from improper individuals. It is said in the Hsiâo Yâ (II, vi, ode 3, 4),

"Your duties quietly fulfil,
And hold the upright in esteem,
With friendship fast;
So shall the Spirits hear your cry,
You virtuous make, and good supply In measure vast."'

38. The Master said, 'In the service of a ruler, for (a minister) whose place is remote from (the court), to remonstrate is an act of sycophancy; for one whose place is near the ruler,

not to remonstrate is to hold his office idly for the sake of gain.'

39. The Master said, 'Ministers near (the ruler) should (seek to) preserve the harmony (of his

[1. See the Thwan, or first of the appendixes of the Yî, on Hexagram 26, vol. xvi, page 234.]

virtues). The chief minister should maintain correctness in all the departments. Great ministers should be concerned about all parts (of the kingdom).'

40. The Master said, 'In the service of a ruler there should be the wish to remonstrate, but no wish to set forth (his faults). It is said in the Book of Poetry (II, viii, ode 4, 4),

"I cherish those men in my heart;—
Might not my words my love impart?
No;—if the words were once but spoken,
The charm of love might then be broken.
The men shall dwell within my heart,
Nor thence with lapse of time depart."'

41. The Master said, 'In the service of a ruler, when it is difficult to advance and easy to retire, there is a proper order maintained in the occupancy of places (according to the character of their holders). If it were easy to advance and difficult to retire, there would be confusion. Hence a superior (visitor) advances (only) after he has been thrice bowed to, while he retires after one salutation on taking leave; and thus confusion is prevented.,'

42. The Master said, 'In the service of a ruler, if (an officer), after thrice leaving the court (on his advice being rejected), do not cross the borders (of the state), he is remaining for the sake of the profit and emolument. Although men say that he is not trying to force (his ruler), I will not believe them.'

43. The Master said, 'In the service of a ruler, (an officer) should be careful at the beginning, and respectful to the end.'

44. The Master said, 'In the service of a ruler, one may be in a high position or a low, rich or poor, to live or to die (according to the will of the ruler), but he should not allow himself to be led to do anything contrary to order or right.'

45. The Master said, 'In the service of a ruler, if it be in the army, (an officer) should not (try to) avoid labour and danger; if it be at court he should not refuse a mean office. To occupy a post and not perform its business is contrary to order and right. Hence, when a ruler employs him on any duty, if it suit his own mind, he thinks carefully of what it requires, and does it; if it do not suit his own mind, he thinks the more carefully of what it requires, and does it. When his work is done, he retires from Office:—such is an officer who well discharges his duty. It is said in the Yî (vol. xvi, p. 96), "He does not serve either king or feudal lord, but in a lofty spirit prefers (to attend to) his own affairs."'

46. The Master said, 'It is only the son of Heaven who receives his appointment from Heaven; officers receive their appointments from the ruler. Therefore if the ruler's orders be conformed (to the mind of Heaven), his orders to his ministers are also conformed to it; but if his orders be contrary (to that mind), his orders to them are also contrary to it. It is said in the Book of Poetry (I, iv, ode 5, 2),

"How strong the magpies, battling fierce,
Each one to keep his mate!
How bold the quails together rush,
Upon the same debate!
This woman, with no trait that's good,
Is stained by vicious crime,
Yet her I hail as marchioness;—
Alas! woe worth the time!"'

47. The Master said, 'The superior man does not consider that his words (alone) show fully what a man is. Hence when right ways prevail in the kingdom, the branches and leaves (from the stem) of right conduct appear; but when there are not right ways in the kingdom, the branches and leaves of (mere) words appear.

'In accordance with this, when a superior man is by the side of one occupied with the mourning rites, and cannot contribute to assist him in his expenditure, he does not ask him what it is; when he is by the side of one who is ill, and cannot supply him with food, he does not ask what he would like; when he has a visitor for whom he cannot provide a lodging, he does not ask where he is staying. Hence the intercourse of a superior man may be compared to water, and that of a small man, to sweet wine. The superior man seems insipid, but he helps to perfection; the small man seems sweet, but he leads to ruin. It is said in the Hsiâo Yâ (II, v, ode 4, 3),

"He trusts the rogues that lie and sneak,
And make things worse;
Their duties shirked, their words so meek
Prove but a curse."'

48. The Master said[1], 'The superior man does not confine himself to praising men with his words; and so the people prove loyal to him. Thus, when he asks about men who are suffering from cold, he clothes them; or men who are suffering from want, he feeds them; and when he praises a man's good qualities, he (goes on to) confer rank on him. It

[1. With this commences the 7th section of the Book, but it commences irregularly with 'the Master said,' instead of 'The words of the Master were;' see note above, on page 344.]

is said in the Lessons from the States (I, xiv, ode 1, 3),

"I grieve; would they but lodge with me!"'

49. The Master said, 'Dissatisfaction and calamity will come to him whose lip-kindness is not followed by the corresponding deeds. Therefore the superior man will rather incur the resentment arising from his refusal than the charge of promising (and then not fulfilling). It is said in the Lessons from the States (V, ode 4, 6),

"I wildly go; I'll never know
Its smiles and chat again,
To me you clearly swore the faith,
Which now to break you're fain.
Could I foresee so false you'd be?
And now regrets are vain."'

50. The Master said, 'The superior man is not affectionate to others with his countenance (merely) as if, while cold in feeling, he could assume the appearance of affection. That belongs to the small man, and stamps him as no better than the thief who makes a hole in the wall.'

51. The Master said, 'What is required in feeling is sincerity; in words, that they be susceptible of proof[1].'

52. These were the words of the Master:—'The ancient and intelligent kings of the three dynasties all served the Spiritual Intelligences of heaven and earth, but invariably used the tortoise–shell and divining stalks. They did. not presume to employ their own private judgment in the service of God.

[1. Here ends the 7th section, showing how the superior man strives to be sincere in his words and looks.]

In this way they did not transgress in the matter of the day or month, for they did not act contrary to the result of the divination. The tortoise and the shell were not consulted in succession on the same point.

53. 'For the great (sacrificial) services there were (fixed) seasons and days; for the smaller services these were not fixed. They fixed them by divination (near the time). (In divining) about external affairs they used the odd days; and for internal affairs, the even. They did not go against the (intimations of the) tortoise–shell and stalks.'

54. The Master said, 'With the victims perfect, the proper ceremonies and music, and the vessels of grain, (they sacrificed); and thus no injury was received from the Spiritual Powers, and the people had no occasion for dissatisfaction.'

55. The Master said, 'The sacrifices of Hâu Kî were easily provided. His language was reverential; his desires were restricted; and the blessings received extended down to his descendants. It is said in the Book of Poetry (III, ii, ode 1, 8),

"Hâu Kî founded the sacrifice;
No one has failed in it,
Down to the present day."'

56. The Master said, 'The shell and stalks employed by the great men[1] must be held in awe and reverence. But the son of Heaven does not divine by the stalks. While the princes are keeping guard in their states, they divine by the stalks. When the son of Heaven is on the road (travelling), he (also) divines by the stalks. In any other state but their

[1. The king and feudal lords.]

own they do not divine by the stalks. They consult the tortoise–shell about the chambers and apartments of the houses (where they lodge). The son of Heaven does not so consult the tortoise–shell he stays always in the grand ancestral temples.'

57. The Master said, 'The men of rank, on occasions of special respect, use their sacrificial vessels. On this account they do not fail to observe the set seasons and days, and do not act contrary to the intimations of the shell and stalks; thus seeking to serve with reverence the ruler and their superiors. In this way superiors are not troublesome to the people, and the people do not take liberties with their superiors[1].'

BOOK XXX. SZE Î, OR THE BLACK ROBES[1].

1. These were the words of the Master[2]: 'When the superior is easily served, his inferiors are easily known[3], and in this case punishments are not numerous (in the state).'

2. The Master said, 'When (the superior) loves the worthy as (the people of old loved him of) the black robes (Shih, I, vii, ode 1), and hates the bad as Hsiang–po (hated them;—II, v, ode 6), then without the frequent conferring of rank the people are stimulated to be good, and without the use of punishments they are all obedient to his orders. It is said in the Tâ Yâ (III, i, ode 1, 7),

"From Wan your pattern you must draw,
And all the states will own your law."'

3. The Master said, 'If the people be taught by lessons of virtue, and uniformity sought to be given to them by the rules of ceremony, their minds will go on to be good. If they be

taught by the laws, and uniformity be sought to be given to them by punishments, their minds will be thinking of how

[1. See the introductory notice, vol. xxvii, pp. 45, 46.

2. Thus the Book begins as if it were another section of the preceding Treatise.

3. They are 'easily known,' there being nothing in the ruler's method to make them deceitful.]

they can escape (the punishment;—Analects, II, iii). Hence, when the ruler of the people loves them as his sons, they feel to him as a parent; when he binds them to himself by his good faith, they do not turn away from him; when he presides over them with courtesy, their hearts are docile to him. It is said in the Punishments of Fû (Shû, V, xxvii, 3), "Among the people of Miâo they did not use orders simply, but the restraints of punishment. They made the five punishments engines of oppression, calling them the laws." In this way their people became bad, and (their rulers) were cut off for ever (from the land).'

4. The Master said, 'Inferiors, in serving their superiors, do not follow what they command, but what they do. When a ruler loves anything, those below him are sure to do so much more. Therefore the superior should by all means be careful in what he likes and dislikes. This will make him an example to the people[1].'

5. The Master said, 'When Yü had been on the throne three years, the humanity of the common people was in accordance with his;—was it necessary that all (at court) should be perfectly virtuous? It is said in the Book of Poetry (II, v, ode 7, 1),

"Awe–inspiring are you, O (Grand–)Master Yin,
And the people all look up to you."

It is said in the Punishments of Fû (V, xxvii, 13), "I, the One man, will have felicity, and the millions of the people will look to you as their sure dependence." It is said in the Tâ Yâ (III, i, ode 9, 3),

[1. This again looks very much as if this Treatise were a continuation of the last.]

"King Wû secured the people's faith,
And gave to all the law."'

6. The Master said, 'When superiors are fond of showing their humanity, inferiors strive to outstrip one another in their practice of it. Therefore those who preside over the people should cherish the clearest aims and give the most correct lessons, honouring the requirement of their humanity by loving the people as their sons; then the people will use their utmost efforts with themselves to please their superiors. It is said in the Book of Poetry (III, iii, ode 2, 2),

"Where from true virtue actions spring,
All their obedient homage bring."'

7. The Master said, 'The kings words are (at first) as, threads of silk; but when given forth, they become as cords. Or they are (at first) as cords; but when given forth, they become as ropes. Therefore the great man does not take the lead in idle speaking. The superior does not speak words which may be spoken indeed but should not be embodied in deeds; nor does he do actions which may be done in deed but should not be expressed in words. When this is the case, the words of the people can be carried into action without risk, and their actions can be spoken of without risk. It is said in the Book of Poetry (III, iii, ode 2, 8),

"Keep on your acts a watchful eye,
That you may scrutiny defy."'

8. The Master said, 'The superior man leads men on (to good) by his words, and keeps them (from evil) by (the example of) his conduct. Hence, in speaking, he must reflect on what may be the end of his words, and examine whether there may not be some error in his conduct; and then the people will be attentive to their words, and circumspect in their conduct. It is said in the Book of Poetry (III, iii, ode 2, 5),

"Be circumspect in all you say,
And reverent bearing still display."

It is said in the Tâ Yâ (III, i, ode 1, 4),

"Deep were Wan's thoughts, unstained his ways;
His reverence lit its trembling rays."'

9. The Master said, 'When the heads of the people use no (improper) variations in their dress, and their manners are always easy and unconstrained, and they seek thus to give uniformity to the people, the virtue of the people does become uniform. It is said in the Book of Poetry (II, viii, ode i, i),

"In the old capital they stood,
With yellow fox–furs plain;
Their manners all correct and good,
Speech free from vulgar stain.
Could we go back to Kâu's old days,
All would look up to them with praise."'

10. The Master said, 'When (the ruler) above can be known by men {???} looking at him, and (his ministers) below can have their doings related and remembered, then the ruler has no occasion to doubt his ministers, and the ministers are not led astray by their ruler. The Announcement of Yin says (Shû, IV, vi, 3), "There were I, Yin, and Thang; both possessed the same pure virtue." It is said in the Book of Poetry (I, xiv, ode 3, 3),

"In soul so steadfast is that princely man,
Whose course for fault or flaw we vainly scan."'

11. The Master said, 'When the holders of states and clans give distinction to the righteous and make it painful for the bad, thus showing the people the excellence (they should cultivate), then the feelings of the people do not swerve (to what is evil). It is said in the Book of Poetry (II, vi, ode 3, 5),

"Your duties quietly fulfil,
And hold the upright in esteem,
With earnest love."'

12. The Master said, "when the highest among men has doubts and perplexities, the common people go astray. When (the ministers) below him are difficult to be understood, the toil of the ruler is prolonged. Therefore when the ruler exhibits clearly what he loves,

and thus shows the people the style of manners (they should aim at), and is watchful against what he dislikes, and thereby guards the people against the excesses (of which they are in danger), then they do not go astray.

'When the ministers are exemplary in their conduct, and do not set a value on (fine) speeches; when they do not try to lead (the ruler) to what is unattainable, and do not trouble him with what cannot be (fully) known, then he is not toiled. It is said in the Book of Poetry (III, ii, ode 10, i),

"Reversed is now the providence of God;
The lower people groan beneath their load."

It is said in the Hsiâo Yâ (II, v, ode 4, 4),

"They do not discharge their duties,
But only cause distress to the king."'

13. The Master said, 'When (the measures of) government do not take effect, and the lessons of the ruler do not accomplish their object, (it is because) the giving of rank and emoluments is unfit to stimulate the people to good, and (the infliction of) punishments and penalties is unfit to make them ashamed (of evil). Therefore (the ruler) above must not be careless in punishing, nor lightly confer rank. It is said in the Announcement to the Prince of Khang (Shû, V, ix, 8), "Deal reverently and understandingly in your infliction of punishments;" and in the Punishments of Fû (Shû, V, xxvii, 12), "He spreads abroad his lessons to avert punishments."'

14. The Master said, 'When the great ministers are not on terms of friendly intimacy (with the ruler), and the common people consequently are not restful, this is because the loyalty (of the ministers) and the respect (of the ruler) are not sufficient, and the riches and rank conferred (on the former) are excessive. (The consequence is, that) the great ministers do not discharge their functions of government, and the ministers closer (to the ruler) form parties against them. Therefore the great ministers should by all means be treated with respect; they are examples to the people; and ministers nearer (to the ruler) should by all means be careful;—they direct the way of the people. Let not the ruler consult with inferior officers about greater, nor with those who are from a distance about those who are near to him, nor with those who are beyond the court about those who belong to it. If

he act thus, the great ministers will not be dissatisfied; the ministers closer to him will not be indignant; and those who are more remote will not be kept in obscurity. The duke of Sheh in his dying charge said, "Do not by little counsels ruin great enterprises; do not for the sake of a favourite concubine provoke queen Kwang; do not for the sake of a favourite officer provoke your grave officers,—the Great officers or high ministers[1].'"

15. The Master said, 'If the great man be not in affectionate sympathy with (his officers) whom he considers worthy, but give his confidence to others whom he despises, the people in consequence will not feel attached to him, and the lessons which he gives them will be troublesome (and ineffective). It is said in the Book of Poetry (II, ii, ode 8),

"As if I were hidden they sought me at first,
At court for a pattern to shine;
'Tis with hatred intense they now bend their scowls,
And my services curtly decline."

It is said in the Kün-khan (Shû, V, xxiv, 4), "While they have not seen a sage, (they are full of desire) as if they could not get a sight of him; but after they have seen him, they are still unable to follow him."'

16. The Master said, 'A small man is drowned in the water; a superior man is drowned or ruined by his mouth; the great man suffers his ruin from the people;—all suffer from what they have played and taken liberties with. Water is near to men, and yet it drowns them. Its nature makes it easy to play with, but dangerous to approach;—men are easily drowned in it. The mouth is loquacious and

[1. This is an error. The dying counsels referred to were not given by any duke of Sheh (a dependency of Khû), but by Wan-fû, duke of Zâi, to king Mû of Kâu. They are found with some slight alterations in the Apocryphal Books of Kâu, Book VIII, article 1. Confucius would not have fallen into such a mistake.]

troublesome; for words once uttered there is hardly a place of repentance;—men are easily ruined by it. The people, restricted in their humanity, have vulgar and rude minds; they should be respected, and should not be treated with contempt;—men are easily ruined by them. Therefore the superior man should by all means be careful in his dealings with them. It is said in the Thâi Kiâ (Shû, III, v, sect. 1, 5, 7), "Do not frustrate the charge to me, and bring on yourself your own overthrow. Be like the forester, who, when he has adjusted the string, goes to examine the end of the arrow, whether it be placed according to rule, and then lets go." It is said in the Charge to Yüeh (III, viii, Sect. 2, 4), "It is the mouth which gives occasion to shame; they are the coat of mail and helmet which give occasion to war. The upper robes and lower garments (for reward) should not be taken (lightly from) their chests; before spear and shield are used, one should examine himself." It is said in the Thâi Kiâ (Shû, III, v, sect. 2, 3), "Calamities sent by Heaven may be avoided; but from those brought on by one's self there is no escape." It is said in the Announcement of Yin (Shû, III, v, sect. 1, 3), "I have seen it myself in Hsiâ with its western capital, that when its sovereigns went through a prosperous course to the end, their ministers also did the same."'

17. The Master said, 'To the people the ruler is as their heart; to the ruler the people are as his body. When the heart is composed, the body is at ease; when the heart is reverent, the body is respectful; when the heart loves anything, the body is sure to rest in it. (So), when the ruler loves anything, the people are sure to desire it. The body is the complement of the heart, and a wound in it makes the heart also suffer. So the ruler is preserved by the people, and perishes also through the people. It is said in an ode,

"Once we had that former premier,
His words were wise and pure;
The states and clans by him were at rest,
The chief cities and towns by him were well regulated,
All the people by him enjoyed their life.
Who (now) holds the ordering of the kingdom?
Not himself attending to the government,
The issue is toil and pain to the people[1]."

It is said in, the Kün-yâ (Shû, V, xxv, 5), "In the heat and rain of summer days the inferior people may be described as murmuring and sighing. And so it may be said of them in the great cold of winter."'

18. The Master said, 'In the service by an inferior of his superior, if his personal character be not correct, his words will not be believed; and in this case their views will not be the same, and the conduct (of the superior) will not correspond (to the advice given to him)[2].'

19. The Master said, 'Words should be capable of proof by instances, and conduct should be conformed to rule; when the case is so, a man's aim cannot be taken from him while he is alive, nor can his good name be taken away when he is dead. Therefore the superior man, having heard much, verifies it by

[1. This is from an ode not in the Shih, and only preserved, so far, here. The three concluding lines, however, are also found in the Shih, II, iv, ode 7, 6.

2. The meaning of this latter part is matter of dispute.]

inquiry, and firmly holds fast (what is proved); he remembers much, verifies it by inquiry, and makes it his own; when he knows it exactly, he carries the substance of it into practice. It is said in the kün-khan (Shû, V, xxi, 5), "Going out and coming in, seek the judgment of the people about things, till you find a general agreement upon them." It is said in the Book of Poetry (I, xiv, ode 3, i),

"The virtuous man, the princely one,
Is uniformly correct in his deportment."'

20. The Master said, 'It is only the superior man who can love what is correct, while to the small man what is correct is as poison. Therefore the friends of the superior man have the definite aims which they pursue, and the definite courses which they hate. In consequence, those who are near at hand have no perplexities of thought about him, and those who are far off, no doubts. It is said in the Book of Poetry (I, i, ode 1, 1),

"For our prince a good mate."'

21. The Master said, 'When a man on light grounds breaks off his friendship with the poor and mean, and only on great grounds with the rich and noble, his love of worth cannot be great, nor does his hatred of evil clearly appear. Though men may say that he is not influenced by (the love of) gain, I do not believe them. It is said in the Book of Poetry (III, ii, ode 3, 4),

"And all the friends assisting you
Behave with reverent mien."'

21). The Master said, 'The superior man will not voluntarily remain to share in private acts of kindness not offered on grounds of virtue. In the Book of Poetry it is said (II, i, ode 1, 1),

"They love me, and my mind will teach
How duty's highest aim to reach."'

23. The Master said, 'If there be a carriage (before you), you are sure (by-and-by) to see the cross-board (in front); if there be a garment, you are sure (in the same way) to see (the traces of) its being worn; if one speaks, you are sure to hear his voice; if one does anything, you are sure to see the result. It is said in the Book of Poetry (I, i, ode 2, 2),

"I will wear them without being weary of them."'

24. The Master said, 'When one says anything, and immediately proceeds to act it out, his words cannot embellish it; and when one does anything, and immediately proceeds to describe it, the action cannot be embellished. Hence the superior man saying little, and acting to prove the sincerity of his words, the people cannot make the excellence of their deeds greater than it is, nor diminish the amount of their badness[1]. It is said in the Book of Poetry (III, iii, ode 2, 5),

"A flaw in mace of white jade may
By patient toil be ground away;
But for a flaw we make in speech,
What can be done? 'Tis past our reach."

[1. The excellence and the badness would seem, in the text, to belong to the conduct of the superior man; but to predicate badness of him would be too daring. To justify the view which appears in my translation, the Khien-lung editors, in their expansion of the meaning, after 'the people,' interpolate 'who come under the transforming influence of his example.']

It is said in the Hsiâo Yâ (II, iii, ode 5, 8),

"Well does our lord become his place,
And high the deeds his reign have crowned."

It is said to the Prince Shih (Shû, V, xvi, 11), "Aforetime, when God beheld the virtue of king Wan in the fields of Kâu, he made the great decree light on his person."'

25. The Master said, 'The people of the south have a saying that "A man without constancy cannot be a diviner either with the tortoise–shell or the stalks." This was probably a saying handed down from antiquity. If such a man cannot know the tortoise–shell and stalks, how much less can he know other men[1]? It is said in the Book of Poetry (II, v, ode 1, 3),

"Our tortoise–shells are wearied out,
And will not tell us anything about the plans."

The Charge to Yüeh says (Shû, IV, Viii, sect. 2, 5, 11), "Dignities should not be conferred on men of evil practices. (If they be), how can the people set themselves to correct their ways? If this be sought merely by sacrifices, it will be disrespectful (to the spirits). When affairs come to be troublesome, there ensues disorder; when the spirits are served so, difficulties ensue[2]."

It is said in the Yî, "When one does not continuously

[1. I cannot make anything but this of this sentence, though Khung Ying–tâ takes it differently. The whole paragraph is evidently very corrupt, and even the Khien–lung editors have put forth all their strength upon it in vain.

2. We have here a quotation from the Shû, IV, viii, sect. 2; but it is very different from the textus receptus. All the commentators and critics are at fault upon it; see vol. iii, pp. 115, 116.]

maintain his virtue, some will impute it to him as a disgrace[1];—(in the position indicated in the Hexagram.) When one does maintain his virtue continuously (in the other position indicated), this will be fortunate in a wife, but in a husband evil."'

BOOK XXXI. PAN SANG, OR RULES ON HURRYING TO MOURNING RITES[1].

1. According to the rules for hurrying to attend the mourning rites, when one first heard that the mourning rites for a relative were going on, he wailed as he answered the messenger, and gave full vent to his sorrow. Having asked all the particulars, he wailed again,—with a similar burst of grief, and immediately arranged to go (to the place). He went 100 lî a day, not travelling in the night.

2. Only when the rites were those for a father or a mother did he travel while he could yet see the stars, and rested when he (again) saw them[3]. If it was impossible for him to go (at once)[4], he assumed the mourning dress, and then went (as soon as he could). When he had passed through be state (where he was), and reached its frontier, he stopped and wailed, giving full vent to his sorrow. He avoided wailing in the market–place and when near the court. He looked towards the frontier of his own state when he wailed.

[1. See the introductory notice, vol. xxvii, pp. 46, 47.

2. The mourner is absent from his state, and a messenger his been sent to tell him of the death. The relative, it is argued, may. have been any one within the 'five degrees' of consanguinity.

3. That is, from peep of dawn till the stars came out again after sunset.

4. Being restrained by the duties of the commission, with which he was charged by the ruler.]

3. When he came to the house, he entered the gate at the left side of it, (passed through the court), and ascended to the hall by the steps on the west. He knelt on the east of the coffin, with his face to the west, and wailed, giving full vent to his grief. He (then) tied up his hair in a knot, bared his arms, and went down from the hall, proceeding to his place on the cast, where he wailed towards the west. Having completed the leaping, he covered his arms and put on his sash of sackcloth in the corridor on the east; and after tucking up the ends of his sash, he returned to his place. He bowed to the visitors, leaping with them, and escorted them (to the gate), returning (afterwards) to his place. When other visitors arrived, he bowed to them, leaped with them, and escorted them;—all in the same way.

4. (After this), all the principal mourners[1], with their cousins, went out at the gate, stopping there while they wailed. The gate was then closed, and the director told them to

go to the mourning shed[2].

5. At the next wailing, the day after, they tied up their hair, bared their arms, and went through the leaping. At the third wailing next day, they again tied up their hair, bared their arms, and went through the leaping. On these three days, the finishing the mourning dress, bowing to and escorting the visitors, took place as in the first case.

6. If he who has hurried to be present at the

[1. This seems to mean 'all the sons of the departed.' Of course there was really but one 'chief or host–man,' as in par. 6.

2. This takes us by surprise. Did all go to the shed? Were there many sheds?]

rites were not the presiding mourner on the occasion[1], then that presiding mourner, instead of him, bowed to the visitors and escorted them.

7. When one hurried to the rites, even where they were less than those for a mother or father, which required the wearing of sackcloth, with even edge or frayed, he entered the gate at the left side of it, and stood in the middle of the court–yard with his face to the north, wailing and giving full vent to his sorrow. He put on the cincture for the head and the sackcloth girdle in the corridor on the east, and repaired to his place, where he bared his arms. Then he wailed along with the presiding mourner, and went through the leaping. For the wailing on the second day and the third, they wore the cincture and bared the arms. If there were visitors, the presiding mourner bowed to them on their arrival, and escorted them.

The husbands and wives (of the family) waited for him at the wailing–places for every morning and evening, without making any change.

8. When one hurries to the mourning rites for a mother, he wails with his face to the west, giving full vent to his sorrow. He then ties up his hair, bares his arms, descends from the hall, and goes to his station on the east, where, with his face to the west, he wails and goes through the leaping. After that, he covers his arms and puts on the cincture and sash in the corridor on the east. He bows to the visitors, and escorts them (to the gate) in the same way as if he had hurried to the rites for his

[1. This seems to imply that, in the preceding paragraphs, he had been the principal mourner.]

father. At the wailing on the day after, he does not tie up his hair.

9. When a wife[1] hurried to the mourning rites, she went up to the hall by the (side) steps on the east, and knelt on the east of the coffin with, her face to the west. There she wailed, giving full vent to her grief. Having put on the lower cincture on the east[2], she went to the station (for wailing), and there leaped alternately with the presiding mourner.

10. When one, hurrying to the mourning rites, did not arrive while the coffin with the body was still in the house, he first went to the grave; and there kneeling with his face to the north, he wailed, giving full vent to his sorrow. The principal mourners have been waiting for him (at the grave), and have taken their stations,—the men on the left of it, and the wives on the right. Having gone through the leaping, and given full expression to his sorrow, he tied up his hair, and went to the station of the principal mourners on the east. In his headband of sackcloth, and sash with the ends tucked up, he wailed and went through the leaping. He then bowed to the visitors, and returned to his station, going (again) through the leaping, after which the director announced that the business was over[3].

11. He then put on the cap, and returned to the

[1. An aunt, sister, or daughter of the family, who was married., and hurried to the family home from her husband's.

2. I suppose this was in the corridor on the east. The rule was for the women to dress in an apartment; but a distinction was made between those residing in the house, and those who returned to it for the occasion.

3 It is understood that this mourner was the eldest and rightful son of the deceased.]

house. There he entered at the left side of the door, and, with his face to the north, wailed and gave full vent to his sorrow. He then tied up his hair, bared his arms, and went through the leaping. Going to his station on the east, he bowed to the visitors, and went through the leaping. When the visitors went out, the presiding mourner bowed to them, and escorted them. When other visitors afterwards arrived, he bowed to them, went through the leaping, and escorted them in the same way. All the principal mourners and their cousins went out at the gate, wailed there and stopped, when the directors instructed them to go to the shed. At the wailing next day, he bound up his hair and went through the leaping. At the third wailing, he did the same. On the third day he completed his mourning dress (as was required). After the fifth wailing, the director announced that the business was over.

12. Wherein the usages at the rites for a mother differed from those at the rites for a father, was that there was but one tying up of the hair. After that the cincture was worn to the end of the business. In other respects the usages were the same as at the rites for a father.

13. At the rites for other relations, after those for the mother or father, the mourner who did not arrive while the coffin was in the house, first went to the grave, and there wailed with his face to the west, giving full vent to his sorrow. He then put on the cincture and hempen sash, and went to his station on the east, where he wailed with the presiding mourner, and went through the leaping. After this he covered his arms; and if there were visitors, the presiding mourner bowed to them and escorted them away.

If any other visitors afterwards came, he bowed to them, as in the former case, and the director announced that the business was over.

Immediately after he put on the cap, and returned to the house. Entering at the left side of the door, he wailed with his face to the north, giving full vent to his sorrow. He then put on the cincture, bared his arms, and went through the leaping. Going then to the station on the east, he bowed to the visitors, and went through the leaping again. When the visitors went out, the presiding mourner bowed to them and escorted them.

At the wailing next day, he wore the cincture, bared his arms, and went through the leaping. At the third wailing he did the same. On the third day, he put on his mourning–garb; and at the fifth wailing, the director announced that the business was over.

14. When one heard of the mourning rites, and it was impossible (in his circumstances) to hurry to be present at them, he wailed and gave full vent to his grief. He then asked the

particulars, and (on hearing them) wailed again, and gave full vent to his grief. He then made a place (for his mourning) .where he was, tied up his hair, bared his arms, and went through the leaping. Having covered his arms, and put on the higher cincture and his sash with the ends tucked up, he went (back) to his place. After bowing to (any visitors that arrived), he returned to the place, and went through the leaping. When the visitors went out, he, as the presiding mourner, bowed to them, and escorted them outside the gate, returning then to his station. If any other visitors came afterwards, he bowed to them and went through the leaping, then escorting them as before.

At the wailing next day, he tied up his hair, bared his arms, and went through the leaping. At the third wailing he did the same. On the third day, he put on his mourning–garb, wailed, bowed to his visitors, and escorted them as before.

15. If one returned home after the mourning rites had been completed, he went to the grave, and there wailed and went through the leaping. On the east of it, he tied up his hair, bared his arms, put on the cincture for the head, bowed to the visitors, and went (again) through the leaping. Having escorted the visitors, he returned to his place, and again wailed, giving full vent to his grief With this he put off his mourning. In the house he did not wail. The principal mourner, in his treatment of him, made no change in his dress; and though he wailed with him (at the grave), he did not leap.

16. Wherein at other observances than those for the death of a mother or father, the usages (of such a mourner) differed from the above, were in the cincture for the head and the hempen sash.

17. In all cases where one made a place for his mourning (away from home), if it were not on occasion of the death of a parent, but for some relative of the classes not so nearly related, he went to the station, and wailed, giving full vent to his sorrow. Having put on the cincture for the head and the girdle on the east, he came back to the station, bared his arms, and went through the leaping. He then covered his arms, bowed to the visitors, went back to the station, wailed, and went through the leaping. (After this), he escorted the guests away, and came back to the station, when the director told him to go to the shed. When the fifth wailing was ended, on the third day, the presiding mourner came forth and escorted the visitors away. All the principal mourners and their cousins went out at the gate, wailed, and stopped there. The director announced to them that the business was ended. He put on his full mourning–garb, and bowed to the visitors[1].

18. If the home were far distant from the place which an absent mourner has selected (for his wailing), they completed all their arrangements about dress before they went to it.

19. One hurrying to mourning rites, if they were for a parent, wailed when he looked towards the district (where they had lived); if they were for a relation for whom nine months' mourning was due, he wailed when he could see the gate of his house; if for one to whom five months' mourning was due, he wailed when he got to the door; if for one to whom but three months' mourning was due, he wailed when he took his station.

20. For one of his father's relations (for whom he did not need to go into mourning) a man wailed in the ancestral temple; for one of his mother or wife's relatives, in the back chamber of the temple; for his teacher, outside the gate of the temple; for a friend, outside the door of the back–chamber; for an acquaintance, in the open country, having pitched a tent for the occasion. Some say the wailing for a mother's relation was in the temple.

[1. The Khien–lung editors think that this last sentence is an erroneous addition to the paragraph. But with other parts of it there are great difficulties, insoluble difficulties, as some of the commentators allow.]

21. In all cases where a station was selected, away from the house of mourning, for paying funeral rites, no offerings were put down (for the departed).

22. For the son of Heaven they wailed nine days; for a feudal prince, seven; for a high minister and Great officer, five; for another officer, three.

23. A Great officer, in wailing for the ruler of his state, did not presume to bow to the visitors.

24. Ministers in other states, when they selected a station (for their wailing), did not presume to bow to the visitors.

25. Officers, of the same surname with a feudal prince, (but who were serving in other states), also made a place at which to wail for him (on his death).

26. In all cases where one made a place (at a distance) at which to wail, he bared his arms (only) once.

27. In condoling with (the relations of) an acquaintance (after he has been buried), one first wailed in his house, and afterwards went to the grave, in both cases accompanying the wailing with the leaping. He alternated his leaping with that of the presiding mourner, keeping his face towards the north.

28. At all mourning rites (in a household), if the father were alive, he acted as presiding mourner; if he were dead, and brothers lived together in the house, each presided at the mourning for one of his own family-circle. If two brothers were equally related to the deceased for whom rites were necessary, the eldest presided at those rites; if they were not equally related, the one most nearly so presided.

29. When one heard of the death of a brother or cousin at a distance, but the news did not arrive till the time which his own mourning for him would have taken had expired[1], he (notwithstanding) put on the mourning cincture, bared his arms, and went through the leaping. He bowed to his visitors, however, with the left hand uppermost[2].

30. The only case in which a place was chosen in which to wail for one for whom mourning was not worn, was the death of a sister-in-law, the wife of an elder brother. For a female member of the family who had married, and for whom therefore mourning was not worn, the hempen sash was assumed.

31. When one had hurried to the mourning rites, and a Great officer came (to condole with him), he bared his arms, and bowed to him. When he had gone through the leaping, he covered his arms. In the case of a similar visit from an ordinary officer, he covered his arms, and then bowed to him.

[1. The deceased would have been only in the degree of relationship, to which five months' mourning was assigned.

BOOK XXXII. WAN SANG, OR QUESTIONS ABOUT MOURNING RITES[1]

1. Immediately after his father's death, (the son put off his cap, and) kept his hair, with the pin in it, in the bag (of silk); went barefoot, with the skirt of his dress tucked up under his girdle; and wailed with his hands across his breast. In the bitterness of his grief, and

the distress and pain of his, thoughts, his kidneys were injured, his liver dried up, and his lungs scorched, while water or other liquid did not enter his mouth, and for three days fire was not kindled (to cook anything for him). On this account the neighbours prepared for him gruel and rice–water, which were his (only) meat and drink. The internal grief and sorrow produced a change in his outward appearance; and with the severe pain in his heart, his mouth could not relish any savoury food, nor his body find ease in anything pleasant.

2. On the third day there was the (slighter) dressing (of the corpse). While the body was on the couch it was called the corpse; when it was put into the coffin, it was called kiû. At the moving of the corpse, and lifting up of the coffin, (the son) wailed and leaped, times without number. Such was the bitterness of his heart, and the pain of his thoughts, so did his grief and sorrow fill his mind and

[1. See the introductory notice, vol. xxvii, pp. 47, 48.]

agitate his spirit, that he bared his arms and leaped, seeking by the movement of his limbs to obtain some comfort to his heart and relief to his spirit.

The women could not bare their arms, and therefore they (merely) pushed out the breast, and smote upon their hearts, moving their feet with a sliding, hopping motion, and with a constant, heavy sound, like the crumbling away of a wall. The expression of grief, sorrow, and deep–seated pain was extreme; hence it is said, 'With beating of the breast and movement of the feet, did they sorrowfully accompany the body; so they escorted it away, and so did they come back to meet its essential part.'

When (the mourners) went, accompanying the coffin (to the grave), they looked forward, with an expression of eagerness, as if they were following some one, and unable to get up to him. When returning to wail, they looked disconcerted, as if they were seeking some one whom they could not find. Hence, when escorting (the coffin), they appeared full of affectionate desire; when returning, they appeared full of perplexity. They had sought the (deceased), and could not find him; they entered the gate, and did not see him; they went up to the hall, and still did not see him; they entered his chamber, and still did not see him; he was gone; he was dead; they should see him again nevermore. Therefore they wailed, wept, beat their breasts, and leaped, giving full vent to their sorrow, before they ceased. Their minds were disappointed, pained, fluttered, and indignant. They could do nothing more with their wills; they could do nothing but continue sad.

3. In presenting the sacrifice (of repose) in the (to his parent) ancestral temple[1], (the son) offered it in his disembodied state, hoping that his shade would peradventure return (and enjoy it). When he came back to the house from completing the grave, he did not venture to occupy his chamber, but dwelt in the mourning shed, lamenting that his parent was now outside. He slept on the rushes, with a clod for his pillow, lamenting that his parent was in the ground. Therefore he wailed and wept, without regard to time; he endured the toil and grief for three years. His heart of loving thoughts showed the mind of the filial son, and was the real expression of his human feelings.

4. Some one may ask, 'Why does the dressing not commence till three days after death?' and the answer is:—When his parent is dead, the filial son is sad and sorrowful, and his mind is full of trouble. He crawls about and bewails his loss, as if the dead might come back to life;—how can he hurriedly take (the corpse) and proceed to dress it? Therefore, when it is said that the dressing does not begin till after three days, the meaning is, that (the son) is waiting that time to see if (his father) will come to life. When after three days there is no such return, the father is not alive, and the heart of the filial son is still more downcast. (During this space, moreover), the means of the family can be calculated, and the clothes that are necessary can be provided and made accordingly; the relations and connexions who live at a distance can also arrive. Therefore the sages decided in the case

[1. 'Not the structure so called,' says Khung Ying–tâ, 'but the apartment where the coffin had been;'—now serving for the occasion as a temple.]

that three days should be allowed, and the rule was made accordingly.

5. Some one may ask, 'How is it that one with the cap on does not bare his arms, and show the naked body?' and the answer is:—The cap is the most honourable article of dress, and cannot be worn where the body is bared, and the flesh exposed. Therefore the cincture for the head is worn instead of the cap, (when the arms are bared).

6. And so, when a bald man does not wear the cincture, and a hunchback does not bare his arms, and a lame man does not leap, it is not that they do not feel sad, but they have an infirmity which prevents them from fully discharging the usages. Hence it is said that in the rites of mourning it is the sorrow that is the principal thing. When a daughter wails,

weeps, and is sad, beats her breast, and wounds her heart; and when a son wails, weeps, is sad, and bows down till his forehead touches the ground, without regard to elegance of demeanour, this may be accepted as the highest expression of sorrow.

7. Some one may ask, 'What is the idea in the cincture?' and the reply is:—The cincture is what is worn while uncapped. The Rule says, 'Boys do not wear (even) the three months' mourning; it is only when the family has devolved on one that he does so.' The cincture, we may suppose, was what was worn in the three months' mourning (by a boy). If he had come to be the representative of the family, he wore the cincture, and carried the staff.

8. Some one may ask, 'What is meant by (using) the staff?' and the answer is:—The staff of bamboo and that of elaeococcus wood have the same meaning. Hence, for a father they used the black staff of bamboo; and for a mother, the square–cut staff, an elaeococcus branch[1].

9. Some one may say, (What is meant by (using) the staff?' and the answer is:—When a filial son mourns for a parent, he wails and weeps without regard to the number of times; his endurances are hard for three years; his body becomes ill and his limbs emaciated; and so he uses a staff to support his infirmity.

10. Thus, while his father is alive he does not dare to use a staff, because his honoured father is still living. Walking in the hall, he does not I use the staff;—refraining from doing so in the place where his honoured father is. Nor does he walk hastily in the hall,—to show that he is not hurried. Such is the mind of the filial son, the real expression of human feeling, the proper method of propriety and righteousness. It does not come down from heaven, it does not come forth from the earth; it is simply the expression of the human feelings.

BOOK XXXIII. FÛ WAN, OR SUBJECTS FOR QUESTIONING ABOUT THE MOURNING DRESS[1].

1. The Directory for Mourning says, 'There are cases in which parties wear deep mourning, while those, in consequence of their connexion with whom they assume it,

wear only light.' Such is the mourning for her husband's mother by the wife of the son of a ruler (by a concubine)[2].

2. 'There are cases in which parties wear light mourning, while those, in consequence of their connexion with whom they assume it, wear deep mourning.' Such is the mourning of a husband for the father or mother of his wife[3].

3. 'There are cases in which parties wear mourning, while those, in consequence of their connexion with whom they have a relation with the deceased, wear none.' Such is the case of the wife of a ruler's

[1. See the introductory notice, vol. xxvii, page 48.

2. Such a son of a ruler could wear for his mother only the nine months' mourning, as she was but a concubine with an inferior position in the family; but his wife wore mourning for her for a whole year. She was her husband's mother, and the general rule for mourning in such a relation was observed by the wife, without regard to the deceased being only a concubine, and whether the ruler were alive or dead.

3. The wife, of course, observed the three years' mourning for her father or mother; the husband only the three months.]

son with the cousins of her husband on the female side[1].

4. There are cases in which parties wear no mourning, while those, in consequence of their connexion with whom they have a relation with the deceased, do wear mourning.' Such is the case of a ruler's son with regard to the father and mother of his wife.

5. The Directory of Mourning says, 'When his mother has been divorced, the son wears mourning for the relatives of the wife whom his father has taken in his mother's place.' When his mother has died[2] (without being divorced), a son wears mourning for her relatives. Wearing mourning for his own mother's relatives, he does not do so for those of the step–mother, whom his father may have taken in her place.

6. After the sacrifice at the end of the first year, during the three years' rites, and after the interment has taken place, during those of one year (occurring at the same time), the

mourner puts on the old sash of dolychos cloth, and the headband of the one year's mourning, wearing (at the same time) the sackcloth of the mourning for nine months.

7. The same thing is done (after the interment) during the nine months' mourning.

8. No change is made (after the interment) during the five months' mourning.

[1. There is no satisfactory account of this case.

2. Khan Hâo supposed that this mother 'dying' is the wife whom his father has taken in the place of the son's divorced mother. The Khien–lung editors rightly point out his error; but it shows how these notices are perplexing, not only to foreigners, but also to native scholars.]

9. Where they wore the sash with the roots of hemp wrought into the cloth[1], they changed it for the dolychos cloth of the three years' mourning[2].

10. After the sacrifice at the end of a year, if there occurred an occasion for using the hempen sash with the roots cut off, (the mourner) put on the proper band along with the higher cincture. When the cincture was no longer worn, he put off the band. When it was proper to use the band, the rule was to wear it; and when the occasion for it was over, it was put off[3].

11. In the mourning for five months they did not change the cap worn for the sacrifice at the end of a year. If there were occasion to wear the cincture, then they employed the band proper for the mourning of three months or five months; still keeping on the first dolychos sash. The linen of the three months' mourning did not make it necessary to change the dolychos cloth of the five months; nor the linen of the five months to change the dolychos cloth of the nine months. Where the roots were woven with the cloth, they made a change.

12. On occasion of mourning for a minor, if he were of the highest grade or the middle, they changed the dolychos cloth of the three years' mourning, assuming it when they had completed the months of these intervening rites. This was done not because of the value set on the linen, but because no change was made at the conclusion of

[1. This was done in the mourning for nine months and for one year; not in that for five months and for three.

2. That is, after the sacrifice at the end of the first year.

3. This is supplementary, say the Khien-lung editors, to paragraph 8.]

the wailing. They did not observe this rule on the death of a minor of the third or lowest grade.

13. The ruler of a state mourned for the son of Heaven for the three years. His wife observed the rule of a lady of her husband's house who had gone to her own married home in mourning for the ruler[1].

14. The heir-son of a ruler did not wear mourning for the son of Heaven[2].

15. A ruler acted as presiding mourner at the mourning rites for his wife, his eldest son, and that son's wife.

16. The eldest son of a Great officer, by his proper wife, wore the mourning of an ordinary officer for the ruler, and for the ruler's wife and eldest son.

17. When the mother of a ruler had not been the wife (of the former ruler)[3], the body of the ministers did not wear mourning (on her death). Only the officers of the harem, the charioteer and the man-at-arms who sat on the left, followed the example of the ruler, wearing the same mourning as he did.

18. For a high minister or Great officer, (during the mourning rites for him), the ruler wore in his place the coarse glazed linen, and also when he went out (on business not connected with the rites). If it were on business connected with them, he wore also the skin-cap and the band round it. Great officers dressed in the same way for one another. At the mourning rites for their wives, they wore the same dress, when they were going to be present at

[1. That is, for a year.

2. To avoid suspicion, say the commentators. I do not see it.

3. She must have been a concubine, or some inferior member of the harem. Various circumstances might have concurred to lead to her son's succession to the state.]

those rites; if they went out (on other business), they did not wear it.

19. In all cases of going to see others, the visitor (being in mourning for his parents) did not put off his headband. Even when he was going to the ruler's court, he did not put it off; it was only at the ruler's gate that (in certain circumstances) he put off his sackcloth. The Directory of Mourning says, 'A superior man will not take away from others their mourning rites;' and so it was deemed wrong to put off this mourning.

BOOK XXXIV. KIEN KWAN, OR TREATISE ON SUBSIDIARY POINTS IN MOURNING USAGES[1].

1. What is the reason that the headband worn with the frayed sackcloth, for a father, must be made of the fibres of the female plant?

Those fibres have an unpleasant appearance, and serve to show outwardly the internal distress. The appearance of (the mourners), wearing the sackcloth for a father with its jagged edges, corresponds to those fibres. That of one wearing the sackcloth for a mother with its even edges, corresponds to the fibres of the male plant. That of one wearing the mourning of nine months looks as if (the ebullitions of sorrow) had ceased. For one wearing the mourning of five months or of three, his (ordinary) appearance is suitable.

These are the manifestations of sorrow in the bodily appearance[2].

2. The wailing of one wearing the sackcloth for his father seems to go forth in one unbroken strain;

[1. See the introductory notice, vol. xxvii, pp. 48, 49.

2 The Zsü is commonly understood to be the female plant of hemp, and the hsî the male plant; though some writers reverse the application of the names. The fibres of both are

dark coloured, those of the female plant being the darker. The cloth woven of them was also of a coarser texture. All admit that the subject here is the mourning band for the head; the staffs borne in the two cases corresponded in colour to the band.]

that of one wearing the sackcloth for a mother is now and then broken; in the mourning of nine months, after the first burst there are three quavers in it, and then it seems to die away; in the mourning of five and three months, an ordinary wailing is sufficient.

These are the manifestations of sorrow in the modulations of the voice[1].

3. When wearing the sackcloth for a father, one indicates that he hears what is said to him, but does not reply in words; when wearing that for a mother, he replies, but does not speak of anything else. During the nine months' mourning, he may speak of other things, but not discuss them; during that for five months or three months, he may discuss other things, but does not show pleasure in doing so.

These are the manifestations of sorrow in speech.

4. When a mourner has assumed the sackcloth for a father, for three days he abstains from food; for a mother, for two days. When he has commenced the nine months' mourning, he abstains from three meals; in that of five months or of three, for two. When an ordinary officer takes part in the dressing (of a friend's corpse), he abstains from one meal. Hence at the mourning rites for a father or mother, when the coffining takes place, (the children) take gruel made of a handful of rice in the morning, and the same quantity in the evening. During all the rites for a mother, they eat coarse rice, and drink only water, not touching vegetables or fruits. During the nine months' mourning (the mourners) do not eat pickles of sauces; during that of five months or three, they do not drink. prepared liquor, either new or old.

[1. I have read something of the same kind as this account of the 'wailing' in descriptions of the 'keening' at an Irish wake.]

These are the manifestations of sorrow in drinking and eating.

5. In the mourning rites for a parent, when the sacrifice of repose has been presented, and the wailing is at an end, (the mourners) eat coarse rice and drink water, but do not take

vegetables or fruits. At the end of a year, when the smaller felicitous sacrifice has been offered, they eat vegetables and fruits. After another year, when the greater sacrifice has been offered, they take pickles and sauces. In the month after, the final mourning sacrifice is offered, after which they drink the must and spirits. When they begin to drink these, they first use the must; when they begin to eat flesh, they first take that which has been dried.

6. During the mourning rites for a parent, (the son) occupied the mourning shed, and slept on straw with a clod for his pillow, without taking off the headband or girdle. If they were for a mother (only, and the father were still alive), be occupied the unplastered chamber, (sleeping on) typha rushes with their tops cutoff, but not woven together. During the mourning for nine months, there was a mat to sleep on. In that for five months or for three, it was allowed to use a bedstead.

These were the manifestations of sorrow given in the dwelling–places.

7. At the mourning rites for a parent, after the sacrifice of repose, and when the wailing was concluded, the (inclined) posts of the shed were set up on lintels, and the screen (of grass) was clipped, while typha rushes, with the tops cut off, but not woven together, (were laid down for a mat). At the end of a year, and when the smaller felicitous sacrifice had been offered, (the son) occupied the unplastered chamber, and had a mat to sleep on. After another year, and when the greater felicitous sacrifice had been offered, he returned to his old sleeping apartment. Then, when the final mourning sacrifice was offered, he used a bedstead.

8. The mourning with jagged edges was made with 3 shang of hempen threads, each shang containing 81 threads; that with even edge, with 4, 5, or 6 shang; that for the nine months' mourning with 7, 8, or 9 shang; that for the five months, with 10, 11, or 12 shang; that for the three months, with 15 shang less the half[1]. When the thread was manipulated and boiled, no such operation was performed on the woven cloth, and it was called sze (or the material for the mourning of three months).

These were the manifestations of sorrow shown in the fabrics of the different mournings.

9. The sackcloth with jagged edges (worn at first) was made with 3 shang, but after the sacrifice of repose when the wailing was over, this was exchanged for a different fabric

made with 6 shang, while the material for the cap was made with 7 shang. The coarse sackcloth for a mother was made with 4 shang, exchanged for a material made with 7 shang, while the cap was made with one of 8 shang.

When the hempen dress is put away (after the burial), grass–cloth is worn, the sash of it being made of triple twist. At the end of the year, and when the first felicitous sacrifice has been offered, (the son) pas on the cap of dyed silk proper to that

[1. Kû Hsî says, 'Inexplicable!']

sacrifice, and the red collar, still retaining the sash and headband. A son begins at the head, and a woman with the girdle, in. putting off their mourning. What is the reason? Because a man considers the head the most important to him, and a woman the waist. In laying aside the mourning, they began with the most important; in changing it, with what was least.

At the end of the second year, and when the greater felicitous sacrifice had been offered, the cap and dress of plain hempen cloth was assumed. After the concluding sacrifice of mourning, in the next month, the black cap and silk of black and white were put on, and all the appendages of the girdle were assumed.

10. Why is it that in changing the mourning they (first) changed what was the lightest? During the wearing of the sackcloth with jagged edges for a father, if when, after the sacrifice of repose and the end of the wailing, there came occasion to wear the even–edged sackcloth for a mother, that, as lighter, was considered to be embraced in the other, and that which was most important was retained.

After the sacrifice at the end of the year, when there occurred. occasion for the mourning rites of nine months, both the sackcloth and grass–cloth bands were worn.

During the wearing of the sackcloth for a mother, when, after the sacrifice of repose and the end of the wailing, there came occasion to wear the mourning for nine months, the sackcloth and grasscloth bands were worn together.

BOOK XXXV. SAN NIEN WAN, OR QUESTIONS ABOUT THE MOURNING FOR THREE YEARS[1].

1. What purposes do the mourning rites for three years serve?

The different rules for the mourning rites were established in harmony with (men's) feelings. By means of them the differences in the social relations are set forth, and the distinctions shown of kindred as nearer or more distant, and of ranks as more noble or less. They do not admit of being diminished or added to; and are therefore called 'The unchanging rules.'

2. The greater a wound is, the longer it remains; and the more. pain it gives, the more slowly is it healed. The mourning of three years, being appointed with its various forms in harmony with the feelings (produced by the occasion of it), was intended to mark the greatest degree of grief. The sackcloth with jagged edges., the dark colour of the sackcloth and the staff, the shed reared against the wall, the gruel, the sleeping on straw, and the clod of earth for a pillow:—these all were intended to set forth the extremity of the grief.

3. The mourning of the three years came really to an end with (the close of) the twenty–fifth month. The sorrow and pain were not yet ended, and the

[1. See the introductory notice, vol. xxvii, pp. 49, 50.]

longing loving thoughts were not yet forgotten; but in the termination of the mourning dress in this way, was it not shown that there should be an end to the duties rendered to the dead, and that the time was come for the resumption of their duties to the living?

4. All living creatures between heaven and earth, being endowed with blood and breath, have a certain amount of knowledge. Possessing that amount of knowledge, there is not one of them but knows to love its species. Take the larger birds and beasts:—when one of them has lost its mate, after a month or a season, it is sure to return and go about their old haunts. It turns round and round, utters its cries, now moves, now stops, and looks quite embarrassed and uncertain in its movements, before it can leave the place. Even the smaller birds, such as swallows and sparrows, chatter and cry for a little before they can

leave the place. But among all creatures that have blood and breath, there is none which has intelligence equal to man; and hence the feeling of man on the death of his kindred remains unexhausted even till death.

5. Will any one follow the example of those men who are under the influence of their depraved lusts? In that case, when a kinsman dies in the morning, he will forget him by the evening. But if we follow the course of such men, we shall find that they are not equal to the birds and beasts. How can they live with their kindred, and not fall into all disorders?

6. Will he rather follow the example of the superior man who attends to all the methods by which the feeling of grief is set forth? In that case, the twenty–five months, after which the mourning of three years comes to an end, will seem to pass as quickly as a carriage drawn by four horses is whirled past a crevice. And if we continue to indulge the feeling, it will prove to be inexhaustible.

7. Therefore the ancient kings determined the proper medium for mourning, and appointed its definite terms. As soon as it was sufficient for the elegant expression of the varied feeling, it was to be laid aside.

8. This being the case, how is it that (in certain cases the mourning lasts) only for a year? The answer is, that in the case of the nearest kindred, there is a break in it at the end of a year.

9. How is that? The answer is:—The interaction of heaven and earth has run its round; and the four seasons have gone through their changes. All things between heaven and earth begin their processes anew. The rules of mourning are intended to resemble this.

10. Then how is it that there are three years' mourning (for a parent)? The answer is:—From the wish to make it greater and more impressive, the time is doubled, and so embraces two round years.

11. What about the mourning for nine months' and the shorter periods? The answer is:—It is to prevent such mourning from reaching (the longer periods).

12. Therefore the three years should be considered as the highest expression of grief in mourning; the three months, and five months, as the lowest; while the year and the nine months are between them. Heaven above gives an example; earth beneath, a law; and man between, a pattern. The harmony and unity that should characterise men living in their kinships are hereby completely shown.

13. Thus it is that in the mourning of three years the highest forms that vary and adorn the ways of men are displayed. Yes, this is what is called the richest exhibition (of human feelings).

14. In this the hundred kings (of all the dynasties) agree, and ancient and modern customs are one and the same. But whence it came is not known.

BOOK XXXVI. SHAN Î, OR THE LONG DRESS IN ONE PIECE[1].

1. Anciently the long dress had definite measurements, so as to satisfy the requirements of the compass and square, the line, the balance, and the steelyard. It was not made so short as to show any of the skin, nor so long as to touch the ground. The outside pieces of the skirt joined, and were hooked together at the side; (the width of) the seam at the waist was half that at the bottom (of the skirt).

2. The sleeve was joined to the body of the dress at the arm–pit, so as to allow the freest movement of the elbow–joint; the length of the lower part admitted of the cuffs being turned back to the elbow. The sash was put on where there were no bones, so as not to interfere with the action of the thighs below or of the ribs above.

3. In the making (of the garment) twelve strips (of the cloth) were used, to correspond to the twelve months. The sleeve was made round, as if fashioned by a disk. The opening at the neck was square, as if made by means of that instrument so named. The cord–like (seam) at the back descended to the ankles, as if it had been a straight line. The edge at the bottom was like the steelyard of a balance, made perfectly even.

4. In this way through the rounded sleeves the arms could be lifted up in walking (for the purpose of salutation) in the most elegant form. The

[1. See the introductory notice, vol. xxvii, p. 50.]

cord–like seam of the back and the square–shaped collar about the neck in front, served to admonish (the wearer) how his government should be correct and his righteousness on the square. It is said in the Yî, 'The movement indicated by the second line in Khwan, divided, is "from the straight (line) to the square[1]."' The even edge at the bottom, like the steelyard and balance, admonished him to keep his will at rest, and his heart even and calm.

5. These five rules being observed in the making (of the dress), the sages wore it. In its squareness and roundness they saw its warning against selfishness; in its line–like straightness they saw its admonition to be correct, and in its balance–like evenness they saw its lesson of impartiality. Therefore the ancient kings attached a high value to it; it could be worn in the discharge of both their civil and military duties; in it they could receive visitors and regulate the cohorts of their armies. It was complete, but not extravagant; it ranked in the second class of good dresses[2].

6. For ornament, while his parents and grandparents were alive, (a son) wore the dress with its border embroidered. If (only) his parents were alive, the ornamental border was blue. In the case of an orphan son[3], the border was white. The border round the mouth of the sleeves and all the edges of the dress was an inch and a half wide.

[1. See the symbolism of the second line of the 2nd Hexagram, and especially the lesser symbolism in the 2nd Appendix, from which the quotation is made;—vol. xvi, pages 60 and 268.

2. That is, next after the court and sacrificial robes.

BOOK XXXVII. THÂU HÛ, OR THE GAME OF PITCH–POT[1].

1. According to the rules for Pitch–pot, the host carries the arrows in both his hands put together; the superintendent of the archery carries in the same way the stand[2] on which the tallies were placed; and an attendant holds in his hand the pot.

2. The host entreats (one of the guests), saying, 'I have here these crooked[3] arrows, and this pot with its wry[3] mouth; but we beg you to amuse yourself with them.' The guest says, 'I have partaken, Sir, of your excellent drink and admirable viands; allow me to decline this further proposal for my pleasure.' The host rejoins, 'It is not worth the while for you to decline these poor arrows and pot; let me earnestly beg you to try them.' The guest repeats his refusal, saying, 'I have partaken (of your entertainment), and you would still further have me enjoy myself;—I venture firmly to decline.' The host again addresses his request in the same words, and then the guest says, 'I have firmly declined what you request, but you will not allow me to refuse;—I venture respectfully to obey you.'

[1. See the introductory notice, vol. xxvii, pp. 50, 51.

2. This was a small stand or tray, with the figure of a stag (or some other animal, according to the rank of the party) carved in wood and put down on it, with a tube by its side in which the tallies were to be placed.

3. These are merely the customary terms of depreciation in which a Chinese speaks of his own things.]

The guest then bows twice, and signifies that he will receive (the arrows). The host wheels round, saying, 'Let me get out of the way;' and then at the top of the steps on the east, he bows to the guest and gives him the arrows. The guest wheels round, and says, 'Let me get out of the way[1].'

3. (The host) having bowed, and received the arrows (for himself), advances to the space between the two pillars. He then retires, and returns to his station, motioning also to the guest to go to his mat (for pitching from).

4. The superintendent of the archery comes forward, and measures the distance of the pot (from the mats), which should be a space of the length of two and a half arrows. He then returns to his station, sets forth the stand for the tallies, and with his face to the east, takes eight counters and stands up. He asks the guest to pitch, saying, 'When the arrow goes straight in, it is reckoned an entry. If you throw a second (without waiting for your opponent to pitch), it is not reckoned.' The victor gives the vanquished a cup to drink; and when the cups of decision have been dispatched, the superintendent begs to set up what he calls 'a horse' for the victor. If he set up one horse, then a second, and finally a third,

he begs to congratulate the thrower on the number of his horses. He asks the host to pitch in the same way, and with the same words.

5. He orders the cithern–players to strike up

[1. From this point to the end of the paragraph, it is very difficult to make out from the text the sequence of proceedings between the host and guest.

'The pitching,' say the Khien–lung editors, 'has been agreed on.']

'The Fox's Head,' with the same interval between (each repetition of the tune), and the director of the music answers, 'Yes.'

6. When the superintendent announces to them on the left and right that the arrows are all used up, he requests them to pitch again. When an arrow enters, he kneels, and puts down a counter. The partners of the guest are on the right, and those of the host on the left.

7. When they have done pitching, he takes up the counters, and says, 'They have done pitching, both on the left and right; allow me to take the numbers.' He then takes the numbers two by two, and leaves the single counters. After this he takes the single counters, and gives the announcement, saying, "Such and such a side has the better by so many doubles, or naming the number of the singles.' If they are equal, he says, 'Left and right are equal.'

8. He then orders the cups to be filled, saying, 'Let the cup go round,' and the cup–bearer (of the successful side) replies, 'Yes.' Those who have to drink all kneel, and raising their cups with both hands, say, 'We 'receive what you give us to drink.' The victors (also) kneel and say, 'We beg respectfully to refresh you.'

9. When this cup has gone round, according to rule, (the superintendent) asks leave to exhibit the 'horses' (of the victorious side). Each 'horse' stands for so many counters. (He who has only) one 'horse' gives it to him who has two, to congratulate him (on his superiority). The usage in congratulating (the most successful) is to say, 'Your three "horses" are all here; allow me to congratulate you on their number.' The guests and host all express their assent. The customary cup goes round, and the superintendent asks leave to remove the 'horses.'

10. The number of the counters varies according to the place in which they kneel (when playing the game). (Each round is with 4 arrows.) (If the game be in) the chamber, there are 5 sets of these; if in the hall, 7; if in the courtyard, 9. The counters are 1 cubit 2 inches long. The neck of the pot is 7 inches long; its belly, 5; and its mouth is 2½ inches in diameter. It contains a peck and 5 pints. It is filled with small beans, to prevent the arrows from leaping out. It is distant from the mats of the players, the length of 2½ arrows. The arrows are made of mulberry wood, or from the zizyphus, without the bark being removed.

11. In Lû, the young people (taking part in the game) were admonished in these words, 'Do not be rude; do not be haughty; do not stand awry; do not talk about irrelevant matters; for those who stand awry, or speak about irrelevant matters, there is the regular (penal) cap.' A similar admonition in Hsieh was to this effect:—'Do not be rude; do not be haughty; do not stand awry; do not speak about irrelevant matters. Those who do any of these things must pay the penalty.'

12. The superintendent of the archery, the overseer of the courtyard, and the capped officers who stood by, all belonged to the party of the guest. The musicians and the boys who acted as attendants, all belonged to the party of the host.

[13. There follows after this what appears to be a representation of the progress of a game by means of small circles and squares. The circles {here represented by O} indicating blows on a small drum called phî, and the squares {here represented by X}, blows on the larger drum (kû);—according, we may suppose, to certain events in the game. The 'drum' marks are followed by what are called 'halves' or semis. The representation is:—

Semis.

O	O	X	O
X	X	O	X
O	X	O	O

Drums.

O	O	O	O
X	X	X	X
	O	X	O

Then follows the representation of a game in Lû:–

Semis.

O	O
X	X
X	O
O	O

Lû drums.

O	X	X	O	O
X	O	O	X	X
X	X	O	X	O
O	O	X	O	O

There is then a remark that in the Hsieh drums the semi marks were used for the game of pitch–pot, and all the marks for the archery game; and then we have:—

Semis.

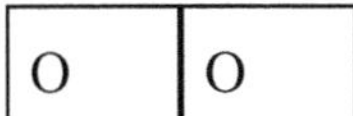

O	O

O	X
O	O
X	X
O	O

Hsieh drums.

O	O	X	O	O
	X	O	X	X
	O	O	O	O
	O	O	X	O
	X	X	O	O

Semis.

O	O	O
X	O	X
O	O	O
	O	O
	X	X

Lû drums.

X	O

O	X
O	O
	O
	X

BOOK XXXVIII. ZÛ HSING, OR THE CONDUCT OF THE SCHOLAR[1].

1. Duke Âi of Lift asked Confucius, saying, 'Is not the dress, Master, which you wear that of the scholar[2]?' Confucius replied, 'When I was little, I lived in Lû, and wore the garment with large sleeves; when I was grown up, I lived in Sung, and was then capped with the kang–fû cap[3]. I have heard that the studies of the scholar are extensive, but his dress is that of the state from which he sprang. I do not know any dress of the scholar.'

2. The duke said, 'Allow me to ask what is the conduct of the scholar.' Confucius replied, 'If I were to enumerate the points in it summarily, I could not touch upon them all; if I were to go into details on each, it would take a long time. You would have changed all your attendants–in–waiting before I had concluded[4].' The duke–ordered a mat

[1. See the introductory notice, vol. xxvii, pp. 51, 52.

2. Callery renders Zû here by 'le Philosophe.' Evidently there was in Confucius' time a class of men, thus denominated, distinguished by their learning and conduct. The name first occurs in the Kâu Lî. It is now used for the literati of China, the followers of Confucius, in distinction from Tâoists and Buddhists.

3. See vol. xxvii, page 438, paragraph 3. Confucius' ancestors belonged to the state of Sung, the representative of the ancient Yin.

4. It was the custom for a ruler to change his attendants–in–waiting, so as not to overtire any.]

to be placed for him, and Confucius took his place by his side.

3. He then said, 'The scholar has a precious gem placed upon its mat, with which he is waiting to receive an invitation (from some ruler)[1]; early and late he studies with energy, waiting to be questioned. He carries in his bosom leal–heartedness and good faith, waiting to be raised (to office); he is vigorous in all his doings, waiting to be chosen (to employment): so does he establish his character and prepare himself (for the future).

4. 'The scholar's garments and cap are all fitting and becoming; he is careful in his undertakings and doings: in declining great compliments he might seem to be rude, and in regard to small compliments, hypocritical; in great matters he has an air of dignity, and in small matters, of modesty; he seems to have a difficulty in advancing, but retires with ease and readiness; and he has a shrinking appearance, as if wanting in power:—such is he in his external appearance.

5. 'The scholar, wherever he resides, ordinarily or only for a time, is grave as if he were apprehensive of difficulties; when seated or on foot, he is courteous and respectful; in speaking, his object is, first of all, to be sincere; in acting, he wishes to be exact and correct; on the road, he does not strive about the most difficult or easiest places; in winter and summer, he does not strive about the temperature, the light and shade; he guards against death that he may be in waiting (for whatever he may be called to); he attends well to his person that he maybe

[1. Compare Analects IX, 12. The gem is the scholar's virtue,—his character and capacities.]

ready for action:—such are his preparations and precautions for the future.

6. 'The scholar does not consider gold and jade to be precious treasures, but leal–heartedness and good faith; he does not desire lands and territory, but considers the establishment of righteousness as his domain; he does not desire a great accumulation of wealth, but looks on many accomplishments as his riches; it is difficult to win him, but easy to pay him; it is easy to pay him, but difficult to retain him. As he will not show himself when the time is not proper for him to do so, is it not difficult to win him? As he will have no fellowship with what is not righteous, is it not difficult to retain him? As he must first do the work, and then take the pay, is it not easy to pay him?—such are the

conditions of his close association with others.

7. 'Though there may be offered to the scholar valuable articles and wealth, and though it be tried to enervate him with delights and pleasures, he sees those advantages without doing anything contrary to his sense of righteousness; though a multitude may attempt to force him (from his standpoint), and his way be stopped by force of arms, he will look death in the face without changing the principles (which) be maintains; (he would face) birds and beasts of prey with their talons and wings, without regard to their fierceness; he would undertake to raise the heaviest tripod, without regard to his strength; he has no occasion to regret what he has done in the past, nor to make preparations for what may come to him in the future; he does not repeat any error of speech; any rumours against him he does not pursue up to their source; he does not allow his dignity to be interrupted; he does not dread to practise (beforehand) the counsels (which he gives):—such are the things in which he stands out and apart from other men.

8. 'With the scholar friendly relations may be cultivated, but no attempt must be made to constrain him; near association with him can be sought, but cannot be forced on him; he may be killed, but he cannot be disgraced; in his dwelling he will not be extravagant; in his eating and drinking he will not be luxurious; he may be gently admonished of his errors and failings, but he should not have them enumerated to him to his face:—such is his boldness and determination.

9. 'The scholar considers leal-heartedness and good faith to be his coat-of-mail and helmet; propriety and righteousness to be his shield and buckler; he walks along, bearing aloft over his head benevolence; he dwells, holding righteousness in his arms before him; the government may be violently oppressive, but he does not change his course:—such is the way in which he maintains himself.

10. 'The scholar may have a house in (only) a mâu of ground,—a (poor) dwelling each of whose (surrounding) walls is (only) ten paces long, with an outer door of thorns and bamboos, and openings in the wall, long and pointed; within, the inner door stopped up by brushwood, and little round windows like the mouth of a jar[1]; the inmates may have to

[1. This is a picture of squalid poverty, in which it is not easy to understand all the details without a discussion of the force of the Chinese characters, on which it is impossible to enter here. With all the discussion which they have received from the critics, there are still difficulties in interpreting the paragraph.]

exchange garments when they go out; they may have to make one day's food serve for two days; if the ruler respond to him, he does not dare to have any hesitation (in accepting office); if he do not respond, he does not have recourse to flattery:—such is he in the matter of taking office, (however small).

11. 'The scholar lives and has his associations with men of the present day, but the men of antiquity are the subjects of his study. Following their (principles and example) in the present age, he will become a pattern in future ages. If it should be that his own age does not understand and encourage him, that those above him do not bring him, and those below him do not push him, forward, or even that calumniators and flatterers band together to put him in danger, his person may be placed in peril, but his aim cannot be taken from him. Though danger may threaten him in his undertakings and wherever he is, he will still pursue his aim, and never forget the afflictions of the people, (which he would relieve):—such is the anxiety which he cherishes.

12. 'The scholar learns extensively, but never allows his researches to come to an end; he does what he does with all his might, but is never weary; he may be living unnoticed, but does not give way to licentiousness; he may be having free course in his acknowledged position, but is not hampered (by it); in his practice of ceremonial usages he shows the value which he sets on a natural ease; in the excellence of his leal–heartedness and good faith, he acts under the law of a benignant playfulness; he shows his fond regard for men of virtue and ability, and yet is forbearing and kind to all; he (is like a potter who) breaks his square (mould), and his tiles are found to fit together:—such is the largeness and generosity of his spirit.

13. 'The scholar recommends members of his own family (to public employment), without shrinking from doing so, because of their kinship, and proposes others beyond it, without regard to their being at enmity with him; he estimates men's merits, and takes into consideration all their services, selecting those of virtue and ability, and putting them forward, without expecting any recompense from them; the ruler thus gets what he wishes, and if benefit results to the state, the scholar does not seek riches or honours for himself:—such is he in promoting the employment of the worthy and bringing forward the able.

14. 'The scholar when he hears what is good, tells it to (his friends), and when he sees what is good, shows it to them; in the view of rank and position, he gives the precedence to them over himself; if they encounter calamities and hardships, he is prepared to die with them; if they are long (in getting advancement), he waits for them; if they are far off, he brings them together with himself:—such is he in the employment and promotion of his friends.

15. 'The scholar keeps his person free from stain, and continually bathes (and refreshes) his virtue; he sets forth what he has to say (to his superior by way of admonition), but remains himself in the back–ground, trying thus quietly to correct him; if his superior do not acknowledge (his advice), he more proudly and clearly makes his views known, but still does not press them urgently; he does not go among those who are low to make himself out to be high, nor place himself among those who have little (wisdom) to make himself out to have much; in a time of good government, he does not think little (of what he himself can do); in a time of disorder, he does not allow his course to be obstructed; he does not (hastily) agree with those who think like himself, nor condemn those who think differently:—so does he stand out alone among others and take his own solitary course.

16. 'The scholar sometimes will not take the high office of being a minister of the son of Heaven, nor the lower office of serving the prince of a state; he is watchful over himself in his retirement, and values a generous enlargement of mind, while at the same time he is bold and resolute in his intercourse with others; he learns extensively that he may know whatever should be done; he makes himself acquainted with elegant accomplishments, and thus smoothes and polishes all his corners and angles; although the offer were made to share a state with him, it would be no more to him than the small weights of a balance; he will not take a ministry, he will not take an office:—such are the rules and conduct he prescribes to himself.

17. 'The scholar has those with whom he agrees in aim, and pursues the same objects, with whom he cultivates the same course, and that by the same methods; when they stand on the same level with him, he rejoices in them; if their standing be below his, he does not tire of them; if for long he has not seen them, and hears rumours to their prejudice, he does not believe them; his actions are rooted in correctness, and his standing in what is right[1]; if they proceed in the same direction with him, he goes forward with them, if not in the same direction, he withdraws from them:—so is he in his intercourse with his friends.

18. 'Gentleness and goodness are the roots of humanity; respect and attention are the ground on which it stands; generosity and large–mindedness are the manifestation of it; humility and courtesy are the ability of it; the rules of ceremony are the demonstration of it; speech is the ornament of it; singing and music are the harmony of it; sharing and distribution are the giving of it. The scholar possesses all these qualities in union and has them, and still he will not venture to claim a perfect humanity on account of them:—such is the honour (he feels for its ideal), and the humility (with which) he declines it (for himself).

19. 'The scholar is not cast down, or cut from his root, by poverty and mean condition; he is not elated or exhausted by riches and noble condition; he feels no disgrace that rulers and kings (may try to inflict); he is above the bonds that elders and superiors (may try to impose); and superior officers cannot distress him. Hence he is styled a scholar. Those to whom the multitude now–a–days give that name have no title to it, and they constantly employ it to one another as a term of reproach.'

When Confucius came (from his wanderings to Lû) to his own house, duke Âi gave him a (public) lodging. When the duke heard these words, he became more sincere in his speech, and more

[1. I suspect there is here some error in the text.]

righteous in his conduct. He said, 'To the end of my days I will not presume to make a jest of the name of scholar[1].'

BOOK XXXIX. TÂ HSIO, OR THE GREAT LEARNING[1].

1. What the Great Learning teaches, is to illustrate illustrious virtue; to love the people[2]; and to rest in the highest excellence.

The point where to rest being known, the object of pursuit is then determined; and, that being determined, a calm unperturbedness may be attained to. To that calmness there will succeed a tranquil repose. In that repose there will be careful deliberation, and that deliberation will be followed by the attainment (of the desired end).

Things have their root and their branches; affairs have their end and their beginning. To know what is first and what is last will lead near to what is taught (in the Great Learning).

2. The ancients who wished to illustrate illustrious virtue throughout the kingdom, first ordered well their states. Wishing to order well their states, they first regulated their families. Wishing to regulate their families, they first cultivated their persons. 'Wishing to cultivate their persons, they

[1. See the introductory notice, vol. xxvii, pp. 53, 54.

2. The text of the Tâ Hsio, since the labours of Kû Hsî upon it, reads here—'to renovate,' instead of 'to love,' the people. Kû adopted the alteration from Po-shun, called also Ming-tâo, one of his 'masters,' the two brothers Khang; but there is really no authority for it.]

first rectified their hearts. Wishing to rectify their hearts, they first sought to be sincere in their thoughts. Wishing to be sincere in their thoughts, they first extended to the utmost their knowledge.

3. The extension of knowledge is by the investigation of things[1].

4. Things being investigated, their knowledge became complete. Their knowledge being complete, their thoughts were sincere. Their thoughts being sincere, their hearts were then rectified. Their hearts being rectified, their persons were cultivated. Their persons being cultivated, their families were regulated. Their families being regulated, their states were rightly governed. Their states being rightly governed, the whole kingdom was made tranquil and happy.

From the son of Heaven down to the multitudes of the people, all considered the cultivation of the person to be the root (of everything besides). It cannot be, when the root is neglected, that what should spring from it will be well ordered. It never has been the case that what was of great importance has been slightly cared for, and at the same time what was of slight importance has been greatly cared for[2].

[1. There is great difficulty in determining the meaning of this short sentence. What Kang and Khung Ying-tâ say on it is unsatisfactory. Kû introduces a long paragraph explaining it from his master Khang;—see Chinese Classics, vol. i, pp. 229, 239.

2. Here ends the first chapter of the Book according to the arrangement of Kû Hsî. He says that it is 'the words of Confucius, handed down by Zang–dze,' all the rest being the commentary of Zang–dze, recorded by his disciples. The sentiments in this chapter are not unworthy of Confucius; but there is no evidence that they really proceeded from him, nor of the other assertions of Kû. See what is said on the subject in the introductory notice.]

This is called 'knowing the root,' this is called 'the perfection of knowledge.'

5. What is called 'making the thoughts sincere' is the allowing no self–deception;—as when we hate a bad smell and love what is beautiful, naturally and without constraint. Therefore the superior man must be watchful over himself when he is alone. There is no evil to which the small man, dwelling retired, will not proceed; but when he sees a superior man, he tries to disguise himself, concealing his evil, and displaying what is good. The other beholds him as if he saw his heart and reins;—of what use (is his disguise)? This is an instance of the saying, 'What truly is within will be manifested without.' Therefore the superior man must be watchful over himself when he is alone.

6. Zang–dze said, 'What ten eyes behold, what ten hands point to, is to be regarded with reverence[1]. (As) riches adorn a house, so virtue adorns the person. When the mind becomes enlarged, the body appears at ease. Therefore the superior man is sure to make his thoughts sincere.

[1. This saying is from Zang–dze; but standing as it does alone and apart, it gives no sanction to the view that the first chapter was handed down by him, or the rest of the Book compiled by his disciples. Rather, the contrary. 'The ten eyes and ten hands,' says Lo Kung–fân, 'indicate all the spirits who know men's inmost solitary thoughts.']

7. It is said in the Book of Poetry (I, v, ode 1, 1),

'How rich the clumps of green bamboo,
Around each cove of Khî!
They lead my thoughts to our duke Wû;—
Of winning grace is he!

As knife and file make smooth the bone,
As jade by chisel wrought and stone,
Is stamp upon him set.
Grave and of dignity serene;
With force of will as plainly seen;
Accomplished, elegant in mien,
Him we can ne'er forget.'

(That expression), 'as knife and file make smooth the bone,' indicates the effect of learning. 'Like jade by chisel wrought and stone' indicates that of self–culture. 'Grave and of dignity serene' indicates the feeling of cautious reverence. 'With force of will as plainly seen' indicates an awe–inspiring deportment. (The lines),

'Accomplished, elegant in mien,
Him can we ne'er forget,'

indicate how when virtue is complete, and excellence extreme, the people cannot forget them.

8. It is said in the Book of Poetry (IV, i, ode 4),

'The former kings in mind still bear,
What glory can with theirs compare?'

Superior men deem worthy whom they deemed worthy, and love whom they loved. The inferior people delight in what they delighted in, and are benefited by their beneficial arrangements. It is on this account that the former kings, after they have quitted the world, are not forgotten.

9. It is said in the Announcement to the Prince of Khang (Shû, V, ix, 3),

'He was able to make his virtue illustrious.'

It is said in the Thâi Kiâ, 'He kept his eye continually on the bright requirements of Heaven' (Shû, III, v, sect. 1, 2).

It is said in the Canon of the Tî (Yâo), 'He was able to make illustrious his lofty virtue' (Shû, I, 2).

These (passages) all show how (those sovereigns) made themselves illustrious.

10. On the bathing-tub of Thang[1], the following words were engraved, 'If you can one day renovate yourself, do so from day to day. Yea, daily renovate yourself.'

In the Announcement to the Prince of Khang it is said, 'Stir up the new people' (Shû, V, ix, 7).

In the Book of Poetry it is said (III, i, 1, 1),

'The state of Kâu had long been known;
Heaven's will as new at last was shown.'

Therefore the superior man in everything uses his utmost endeavours[2].

11. It is said in the Book of Poetry (IV, iii, 3),

'A thousand lî extends the king's domain,
And there the people to repose are fain.'

And in another place (II, viii, i),

'Twitters fast the oriole
Where yonder bends the mound,
The happy little creature
Its resting-place has found.'

The Master said, 'Yes, it rests; it knows where

[1. A fact not elsewhere noted. But such inscriptions are still common in China.

2. The repeated use of 'new,' 'renovated,' in this paragraph, is thought to justify the change of 'loving the people,' in paragraph 1, to 'renovating the people;' but the object of

the renovating here is not the people.]

to rest. Can one be a man, and yet not equal (in this respect) to this bird?'

12. It is said in the Book of Poetry (III, i, 1, 4),

'Deep were Wan's thoughts, sustained his ways;
And reverent in each resting–place.'

As a ruler, he rested in benevolence; as a minister, he rested in respect; as a son, he rested in filial piety; as a father, he rested in kindness; in intercourse with his subjects, he rested in good faith.

13. The Master said, 'In hearing litigations, I am like any other body.' What is necessary is to cause the people to have no litigations, so that those who are devoid of truth shall find it impossible to carry out their speeches, and a great awe be struck into the minds of the people.

14. This is called 'knowing the root[1].'

15. What is meant by 'The cultivation of the person depends on the rectifying of the mind' (may be thus illustrated):—If a man be under the influence of anger, his conduct will not be correct. The same will be the case, if he be under the influence of terror, or of fond regard, or of sorrow and distress. When the mind is not present, we look and do not see; we hear and do not understand; we eat and do not know the taste of what we eat. This is what is meant by saying that 'the cultivation of the person depends on the rectifying of the mind.'

16. What is meant by 'The regulation of the family depends on the cultivation of the person'

[1. It is certainly difficult to see bow paragraphs 13, 14 stand where they do. Lo Kung–fân omits them.]

is this:—Men are partial where they feel affection and love; partial where they despise and dislike; partial where they stand in awe and with a feeling of respect; partial where they feel sorrow and compassion; partial where they are arrogant and rude. Thus it is that there are few men in the world who love and at the same time know the bad qualities (of the object of their love), or who hate and yet know the good qualities (of the object of their hatred). Hence it is said, in the common adage, 'A man does not know the badness of his son; he does not know the richness of his growing corn.' This is what is meant by saying, that 'if his person be not cultivated, a man cannot regulate his family.'

17. What is meant by 'In order to govern well his state, it is necessary first to regulate his family' is this:—It is not possible for one to teach others while he cannot teach his own family. Therefore the superior man (who governs a state), without going beyond his family, completes the lessons for his state. There is filial piety;—it has its application in the service of the ruler. There is brotherly obedience;—it has its application in the service of elders. There is kindly gentleness;—it has its application in the employment of the multitudes. It is said in the Announcement to the Prince of Khang (Shû, V, ix, 9), '(Deal with the people), as if you were watching over an infant.' If (a mother) be really anxious about it, though she may not hit (exactly the wants of her infant), she will not be far from doing so. There never has been (a girl) who learned (first) to bring up an infant that she might afterwards be married.

18. From the loving (example) of one family, a whole state may become loving, and from its courtesies, courteous, while from the ambition and perverseness of the One man, the whole state may be thrown into rebellious disorder;—such is the nature of the influence. This is in accordance with the saying, 'Affairs may be ruined by a single sentence; a state may be settled by its One man.'

19. Yâo and Shun presided over the kingdom with benevolence, and the people followed them. Kieh and Kâu did so with violence, and the people followed them. When the orders of a ruler are contrary to what he himself loves to practise the people do not follow him.

20. Therefore the ruler must have in himself the (good) qualities, and then he may require them in others; if they are not in himself, he cannot require them in others. Never has there been a man who, not having reference to his own character and wishes in dealing with others, was able effectually to instruct them. Thus we see how 'the government of the state depends on the regulation of the family.'

21. In the Book of Poetry it is said (I, i, 6, 3),

'Graceful and young the peach–tree stands,
Its foliage clustering green and full.
This bride to her new home repairs;
Her household will attest her rule.'

Let the household be rightly ordered, and then the people of the state may be taught.

In another ode it is said (II, ii, 9, 3),

'In concord with their brothers may they dwell!'

Let rulers dwell in concord with all their brethren, and then they may teach the people of their states.

In a third ode it is said (I, xiv, 3, 3),

'His movements without fault or flaw beget
Good order for his rule throughout the state.'

When the ruler as a father, a son, an elder brother or a younger, is a model for imitation, then the people imitate him. These (passages) show how 'the government of a state depends on the regulation of the family.'

22. What is meant by 'The making the whole kingdom peaceful and happy depends on the government of its states' is this:—When the superiors behave to their aged as the aged should be behaved to, the people become filial; when they behave to their elders as elders should be behaved to, the people learn brotherly submission; when they treat compassionately the young and helpless, the people do the same. Thus the superior man has a principle with which, as with a measuring square, to regulate his course.

23. What a man dislikes in his superiors, let him not display in his treatment of his inferiors; and what he dislikes in his inferiors, let him not display in his service of his superiors: what he dislikes in those who are before him, let him not therewith precede those who are behind him; and what he dislikes in those who are behind him, let him not therewith follow those who are before him: what he dislikes to receive on the right, let him not bestow on the left; and what he dislikes to receive on the left, let him not bestow

on the right:—this is what is called 'The Principle with which, as with a measuring square, to regulate one's course.'

24. In the Book of Poetry it is said (II, ii, 7, 3),

'To be rejoiced in are these noble men,
The parents of the people!'

When (a ruler) loves what the people love, and hates what the people hate, then is he what is called 'The Parent of the People.'

25, In the Book of Poetry it is said (II, iv, 7, 1),

'That southern hill, sublime, uprears its craggy height;
Such thou, Grand–master Yin, before the nation's sight!'

Rulers of states should not neglect to be careful. If they deviate (to a selfish regard only for themselves), they will be counted a disgrace throughout the kingdom.

26. In the Book of Poetry it is said (III, i, 1, 6),

'Ere Shang had lost the nation's heart,
Its monarchs all with God had part
In sacrifice. From them we see
'Tis hard to keep High Heaven's decree.'

This shows that by gaining the people, the state is gained; and by losing the people, the state is lost.

Therefore the ruler should first be careful about his (own) virtue. Possessing virtue will give him the people. Possessing the people will give him the territory. Possessing the territory will give him its wealth. Possessing the wealth, he will have resources for expenditure.

Virtue is the root; wealth is the branches. If he make the root his secondary object, and the branches his primary object, he will only quarrel with the people, and teach them rapine. Hence the accumulation of wealth is the way to scatter the people, and the distribution of his wealth is the way to collect the people. Hence (also), when his words go forth contrary to right, they will come back to him in the same way, and wealth got by improper ways will take its departure by the same.

27. It is said in the Announcement to the Prince of Khang (Shû, V, ix, 2, 3), 'The decree (of Heaven) is not necessarily perpetual.' That is, goodness obtains the decree, and the want of goodness loses it.

28. In a Book of Khû it is said[1], 'The state of Khû does not consider (such a toy) to be precious. Its good men are what it considers to be precious.'

29. Fan, the maternal uncle (of duke Wan of Zin), said, 'A fugitive (like you) should not account (that) to be precious. What he should consider precious is the affection due (even) to his (deceased) parent[2].'

30. It is said in the Speech of (duke Mû of) Khin (Shû, V, xxx, 6, 7), Let me have but one minister, plain and sincere, not possessed of other abilities, but with a simple, upright, and at the same time a generous, mind, regarding the talents of others as if they were his own; and when he finds accomplished and perspicacious men, loving them in his heart more than his mouth expresses, and really showing himself able to bear them (and employ them),—such a minister will be able to preserve my sons and grandsons, and other benefits (to the state) may well be expected from him. But if (it be his character), when he finds men of ability, to be

[1. The narratives about Khû, Section II, Article 5, in the 'Narratives of the States.' The exact characters of the text are not found in the article, but they might easily arise from what we do find. An officer of Zin is asking Wang-sun Wei, an envoy from Khû, about a famous girdle of that state. The envoy calls it a toy, and gives this answer.

2. See vol. xxvii, page 165, paragraph 19.]

jealous of them and hate them; and, when he finds accomplished and perspicacious men, to oppose them, and not allow their advancement, showing himself really not able to bear them,—such a man will not be able to protect my sons and grandsons, and black-haired people; and may he not also be pronounced dangerous (to the state)?'

31. It is only the truly virtuous man that can send away such a man and banish him, driving him out among the barbarous tribes around, determined not to dwell with him in the Middle states. This is in accordance with the saying, 'It is only the truly virtuous man who can love others or can bate others.'

32. To see men of worth, and not be able to raise them to office; to raise them to office, but not to do so quickly:—this is treating them with disrespect. To see bad men, and not to be able to remove them; to remove them, but not to do so to a distance:—this is weakness.

33. To love those whom men hate, and to hate those whom men love:—this is to outrage the natural feeling of men. Calamities are sure to come on him who does so.

34. Thus we see that the ruler has a great course to pursue. He must show entire self–devotion and sincerity to succeed, and by pride and extravagance he will fail.

35. There is a great course (also) for the production of wealth. Let the producers be many, and the consumers few. Let there be activity in the production, and economy in the expenditure. Then the wealth will always be sufficient.

36. The virtuous (ruler) uses his wealth so as to make himself more distinguished. The vicious ruler will accumulate wealth, even though it cost him his life.

37. Never has there been a case of the superior loving benevolence, and his inferiors not loving righteousness. Never has there been a case where (his inferiors) loved righteousness, and the business (of the superior) has not reached a happy issue. Never has there been a case where the wealth accumulated in the treasuries and arsenals (of such a ruler and people) did not continue to be his.

38. Mang Hsien–dze[1] said, 'He who keeps his team of horses[2] does not look after fowls and pigs. The family which has its stores of ices[3] does not keep cattle or sheep. The house which possesses a hundred chariots[4] should not keep a grasping minister to gather up all the taxes for it. Than have such a minister, it would be better to have one who would rob it of its revenues. This is in accordance with the saying, 'In a state gain should not be considered prosperity; its prosperity lies in righteousness.'

39. When he who presides over a state or a family makes his revenues his chief business, he must be under the influence of some small man. He may consider him to be good; but when such a person is employed in the administration of a state

[1. The worthy minister of Lû, mentioned in vol. xxvii, p. 154, et al. His name was Kung-sun Mieh. Hsien was his posthumous title.

2. An officer who has just attained to be a Great officer, and received from the ruler the carriage of distinction.

3. To be used in sacrificing; but, we may suppose, for other uses as well.

4. A dignitary, possessing an appanage.]

BOOK XL. KWAN Î, OR THE MEANING OF THE CEREMONY OF CAPPING[1].

1. Generally speaking, that which makes man man is the meaning of his ceremonial usages. The first indications of that meaning appear in the correct arrangement of the bodily carriage, the harmonious adjustment of the countenance, and in the natural ordering of the speech. When the bodily carriage is well arranged, the countenance harmoniously adjusted, and speech naturally ordered, the meaning of the ceremonial usages becomes complete, and serves to render correct the relation between ruler and subject, to give expression to the affection between father and son, and to establish harmony between seniors and juniors. When the relation between ruler and subject is made correct, affection secured between father and son, and harmony shown between seniors and juniors, then the meaning of those usages is established. Hence after the capping has taken place, provision is made for every other article of dress. With the complete provision of the dress, the bodily carriage becomes (fully) correct, the harmonious expression of the countenance is made perfect, and the speech is all conformed to its purposes. Hence it is said that in capping we have the first indications of (the meaning of the) ceremonial usages. It was on this account that the sage

[1. See the introductory notice, vol. xxvii, pp. 54, 55.]

kings of antiquity made so much as they did of the capping.

2. Anciently, when about to proceed to the ceremony of capping, they divined for the day by the stalks, and also for the guests (who should be present). In this way did they manifest the value which they attached to capping. Attaching such a value to it, they made the ceremony very important. They made the ceremony so important, showing how they considered it to lie at the foundation of the state's (prosperity).

Hence (also) the capping took place at the top of the eastern steps, (appropriate to the use of the Master);—to show that the son would (in due time) take his place. (The father) handed him a (special) cup in the guests' place. Three caps were used in the ceremony, each successive one more honourable, and giving the more importance to his coming of age. When the capping was over, he received the name of his maturity. So was it shown that he was now a full-grown man[1].

4. He presented himself before his mother, and his mother bowed to him; he did the same before his brothers and cousins, and they bowed to him:—he was a man grown, and so they exchanged courtesies with him. In the dark-coloured cap, and the dark-coloured square-cut robes, he put down his gift of introduction before the ruler, and then proceeded with the proper gifts to present himself to the high ministers and Great officers, and to the old gentlemen of the country:—appearing before them as a man grown.

[1. Compare paragraph 2 on pages 437, 438, vol. xxvii.]

5. Treating him (now) as a grown-up man, they would require from him all the observances of a full-grown man. Doing so, they would require from him the performance of all the duties of a son, a younger brother, a subject, and a junior. But when these four duties or services were required from him, was it not right that the ceremony by which he was placed in such a position should be considered important?

6. Thus when the discharge of filial and fraternal duties, of loyal service, and of deferential submission was established, he could indeed be regarded as a (full-grown) man. When he could be regarded as such, he could be employed to govern other men. It was on this account that the sage kings attached such an importance to the ceremony, and therefore it was said, that in capping we have the introduction to all the ceremonial

usages, and that it is the most important of the festive services.

BOOK XLI. HWAN Î, OR THE MEANING OF THE MARRIAGE CEREMONY[1].

1. The ceremony of marriage was intended to be a bond of love between two (families of different) surnames, with a view, in its retrospective character, to secure the services in the ancestral temple, and in its prospective character, to secure the continuance of the family line. Therefore the superior men, (the ancient rulers), set a great value upon it. Hence, in regard to the various (introductory) ceremonies,—the proposal with its accompanying gift[2]; the inquiries about the (lady's) name; the intimation of the approving divination[3]; the receiving the special offerings[4]; and the request to fix the day[5]:—these all were received by the principal party (on the lady's side), as he rested on his mat or leaning-stool in the ancestral temple, (When they arrived), he met the messenger, and greeted him outside the gate, giving place to him as he entered, after which they ascended to the hall. Thus were the instructions

[1. See the introductory notice, vol. xxvii, page 55.

2. This gift was always a goose; into the reasons for which it is not necessary to enter.

3. The gentleman's family had divined on the proposal.

4. These were various.

5. The lady's family fixed this. The first proposal was made, and perhaps those which followed also, by that important functionary in Chinese life, 'the go-between,' or a friend acting in that capacity.]

received in the ancestral temple[1], and in this way was the ceremony respected, and watched over, while its importance was exhibited and care taken that all its details should be correct.

2. The father gave himself the special cup[2] to his son, and ordered him to go and meet the bride; it being proper that the male should take the first step (in all the arrangements).

The son, having received the order, proceeded to meet his bride. Her father, who had been resting on his mat and leaning-stool in the temple, met him outside the gate and received him with a bow, and then the son-in-law entered, carrying a wild goose. After the (customary) bows and yieldings of precedence, they went up to the hall, when the bridegroom bowed twice and put down the wild goose. Then and in this way he received the bride from her parents.

After this they went down, and he went out and took the reins of the horses of her carriage, which he drove for three revolutions of the wheels, having handed the strap to assist her in mounting. He then went before, and waited outside his gate, When she arrived, he bowed to her as she entered. They ate together of the same animal, and joined in sipping from the cups made of the same melon[3];

[1. Thus a religious sanction entered into the idea of marriage.

2. The same cup that is mentioned in the last chapter, paragraph 3; the son received it and gave no cup to the father in return. This was its speciality. In the capping ceremonies it was given 'in the guests' place;' in those of marriage, in the son's chamber.

3. Once when I was permitted to witness this part of a marriage ceremony, the bridegroom raised his half of the melon, with the spirit in it, to the bride's lips, and she raised her half to his. Each sipped a little of the spirit.]

thus showing that they now formed one body, were of equal rank, and pledged to mutual affection.

3. The respect, the caution, the importance, the attention to secure correctness in all the details, and then (the pledge of) mutual affection,—these were the great points in the ceremony, and served to establish the distinction to be observed between man and woman, and the righteousness to be maintained between husband and wife. From the distinction between man and woman came the righteousness between husband and wife. From that righteousness came the affection between father and son; and from that affection, the rectitude between ruler and minister. Whence it is said, 'The ceremony of marriage is the root of the other ceremonial observances.'

4. Ceremonies (might be said to) commence with the capping; to have their root in marriage; to be most important in the rites of mourning and sacrifice; to confer the greatest honour in audiences at the royal court and in the interchange of visits at the feudal courts; and to be most promotive of harmony in the country festivals and celebrations of archery. These were the greatest occasions of ceremony, and the principal points in them.

5. Rising early (the morning after marriage), the young wife washed her head and bathed her person, and waited to be presented (to her husband's parents), which was done by the directrix, as soon as it was bright day. She appeared before them, bearing a basket with dates, chestnuts, and slices of dried spiced meat. The directrix set before her a cup of sweet liquor, and she offered in sacrifice some of the dried meat and also of the liquor, thus performing the ceremony which declared her their son's wife[1].

6. The father and mother–in–law then entered their apartment, where she set before them a single dressed pig,—thus showing the obedient duty of (their son's) wife[1].

7. Next day, the parents united in entertaining the young wife, and when the ceremonies of their severally pledging her in a single cup, and her pledging them in return, had been performed, they descended by the steps on the west, and she by those on the east,—thus showing that she would take the mother's place in the family[1].

8. Thus the ceremony establishing the young wife in her position; (followed by) that showing her obedient service (of her husband's parents); and both succeeded by that showing how she now occupied the position of continuing the family line:—all served to impress her with a sense of the deferential duty proper to her. When she was thus deferential, she was obedient to her parents–in–law, and harmonious with all the occupants of the women's apartments; she was the fitting partner of her husband, and could carry on all the work in silk and linen, making cloth and silken fabrics, and maintaining a watchful care over the various stores and depositories (of the household).

9. In this way when the deferential obedience of the wife was complete, the internal harmony was

[1. The details of the various usages briefly described in these paragraphs are to be found in the 4th Book of the Î Lî, the 2nd of those on the scholar's marriage ceremonies:

paragraphs 1–10; 11–17; 18–20. There were differences in the ceremonies according to the rank of the parties; but all agreed in their general character.]

secured; and when the internal harmony was secured, the long continuance of the family could be calculated on. Therefore the ancient kings attached such importance (to the marriage ceremonies).

10. Therefore, anciently, for three months before the marriage of a young lady, if the temple of the high ancestor (of her surname) were still standing (and she had admission to it), she was taught in it, as the public hall (of the members of her surname); if it were no longer standing (for her), she was taught in the public hall of the Head of that branch of the surname to which she belonged;—she was taught there the virtue, the speech, the carriage, and the work of a wife. When the teaching was accomplished, she offered a sacrifice (to the ancestor), using fish for the victim, and soups made of duckweed and pondweed. So was she trained to the obedience of a wife[1].

11. Anciently, the queen of the son of Heaven divided the harem into six palace–halls, (occupied) by the 3 ladies called fû–zan, the 9 pin, the 27 shih–fû, and the 81 yü–khî. These were instructed in the domestic and private rule which should prevail throughout the kingdom, and how the deferential obedience of the wife should be illustrated; and thus internal harmony was everywhere secured, and families were regulated. (In the same way) the son of Heaven established six official departments, in

[1. There is supposed to be an allusion to this custom in the Shih, I, ii, 4, beginning,

'She gathers fast the large duckweed,
From valley stream that southward flows;
And for the pondweed to the pools
Left on the plains by floods she goes.'

]

which were distributed the 3 kung, the 9 khing, the 27 tâ fû, and the 81 sze of the highest grade. These were instructed in all that concerned the public and external government of the kingdom, and how the lessons for the man should be illustrated; and thus harmony was secured in all external affairs, and the states were properly governed.

It is therefore said, 'From the son of Heaven there were learned the lessons for men; and from the queen, the obedience proper to women.' The son of Heaven directed the course to be pursued by the masculine energies, and the queen regulated the virtues to be cultivated by the feminine receptivities. The son of Heaven guided in all that affected the external administration (of affairs); and the queen, in all that concerned the internal regulation (of the family). The teachings (of the one) and the obedience (inculcated by the other) perfected the manners and ways (of the people); abroad and at home harmony and natural order prevailed; the states and the families were ruled according to their requirements:—this was what is called 'the condition of complete virtue.'

12. Therefore when the lessons for men are not cultivated, the masculine phenomena in nature do not proceed regularly;–as seen in the heavens, we have the sun eclipsed. When the obedience proper to women is not cultivated, the feminine phenomena in nature do not proceed regularly;–as seen in the heavens, we have the moon eclipsed. Hence on an eclipse of the sun, the son of Heaven put on plain white robes, and proceeded to repair what was wrong in the duties of the six official departments, purifying everything that belonged to the masculine sphere throughout the kingdom; and on an eclipse of the moon, the queen dressed herself in plain white robes, and proceeded to repair what was wrong in the duties of the six palace–halls, purifying everything that belonged to the feminine sphere throughout the kingdom. The son of Heaven is to the queen what the sun is to the moon, or the masculine energy of nature to the feminine. They are necessary to each other, and by their interdependence they fulfil their functions.

BOOK XLII. HSIANG YIN KIÛ Î, OR THE MEANING OF THE DRINKING FESTIVITY IN THE DISTRICTS[1].

1. The meaning of the drinking in the country districts may be thus described:—The president on the occasion bows to the (coming) guest as he receives him outside the college gate. They enter and thrice salute each other till they come to the steps. There each thrice yields the precedence to the other, and then they ascend. In this way they carry to the utmost their mutual demonstrations of honour and humility. (The host) washes his hands, rinses the cup, and raises it,—to give the highest idea of purity. They bow on the guest's arrival; they bow as (the cup) is washed; they bow when the cup is

received, and when it is presented (in return); they bow when the drinking it is over:—in this way carrying to the utmost their mutual respect.

2. Such giving of honour, such humility, such purity, and such respect belonged to the intercourse of superior men with others. When they gave honour and showed humility, no contentions arose. When they maintained purity and respect, no indifference or rudeness arose. When there was no rudeness or contention, quarrels and disputations were kept at a distance. When men did not quarrel

[1. See the introductory notice, vol. xxvii, page 56.]

nor dispute, there came no evils of violence or disorder. It was thus that superior men escaped suffering calamity from other men; and therefore the sages instituted the observances in this ceremony to secure such a result.

3. The chief of the district with the accomplished and virtuous men belonging to it had the vessel of liquor placed between the room (on the cast), and the door (leading to the apartments on the west), host and guests sharing it between them. The vessel contained the dark–coloured liquor (of pure water);—showing the value, they attached to its simplicity. The viands came forth from the room on the east;—being supplied by the host. All washing, took place (in the courtyard) opposite the eastern wing;—showing how the host purified himself and made himself ready to serve the guests.

4. The (principal) guest and the host represented heaven and earth; the attendants of the guest and host respectively represented the forces inherent in nature in their contracting and expanding operations; the three (heads of the) guests (in their threefold division) represented the three (great) luminaries; the precedence thrice yielded (to the guest) represented the three days when the moon is invisible till it begins to reappear; the seating of the parties present (all round or) on the four sides represented the four seasons[1].

[1. P. Callery says:—'There were at this ceremony, 1. the chief and his assistant; 2. the principal guest who was supposed to represent all the other guests, and who also had his assistant; 3. three guests who formed a second category; 4. finally, the crowd of guests, a number not fixed, to whom no honour was paid directly, since they were held to receive all the honours rendered to the principal guest.' Khan Hâo quotes an opinion that the principal guest was made to represent heaven, to do him the greater honour; and the host to represent the earth, because he was the entertainer and nourisher; and that their assistants represented the yin and yang, because they assisted their principals as these energies in nature assist heaven and earth.

On 'the three Luminaries,' Callery says:—'Ordinarily the name of "the three Luminaries" belongs to the sun, the moon, and the stars, but par. 16 below does not allow us to take it so here. The commentators say that we are to understand the three most brilliant constellations in the firmament, which they call Hsin, Fâ, and Po-khan, corresponding, I believe, in part to Orion, Scorpio, and Argo or the Ship.' So also Khan Hâo's authority. Hsin is generally understood to be Scorpio (Antares, {sigma}, {tau}, and two c. 3584 and 3587); Fâ to be {upsilon} Orion; and Po-khan to be the north polar star.

On the 'thrice-yielded precedence to the guest,' Callery says:—'The comparison is far-fetched; it is intended to say that as the moon would not receive light if the sun did not accord it, so the guest would not receive such honours if the host did not render them.' So the commentators certainly try to explain it.]

5. The snell and icy wind (that blows between) heaven and earth begins in the south-west and is strongest in the north-west. This is the wind that represents the most commanding severity of heaven and earth;—the wind of their righteous justice. The warm and genial wind (that blows between) heaven and earth begins in the north-east and is strongest in the south-east. This is the wind that represents the abundant virtue of heaven and earth;—the wind of their benevolence. The host, wishing to do honour to his guest, assigns him his seat on the north-west, and that of his attendant on the south-west, that he may there (most conveniently) assist him. The guest (represents) the treatment of others according to justice, and therefore his seat is on the north-west; the host (represents) the treatment of others according to benevolence and a genial kindness, and therefore his seat is on the southeast, and his attendant is seated on the north-east, that he may there (most conveniently) assist him[1].

6. That intercourse according to benevolence and righteousness being established, so as to show the respective duties of host and guest, and the number of stands and dishes being properly fixed;—all this must be the result of sage intelligence. That intelligence established the arrangements, and each one being carried through with respect, it became a ceremonial usage. That usage proceeding to mark and embody the distinction between

old and young, it became a virtue. Virtue is that which is the characteristic of the person. Therefore we have the saying, 'In the learning of antiquity, the methods by which they pursued the course adopted were intended to put men in possession of their proper virtue.' On this account the sages employed their powers (on its lessons)[2].

[1. P. Callery observes on this paragraph:—'The meteorological observations on which these statements rest must have been made very long ago in the interior of the country, there where the winds come under the influence of the icy plains of Tartary and the high mountains which separate China from Thibet; for on the seacoasts of China, exactly the contrary has place. During the winter the north–east monsoon prevails, varying sometimes to the north and sometimes to the east, rarely to the north–west; while during the heats of summer the wind blows from the south–west, bending a little towards the south or towards the east, according as the monsoon is in the period of its increase or decline. It is generally in the course of this monsoon that there takes place the terrible storms known by the name of typhoons.'

2. The Khien–lung editors do their best to elucidate this difficult and obscure paragraph; but are obliged to quote in the end the judgment of Kû Hsî' that 'it is vague and intractable, and not worth taking much trouble about.']

7. When (the guest) offers in sacrifice some of the things that have been set before him, and some of the liquor, he showed how he respected (the host) for his courtesy; when he proceeded to take some of the lungs in his teeth, he thereby tasted (the host's) courtesy; when he then sipped some of the liquor, that was his last step in acknowledgment thereof. This last act was done at the end of his mat, showing that the mat was spread straight before him, not only for the purpose of eating and drinking, but also for the performance of the (proper) rites. In this was shown how it was the ceremony that was valued, while the wealth was made little account of. Finally, when the host filled their cups from the horn, they drained them at the top of the western steps;—showing how the mat was set not (merely) for the purpose of eating and drinking, and how the idea was that of giving to the ceremony the first place, and to wealth the last. But when the ceremony has the first place, and wealth the last, the people become respectful and yielding, and are not contentious with one another.

8. At the ceremony of drinking in the country districts, those who were sixty years old sat, and those who were (only fifty) stood, and were in waiting to receive any orders and

perform any services;—thus illustrating the honour which should be paid to elders.

Before those who were sixty, three dishes were placed; before those of seventy, four; before those of eighty, five; before those of ninety, six:—thus illustrating how the aged should be cherished and nourished.

When the people knew to honour their elders and nourish their aged, then at home they could practise filial piety and fraternal duty. Filial and fraternal at home and abroad, honouring elders and nourishing the aged, then their education was complete, and this led to the peace and tranquillity of the state. What the superior man calls filial piety, does not require that (every) family should be visited and as members daily taught; if (the people) be assembled at the archery meetings in the districts, and taught the usages at the district–drinkings, their conduct is brought to be filial and fraternal.

9. Confucius said, 'When I look on at the festivity in the country districts, I know how easily the Royal way may obtain free course.

10. 'The host in person invites the principal guest and his attendant, and all the other guests follow them of themselves. When they arrive outside the gate, he bows (and welcomes) the chief guest and his attendant, and all the others enter of themselves. In this way the distinction between the noble and the mean is exhibited.

11. 'With the interchange of three bows (the host and guest) arrive at the steps; and after precedence has been thrice yielded to him, the guest ascends. In bowing to him (on the hall), (the host) presents to him the cup, and receives the cup from him in return. The usages between them, now declining, now yielding, the one to the other, are numerous; but the attention paid to the assistant is less. As to the crowd of guests, they ascend, and receive the cup. Kneeling down they offer some of it in sacrifice; they rise and drink it; and without pledging the host in the return–cup, they descend. In this way the proper distinction is made between the different parties by the multitude or paucity of the observances paid to them.

12. 'The musicians enter, ascend the hall, and sing the three pieces which complete their performance, after which the host offers to them the cup. The organists enter, and (below the hall) play three tunes, which complete their part of the performance, after which the host offers to them (also) the cup. Then they sing and play alternately other three pieces

and tunes; and also thrice again they sing and play in concert. When this is finished, the musicians announce that the music is over, and go out.

'At the same time a person (as instructed by the host) takes up the horn, and one is appointed to superintend the drinking, and see that it proceeds correctly. From this we know how they could be harmonious and joyful, without being disorderly.

13. 'The (principal) guest pledges the host, the host pledges the attendants, the attendants pledge all the guests. Young and old pledge one another according to their age, and the cup circulates on to the keepers of the vases and the cup–washers. From this we know how they could practise brotherly deference to their elders without omitting any one.

14. 'Descending (after this), they take off their shoes; ascending again, and taking their seats, they take their cups without any limit as to number. But the regulations of the drinking do not allow them to neglect the duties either of the morning or evening. When the guests go out, the host bows to each as he escorts him away. The regulations and forms are observed to the end; and from this we know how they could enjoy the feast without turbulence or confusion.

I5. 'The distinction between the noble and mean thus exhibited; the discrimination in the multitude or paucity of the observances to different parties; the harmony and joy without disorder; the brotherly deference to elders without omitting any; the happy feasting without turbulence or confusion;—the observance of these five things is sufficient to secure the rectification of the person, and the tranquillity of the state. When that one state is tranquil, all under heaven will be the same. Therefore I say that when I look on at the festivity in the country districts, I know how easily the Royal Way may obtain free course[1].'

16. According to the meaning attached to the festivity of drinking in the country districts, the principal guest was made to represent heaven; the host, to represent earth; their attendants respectively to represent the sun and moon; and the three head guests (according to the threefold division of them) to represent the three (great) luminaries. This was the form which the festivity received on its institution in antiquity: the presiding idea was found in heaven and earth; the regulation of that was found in the sun and moon; and the three luminaries were introduced as a third feature. (The

[1. I have supposed that all from paragraph 9 to this is the language of Confucius, and translated in the present tense as he would speak. Possibly, however, after par. 9 the compiler of the Book may be giving his own views of the different parts of the festivity (which would in that case have to be translated in the past tense), and then winds up with therefore 'He—Confucius—said,' &c.]

whole represented) the fundamental principles in the conduct of government and instruction.

17. The dogs were boiled on the eastern side (of the courtyard[1]);—in reverential acknowledgment of the fact that the vivifying and expanding power in nature issues from the east.

The washings took place at the eastern steps, and the water was kept on the east of the washing–place;—in reverential acknowledgment of the fact that heaven and earth have placed the sea on the left.

The vessel contained the dark–coloured liquid;—teaching the people not to forget the original practice (at ceremonies).

18. The rule was that the (principal) guest should face the south. The quarter of the east suggests the idea of the spring, the name of which (also) denotes the appearance of insects beginning to move:—(there is then at work that mysterious) intelligence which gives birth to all things. The quarter of the south suggests the idea of the summer, the name of which (also) denotes what is great:—what nourishes things, encourages their growth, and makes them great is benevolence. The quarter of the west suggests the idea of the autumn, the name of which also denotes gathering or collecting:—the fruits of the earth are gathered at this season, suggesting the idea of justice in discriminating

[1. Compare the statement in paragraph 3, that 'the viands come forth from the room on the east.' Khan Hsiang–tâo says:—'The dog is a creature that keeps watch, and is skilful in its selection of men;–it will keep away from any one who is not what he should be. On this account the ancients at all their festive occasions of eating and drinking employed it.']

and guarding. The quarter of the north suggests the idea of winter, the name of which denotes also what is kept within:—and the being within leads us to think of being stored up. On this account, when the son of Heaven stands up, he keeps (the quarter of the life–giving) intelligence on his left hand, faces (the quarter of) benevolence, has that of justice on his right hand, and that of depositing behind him[1].

19. It was the rule that his attendants should face the east; thus (making) the principal guest to be the chief (party) at the festivity.

[1. The Khien–lung editors say that portions of this paragraph have been lost, and that other parts are out of their proper place; and they suggest the additions and alterations necessary to make it right. It is not worth while, however, to consider their views. No alterations will remedy its incurable defects or reverse the severe judgment passed on it by P. Callery:—'The method,' he says, 'by which the author proceeds is exceedingly eccentric, and partakes at once of the nature of the pun, of allegory, and of mysticism. He begins by basing his comparisons on the resemblance of certain sounds, or the homophony of certain words. Then he seeks to find in the sense, proper to those words that are homophonous or nearly so, connexions with the principal word in the text; and as those connexions are far from being natural or simply plausible, he puts his spirit to the torture, and goes to seek in the mysterious action of nature points of contact of which no one would think. Thus in the sound khun he finds a natural analogy between the slow and gradual movement of a worm without eyes, and the march, equally slow and gradual, of vegetation in spring; in the sounds hsiâ and kiâ he finds a direct connexion between greatness and the action which makes plants become great in summer. So in the same way with the other sounds which he deals with. To many Chinese this fashion of reasoning appears to be very profound; but, as I think, it is nothing but a childish play on words and hollow ideas.']

It was the rule that the host should be in the eastern quarter. The eastern quarter suggests the idea of spring, the name of which (also) denotes the appearance of insects beginning to move, and (it is spring) which produces all things. The host makes the festivity; that is, he produces all things.

BOOK XLIII. SHÊ Î, OR THE MEANING OF THE CEREMONY OF ARCHERY[1].

1. Anciently it was the rule for the feudal lords, when they would practise archery, first to celebrate the ceremony of the Banquet, and for the Great officers and ordinary officers, when they would shoot, first to celebrate the ceremony of the Drinking in the country districts. The ceremony of the Banquet served to illustrate the relation between ruler and subject; that of the District–drinking, to illustrate the distinction between seniors and juniors.

2. The archers, in advancing, retiring, and all their movements, were required to observe the rules. With minds correct, and straight carriage of the body, they were to hold their bows and arrows skilfully and firmly; and when they did so, the), might be expected to hit the mark. In this way (from their archery) their characters could be seen[1].

3. To regulate (the discharging of the arrows), there was,—in the case of the son of Heaven, the playing of the Zâu–yü; in the case of the feudal lords, that of the Lî–shâu; in the case of the dignitaries, the Great officers, that of the Zhâi–pin; and in the case of officers, that of the Zhâi–fân[2].

[1. See introductory notice, vol. xxvii, pages 56, 57.

2. Each archer discharged four arrows at the target. According to the account of the duties of the superintendent of archery in the Kâu Lî (Book XXX, paragraphs 54–67, especially 57), the Zâu–yü was played or sung nine times; the Li–shâu seven times; and the two other pieces five times. When the king was shooting therefore, he began to shoot after the fifth performance, and had all the previous time to prepare himself; a prince began to shoot after the third performance; and in the two other cases there was only the time of one performance for preparation.]

The Zâu–yü[1] is expressive of joy that every office is (rightly) filled; the Lî–shâu is expressive of the joy at audiences of the court; the Zhâi–pin is expressive of the joy in observing the laws (which have been learned); and the Zhâi–fân is expressive of the joy in being free from all failures in duty. Therefore the son of Heaven regulated his shooting by keeping in his mind the right feeling of all officers; a feudal prince, by keeping in his mind the times of his appearing before the son of Heaven; a dignitary, being a Great officer, by keeping in his mind the observing of the laws (which he had learned); and an officer, by keeping in his mind that he must not fail in the duties of his office.

In this way, when they clearly understood the meaning of those regulating measures, and were thus able to avoid all failure in their services, they were successful in their undertakings, and their character

[1. The Zâu-yü is the last piece in the 2nd Book of the first part of the Book of Poetry; supposed to celebrate the benevolence of the king; here seen in his delight at every office being rightly filled. The Li-shâu, 'Fox's Head,' or 'Wild Cat's Head,' has not come down to us;—see note 2, page 124. The Zhâi-pin and Zhâi-fân are the fifth and second pieces of the same Book and same part of the Shih as the Zâu-yü. The regulating the discharge of the arrows by the playing of these pieces was part of the moral discipline to which it was sought to make the archery subservient.]

and conduct were established. When their characters were established, no such evils as oppression and disorder occurred; and when their undertakings were successful, the states were tranquil and happy. Hence it is said that 'the archery served to show the completeness of (the archer's) virtue.'

4. Therefore, anciently, the son of Heaven chose the feudal lords, the dignitaries who were Great officers, and the officers, from their skill in archery. Archery is specially the business of males, and there were added to it the embellishments of ceremonies and music. Hence among the things which may afford the most complete illustration of ceremonies and music, and the frequent performance of which may serve to establish virtue and good conduct, there is nothing equal to archery: and therefore the ancient kings paid much attention to it.

5. Therefore, anciently, according to the royal institutes, the feudal princes annually presented the officers who had charge of their tribute to the son of Heaven, who made trial of them in the archery-hall. Those of them whose bodily carriage was in conformity with the rules, and whose shooting was in agreement with the music, and who hit the mark most frequently, were allowed to take part at the sacrifices. When his officers had frequently that privilege, their ruler was congratulated; if they frequently failed to obtain it, he was reprimanded. If a prince were frequently so congratulated, he received an

increase to his territory; if he were frequently so reprimanded, part of his territory was taken from him. Hence came the saying, 'The archers shoot in the interest of their princes.' Thus, in the states, the rulers and their officers devoted themselves to archery, and the practice in connexion with it of the ceremonies and music. But when, rulers and officers practise ceremonies and music, never has it been known that such practice led to their banishment or ruin.

6. Hence it is said in the ode (now lost),

'The long–descended lord
Presents your cups of grace.
His chiefs and noble men
Appear, all in their place;
Small officers and Great,
Not one will keep away.
See them before their prince,
All in their full array.
They feast, and then they shoot,
Happy and praised to boot.'

The lines show how when rulers and their officers earnestly devoted themselves together to archery, and the practice in connexion with it of ceremonies and music, they were happy and got renown. It was on this account that the son of Heaven instituted the custom, and the feudal lords diligently attended to it. This was the way in which the son of Heaven cherished the princes, and had no need of weapons of war (in dealing with them); it furnished (also) to the princes an instrument with which they trained themselves to rectitude.

7. (Once), when Confucius was conducting an archery meeting in a vegetable garden at Kio–hsiang, the lookers–on surrounded it like a wall. When the proceedings reached the point when a Master of the Horse should be appointed, he directed Dze–lû to take his bow and arrows, and go out to introduce those who wished to shoot, and to say, 'The general of a defeated army, the Great officer of a ruler–less state, and any one who (has schemed to be) the successor and heir of another, will not be allowed to enter, but the rest may all enter.' On this, one half went away, and the other half entered.

After this, (wishing to send the cup round among all the company), he further directed Kung-wang Khiû and Hsü Tien to raise the horns of liquor, and make proclamation. Then Kung-wang Khiû raised his horn, and said, 'Are the young and strong (here) observant of their filial and fraternal duties? Are the old and men of eighty (here) such as love propriety, not following licentious customs, and resolved to maintain their characters to death? (If so), they may occupy the position of guests.' On this, one half (of those who had entered) went away, and the other half remained.

Hsü Tien next raised his horn, and proclaimed, 'Are you fond of learning without being tired? are you fond of the rules of propriety, and unswerving in your adherence to them? Do those of you who are eighty, ninety, or one hundred, expound the way (of virtue) Without confusion or error? If so, you can occupy the position of visitors.' Thereupon hardly any remained[1].

8. To shoot means to draw out to the end, and some say to lodge in the exact point. That drawing

[1. The authenticity of what is related in this paragraph, which is not in the expurgated edition of the Lî Kî, may be doubted. But however that be, it is evidently intended to be an illustration of what did, or might, take place at meetings for archery in the country. Kio-hsiang is understood to be the name of some place in Lû.]

out to the end means every one unfolding his own idea; hence, with the mind even-balanced and the body correctly poised, (the archer) holds his bow and arrow skilfully and firmly. When he so holds them, he will hit the mark. Hence it is said, 'The father (shoots) at the father-mark; the son, at the son-mark; the ruler, at the ruler-mark; the subject, at the subject-mark.' Thus the archer shoots at the mark of his (ideal) self; and so the Great archery of the son of Heaven is called shooting at (the mark of) the feudal prince. 'Shooting at the mark of the feudal prince' was shooting to prove himself a prince. He who hit the mark was permitted to be, that is, retain his rank as) a prince; he who did not hit the mark was not permitted to retain his rank as a prince[1].

9. When the son of Heaven was about to sacrifice, the rule was that he should celebrate the archery at the pool, which name suggested the idea of selecting the officers (by their shooting)[2]. After

[1. In this paragraph we have a remarkable instance of that punning or playing on words or sounds, which Callery has pointed out as a 'puerility' in Chinese writers, and of which we have many examples in the writers of the Han dynasty. The idea in the paragraph is good, that when one realises the ideal of what he is, becoming all he ought to be, he may be said to hit the mark. But to bring out this from the character, which is the symbol of shooting with the bow, the author is obliged to give it two names,—yî (=, drawing out or unwinding the thread of a cocoon, or clue of silk, to the end) and shê (a cottage or booth, a place to lodge in). The latter is the proper name for the character in the sense of shooting.

2. Here there is another play on names,—zeh, in Pekinese kâi, 'a pond or pool,' suggesting the character, which has the same name, and means 'to choose, select.' There were two places for the archery, one called the Kâi Kung, 'Palace or Hall by the pool,' and the other, Shê Kung, 'Palace or Hall of Archery,' which was, says Callery, 'a vast gallery in the royal college.']

the archery at the pool came that in the archery hall. Those who hit the mark were permitted to take part in the sacrifice; and those who failed were not permitted to do so. (The ruler of those) who did not receive the permission was reprimanded, and had part of his territory taken from him. The ruler of those who were permitted was congratulated, and received an addition to his territory. The advancement appeared in the rank; the disapprobation, in the (loss of) territory.

10. Hence, when a son is born, a bow of mulberry wood, and six arrows of the wild raspberry plant (are placed on the left of the door) for the purpose of shooting at heaven, earth, and the four cardinal points. Heaven, earth, and the four points denote the spheres wherein the business of a man lies. The young man must first give his mind to what is to be his business, and then he may venture to receive emolument, that is, the provision for his food.

11. Archery suggests to us the way of benevolence. (The archer) seeks to be correct in himself, and then discharges his arrow. If it miss the mark, he is not angry with the one who has surpassed himself, but turns round and seeks (for the cause of failure) in himself[1]. Confucius said, 'The student of virtue has no contentions. If it be said that he cannot avoid them, shall this be in archery? (But) he bows complaisantly to his competitor, ascends

[1. Compare above, page 307, paragraph 40, where we have 'the way of the superior man' instead of the way of benevolence, or perfect virtue.']

(the hall), descends (again), and exacts the forfeit of drinking. In his contention, he is still the superior man[1].'

12. Confucius said, 'How difficult it is to shoot! How difficult it is to listen (to the music)! To shoot exactly in harmony with the note (given) by the music, and to shoot without missing the bull's–eye on the target:—it is only the archer of superior virtue who can do this! How shall a man of inferior character be able to hit the mark? It is said in the Book of Poetry (II, viii, ode 6, 1),

'"Now shoot," he says, "and show your skill."
The other answers, "Shoot I will,
And hit the mark;—and when you miss,
Pray you the penal cup to kiss."'

'To pray' is to ask. The archer seeks to hit that he may decline the cup. The liquor in the cup is designed (properly) to nourish the aged, or the sick. When the archer seeks to hit that he may decline the cup, that is declining what should serve to nourish (those that need it).

BOOK XLIV. YEN Î, OR THE MEANING OF THE BANQUET[1].

1. Anciently, among the officers of the kings of Kâu, there was one called the shû–dze. He was charged with the care of the sons of the feudal lords, the high dignitaries who were the Great officers, and (other) officers,—the eldest sons who occupied the next place to their fathers. He managed (the issuing) to them of (all) cautions and orders; superintended their instruction in all they had to learn and (the art of self–)government; arranged them in their different classes; and saw that they occupied their correct positions. If there were any grand solemnity (being transacted) in the kingdom, he conducted them–these sons of the state–and placed them under the eldest son, the heir–apparent, who made what use of them he thought fit. If any military operations were being undertaken, he provided for them their carriages and coats of mail, assembled for

them the companies of a hundred men and of five men (of which they should have charge), and appointed their inferior officers, thus training them in the art of war:—they were not under the jurisdiction of the minister of War. In all (other) governmental business of the state, these sons of it were left free, their fathers' eldest sons, without public occupation,

[1. See introductory notice, vol. xxvii, pages 57, 58.]

and were made to attend to the cultivation of virtuous ways. In spring, (the shû–dze) assembled them in the college; and in autumn, in the archery (hall), that he might examine into their proficiency, and advanced or degraded them accordingly.

2. The meaning of the ceremony of the banquet at the feudal courts (may be thus described):–The ruler stood on the south–east of (his own) steps on the east, having his face towards the south, fronting the ministers or dignitaries who were nearest to him. They and all the (other) Great officers came forward a little, taking each his proper station. The ruler's mat is placed at the top of the eastern steps:—there is the station of the host. The ruler alone goes up and stands on his mat; with his face to the west he stands there by himself:—showing that no one presumes to place himself on a par with him.

3. Guests and host having been arranged, according to the rules for the ceremony of drinking in the country districts, (the ruler) makes his chief cook act for him in presenting (the cup):—a minister may not presume to take on himself any usage proper to the ruler. None of the (three) kung and no high minister has the place of a guest; but the Great officers are among the guests,–because of the doubts that might arise, and to show the jealousy (which such great men in that position might create).

When the guests have entered to the middle of the courtyard, the ruler descends a step and bows to them:—thus courteously receiving them.

4. The ruler sends the cup round among the guests in order; and when he has given a special cup to any, they all descend, and bow twice, laying at the same time their heads to the ground; after which they ascend, and complete their bowing:—thus showing the observance due from subjects. The ruler responds to them, for every act of courtesy must be responded to:—illustrating the observances due from the ruler and superiors. When ministers and inferiors do their utmost to perform service for the state, the ruler must

recompense them with rank and emoluments. Hence all officers and inferiors endeavour with their utmost strength and ability to establish their merit, and thus the state is kept in tranquillity, and the ruler's mind is at rest.

(The principle) that every act of courtesy must be responded to, showed that rulers do not receive anything from their inferiors without sufficient ground for doing so. The ruler must illustrate the path of rectitude in his conduct of the people; and when the people follow that path and do good service (for the state), then he may take from them a tenth part (of their revenues). In this way he has enough, and his subjects do not suffer want. Thus harmony and affection prevail between high and low, and they have no mutual dissatisfactions. Such harmony and rest are the result of the ceremonial usages. This is the great idea in the relation between ruler and subject, between high and low:—hence it is said that the object of the banquet was to illustrate the idea of justice between ruler and subject.

5. The mats were arranged so that the dignitaries of smaller rank occupied the place next (in honour) to those of higher; the Great officers, the place next to the lower dignitaries. The officers and sons of concubines[1] (also) took their places below in their regular order. The cup being presented to the ruler, he begins the general pledging, and offers the cup to the high dignitaries[2]. They continue the ceremony, and offer the cup to the Great officers, who offer it in turn to the (other) officers, and these finally offer it to the sons of concubines. The stands and dishes, with the flesh of the animals[3], and the savoury viands, were all proportioned to the differences of rank in the guests:–and thus the distinction was shown between the noble and the mean.

[1. This is a common meaning of the phrase shû–dze. We cannot suppose that there is a reference to the officer so called in paragraph 1. He was of too high a rank to be placed after the officers, who ranked below the Great officers. Nor can we suppose that it denotes here 'the sons of the state' under his charge.

2. The ruler did this by his deputy, the chief cook, who officiated for him on the occasion. All the different offerings are said to have been made by him indeed; but that is not the natural interpretation of the text.

BOOK XLV. PHING Î, OR THE MEANING OF THE INTERCHANGE OF MISSIONS BETWEEN DIFFERENT COURTS[1].

1. According to the ceremonies in missions, a duke of the highest grade sent seven attendants with (his representative); a marquis or earl, five; and a count or baron, three. The difference in number served to show the difference in rank of their principals[2].

2. The messages (between the visitor and the host) were passed through all the attendants, from one to another. A superior man, where he wishes to do honour, will not venture to communicate directly and in person. This was a high tribute of respect.

3. The message was transmitted (only) after the messenger had thrice declined to receive (the courtesies offered to him at the gate); he entered the gate of the ancestral temple after thrice in the same way trying to avoid doing so; thrice he exchanged bows with his conductor before they arrived at the steps; and thrice he yielded the precedence offered to him before he ascended the hall:—so did he carry to

[1. See introductory notice, vol. xxvii, pages 58, 59.

2. If the ruler went in person on the mission, he had in every case, according to his rank, two attendants more than the number specified for his representative.]

the utmost his giving of honour and yielding courtesy.

4. The ruler sent an officer to meet (the messenger) at the border (of the state), and a Great officer to offer him the customary presents and congratulations (after the toils of the journey) in the suburb (near the capital); he himself met him and bowed to him inside the great gate, and then received him in the ancestral temple; with his face to the north he bowed to him when the presents (which he brought) were presented, and bowed again (when his message was delivered), in acknowledgment of its condescension:—in this way did he (on his part) testify his respect.

5. Respectfulness and yielding courtesy mark the intercourse of superior men with one another. Hence, when the feudal lords received one another with such respectfulness and yielding courtesy, they would not attack or encroach on one another.

6. A high minister is employed as principal usher (for the messenger), a Great officer as the next, and (ordinary) officers acted as their attendants. (When he had delivered his message), the ruler himself showed him courtesy, (and presented to him the cup of new liquor). He had his private interviews (with the dignitaries and Great officers of the court), and also with the ruler[1]. (After this), supplies of animals, slaughtered and living, were sent (to his hotel). (When he was about to take his departure), the jade–symbols (by which he was accredited) were returned to him, and the return

[1. At these interviews, after he had discharged his mission and presented the gifts from his ruler, he presented other gifts on his own account.]

gifts (of silk and other things) presented at the same time. He had been entertained and feasted. All these observances served to illustrate the idea underlying the relations between ruler and minister in receiving visitors and guests[1].

7. Therefore it was a statute made by the son of Heaven for the feudal lords, that every year they should interchange a small mission, and every three years a great one:—thus stimulating one another to the exercise of courtesy. If the messenger committed any error in the exchange of his mission, the ruler, his host, did not personally entertain and feast him:—thereby making him ashamed, and stimulating him.

When the princes thus stimulated one another to the observance of the ceremonial usages, they did not make any attacks on one another, and in their states there was no oppression or encroachment. In this way the son of Heaven cherished and nourished them; there was no occasion for any appeal to arms, and they were furnished with an instrument to maintain themselves in rectitude.

8. (The commissioners) carried with them their jade–symbols, the sceptre and half–sceptre:—showing the importance of the ceremony. On the completion of their mission, these were returned to them:—showing the small importance to be attached to their value, and the great importance of the ceremony. When the princes thus stimulated one another, to set light by the value of the articles, and recognise the importance of the

ceremony, the people learned to be yielding and courteous.

[1. The entertainment took place in the open court; the banquet in the banqueting chamber.]

9. The prince of the state to which the mission was sent treated his guests in this way:—Till their departure from their coming, they were supplied from the three stores (provided for such purposes). Living animals were sent to them at their lodging. A provision of five sets of the three animals for slaughter was made inside. Thirty loads of rice, the same number of grain with the straw, and twice as many of fodder and firewood were provided outside. There were five pairs of birds that went in flocks every day. All the attendants had cattle supplied to them for their food. There was one meal (a day in the court), and two (spare) entertainments (in the temple). The banquets and occasional bounties were without any definite number. With such generosity was the importance of the ceremony indicated[1].

10. They could not always be so profuse as this in antiquity in the use of their wealth; but their employment of it thus liberally (in connexion with these missions) showed how they were prepared to devote it to the maintenance of the ceremonies. When they expended it as they did on the ceremonies, then in the states ruler and minister did not encroach on one another's rights and possessions, and different states did not attack one another. It was on this account that the kings made their statute about these missions, and the feudal lords did their utmost to fulfil it[2].

[1. The particulars here briefly mentioned and many others are to be found in great detail in the 8th division of the Î Lî, Books 15–18. which are on the subject of these missions.

2. About twenty years ago, when I had occasion to accompany a mandarin from Canton to a disturbed district in the interior, he introduced one day in conversation the subject of these missions, saying that they must have been a great drain on the revenues of the ancient states, and that in the same way in the present day the provincial administrations were burdened with many outlays which should be borne by the imperial treasury. As resident ambassadors from foreign nations had then begun to be talked about, he asked whether China would have to pay their expenses, or the countries which they represented would do so, and was greatly relieved when I told him that each nation would pay the expenses of its embassy.]

11. The archery in connexion with these missions was a very great institution. With the early dawn they commenced it, and it was nearly midday before the whole of the ceremonies were concluded:—it required men of great vigour and strength to go through with it.

And further, when such men were about to engage in it, though the liquor might be clear and they were thirsty, they did not venture to drink of it; though the stalks of flesh were dry (and ready to their hand), and they were hungry, they did not venture to eat of them; at the close of the day, when they were tired, they continued to maintain a grave and correct deportment. So they carried out all the details of the ceremonies; so they maintained correctly the relation between ruler and subject, affection between father and son, and harmony between seniors and juniors. All this it is difficult for the generality of men to do, but it was done by those superior men; and on this account they were called men possessed of great ability in action. The ascribing to them such ability in action implied their possession of the sense of righteousness; and their possession of that sense implied that they were valiant and daring. The most valuable quality in a man who is bold and daring is that he can thereby establish his sense of righteousness; the most valuable quality in him who establishes that sense is that he can thereby show his great ability in action; the most valuable quality in him who has that ability is that he can carry all ceremonies into practice. In this way, the most valuable quality in valiant daring is that its possessor dares to carry into practice the rules of ceremony and righteousness.

It follows from this that such men, bold and daring, full of vigour and strength, when the kingdom was at peace, employed their gifts in the exercise of propriety and righteousness; and, when there was trouble in the kingdom, employed them in the battle–field and in gaining victory. When they employed them to conquer in battle, no enemies could resist them; when they employed them in the exercise of propriety and righteousness, then obedience and good order prevailed. No enemies abroad, and obedience and good order at home:—this was called the perfect condition for a state. But when men, so endowed, did not use their valour and strength in the service of propriety and righteousness, and to secure victory, but in strifes and contentions, then they were styled men of turbulence or disorder. Punishments were put in requisition throughout the kingdom, and the (first) use of them was to deal with those same men, and take them off. In this way (again), the people became obedient and there was good order, and the state was tranquil and happy.

12. Dze-kung asked Confucius, saying, 'Allow me to ask the reason why the superior man sets a high value on jade, and but little on soapstone? Is it because jade is rare, and the soapstone plentiful?'

13. Confucius replied, 'It is not because the soapstone is plentiful that he thinks but little of it, and because jade is rare that he sets a high value on it. Anciently superior men found the likeness of all excellent qualities in jade. Soft, smooth, and glossy, it appeared to them like benevolence; fine, compact, and strong,—like intelligence; angular, but not sharp and cutting,—like righteousness; hanging down (in beads) as if it would fall to the ground,—like (the humility of) propriety; when struck, yielding a note, clear and prolonged, yet terminating abruptly,—like music; its flaws not concealing its beauty, nor its beauty concealing its flaws,—like loyalty; with an internal radiance issuing from it on every side,—like good faith; bright as a brilliant rainbow,—like heaven; exquisite and mysterious, appearing in the hills and streams,—like the earth; standing out conspicuous in the symbols of rank,—like virtue; esteemed by all under the sky,—like the path of truth and duty. As is said in the ode (I, xi, ode 3, 1),

"Such my lord's car. He rises in my mind,
Lovely and bland, like jade of richest kind."

BOOK XLVI. SANG FÛ SZE KIH, OR THE FOUR PRINCIPLES UNDERLYING THE DRESS OF MOURNING[1].

1. All ceremonial usages looked at in their great characteristics are the embodiment of (the ideas suggested by) heaven and earth; take their laws from the (changes of the) four seasons; imitate the (operation of the) contracting and developing movements in nature; and are conformed to the feelings of men. It is on this account that they are called the Rules of Propriety; and when any one finds fault with them, he only shows his ignorance of their origin.

2. Those usages are different in their applications to felicitous and unfortunate occurrences; in which they should not come into collision with one another:—this is derived from (their pattern as given by) the contracting and developing movements in

nature.

3. The mourning dress has its four definite fashions and styles, the changes in which are always according to what is right:—this is derived from the (changes of the) four seasons.

Now, affection predominates; now, nice distinctions; now, defined regulations; and now, the consideration of circumstances:—all these are

[1. See the introductory notice, vol. xxvii, pp. 59, 60.]

derived from the human feelings. In affection we have benevolence; in nice distinctions, righteousness; in defined regulations, propriety; and in the consideration of circumstances, knowledge. Benevolence, righteousness, propriety, and knowledge;—these make up the characteristic attributes of humanity.

4. Where the affection has been great, the mourning worn is deep. On this account the sackcloth with jagged edges is worn for the father for three years:—the regulation is determined by affection.

5. In the regulation (of the mourning) within the family circle, the, affection throws the (duty of public) righteousness into the shade[1]. In the regulation (of that which is) beyond that circle, the (duty of public) righteousness cuts the (mourning of) affection short[1]. The service due to a father is employed in serving a ruler, and the reverence is the same for both:—this is the greatest instance of (the conviction of the duty of) righteousness, in all the esteem shown to nobility and the honour done to the honourable. Hence the sackcloth with jagged edges is worn (also) for the ruler for three years:—the regulation is determined by righteousness.

6. The eating after three days; the washing the head after three months; the sacrifice and change of dress at the end of the first year; the not carrying the emaciation to such an extent as to affect life:—these regulations were to avoid doing harm to the living

[1. A son, on his father's death, is exempted from official duties for a time; but this exemption is suspended on occasions of pressing exigency.]

(by the mourning) for the dead. Not protracting the mourning rites beyond three years; not mending even the coarsest sackcloth; making no addition to the mound (raised at first) over the grave; fixing the day for the sacrifice at the end of the second year; playing (at first, on the conclusion of the rites) on a plain, unvarnished lute:—all these things were to make the people aware of the termination (of the several rites), and constituted the defined regulations.

The service due to a father is employed in serving a mother, and the love is the same for both. (But) in the sky there are not two suns, nor in a land two kings, nor in a state two rulers, nor in a family two equally honourable:—one (principle) regulates (all) these conditions. Hence, while the father is alive, the sackcloth with even edges is worn (for a mother), (and only) for a year,—showing that there are not (in the family) two equally honourable.

7. What is meant by the use of the staff? It is (a symbol of) rank. On the third day it is given to the son; on the fifth day, to Great officers; and on the seventh day, to ordinary officers;—(at the mourning rites for a ruler). Some say that it is given to them as the presiding mourners; and others, that it is to support them in their distress.

A daughter (not yet fully grown) and a son (while but a lad), do not carry a staff;—(being supposed) not to be capable of (extreme) distress.

When all the array of officers is complete, and all things are provided, and (the mourner) cannot speak (his directions), and things must (still) proceed, he is assisted to rise. If he be able to speak, and things will proceed (as he directs), he rises by the help of the staff. Where (the mourner) has himself to take part in what is to be done, he will have his face grimed (as if black with sorrow). Women who are bald do not use the coiffure; hunchbacks do not unbare their arms; the lame do not leap; and the old and ill do not give up the use of liquor and flesh. All these are cases regulated by the consideration of circumstances.

8. After the occurrence of the death, the (wailing for) three days, which left no leisure for anything else; the not taking off (the headband or girdle) for three months; the grief and lamentation for a whole year; and the sorrow on to the three years: (in all these things) there was a gradual diminution of the (manifestation of) affection. The sages, in accordance with that diminution of the natural feeling, made their various definite

regulations.

9. It was on this account that the mourning rites were limited to three years. The worthiest were not permitted to go beyond this period, nor those who were inferior to them to fall short of it. This was the proper and invariable time for those rites, what the (sage) kings always carried into practice.

When it is said in the Shû (Part IV, Book VIII, i, 1), that Kâo Zung, while occupying the mourning shed, for three years did not speak, this expresses approval of that sovereign. But the kings all observed this rule;—why is the approval only expressed in connexion with him? It may be replied, 'This Kâo Zung was Wû Ting.' Wû Ting was a worthy sovereign of Yin. He had come to the throne in the due order of succession, and was thus loving and good in his observance of the mourning rites. At this time Yin, which had been decaying, revived again; ceremonial usages, which had been neglected, came again into use. On this account the approval of him was expressed, and therefore it was recorded in the Shû, and he was styled Kâo (The Exalted), and designated Kâo Zung (The Exalted and Honoured Sovereign). (The rule was that), during the three years' mourning, a ruler should not speak; and that the Shû says, 'Kâo Zung, while he occupied the mourning shed, for the three years did not speak,' was an illustration of this. When it is said (in the Hsiâo King, chapter 18th), 'They speak, but without elegance of phrase,' the reference is to ministers and inferior (officers).

10. According to the usages, when wearing the sackcloth with jagged edges (for a father), (a son) indicated that he heard what was said to him, but did not reply in words; when wearing that with even edges (for a mother), he replied, but did not speak (of anything else); when wearing the mourning of nine months, he might speak (of other things), but did not enter into any discussion; when wearing that of five months, or of three, he might discuss, but did not show pleasure in doing so.

11. At the mourning rites for a parent, (the son) wore the cap of sackcloth, with strings of cords, and sandals of straw; after the third day, he (began to) take gruel; after the third month, he washed his head; at the end of the year, in the thirteenth month, he put on the mourning silk and cap proper after the first year; and when the three years were completed, he offered the auspicious sacrifice.

BOOK XLVI. SANG FÛ SZE KIH, OR THE FOUR PRINCIPLES UNDERLYING THE DRESS OF MOURNING[1].

1. All ceremonial usages looked at in their great characteristics are the embodiment of (the ideas suggested by) heaven and earth; take their laws from the (changes of the) four seasons; imitate the (operation of the) contracting and developing movements in nature; and are conformed to the feelings of men. It is on this account that they are called the Rules of Propriety; and when any one finds fault with them, he only shows his ignorance of their origin.

2. Those usages are different in their applications to felicitous and unfortunate occurrences; in which they should not come into collision with one another:—this is derived from (their pattern as given by) the contracting and developing movements in nature.

3. The mourning dress has its four definite fashions and styles, the changes in which are always according to what is right:—this is derived from the (changes of the) four seasons.

Now, affection predominates; now, nice distinctions; now, defined regulations; and now, the consideration of circumstances:—all these are

[1. See the introductory notice, vol. xxvii, pp. 59, 60.]

derived from the human feelings. In affection we have benevolence; in nice distinctions, righteousness; in defined regulations, propriety; and in the consideration of circumstances, knowledge. Benevolence, righteousness, propriety, and knowledge;—these make up the characteristic attributes of humanity.

4. Where the affection has been great, the mourning worn is deep. On this account the sackcloth with jagged edges is worn for the father for three years:—the regulation is determined by affection.

5. In the regulation (of the mourning) within the family circle, the, affection throws the (duty of public) righteousness into the shade[1]. In the regulation (of that which is) beyond that circle, the (duty of public) righteousness cuts the (mourning of) affection short[1]. The service due to a father is employed in serving a ruler, and the reverence is the same for both:—this is the greatest instance of (the conviction of the duty of) righteousness, in all the esteem shown to nobility and the honour done to the honourable. Hence the sackcloth with jagged edges is worn (also) for the ruler for three years:—the regulation is determined by righteousness.

6. The eating after three days; the washing the head after three months; the sacrifice and change of dress at the end of the first year; the not carrying the emaciation to such an extent as to affect life:—these regulations were to avoid doing harm to the living

[1. A son, on his father's death, is exempted from official duties for a time; but this exemption is suspended on occasions of pressing exigency.]

(by the mourning) for the dead. Not protracting the mourning rites beyond three years; not mending even the coarsest sackcloth; making no addition to the mound (raised at first) over the grave; fixing the day for the sacrifice at the end of the second year; playing (at first, on the conclusion of the rites) on a plain, unvarnished lute:—all these things were to make the people aware of the termination (of the several rites), and constituted the defined regulations.

The service due to a father is employed in serving a mother, and the love is the same for both. (But) in the sky there are not two suns, nor in a land two kings, nor in a state two rulers, nor in a family two equally honourable:—one (principle) regulates (all) these conditions. Hence, while the father is alive, the sackcloth with even edges is worn (for a mother), (and only) for a year,—showing that there are not (in the family) two equally honourable.

7. What is meant by the use of the staff? It is (a symbol of) rank. On the third day it is given to the son; on the fifth day, to Great officers; and on the seventh day, to ordinary officers;—(at the mourning rites for a ruler). Some say that it is given to them as the presiding mourners; and others, that it is to support them in their distress.

A daughter (not yet fully grown) and a son (while but a lad), do not carry a staff;—(being supposed) not to be capable of (extreme) distress.

When all the array of officers is complete, and all things are provided, and (the mourner) cannot speak (his directions), and things must (still) proceed, he is assisted to rise. If he be able to speak, and things will proceed (as he directs), he rises by the help of the staff. Where (the mourner) has himself to take part in what is to be done, he will have his face grimed (as if black with sorrow). Women who are bald do not use the coiffure; hunchbacks do not unbare their arms; the lame do not leap; and the old and ill do not give up the use of liquor and flesh. All these are cases regulated by the consideration of circumstances.

8. After the occurrence of the death, the (wailing for) three days, which left no leisure for anything else; the not taking off (the headband or girdle) for three months; the grief and lamentation for a whole year; and the sorrow on to the three years: (in all these things) there was a gradual diminution of the (manifestation of) affection. The sages, in accordance with that diminution of the natural feeling, made their various definite regulations.

9. It was on this account that the mourning rites were limited to three years. The worthiest were not permitted to go beyond this period, nor those who were inferior to them to fall short of it. This was the proper and invariable time for those rites, what the (sage) kings always carried into practice.

When it is said in the Shû (Part IV, Book VIII, i, 1), that Kâo Zung, while occupying the mourning shed, for three years did not speak, this expresses approval of that sovereign. But the kings all observed this rule;—why is the approval only expressed in connexion with him? It may be replied, 'This Kâo Zung was Wû Ting.' Wû Ting was a worthy sovereign of Yin. He had come to the throne in the due order of succession, and was thus loving and good in his observance of the mourning rites. At this time Yin, which had been decaying, revived again; ceremonial usages, which had been neglected, came again into use. On this account the approval of him was expressed, and therefore it was recorded in the Shû, and he was styled Kâo (The Exalted), and designated Kâo Zung (The Exalted and Honoured Sovereign). (The rule was that), during the three years' mourning, a ruler should not speak; and that the Shû says, 'Kâo Zung, while he occupied the mourning shed, for the three years did not speak,' was an illustration of this. When it is said (in the Hsiâo King, chapter 18th), 'They speak, but without elegance of phrase,' the reference is to ministers and inferior (officers).

10. According to the usages, when wearing the sackcloth with jagged edges (for a father), (a son) indicated that he heard what was said to him, but did not reply in words; when wearing that with even edges (for a mother), he replied, but did not speak (of anything else); when wearing the mourning of nine months, he might speak (of other things), but did not enter into any discussion; when wearing that of five months, or of three, he might discuss, but did not show pleasure in doing so.

11. At the mourning rites for a parent, (the son) wore the cap of sackcloth, with strings of cords, and sandals of straw; after the third day, he (began to) take gruel; after the third month, he washed his head; at the end of the year, in the thirteenth month, he put on the mourning silk and cap proper after the first year; and when the three years were completed, he offered the auspicious sacrifice.

CPSIA information can be obtained
at www.ICGtesting.com
Printed in the USA
LVHW061105220422
716949LV00006B/456